8°

La Coruña

Avilés Gijón

Golfo de Viscaya

FRANCIA

Montpellier

Santander

Santiago

Oviedo

Bilbao

San
Sebastián

Narbonne

PRINCIPADO DE ASTURIAS

CANTABRIA

PAÍS
VASCO

Vitoria

GALICIA

Ponferrada

Pamplona

ANDORRA

Orense

CASTILLA Y LEÓN

Logroño

COM. FORAL DE NAVARRA

CATALUÑA

Verín

LA RIOJA

Burgos

Zaragoza

Lérida

Benavente

Badalona

Porto

Tordesillas

Valladolid

ARAGÓN

Barcelona

Salamanca

Medina del
Campo

Segovia

Golfo de Valencia

Aveiro

Ávila

COM. DE MADRID

Menorca

Palma de
Mallorca

Coimbra

MADRID

Mallorca

40°

PORTUGAL

Toledo

Aranjuez

40°

CASTILLA–LA MANCHA

Valencia

Ibiza

ISLAS
BALEARES

Lisboa

EXTREMADURA

Cascais

Mérida

Ciudad
Real

Albacete

COM. VALENCIANA

Formentera

Mar Mediterráneo

Córdoba

REGIÓN DE
MURCIA

Alicante

Huelva

Sevilla

Carmona

Murcia

ANDALUCÍA

Cartagena

Faro

Granada

Málaga

Motril

Almería

Cádiz

San
Fernando

36°

Algeciras

GIBRALTAR (U.K.)

Mar de
Alborán

Esrecho de
Gibraltar

CEUTA (Sp.)

Soberanía en África

MELILLA (Sp.)

OCÉANO
ATLÁNTICO

MARRUECOS

0   100   200   300 Kilómetros

0   50   100   150 Millas

8°

4°

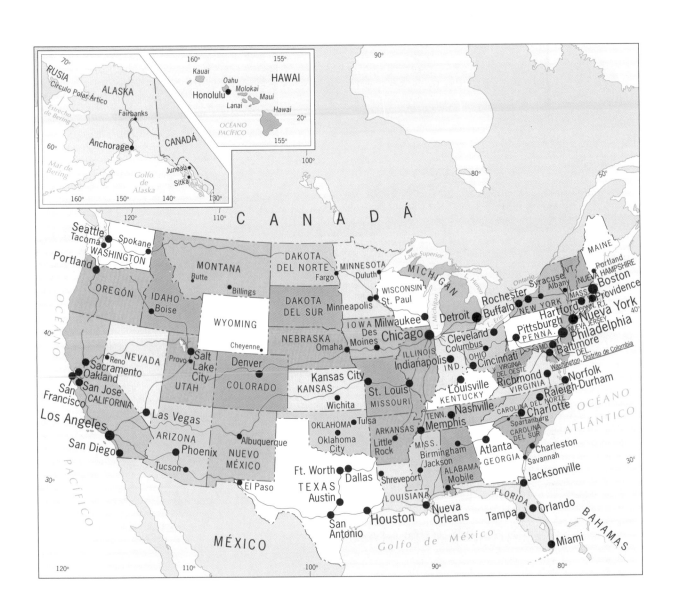

Dicho y hecho

Seventh Edition

Beginning Spanish

Laila M. Dawson

Joseph R. Farrell
California State Polytechnic University

Trinidad González
California State Polytechnic University

WILEY

VICE PRESIDENT/PUBLISHER	Anne Smith
ACQUISITIONS EDITOR	Helene Greenwood
DEVELOPMENT EDITOR	María F. García
DEVELOPMENT PROGRAM ASSISTANT	Kristen Babroski
EDITORIAL ASSISTANT	Christine Cordek
MARKETING MANAGER	Gitti Lindner
NEW MEDIA EDITOR	Lisa Schnettler
SENIOR PRODUCTION EDITOR	Christine Cervoni
PHOTO EDITOR	Hilary Newman
PHOTO RESEARCHER	Elyse Rieder
TEXT DESIGNER	Word & Image Design Studio, Inc.
COVER DESIGN	Kevin Murphy, Senior Designer; Sue Noli
COVER IMAGE	© Jose Ortega/Stock Illustration Source/Images.com
ILLUSTRATORS	Josée Morin, Paul McCusker, Peter Grau, Deborah Crowle

This book was set in 11/15 EideticNeo Regular by Word and Image Design Studio, Inc. and printed and bound by VonHoffmann Press, Inc. The cover was printed by VonHoffmann Press, Inc.

This book is printed on acid free paper.

To order books please call 1-800-CALL WILEY (225-5945).

Student Book ISBN: 0-471-26886-0
AIE ISBN: 0-471-47656-0

Printed in the United States of America
10 9 8 7 6 5 4

To Al,
my life-long companion,
for his love, patience, constant
support, and invaluable assistance
throughout this project.

L. M. D.

To Darla,
my soul mate,
for her encouragement, unconditional
love, and boundless confidence in me.

J. R. F.

To Gregory Bradford Jr.,
my guardian angel
for over a quarter century.

T. G.

Preface

Carefully crafted and sequenced, pedagogically sound, student-centered and user-friendly, *Dicho y hecho* is an interactive Beginning Spanish program that has been enthusiastically praised by countless instructors and over 250,000 students since its first edition in 1981. Straightforward, easy-to-implement, and highly successful, its lively classroom-tested approach makes both learning and teaching Spanish not only an attainable goal but also an enjoyable experience. Over the years, teachers—both users and non-users of the text—and students have collaborated with the authors in fine-tuning this well-balanced, four-skills program. And while each new edition incorporates important, exciting improvements that respond both to recent advances in pedagogy and to the changing needs of students and teachers, *Dicho y hecho* never deviates from its original objective: to be the easiest to understand, easiest to use, and easiest to adapt Beginning Spanish program available.

A TRADITION OF EXCELLENCE: Hallmarks of the *Dicho y hecho* program

- **EASY TO UNDERSTAND** Carefully sequenced step-by-step grammar presentations with contextualized examples make *Dicho y hecho* an effective out-of-class study guide that facilitates student preparation for classroom activities. Uncluttered pages and a stunningly contemporary, student-friendly new design highlight the text's key features and further enhance the learning process.

- **EASY TO USE** Its streamlined and consistent chapter organization makes *Dicho y hecho* the most accessible Spanish program available today. Every aspect of each chapter is carefully developed, well-integrated, and thoroughly class-tested with successful results.

- **EASY TO SUPPLEMENT** While it focuses on the essentials that beginning students need to master, *Dicho y hecho* is flexible enough to adapt to any kind of course in the curriculum. Whether supplemented with transparencies or cutting-edge technology, it maintains a clear direction for students, who remain solidly grounded in the basics.

- **PRACTICAL, CONTEXTUALIZED, ACTIVE VOCABULARY** *Dicho y hecho* offers the most thorough and varied practice of vocabulary of any text available today. Thematic vocabulary is presented visually and contextually and then activated through multiple, progressive phases of application that range from identification in the chapter opening art scenes to personal expression and situational conversations.

- **AMPLE OPPORTUNITIES FOR VARIOUS TYPES OF PRACTICE: STRUCTURED, GUIDED, AND OPEN-ENDED** *Dicho y hecho* combines a broad array of time-tested exercises with innovative, original activities, and it presents them in a way that imparts a varied pace and rhythm to every class meeting: whole-class exercises interwoven with individual, paired, and small group activities.

- **WEB-EXTENDED PANORAMAS CULTURALES** Each country has its own unique home page, with a mix of textual information, maps and graphics, and Web-based discussion and research activities. Numerous authentic links on every page provide access to virtual experiences in any land and culture.

DICHO Y HECHO: Features of the Seventh Edition

- **NEW,** more varied, and more communicative activities and exercises provide greater opportunity for interaction, feedback, and creative expression. New pair and group activities ② ③ ④ ⑤, role playing, class projects, and interviews enhance student communication in an enjoyable way. Clear, concise direction lines (English in Chapters P–5, Spanish in Chapters 6–14) and increased focus on recycling of vocabulary and structures are featured throughout.

- **REVISED** scope and sequence results in fewer tenses presented in the last two chapters, adds the **se impersonal**, and introduces several structures (such as the reflexives, the preterit, and the subjunctive) earlier in the text.

- **DRAMATIC NEW** two-page art openers and contextualized short readings featuring the *Dicho y hecho* cast of characters present the majority of active vocabulary in each chapter. Supplementary vocabulary lists have been virtually eliminated. Three new chapter themes (*La salud, Aventuras al aire libre,* and *El mundo en las noticias*) and modification of former themes update the text.

- **REVISED** grammar presentations result in simpler, clearer, and more precise formats; for example, **gustar, ser/estar,** and preterit/imperfect presentations are reconfigured for greater visual impact and clarity. *Dicho y hecho* exemplifies the best application of the eclectic pedagogy favored by large and ever-increasing numbers of experienced teachers and linguists.

- **CULTURAL** readings have been simplified and shortened, especially in the earlier chapters. Several have been replaced, while others have been updated to reflect current political, social, and geographic changes.

- **¡QUÉ DILEMA!**, informal, interactive problem-solving situations that require students to create brief original dialogs, appear in every chapter.

- **PERSON@JE DEL MOMENTO** accompanies most *Panorama cultural* sections. Students identify a photo of a famous Hispanic person and then share with the class pertinent information from the Internet.

- **ENHANCED** story line features a group of easily recognizable characters who appear throughout the entire text in art spots, vocabulary presentations, conversations, activities, and exercises. It culminates in an Epilogue at the end of the last chapter.

- **NEW** appendix adds substantial supplementary vocabulary for **países y nacionalidades, las profesiones**, and **materias académicas**.

- **OUTSTANDING NEW** 60-minute video complements the carefully developed supplements, which have been revised and updated. Pre-viewing, while-viewing, and post-viewing activities are provided on worksheets for students. Video resources for instructors include a videoscript and answer key plus suggested expansion activities.

CHAPTER ORGANIZATION

Each of the fourteen chapters of *Dicho y hecho* includes the following components.

Overview presents the chapter's goals for communication, structures, vocabulary theme, and the cultural focus within which these elements will be presented.

Así se dice introduces most of the chapter's vocabulary visually in a beautiful two-page art illustration. Items are identified both in Spanish and English. The *Práctica y comunicación* activities that immediately follow, practice and reinforce the vocabulary.

Escenas are brief, situational conversations that employ authentic language to provide concise, practical, and natural contexts in which to apply the chapter's vocabulary and grammar. Designed for oral practice, they are followed by a short comprehension exercise.

Estructuras are the grammar structures, presented in functional, clear, and concise language, and introduced by an icon to enable students to find them easily for study and review. Usually accompanied by a relevant visual, they are always followed by contextualized models that integrate the chapter's vocabulary and theme. Structures are reintroduced, recycled, and practiced in subsequent chapters.

Práctica y comunicación exercises and activities always follow vocabulary or grammar presentations, and move students gradually from controlled to open-ended communication. The variety of these activities, both prepared and spontaneous, provides ample opportunity for individual student feedback as well as interaction in pairs and groups.

Noticias culturales are short readings in Spanish that focus on cultural attitudes and behaviors, and expand one cultural aspect of the chapter theme. They are followed by questions or a brief comprehension activity that reinforces the content of the passage. A concluding section, *Conexiones y contrastes*, requires students to make cultural contrasts and comparisons that develop an appreciation of their own heritage and culture, as well as those of others.

Así se pronuncia is a pronunciation component in Chapters 1–6 only that systematically reviews key points presented in the preliminary pronunciation section of the book.

Dicho y hecho, acclaimed by users and reviewers as a *Dicho* hallmark, reviews, integrates, and puts into practice all components of the chapter. It features guided conversations, role play and situational dramatizations (*Conversando* 🔲), lively listening activities (*¡A escuchar!* 🎧), and varied individual and group writing practice (*De mi escritorio* ✏️).

Panorama cultural, now Web-expanded www.wiley.com/college/panoramas, is an appealing combination of readings, maps, photos, realia, and intriguing *Curiosidades* that acquaint students with the geography, history, and other aspects of the various countries and peoples of the Spanish-speaking world. In-text and Web discovery activities and *Adivinanzas* enable students to synthesize and apply the information.

Encuentro cultural allows students to experience cultures different from their own by introducing them to a wide variety of Hispanic creative expression through a rich array of authentic materials, including literary, visual, textile, folk, and culinary arts.

Repaso de vocabulario activo presents, at the end of each chapter, an alphabetized list of active Spanish vocabulary words and phrases introduced in the chapter, grouped by parts of speech. This list is also recorded on the audio program.

Autoprueba y repaso review exercises at the end of each chapter and on the Web are an effective format for reviewing material and preparing for tests. The answer key that appears in an appendix provides instant feedback.

THE *DICHO Y HECHO* PROGRAM

Dicho y hecho is a complete teaching and learning program that includes the following components. Please check the *Dicho y hecho* Book Companion Site at www.wiley.com/college/dawson for updates and availability of components for both students and instructors.

For the student:

- The **Student Textbook** of 14 chapters, accompanied by a **student audiocassette** or **audio CD** that includes the pronunciation materials from the *Así se pronuncia* at the beginning of the text and the *¡A escuchar!* listening activities from the *Dicho y hecho* sections of every chapter.

- A **Workbook**, designed to practice writing skills and to reinforce classroom materials, also contains Internet Discovery activities. The answer key at the end encourages students to monitor and evaluate their work.

- A **Laboratory Manual** coordinates with the **laboratory audio program** to provide practice and reinforcement of the vocabulary and grammar for each chapter, as well as extensive practice in listening comprehension.

- An **Activities Manual** combines the **workbook** and **laboratory manual** in one convenient volume.

- The **Electronic Workbook, Laboratory Manual,** and **Activities Manual,** available on CD-ROM and online, provide an electronic version of the print components.

- *Panoramas culturales* **Web Site** allows students to interact with authentic cultural materials at www.wiley.com/college/panoramas. The site, developed by John Wiley and Sons, Inc., features geographical, cultural, and political content on the twenty-one Spanish-speaking countries.

- The **Autopruebas** (*Self-tests*) allow students to practice online vocabulary and grammatical structures from each chapter section and receive instant feedback. These will provide additional preparatory work for tests.

For the instructor:

- The **Annotated Instructor's Edition (AIE)** includes the audioscript for the *¡A escuchar!* activities, as well as teaching suggestions for presentation and reinforcement of material. Answers are also provided for all discrete point activities. The **AIE** is accompanied by the **Instructor's Audio CD** which includes the *Escenas* from each chapter.

- The **Instructor's Resource Manual** includes the printed Testing Program, Tapescripts, Video Resources, Answer Key for the Laboratory Manual, and numerous tips and strategies for using **Dicho y hecho.**

- The **Transparency program,** a unique full-color visual component, includes drawings and maps used in exercises and activities, including the chapter-opener illustrations without the vocabulary labels. Transparencies may also be used as an effective means of testing. Annotations in the margins of the **AIE** indicate all text exercises that are accompanied by transparencies.

- The **Audio Program** coordinates with the listening activities in the Laboratory Manual. Also included are the *Repaso de vocabulario activo* sections from the main text. This audio program is available on CD or cassette.

- The **Testing Program** has been completely rewritten and consists of 15 chapter tests, each having alternate A and B versions. There are additional longer exams for use after Chapter 7 and Chapter 14. The test items range from single response to short answer, culminating in open-ended responses for the communicative section. Tests are available in hard copy and also online through the Instructor's Resources section of the Book Companion Site.

- **Supplementary Oral Exercises and Activities** are available online through the Instructor's Resources section of the Book Companion Site for use in class and in small-group practice sessions.

ACKNOWLEDGMENTS

No project of the scope and complexity of *Dicho y hecho, Seventh Edition* could have materialized without the collaboration of numerous people. The author team gratefully acknowledges the contributions of the many individuals who were instrumental in the development of this work.

The professionalism, dedication, and expertise of the John Wiley & Sons, Inc. staff who worked with us have been both indispensable and inspirational. To Anne Smith, Publisher, who oversaw the administrative aspects of the entire project, bore the ultimate responsibility for its completion, and never failed to be approachable, we are very grateful. We are also most grateful to Christine Cervoni, Senior Production Editor, for her expertise, flexibility, creativity, inordinate patience, and dedication to the project. We extend our thanks and appreciation to Hilary Newman, Photo Editor, for facilitating the photo selections that enhance the text. Nor can we neglect to thank Gitti Lindner, Marketing Manager, for creating a brilliant advertising program that will position *Dicho y hecho* favorably in the marketplace. We thank Harriet Dishman for her creativity in coordinating the outstanding print and media ancillaries that supplement the text, Grisel Lozano-Garcini for her careful and insightful manuscript editing, Janice Baillie, our meticulous and tactful copyeditor, and Kristen Babroski, Development Program Assistant, for keeping track of us and maintaining order in the midst of the myriad details of the project. We would also like to acknowledge our cover designer, Kevin Murphy, Senior Designer; the text designer, compositor, and everyone at Word & Image Design Studio; and Josée Morin, the illustrator. Most of all, the authors extend our heartfelt appreciation and most profound gratitude to our wonderful Development Editor, María F. García, for her unfaltering devotion to *Dicho y hecho*, her tireless hands-on involvement with us on a daily basis since initial conceptualization of the *Seventh Edition*, her talent, expertise, and diligence in turning a manuscript into a book, her relentless pursuit of perfection, and—most importantly—her friendship and confidence in us as authors.

For their generous and invaluable assistance, we acknowledge and thank: Dr. Isabel Bustamante-López, California State University, Pomona, for her dependable input regarding vocabulary, linguistic authenticity, and cultural matters; Dr. Carlos Schwalb for his excellent suggestions in the areas of culture and language; Professor Ted Peebles, Dr. Claudia Ferman, and colleagues at the University of Richmond for their on-going support and willingness to respond to multiple cultural and linguistic queries; Victoria Mujica and Ana Mujica Baquerizo for their extensive contributions to the Lambayeque gold reading; María Odette from Florida Atlantic University for her special attention to manuscript details; Professor Greg Briscoe at Utah Valley State College for his "Lost luggage" activity and the concept behind the *¡Qué dilema!* sections; Alfonzo Fernández for his timely input regarding the "Torch of Friendship" sculpture and suggestions for *Person@je del momento*; Paul and Sheila Caputo for their insightful design/art contributions; and Eric Dawson and Rick Baldacci for their humorous *¡Qué dilema!* suggestions.

We are grateful to the loyal users of **Dicho y hecho**, who over the years have continued to provide valuable insights and suggestions. And finally, for their candid observations, their critically important scrutiny, and their creative ideas, we wish to thank the following reviewers from across the nation:

Sharon Abernethy, *University of Alabama in Huntsville*; Joanne M. Olson-Biglieri, *Lexington Community College*; Christine Bridges, *Lamar University*; June Chatterjee, *Contra Costa College*; Ivana Cuvalo, *South Suburban College*; John Ellis, *Scottsdale Community College*; Heather Fernandez, *Asheville-Buncombe Technical Community College*; Anthony J. Farrell, *Saint Mary's University*; Tracy Ferrell, *Rocky Mountain College*; Sergio A. Guzman, *Community College of Southern Nevada*; Anne E. Hardcastle, *Millsaps College*; Martine Howard, *Camden County College*; Melinda Johansson, *University of North Carolina at Wilmington*; Steven Konopacki, *Palm Beach Community College*; Helen L. Levin, *Santa Rosa Jr. College*; Tom Manzo, *San Antonio College*; Susan D. Martín, *Northern Michigan University*; Timothy B. Messick, *Mohawk Valley Community College*; Maria de los Santos Onofre-Madrid, *Angelo State University*; Marilyn Palatinus, *Pellissippi State Technical Community College*; Jennifer Pedersen, *Omaha Public Schools*; Gema Mayo Pushee, *Dartmouth College*; Nori E. Mejia, *San Bernardino Valley College*; Mayela Vallejos Ramírez, *University of Nebraska-Lincoln*; Valerie Rider, *University of North Carolina at Wilmington*; José A. Sandoval, *Des Moines Area Community College*; Sylvia Santaballa, *University of North Carolina at Wilmington*; March Jean Sustarsic, *Community College of Southern Nevada*; Luis Torres, *University of Calgary*; Vicki L. Trylong, *Olivet Nazarene University*; John H. Twomey, Jr., *University of Massachusetts-Dartmouth*; Miguel Ángel Vázquez, *Indiana University*; Harriet L. Wiles, *Honors College-Florida Atlantic University*; Myrna A. Vélez, *Dartmouth College*; Mary Frances Wadley, *Jackson State Community College*; Burl J. Walker, Jr., *Ozarks Technical Community College*; Dana Derrick Ward, *Arkansas Technical University*; Valerie K. Watts, *Asheville-Buncombe Technical Community College*.

Laila Dawson

Joseph Farrell

Trinidad González

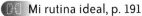

Así se pronuncia

It's pronounced like this

Becoming familiar with the sounds of Spanish is the first step to an exciting encounter with the world of Spanish language and Hispanic cultures. The information recorded on the tape or CD that accompanies your textbook will help you absorb the basic rules in this section. Soon you will be able to pronounce most Spanish words correctly.

1 Vowels

Each Spanish vowel has only *one* basic sound and is represented with *one* symbol. Spanish vowels are short and clipped, never drawn out. Listen carefully and repeat each sound and the corresponding examples.

a   Panamá, ala
e   bebe, lee
i   sí, ni
o   solo, loco
u   Lulú, cucú

A. Now listen to and repeat the following words, focusing on the vowels. Do not worry about the meaning.

peso, piso, puso, pasa, pesa, pisa, misa, mesa, musa, usa, eso, liso, lisa, lupa

B. Line by line, repeat the following children's verse, "Arbolito del Perú" (*Little Tree from Peru*). Focus on the vowel sounds.

> a, e, i, o, u
> Arbolito del Perú.
> Yo me llamo... (*add your name*)
> ¿Cómo te llamas tú?

2 Diphthongs

A diphthong is a combination of two vowels. In Spanish, the possibilities include: **a, e, o + i, u**; or **i + u**; or **u + i**. The consonant **y** also forms a diphthong when it occurs at the end of a word. Diphthongs constitute one unit of sound. Listen to and repeat the following examples. The symbol in brackets represents the sound of the diphthong.

Sound	Spelling	Examples
[ay]	ai/ay	aire, traigo, caray
[ye]	ie	cielo, Diego, siempre
[oy]	oi/oy	oigo, doy, soy
[ew]	eu	euro, Europa, Eugenia
[aw]	au	aula, Paula
[ey]	ei/ey	reina, rey
[yu]	iu	ciudad, viuda
[wy]	ui/uy	cuidado, muy

C. Let's learn to greet people and ask how they are. Repeat the following conversation, paying special attention to the diphthongs.

STUDENT 1: Buenos días. ¿Cómo está?

STUDENT 2: Muy bien gracias. ¿Y usted?

STUDENT 1: Bien, gracias.

3 Consonants

Below you will find general guidelines for pronouncing Spanish consonants. The symbol in brackets represents the sound, followed by a brief explanation of its pronunciation. Listen carefully and repeat the examples. Before you know it, you will be surprised at how proficient you are.

Sound	Spelling	Position	Examples
[b] as in English *boy*	b, v	begins word after *m, n*	bote, vote sombrero, enviar
[ß] a *b* with lips half-open	b, v	other positions	liberal, avaro
[s] as in English *son*	ce, ci z[1]	begins syllable all positions	cero, gracias pez, zapato, retazo
	s	all positions	seta, solo, susto, dos
[k] very similar to English	qu + e, i c + a, o, u	begins syllable begins syllable	queso, quiso saca, cosa, cuna
[d] as in English	d	begins word after *n, l*	doctor, dentista banda, caldo, saldo
[đ] as in *th* in *other*	d	other positions	ido, salud, nado
[h]	j ge, gi	all positions begins syllable	jamás, reloj, ajo gente, gitano, agente

---

[1] In many regions of Spain, the letter *c* before *e* or *i*, and the letter *z* are pronounced like the English *th* in the words *thin, thanks*.

D. Read each sentence on your own. Focus on the hightlighted consonants or consonant-vowel combinations. Then listen to the recorded pronunciation.

b/v	**V**endo **v**einte **v**acas y un **b**urro.
	Un a**v**e li**b**re **v**uela.
c/**que, qui**	**C**ompro **c**ator**c**e **c**ocos y **qui**nce **que**sos.
c/**ce, ci**	**Ci**nco chimpan**c**és **c**ómicos **ce**lebran sus **c**umpleaños.
z/s	La **s**eñorita **s**irve **z**umo de **z**anahorias.
d/d̶	¡**D**octor! ¡Me **d**uele el **d**ed̶o!
j/**ge, gi**	**J**erónimo es **j**oven, á**gi**l e inteli**ge**nte.

More consonants

Repeat the examples.

[y] as in English²	ll, y + *vowel*	begins syllable	llanto, yeso, allí
[g] as in English	g + a, o, u	begins syllable	gato, gusto, gota
	gu + e, i	begins syllable	guitarra, guerra
[gw] rare in English	gu + a, o	begins syllable	agua, antiguo
	gü + e, i	begins syllable	pingüino, averigüe
[r] as in Be*tt*y, E*dd*y	r	middle and end of a word	aro, verdad, bar
[rr] trilled, rolled sound	r + *vowel*	begins word	rifle, rato
	n, s, l + r		enredo, alrededor
	vowel + rr + *vowel*		perro, corro

- The letter **h** is always silent: **hotel, hospital, deshonesto**
- The **ñ** is similar to the *ny* in the word *canyon*: **montaña, cañón, mañana**
- Double **cc** and **x** are pronounced [ks]: **examen, acción**

E. Read each sentence on your own. Focus on the highlighted consonants or consonant-vowel combinations. Then listen to the recorded pronunciation.

ll/y	Un mi**ll**ón de **ll**amas **y**acen en la **ll**anura.
g/**gue, gui**	El **g**urú, el **gue**rrero y el **guí**a son **g**olosos.
g/**güe, güi**	Ana es bilin**güe**.
	El pin**güi**no está en el a**g**ua.
g/**ge, gi**	El **gi**tano es **g**uapo y **ge**neroso.
r/rr	**R**ita co**rr**e por la ca**rr**etera.
	El pirata **r**inde el teso**r**o.
h̶	**H**éctor es un **h**otelero **h**olandés.
h̶/j	**H**ernán es **j**oven.
ñ	Ma**ñ**ana el ni**ñ**o va a las monta**ñ**as y al ca**ñ**ón.

---

² This sound varies in different regions of the Spanish-speaking world.

4 The alphabet

The letters of the alphabet and their names follow. Repeat each letter.

a (a)	j (jota)	r (ere)
b (be)	k (ka)	s (ese)
c (ce)	l (ele)	t (te)
d (de)	m (eme)	u (u)
e (e)	n (ene)	v (ve, uve)
f (efe)	ñ (eñe)	w (doble ve, doble uve)
g (ge)	o (o)	x (equis)
h (hache)	p (pe)	y (i griega)
i (i)	q (cu)	z (zeta)

In the past, three two-letter combinations—**ch** (che), **ll** (elle), **rr** (erre)—were part of the Spanish alphabet. Now they are considered part of the letters **c**, **l**, and **r**.

F. Spell the following words aloud using the Spanish alphabet. Listen for confirmation.

1. general   **3.** señorita   **5.** yo   **7.** examen

2. hotel   **4.** ejercicio   **6.** quince   **8.** voz

5 Accents and stress

Listen carefully and repeat the examples.

- If a word has a written accent mark (called **acento** in Spanish), the accented syllable is stressed.

  ca-**fé**   ma-**má**   **á**-ri-do

- In words without a written accent, the next to the last syllable is stressed if the word ends in a *vowel*, *n*, *or s*.

  pa-tio   re-**su**-men   **gra**-cias

- The last syllable is stressed if the word ends in a *consonant other than n or s*.

  a-ni-**mal**   doc-**tor**   u-ni-ver-si-**dad**

- A stress mark over the **i** or the **u** in a two-vowel combination indicates that both vowels are pronounced separately.

  dí-a   ba-**úl**

G. Pronounce the following words, stressing the correct syllable. Listen for confirmation.

1. pro-fe-sor   **4.** Ma-rí-a   **7.** di-fí-cil

2. den-tis-ta   **5.** di-ná-mi-co   **8.** se-cre-ta-ria

3. pre-si-den-te   **6.** es-pa-ñol   **9.** flo-res

Para empezar: Nuevos encuentros

Goals for communication

- To meet and greet each other
- To state where you are from and learn the origins of others
- To describe yourself and others
- To exchange phone numbers, e-mail addresses, and birthdays
- To tell time

Así se dice

Informal greetings and introductions (used in most first-name basis relationships)

1. Hi, how are you? My name is Linda. What's your name?
2. My name is Manuel.
3. Pepita, I want to introduce you to my friend (*f.*) Natalia.
4. Delighted (*f.*) to meet you. **Encantado** (*m.*).
5. Nice meeting you too.
6. Where are you from?
7. I'm from New Mexico. And you?
8. I'm from Los Angeles.

Formal greetings and introductions (used in most last-name basis relationships)

9. Good morning. My name is Alfonso Lema. What's your name, ma'am?
10. My name is Carmen Sábato.
11. Professor Falcón, I would like to introduce you to my friend (*m.*) Octavio.
12. Pleased to meet you, Octavio.
13. The pleasure is mine.
14. Where are you from, professor?
15. I'm from Colombia. And you?
16. I'm from Mendoza, Argentina.

Práctica y comunicación

A. Nuestros personajes (*Our characters*). In this exercise you will become acquainted with some of the characters whose activities you will follow throughout this text. Answer the questions, referring to the drawing on pages 8-9.

1. ¿Qué dice Linda (*What does Linda say*)? **Linda dice...**
   ¿Qué responde Manuel (*How does Manuel answer*)? **Manuel responde...**
2. ¿Qué dice Javier?
   ¿Qué dice Pepita?
   ¿Qué responde Natalia?
3. ¿De dónde es Natalia? **Es de...** ¿Y Pepita?
4. ¿Qué dice Alfonso?
   ¿Qué responde Carmen?
5. ¿Cómo se llama la profesora (*What is the professor's name*)? **Se llama...**
6. ¿Qué dice Inés?
   ¿Qué dice la profesora Falcón?
   ¿Qué responde Octavio?
7. ¿De dónde es la profesora? ¿Y Octavio?

B. Las presentaciones. Move about the classroom introducing yourself and learning the names of at least five of your classmates and your instructor.

1. With your classmates, use the expressions **Hola, me llamo...**, **¿Cómo te llamas?**, and **Encantado** (*said by males*)/**Encantada** (*said by females*). Shake hands as you say that you are delighted to meet him or her.
2. With your instructor, use the expressions **Buenos días, Me llamo...**, **¿Cómo se llama usted?**, and **Mucho gusto**. Shake hands as you say that you are pleased to meet him or her.

Can you identify your classmates? Respond as your instructor indicates various students and asks their names.

> **Modelo:** ¿Cómo se llama?
> **Se llama Kevin.**

C. Más presentaciones. Now, moving about the classroom, introduce your partner to several classmates and to the instructor.

> **Modelo:** (*A classmate's name*), te presento a mi amigo/a (*partner's name*).
> Profesor/a..., le presento a mi amigo/a (*partner's name*).

Each party should respond to the introduction appropriately.

D. ¿De dónde eres? Move about the classroom learning the origin of at least five of your classmates and your instructor. Use the informal question (**¿De dónde eres?**) with your classmates and the formal question (**¿De dónde es usted?**) with your instructor. Write down the information. Once you have finished, your instructor will ask you where some of your classmates are from.

> **Modelo:** ¿De dónde es...?
> Es de...

Turn in the information you have gathered for possible inclusion in the Class Directory.

Los cognados

> Me llamo Pepita. Soy dinámica, atlética y extrovertida. Ah... y soy muy puntual.

Cognates are words that are identical or similar in two languages and have the same meaning. Repeat the following cognates, imitating your instructor's pronunciation.

Adjectives that may be used to describe males or females:

admirable	flexible	materialista	rebelde
arrogante	independiente	optimista	responsable
conformista	inteligente	paciente	sentimental
eficiente	irresponsable	pesimista	terrible
egoísta	liberal	puntual	tolerante

Adjectives that change **-o** to **-a** when referring to a female:

ambicioso/a	dinámico/a	introvertido/a	religioso/a
atlético/a	extrovertido/a	modesto/a	romántico/a
cómico/a	generoso/a	organizado/a	serio/a
creativo/a	impulsivo/a	práctico/a	tranquilo/a

To describe more than one person, add **-s** to adjectives that end in a vowel and **-es** to those ending in a consonant (admirable ➔ admirable**s**; sentimental ➔ sentimental**es**).

Estructuras

Identifying and describing people: Subject pronouns and the verb *ser*

Natalia y yo somos amigas.

Me llamo Natalia. Soy estudiante y soy de Nuevo México. Soy responsable, generosa y muy independiente.

You have just used some forms of the verb **ser** (*to be*) in the previous section (**¿De dónde *es* usted? ¿De dónde *eres*? *Soy* de...**). Now observe the subject pronouns and the other forms of **ser**.

Subject pronouns	**ser** *to be*
yo (*I*)	**Soy** estudiante.
tú (*you, singular informal*)	**Eres** inteligente.
él (*he*)	**Es** profesor.
ella (*she*)	**Es** profesora.
usted[1] (*you, singular formal*)	**Es** de Bolivia.
nosotros/as (*we*)	**Somos** estudiantes.
vosotros/as (*you, plural informal*)	**Sois** inteligentes.
ustedes[1] (*you, plural*)	**Son** profesores.
ellos (*they, masculine*)	**Son** de Panamá.
ellas (*they, feminine*)	**Son** dinámicas.

- **Vosotros/as** is used only in Spain. **Ustedes** is formal in Spain but both formal and informal in Hispanic America.

- Use Spanish subject pronouns only *to emphasize, to contrast,* or *to clarify.* Otherwise avoid them, since Spanish verbs indicate the subject.

Yo soy de Cuba y **él** es de Chile.	*I am from Cuba and **he** is from Chile.*
Somos estudiantes.	*We are students.*

- Use the verb **ser** to tell who a person is, where a person is from, and what a person is like.

Natalia **es** estudiante.	*Natalia is a student.*
Es de Nuevo México.	*She is from New Mexico.*
Es muy independiente.	*She is very independent.*

---

[1] **Usted** and **ustedes** may be abbreviated to **Ud.** and **Uds.**, respectively.

Práctica y comunicación

E. Personas famosas. Using the information provided, tell about the persons in the photos. Include descriptive adjectives from the following list.

atlético/a	creativo/a	famoso/a	popular
bello/a (*beautiful*)	dinámico/a	fuerte (*strong*)	romántico/a

Modelo: Salma Hayek / actriz / México
Salma Hayek es actriz, es de México y es muy (*very*) **dinámica.**

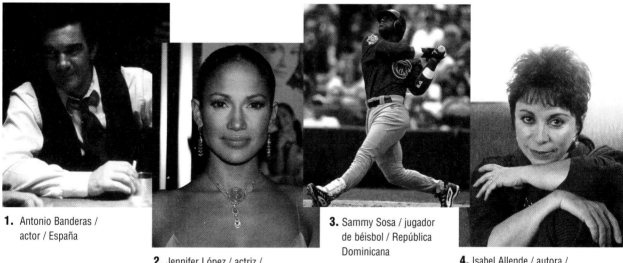

1. Antonio Banderas / actor / España

2. Jennifer López / actriz / Estados Unidos

3. Sammy Sosa / jugador de béisbol / República Dominicana

4. Isabel Allende / autora / Chile

Now name another famous person and state what he/she does, where he/she is from, and what he/she is like.

To make a negative statement, place **no** before the verb.
No soy estudiante.   *I am not a student.*

In answering yes/no questions, repeat the **no**.

¿Es usted pesimista?[2]   *Are you a pessimist?*
¡**No, no** soy pesimista![2]   *No, I'm not a pessimist!*
¡Soy optimista!   *I'm an optimist!*

---

[2] Spanish uses an upside-down question mark at the beginning of a question and an upside-down exclamation point to mark the beginning of an exclamation. ¿? = **signos de interrogación**; ¡! = **signos de exclamación.**

2 **F. Mi personalidad.** Ask each other yes/no questions to determine personality traits. Use the cognates on page 11. Remember traits that you have in common, as you will need them for Exercise G.

> **Modelo:** (*to a male*) ¿Eres (muy) romántico?
>
> Sí, soy muy romántico. *o* (*or*)
>
> No, no soy (muy) romántico. ¿Y tú?
>
> (*female responds*) Sí, soy (muy) romántica. *o*
>
> No, no soy (muy) romántica.

2 **G. ¿Algo en común (*Something in common*)?** Tell the class one difference between you and your classmate and two things you have in common. Remember to add **-s** or **-es** to the adjective to make it plural.

> **Modelo:** (*Partner's name*) es... y yo soy...
>
> Él/Ella y yo somos... y...

H. Mi amigo/a. Walking around the classroom, introduce your classmate to three other students. Tell her/his name, origin, and two personality traits.

> **Modelo:** Mi amigo/a se llama... *o* Te presento a mi amigo/a...
>
> Es de...
>
> Es... y...

Así se dice

Greetings and expressions of well-being and farewell

Examine the following two conversations. The first introduces certain formal greetings (**los saludos**) and expressions of well-being (**el bienestar**). The second presents their informal equivalents, as well as expressions of farewell (**las despedidas**). Expressions in parentheses are possible alternatives (for example, *Good morning* vs. *Good afternoon*).

Formal

EL PROF. RUIZ:	Buenos días, señorita.	*Good morning, Miss.*
	(Buenas tardes, señora.)	*(Good afternoon, Ma'am.)*
	(Buenas noches, señor.)	*(Good evening, Sir.)*
SUSANA:	Buenos días. ¿Cómo está usted?	*Good morning. How are you?*
EL PROF. RUIZ:	Muy bien, gracias. ¿Y usted?	*Very well, thanks. And you?*
SUSANA:	Bien, gracias.	*Fine, thanks.*

Informal

LUIS:	¡Hola!	*Hello!/Hi!*
OLGA:	¡Hola! ¿Cómo estás? (¿Qué tal?)	*How are you? (How's it going?)*
LUIS:	Fenomenal. ¿Y tú?	*Terrific. And you?*
OLGA:	Regular.	*Okay./So-so.*
LUIS:	¿Qué pasa? (¿Qué hay de nuevo?)	*What's happening? (What's new?)*
OLGA:	Pues nada. Voy a la clase de historia.	*Not much. I'm going to history class.*
LUIS:	Bueno (Pues), hasta luego. (Hasta mañana.) (Hasta pronto.) (Chao.)	*Well, see you later. (See you tomorrow.) (See you soon.) (Bye./So long.)*
OLGA:	Adiós.	*Good-bye.*

> You may have noticed that Spanish has two verbs expressing *to be*:
>
> **ser → Soy** de México. **estar → ** ¿Cómo **está** usted?
>
> You will study **estar** and the differences between **ser** and **estar** in later chapters.

Práctica y comunicación

 I. ¿Cómo estás? Practice the formal and informal conversations presented above. Read expressively! Use some of the alternate expressions in parentheses where appropriate. When you conclude each conversation, switch roles.

J. ¿Cómo contestas (*How do you answer*)? Your instructor arrives on the first day of class. Give an appropriate response to each of her/his greetings or inquiries.

1. Buenos días, señorita/ señora/ señor.
2. ¿Cómo está usted?
3. ¿Cómo se llama usted?
4. ¿De dónde es usted?
5. Le presento a...
6. Hasta luego.

(continued)

A student from Bolivia joins your group. Respond appropriately to each of her/his greetings or inquiries.

7. ¡Hola!

8. ¿Qué tal?

9. ¿Cómo te llamas?

10. ¿De dónde eres?

11. Te presento a...

12. ¿Qué pasa?

13. Hasta pronto.

Can you guess what the note cards say? **¿Cómo te va? Una nota para ti. Con amor.** Which cards would you like to purchase?

Expressions of courtesy

Con permiso.	*Pardon me, excuse me. (to seek permission to pass by someone or to leave)*
Perdón/ Disculpe.	*Pardon me, excuse me. (to get someone's attention or to seek forgiveness)*
Por favor.	*Please.*
Lo siento (mucho).	*I'm (so/very) sorry.*
(Muchas) Gracias.	*Thank you (very much).*
De nada.	*You're welcome.*

Práctica y comunicación

K. ¡Son muy corteses! Determine what expression of courtesy each character should be saying in the following situations.

1. El profesor Marín-Vivar a Natalia y Alfonso

2. Rubén a Camila

3. Esteban a Inés y Pepita

4. Linda a Manuel / Manuel a Linda

L. Soy muy cortés. Moving around the classroom, perform each of the following tasks. Use the correct expression.

1. Walk in front of someone and excuse yourself.
2. Lightly bump into someone and seek his/her forgiveness.
3. Get someone's attention and ask the person how you say *please* in Spanish (**¿Cómo se dice… en español?**).
4. Give a classmate something of yours, saying **Para ti** (*For you*). Expect a thanks and say *You're welcome.*
5. Get someone's attention and ask the person his/her name and where he/she is from.

M. Situaciones. Imagine that you find yourself in the following situations. What might you say? With a classmate, create a conversation appropriate to each setting. Begin with an expression of courtesy (**Perdón…**) and/or a greeting, and end with good-bye.

1. At the university, you and a friend converse. **¡Hola!**…
2. At a conference in Mexico City, you and a colleague converse. It's 9:00 A.M.
3. At the university, you want to meet (get to know) professor García. It's 4:00 P.M.
4. You're at a party and want to meet Jaime, a student from Peru. It's 10:00 P.M.

N. Conociéndonos (*Getting to know each other*). Write a dialog that takes place between yourself and a person your age that you want to get to know. Begin with a greeting and end with good-bye.

Noticias culturales

among

Los saludos entre° hispanos

Los saludos son muy importantes en la cultura hispana. Generalmente las personas se saludan° con contacto físico y hay° diversas maneras de saludarse:

among

se... greet one another / there are

shake hands

Es muy común **darse la mano°**.

women
man
to give each other a soft kiss on the cheek

Entre las mujeres°, o entre un hombre° y una mujer, es usual **darse un beso suave en la mejilla°**.

even
to hug each other
little pats on the back

Entre amigos, y aun° entre hombres, también es común **darse un abrazo°** y **palmaditas en la espalda°**.

¿Qué recuerda (*What do you remember*)? Indicate if the statements are true (**cierto**) or false (**falso**). If the information is false, provide the correct information.

1. Los saludos son muy importantes en la cultura hispana.
2. Por lo general, los hombres se saludan con un beso suave en la mejilla.
3. Las mujeres se dan palmaditas en la espalda.
4. Los hispanos se dan la mano.

2 Dramatize as appropriate the following: **darse la mano, darse un abrazo, darse palmaditas en la espalda, darse un beso suave en la mejilla.** Accompany each physical expression with appropriate verbal greetings and questions.

B	I	N	G	O		
0 cero	1 uno	2 dos	3 tres	4 cuatro	5 cinco	6 seis
7 siete	8 ocho	9 nueve	10 diez	11 once	12 doce	13 trece
14 catorce	15 quince	16 dieciséis	17 diecisiete	18 dieciocho	19 diecinueve	20 veinte
21 veintiuno	22 veintidós	30 treinta	31 treinta y uno	32 treinta y dos	40 cuarenta	50 cincuenta
60 sesenta	70 setenta	80 ochenta	90 noventa...	99 noventa y nueve		

- **Uno** is used for counting. When **uno** modifies a masculine noun, use **un**. When it modifies a feminine noun, use **una**. The same holds true for **veintiuno**, **treinta y uno**, and so on.

  Un profesor es de Nuevo México.
  One professor (m.) is from New Mexico.

  Una profesora y **veintiún** estudiantes son de Tejas.
  *One professor (f.) and **twenty-one** students are from Texas.*

- The numbers from 16 to 29 are usually written as one word. Those from 31 on are written as three words. Note the numbers that carry accent marks: **dieciséis, veintidós, veintitrés, veintiséis.**

Práctica y comunicación

2 **O. Una rima.** Repeat the following children's verse several times, then recite it to a classmate.

Dos y dos son cuatro,
cuatro y dos son seis,
seis y dos son ocho,
y ocho dieciséis.

Palabras útiles	
y	+
menos	−
son	=

2 **P. Las matemáticas.** Read the following math problems aloud. Then give the answer.

1. 9 + 5 =   **7.** 31 + 18 =

2. 7 + 4 =   **8.** 40 + 10 =

3. 8 + 7 =   **9.** 60 – 9 =

4. 6 + 6 =   **10.** 80 – 14 =

5. 15 + 13 =   **11.** 99 – 12 =

6. 17 + 16 =   **12.** 50 + 20 =

5 **Q. Mi nombre (*name*) y mi número de teléfono.** Ask for and give each other your names and phone numbers. If necessary, confirm the spelling of names using the Spanish alphabet. In Spanish, the digits of phone numbers are usually given in pairs: 4-86-05-72. Write the information accurately, as it will be used later to form a Class Directory.

> **Modelo:**
> Estudiante 1: ¿Cómo te llamas?
> Estudiante 2: Me llamo...
> Estudiante 1: ¿Cuál es tu (*your*) número de teléfono?
> Estudiante 2: Es el cuatro ochenta y seis cero cinco setenta y dos.

Respond as your instructor asks for the phone numbers of certain students.

> **Modelo:**
> ¿Cuál es el número de teléfono de...?
> Es el...

5 **R. Mi dirección electrónica (*e-mail address*).** Remain in your groups. Ask for and give each other your e-mail addresses, using the Spanish alphabet. Write the information carefully for later inclusion in the Class Directory.

> **Modelo:** ¿Cuál es tu dirección electrónica?
> Es monica3@dicho.com.

One student from each group turns in the information from Exercises Q and R to the instructor for later inclusion in the Class Directory.

Palabras útiles

@ = arroba

. = punto

Indicating days of the week

¡Ay de mí! ¡Es lunes!

¿Qué día es hoy?

JUNIO

lunes[3]	martes	miércoles	jueves	viernes	sábado	domingo
					1	2
3	4	5	6	7	8	9
10	11	12	13	14	LA 15	London 16
England 17	Paris 18	Amsterdam 19 Berlin 20	LA 21		22	23
24	25	26	27	28	29	30

└─ el **día** ─┘   └─ el **fin de semana** ─┘
└────────────────── la **semana** ──────────────────┘

- The days of the week are not capitalized in Spanish.
- With the day of the week, the definite article **el** (singular) or **los** (plural) is used to indicate *on.*

  El sábado vamos a una gran fiesta. *On Saturday we are going to a big party.*
  Los miércoles vamos al gimnasio. *On Wednesdays we go to the gym.*

- The plural of **el sábado** and **el domingo** is **los sábados** and **los domingos**. The other days use the same form in the singular and in the plural:

  el lunes → los lunes.

---

[3] In Hispanic calendars, the week usually begins on Monday.

Práctica y comunicación

S. El mes de junio. Look at the calendar on page 21 and as your instructor calls out the day of the month, indicate on what day of the week it falls.

> **Modelo:** Es el catorce de junio. ¿Qué día es?
> Es viernes.

2 Following the same pattern, practice the numbers and days of the week in pairs.

T. ¿Qué día es? Complete the statements with the appropriate day/s.

1. ¿Qué día es hoy? Hoy es...
2. Pasado mañana es...
3. Los días preferidos de los estudiantes son...
4. El peor (*worst*) día para los estudiantes es...
5. En los Estados Unidos, el peor día para los supersticiosos es el... 13.
6. Un día bueno para hacer fiestas es...
7. Un día bueno para ir (*to go*) a la iglesia (*church*)/ sinagoga es...
8. La clase de español es...
9. Mi (*My*) día favorito es...

Indicating months, dates, and birthdays

¿Cuál es la fecha de hoy? ¿Qué fecha es hoy? (*What's today's date?*)

- To express what day of the month it is, use cardinal numbers (**dos**, **tres**, **cuatro,**...). In Latin America, the first of the month is always expressed with **el primero**. In Spain **el uno** is used.

    Hoy es (el)[4] cuatro de julio.
    Mañana es (el) primero de abril. (Latin America)
    Mañana es el uno de abril. (Spain)

---

[4] The word **el** is optional.

- To express the month in a date, use **de** before the month. Months are not generally capitalized in Spanish.

  el **25 de** diciembre   el cinco **de** mayo

- When dates are given in numbers, the day precedes the month.

  4/7 = **el cuatro de julio**

ENERO	200_	FEBRERO	200_	MARZO	200_	ABRIL	200_

ENERO 200_
L M M J V S D
1 2 3 4 5 6
7 8 9 10 11 12 13
14 15 16 17 18 19 20
21 22 23 24 25 26 27
28 29 30 31

FEBRERO 200_
L M M J V S D
1 2 3
4 5 6 7 8 9 10
11 12 13 14 15 16 17
18 19 20 21 22 23 24
25 26 27 28

MARZO 200_
L M M J V S D
1 2 3
4 5 6 7 8 9 10
11 12 13 14 15 16 17
18 19 20 21 22 23 24
25 26 27 28 29 30 31

ABRIL 200_
L M M J V S D
1 2 3 4 5 6 7
8 9 10 11 12 13 14
15 16 17 18 19 20 21
22 23 24 25 26 27 28
29 30 31

MAYO 200_
L M M J V S D
1 2 3 4 5
6 7 8 9 10 11 12
13 14 15 16 17 18 19
20 21 22 23 24 25 26
27 28 29 30 31

JUNIO 200_
L M M J V S D
1 2
3 4 5 6 7 8 9
10 11 12 13 14 15 16
17 18 19 20 21 22 23
24 25 26 27 28 29 30

JULIO 200_
L M M J V S D
1 2 3 4 5 6 7
8 9 10 11 12 13 14
15 16 17 18 19 20 21
22 23 24 25 26 27 28
29 30 31

AGOSTO 200_
L M M J V S D
1 2 3 4
5 6 7 8 9 10 11
12 13 14 15 16 17 18
19 20 21 22 23 24 25
26 27 28 29 30 31

SEPTIEMBRE 200_
L M M J V S D
1
2 3 4 5 6 7 8
9 10 11 12 13 14 15
16 17 18 19 20 21 22
23 24 25 26 27 28 29
30

OCTUBRE 200_
L M M J V S D
1 2 3 4 5 6
7 8 9 10 11 12 13
14 15 16 17 18 19 20
21 22 23 24 25 26 27
28 29 30 31

NOVIEMBRE 200_
L M M J V S D
1 2 3
4 5 6 7 8 9 10
11 12 13 14 15 16 17
18 19 20 21 22 23 24
25 26 27 28 29 30 31

DICIEMBRE 200_
L M M J V S D
1
2 3 4 5 6 7 8
9 10 11 12 13 14 15
16 17 18 19 20 21 22
23 24 25 26 27 28 29
30 31

Práctica y comunicación

2 **U. Los meses y las fechas.** With the help of a classmate, first identify the month of the following celebrations.

Modelo: El Día de Acción de Gracias es en noviembre.

1. el Día de Acción de Gracias (*Thanksgiving*)
2. la Navidad (*Christmas*)
3. el Año Nuevo (*New Year's Day*)
4. el Día de los Reyes Magos[5]
5. el Día de los Enamorados (*Valentine's Day*)
6. el Día de San Patricio
7. el Día de los Inocentes[6] (en los Estados Unidos, *equivalent of April Fools' Day*)
8. el Día de la Madre (*Mother's Day*)
9. el Día del Padre
10. el Día de la Independencia de los Estados Unidos
11. el Día del Trabajo (*Labor Day*) en los Estados Unidos

For how many of the above holidays can you give the date? **La Navidad es el... de...**

---

[5] The religious celebration of the Epiphany, honoring the visit of the Three Wise Men. In the Hispanic world the Magi bring gifts to the children on this day.

[6] Celebrated on December 28 in Hispanic countries, it commemorates King Herod's slaughter of the innocent children of Bethlehem.

V. Los cumpleaños. Ask each other the dates of your birthdays. Write down names and dates. Have one person from each group turn in the list of birthdays to the instructor.

> **Modelo:** Estudiante 1: **¿Cuándo es tu (*your*) cumpleaños?**
>
> Estudiante 2: **Mi cumpleaños es el ocho de octubre.**

Answer your instructor's questions.

1. ¿Cuándo es el cumpleaños de...? ¿Y de...?
2. ¿Cuándo es el cumpleaños de la profesora/del profesor? (*Guess it!*)

¡Dicho y hecho! Now it is time for the person in charge of compiling the Class Directory to finalize it and distribute it to the class. Be sure to include names, telephone numbers, e-mail addresses, birthdays, and origins.

In most Hispanic countries it is common to celebrate your birthday and your saint's day (based on the Catholic tradition). If your parents give you the name of the saint honored on the day of your birth, then your birthday and your saint's day are one and the same. If they give you the name of a saint honored on a different day of the year, you have two celebrations! Observe the names of the saints on the January calendar.

ENERO

LUNES MONDAY	MARTES TUESDAY	MIÉRCOLES WEDNESDAY	JUEVES THURSDAY	VIERNES FRIDAY	SÁBADO SATURDAY	DOMINGO SUNDAY
◯ LUNA LLENA FULL MOON 1st-31st ~ DIA 1-31	◑ C. MENGUANTE LAST QUARTER 9th ~ DIA 9	◯ LUNA NUEVA NEW MOON 17th ~ DIA 17	◐ C. CRECIENTE FIRST QUARTER 24th ~ DIA 24	**1** LA CIRCUNCISION NEW YEAR'S DAY	**2** SAN BASILIO M.	**3** S. ANTERO PAPA
4 SAN PRISCO	**5** S. TELESFORO	**6** LOS S. REYES EPIPHANY	**7** SAN RAYMUNDO	**8** SAN APOLINAR	**9** SAN MARCELINO	**10** SAN GONZALO
11 S.HIGINIO PAPA	**12** S. ARCADIO M.	**13** S. HILARIO OB.	**14** SAN FELIX M.	**15** S. MAURO ABAD ADULT'S DAY	**16** SAN MARCELO	**17** S. ANTONIO ABAD
18 STA. PRISCA V. MARTIN L. KING DAY (US)	**19** SAN MARIO (EID) AL FITR (END OF RAMADAN)	**20** SAN FABIAN	**21** SAN FRUCTUOSO	**22** SAN VICENTE M.	**23** SAN ALBERTO	**24** SAN FRANCISCO DE S.
25 STA. ELVIRA V.	**26** S. TIMOTEO OB.	**27** STA. ANGELA V.	**28** STO. TOMAS DE A.	**29** SAN VALERIO	**30** STA. MARTINA	**31** S. JUAN BOSCO

If your friend's name is Ángela, what is her saint's day? What about Elvira/ Alberto/ Martina/ Tomás? Can you find a saint's day that corresponds to someone you know? Share the date with the class.

Telling time

- When you want to know what time it is, ask **¿Qué hora es?** For telling time on the hour, use **es** for *one o'clock* only. Use **son** for all other times.

Es la una.

Son las ocho.

- To state the number of minutes past the hour, say the name of that hour plus (**y**) the number of minutes.

Es la una **y** diez.   Son las cuatro **y** cuarto.   Son las diez **y** media.   Son las once **y** cuarenta.[7]

Son las cuatro **y** quince.   Son las diez **y** treinta.

- To state the number of minutes before the coming hour, give the next hour less (**menos**) the number of minutes to go before that hour.

Es la una **menos** diez.   Son las nueve **menos** veinticinco.

- To differentiate between hours in the morning, afternoon, and evening, use the following expressions.

de la mañana   de la tarde[8]   de la noche

For 12:00 noon use: For 12:00 midnight use:

Es mediodía.   **Es medianoche.**

---

[7] In Spanish, trends in telling time have been affected by the popularity of digital watches and clocks. This presentation on telling time reflects these changes.

[8] In most Spanish-speaking countries, **tarde** is used while there is still daylight, and thus may extend until 7:00 P.M. or even 8:00 PM.

Práctica y comunicación

W. ¿Qué hora es? First your instructor will tell the time on each clock in random order. Identify the clock that tells the given time.

> **Modelo:** Son las ocho y media de la mañana.
> **Reloj** (*Clock*) 3.

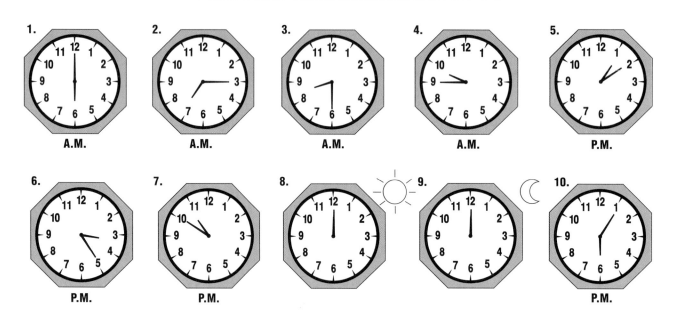

2 Now practice telling each other the time on each of the clocks. Where applicable, say each time as many ways as you can.

X. El mundo (*The world*). Times on the map on page 27 are given according to the 24-hour clock, often used for transportation schedules, TV and movie times, class schedules, etc.[9]

Tell what time it is in the cities that follow, according to the information on the map.

> **Modelo:** ¿Qué hora es en Tokio?
> **Son las 22 horas.** *o* **Son las 10:00 de la noche.**

1. ¿Qué hora es en Toronto, Canadá?
2. ¿Qué hora es en Los Ángeles, California? ¿Y en Nueva York?
3. ¿Qué hora es en Buenos Aires, Argentina? ¿Y en Madrid, España?
4. ¿Qué hora es en Moscú, Rusia? ¿Y en Beijing, China?

---

[9] To convert from the 24-hour clock to a 12-hour clock, subtract 12. For example: 14:00 minus 12 equals 2:00 P.M. All A.M. times are the same in both systems.

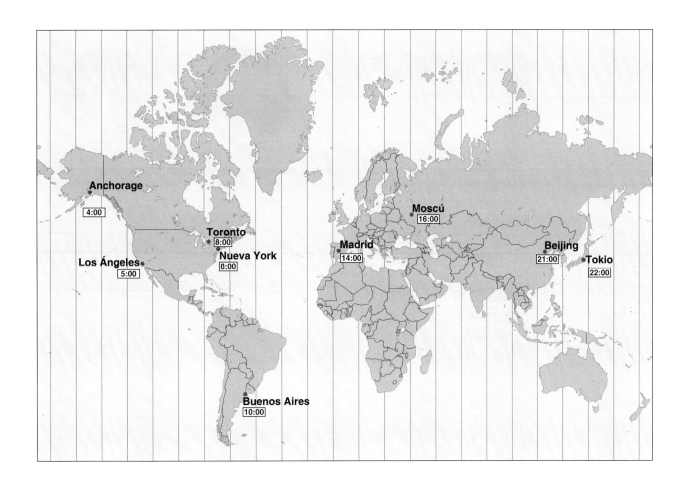

Nationalities of the Hispanic world

Soy española.

Y yo soy argentino.

Following (on pages 28–29) are the nationalities of the Spanish-speaking world, including the United States, where soon about 20 percent of the population will be of Hispanic origin. Pay attention to the first three examples and fill in the blanks. Your instructor will help you.

Las nacionalidades

País	masculino	femenino
Argentina	argentino	argentina
Bolivia	boliviano	boliviana
Chile	chileno	chilena
Colombia	colombiano	_____
Cuba	_____	cubana
La República Dominicana	dominicano	_____
Ecuador	_____	ecuatoriana
Guatemala	guatemalteco	_____
Guinea Ecuatorial	guineano	_____
Honduras	_____	hondureña
México	mexicano[10]	_____
Panamá	_____	panameña
Paraguay	paraguayo	_____
Perú	_____	peruana
Puerto Rico	puertorriqueño	_____
El Salvador	_____	salvadoreña
Uruguay	uruguayo	_____
Venezuela	_____	venezolana

---

[10] In modern Spanish, the letter **x** in **mexicano/México** is pronounced like a Spanish **j**.

España	español	española
Costa Rica	costarricense	costarricense
Nicaragua	nicaragüense	nicaragüense
Estados Unidos [EE.UU]	estadounidense[11]	estadounidense

For a complete listing of nationalities from around the world, see **Apéndice 3**, page A-14.

> You have discovered that in Spanish, feminine nationalities are usually indicated by a final **a**, and the masculine forms by **o**. When the masculine form ends in a consonant, add **-a** to form the feminine (**español → española**). Also notice that nationalities that end in **-e** do not change.

Práctica y comunicación

Y. Las nacionalidades. Read aloud the statements that indicate the country where each person is from. Then give the nationality.

> **Modelo:** La artista Frida Kahlo es de México.
> **Es mexicana.**

1. El cantante Marc Anthony es de Puerto Rico.
2. El ganador (*winner*) del Premio Nobel de la Paz, Óscar Arias, es de Costa Rica.
3. La cantante Shakira es de Colombia.
4. La actriz Jennifer López es de los Estados Unidos.
5. El rey (*king*) Juan Carlos es de España.
6. La actriz Penélope Cruz es de España.
7. La presidenta Mireya Moscoso es de Panamá.
8. El escritor Gabriel García Márquez es de Colombia.
9. El jugador de fútbol Enzo Francescoli es de Uruguay.
10. La activista Elvia Alvarado es de Honduras.

---

[11] Although in Spanish the nationality of a person from the United States is officially **estadounidense**, in colloquial Spanish **americano/a** is often used, and may refer to anyone who lives in the New World.

Since you have already encountered the following vocabulary words throughout the chapter, English translations do not appear here. Test your knowledge of the following expressions.

Saludos y expresiones comunes

Buenos días, señorita/ señora/ señor.
Buenas tardes.
Buenas noches.
¡Hola!
¿Cómo está usted? ¿Cómo estás?
¿Qué tal?
Muy bien, gracias.
Fenomenal.
Regular.
¿Qué pasa?
¿Qué hay de nuevo?
Pues nada.
Le presento a… (*formal*)
Te presento a… (*informal*)
Mucho gusto.
Encantado/a.
Igualmente.
El gusto es mío.
¿Cómo se llama usted? ¿Cómo te llamas?
Me llamo…
¿De dónde es usted? ¿De dónde eres?
Soy de…
Perdón./ Disculpe.
Lo siento (mucho).
Con permiso.
Por favor.
(Muchas) gracias.
De nada.
Adiós.
Hasta luego.
Hasta pronto.
Hasta mañana.
Chao.

Verbo

ser

Nacionalidades del mundo hispano

argentino/a
boliviano/a
chileno/a
colombiano/a
costarricense
cubano/a
dominicano/a
ecuatoriano/a
español/española
estadounidense
guatemalteco/a
guineano/a
hondureño/a
mexicano/a
nicaragüense
panameño/a
paraguayo/a
peruano/a
puertorriqueño/a
salvadoreño/a
uruguayo/a
venezolano/a

Los días de la semana

lunes
martes
miércoles
jueves
viernes
sábado
domingo

¿Qué día es hoy?
el día
la semana
el fin de semana

Los meses

enero
febrero
marzo
abril
mayo
junio
julio
agosto
septiembre
octubre
noviembre
diciembre

¿Cuál es la fecha de hoy?/ ¿Qué fecha es hoy?

¿Qué hora es?

la hora
y/ menos
cuarto/ media
de la mañana/ tarde/ noche
Es mediodía/ medianoche.

I. Meeting and greeting each other. Complete the conversations. In some cases, there is more than one possible answer.

1. PROFESORA: Buenos días. ¿Cómo está usted?

   PEPITA: _____. ¿Y usted?

   PROFESORA: _____.

2. PROFESORA: ¿_____?

   PEPITA: Me llamo Pepita.

3. CARMEN: ¡Hola, Pepita! ¿_____?

   PEPITA: Regular. ¿Y tú?

   CARMEN: _____.

4. PEPITA: Profesora, le presento a Carmen Martínez.

   PROFESORA: _____.

   CARMEN: _____.

5. PEPITA: ¿Cómo te llamas?

   MANUEL: _____. ¿Y tú?

   PEPITA: _____.

   MANUEL: Encantado, Pepita.

   PEPITA: _____.

6. CARMEN: ¿_____?

   PEPITA: Son las 9:30.

   CARMEN: Pues, tengo una clase ahora. Hasta luego.

   PEPITA: _____.

II. Subject pronouns and the verb *ser*. Tell where the people are from. Write sentences using the correct form of the verb **ser**.

> **Modelo:**   yo / de México; ella / de Panamá
> **Yo soy de México pero (*but*) ella es de Panamá.**

1. ellos / de Chile; nosotras / de México
2. tú / de Colombia; ustedes / de España
3. Luis / de El Salvador; Juan y Elena / de Honduras

III. Counting from 0 to 99. Tell how much each item costs. Write out the numbers ($ = **dólar/ dólares**).

1. los jeans $35.00
2. el suéter $57.00
3. la chaqueta $72.00
4. el sombrero $26.00
5. el video $15.00
6. el CD $9.00

IV. The days of the week. Complete the sentences.

1. Vamos (*We go*) a la clase de español los _____,

   _____ _____, _____ _____…

2. Muchos estudiantes van (*go*) a fiestas_____

   _____ y _____ _____.

V. Indicating dates. Write the dates in Spanish. Include only the day and the month.

> **Modelo:**   2/1/04 (día/mes/año)
> **Es el dos de enero.**

1. 14/2/01
2. 1/4/02
3. 4/7/03
4. 23/11/04
5. 25/12/05

VI. Telling time. What time is it?

> **Modelo:**   1:10 P.M.
> **Es la una y diez de la tarde.**

1. 1:15 P.M. (*Give two ways.*)
2. 9:30 P.M. (*Give two ways.*)
3. 5:50 A.M. (*Give two ways.*)
4. 11:40 P.M. (*Give two ways.*)
5. 12:00 P.M.

VII. Nationalities. Indicate the nationality.

> **Modelo:**   Marta es de San José.
> **Es costarricense.**

1. Aurora es de Madrid.
2. Eduardo es de Washington, D.C.
3. Dulcinea es de la Habana.
4. Claudia es de Buenos Aires.
5. Ricardo es de San Salvador.

VIII. General review. Answer the questions in complete sentences.

1. ¿Cómo se llama usted?
2. ¿Es usted inflexible y arrogante? ¿Es usted responsable y generoso/a?
3. ¿Cómo está usted?
4. ¿De dónde es usted?
5. ¿De qué nacionalidad es usted?
6. ¿Cuál es la fecha de su cumpleaños?
7. ¿Qué día es hoy?
8. ¿Qué hora es?

Answers to the *Autoprueba y repaso* are found in **Apéndice 2**.

La vida universitaria

Goals for communication

- To talk about computers, the language lab, and the "smart" classroom
- To talk about where you are going on campus
- To talk about your class schedule
- To talk about activities related to university life

Así se dice

La vida universitaria

1. En el laboratorio
2. la impresora
3. imprimir
4. el trabajo escrito
5. la hoja de papel
6. la papelera

Alfonso

7. los audífonos
8. escuchar
9. el disco compacto/ el CD

Carmen

10. navegar por la red
11. buscar información
12. la página web, el sitio web
13. el ratón

Natalia

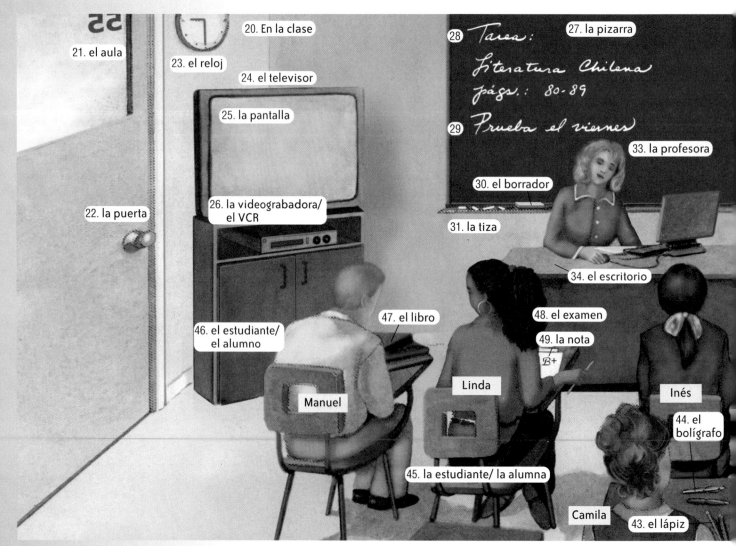

20. En la clase
21. el aula
22. la puerta
23. el reloj
24. el televisor
25. la pantalla
26. la videograbadora/ el VCR
27. la pizarra
28. Tarea: Literatura Chilena págs.: 80-89
29. Prueba el viernes
30. el borrador
31. la tiza
33. la profesora
34. el escritorio
46. el estudiante/ el alumno
47. el libro
48. el examen
49. la nota
44. el bolígrafo
45. la estudiante/ la alumna
43. el lápiz

Manuel

Linda

Inés

Camila

14. usar

15. la computadora

16. el teclado

Javier

17. el correo electrónico

18. la dirección electrónica

19. mandar un mensaje electrónico

Pepita

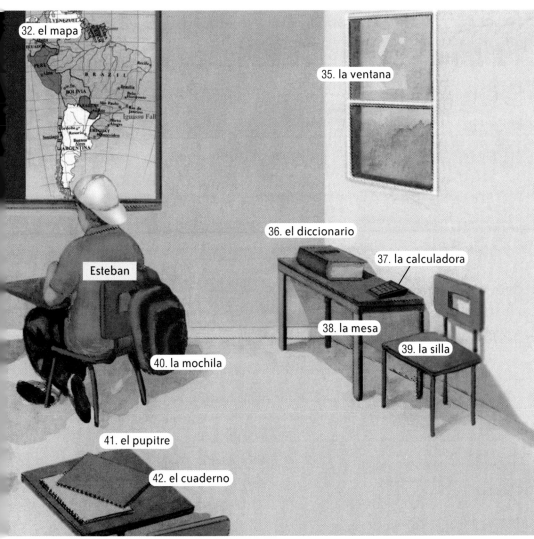

32. el mapa

35. la ventana

36. el diccionario

37. la calculadora

Esteban

38. la mesa

39. la silla

40. la mochila

41. el pupitre

42. el cuaderno

1. In the laboratory
2. printer
3. to print
4. term paper, academic paper
5. sheet of paper
6. wastebasket
7. headphones
8. to listen to
9. CD
10. to explore (surf) the Web
11. to look for information
12. Web page, Web site
13. mouse
14. to use
15. computer
16. keyboard
17. e-mail
18. e-mail address
19. to send an e-mail
20. In class
21. classroom
22. door
23. clock
24. television set
25. screen
26. VCR
27. chalkboard
28. homework, assignment, task
29. quiz
30. eraser
31. chalk
32. map (*m.*)
33. professor (*f.*); **el profesor** (*m.*)
34. (teacher's) desk
35. window
36. dictionary
37. calculator
38. table
39. chair
40. backpack
41. classroom desk
42. notebook
43. pencil; **los lápices** (*pl.*)
44. ballpoint pen
45. student (*f.*)
46. student (*m.*)
47. book
48. exam
49. grade, score

Práctica y comunicación

1-1. **¡Todos están ocupados (*Everyone is busy*)!** Study the vocabulary presented on pages 34-35. Then, with a classmate, answer the questions that follow.

En el laboratorio

1. ¿Qué usa Alfonso para (*in order to*) imprimir su (*his*) trabajo?
2. ¿Hay (*Are there*) hojas de papel en la papelera?
3. Carmen practica español. ¿Qué usa para escuchar la lección? (Mencione dos objetos.)
4. Natalia navega por la red para buscar información. ¿Qué usa para navegar por la red?
5. Javier está muy ocupado. ¿Qué usa?
6. ¿Qué tipo de mensaje manda Pepita?

En la clase

7. ¿Qué usa la profesora Falcón para enseñar (*to teach*) la clase?
8. ¿Hay tarea para mañana? ¿Qué día es la prueba?
9. ¿Cuántos (*How many*) pupitres hay en el aula? ¿Y cuántos estudiantes hay?
10. ¿Cuántos libros hay en el pupitre de Manuel?
11. ¿Cuántos lápices hay en el pupitre de Camila? ¿Y bolígrafos?
12. ¿Cuántos cuadernos hay en el pupitre?
13. ¿Quién tiene (*Who has*) una mochila?
14. ¿Cuál es el número del aula?
15. ¿Qué hora es?

Hay means *there is* or *there are* in a statement, and *is there* or *are there* in a question. It is used with singular and plural forms.

Hay una ventana en el aula.	***There is*** *a window in the classroom.*
Hay treinta pupitres.	***There are*** *thirty desks.*
¿Hay mucha tarea?	***Is there*** *much homework?*

1-2. **¿Cuántos hay?** Make a list of the number of students, desks, windows, backpacks and chalkboards in the classroom. Your professor will ask you about the number of students, desks, etc. that you counted.

> **Modelo:** En la clase hay...

Capítulo 1

1-3. Juego de palabras (Word game). What words do you associate with each of the following?

Modelo: el estudiante ➔ el profesor, la clase

1. la impresora
2. el examen
3. la mochila
4. la computadora

5. el video
6. la puerta
7. la mesa
8. la tiza

9. el bolígrafo
10. el correo electrónico
11. el laboratorio
12. el aula

READING STRATEGY

Scanning for cognates
Glean information about the content of this ad by finding words that are cognates—words that are identical or similar in the two languages and have the same meaning. How many can you find?

1-4. Internet para todos. Study the following ad. Then answer the questions.

1. El servicio Internet de Telmex ofrece muchas ventajas (*advantages*). ¿Qué ventajas del servicio son importantes para (*for*) ustedes? Mencionen tres o cuatro.
2. ¿Qué sitios web o tipo de información en la red representan las imágenes que aparecen en el anuncio? Identifiquen las categorías: **naturaleza, historia, tecnología y espacio, música, teatro, aviación y deportes** (*sports*).
3. ¿Qué sitios web son interesantes para ustedes?
4. ¿Cuál es la dirección electrónica de Telmex?

¿Qué dicen los profesores? (*What do professors say?*)

Abra la puerta/ la ventana.	*Open (to one person) the door/window.*
Abran el libro en la página...	*Open (to more than one person) your book to page . . .*
Lea/n las instrucciones del ejercicio...	*Read the instructions/directions for exercise . . .*
Lea/n en voz alta.	*Read aloud.*
Cierre/n el libro/ el cuaderno.	*Close your book/notebook.*
Escuche/n.	*Listen.*
Repita/n la palabra...	*Repeat the word . . .*
Traduzca/n la palabra...	*Translate the word . . .*
Vaya/n a la pizarra, por favor.	*Go to the chalkboard, please.*
Escriba/n la siguiente oración: ...	*Write the following sentence: . . .*
Conteste/n la siguiente pregunta: ...	*Answer the following question: . . .*
Estudie/n los verbos.	*Study the verbs.*
Siéntese/ Siéntense, por favor.	*Please sit down.*
Trabaje/n con un/a compañero/a.	*Work with a classmate.*
Trabaje/n en grupos de cuatro.	*Work in groups of four.*

¿Qué dicen los estudiantes? (*What do students say?*)

Profesor/a, tengo una pregunta.	*Professor, I have a question.*
¿Cómo se dice ... en español/ inglés?	*How do you say . . . in Spanish/in English?*
¿Qué significa la palabra...?	*What does the word . . . mean?*
Perdón, repita la palabra/ la oración/ la pregunta/ la respuesta, por favor.	*Pardon me, please repeat the word/sentence/question/answer.*
Perdón, ¿en qué página/ ejercicio/ lección/ capítulo estamos?	*Pardon me, what page/exercise/ lesson/chapter are we on?*
Más despacio, por favor.	*More slowly, please.*

Práctica y comunicación

1-5. **Usted es el/la profe.** Student 1 reads several commands in Spanish (one at a time, randomly) from the first list above, and Student 2 acts or carries them out. Your instructor will then give commands to the entire class, or to individual students. To be polite, answer: **Cómo no** or **Con mucho gusto**—equivalents of *Gladly.*

1-6. *¿Cómo reaccionan (react) ustedes?* After studying the Spanish expressions in the second list, decide what the two of you would say in the following situations.

1. There is a word you would like to learn in Spanish.

2. You did not understand, and you want your professor to repeat the sentence.

3. You have a question.

4. The professor uses the word **tiza**, but you do not remember what it means.

5. The professor is speaking very, very fast.

6. You have lost your place in the textbook and want to know what page the class is on.

Escenas

Un pequeño° accidente

Alfonso   Camila

small

En un corredor de la universidad. Alfonso va muy de prisa° y choca° con Camila. Sus libros, cuadernos y otras cosas caen° al suelo°.

va... is in a big hurry / collides
fall / to the floor

ALFONSO Y CAMILA:	¡Ay!
CAMILA:	¡Hombre! ¡Qué rápido vas!°
ALFONSO:	Perdón, Camila. Es que hoy llego tarde a clase.
CAMILA:	No es tarde. Son las 9:20. ¿Adónde vas?
ALFONSO:	Voy° al laboratorio. Tengo° una clase de computación a las 9:30.
CAMILA:	Hum... Yo necesito imprimir un trabajo de historia del arte. ¿Hay una impresora en el laboratorio?
ALFONSO:	Sí, hay dos.

¡Qué... You are going so fast!

I am going / I have

(*Comienzan a recoger° las cosas del suelo.*)

pick up

CAMILA:	Estos son mis bolígrafos.
ALFONSO:	Aquí está el libro de matemáticas.
CAMILA:	Gracias.
ALFONSO:	Bueno. Vamos° al laboratorio.
CAMILA:	¡Yo necesito un café! ¿Vamos a la cafetería un momento?
ALFONSO:	¡Ay, Camila! Lo siento, pero tengo una clase ahora°.

Let's go

now

¿Qué pasa?

1. ¿Quién llega tarde a clase?

2. ¿Qué hora es?

3. ¿Qué trabajo necesita imprimir Camila?

4. ¿Hay impresoras en el laboratorio?

5. ¿Alfonso va con Camila a la cafetería?

Estructuras

1 **Identifying gender and number: Nouns and definite and indefinite articles**

Observe the following sentences:

Los estudiant**es** están en clase. **Un** alumn**o** escribe en **el** cuaderno. Dos alumnos escriben en **la** pizarra. **La** profesora conversa con **unas** alumnas. Hay **una** computadora y **unos** libros en **el** escritorio.

All nouns in Spanish, even those referring to nonliving things, are either masculine or feminine (gender) and singular or plural (number). The definite article (*the*) or indefinite article (*a, an*) that accompanies each noun must also be either masculine or feminine and singular or plural to agree with the noun.

Artículos definidos			**Artículos indefinidos**		
el, la, los, las = *the*			un, una = *a, an, one*; unos, unas = *some*		
	singular	plural		singular	plural
masculino	**el** alumno	**los** alumnos	masculino	**un** alumno	**unos** alumnos
femenino	**la** alumna	**las** alumnas	femenino	**una** alumna	**unas** alumnas

Masculine and feminine nouns

- Nouns referring to a male are masculine; those referring to a female are feminine.

    el estudiante   **el** profesor   **el** señor   **la** estudiante   **la** profesora   **la** señora

- 99.7% of Spanish nouns that end in **-o** and 99.2% of those that end in **-r** or **-l** are masculine.

    el escritori**o**   **el** diccionari**o**   **el** televiso**r**   **el** borrado**r**   **el** pape**l**

- 98.9% of nouns that end in **-a** and practically 100% of those that end in **-ión** and **-d** are feminine.

    la impresor**a**   **la** puert**a**   **la** informac**ión**   **la** orac**ión**   **la** actitu**d**

- Note that some nouns that end in **-a** are actually masculine: **el mapa, el día, el problema, el programa**. Other exceptions will be pointed out as they appear in the textbook.[1]

> **HINT** If you memorize the article when you learn a new noun, you will remember its gender. For example: **la** clas**e** (feminine), but **el** pupitr**e** (masculine).

---

[1] **Aula** is feminine even though it uses the article **el**. The plural form is **las aulas**.

Plural forms of nouns

Singular nouns ending in a vowel add **-s**. Those ending in consonants add **-es**.

un estudiante

dos estudiante**s**

un lápiz

dos lápi**ces**[2]

Práctica y comunicación

1-7. **¡Hay mucha tarea!** Complete the instructions. Use the definite article **el** or **la**.

> **Modelo:** Escriba... (ejercicio)
> **Escriba el ejercicio.**

1. Escriba... (palabra, respuesta, dirección electrónica)
2. Estudie... (vocabulario, lección, mapa, capítulo)
3. Lea... (pregunta, diálogo, oración, párrafo)
4. Use... (computadora, teléfono, diccionario, impresora)

1-8. **Más tarea.** Complete the instructions, selecting words from the list. Use the definite article **los** or **las** and the plural form of the noun selected. Give several options.

bolígrafo	calculadora	cuaderno	ejercicio	lápiz	libro
oración	palabra	pregunta	respuesta	verbo	vocabulario

> **Modelo:** Escriban...
> **Escriban los ejercicios,...**

1. Escriban...   **2.** Estudien...   **3.** Traigan (*Bring*) a clase...

1-9. **¿Qué hay en la mochila de Esteban?** Identify the contents of Esteban's backpack, using **un/ una/ unos/ unas.**

En la mochila de Esteban hay ___ bolígrafo, ___ lápices, ___ diccionario, ___ cuadernos, ___ calculadora, ___ libro de texto, ___ hojas de papel y ___ discos compactos.

Now tell each other what is in your backpacks: **En mi mochila hay...** (Use words you already know.)

---

[2] Singular nouns ending in the letter **z** change the **z** to **c** before adding **-es**.

2 Talking about going places: *Ir + a + destination*

To state where you are going, use a form of the verb **ir** (*to go*) + **a** (*to*) + *destination*.

ir	*to go*	
(yo)	**voy**	**Voy** a la clase todos los días (*every day*).
(tú)	**vas**	¿**Vas** al teatro con frecuencia?
(usted, él, ella)	**va**	Ella **va** a la universidad
(nosotros/as)	**vamos**[3]	**Vamos** al restaurante.
(vosotros/as)	**vais**	¿**Vais** al café?
(ustedes, ellos/as)	**van**	Ellas **van** al gimnasio.

The present tense in Spanish is used to talk about actions that occur in the present or that commonly reoccur. The forms of **ir** can be translated according to context in three different ways (*I go, I do go, I am going*).

Voy al gimnasio todos los días.	*I go to the gym every day.*
Voy al gimnasio ahora.	*I'm going to the gym now.*
¿**Vas** con frecuencia?	*Do you go frequently?*

The present tense, accompanied by phrases indicating future time, may also be used to talk about actions in the near future.

María **va** a una fiesta esta noche.	*María **will go/is going** to a party tonight.*

---

[3] **¡Vamos!** also means *Let's go!*

Así se dice

Vamos a la clase de...

Vamos...

español/ inglés/ francés	a la residencia estudiantil (*to the dorm*)
italiano/ alemán (*German*)	a la biblioteca (*to the library*)
ruso/ japonés	a la librería (*to the bookstore*)
arte/ música/ literatura	al restaurante/ a la cafetería
religión/ filosofía	a la oficina del profesor/ de la profesora
historia/ ciencias políticas	a la universidad
psicología/ sociología	a la fiesta
biología/ física/ química (*chemistry*)	al cuarto (*to the room*)
matemáticas/ álgebra/ cálculo	al apartamento
computación, informática	al centro estudiantil
(*computer science*)	al gimnasio
contabilidad (*accounting*)	al centro
economía	a casa (*home*)

¿Cuándo (*When*) vamos?

ahora/ más tarde	*now/later*
después (de clase)	*after (class)*
esta mañana/ tarde/ noche	*this morning/this afternoon/tonight*

---

a (*to*) combines with **el** (*the*) to become **al**. In the combinations **a + la, los, las,** no change takes place.

a + el = al   Vamos **al** cuarto de Anita. vs. Vamos **a la** casa de Anita.

de (*from, about, of*) combines with **el** to become **del**. In the combinations **de + la, los, las,** no change takes place.

de + el = del   Vamos a la oficina **del** profesor. *vs.* Vamos a la oficina **de la** profesora.

Práctica y comunicación

1-10. **La vida universitaria.** Talk with your partner about how often you go to the following places. Start your sentences with **Frecuentemente** (*Frequently*), **A veces** (*Sometimes*), or **Casi nunca** (*Almost never*). Make note of the places you both go to with the same frequency.

> **Modelo:** a la biblioteca
> **A veces voy a la biblioteca.**

1. a la biblioteca
2. al laboratorio para usar las computadoras
3. al centro estudiantil
4. a la oficina del profesor/de la profesora de español
5. a la librería de la universidad
6. al gimnasio
7. al restaurante/ a la cafetería de la universidad
8. a fiestas los sábados

Now share with the class responses that you and your partner have in common: **Pablo y yo casi nunca vamos...**

1-11. **¿A qué clase van?** Guess to what class the following students are going. The object is your clue. You might consult the list of classes on page 43.

> **Modelo:** Manuel / una calculadora
> **Va a la clase de matemáticas.**

1. nosotros / los microscopios
2. Alfonso / un CD-Rom (cederóm) para la computadora
3. Inés / un violín
4. yo / un tubo con ácido sulfúrico
5. Camila / un libro sobre Picasso
6. Natalia y Linda / una copia de *Hamlet*
7. tú / un libro sobre Abraham Lincoln
8. nosotros / los libros sobre Freud
9. Javier / una biblia y un libro sobre Gandhi
10. tú / un libro sobre la política de los EE.UU.
11. yo / un libro sobre finanzas
12. María, Jessica y yo / *Dicho y hecho*

1-12. ¿Adónde vas?

Move about the classroom asking several classmates where they are going after class, this afternoon, etc. Use the following time expressions.

después de clase	más tarde	esta tarde	esta noche

Modelo:
Estudiante 1: ¿Adónde vas después de clase?
Estudiante 2: Voy a la clase de biología.

Now share some of your information with the class: **Después de clase Joe va a...**

To ask *at what time* a class or event takes place or *at what time* someone is going somewhere, use **¿A qué hora...?** Use **A la una/A las dos,...** in your answer.

¿A qué hora es la clase?	Es a las 8:15 de la mañana.
¿A qué hora vas al gimnasio?	Voy a las 5:00 de la tarde.

HINT | Review telling time on pp. 24–25.

1-13. ¿A qué hora es...?

Ask a classmate at what time the following activities usually take place. Take turns.

1. Los sábados, ¿a qué hora son las fiestas en la universidad?
2. Los domingos, ¿a qué hora son los partidos de fútbol americano?
3. ¿A qué hora son los conciertos los viernes?
4. ¿A qué hora vas al laboratorio? ¿Y qué día/s vas?
5. ¿Qué día y a qué hora es tu programa favorito de televisión?

HINT | For additional course names, see **Apéndice 3**, p. A–14.

1-14. Mi horario (*schedule*) de clases.

Give a list of your classes to a classmate. He/She will ask you the days and times of your classes and write them down. Then reverse roles.

Modelo:
Estudiante 1: ¿Qué días vas a la clase de química? ¿Y a qué hora?
Estudiante 2: Voy los martes y los jueves a las 8:15 de la mañana.

Your professor may ask you to read your classmate's schedule to the class.

Modelo:
Elena va a la clase de química los martes y los jueves a las 8:15 de la mañana.

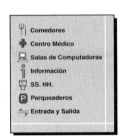

Palabras útiles

Facultad de... *School of...*

invernadero *greenhouse*

Laboratorio de Suelos *Soil Research Laboratory*

1-15. El campus de la PUCE (*Pontificia Universidad Católica del Ecuador*). Imagine that you are new students at this university in Quito, Ecuador. Using the campus map as a guide, answer the following questions.

Campus universitario

1. Departamento de Arqueología
2. Consultorios Jurídicos
3. Bloque No.1
   Facultad de Administración
   Facultad de Enfermería
   Facultad de Psicología
   Relaciones Internacionales
4. Bloque No. 2
   Facultad de Ciencias Humanas
   Facultad de Jurisprudencia
   Facultad de Economía
5. Centro Cultural
6. Edificio Administrativo
7. Departamento de Física y Matemáticas
8. Departamento de Química
9. Facultad de Ciencias de la Educación
10. Ingeniería de Transportes
    Departamento de Biología
    Escuela de Tecnología Médica
11. Audiovisuales
12. Invernadero
13. Departamento de Religión
14. Biblioteca
    Museo Jacinto Jijóny y Camaño
    Archivo Juan José Flores
    Centro de Cómputo
15. Residencia de Profesores
16. Facultad de Lingüística y Literatura
17. Facultad de Teología
18. Aula Magna
19. F.E.U.C.E
20. Ingeniería de Sistemas
21. Coliseo Cerrado
22. Ingeniería Civil
23. Laboratorio de Suelos

1. ¿Adónde van los estudiantes para...

comer (*to eat*), visitar al médico/a la médica, buscar libros, conversar con el rector/la rectora, usar las computadoras, ver obras (*works*) de arte, parquear el auto?

2. ¿Cuántos parqueaderos hay? ¿Cuántas Salas de Computadoras? ¿Cuántas facultades?

3. ¿A qué facultad van los estudiantes para una clase de educación? ¿Y una clase de literatura?

4. ¿Qué departamentos van a visitar los estudiantes si tienen (*if they have*) interés en las ciencias?

5. En la PUCE, ¿hay departamentos, facultades, etc. que no existen en su universidad? ¿Cuáles?

6. ¿Hay residencias estudiantiles en la PUCE? ¿Y residencias de profesores?

1-16. Guía para los visitantes. Using a map of your campus, begin a project to produce a "Guide for Spanish-speaking Visitors" to your school. Select ten important or interesting places and write the corresponding Spanish names. Your professor can provide you with assistance. Be sure to keep your list for inclusion in the guide.

Noticias culturales

La vida universitaria en el mundo hispano

Aunque° la mayoría de las universidades hispanas son instituciones públicas, también existen universidades privadas. En muchos países°, el gobierno° financia el costo de la educación en la universidad pública; los estudiantes sólo compran° los libros.

Frecuentemente, las universidades antiguas° son pequeñas y están en el centro de las comunidades: los edificios° no están todos juntos° en un campus. En las universidades modernas, hay más edificios y están en un campus.

Muchas universidades hispanas tienen más de 15.000 (quince mil) estudiantes. Los universitarios° viven con sus padres, en casa de otros familiares, en pensiones° o en apartamentos porque, por lo general, en las universidades no hay residencias estudiantiles. Las clases son muy especializadas y los programas son muy rígidos; por eso los estudiantes hispanos seleccionan una carrera antes de° comenzar sus estudios.

Although
countries / government
buy

old
buildings / together

university students
boarding houses

antes... before

La Universidad Iberoamericana. México, D.F. ¿Es similar al campus de su universidad?

La Universidad de Barcelona, una de las más antiguas de España. ¿De qué hablan (probablemente) los estudiantes?

¿Qué recuerda (*What do you remember*)? Decide if the statements are true (**cierto**) or false (**falso**). If the information is false, provide the correct information.

1. Generalmente las universidades hispanas son instituciones privadas.
2. Las universidades modernas están en el centro de las comunidades.
3. En muchas universidades hispanas no hay residencias estudiantiles.
4. Los estudiantes financian el costo de sus estudios universitarios.

3 **Conexiones y contrastes.** What are the similarities and differences between your university and Hispanic universities? Write two or three main differences. Later you will add them to the "Guide for Spanish-speaking Visitors" that the class will prepare.

③ Talking about actions in the present: Regular *-ar* verbs

When you look up a Spanish verb in the dictionary, you will find only the infinitive form (the form ending in **-ar**, **-er**, or **-ir**). In this section you will learn to work with regular verbs. They are called regular because they follow a set pattern. First you will become familiar with **-ar** verbs.

Las actividades en la universidad

Observe what Natalia and her friend Camila do.

only

first / there

Natalia y Camila **llegan**(1) a la universidad a las ocho de la mañana. Natalia **desayuna**(2) en la cafetería de la universidad, pero Camila nunca desayuna; sólo° compra°(3) una Pepsi. La primera° clase es la de psicología. Ahí° escuchan al profesor y **toman apuntes**(4). Luego van a la clase de español donde **practican**(5), **hablan**(6) y **estudian**(7) con los compañeros de clase. Por la tarde van a la biblioteca para estudiar y **preparar**(8) sus lecciones. Son excelentes estudiantes. Generalmente **sacan**(9) buenas notas en las pruebas y en los exámenes. Después de **cenar**(10), Camila **trabaja**(11) tres horas en la librería de la universidad. Natalia **regresa**(12) temprano a su casa. Prepara su trabajo para la clase de historia, navega por la red y manda mensajes electrónicos a sus amigos.

(1) **llegar** *to arrive* *(2)* **desayunar** *to have breakfast* *(3)* **comprar** *to buy* *(4)* **tomar apuntes** *to take notes* *(5)* **practicar** *to practice* *(6)* **hablar** *to speak* *(7)* **estudiar** *to study* *(8)* **preparar** *to prepare* *(9)* **sacar... notas** *to get ... grades* *(10)* **cenar** *to have dinner* *(11)* **trabajar** *to work* *(12)* **regresar** *to return, go back*

Now observe what happens when we use **hablar** to talk about the present (*I speak, he speaks, etc.*). Note that you drop the **-ar** from the infinitive and replace it with the endings indicated. The endings correspond to the subject of the verb.

hablar *to speak*	
hablar ➔ habl-	
(yo)	habl**o**[4]
(tú)	habl**as**
(usted, él, ella)	habl**a**
(nosotros/as)	habl**amos**
(vosotros/as)	habl**áis**
(ustedes, ellos/as)	habl**an**

Práctica y comunicación

1-17. **Un sondeo (*poll*) de la clase.** When your professor asks the following questions, raise your hand to answer affirmatively. Count the students who answer affirmatively in each category and write down the numbers.

¿Quién...

1. ... estudia con frecuencia en la biblioteca? _____
2. ... toma muchos apuntes en la clase de español? _____
3. ... llega a clase tarde? _____
4. ... saca buenas notas? _____
5. ... trabaja en la universidad? _____
6. ... desayuna en la cafetería? _____
7. ... usa el correo electrónico <u>frecuentemente</u>? _____
8. ... escucha CDs (ce-des) de música clásica? _____
9. ... compra discos compactos de música popular? _____

2 Now review the numbers with your partner. Follow the model.

Modelo: Cinco estudiantes estudian con frecuencia en la biblioteca. *o*
Nadie (*No one*) estudia con frecuencia en la biblioteca.

---

[4] Unlike nouns, Spanish verbs do not have gender: both males and females say **hablo** (*I speak*).

③ **1-18. Las actividades en la universidad.** Mention at least three activities generally done by each group of people listed. You may use some of the following verbs.

cenar	comprar	desayunar		escuchar	estudiar	hablar
llegar	sacar notas	tomar clases/apuntes		trabajar	ir	usar

Modelo: Nosotros/as... **Cenamos en la cafetería,... ,...**

1. Nosotros/as...
2. Los estudiantes de esta clase...
3. Los profesores de esta universidad...
4. Mis amigos/as...

> The expressions **por/en la mañana/ tarde/ noche** refer to a general period of time. In contrast, **de la mañana/ tarde/ noche** refer to a specific time.
> Trabajo **por la tarde**.
> *vs.*
> Llego a la oficina a las 2:00 **de la tarde**.

Así se dice
¿Cuándo?

Trabajo **por/en la mañana/ tarde/ noche.** — *in the morning/afternoon/at night*
Estudian **toda la mañana/ tarde/ noche.** — *all morning/afternoon/night*
Estudiamos **todas las mañanas/ tardes/ noches.** — *every morning/afternoon/night*

Trabajo **todo el día/ todos los días.** — *all day/every day*
Van a fiestas **los fines de semana.** — *on weekends*
Llegan a clase **tarde/ temprano/ a tiempo.** — *late/early/on time*

Práctica y comunicación

1-19 **¿Cuándo llegan?** Answer the questions that follow according to the drawings.

Natalia

Pepita

Esteban

1. La clase comienza a las 9:00 de la mañana. ¿Quién llega tarde? ¿A qué hora llega?
2. ¿Quién llega temprano? ¿A qué hora llega?
3. ¿Quién llega a tiempo? ¿A qué hora llega?
4. A la clase de español, ¿quiénes generalmente llegan temprano? ¿Tarde?

1-20. **Cosas en común (*Things in common*).** Ask each other questions using the cues provided. If both of you answer affirmatively, write the number of the question to identify what the two of you do in common.

> **Modelo:** desayunar / todas las mañanas
>
> Estudiante 1: **¿Desayunas todas las mañanas?**
>
> Estudiante 2: **Sí, desayuno todas las mañanas en la cafetería. ¿Y tú?**
> *o* **No, no desayuno todas las mañanas. ¿Y tú?**

1. tomar / Coca-Cola o Pepsi por la mañana
2. llegar a clase a tiempo / todos los días
3. ir al gimnasio / por la tarde
4. tomar siestas / por la tarde
5. estudiar / casi toda la noche cuando hay un examen
6. navegar por la red / en la noche
7. usar el correo electrónico / casi todos los días
8. escuchar discos compactos / con mucha frecuencia

Now present to the class a list of your common activities: **Susana y yo tomamos Coca-Cola por la mañana.**

1-21. **Usted y sus amigos/as.** Take turns asking questions and answering them.

> **Modelo:** ¿Dónde? / trabajar
>
> Estudiante 1: **¿Dónde trabajas?**
>
> Estudiante 2: **Trabajo en la biblioteca. ¿Y tú?** *o*
> **No trabajo. ¿Y tú?**

1. ¿Dónde? / trabajar, estudiar, desayunar, cenar
2. ¿Cuándo? / estudiar, desayunar, cenar
3. ¿Qué? / estudiar
4. ¿Qué notas? / sacar en la clase de...
5. ¿Qué tipo de música? / escuchar
6. ¿Qué tipo de computadora? / usar

Es el segundo día de clases. Son las 9:15 de la mañana y la profesora de español habla con los estudiantes. De repente (Suddenly) te das cuenta (you realize) que estás en la clase equivocada (wrong). Habla con la profe: **Perdón…**

Palabras útiles: mi *(my)*, su *(your)*

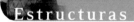

Estructuras

4 **Talking about actions in the present: Regular *-er* and *-ir* verbs; *hacer* and *salir***

Más actividades en la universidad

Read what Octavio has to say about his university life.

Soy de Mendoza, Argentina y **asisto**[1] a la Universidad Politécnica de California. **Vivo**[2] en la residencia estudiantil. Tomo cursos de informática, de ciencias políticas y de literatura latinoamericana. En mis clases de ciencias políticas y literatura **leemos**[3] y **escribimos**[4] mucho y yo participo con frecuencia en las discusiones. En la clase de informática analizamos sistemas de computadoras y **aprendemos**[5] a usar *software*. Me gustan° mucho mis clases. Al mediodía voy con mis compañeros al restaurante de la universidad. Ahí **comemos**[6], **bebemos**[7] y conversamos de mil cosas°. La comida del restaurante no es excelente pero tampoco° es terrible. Los sábados por la mañana voy al gimnasio y por la noche **salgo**[8] con mis amigos. No **hago**[9] mucho los domingos.

Me… I like

mil… a thousand things

neither

(1) **asistir a** *to attend* *(2)* **vivir** *to live* *(3)* **leer** *to read* *(4)* **escribir** *to write* *(5)* **aprender** *to learn* *(6)* **comer** *to eat* *(7)* **beber** *to drink* *(8)* **salir** *to go out, leave;* **salgo** *I leave* *(9)* **hacer** *to do, to make;* **hago** *I do, make*

Regular -er and -ir verbs

Now observe what happens when you use **comer** and **vivir** to talk about the present. Note that you drop the **-er/-ir** from the infinitive and replace it with the endings indicated. The endings correspond to the subject of the verb.

	comer to eat comer → com-	**vivir** to live vivir → viv-
(yo)	com**o**	viv**o**
(tú)	com**es**	viv**es**
(usted, él, ella)	com**e**	viv**e**
(nosotros/as)	com**emos**[5]	viv**imos**
(vosotros/as)	com**éis**	viv**ís**
(ustedes, ellos, ellas)	com**en**	viv**en**

Hacer and *salir*

The verbs **hacer** (*to do, make*) and **salir** (*to leave, go out*) are irregular only in the **yo** form.

> **hacer: hago**, haces, hace, hacemos, hacéis, hacen
> **salir: salgo**, sales, sale, salimos, salís, salen

Hago la tarea todas las noches.   *I do homework every night.*

Salgo con mis amigos los fines de semana.   *I go out with my friends on weekends.*

Práctica y comunicación

1-22. **¿Sí o no?** Tell if the following activities occur or not in Spanish class or in the language lab.

> **Modelo:** En la clase de español... aprender muchos verbos
> **Sí, aprendemos muchos verbos.** *o* No, no aprendemos muchos verbos.

En la clase de español...

1. ... aprender muchas palabras útiles (*useful*)
2. ... leer novelas
3. ... beber Pepsi-Cola
4. ... escribir composiciones
5. ... tomar apuntes constantemente
6. ... hablar inglés
7. ... salir temprano

En el laboratorio...

8. ... escuchar discos compactos
9. ... imprimir los trabajos escritos
10. ... hacer actividades en la red
11. ... comer
12. ... usar las computadoras

---

[5] Note that **-er** and **-ir** verbs have identical endings except in the **nosotros** and **vosotros** forms.

1-23. **Muchas actividades.** Work together to make a list of possible activities that occur in the places below.

> **Modelo:** En el laboratorio... **los estudiantes usan las computadoras.**

1. En el laboratorio...
2. En la clase...
3. En la biblioteca...
4. En la librería de la universidad...
5. En el restaurante/ la cafetería de la universidad...
6. En el centro estudiantil...

Now select a member of your group to read your list to the class.

1-24. **Sondeo: preferencias.** Walking about the classroom, poll your classmates using the questions in the **Sondeo de la clase**. When someone answers affirmatively, write on a sheet of paper her/his name and what she/he does. How many affirmative answers can you get in ten minutes? Later, your professor may ask you to read your affirmative answers to the class.

> **Modelo:** (*talking to George*): George, ¿asistes a los conciertos de *rock*?
> George: **Sí, asisto a los conciertos de *rock*.**
> *Now you write:* **George asiste a los conciertos de *rock*.**

Sondeo de la clase

1. *¿ASISTIR A...?* ¿ASISTES A...?
   LOS CONCIERTOS DE MÚSICA CLÁSICA
   LOS CONCIERTOS DE «ROCK»

2. *¿COMPRAR...?*
   LA PIZZA DE DOMINO'S
   LA PIZZA DE MAMA CELESTE

3. *¿BEBER...?*
   PEPSI-COLA
   SPRITE
   MOUNTAIN DEW

4. *¿COMER* (NORMALMENTE)...?
   EN EL RESTAURANTE/LA CAFETERÍA DE LA U.
   EN CASA/EN TU APARTAMENTO

5. ¿*VIVIR*...?

    EN UNA RESIDENCIA ESTUDIANTIL

    EN UN APARTAMENTO

    EN UNA CASA

6. ¿*LEER* NOVELAS...?

    DE CIENCIA FICCIÓN

    ROMÁNTICAS

    DE MISTERIO

    POLICÍACAS (*DETECTIVE*)

7. ¿*HACER* EJERCICIO...?

    CASI (*ALMOST*) TODOS LOS DÍAS

    CON MUY POCA FRECUENCIA

8. ¿*IR* (FRECUENTEMENTE)...?

    A FIESTAS

    AL CINE

    A DISCOTECAS

9. ¿*SALIR* CON TUS AMIGOS/AS...?

    TRES O CUATRO NOCHES POR SEMANA

    UNA O DOS NOCHES POR SEMANA

Así se pronuncia

The consonant *d*

Remember that the Spanish **d** has two sounds. At the beginning of a phrase or sentence, and after **n** or **l**, it is pronounced like the English *d* in the word *door*.

    ¿**D**ónde está el **d**iccionario?   **d**esayunar   apren**d**er   el **d**ía   un **d**isco

In most other positions, particularly between vowels and at the end of a word, Spanish **d** has a slight *th* sound, as in *this* or *brother*.

    ¿De **d**ónde es **D**avi**d**?   borra**d**or   re**d**   resi**d**encia   vi**d**eograba**d**ora

Repeat the following children's verse, paying close attention to the **d** with a slight *th* sound.

...Y aserrín°	*sawdust*
aserrán	
los ma**d**eros° **d**e San Juan	*clumsy fools*
pi**d**en queso°	piden... *ask for cheese*
pi**d**en pan°.	*bread*

Dicho y hecho

 Conversando

5 **Su universidad.** Talk about your campus. Include the categories listed. Take notes: You will need them later to complete the class project.

- lugares (*places*) interesantes o famosos
- restaurantes o cafés cerca de (*near*) la universidad
- el equipo de básquetbol/ fútbol americano, etc.
- clubes y organizaciones
- actividades: lo que (*what*) hacen los estudiantes

¡A escuchar!

Computadoras de Compulandia. You need to buy a computer and class materials for the new school term. Listen to the **Compulandia** advertisement and mark the correct answers for numbers 1 and 2.

1. El anuncio es para: ❑ estudiantes ❑ el público en general.

2. Venden (*They sell*) sólo (*only*) computadoras y accesorios: ❑ sí ❑ no

Now listen to the advertisement again and complete the rest of the sentences.

3. Ofrecen computadoras con

_____, _____ e

impresora por sólo _____

al mes.

4. Hay un descuento especial

para las _____ a color.

5. Para las clases venden

_____, _____ y

bolígrafos.

¿Qué tipo de computadora usa usted?

De mi escritorio

Guía para los visitantes. Now it is time to write and compile the "Guide for Spanish-speaking Visitors" for your university. Your professor will divide the class into five groups, assigning one of the categories listed below to each group. After completion of the assigned task, each group should type its section for incorporation into the total class project. Use your notes from Exercise 1-16 and *Conversando*.

HINT Use structures and words you have studied. If you look up additional words in a dictionary, seek guidance from your instructor.

¡Bienvenidos a (*add the name of your university or institution*)!

Include a map of the campus with the names (in Spanish) of the main buildings. Include some differences between United States and Hispanic universities. (See *Noticias culturales*, p. 47 and Exercise 1-15.)

Lugares que usted debe (*should*) visitar

Describe things that are a "must" to visit—a gallery (**galería**) or museum (**museo**), the student union, gymnasium, bookstore, some good places to eat on campus or near campus, etc.

Los cursos académicos

Mention some of the more popular or interesting classes at your university. Talk about the university computer facilities, library, and where/when students generally study.

HINT For additional course names, see **Apéndice 3**, p. A–14.

Clubes, organizaciones y equipos (*teams*) de la universidad

Mention some clubs, fraternities, sororities, and other important organizations on your campus.

Highlight some of the university sports teams (**fútbol americano, básquetbol, béisbol,**...).

Indicate if they win (**ganar**) frequently or are famous. Don't forget **la mascota de la universidad**.

La vida (*life*) universitaria y qué hacer en la universidad

Indicate where students live, where students go on campus, and what they frequently do in the mornings, afternoons, evenings, and on weekends.

Panorama cultural

El mundo hispano*

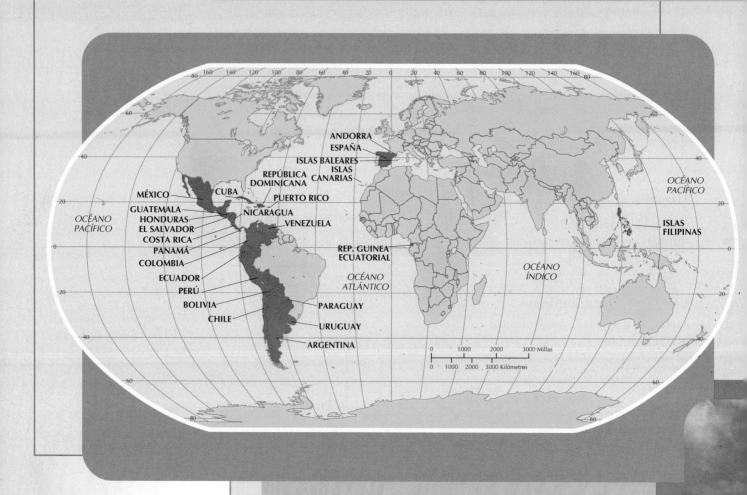

Preguntas sobre el mapa

1. ¿Cuáles son tres países (*countries*) sudamericanos donde hablan español? ¿Y tres centroamericanos? ¿Y tres en el mar Caribe?

2. ¿De dónde es el tango? ¿Y cuál es el país de Don Quijote?

3. ¿Qué países hispanos son famosos por sus vinos?

4. ¿De dónde son los mariachis?

5. ¿De qué país son muchos jugadores de béisbol?

6. Con un/a compañero/a de clase, identifique la nacionalidad que le corresponde a cada (*each*) país de la América Central y de la América del Sur.

*The Hispanic World

¿Sabía usted que...?[1]

- El español es una de las cinco lenguas[2] más importantes del mundo[3].
- Existen cuatrocientos millones de hispanohablantes[4] en el mundo.
- En los Estados Unidos hay más de treinta y siete millones de hispanohablantes.
- El español es la lengua oficial de veintiún países: Argentina, Bolivia, Chile, Colombia, Costa Rica, Cuba, Ecuador, El Salvador, España, Guinea Ecuatorial, Guatemala, Honduras, México, Nicaragua, Panamá, Paraguay, Perú, Puerto Rico, la República Dominicana, Uruguay y Venezuela.
- En España hay influencias africanas, judías[5] y árabes. En Bolivia y Guatemala, la población[6] indígena representa más del 50% de los habitantes.
- En muchos países de Centroamérica, Sudamérica y el Caribe hay una importante influencia africana.

[1]Did you know that
[2]languages [3]world
[4]Spanish speakers
[5]Jewish [6]population

Estatua de Don Quijote, Sancho Panza y Cervantes. Plaza de España, Madrid.

Grupo de mariachis mexicanos.

Bailando un tango. Buenos Aires, Argentina.

¿Qué descubrimos (*What did we discover*)?

Provide the missing information.

1. El español es una de las _____ lenguas más importantes del mundo.

2. El español es la lengua de _____ países.

3. En los Estados Unidos hay más de _____ millones

de hispanohablantes.

4. En España hay influencias _____, _____ y _____.

5. En Guatemala más del 50% de la población es _____.

¡Interesante! En 1492 había aproximadamente 1.000 lenguas indígenas en Norteamérica y más de dos mil en Sudamérica.

Así también se dice

Hay muchos dialectos y variaciones de vocabulario en los veintiún países del mundo hispano. Por ejemplo, se dice (*One says*) **autobús** en España, **camión** en México, **guagua** en el Caribe, **colectivo** en Argentina y **bus** en otros. ¿Tienes **computadora**? En algunos países de latinoamérica se dice **computador**, y en España, **ordenador**.

En Venezuela tu **mochila** es **morral**.

¿Y el **suéter**? Es **chompa** en la región andina y **púlover** o **jersey** en España. ¡Qué variedad!

Encuentro cultural
Artes pictóricas

Diego Rivera

Diego Rivera, famoso pintor[1], muralista y activista mexicano, nació[2] en Guanajuato el 13 de diciembre de 1892 (mil ochocientos noventa y dos) y murió[3] en la Ciudad de México en el año 1957 (mil novecientos cincuenta y siete). Observe la pintura al óleo[4] *Día de las flores*[5]. Note la influencia indígena.

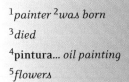

[1]*painter* [2]*was born*
[3]*died*
[4]**pintura...** *oil painting*
[5]*flowers*

Diego Rivera, *Flower Day, Día de las flores*, 1925. Oil on canvas (58x47.5 inches). Photograph ©2003 Museum Associates/LACMA/Los Angeles County Museum of Art, Los Angeles County Fund.

Preguntas

1. ¿Cuándo nació Diego Rivera?
2. ¿Cuál es la nacionalidad de Diego Rivera?
3. ¿Por qué (*Why*) es Diego Rivera famoso?
4. ¿Cómo se llama la pintura?
5. ¿Cuántas personas hay en la pintura? ¿Cuántas flores hay?

Adverbios y expresiones adverbiales

ahora/ más tarde

a tiempo/ temprano/
   tarde

después (de clase)

esta mañana/ tarde/
   noche

los fines de semana

por/en la mañana/ tarde/
   noche

toda(s) la(s) mañana(s)/
   tarde(s)/ noche(s)

todo el día/ todos los
   días

Sustantivos (Nouns)

En el aula

la alumna/ la estudiante

el alumno/ el estudiante

los apuntes

el bolígrafo

el borrador

la calculadora

el cuaderno

el diccionario

el escritorio

el examen

la hoja de papel

el lápiz

el libro

el mapa

la mesa

la mochila

la nota

la papelera

la pizarra

el profesor

la profesora

la prueba

la puerta

el pupitre

el reloj

la silla

la tarea

la tiza

el trabajo escrito

la ventana

En el laboratorio

los audífonos

la computadora

el correo electrónico

la dirección electrónica

el disco compacto/ el CD

la impresora

el mensaje electrónico

la página web

la pantalla

el ratón

el sitio web

el teclado

el televisor

el VCR

la videograbadora

La clase de...

alemán

álgebra

arte

biología

cálculo

ciencias políticas

computación/ informática

contabilidad

economía

español

filosofía

física

francés

historia

inglés

italiano

japonés

literatura

matemáticas

música

psicología

química

religión

ruso

sociología

Destinos

a casa

el apartamento

la biblioteca

la cafetería

el centro

el centro estudiantil

el cuarto

la fiesta

el gimnasio

la librería

la oficina

la residencia estudiantil

el restaurante

la universidad

Verbos y expresiones verbales

aprender

asistir a

beber

buscar

cenar

comer

comprar

desayunar

escribir

escuchar

estudiar

hablar

hacer

hay

imprimir

ir

leer

llegar

mandar

practicar

preparar

regresar

salir

ser

tomar

   tomar apuntes

trabajar

usar

vivir

navegar por la red

sacar una nota

Palabras interrogativas

¿Cuándo?

¿Adónde?

Expresiones útiles

¿Cómo se dice... en
   español/ inglés?

Más despacio, por favor.

Perdón, ¿en qué página/
   ejercicio/ lección/
   capítulo estamos?

Perdón, repita la palabra/
   la oración/ la pregunta/
   la respuesta, por favor.

¿Qué significa la
   palabra...?

Tengo una pregunta.

I. Nouns and definite and indefinite articles.

A. Professor B is more demanding than Professor A, and she always gives more homework. Complete each professor's assignment with the appropriate definite article (**el, la, los, las**). Change nouns to the plural when necessary.

> **Modelo:** Profesor A: Contesten __la__ pregunta nº 1.
> Profesor B: Contesten _las preguntas_ del nº 1 al 10.

1. PROF. A: Escriban _____ ejercicio A.
   PROF. B: Escriban _____ _____ A y B.
2. PROF. A: Estudien _____ lección 1.
   PROF. B: Estudien _____ _____ 1 y 2.
3. PROF. A: Lean _____ página 40.
   PROF. B: Lean _____ _____ 40 y 41.
4. PROF. A: Completen _____ Capítulo 3.
   PROF. B: Completen _____ _____ 3 y 4.

B. Describe the university by completing the sentences with **un, una, unos,** or **unas**.

En la universidad hay _____ centro estudiantil con _____ librería grande. Tenemos _____ laboratorio con _____ impresora y _____ computadoras nuevas. Hay _____ biblioteca grande con _____ libros muy antiguos e interesantes.

II. _Ir + a + destination_. Tell where the following people go to carry out the indicated activities. Avoid subject pronouns.

> **Modelo:** Esteban / estudiar
> **Va a la biblioteca.**

1. yo / desayunar
2. nosotros / trabajar en la computadora
3. mis amigos y yo / hacer ejercicio
4. los estudiantes/ hablar con el profesor
5. tú / comprar libros y cuadernos
6. Susana / tomar una siesta

III. The present tense of regular _-ar_ verbs. Indicate or ask questions about what university students do. Change the verbs to correspond to the subjects given in parentheses. Avoid the use of subject pronouns.

> **Modelo:** navegar por la red con frecuencia (yo)
> **Navego por la red con frecuencia.**

1. comprar libros y cuadernos en la librería (yo)
2. llegar a clase a tiempo (todos los estudiantes)
3. ¿estudiar en la biblioteca por la tarde (tú)?
4. ¿trabajar por la noche (usted)?

5. usar el correo electrónico todos los días (nosotros)
6. escuchar música clásica por la noche (Ana)

IV. The present tense of regular _-er_ and _-ir_ verbs; _hacer_ and _salir_. Indicate or ask questions about what university students do. Change the verbs to correspond to the subjects given in parentheses. Avoid the use of subject pronouns.

> **Modelo:** hacer muchos exámenes y escribir muchas composiciones (ella)
> **Hace muchos exámenes y escribe muchas composiciones.**

1. asistir a una universidad buena y aprender mucho (nosotros)
2. vivir en la residencia y estudiar en la biblioteca (yo)
3. comer en la cafetería y tomar café en el centro estudiantil (los estudiantes)
4. leer libros interesantes y escribir muchas composiciones (nosotros)
5. imprimir los trabajos y usar las computadoras en el laboratorio (tú)
6. hacer la tarea y después salir con mis amigos/as (yo)

V. General review. Answer the questions about your daily routine at the university.

1. ¿Va usted a clase todos los días?
2. ¿A qué hora es su primera (_your first_) clase?
3. ¿Cuántos estudiantes hay en la clase de español?
4. ¿Hay tarea todas las noches? (¿Mucha tarea?)
5. ¿Escriben ustedes en el _Cuaderno de ejercicios_ todas las noches?
6. ¿Adónde va usted para comprar libros interesantes? ¿Y para usar las computadoras?
7. ¿Adónde va usted a conversar con sus amigos?
8. ¿A qué hora cena usted?
9. ¿Dónde come usted normalmente?

Answers to the _Autoprueba y repaso_ are found in **Apéndice 2**.

Capítulo 2

Así es mi familia

Goals for communication

- To talk about the family
- To tell age
- To indicate possession
- To describe people and things
- To indicate location
- To describe mental and physical conditions

Así se dice

Así es mi familia

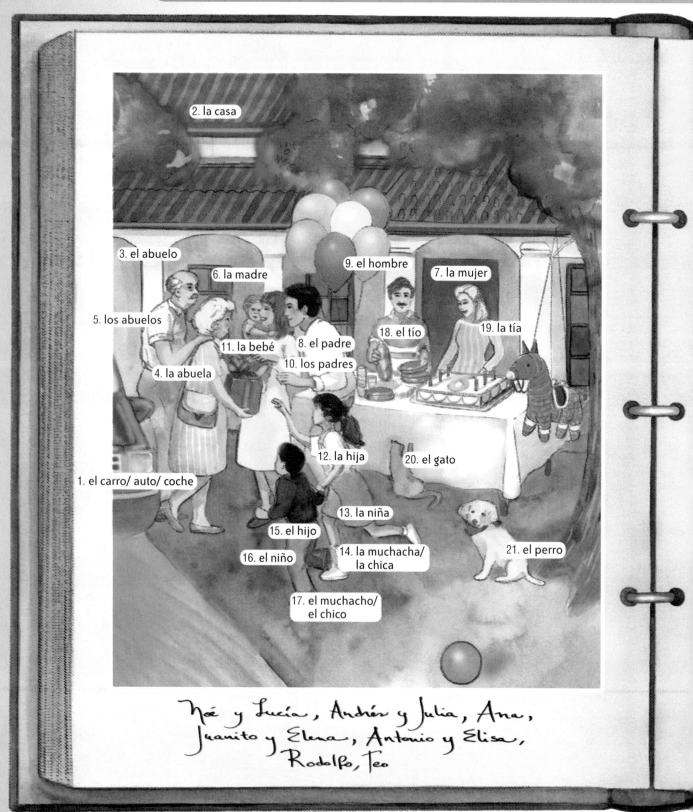

2. la casa

3. el abuelo

6. la madre

9. el hombre

7. la mujer

5. los abuelos

11. la bebé

8. el padre

18. el tío

19. la tía

4. la abuela

10. los padres

12. la hija

20. el gato

1. el carro/ auto/ coche

13. la niña

21. el perro

15. el hijo

16. el niño

14. la muchacha/ la chica

17. el muchacho/ el chico

Noé y Lucía, Andrés y Julia, Ana, Juanito y Elena, Antonio y Elisa, Rodolfo, Teo

22. el novio

23. la novia

24. mi pareja

Andrés y Julia

25. el esposo/ el marido

26. la esposa/ la mujer

28. la suegra

27. el suegro

Andrés y Julia
con Tomás, Tina, Silvia y José

la nieta

30. el nieto

...a, Noé y Juanito

31. el primo

32. la prima

Ricardo, Juanito y Tere

33. el hermano

34. la hermana

Juanito, Elena

1. car
2. house
3. grandfather
4. grandmother
5. grandparents
6. mother
7. woman
8. father
9. man
10. parents
11. baby (f.); **el bebé** (m.)
12. daughter
13. child (f.)
14. girl
15. son
16. child (m.)
17. boy
18. uncle
19. aunt
20. cat
21. dog
22. boyfriend
23. girlfriend
24. my partner, significant other
25. husband
26. wife
27. father-in-law
28. mother-in-law
29. granddaughter
30. grandson
31. cousin (m.)
32. cousin (f.)
33. brother
34. sister

Práctica y comunicación

2-1. **La familia.** Answer the questions, based on the family album on pages 66–67.

En la fotografía grande...

1. Los abuelos[1] llegan en coche para celebrar el cumpleaños de Juanito. ¿Cómo se llama el abuelo? ¿Y la abuela?
2. ¿Quién es la mujer con la bebé? ¿Quién es el hombre? ¿Quiénes son Andrés y Julia?
3. ¿Quién es Ana? ¿Cómo se llama la otra (*other*) hija? ¿Y el hijo?
4. ¿Cuántas velas (*candles*) hay en la torta de cumpleaños de Juanito?
5. ¿Hay una piñata?
6. ¿Quién es Antonio? ¿Y Elisa?
7. El gato se llama Rodolfo. ¿Cómo se llama el perro?
8. ¿Cuántas personas hay en la familia? ¿Cuántos niños hay?
9. La arquitectura de la casa, ¿es colonial o contemporánea?
10. ¿Viven todos en la casa?

En las fotografías pequeñas de la familia...

11. Andrés es el novio. ¿Quién es Julia?
12. Julia es la esposa. ¿Quién es Andrés?
13. ¿Cómo se llaman los suegros?
14. Noé es el abuelo. ¿Quién es Elena? ¿Y Juanito?
15. ¿Son Juanito y Ricardo hermanos? ¿Qué son? ¿Y quién es Tere?
16. ¿Son Elena y Juanito primos? ¿Qué son?

DICHOS

stick / splinter

De tal palo°, tal astilla°. De tal padre, tal hijo.

¿Cuál es el dicho (*saying*) equivalente en inglés? ¿Se aplica a su familia? ¿Es usted como (*like*) su madre o padre?

---

[1] In Spanish, the masculine plural can refer to a group of both males and females. Examples: **padres** = *parents*, **abuelos** = *grandparents*, **tíos** = *aunts and uncles*, **hermanos** = *brothers and sisters (siblings)*.

Así se dice

La familia, los parientes(1) y los amigos

Inés tells us about her family, relatives, and friends.

Me llamo Inés, y soy española. Ahora vivo aquí en los Estados Unidos. Tengo° *I have*
una familia interesante porque mis padres son divorciados y ahora mi madre
tiene° otro esposo: mi **padrastro**(2). De ese matrimonio tengo un **hermanastro**(3) *has*
y una **hermanastra**(4), pero no tengo **medio hermanos**(5). El resto de mi familia, es
decir°, un hermano **mayor**(6), la esposa de mi hermano (mi **cuñada**(7)), las dos niñas *es... that is*
de mi hermano (mis **sobrinas**(8)) y mi hermana **menor**(9) viven en España, en León.
También están allá mi padre, los cuatro abuelos y mi **bisabuela**(10). Mi **mejor**
amiga(11), Pilar, es de León también. Sin embargo°, ya° tengo excelentes amigos *However / already*
aquí en los Estados Unidos. Bueno, así es mi familia.

¿**Cuántos**(12) hermanastros tiene Inés? ¿**Cuántas** personas de su familia viven
en León? ¿**Quién**(13) es su mejor amiga?¿**Dónde**(14) vive?

(1) relatives (m.) (2) stepfather; **la madrastra** *stepmother (3) stepbrother (4) stepsister (5) half-
brothers and sisters;* **el medio hermano/la media hermana** *(6) older (7) sister-in-law;* **el
cuñado** *brother-in-law (8) nieces;* **el sobrino** *nephew (9) younger (10) great-grandmother;* **el
bisabuelo** *great-grandfather (11) best friend (f.) (12)* **¿Cuántos/Cuántas?** *How many?*
(13) **¿Quién/Quiénes?** *Who? (14) Where?*

2-2. **Mi familia y mis amigos.** Ask each other the following questions
about your families and friends. Write down some of the information
about your classmate's relatives to report back to the class.

1. ¿Dónde vive tu familia?
2. ¿Cómo se llama tu madre/padre? ¿De dónde es? ¿Dónde trabaja?
3. ¿Cuántos hermanos o hermanas tienes? **Tengo...** o **No tengo hermanos/as.**
   (¿Son mayores o menores?)
4. ¿Tienes madrastra o padrastro? (¿Hermanastro o hermanastra?) (¿Medio
   hermano o media hermana?)
5. ¿Tienes primos? (¿Cuántos?)
6. ¿Tienes abuelos o bisabuelos? (¿Dónde viven?)
7. ¿Quiénes son tus parientes favoritos?
8. ¿Tienes cuñados? ¿Sobrinos? (¿Cuántos?)
9. ¿Tienes esposo/a? ¿Novio/a? ¿Pareja? (¿De dónde es?)
10. ¿Tienes hijos? (¿Cuántos?) (¿Y nietos?)
11. ¿Quién es tu mejor amigo/a? (¿De dónde es?)
12. ¿Tienes perro o gato? (¿Cómo se llama/n?)

Escenas

Para eso están los amigos°

Pepita   Inés   Octavio

Para... *That's what friends are for*

En la cafetería de la universidad. Inés está sola en una mesa tomando su café. Llega Pepita con Octavio.

PEPITA:	¡Hola, Inés!
INÉS:	Pepita, ¡qué sorpresa! (*Se dan un beso en la mejilla.*) ¿Cómo estás?
PEPITA:	Muy bien. Quiero presentarte a Octavio. Es el compañero de cuarto° de Manuel.
INÉS:	(*Inés y Octavio se dan la mano.*) Mucho gusto, Octavio. ¿Eres nuevo en la universidad?
OCTAVIO:	Sí, soy de Mendoza, Argentina. Estudio informática. ¿De dónde eres tú?
INÉS:	Soy española, de León. La mayoría de mi familia todavía° vive allá, pero mi madre y mi padrastro viven aquí. Estudio economía. ¿Así que° eres un viejo amigo de Manuel?
OCTAVIO:	En realidad no. Tengo un primo en Buenos Aires que es amigo de Manuel desde hace años°. Yo sólo conocí° a Manuel hace un mes°.
INÉS:	¡Manuel y su familia tienen amigos en todo el mundo!
PEPITA:	A propósito, Inés, ¿tienes planes para este fin de semana? El sábado mi madre prepara una fiesta de cumpleaños para mi tía Rosita. ¿Puedes ir°?
INÉS:	¡Por supuesto!° Gracias por la invitación.
PEPITA:	¡Qué bueno! Manuel, su novia y Octavio también° están invitados.
OCTAVIO:	Inés, tenemos espacio en el auto. ¿Por qué no vamos todos juntos° a la fiesta el sábado?
INÉS:	¡Estupendo! Es un buen plan. Gracias, Octavio.
OCTAVIO:	De nada. Para eso están los amigos.

compañero... *roommate*

still

Así... *So*

desde... *for years / I met / hace... a month ago*

Puedes... *Can you come/go?*

Por... *Of course*

also

together

¿Qué pasa?

1. ¿Quién es Octavio?
2. ¿Quién tiene familia en España?
3. ¿Dónde vive el primo de Octavio?
4. ¿Para quién es la fiesta del sábado?
5. ¿Quiénes están invitados?
6. ¿Cómo responde Inés a la oferta (*offer*) de Octavio? ¿Acepta?

Estructuras

1 **Indicating possession and telling age: The verb *tener* and *tener... años***

Abuelo, ¿cuántos años tienes?

¡Tengo ochenta y un años!

The verb *tener*

You have already informally used **tener** to express possession, as in **tengo dos hermanos**. Now observe the following forms:

tener *to have*		
(yo)	tengo	**Tengo** un hermano.
(tú)	tienes	**¿Tienes** bisabuelos?
(usted, él, ella)	tiene	Mi madre **tiene** cuatro hermanas.
(nosotros/as)	tenemos	Mi hermano y yo **tenemos** un perro.
(vosotros/as)	tenéis	**¿Tenéis** coche?[2]
(ustedes, ellos, ellas)	tienen	Mis tíos **tienen** una casa nueva.

To be . . . years old   *Tener... años*

Whereas English uses *to be* . . . to tell age (*She is eighteen years old.*), Spanish uses **tener... años**. To inquire about age, the question **¿Cuántos años...?** (*How many years . . . ?*) is used with **tener**.

—¿Cuántos años tiene él?   *How old is he?*
—Tiene veintiún años.   *He is twenty-one years old.*

---

[2] Observe the English equivalents of the two Spanish sentences: **¿Tenéis coche?** *Do you have a car?* **¿Tenéis un coche?** *Do you have one car?*

Así es mi familia

Práctica y comunicación

2-3. **¿Qué tiene el profesor/la profesora?** Try to guess the eight items your professor has in the bag. Make a written list of your guesses. Then check off the items you guessed according to your professor's responses. The group that guesses the most objects correctly is the winner.

> **Modelo:** Profesor/a: ¿Qué tengo en la bolsa?
>
> Estudiante: **En la bolsa usted tiene un/una...**
>
> Profesor/a: **Sí, tengo un/una...** *o* **No, no tengo un/una...**

2-4. **¿Cuántos años tiene?** Moving about the classroom, find out how old your classmates and their relatives are. Ask the following questions and jot down interesting information (unusually young/old relatives, etc.).

1. ¿Cuántos años tienes? **Tengo... años.**
2. ¿Tienes una hermana o un hermano mayor? ¿Cuántos años tiene?
3. ¿Cuántos años tiene tu mejor amigo/a?
4. ¿Cuántos años tiene tu madre o tu padre?
5. ¿Tienes abuelos? ¿Cuántos años tiene tu abuelo favorito o tu abuela favorita?
6. ¿Tienes bisabuelos? ¿Cuántos años tiene tu bisabuelo o tu bisabuela?

Now report back to the class: **¡El bisabuelo de (*classmate's name*) tiene...!**

2-5. **Mi árbol genealógico (*My family tree*).** This is the first step in the creation of a chapter project. Produce a chart of your family tree. Then, after adding some other details, share it with a classmate.

> **Modelo:** **Tengo una tía y dos tíos. Mi tía se llama..., y tiene... años. Es divorciada, pero vive con su novio en...** etc.

Así se dice

Relaciones personales

Todas las mañanas Carmen besa y abraza a sus hijas.

See what an important role Carmen's family plays in her very busy lifestyle.

Carmen trabaja, estudia y es madre soltera°. Sus gemelas°, Tina y Mari, tienen tres años. Carmen **ama**[1] *a* sus hijas con todo el corazón°. Cuando va al trabajo o a la universidad, su tía o la niñera° **cuida**[2] *a* las niñas. Todas las mañanas, al salir de la casa, Carmen **besa**[3] y **abraza**[4] *a* Tina y *a* Mari. Con frecuencia **llama**[5] *a* sus padres y abuelos, que viven en Ponce, Puerto Rico. Ellos **visitan**[6] *a* Carmen y *a* las nietas dos veces al año.

single / twins

heart

babysitter

(1) amar *to love* *(2)* cuidar *to take care of* *(3)* besar *to kiss* *(4)* abrazar *to hug* *(5)* llamar *to call* *(6)* visitar *to visit*

> Observe the use of the word **a** in the above description of Carmen's life. It does not have an English equivalent; its only function is to indicate that the direct object noun that immediately follows it refers to a specific person or persons. It is called the "personal *a*."
>
> —¿**A** quién buscas?   *Who(m) are you looking for?*
> —Busco **a** mi amigo.   *I am looking for my friend.*
> —También busco su apartamento.   *I am also looking for his apartment.*

(2) **2-6. Preguntas personales.** Take turns asking and answering the following questions.

1. ¿A quién en tu familia amas mucho?
2. ¿Llamas a tus amigos o a tu familia por teléfono con frecuencia? ¿A quién llamas con más frecuencia?
3. ¿A quién abrazas con frecuencia?
4. ¿Qué parientes visitas con más frecuencia?
5. ¿Tienes niños? (¿Quién cuida a los niños?)

② Indicating possession: Possessive adjectives and possession with *de*

A. Possessive adjectives

Ricardo y Tere son mis primos.

In addition to using **tener** to express possession (**tengo abuelos**), possession may also be expressed with possessive adjectives, which you have previously seen and used: *Mis* abuelos viven en España. As with the verb **tener**, possessive adjectives show ownership (*my house*) or a relationship between people (*my boyfriend*). Observe the varying forms of the possessive adjectives in the following chart.

Los adjetivos posesivos	
mi tío, **mis** tíos	*my*
tu[3] hermana, **tus** hermanas	*your (informal)*
su abuelo, **sus** abuelos	*his, her, its, their, your (formal)*
nuestro/a amigo/a, **nuestros/as** amigos/as	*our*
vuestro/a primo/a, **vuestros/as** primos/as	*your (informal, Spain)*

- In Spanish, possessive adjectives agree with the thing possessed or person related, *not* with the possessor.

  Susana tiene **nuestros libros**[4].   *Susana has our books.*

  Mis padres y yo vivimos en   *My parents and I live in our*
  nuestra casa[5].   *house.*

- If the ownership referred to by **su/sus** is not clear from the context, you may use an alternate form for clarity: **de** + *pronoun* or **de** + *person's name*.

  Es **su** carro. *o* Es el carro **de** él/ ella/ usted/ ellos/ ellas/ ustedes.
  Es el carro **de** Elena.

---

[3] **Tú** (with written accent) = *you*; **tu** (without written accent) = *your*. **Tú** tienes **tu** libro, ¿verdad? (*You have your book, right?*)
[4] **Susana** is a feminine singular noun, but **libros** is masculine plural.
[5] **Mis padres y yo** is masculine plural, but **casa** is feminine singular.

Práctica y comunicación

2-7. **Álbumes de fotos.** Imagine that you are showing photos in a family album to a friend. Tell who is in each picture.

Modelo: Tengo una foto de... (abuelos)
Tengo una foto de mis abuelos.

1. Tengo una foto de... (primos, padres, hermano, gato)
2. Mi madre tiene una foto de... (tía, hijas, abuelos)
3. Mis hermanas tienen una foto de... (perro, novios, primos, amigos)
4. Tenemos una foto de... (casa, abuelos, familia, tíos)

2-8. **Mis fotos.** Tell a classmate what photos you have of your favorite relatives, movie or TV stars, singers, etc. Describe at least three pictures.

Modelo: Estudiante 1: ¿Qué fotos especiales tienes en tu álbum de fotos o en tu cuarto?

Estudiante 2: En mi álbum de fotos/En mi cuarto tengo una foto de.../de mi(s)...

Estructuras

B. Possession with *de*

Where English uses an '*s* (or *s*') with a noun to indicate possession, Spanish uses **de** + *noun*.

HINT | de + el = del

Es la casa **de** mi abuela.	*It's my grandmother's house.*
Es la casa **de** mis abuelos.	*It's my grandparents' house.*
Las hijas **de** Carmen son simpáticas.	*Carmen's daughters are nice.*
Las fotos **del** señor Soto son interesantes.	*Mr. Soto's photos are interesting.*

To express the equivalent of the English *Whose?*, Spanish uses **¿De quién?**

—**¿De quién** es el álbum?	*Whose album is it?*
—**Es de** Susana.	*It's Susana's.*

Práctica y comunicación

2-9. **¿De quién es?** Close your eyes. Your instructor will "borrow" a few items from random students and will place them on her/his desk. One student will ask to whom an item on the desk belongs. Another will try to guess the owner.

> **Modelo:** Estudiante 1: ¿De quién es el libro de español?
>
> Estudiante 2: Es de Rita.

2-10. **Mis parientes favoritos.** Describe to your classmate three of your favorite relatives. Define the family relationship.

> **Modelo:** Mi abuelo favorito se llama...
>
> Tiene... años.
>
> Es el padre de mi madre.

You may be called upon to share information about your classmate with the class:
El abuelo favorito de (*classmate*) se llama...

> **② ¡Qué dilema!** *Hablas con tu novio/a y ¡usas el nombre de tu ex-novio/a!* **Hola,...**

Estructuras

③ Describing people and things: Descriptive adjectives

Soy muy artística, ¿no?

Adjectives in Spanish agree in gender (masculine or feminine) and number (singular or plural) with the nouns or pronouns they describe. You have already learned some adjectives of nationality as well as adjectives that are cognates (**romántico/a**) in the **Para empezar** chapter.

76 setenta y seis **Capítulo 2**

Formation of adjetives

Adjectives that end in **-o** have four possible forms (masculine or feminine, singular or plural) to indicate agreement.

	singular	plural
masculine	Él es honest**o**.	Ellos son honest**os**.
feminine	Ella es honest**a**.	Ellas son honest**as**.

Adjectives ending in **-e** or **-ista**, and most that end in a consonant, have only two possible forms: singular or plural. (Adjectives of nationality that end in a consonant are one exception. See page 29.)

singular	plural
Él/Ella es inteligent**e**.	Ellos/Ellas son inteligent**es**.
… ideal**ista**.	… idealista**s**.
… sentiment**al**.	… sentiment**ales**.

To make a singular adjective plural, add **-s** to the vowel or **-es** to the consonant, as is done with nouns.

americano **➔** americano**s**   español **➔** español**es**

Adjective position

- In contrast to English, Spanish descriptive adjectives usually follow the noun they describe.

   Marta es una **estudiante responsable**.   *Marta is a responsible student.*

- Adjectives of quantity (such as numbers) precede the noun, as in English.
   Tres estudiantes son de Nuevo México.
   Muchos estudiantes van al concierto.

You often use more than one adjective when describing a person. In doing so, note the following:

Y (*And*) becomes **e** before words beginning with **i** or **hi**.
   Mi madre es bonita **e** inteligente.

O (*Or*) becomes **u** before words beginning with **o** or **ho**.
   ¿El presidente es deshonesto **u** honesto?

Así se dice

Adjetivos descriptivos

The following descriptive adjectives are most commonly used with the verb **ser** to indicate characteristics or qualities that are considered inherent or natural to the person or thing described. They indicate what the person or thing *is like.*

alto(a) ➔ bajo(a) (1)

fuerte ➔ débil (2)

joven* ➔ mayor (3)

tonto(a) ➔ inteligente (4)

**perezoso(a) ➔ trabajador(a)/
serio(a)/ responsable** (5)

difícil ➔ fácil (6)

pobre ➔ rico(a) (7)

**bonito(a)/ hermoso(a)/
guapo(a) ➔ feo(a)** (8)

flaco(a)/ delgado(a) ➔ gordo(a) (9)

malo(a) ➔ bueno(a) (10)

pequeño(a) ➔ grande (11)
viejo(a) ➔ nuevo(a) (12)

---

* The plural of **joven** is **jóvenes**.
** Although the most common Spanish word for *old* is **viejo**, it is not polite to use it to describe people. Use **mayor** instead.

Observe how Pepita describes her cousins Luis and Alberto.

Tengo dos primos que son completamente diferentes. Luis es **moreno**(13), bajo, con unos kilos de más. Alberto es **rubio**(14), alto, delgado y guapo. Luis es **muy**(15) **amable**(16); tiene un carácter agradable. Es **divertido**(17) y **simpático**(18). Alberto no habla mucho; es serio, **un poco**(19) egoísta y un poco **aburrido**(20). La verdad es que a veces es **antipático**(21). Los dos son mis primos, **pero**(22) ¡qué contraste!

(1) tall → short (2) strong → weak (3) young → old (4) foolish, silly → intelligent (5) lazy → hardworking/serious, dependable/responsible (6) difficult → easy (7) poor → rich (8) pretty/ beautiful/good-looking, handsome → ugly (9) skinny/slender → fat (10) bad → good (11) small, little → large (12) old → new (13) brunet(te), dark-skinned (14) blond(e) (15) very (16) friendly, kind (17) amusing, fun, funny (18) nice, likeable (19) a bit, somewhat (20) boring (21) unpleasant, disagreeable (22) but

> **Bueno/a** and **malo/a** may be placed either before or after a noun. When placed before a masculine singular noun, **bueno** becomes **buen**, and **malo** becomes **mal**.
>
> Es un estudiante **bueno/malo**.   *o*   Es un **buen/mal** estudiante.
>
> Es una profesora **buena/mala**.   *o*   Es una **buena/mala** profesora.
>
> Adjectives ending in **-dor** add **-a** to agree with a feminine singular noun:
>
> trabajador → trabajador**a**   conservador → conservador**a**

Práctica y comunicación

2–11. **¿Cómo son (*What are they like*)?** Describe the people and things in the drawings on page 78.

Modelo: Pepita

Es baja.

¿Y Javier? ¿Y Alfonso, Octavio… (etc.)?

2–12. **¿Cómo soy?** Referring to the adjectives presented in the drawings and in the paragraph "**Los opuestos**", tell your classmate which traits best describe you. Then describe your favorite person. Take turns.

1. Soy…
2. Mi persona favorita se llama… Es…

2-13. **El espejo (mirror) mágico.** Using adjectives from the previous *Así se dice* sections, first indicate what you don't want to be like. Then, using contrasting adjectives and the help of the "magic mirror," indicate your "transformation." Begin with personality traits. You may be asked to share your magical transformation with the class.

No quiero (*I don't want*) ser...	Quiero ser...
1. No quiero ser antipático/a.	Quiero ser simpático/a.
2.	
3.	
4.	
5.	

2-14. **Los opuestos.** Write three sentences describing contrasts that exist within your family. Then share your sentences with a classmate.

Modelo: Mi madre es... pero mi padre es...

1. _____

2. _____

3. _____

2-15. **Descripciones.** First review the new expressions and then describe the people or things that follow.

1. Soy... Tengo pelo... y ojos...
2. Mi padre es...Tiene pelo... y ojos...
3. Mi madre es...Tiene pelo... y ojos...
4. Mi hermano/a mayor es... *o* Mi hermano/a menor es...
5. Mi novio/a es...Tiene pelo... y ojos... *o*
6. Mi mejor amigo/a es...
7. Mis amigos y yo somos...
8. Mi profesor/a de español es...
9. Nuestra clase de español es...
10. Mis clases, en general, son...

Palabras útiles

Tiene pelo (*hair*)
  negro/ rubio/
  castaño (*brown*)/ canoso (*grey*).

Es pelirrojo (*redhead*).

Tiene ojos (*eyes*)
  azules (*blue*)/
  verdes (*green*)/
  negros/ café.

5 **2-16.** **Adivinanza (*Guessing game*).** One student will assume the role of a well-known personality but will not divulge his/her identity. The other members will ask questions to discover his/her identity. Use the adjectives on page 78 and those from the list that follows. The mystery personality may respond only with a **sí** or a **no**. You have four minutes to guess.

> Possible categories: **político/a** **actor/actriz** **cantante (*singer*)**

> **Modelo:** ¿Eres actor? ¿Eres joven/mayor? ¿Eres cómico?

More descriptive words and their opposites

amable ➔ cruel

ambicioso/a ➔ perezoso/a

conservador/a ➔ liberal

decente ➔ grosero/a

egoísta ➔ modesto/a

enérgico/a ➔ tranquilo/a

exótico/a ➔ ordinario/a

honesto/a ➔ deshonesto/a

moral ➔ inmoral

optimista ➔ pesimista

práctico ➔ idealista

responsable ➔ irresponsable

serio/a ➔ cómico/a

tolerante ➔ intolerante

2-17. **Mi anuncio personal.** Read the personal ads, and then write one of your own. Later several volunteers will be asked to read their ads to the class.

> **Modelo:** Busco[6] compañero/a (esposo/a) amable,...

_____

_____

_____

_____

_____

_____

_____

Caballero
39, busca amiga sincera, simpática independiente. Apdo. 2151-1002

Norteamericano
desea conocer Srta. sincera, 25-32 años. Telf: 276-6660.

---

[6] The personal **a** is used with **buscar** when you are looking for a specific person: **Busco a mi novio.** It is not used in more general contexts: **Busco novio, amigos nuevos,** etc., as you see in personal ads.

Noticias culturales

La familia hispana

Para la mayoría de los hispanos la familia es una pequeña comunidad unida por la solidaridad y el cariño°. El concepto hispano de la familia incluye a los parientes más inmediatos (madre, padre, hijos, hermanos) y también a los abuelos, tíos, primos y numerosos otros parientes. En la familia tradicional, y especialmente en las zonas rurales, es común tener muchos niños.

En los países hispanos, los padres, los hijos y los abuelos con frecuencia viven en la misma° casa. Los abuelos son muy importantes en la crianza° de sus nietos y normalmente los cuidan cuando los padres salen. Tradicionalmente, el padre trabaja y la madre cuida de la casa y de los niños. Los hijos solteros° generalmente viven en la casa de sus padres mientras° asisten a la universidad o trabajan.

Sin embargo°, hoy en día el concepto de la familia hispana está cambiando°. Dos de los cambios más notables son que la familia es más pequeña y que muchas mujeres trabajan fuera de° casa.

affection

same / upbringing

single, unmarried

while

Sin... *Nevertheless*

changing

fuera... *outside of*

Una de las celebraciones es la fiesta de los quince años. Aquí vemos a una quinceañera a la salida de la iglesia (*church*), rodeada de mariachis. México.

Por lo general la familia, sea tradicional o moderna, es el núcleo de la vida social. Abuelos, nietos, padres, tíos, padrinos° y primos se reúnen con frecuencia para celebrar los cumpleaños, bautizos°, comuniones y otras fiestas. Las relaciones familiares ocupan un lugar° esencial en la sociedad hispana.

godparents

baptisms

place

¿Qué recuerda?

1. ¿Qué palabras describen a la familia hispana?
2. ¿Cuáles son algunas de las características de la familia hispana tradicional?
3. ¿Qué cambios existen en la familia hispana de hoy?
4. ¿Cómo sabemos (*How do we know*) que la familia es el núcleo de la vida social hispana?

3 **Conexiones y contrastes.** Discuss the following questions.

1. ¿Qué diferencias existen entre las familias hispanas y algunas familias típicas de su país? Mencionen tres.
2. ¿Se reúne su familia con frecuencia? ¿Para qué ocasiones?
3. En su país, ¿hay un equivalente a la quinceañera o la fiesta de los quince?

Así se dice

Algunas profesiones

el señor Vega

el **abogado**/ la **abogada** (1)

la señora Vega

la **mujer de negocios**/ el **hombre de negocios** (2)

el Dr. López

el **médico**/ la **médica**
el **doctor**/ la **doctora** (3)

la señorita Rojas

la **enfermera**/ el **enfermero** (4)

la señora Ruíz

la **programadora**/
el **programador** (5)

el señor Gómez

el **contador**/ la **contadora** (6)

la señorita Cortés

la **maestra**/ el **maestro** (7)

la señora Casona

el **ama de casa**/ el **amo de casa** (8)

(1) lawyer (m./f.) (2) businesswoman/man (3) doctor (m./f.) (4) nurse (f./m.) (5) computer programmer (f./m.) (6) accountant (m./f.) (7) teacher (f./m.) (8) homemaker (f./m.)

> Many feminine nouns that start with a stressed **a** require the article **el** in the singular. It is easier to link **el** to the noun than **la**. However, in the plural, **las** is used rather than **los**.
>
> el **a**ma de casa   *but*   **las** amas de casa
> el **a**ula   *but*   **las** aulas
>
> When stating a person's profession or vocation without further qualifiers or description, the indefinite article **un** or **una** is not used. When an adjective is added, the indefinite article is used.
>
> Mi madre es **abogada**.   *but*   Mi madre es **una abogada** excelente.

Práctica y comunicación

2-18. **¿Quién es? ¿Y cuál es la profesión?** Referring to the following descriptions and to the drawings on page 83, identify each person and his/her profession.

> **Modelo:** Trabaja con computadoras.
>
> Es la[7] señora Ruíz. Es programadora.

1. Trabaja en un hospital y cuida a los pacientes día y noche.
2. Trabaja con cifras (*figures*) grandes y escribe informes sobre la situación económica de una compañía.
3. Trabaja para una compañía grande.
4. Defiende a los «inocentes».
5. Pasa el día en la sala de clase de una escuela primaria. Tiene muchos alumnos.
6. Trabaja en una clínica o en el hospital. Tiene muchos pacientes.
7. Trabaja en casa.

2-19. **Preguntas personales.** Review the list of additional professions found in **Apéndice 3**, page A-14. Then find out more about your partner and his/her family by asking the questions that follow.

1. ¿Cuál es la profesión o vocación de tu madre? ¿Y la de tu padre? **Mi madre...**
2. ¿Cuál es la profesión de tu tío favorito? ¿Y de tu tía favorita?
3. ¿Trabajas? (¿En qué tipo de trabajo?)
4. En el futuro, ¿quieres (*do you want*) ser abogado/a? **Sí, quiero ser...** *o* **No, no quiero ser...** ¿Quieres ser militar? ¿Profesor/a de español? ¿Hombre/Mujer de negocios? ¿...? ¿...?

Estructuras

 Indicating location and describing conditions: The verb *estar*

A. Indicating location of people, places, and things

You have used the two Spanish verbs that mean *to be*: **ser** and **estar**. So far, you have used **ser** to tell origin, to indicate days of the week, dates and time, to describe inherent personality and physical characteristics, and to indicate profession. You have used **estar** with the expressions **¿Cómo está usted?** and **¿Cómo estás?** When **estar** is used with the preposition **en** (*in, at*), it indicates the location of people, places, or objects.

---

[7] The definite article **el/ la/ los/ las** must precede titles when talking *about* a person. Examples: **Los** señores Ríos son abogados. **La** doctora Artavia es excelente. The article is not used when talking *to* a person: **Buenos días, señor(a)/ doctor(a) Ríos.**

Study the forms of the present tense of the verb **estar** (*to be*), as well as the sample sentences.

estar *to be*		
(yo)	estoy	**Estoy** en la universidad.
(tú)	estás	¿**Estás** en casa?
(usted, él, ella)	está	Acapulco **está** en México.
(nosotros/as)	estamos	**Estamos** en clase.
(vosotros/as)	estáis	¿**Estáis** en el apartamento de Beatriz?
(ustedes, ellos, ellas)	están	Mis amigas **están** en clase.

Así se dice
¿Dónde están?

Fotos del álbum familiar

Mi prima Anita está **en el trabajo**(3).

Mi prima Susana cstá **en el colegio**(2)*.

Mi hermano Ricardo está **en la escuela**(1).

Mis tíos están **en casa**(4).

Mi primo y yo estamos **en la playa**(5).

(1) at, in school (elementary school) (2) at, in school (high school) (3) at work (4) at home (5) at the beach

---

* **El colegio, el liceo,** or **la preparatoria** (Mexico) refer to secondary school. Use **universidad** for university or college.

Así es mi familia

HINT | Note that **en** = *in* or *at*; **a** = *to*. **Vamos *a* la playa. Están *en* la playa.**

¿Dónde están?

Estamos **en el campo**(6).

Aquí(7), estoy **en las montañas**(8) de Colorado.

Estamos **en la ciudad**(9) de Los Ángeles. ¡Hay much tráfico **allí**(10)!

(6) in the country (7) Here (8) in the mountains (9) in the city (10) there

Práctica y comunicación

2-20. **¿Dónde están?** Guess where the following people are according to the information given.

> **Modelo:** Juanito está en clase con su maestra. Tiene seis años.
>
> Está en la escuela.

1. Sandra toma varias clases. Tiene muchos maestros. **Está...**

2. Tenemos varios profesores. Somos adultos. Las clases son difíciles. **Estamos...**

3. Trabajamos desde las 9:00 de la mañana hasta las 5:00 de la tarde. **Estamos...**

4. Tomo una siesta. Miro la televisión, hablo por teléfono. **Estoy...**

5. Estás de vacaciones. El océano es muy bonito. **Estás...**

6. Estás de vacaciones. Usas tus suéteres y tus esquís. **Estás...**

7. Los González dicen (*say*) que hay mucho tráfico allí. **Están...**

8. Los Martínez dicen que hay animales, flores y mucha tranquilidad allí. **Están...**

2 Now tell a classmate where some of the most important people in your life are right now. **Mi pareja/ mi mejor amigo/a...**

2-21. **¿Dónde estás?** Walking around the classroom, ask six of your classmates where they normally are on the days and at the times indicated. Be prepared to report back to the class.

Modelo: Normalmente, ¿dónde estás los lunes a las ocho de la mañana?
José responde: **Estoy en casa.**

José						
lunes 8:00 A.M.	martes 9:30 A.M.	miércoles 10:45 A.M.	jueves 1:30 P.M.	viernes 3:00 P.M.	sábado 10:00 P.M.	domingo 8:00 A.M.
Está en casa.						

Estructuras

B. Describing conditions

Estar can also be used with descriptive words to indicate the mental, emotional, or physical condition in which the subject is found at a given time.

Estoy cansado/a.	*I'm tired.* (physical)
¿**Estás** preocupado?	*Are you worried?* (mental/emotional)
¡Carlos **está** furioso!	*Carlos is furious!* (emotional)

Así se dice

¿Cómo están?

Rubén

aburrido/a(1)

Camila

enojado/a(2)

Octavio

cansado/a(3)

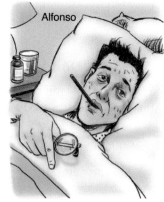

Alfonso

enfermo/a(4)

Carmen

nervioso/a(5)
preocupado/a(6)
estresado/a(7)

Manuel

Linda

contento/a ➜ triste (8)
bien ➜ mal (9)

Natalia

ocupado/a(10)

la ventana

la puerta

el libro

el cuaderno

cerrado/a ➜ abierto/a (11)

(1) bored (2) angry (3) tired (4) sick (5) nervous (6) worried (7) stressed (8) happy ➜ sad
(9) well ➜ bad, badly, sick (10) busy (11) closed ➜ open

> **Bien** and **mal** are *adverbs* and do not change in gender (masculine/feminine) or number (singular/plural) as adjectives do. **Bien** and **mal** are often used with **estar**.
> **Estoy** muy **bien**, gracias.

Práctica y comunicación

2-22. **Condiciones.** Describe the people and things in the drawings on page 88.

page 88.

> **Modelo:** Rubén
> Está aburrido.

¿Y Camila? ¿Y Octavio? ¿Y ...?

2 **2-23.** **¿Dónde estás? ¿Cómo estás?** Describe to each other where you are and how you normally feel in each of the following circumstances.

	¿Dónde estás?	¿Cómo estás normalmente?
1. los lunes temprano por la mañana	Estoy en...	Estoy...
2. los viernes por la tarde		
3. de lunes a viernes		
4. la noche antes de (*before*) un examen final		
5. los fines de semana		
6. …		

Now report back to the class one statement about your partner.

3 **2-24.** **Nuestro amigo Javier.** Describe what Javier is like (**ser** + *characteristics*) and/or imagine how he is feeling (**estar** + *condition*) according to the circumstances. Use the adjectives provided. In some cases there can be more than one possible answer.

> cansado   contento   enfermo   estresado   fuerte
> inteligente   ocupado   preocupado   trabajador

> **Modelo:** Javier juega al tenis toda la mañana.
> Está muy cansado.

1. Saca buenas notas.
2. Va al gimnasio y levanta pesas.
3. Hoy está en la clínica.
4. Toma cinco clases, es voluntario y trabaja en el laboratorio por la noche.
5. Tiene dos exámenes mañana.
6. ¡Marlena, su mejor amiga, llega este fin de semana!

2-25. La familia: ¿Cómo son? ¿Cómo están? You and your classmate have just received a photo of the López family, with whom you will be staying during your upcoming trip to New York. Describe the family: number of children; what the mother, the father, the youngest/oldest daughters, etc. are like (**ser** + *characteristics*). Talk about where they are now and how they are feeling (**estar** + *location/condition*).

Los López. Long Island, Nueva York.

Así se pronuncia

The pronunciation of *h* and *j*

h Remember that the Spanish **h** is never pronounced.

hermana **h**ombre **h**ermanastro **h**ermoso

j The Spanish **j** is pronounced like the *h* in the English word *help*.

vie**j**o   **j**oven   mu**j**er de negocios

Repeat the following sentences to help perfect your pronunciation. Focus on the letters **h** and **j**.

h **H**éctor y **H**elena tienen **h**ijos muy **h**onrados.

j **J**osé y **J**uana tienen hi**j**os muy traba**j**adores.

Dicho y hecho

◀▶ Conversando

③ Una persona muy especial. Bring to class a photo of a family member, your partner, or a friend. Describe the person in detail, including origin/nationality (see **Apéndice 3**, p. A-14), age, physical and personality traits, where he/she is right now, etc.

Your classmates will ask you questions to elicit more information.

🎧 ¡A escuchar!

Linda conversa con su padre. Linda comes from a very traditional Hispanic family. She is getting ready for her first date with Manuel, and of course her father wants to know all about Manuel's background. Listen to the conversation between father and daughter; then answer the first two questions.

1. ¿Quién hace la mayoría (*majority*) de las preguntas?
   ❏ el padre   ❏ Linda
2. ¿A quién describe Linda más (*more*)?
   ❏ a Manuel   ❏ a la familia de Manuel

Now listen to the conversation again, and then select the correct answers.

3. Linda dice (*says*) que Manuel es:
   ❏ trabajador y un buen estudiante   ❏ muy simpático y divertido
4. La madre de Manuel es de:
   ❏ San Francisco ❏ Los Ángeles   ❏ Perú
5. La madre es: ❏ alta   ❏ baja   ❏ rubia   ❏ morena
6. El padre es: ❏ alto   ❏ bajo   ❏ gordo   ❏ delgado
7. El padre es: ❏ profesor de español   ❏ hombre de negocios

✍ De mi escritorio

Así es mi familia. This is the final phase of your chapter project. Start by including your family tree and the information you prepared earlier (see Exercise 2-5). Then write about your family: What are your grandparents, parents, siblings, and other relatives like? Include: origin and nationality/ies, profession, age, physical and personality traits, and any other interesting details. Conclude by writing about yourself. You might want to add some family photos. Your professor will ask for volunteers to present their work to the class.

HINT | To describe deceased relatives, use: **era** (*he/she was*) or **eran** (*they were*). Refer to **Apéndice 3** for a listing of nationalities and professions.

Panorama cultural

Los hispanos en los Estados Unidos

CANADÁ

WASHINGTON
MONTANA
DAKOTA DEL NORTE
MINNESOTA
NEW HAMPSHIRE VERMONT
MAINE
OREGÓN
IDAHO
DAKOTA DEL SUR
WISCONSIN
MICHIGAN
MASSACHUSETTS
NUEVA YORK
RHODE ISLAND CONNECTICUT
WYOMING
NEBRASKA
IOWA
Chicago
INDIANA
OHIO
PENSILVANIA
Nueva York
NUEVA JERSEY
NEVADA
UTAH
ESTADOS UNIDOS
ILLINOIS
DELAWARE
MARYLAND
Washington, D.C.
San José
CALIFORNIA
COLORADO
KANSAS
MISURI
VIRGINIA OCCIDENTAL
VIRGINIA
Los Ángeles
ARIZONA
Albuquerque
NUEVO MÉXICO
Phoenix
OKLAHOMA
ARKANSAS
KENTUCKY
TENNESSEE
CAROLINA DEL NORTE
CAROLINA DEL SUR
OCÉANO ATLÁNTICO
San Diego
El Paso
TEXAS
Dallas
MISISIPÍ
ALABAMA
GEORGIA
San Antonio
Houston
LUISIANA
OCÉANO PACÍFICO
Corpus Christi
MÉXICO
GOLFO DE MÉXICO
FLORIDA
Miami

ALASKA
HAWAI

0   250   500 Millas
0   250   500 Kilómetros

■ Estados que tienen más del 15.1% de población hispana
■ Estados que tienen 5.1-15.1% de población hispana
■ Estados que tienen 2-5% de población hispana
★ Ciudades indicadas tienen más de 100.000 hispanos

Población hispana total en los Estados Unidos según el censo de 2000 = aproximadamente 35.3 millones

Person@je del momento

¿Sabe usted (*Do you know*) quién es Salma Hayek? Busque información en el Internet y compártala (*share it*) con sus compañeros/as de clase. ¡En español, por favor!

Preguntas sobre el mapa

1. ¿Cuáles son los estados con mayor concentración hispana (más del 15.1%)?
2. ¿Cuáles son los estados que tienen de 5.1% a 15.1% de población hispana?
3. ¿Sabe usted (*Do you know*) en qué estados viven muchas personas de origen mexicano? ¿De origen cubano? ¿De origen puertorriqueño?

¿Cuántos hispanos hay?

¿Sabe usted que hoy los hispanos representan aproximadamente el 15% (por ciento) de la población de los Estados Unidos (EE.UU.)? La comunidad hispana es una de las más importantes del país. Aproximadamente el 70% de la población hispana se concentra en cuatro estados: California, Tejas, Nueva York y la Florida. Gran parte de esta población vive en áreas metropolitanas como[1] Los Ángeles, Nueva York, Miami, Chicago, Washington, D.C. y San Antonio. También existen comunidades hispanas importantes en ciudades más pequeñas como Santa Fe (NM), Pueblo (CO), Yuma (AZ), Hialeah (FL), Trenton (NJ), Gary (IN), Racine (WI) y Cheyenne (WY).

¡Qué enchilada! La enchilada más grande del mundo se hace en Nuevo México; 75 personas la preparan ¡y 8.500 personas la comen!

¿De dónde son?

La mayoría de los hispanos en los EE.UU. son de México (60+%), Puerto Rico (10+%) y Cuba (5+%). Gran parte de los nuevos inmigrantes hispanos de los últimos[2] treinta años son de Centroamérica —salvadoreños, nicaragüenses, hondureños y guatemaltecos— y también de la República Dominicana. Viven en diversas zonas del país.

[1]*like* [2]*last* [3]*southwest* [4]*arrival* [5]*English-speaking* [6]*friendship* [7]*southeast*

En el suroeste[3] del país la presencia de la población hispana de origen mexicano es anterior a la llegada[4] de la población angloparlante[5]. Hoy la amistad[6] entre México y los Estados Unidos se representa en la escultura *Torch of Friendship* en San Antonio, Tejas. El escultor es un famoso artista mexicano. ¿En qué estados de los Estados Unidos hay muchos mexicano-americanos?

A partir de 1959, como resultado de la revolución cubana, muchos cubanos inmigraron al sureste[7] de los EE.UU., especialmente a Tampa y Miami. Hoy, medio millón de cubanos y cubanoamericanos viven en Miami. En la foto, ¿quienes juegan (*play*) al dominó en el parque?

Su influencia

- Los nombres de varias ciudades y estados son la evidencia más notable de la presencia hispana en la historia del país.
- La ciudad más antigua en el territorio continental de los EE.UU. tiene un nombre hispano (San Agustín, FL).
- La vida diaria[8] de los EE.UU. integra numerosos elementos de las artes, la comida[9] y el idioma de la cultura hispana.
- Los hispanos también hacen contribuciones muy valiosas[10] a la política, las ciencias y la economía del país.

Hoy hay más de un millón de puertorriqueños en Nueva York. La comunidad dominicana más grande del país también reside en esta ciudad. ¿Cómo se llama este mercado en Spanish Harlem, Nueva York?

¿Cuáles son las atracciónes de este restaurante en la pequeña Habana?

[8]*daily* [9]*food*
[10]*valuable*

¿Qué descubrimos?

1. El 70% de la población hispana se concentra en…
2. … son tres ciudades donde hay comunidades hispanas importantes.
3. Muchos de los hispanos en los EE.UU. son de…, … y…
4. La población hispana del suroeste es de origen…
5. Gran parte de la población cubana vive en el… del país.
6. En Nueva York dos comunidades hispanas importantes son los… y los…
7. … son evidencia de la importancia histórica de los hispanos en los EE.UU.
8. Los hispanos son participantes muy activos en…

② Preguntas

Explore the impact of Hispanic culture in the United States by answering the following questions.

1. ¿Cuáles son algunos nombres de ciudades y estados que indican la presencia hispana en la historia de los EE.UU.?
2. ¿Cuáles son algunos ejemplos de la comida hispana en los EE.UU.? ¿Cuál es su favorita?
3. ¿Existen otras influencias hispanas en su comunidad?
4. ¿Conoce usted (*Are you acquainted with*) a algunos hispanos famosos que viven en los Estados Unidos? ¿Actores/Actrices? ¿Cantantes (*Singers*)? ¿Políticos/as? ¿Autores/Autoras? ¿Atletas?

Encuentro cultural

Artes populares

Los murales

Los murales son creaciones que inspiran la imaginación y estimulan la conciencia. Los primeros[1] murales tienen miles[2] de años: están en las cuevas[3] de Lascaux (Francia) y Altamira (España). Históricamente, en los EE.UU., los murales son la auto-expresión y la auto-definición de muchas comunidades, especialmente en el oeste y el suroeste del país. La creación de murales en las ciudades más importantes de California en los años 60 y 70 es labor de jóvenes chicanos[4]. Muchos murales presentan panoramas de la historia mexicano-americana. Los murales más recientes también manifiestan los intereses y preocupaciones de cada comunidad.

California es la capital del arte mural en los EE.UU. El sol[5], las numerosas paredes[6] de cemento y estuco, la influencia de la tradición muralista mexicana y la buena recepción que tiene el arte popular entre los californianos contribuyen a la preservación de la colección de arte público más impresionante de la nación. Examine los siguientes murales y conteste las preguntas.

[1] first [2] thousands [3] caves
[4] Mexican-Americans [5] sun
[6] walls

Mural «Siete punto uno» de John Pugh. Los Ángeles, California. ¿Ruinas mayas en Los Ángeles? En realidad es un mural pintado en el exterior de un restaurante hispano.

«La ofrenda» de Yreina Cervantes. Los Ángeles, California. En el centro está Dolores Huerta, fundadora del sindicato (union) United Farm Workers.

Preguntas

1. ¿Cuál de los murales celebra el activismo de la mujer hispana? ¿Cuál hace referencia a una cultura precolombina? ¿Qué cultura?
2. Mural 1: ¿Qué elementos históricos hay en el mural?
3. Mural 2: ¿Qué simbolizan las manos (hands) grandes? ¿Representan los siguientes símbolos un elemento positivo o un elemento negativo en el mural? Símbolos: el grupo de hombres tristes; las manos grandes; el hombre que cultiva las plantas; las flores; la sangre (blood); Dolores Huerta.

Adjetivos

abierto/a
aburrido/a
alto/a
amable
antipático/a
bajo/a
bonito/a
bueno/a
cansado/a
cerrado/a
contento/a
débil
delgado/a
difícil
divertido/a
enfermo/a
enojado/a
estresado/a
fácil
feo/a
flaco/a
fuerte
gordo/a
grande
guapo/a
hermoso/a
inteligente
joven
malo/a
mayor
menor
moreno/a
nervioso/a
nuevo/a
ocupado/a
pequeño/a
perezoso/a
pobre
preocupado/a
responsable
rico/a
rubio/a
serio/a
simpático/a
tonto/a
trabajador/a

triste
viejo/a

Adverbios

allí
aquí
bien
mal
muy
un poco

Conjunciones

o/u
pero
y/e

Sustantivos (*Nouns*)

La familia

la abuela
el abuelo
los abuelos
la bisabuela
el bisabuelo
la cuñada
el cuñado
la esposa
el esposo/el marido
la hermana
la hermanastra
el hermanastro
el hermano
la hija
el hijo
la madrastra
la madre
la media hermana
el medio hermano
la nieta
el nieto
el padrastro
el padre
los padres
el pariente
la prima
el primo
la sobrina

el sobrino
la suegra
el suegro
la tía
el tío

Otras personas

la amiga
el amigo
  mi mejor amigo/a
el/la bebé
la chica
el chico
el hombre
la muchacha
el muchacho
la mujer
la niña
el niño
la novia
el novio
mi pareja

Las mascotas (pets)

el gato
el perro

Las profesiones

la abogada
el abogado
el ama (*f.*) de casa
el amo de casa
el contador
la contadora
la enfermera
el enfermero
el hombre de negocios
la maestra
el maestro
la médica/ la doctora
el médico/ el doctor
la mujer de negocios
el programador
la programadora

Cosas (Things) y lugares (places)

el auto
el campo
el carro
la casa
  en casa
la ciudad
el coche
el colegio
la escuela
las montañas
la playa
el trabajo

Verbos y expresiones verbales

abrazar
amar
besar
cuidar
estar
llamar
tener
  tener… años
  ¿Cuántos años tienes?
visitar

Palabras interrogativas

¿Cuántos/as?
¿Dónde?
¿Quién/es?

I. The verb *tener*. Use the correct form of **tener**.

1. Yo _____ tres hermanos.
2. Mi hermano mayor _____ 21 años.
3. Mis padres _____ 55 años.
4. Mi hermano menor y yo _____ un perro.
5. ¿Cuántos años _____ tú?

II. Possessive adjectives. Use possessive adjectives to explain what the persons have.

Modelo: mi hermano / cuadernos
Tiene sus cuadernos.

1. yo / fotos
2. ¿tú / libros?
3. José / diccionario
4. mi hermano y yo / televisor
5. ¿ustedes / calculadoras?

III. Possession with *de*. Indicate to whom each object belongs.

Modelo: la mochila / Juan
Es la mochila de Juan.

1. la foto / Marta
2. los cuadernos / José
3. los exámenes / los estudiantes

IV. Descriptive adjectives. Complete the first sentence in each item with the correct form of the verb **ser**. Then complete the second sentence with the correct form of **ser** and the adjective of opposite meaning.

Modelo: Mi tío Paco ___es___ un poco gordo. Al contrario, mi tía Lisa _es_ _flaca/delgada_ .

1. Yo _____ trabajador/a. Al contrario, algunos de mis amigos _____ _____.
2. Mis padres _____ muy altos. Al contrario, mi hermano _____ _____.
3. Nosotros no _____ antipáticos. Al contrario, _____ muy _____.
4. Nuestra clase de español _____ fácil. Al contrario, nuestras clases de ciencia _____ _____.

V. *Estar* to indicate location. Tell where on campus the students are located according to the activity.

Modelo: Juana estudia mucho.
Está en la biblioteca.

1. Linda y Mónica compran lápices, bolígrafos y sus libros de texto.
2. Octavio y yo hacemos ejercicio.
3. Hablo con mis amigos y compro comida.
4. Mi amiga habla con la profesora Falcón. No están en el aula.

VI. *Estar* to indicate condition. React to the statements with forms of **estar** and appropriate adjectives.

Modelo: Tenemos un problema.
Estamos preocupados.

1. Tengo un examen mañana.
2. Mis amigos tienen mucha tarea.
3. Sancho tiene apendicitis.
4. ¡Tenemos un día sin (*without*) preocupaciones! ¡No hay clases!

VII. General review. Answer the following questions.

1. ¿Cuántos años tiene usted?
2. ¿Cómo es su madre o padre?
3. ¿Cómo son sus amigos/as?
4. ¿Cómo están sus amigos/as?
5. ¿Están usted y sus amigos preocupados por sus notas? ¿En qué materias (*subjects*)?
6. ¿Qué días tienen ustedes clases?
7. ¿Cómo son sus clases?

Answers to the *Autoprueba y repaso* are found in **Apéndice 2**.

Capítulo 3

¡A la mesa!

Goals for communication

- To buy and talk about food in a market, restaurant, etc.
- To express likes and dislikes
- To talk about actions, desires, and preferences in the present
- To express large quantities, prices, and dates
- To ask for specific information

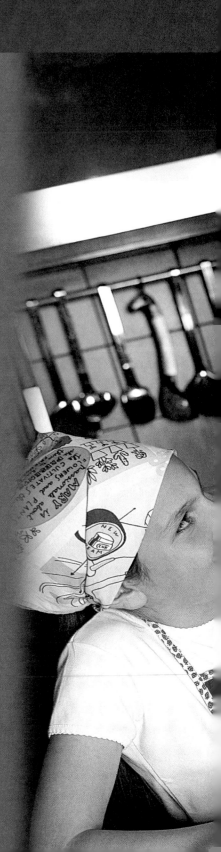

Así se dice

¡A la mesa!

① Mercado Central

② ¿Cuánto cuestan?

③ Frutas

16 ¿Qué desea, señor?

19. vender

18. el pescado

17 Mariscos

4. las piñas

20. la langosta

21. los camarones

5. las bananas/ los plátanos

Seis pesos el kilo.

12 Necesitamos comprar fresas hoy.

6. las manzanas

7. las uvas

15. las sandías

8. las naranjas

13. las fresas

10. las peras

11. las cerezas

14. los melocotones/ los duraznos

9. los limones

Carnes

22

23 Voy a preparar arroz con pollo esta noche.

24. el pollo

26. la salchicha/ el chorizo

31. el ajo

25. el jamón

27. el bistec

29. las chuletas de cerdo/puerco

28. la carne de res

30. la carne de cerdo/puerco

Legumbres Verduras
32

33. el maíz

37. las cebollas

34. papas/ las patatas

38. el brócoli

40. las zanahorias

35. los tomates

36. la lechuga

Frijoles **42**

39. las judías verdes

Arroz **43**

41. los guisantes

1. market
2. How much do they cost?; **¿Cuánto cuesta?** (s.)
3. fruits
4. pineapples
5. bananas
6. apples
7. grapes
8. oranges
9. lemons; **el limón** (s.)
10. pears
11. cherries
12. We need . . . ; **necesitar** to need
13. strawberries
14. peaches; **el melocotón** (s.)
15. watermelons
16. What do you want?; **desear** to want, desire
17. seafood, shellfish
18. fish
19. to sell
20. lobster
21. shrimp
22. meats (f.), beef
23. to prepare
24. chicken
25. ham
26. sausage
27. steak
28. beef
29. pork chops
30. pork
31. garlic
32. vegetables (f.)
33. corn
34. potatoes
35. tomatoes
36. lettuce
37. onions
38. broccoli
39. green beans
40. carrots
41. peas
42. beans
43. rice (m.)

HINT When two Spanish verbs are used consecutively, only the first is conjugated, just as in English.

¿Desea usted **cenar**?

*Do you **want to have dinner**?*

Necesito comprar más tomates.

***I need to buy** more tomatoes.*

Práctica y comunicación

3-1. **En el Mercado Central.** Answer according to the drawing on pages 100–101 and your personal preferences.

1. ¿Qué frutas venden en el mercado? ¿Cuál es su fruta favorita?
2. ¿Cuánto cuestan las naranjas?
3. ¿Qué necesitan comprar Juanito y su madre?
4. ¿Qué pregunta el vendedor de mariscos? ¿Qué mariscos vende? ¿Cuál es su marisco favorito?
5. ¿Qué legumbres venden en el mercado? ¿Cuál es su legumbre favorita? ¿Es usted vegetariano/a?
6. ¿Qué carnes venden? ¿Qué va a comprar la señora? ¿Por qué?
7. ¿Come usted carne? ¿Cuál es su carne favorita?

3-2. **La lista de compras.** Make a shopping list of the ingredients you will need to buy to prepare the following dishes.

Plato

1. una ensalada mixta
2. una ensalada de frutas
3. una sopa muy original

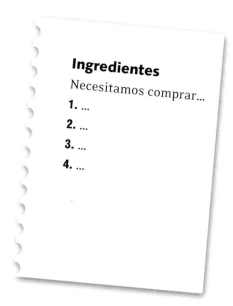

Ingredientes

Necesitamos comprar...

1. ...
2. ...
3. ...
4. ...

3-3. **Vamos al mercado.** Imagine that two of you are customers shopping at an open-air market in Mexico. Using the shopping lists you prepared for Exercise 3–2, inquire about and purchase produce. The third student is the vendor.

Modelo: Vendedor/a: **Buenos días, ¿qué desean ustedes?**

Cliente 1: **Pues, necesitamos...**

Cliente 2: **¿Tienen...?**

El pollo, la carne, o el pescado más exquisito, Usted lo prepara con Chef Merito...

Con los productos **Chef Merito**, Usted no tiene que saber cocinar. Con recetas en cada frasco, **Chef Merito** le ayuda a preparar cualquier platillo. **Chef Merito** tiene un Sazonador para cada ocasión y la **mejor *auténtica Salsa Picante.*** Todos los productos **Chef Merito** tienen sellos protectores y fechas de expiración para garantizar el buen sabor y calidad. Recuerde...**con Chef Merito en la sartén, cualquiera cocina bien.**

Pídalo en su tienda favorita o llame al **800-MERITO-1**
o visítenos en www.chefmerito.com.

READING STRATEGY

Skimming for general content
Read the ad quickly to get a general idea of content. Do not attempt to translate word for word.
What is the principal idea in this ad?

1. Identifiquen las carnes y las legumbres del anuncio.
2. Identifiquen los dos ingredientes que son típicamente mexicanos: los chiles y el nopal (*cactus leaf*).
3. ¿Usan ustedes salsa picante? ¿En qué comidas?
4. Lean la rima que comienza con **El pollo, la carne...** En el contexto de la rima, ¿qué significa **carne**?
5. ¿Qué sazonadores (*seasonings*) desean ustedes comprar para preparar sus comidas favoritas?

Escenas

¿Qué hay de comer?

 Camila   Esteban   Natalia

3 *Frente al restaurante de la universidad. Es hora de cenar y Natalia lee el menú en la entrada. Llegan Camila y Esteban.*

CAMILA Y ESTEBAN:	¡Hola, Natalia! ¿Cómo te va?
NATALIA:	Bastante bien. ¿Qué hay de nuevo?
ESTEBAN:	Pues no mucho. Vamos a comer. ¿Hay algo° bueno en el menú de hoy?
NATALIA:	Depende. ¿Te gusta el arroz con guisantes y pollo frito?
CAMILA:	¿Pollo frito otra vez? ¡No es un plato muy saludable°! ¿Hay ensalada?
NATALIA:	Claro que sí, es tu favorita: ensalada de papa y zanahoria con mayonesa.
CAMILA:	¡Ugh! Esa ensalada tiene mucha grasa° y yo estoy a dieta. Pero hay sopa de verduras, ¿verdad?
NATALIA:	Vamos a ver... Pues, no. Sólo hay sopa de pescado.
ESTEBAN:	Yo quiero comer algo diferente. Quiero unas chuletas de cerdo con puré de papas°, frijoles y arroz...
CAMILA:	Y una ensalada de lechuga fresca, con tomates y aceitunas°...
NATALIA:	¡Y flan° y café para el postre°!

something (algo)
healthy (saludable)
fat (grasa)
puré... mashed potatoes
olives (aceitunas)
caramel custard / dessert (flan / postre)

Todos... They all sigh

(*Todos suspiran°.*)

ESTEBAN:	Bueno, ¿y por qué no vamos al restaurante La Isla?
CAMILA:	Esteban, ir a un restaurante es caro° y no tengo mucho dinero° en este momento.
NATALIA:	Es verdad. ¿Por qué no cocinamos° en mi casa? Las chuletas de cerdo son mi especialidad y son muy fáciles de preparar.
ESTEBAN:	Yo no cocino bien, pero mi especialidad es el flan instantáneo... Camila, tú puedes preparar la ensalada.
CAMILA:	¡Sí! Y también° puedo preparar las papas.
NATALIA:	¡Fantástico! Vamos al supermercado. Mi coche está en el estacionamiento norte.

expensive / money (caro / dinero)
cook (cocinamos)
also (también)

¿Qué pasa?

1. ¿Adónde van Camila y Esteban?
2. ¿Qué hay en el menú de hoy?
3. ¿Por qué no quiere Camila comer la ensalada de papa y zanahoria?
4. ¿Qué desea comer Esteban? ¿Y Camila? ¿Y Natalia?
5. ¿Por qué no van a un restaurante? ¿Qué hacen?

Estructuras

1 **Expressing likes and dislikes: The verb *gustar***

¡Me gustan las fresas!

Read the following dialog between Octavio and Inés. Pay attention to the forms of **gustar**.

INÉS:	¿**Te gusta**° la comida° del restaurante de la U?	*do you like / food*
OCTAVIO:	Sí, **me gusta**° mucho.	*I like it*
INÉS:	¿De veras? A mí **no me gusta** para nada y a mi compañera de cuarto **no le gusta**° tampoco°.	*does not like it / either*
OCTAVIO:	¿Por qué no **les gusta**?	
INÉS:	No **nos gusta** porque no es nutritiva ni muy sabrosa°.	*tasty*
OCTAVIO:	Pero esta sopa de champiñones° está deliciosa. **Me gusta** muchísimo.	*mushrooms*
INÉS:	Sí, está deliciosa, pero el problema es que no tiene champiñones.	
OCTAVIO:	¡Qué horror! ¿Qué son?	
INÉS:	¿Quién sabe?	

Gustar, meaning *to be pleasing* (to someone), is used in a special construction to express the Spanish equivalent of the English *to like*.

		Literal Translation
Me gusta el helado.	*I like ice cream.*	*(Ice cream is pleasing to me.)*
¿Te gustan las fresas?	*Do you like strawberries?*	*(Are strawberries pleasing to you?)*
No le gusta tomar vino.	*He doesn't like to drink wine.*	*(Drinking wine isn't pleasing to him.)*

As you can see in the examples, the subject pronouns (**yo, tú, él,...**) are *not* used in the **gustar** constructions. To express who is doing the liking (or literally, to whom something is pleasing), the forms **me, te, le, nos, os, les**[1] are used. **Gusta** (for single items) and **gustan** (for plural) are the two most commonly used forms of **gustar** in the present tense.

Person(s) doing the liking	+	**gusta / gustan**	+	thing(s) liked

| | | **gusta** | + | el helado / la fruta / comer frutas |
| me / te / le / nos / os / les | + | **gustan** | + | las uvas / las fresas / los camarones |

- Note that the definite article is used with the thing(s) liked: **Me gusta** *el* **helado. Me gustan** *las* **fresas.**

- To express the idea that one *likes to do something*, the singular form **gusta** is used with the infinitive (the **-ar, -er, -ir** form of the verb).

  Nos **gusta comer**.　　　　　　　　*We **like to eat**.*

  Les **gusta cenar** en restaurantes　　*They **like to have dinner** in*
  y **asistir a** conciertos　　　　　　*restaurants and **attend** concerts.*

- To clarify the meaning of **le** and **les**, use **a** + *person*: **a mis padres, a Pedro, a él, a ella, a usted, a ellos**, etc.

  A mis padres les gusta la langosta.　　***My parents** like lobster.*

  A Pedro le gusta tomar café con　　***Pedro** likes to drink coffee*
  leche.　　　　　　　　　　　　　　*with milk.*

  A ella le gusta el té; **a él** no.　　***She** likes tea; he doesn't.*

- For emphasis, use **a mí, a ti, a usted, a nosotros**, etc.

  A mí no me gustan los camarones.　　***I** don't like shrimp.*

  A ti te gustan, ¿verdad?　　　　　***You** like them, right?*

- To ask a follow-up question, use **¿Y a ti?, ¿Y a usted?, ¿Y a él?**, etc.

---

[1] The indirect object pronouns, meaning *to me, to you, to you/him/her, to us, to you, to you/them*, will be studied in detail in **Chapter 7**.

Práctica y comunicación

3-5. **¡Me gusta!** Find out whether your classmate likes the following items or not. Then write down your shared likes and dislikes (**Nos gusta/gustan.../No nos...**) to report back to the class.

> **Modelo:** los tomates
>
> Estudiante 1: **¿Te gustan los tomates?**
>
> Estudiante 2: **Sí, me gustan. ¿Y a ti?** *o* **No, no me gustan.**

1. los duraznos
2. las uvas
3. las cebollas
4. el ajo
5. los camarones
6. la langosta
7. los guisantes
8. la pizza
9. la pasta
10. las fresas
11. el bróculi
12. la carne de res
13. la comida (*food*) china/ italiana/ francesa/ tailandesa/ vietnamita

3-6. **Preguntas para su profesor/a.** Now it is your turn to ask your instructor what he/she likes to do. Use the cues provided.

> **Modelo:** leer novelas (¿Qué tipo?)
>
> Estudiante: **¿Le gusta a usted leer novelas?**
>
> Profesor/a: **Sí, me gusta mucho leer novelas.**
>
> Estudiante: **¿Qué tipo?**
>
> Profesor/a: **Novelas de ciencia ficción.**

1. preparar comida mexicana/española (¿Qué platos prepara?)
2. comer en el restaurante/la cafetería de la universidad (¿Todos los días?)
3. cenar en restaurantes muy buenos (¿Cuáles?)
4. escuchar discos compactos (¿Qué tipo de música?)
5. asistir a conciertos (¿De *rock*? ¿De música clásica?)
6. navegar por la red (¿Con mucha frecuencia?)
7. mandar mensajes electrónicos (¿A quién?)
8. ... (*your own idea*)

3-7. **Los gustos de los estudiantes.** Pablo, a foreign-exchange student from Mexico, asks in an e-mail about the likes/dislikes of students at your university. Respond to him.

Asunto :

Hola, Pablo,
Pues, a mis amigos les.../no les...
A nosotros nos.../no nos...

2 Talking about actions, desires, and preferences in the present: Stem-changing verbs

Rubén, ¿quieres cenar en un restaurante con nosotras esta noche?

Prefiero cenar solo, gracias.

¡Ay de mí!

Stem-changing verbs have the same endings as regular **-ar**, **-er**, and **-ir** verbs. However, they differ from regular verbs in that a change occurs in the stem (**e → ie**, **o → ue**, or **e → i**) in all persons except **nosotros** and **vosotros**. (The stem is the part of the verb that remains after the **-ar**, **-er**, or **-ir** ending is removed.) Study the pattern of change in the following model verbs.

e → ie

querer *to want, to love*	
quer- → quier-	
qui**e**ro	queremos
qui**e**res	queréis
qui**e**re	qui**e**ren

querer (ie)	*to want, to love*	No **quiero** comer ahora.
preferir (ie)	*to prefer*	**Prefiero** comer más tarde.
entender (ie)	*to understand*	¿**Entienden** el problema?
pensar² (ie)	*to think*	¿**Piensas** que hay un problema?

o → ue

dormir *to sleep*	
dorm- → duerm-	
d**ue**rmo	dormimos
d**ue**rmes	dormís
d**ue**rme	d**ue**rmen

---

² When seeking an opinion, ask ¿**Qué piensas de...?** (*What do you think about . . .?*). When giving your opinion, say **Pienso que...** (*I think that . . .*).

dormir (ue)	to sleep	¿**Duermes** bien?
almorzar (ue)	to have lunch	¿A qué hora **almuerzas**?
poder (ue)	to be able, can	¿**Puedes** cenar a las 7:00?
volver (ue)	to return, go back	¿A qué hora **vuelves** a la residencia?

e → i

pedir *to ask for*	
ped- → **pid-**	
pido	pedimos
pides	pedís
pide	piden

| pedir (i) | to ask for, request, order | Ella siempre **pide** pizza. |
| servir (i) | to serve | ¿**Sirven** langosta aquí? |

DICHOS

Querer es poder.

Quien mucho tiene más quiere.

¿Puede usted explicar estos dichos en español?

Práctica y comunicación

2 **3-8. La confesión de Esteban.** Read the following paragraph, paying special attention to the stem-changing verbs.

Sí, es verdad. Soy un poco perezoso —bueno, muy perezoso. Pref**ie**ro estudiar por la noche, cuando estudio. Por la tarde alm**ue**rzo, v**ue**lvo a mi cuarto, y luego d**ue**rmo la siesta. Es mi rutina; de lo contrario no p**ue**do funcionar bien el resto del día. Verdaderamente p**ie**nso que es indispensable recargar° las baterías. No ent**ie**ndo a esa gente que trabaja sin descanso. Es necesario saber° vivir. ¿Para qué s**i**rven las buenas notas cuando uno es infeliz°?

recharge

to know how to

unhappy

Now pretend with a partner that the two of you are as lazy as Esteban. Make his confession yours by making his statements about himself plural. Your instructor will ask some of you to read your "confessions" to the class.

Modelo: Esteban: Soy un poco perezoso.

Estudiantes: **Somos un poco perezosos/as.**

¿Prefieren ustedes la comida de la universidad o la comida rápida (*fast food*)? ¿Por qué?

3-9. **La comida de la universidad.** Your professor wants to know something about the university's food. Answer her/his questions.

1. Por lo general, ¿cómo es la comida que sirven en la universidad?

2. ¿Qué carnes o mariscos sirven con frecuencia?

3. ¿Sirven ensalada y/o sopa todos los días? ¿Qué tipo?

4. ¿Hay frutas frescas todos los días? ¿Qué tipo de frutas?

3-10. **Sondeo alimentario.** Moving about the classroom, conduct the following poll on eating habits. Ask three different classmates each question. Write their answers. Your professor will ask some students to report back to the class.

SONDEO DE LAS COSTUMBRES ALIMENTARIAS

1. ¿Dónde almuerzas?

Almuerzo en...   a. _____   b. _____   c. _____

2. ¿Dónde prefieres cenar?

a. _____   b. _____   c. _____

3. ¿Qué piensas de los restaurantes universitarios?

Pienso que...   a. ❑ son buenos   b. ❑ son malos   c. ❑ son mediocres

4. En general, ¿qué piensas de la «comida rápida»?

a. ❑ es mala   b. ❑ es buena   c. ❑ es mediocre

5. ¿Qué restaurantes prefieres?

a. _____   b. _____   c. _____

6. ¿Qué pides con frecuencia en un restaurante?

a. _____   b. _____   c. _____

7. Cuando vuelves a casa para visitar a tu familia, ¿qué comidas pides?

a. _____   b. _____   c. _____

8. ¿Qué tres platillos (*dishes*) puedes preparar?

a. _____   b. _____   c. _____

3-11. **Las preferencias y necesidades estudiantiles.** Using the cues provided, ask each other questions. To get more information, ask a follow-up question using the interrogative words listed.

> **Modelo:** necesitar dormir más
>
> Estudiante 1: **¿Necesitas dormir más?**
>
> Estudiante 2: **Sí, necesito dormir más. ¡No duermo mucho!**
>
> Estudiante 1: **¿Cuántas horas duermes normalmente?**
>
> Estudiante 2: **Cinco horas.**

> ¿Cuántos/as…? ¿Dónde…? ¿Qué…?
>
> ¿Por qué…? ¿Cuándo…? ¿A qué hora…?

¡Quiero comer!

1. almorzar todos los días
2. cenar en restaurantes con frecuencia
3. pedir pasta en los restaurantes con frecuencia
4. poder cocinar (*to cook*)

¡Quiero dormir!

5. dormir bien o mal
6. necesitar dormir más
7. dormir la siesta casi todos los días
8. querer tomar una siesta ahora

Now tell the class something about your partner, or something you and your partner have in common.

3-12. **Más sobre los gustos.** In a reply to your earlier e-mail, Pablo asks for more information about preferences and customs of students at your university. Respond, using all or most of the following verbs.

> almorzar   cenar   desayunar   dormir   hacer
>
> pedir   poder   preferir   (no) querer   salir

Asunto :

Hola Pablo,
Pues, por lo general los estudiantes...

Así se dice

Más comidas y las bebidas

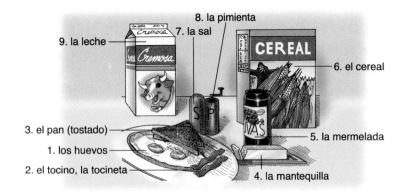

9. la leche
8. la pimienta
7. la sal
6. el cereal
3. el pan (tostado)
1. los huevos
2. el tocino, la tocineta
5. la mermelada
4. la mantequilla

13. el jugo, el zumo (Esp.)
11. la crema
12. el azúcar
10. el café
14. el té

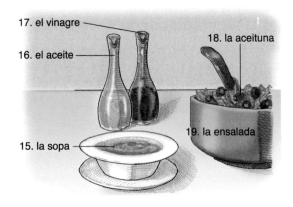

17. el vinagre
16. el aceite
18. la aceituna
19. la ensalada
15. la sopa

23. el refresco
22. el sándwich, el bocadillo (Esp.)
21. las papas fritas
20. la hamburguesa

24. el vino
25. la cerveza
26. el agua
27. el hielo

28. el pastel
29. el queso
32. la torta
30. el helado
31. las galletas

(1) eggs (2) bacon (3) bread (toast) (4) butter (5) jam (6) cereal (7) salt (8) pepper (9) milk (10) coffee (11) cream (12) sugar (13) juice (14) tea (15) soup (16) oil (17) vinegar (18) olive (19) salad (20) hamburger (21) french fries (22) sandwich (23) soft drink (24) wine (25) beer (26) water (27) ice (28) pie, pastry (29) cheese (30) ice cream (31) cookies (32) cake

¿Cuál es tu preferencia?

Imagine that you are studying abroad and staying with a Spanish-speaking family. Shortly after your arrival, your host mother (a great cook) has many questions for you. She aims to please!

Puedes tomar cuatro **comidas**[1] en casa con nosotros: el **desayuno**[2], el **almuerzo**[3], la **merienda**[4] y la **cena**[5]. En la mañana, ¿prefieres **tomar**[6] una **bebida**[7] **fría**[8] (el jugo) o una bebida **caliente**[9] (el café o el té)? ¿Prefieres jugo de naranja o jugo de piña? ¿Tomas el café **con**[10] o **sin**[11] azúcar? ¿Prefieres los huevos **fritos**[12] o **revueltos**[13]? Esta noche voy a preparar sopa, ensalada y pollo con papas fritas. ¿Prefieres el pollo **a la parrilla**[14], frito o **al horno**[15]? ¿Comes **mucha**[16] o **poca**[17] carne? ¿Cuál es tu **postre**[18] favorito? ¿Te gusta la torta de chocolate? ¿El pastel de limón? Como ves, ¡me gusta **cocinar**[19]!

(1) meals; **la comida** *food, meal, main meal (2) breakfast (3) lunch (4) snack (5) dinner (6) to drink, to take (7) drink, beverage (8) cold (9) hot (10) with (11) without (12) fried (13) scrambled (14) grilled (15) baked (16)* **mucho/a/os/as** *much, a lot, many (17)* **poco/a/os/as** *little (quantity), few (18) dessert (19) to cook*

Mucho and **poco** *do not* change in gender and number when they modify verbs.
Comemos **mucho/poco**.　　*We eat a lot/little.*

When they modify nouns, **mucho** and **poco** *do* change in gender and number to agree with the noun.
Comemos **muchas** verduras y **poca** carne.

Spanish uses the preposition **de** (*of*) to join two nouns for the purpose of description.
helado **de** vainilla　　　*vanilla ice cream*
jugo **de** naranja　　　　*orange juice*

How many combinations can you come up with?

DICHOS

Desayuna como un rey°, almuerza como un burgués° y cena como un mendigo°.
¿Cómo puede usted explicar este dicho?

king / middle-class person / beggar

Práctica y comunicación

3-13. **Mi «nueva madre».** One of you plays the role of the host mother/father and asks the questions from the *¿Cuál es tu preferencia?* paragraph on page 113. The other responds. Then switch roles.

3-14. **¡A la mesa!** With what do you associate the following foods? Use the categories listed.

> el desayuno   el almuerzo   la merienda   la cena

Modelo: panes dulces
              el desayuno

¿Desea usted un pan dulce (*sweet*) de esta pastelería mexicana de Los Ángeles?

1. pan tostado con mantequilla y mermelada
2. sopa y ensalada
3. pastel de manzana con helado de vainilla
4. un cóctel de camarones
5. huevos revueltos con tocino
6. jugo/ zumo de naranja
7. un sándwich/ bocadillo de jamón y queso
8. arroz con pollo, pan y vino
9. café caliente con crema y azúcar
10. una hamburguesa con papas fritas
11. bistec a la parrilla con papas al horno y ensalada mixta
12. unas galletas y leche

3-15. Consejos (*Advice*) de los nutricionistas.

3-15. Consejos (*Advice*) de los nutricionistas. Medical studies show that certain foods are beneficial and reduce the risk of cancer and other diseases. Compile two lists of foods for incoming first-year students: those they should consume a lot of to maintain optimum health, and those they should consume less of.

Deben comer/tomar mucho(a)/muchos(as)	Deben comer/tomar poco(a)/pocos(as)
mucha ensalada	poco helado

Now compare your list with that of another team of "nutritionists."

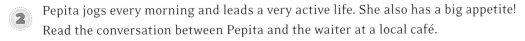

Así se dice

¡Tengo hambre!

(2) Pepita jogs every morning and leads a very active life. She also has a big appetite! Read the conversation between Pepita and the waiter at a local café.

MESERO: ¿Qué desea usted, señorita?

PEPITA: **¡Tengo mucha hambre!**[1] **Quisiera**[2] un sándwich de jamón y queso y **también**[3] una ensalada.

MESERO: ¿Y para tomar?

PEPITA: Una limonada grande, por favor. **Tengo** mucha **sed**[4].

MESERO: A la orden°, señorita.

A... *At your service*

(*Pepita se lo come todo y decide que* **todavía**[5] *tiene hambre. Pide* **más**[6] *comida.*)

MESERO: ¿Desea usted algo más?

PEPITA: Sí, **otro**[7] sándwich, por favor, y otra limonada, pero con **menos**[8] hielo.

MESERO: Con mucho gusto, señorita.

(1) I am very hungry; **tener (mucha) hambre** *to be (very) hungry (2) I would like (polite variation of* **quiero***) (3) also (4) I am very thirsty;* **tener (mucha) sed** *to be (very) thirsty (5) still, yet (6) more (7) another (8) less, fewer*

In Spanish the verb **tener** has many uses. In **Chapter 2** you learned the expression **tener... años** (*to be . . . years old*). **Tener hambre** and **tener sed** follow the same pattern. Whereas English uses *to be* to express age, hunger, and thirst, Spanish uses **tener**, meaning *to have . . . years, hunger,* and *thirst.*

¡Tengo mucha hambre!   *I am very hungry.*

Otro/a does *not* use the indefinite article **un/una.**

Quisiera **otra** limonada, por favor.   *I would like **another** lemonade, please.*

3-16. **¡Qué hambre tenemos!** Two of you have just run a marathon, and you are famished and extremely thirsty. You are now at a restaurant. Following the format of Pepita's conversation on page 115, place your orders. Then say that you are still hungry/thirsty, and ask for another . . . and yet another . . . (food items/beverages). Your third classmate is the waiter. Be sure to thank him/her at the end.

3-17. **Cuando tenemos hambre o sed.** Take turns asking and answering the following questions.

1. En este momento, ¿tienes mucha hambre? (¿Qué quieres comer?)
2. ¿Tienes sed ahora? (¿Qué quieres tomar?)
3. Cuando estás en una fiesta y tienes sed, ¿qué tomas?
4. Después de ir al gimnasio, ¿qué tomas?
5. Cuando estás en tu casa y tienes hambre, ¿qué comes?
6. Cuando estás en la residencia por la noche y tienes hambre, ¿que comes?
7. ¿Qué pides cuando estás en un restaurante de «comida rápida»? ¿Y en un restaurante elegante?

¡Qué dilema!

*Vives con una familia hispana por un semestre. Es la hora de tu primera (first) cena con la familia. La madre sirve su especialidad— lengua (tongue). No te gusta y absolutamente no puedes comerla. La madre dice (says): **¡Buen provecho (Bon appétit)!** Unos minutos más tarde, observa que no comes y pregunta: **¿No te gusta la comida?***

Noticias culturales

Las comidas en el mundo hispano

El desayuno hispano es normalmente entre las 6:00 y las 9:00 de la mañana. Comparado con el desayuno tradicional estadounidense, el desayuno hispano es muy ligero°. Muchos españoles e hispanoamericanos desayunan una taza de café (expreso) con leche y pan con mantequilla o mermelada. En las regiones costeras° de Hispanoamérica, también es común desayunar con plátanos verdes° o tortillas de maíz y café.

El almuerzo generalmente es entre la 1:00 y las 2:00 de la tarde y es la comida más fuerte° del día[3]: puede incluir una ensalada, sopa, arroz o verduras, carne o pescado y postre. En algunos países, a las 5:00 o a las 6:00 de la tarde es común comer la merienda, que consiste en café o té, leche, galletas, pastel o algún bocadillo.

Generalmente los hispanos cenan más tarde que los estadounidenses. La cena hispana típicamente es entre las 8:00 y las 9:00 de la noche, y en España puede ser más tarde, entre las 10:00 y las 12:00 de la noche.

Una parte importante de la comida es «la sobremesa». Este término define la charla° después de la comida. Es cuando se toma el café, a veces seguido° de brandy (coñac), y se conversa de asuntos° serios o triviales.

light

coastal

plátanos... *green plantains*

más... *largest*

chat, conversation /
followed / issues

Algunos platos[4] típicos del mundo hispano

masa... *dough / stuffed*

Los **churros**: masa de harina° cilíndrica frita. Frecuentemente se sirven con café con leche o con chocolate caliente.

La **empanada**: masa de harina rellena° generalmente con carne, cebollas, huevos y aceitunas, frita o al horno.

---

[3] Businesses, particularly in small towns, close down during lunchtime.
[4] These dishes are sometimes associated with a particular country (for example, **la paella** = Spain). Most, however, are popular throughout the Spanish-speaking world.

syrup

El **flan**: un postre de huevos, leche, azúcar y vainilla, cocido en un molde al horno con almíbar° de caramelo.

La **tortilla** (España): fritada que contiene huevos, patatas y cebollas. Se sirve con frecuencia a la hora de la merienda en los bares de España. También se come en casa para la cena.

saffron

La **paella**: plato de arroz con pollo, mariscos y guisantes, sazonado con azafrán°.

Las **quesadillas** (México): tortillas de maíz, fritas, con queso, pollo, champiñones y otros ingredientes al gusto. En el desayuno típico de la foto se sirven con frijoles, papaya, jugo de naranja y café con leche.

¿Qué recuerda?

A. Based on the text in the first part of the *Noticias culturales*, determine if the following meals are typical of the U.S., a Hispanic country, or both.

1. desayuno con pan y café con leche

2. almuerzo con sopa, carne, arroz y postre

3. desayuno con cereal, huevos y tocino

4. cena a la medianoche

5. cena con una pizza y Coca-Cola

6. merienda con leche y galletas

7. almuerzo con un sándwich

B. Can you identify which of the dishes pictured above are made with the following ingredients?

1. huevos

2. masa de harina

3. queso

4. carne y/o mariscos

2 **Conexiones y contrastes.** Discuss the following questions.

1. ¿Cuáles son las horas típicas de las comidas en su país? ¿Y en el mundo hispano?

2. ¿Cómo es un almuerzo típico para ustedes? ¿Es similar o diferente al almuerzo hispano? Expliquen.

3. ¿Cuáles son sus comidas favoritas? ¿Cuáles de los «platos típicos del mundo hispano» quieren ustedes probar (*to sample/try*)? ¿Por qué?

3 Counting from 100 and indicating the year

ochocientos noventa y uno, ...

In Hispanic countries, prices of meals and of everyday items are often expressed in thousands of **pesos**, **colones**, and so on. Therefore, it is important to become accustomed to understanding and using numbers over 100.

cien	100	ochocientos/as	800
ciento uno/a	101	novecientos/as	900
doscientos/as	200	mil	1000
trescientos/as	300	dos mil	2000
cuatrocientos/as	400	cien mil	100.000
quinientos/as	500	doscientos mil	200.000
seiscientos/as	600	un millón (de + *noun*)[5]	1.000.000
setecientos/as	700	dos millones (de + *noun*)	2.000.000

- **Cien** is used before a noun or as the number 100 when counting. **Ciento** is used with numbers 101 to 199.

    Hay **cien** estudiantes en la clase. **Cien, ciento uno,...**
    Sólo tengo **cien** pesos. La torta cuesta **ciento un** pesos.

- In Spanish there is no **y** between hundreds and a smaller number, although *and* is often used in English.

    205 (*two hundred and five*) = **doscientos cinco**

- When the numbers 200–900 modify a noun, they agree in gender.
    trescient**os** alumnos y quinient**as** alumnas

- Years above 1000 are not broken into two-digit groups as they are in English.
    1971 (*nineteen seventy-one*) = **mil novecientos setenta y uno**

- In writing numbers, Spanish commonly uses a period where English uses a comma, and vice-versa.
    English: $121,250.50 = Spanish: $121.250,50

---

[5] When **millón/millones** is immediately followed by a noun, the word **de** must be used: **un millón *de* pesos, dos millones *de* euros**; but **un millón doscientos mil quetzales**.

Práctica y comunicación

3-18. **Vamos a cambiar (*exchange*) dólares.** One of you is the teller at a money exchange booth at the Miami International Airport. For each client headed for a foreign country, you must calculate the currency according to the exchange rates listed in the chart below. The other plays the roles of several tourists who want to exchange U.S. dollars. Switch roles.

> **Modelo:** Destino: Guatemala/$100 (U.S.)
>
> Turista: **Quiero cambiar cien dólares a quetzales, por favor.**
>
> Cajero/a: **Muy bien, señor/señorita.** (*He/She counts the money.*)
>
> **Aquí tiene 800 (ochocientos) quetzales. Buen viaje.**
>
> Turista: **Muchas gracias.**

Cambio	Moneda	Dólar EE.UU.
España	euro	1,15
Guatemala	quetzal	8
Colombia	peso	3
Costa Rica	colón	350
México	peso	10

Destino

1. Guatemala/$175 (U.S.)
2. Colombia/$550
3. España/$2.000
4. Costa Rica/$700
5. México/$900

3-19. **¿Qué vamos a pedir?** You are in a restaurant in San José, Costa Rica, trying to decide what to order. Study the menu below. Prices are in **colones** (1 dollar = 350 **colones** approximately).

El Rincón

DESAYUNO (7 A.M.–10 A.M.)		ALMUERZO (11 A.M.–2 P.M.)		CENA (5 P.M.–10 P.M.)	
Omelete	1.025	Tacos de carne	450	Puerco en salsa verde	2.500
Huevos con tocino	975	Enchiladas suizas	875	Carne de res en salsa	3.500
Huevos revueltos	750	Ensalada el Rincón	900	Pollo a la parrilla	3.000
Pan tostado	100	Tamales	625	Pollo al horno	2.800
Cereal	700			Casado*	1.500

SOPAS		BEBIDAS		POSTRES	
Sopa de legumbres	575	Té helado	450	Helados	700
Sopa de pollo	800	Refrescos	900	Flan	670

PLATO DEL DÍA: Pescado al mojo de ajo 4.800

Bar y Restaurante 225 Paseo Colón Tel. 2-25-44-91

Now discuss your decisions.

Modelo: Estudiante 1: **Pienso pedir... Cuesta... Y tú ¿qué vas a pedir?**

Estudiante 2: **No voy a pedir... porque cuesta... Voy a pedir...**

---

* Un plato de arroz, frijoles negros, huevos y carne de res. Es el plato nacional de Costa Rica.

2

3-20. **¿En qué año?** Following is a list of well-known restaurants with the year they opened. Choose three in which you would like to eat and tell your partner the name and year of each: **Quiero comer en...**

1. Restaurante la Diligencia, originalmente Casa de Postas (Tarragona, España): ¡1515!
2. Casa Botín (Madrid, España): 1725
3. Delmonico's (Nueva York, NY): 1836
4. Venta de Aires (Toledo, España): 1891
5. Restaurante Richmond (Buenos Aires, Argentina): 1917
6. Restaurante El Faro (Nueva York, NY): 1927
7. Restaurante El Quijote (Nueva York, NY): 1930

Now, read the following restaurant names. Share with your partner the names of two restaurants that you want to patronize: **Quiero ir a...** Also indicate what kind of food/beverages you think are served there: **Probablemente sirven...** Be prepared to share information with the class.

8. Restaurante 1800 (Buenos Aires, Argentina)
9. México Lindo 1900 (Panamá, Panamá)
10. Havana '59 (1959) (Richmond, Virginia)
11. Bar Restaurante 1985 (Panamá, Panamá)
12. Cafetería Año 2000 (Tegucigalpa, Honduras)

5

3-21. **¿Cuánto cuesta?** Determine the price of each of the following items and write it down. Later, your professor will ask you to list your answers on the chalkboard to compare them with the "correct" price he/she has previously determined. The group that comes closest to the "correct" price for the most items, without going over, wins. Remember: The teacher is always right!

1. una cena elegante en un restaurante de ☆ ☆ ☆ ☆ ☆ en Nueva York
2. una mansión en Beverly Hills, California
3. un televisor con una pantalla muy grande
4. una computadora con monitor y teclado
5. una cámara digital
6. los libros de texto para un semestre
7. la matrícula de un año en su universidad
8. un *Rolls Royce* nuevo

Estructuras

4 **Asking for specific information: Interrogative words (A summary)**

You have used some interrogative words to ask questions: *¿Cómo* estás? *¿Qué* pasa? *¿De dónde* eres? *¿Adónde* vas después de la clase? *¿Cuántos* años tienes? *¿Cuánto* cuesta? Following are the most commonly used interrogative words in Spanish.

¿Qué?	*What? Which?*	**¿Qué** frutas tienen hoy?
¿Cómo?	*How?*	**¿Cómo** están las fresas hoy?
¿Cuándo?	*When?*	**¿Cuándo** llegan las piñas?
¿Por qué?	*Why?*	**¿Por qué** no hay cerezas?
¿Quién? ¿Quiénes?	*Who?*	**¿Quién** vende mariscos?
¿De quién?	*Whose?*	**¿De quién** es?
¿Cuál?	*Which (one)?*	**¿Cuál** prefieres?
¿Cuáles?	*Which (ones)?*	**¿Cuáles** son tus favoritos?
¿Cuánto? ¿Cuánta?	*How much?*	**¿Cuánto** es en total?
¿Cuántos? ¿Cuántas?	*How many?*	**¿Cuántos** tomates tienes?
¿Dónde?	*Where?*	**¿Dónde** está el vendedor?
¿Adónde?	*(To) where?*	**¿Adónde** va?
¿De dónde?	*From where?*	**¿De dónde** es?

- **¿Qué?** asks for a definition or explanation. Used *in front of a noun*, it seeks a choice.

¿Qué es?	*What is it?* (definition)
¿Qué quieres?	*What do you want?* (explanation)
¿Qué postre deseas?	*What (Which) dessert do you want?* (choice)

- **¿Cuál/Cuáles?** (*Which? Which one/ones?* or *What?*) ask for a choice, and are used in front of a verb or preposition. They are typically not used in front of a noun.

¿Cuáles quieres comprar?	*Which ones do you want to buy?*
¿Cuál es tu postre favorito?	*Which (What) is your favorite dessert?*
¿Cuál de los postres prefieres?	*Which of the desserts do you prefer?*

¡A la mesa!

- When some of the words listed previously appear without a written accent, they connect two separate thoughts within a statement rather than ask a question.

que *that, which, who*	En el mercado **que** está en la plaza venden mariscos.
lo que *what, that which*	Compro **lo que** necesito.
cuando *when*	**Cuando** tengo hambre, voy a la cafetería.
porque *because*	Quiero una pizza grande **porque** tengo mucha hambre.

Práctica y comunicación

3-22. **Pregúntele a su profesor/a.** After your professor makes each of the following statements, use appropriate interrogative words to request more information.

> **Modelo:** Profesor/a: Mi plato favorito no son los raviolis.
>
> Estudiante: **¿Cuál es su plato favorito?**
>
> Profesor/a: Los tamales.

1. No me llamo…

2. No soy de…

3. No tengo… años.

4. No vivo en una residencia estudiantil.

5. No enseño (*teach*) seis clases de español.

6. Pancho Villa no es mi estudiante favorito. (¡Todos son…!)

7. Después de esta clase no voy a la biblioteca.

8. Mi primera clase no es a las ocho de la mañana.

9. Éste (*This*) no es mi libro de español.

10. No me gustan los plátanos.

11. La pizza no es mi comida favorita.

12. No tomo té en la mañana.

3-23. **Una entrevista (*An interview*).** First, you and your partner each decide on your new identity—that of a celebrity or an exotic, imaginary, famous person. Then write eight questions that you will ask each other, using at least eight different interrogative words. Finally, conduct the interview. Some of you may be asked to perform the interview in front of the class.

3-24. **Una cena especial.** Talk to each other about a special dinner that you are planning for your friends. Use interrogative words such as those in parentheses to converse about:

- la fecha y la hora de la cena (¿Cuándo?)
- el número de personas que van a invitar (¿Cuántos/as?)
- lo que van a servir (¿Qué?)
- los ingredientes que van a comprar y las cantidades (*quantities*) (¿Qué?) (¿Cuántos/as?)
- las responsabilidades de las varias personas que van a preparar la comida (¿Quién?)

Así se pronuncia

The pronunciation of *ce/ci*, *gue/gui*, and *que/qui*

Remember that in Latin America **c** before **e** or **i** has the English *s* sound as in *sister*. In most regions of Spain, **c** before **e** or **i** is pronounced with a *th* sound as in *thanks*. Practice these words with both pronunciations.

cena   **ce**real   **ce**rveza   a**ce**ite   **ci**nco   gra**ci**as

In the combinations **gue, gui, que, qui**, remember that the **u** is silent.

hambur**gue**sa   **gui**santes   **que**so   mante**qui**lla

Repeat the following sentences.

ce/ci	**Ce**cilia ne**ce**sita comprar **ci**nco **ce**bollas para la **ce**na.
gue/gui	Al distin**gui**do señor **Gue**rra le gustan los **gui**santes y las fresas con meren**gue**.
que/qui	Ra**que**l **Qui**ntana **qui**ere comprar **que**so y mante**qui**lla.

Dicho y hecho

Conversando

4 **Una cena especial.** Larios' restaurant in Miami Beach serves typical Cuban food. Imagine that one of you is a waiter at the restaurant and the other three are customers. First, read the menu and discuss the dishes. The waiter offers several suggestions. Then decide what you are going to order, and order it.

SOPAS
SOUPS

SOPA DEL DÍA SOUP OF THE DAY	$3.75
SOPA DE POLLO CHICKEN SOUP	$3.50
SOPA DE FRIJOLES NEGROS BLACK BEAN SOUP	$3.50

TORTILLAS
OMELETTES

TORTILLA ESPAÑOLA *CON ARROZ Y PLÁTANOS* SPANISH OMELETTE, RICE & PLANTAINS	$6.75
TORTILLA DE PLÁTANO *CON ARROZ Y FRIJOLES NEGROS* PLANTAIN OMELETTE WITH RICE & BEANS	$5.95

ENSALADAS
SALADS

ENSALADA MIXTA HOUSE SALAD	$4.75
ENSALADA DE SARDINAS SARDINE SALAD	$6.95
ENSALADA DE TOMATE TOMATO SALAD	$3.50
SERRUCHO EN ESCABECHE PICKLED KINGFISH	$8.25
PLATO DE FRUTAS FRUIT PLATTER	$4.95

AVES
CHICKEN

PECHUGA DE POLLO A LA PLANCHA BONELESS GRILLED CHICKEN BREAST	$8.25
POLLO ASADO ROASTED CHICKEN	$7.95
CHICHARRONES DE POLLO DEEP FRIED CHICKEN CHUNKS	$7.95
ARROZ CON POLLO CHICKEN AND YELLOW RICE	$6.95
PECHUGA DE POLLO RELLENA *CON CAMARONES* CHICKEN BREAST STUFFED WITH SHRIMP	$8.95

PESCADOS
FISH

PESCADO EMPANIZADO BREADED FISH	$9.95
PESCADO A LA PLANCHA GRILLED FISH	$9.75
BROCHETA DE CAMARONES SHRIMP KABOB	$11.75
CAMARONES EMPANIZADOS BREADED SHRIMP	$12.25
CAMARONES AL AJILLO SHRIMP IN GARLIC	$12.25
LANGOSTA ENCHILADA LOBSTER CREOLE	$20.50

> **TODOS ESTOS PLATOS SE SIRVEN CON ARROZ Y PLÁTANOS FRITOS**

CARNES
MEATS

BISTEC DE PALOMILLA CUBAN STEAK	$8.95
LOMO DE PUERCO ROAST PORK LOIN-CUBAN STYLE	$9.75
MASAS DE PUERCO FRIED PORK CHUNKS	$9.25
CHULETAS DE PUERCO PORK CHOPS	$8.50
CARNE AL PINCHO SHISH KABOB	$12.95
PICADILLO A LA CUBANA CUBAN GROUND BEEF CREOLE	$6.25

POSTRES
DESSERTS

PUDÍN DE PAN BREAD PUDDING	$3.75
FLAN DE LECHE CUSTARD	$3.75
ARROZ CON LECHE RICE PUDDING	$3.75
COCO RALLADO SHREDDED COCONUT	$3.25

HELADOS
ICE CREAM

COCO	$2.95
MANGO	$2.95
GUANÁBANA SORBET	$2.95
CHOCOLATE	$2.95
VAINILLA	

¡A escuchar!

Un mensaje telefónico. The telephone rings. Nobody is home and the answering machine picks up. Listen to the message and then answer the first two questions.

1. ¿Quién deja el mensaje?
- ❏ la esposa de Pablo
- ❏ la madre de Pablo

2. ¿Quién va a preparar la comida?
- ❏ Pablo
- ❏ ella

Listen to the message again and then complete the following sentences.

3. Puede preparar un sándwich con _____, _____, lechuga y

_____ .

4. Para tomar hay _____.

5. Para el postre hay _____ y _____.

De mi escritorio

Usted es guionista (*screenwriter*). You have been asked to complete the following TV script for a romantic soap opera scene featuring Linda and Manuel celebrating at a restaurant. Use your imagination to write the middle section of the scene.

Estamos en El Madrileño, un elegante restaurante español. Es el cumpleaños de Linda, y Manuel quiere celebrarlo con su novia.

ANFITRIÓN:	Buenas noches, ¿tienen reservaciones?
MANUEL:	Sí, señor, a nombre de Manuel Cervantes.
LINDA:	¡Ay, Manuel, qué restaurante tan elegante!
MANUEL:	Lo mejor para ti en tu día, mi cielo°. Te quiero°.
LINDA:	Yo también te quiero mucho.

darling / Te... I love you

(*Your section goes here: Linda and Manuel review the menu together, talking about their likes, dislikes, and preferences. Then they place their order and enjoy the meal.*)

MANUEL:	La cuenta, por favor.
MESERO:	Aquí tiene, señor.
MANUEL:	¡Dios mío, Linda, se me perdió la billetera°!
LINDA:	No te preocupes°, mi amor. Te ayudo° a lavar° los platos. ¡Ja! ¡Ja!

se... I lost my wallet!

No... Don't worry / Te... I'll help you / wash

Panorama cultural

México: Tradición e innovación

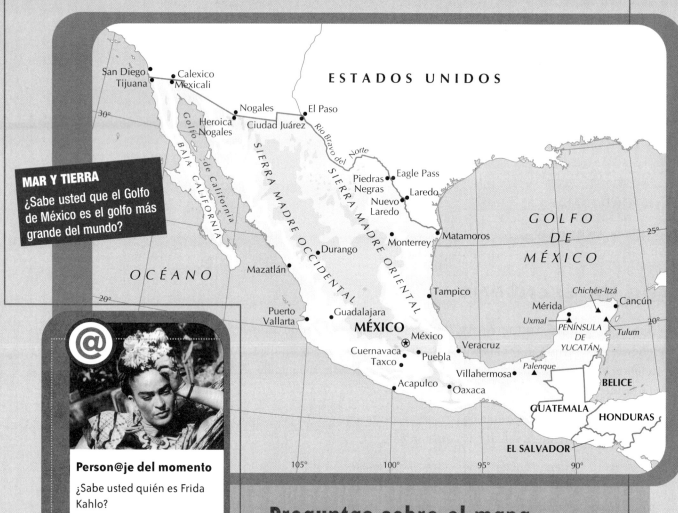

MAR Y TIERRA

¿Sabe usted que el Golfo de México es el golfo más grande del mundo?

Person@je del momento

¿Sabe usted quién es Frida Kahlo?

Busque información en el Internet y compártala con sus compañeros/as de clase. ¡En español, por favor!

Preguntas sobre el mapa

1. ¿Cuáles son cuatro ciudades importantes en la frontera (*border*) entre México y los EE.UU.?

2. ¿Cuáles son dos ciudades importantes en la región del Golfo de México? ¿Y en la costa del Pacífico?

3. ¿Puede usted identificar la capital? ¿Y una ciudad importante que está al noroeste de la capital?

4. ¿Puede usted identificar tres de las ruinas mayas en la Península de Yucatán? ¿Y una ciudad turística muy famosa?

5. ¿Qué montañas separan la región central de las costas?

Un territorio diverso

México es un país muy diverso. El centro del país es una vasta región de valles. La región centro-oeste es una zona fértil con una rica producción agrícola y ganadera[1]. En el sureste está la región más industrializada del país, en el Golfo de México, donde el petróleo y los productos petroquímicos son la industria principal. ¿Conoce usted la frontera[2]? ¿La Península de Yucatán? ¿La «Nueva Riviera»? Vea las siguientes fotos.

ADIÓS, DINOSAURIOS MEXICANOS
Un meteorito que cayó en Yucatán, México, posiblemente fue la razón de la extinción de los dinosaurios en esa zona.

La Península de Yucatán es una área turística importante. Las playas del mar Caribe y las impresionantes ruinas mayas atraen una multitud de turistas a este paraíso tropical. ¿Le gustaría visitar estas ruinas mayas de Tulum, México? ¿Por qué?

Con el Tratado de Libre Comercio entre los EE.UU., México y Canadá (NAFTA, 1994), la frontera entre Tijuana y Matamoros es una región cada vez más[3] fundamental para el comercio y la industria. Miles de fábricas maquiladoras[4] en las ciudades fronterizas de México emplean un millón de mexicanos, y millones vienen a buscar empleo en los Estados Unidos. Mexicanos y norteamericanos cruzan los puentes[5] fronterizos constantemente para ir de compras[6]. Vea la foto del puente entre Nuevo Laredo, México y Laredo, Tejas. ¿Puede usted imaginar cuántas personas pasan por este puente cada día?

En las costas del Pacífico, en la «Nueva Riviera», la belleza[7] natural de las playas contrasta con las estructuras modernas de los hoteles y discotecas. ¿Cuáles son algunas de las atracciones principales de Acapulco, una de las ciudades más famosas del Pacífico? (Vea la foto.)

[1] *cattle-raising*
[2] *border*
[3] *cada... increasingly*
[4] *assembly plants*
[5] *bridges* [6] *shopping*
[7] *beauty*

La capital, México, D.F.

¿Sabe usted que México, D.F. (Distrito Federal) es una de las ciudades más grandes del mundo? Tiene una población de más de 19.750.000 de habitantes. Pero la población de México disminuye un poco cada año con la migración a las ciudades del norte donde hay más trabajo.

Tenochtitlán, capital de los aztecas, era[8] una ciudad esplendorosa. Hoy esta ciudad es la Ciudad de México, la capital actual más antigua[9] de Latinoamérica. La cultura indígena es visible en los murales que decoran la capital. ¿Qué aspectos de la vida azteca puede usted describir en el mural del famoso pintor mexicano, Diego Rivera?

México es una ciudad fascinante donde coexisten la tradición y la modernidad. La Plaza de las Tres Culturas simboliza esta fusión; combina ruinas arqueológicas aztecas, una iglesia[10] colonial y edificios[11] modernos. Según la foto, ¿qué cultura representa la catedral? ¿Las ruinas? ¿La nueva arquitectura?

En las avenidas de la zona céntrica de la ciudad hay muchas tiendas[12], restaurantes, teatros y hoteles elegantes. La impresionante arquitectura es futurista y tradicional. El Ángel de la Independencia domina el Paseo de la Reforma, una de las avenidas principales de la ciudad capital. En su opinion, ¿cuál es más impresionante? ¿El monumento? ¿El tráfico? ¿Los edificios grandes? ¿Las luces[13]?

[8]*was* [9]**más... oldest**
[10]*church* [11]*buildings*
[12]*stores* [13]*lights*

UNA MARCA
La ciudad de México tiene la avenida más larga (*long*) del mundo, Insurgentes. ¡Tiene 25 kilómetros!

¿Qué descubrimos?

Según el mapa y la información presentada en el *Panorama cultural*, identifique la ciudad correspondiente a cada descripción.

> Acapulco   Cancún   Ciudad Juárez   México   Veracruz

1. Está en la «Nueva Riviera», una región turística del Pacífico.
2. Está en la región más cercana (*closest*) a los EE.UU. Existen muchas fábricas maquiladoras allí.
3. Está en la región que tiene playas en el Caribe. Hay muchas ruinas mayas a poca distancia.
4. Está en la región más industrializada de México donde abundan las industrias petroquímicas.
5. La Plaza de las Tres Culturas está en esta ciudad moderna.

Encuentro cultural

Artes culinarias

Las tortillas de maíz

El consumo diario de tortillas en México es de aproximadamente 300 millones. Desde luego[1], para satisfacer una demanda de esta magnitud, existen máquinas que las elaboran[2] en grandes cantidades. Pero en muchas partes del país, especialmente en zonas rurales, hacer las tortillas es el deber cotidiano[3] de las mujeres. La única[4] concesión a los tiempos modernos es el empleo[5] de la pequeña prensa[6] metálica para extender la masa[7]: un instrumento elemental, que se vende en todos los mercados de México y que ha ahorrado[8] incalculables millones de horas de trabajo a millones de manos[9] femeninas. Si usted quiere hacer sus propias[10] tortillas en casa, ponga los siguientes pasos[11] en el orden correcto.

READING STRATEGY

Linking language and visuals

The introductory paragraph and diagram come from a Web site about Mexican cuisine. Skim the passage quickly to find general information about the preparation of tortillas. Then refer to the diagram to help you determine the steps involved in making a homemade tortilla.

Instrucciones:

_____ cerrar la prensa, presionar y luego abrir la prensa

__1__ tomar la masa necesaria y hacer una bolita

_____ cocinar cada lado de la tortilla unos momentos

_____ poner la bolita en el centro de una prensa metálica, entre dos pedazos de plástico transparente

_____ extender la tortilla sobre el comal caliente

_____ separar la tortilla del plástico superior y luego del otro plástico

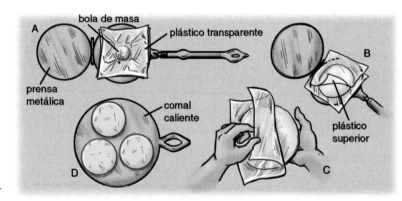

Preguntas

1. ¿Cuál es el consumo diario de tortillas en México?
2. ¿Cómo preparan las tortillas para satisfacer una demanda tan grande?
3. En las zonas rurales, ¿quiénes hacen las tortillas?
4. ¿Para qué usan las mujeres las prensas metálicas? ¿Dónde compran las prensas?
5. En su experiencia, ¿qué platos mexicanos usan las tortillas como base?
6. ¿Qué comidas tienen más consumo diario en su comunidad?

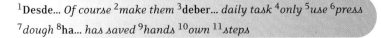

[1]Desde... *Of course* [2]*make them* [3]deber... *daily task* [4]*only* [5]*use* [6]*press* [7]*dough* [8]ha... *has saved* [9]*hands* [10]*own* [11]*steps*

En México, la tortilla es la base de la comida típica y forma parte de muchos platos sabrosos (*tasty*).

Adjetivos y expresiones adjetivales

al horno
a la parrilla
caliente
frío/a
frito/a
mucho/a/os/as
otro/a/os/as
poco/a/os/as

Adverbios

más/menos
mucho/poco
también
todavía

Conjunciones

cuando
lo que
porque
que

Palabras interrogativas

¿Adónde?
¿Cómo?
¿Cuál?/¿Cuáles?
¿Cuándo?
¿Cuánto/a/os/as?
¿De dónde?
¿De quién?
¿Dónde?
¿Por qué?
¿Qué?
¿Quién/es?

Preposiciones

con
sin

Sustantivos

Las comidas del día

el almuerzo
la cena
el desayuno
la merienda

Las legumbres y las verduras en el mercado

el bróculi
la cebolla
los frijoles
los guisantes
las judías verdes
la lechuga
el maíz
la papa/ la patata
  las papas fritas
el tomate
la zanahoria

Las frutas

la banana/ el plátano
la cereza
la fresa
el limón
la manzana
el melocotón/ el durazno
la naranja
la pera
la piña
la sandía
la uva

Las carnes y los mariscos

el bistec
el camarón
la carne de cerdo/ puerco
la carne de res
la chuleta de cerdo/
  puerco
la hamburguesa
el jamón
la langosta
el pescado
el pollo

la salchicha/ el chorizo
la tocineta/ el tocino

Las bebidas

el agua
el café
la cerveza
el jugo/ el zumo
la leche
el refresco
el té
el vino

Los postres

la galleta
el helado
el pastel
la torta

Otras comidas y condimentos

el aceite
la aceituna
el ajo
el arroz
el azúcar
el cereal
la crema
la ensalada
el hielo
el huevo
  los huevos revueltos/
  fritos
la mantequilla
la mermelada
el pan
  el pan tostado
la pimienta
el queso
la sal
el sándwich/ el bocadillo
la sopa
el vinagre

Verbos y expresiones verbales

almorzar (ue)
cocinar
desear
dormir (ue)
entender (ie)
gustar
necesitar
pedir (i)
pensar (ie)
poder (ue)
preferir (ie)
preparar
querer (ie)
servir (i)
tomar
vender
volver (ue)

quisiera
tener (mucha) hambre
tener (mucha) sed

Autoprueba y repaso

I. The verb *gustar*. Write questions according to the model, and then answer them. Use the correct form of **gustar** and the appropriate corresponding pronoun.

> **Modelo:** ¿a su hermano / las legumbres?
> **¿A su hermano le gustan las legumbres?**
> **Sí, le gustan las legumbres.** *o* **No, no le gustan…**

1. ¿A sus padres / tomar café?
2. ¿A ustedes / la comida italiana?
3. ¿A ustedes / desayunar temprano?
4. ¿A su abuela / los postres?
5. ¿A usted / los frljoles negros?

II. Stem-changing verbs. Write questions to your friends using the **ustedes** form of the verb. Then write answers to the questions, using the **nosotros** form.

> **Modelo:** entender el ejercicio
> **¿Entienden el ejercicio?**
> **Sí, entendemos el ejercicio.** *o* **No, no entendemos el ejercicio.**

1. poder cocinar
2. querer ir al supermercado
3. almorzar a las doce todos los días
4. preferir cenar en un restaurante o en la cafetería
5. normalmente pedir postres en los restaurantes

III. Counting from 100 and indicating the year.

A. Mr. Trompa, a very wealthy man, is going to buy everything his two daughters need to start college. How much money does he need to buy two of each of the following items? Follow the model and write out the numbers.

> **Modelo:** Un libro de psicología cuesta $90.
> **Dos cuestan ciento ochenta dólares.**

1. Un libro de arte cuesta $125.
2. Una calculadora excelente cuesta $170.
3. Una impresora cuesta $450.
4. Una computadora con teclado y monitor cuesta $1400.
5. Un televisor para el cuarto cuesta $750.
6. Un coche nuevo cuesta $25.000.

B. Write out the following famous years.

1. Colón llega al Nuevo Mundo: 1492
2. La destrucción de la Armada Invencible de España: 1588
3. La Declaración de Independencia de EE.UU.: 1776
4. La caída (*fall*) del Muro de Berlín: 1989
5. La caída de las Torres Gemelas: 2001

IV. Interrogative words. Use various interrogative words to obtain more information.

> **Modelo:** Ana no come en la cafetería.
> **¿Dónde come?** *o* **¿Por qué no come en la cafetería?**

1. Ana no bebe vino.
2. La sandía no es su fruta favorita.
3. No trabaja por la mañana.
4. No es de Buenos Aires.
5. No tiene veinte años.
6. No vive en la residencia estudiantil.
7. No va a la librería ahora.
8. No está enferma hoy.

V. General review. Answer the following questions about yourself and your friends. Use complete sentences.

1. ¿Qué come usted en el desayuno?
2. ¿Cuál es su postre favorito?
3. ¿Qué frutas le gustan más a usted?
4. ¿Dónde quiere usted cenar esta noche?
5. ¿Cuántas horas duerme (generalmente) por la noche?
6. Usted y sus amigos, ¿pueden estudiar toda la noche sin dormir?

Answers to the *Autoprueba y repaso* are found in **Apéndice 2**.

Recreaciones y pasatiempos

Goals for communication

- To talk about hobbies, pastimes, and activities
- To talk about the weather and the seasons
- To talk about future actions
- To describe an act in progress

Así se dice

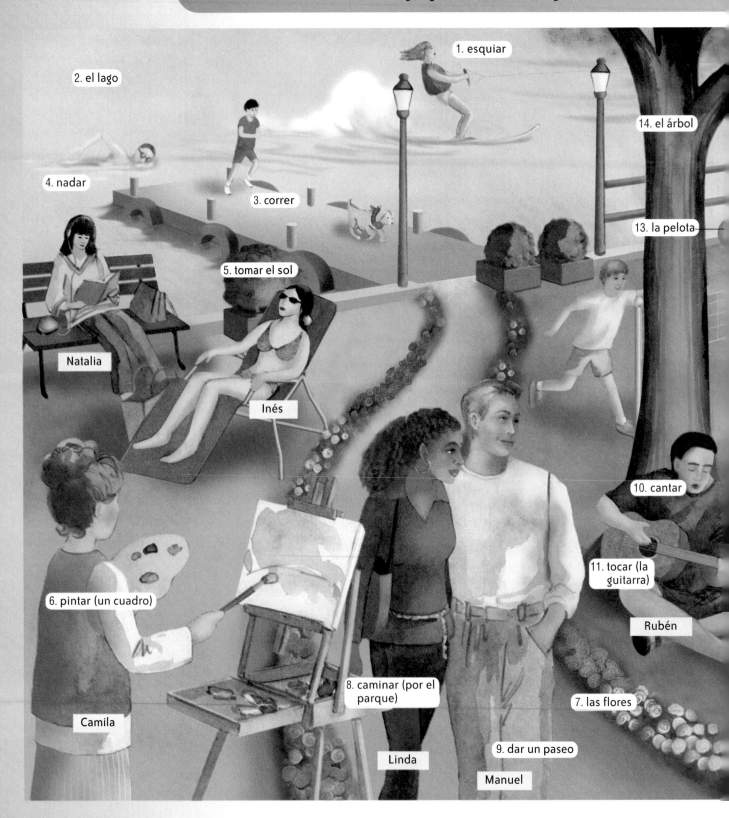

1. esquiar
2. el lago
14. el árbol
4. nadar
3. correr
13. la pelota
5. tomar el sol
Natalia
Inés
10. cantar
6. pintar (un cuadro)
11. tocar (la guitarra)
Rubén
8. caminar (por el parque)
7. las flores
Camila
Linda
9. dar un paseo
Manuel

15. las hojas

16. jugar (ue) al básquetbol/baloncesto

17. practicar

18. jugar (ue) al tenis

19. el partido (de tenis)

20. ganar/perder (ie)

12. jugar (ue) al vólibol

Esteban

Javier

Alfonso

22. levantar pesas

Octavio

21. hacer ejercicio

23. fumar

Pepita

25. montar en bicicleta

Elena

24. descansar

Héctor

1. to ski
2. lake
3. to run
4. to swim
5. to sunbathe
6. to paint (a picture, painting)
7. flowers
8. to walk (through the park)
9. to take a walk/stroll
10. to sing
11. to play (the guitar)
12. to play volleyball
13. ball
14. tree
15. leaves
16. to play basketball
17. to practice, go out for (a sport)
18. to play tennis
19. (tennis) game, match
20. to win/lose
21. to exercise, work out, do exercises
22. to lift weights
23. to smoke
24. to rest
25. to bicycle/ride a bike

Práctica y comunicación

4-1. **Los sábados en el parque.** Answer the following questions, referring to the drawing on pages 136–137.

> **Modelo:** ¿Qué hace la mujer que está en el lago?
>
> Esquía.[1]

1. ¿Qué hace el hombre que está en el lago?
2. ¿Quién corre más rápido, Juanito o su perro Teo?
3. Inés está cerca (*near*) del lago. ¿Qué le gusta hacer?
4. A Natalia le gusta escuchar música con su walkman. ¿Qué más hace?
5. ¿Qué hace Camila, la artista?
6. ¿Qué hacen Linda y Manuel? **Dan...** *o...*
7. A Rubén le gusta la música. ¿Qué hace?
8. La pelota está en el aire. ¿Qué hacen los niños?
9. ¿Qué deporte practica Esteban? ¿Y Javier?
10. ¿Piensa usted que Javier va a ganar o perder el partido?
11. ¿Qué hace Octavio? ¿Y qué hace Alfonso?
12. ¿Qué hace Héctor? ¿Debe (*Should he*) o no debe fumar?
13. Pepita no camina por el parque. ¿Qué hace? ¿Y qué hace Elena?

4-2. **¿Qué te gusta hacer?** Ask each other questions to find out which activities you like. When you agree on an activity, write it down.

> **Modelo:** jugar al vólibol
>
> Estudiante 1: **¿Te gusta jugar al vólibol?**
>
> Estudiante 2: **Sí, me gusta. ¿Y a ti?** *o* No, no me gusta. ¿Y a ti?

1. jugar al tenis/ básquetbol/ vólibol?
2. nadar (¿Prefieres nadar en un lago, un río o en el océano?)
3. tomar el sol (¿Qué playa prefieres?)
4. levantar pesas y/o hacer ejercicio
5. correr (¿Cuántas millas corres?)
6. esquiar en la nieve (*snow*) y/o en el agua (¿Cuál es tu lugar favorito para...?)
7. montar en bicicleta
8. cantar
9. escuchar música (¿Qué tipo?)
10. leer (¿Qué tipo de libros?)

Now tell the class about an interest that you and your classmate have in common:

A Luisa y a mí nos gusta...

---

[1] **Esquiar** requires an accent mark over the **í**, except in the **nosotros** and **vosotros** forms: **esquío, esquías, esquía, esquiamos, esquiais, esquían.**

Así se dice

Los colores

Camila enjoys painting in the park. Observe the colors on her palette.

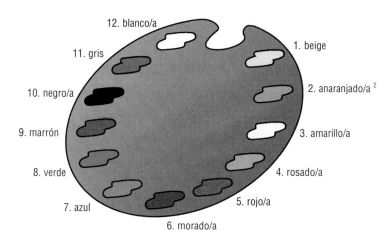

1. beige
2. anaranjado/a [2]
3. amarillo/a
4. rosado/a
5. rojo/a
6. morado/a
7. azul
8. verde
9. marrón
10. negro/a
11. gris
12. blanco/a

> All of the colors above are adjectives. Those that end in **-o** change to reflect both gender and number: **blanco, blanca, blancos, blancas**. Those that end in **-e (verde)** or a consonant **(gris, marrón, azul)** have two forms, singular and plural: **verde, verdes**.
> Las flores son **azules** y **amarillas**.

4–3. De colores.

Identify the following colors. As appropriate, refer to the drawing of the park scene on pages 136–137.

1. ¿De qué color es el agua del lago?
2. ¿De qué color son las hojas de los árboles? ¿Y los troncos?
3. ¿De qué color son las flores? **Hay flores amarillas, ...**
4. ¿Cuáles son tus colores favoritos? ¿Cuáles no te gustan?

Es otoño (*fall*). ¿De qué color son las hojas?

---

[2] Some colors have alternate names that are nouns, and thus *do not change* in gender and number. They are often preceded by the word **color**, or the word is implied. Examples: **(color) naranja; (color) café; (color) rosa; (color) violeta**.

Así se dice

Más actividades y deportes

Read about Manuel's and Linda's interests and activities. What interests do they have in common? What are their differences? Do you think they are compatible?

MANUEL	LINDA
Me gusta mucho **bailar**(1) con Linda.	→ ¡Me encanta° bailar!
También me gusta **ir de compras**(2) con ella.	Vamos de compras casi todos los sábados.
El **fútbol**(3) es mi **deporte**(4) favorito.	Prefiero el **fútbol americano**(5).
Me gusta **ver la tele**(6): partidos de **béisbol**(7), torneos de **golf**(8), ...	Veo partidos de baloncesto o tenis y también me gustan las telenovelas°.
Mi **equipo**(9) favorito son los Padres.	Pues, mi equipo son los Celtas.
Me gusta **manejar**(10)*. ¡Tengo un carro nuevo!	No manejo; prefiero caminar o ir con Inés, que tiene carro.
Soy muy ordenado°. **Limpio**(11) mi apartamento cada semana.	También limpio mi apartamento cada semana.
Generalmente soy puntual. (**Casi**) **siempre**(12) llego a tiempo.	Pues, **a veces**(13) llego tarde, pero **nunca**(14) muy tarde.

I love

soap operas

tidy

(1) *to dance* (2) *to go shopping* (3) *soccer* (4) *sport* (5) *football* (6) *to watch TV*
(7) *baseball* (8) *golf* (9) *team* (10) *to drive* (11) *I clean;* **limpiar** *to clean* (12) *(Almost) always*
(13) *sometimes* (14) *never*

4-4. **Mis hábitos.** Tell each other how often you do the following activities. Use (**casi**) **siempre, a veces,** or **nunca** in your answers.

1. Manejo después de tomar bebidas alcohólicas.
2. Bailo en las fiestas.
3. Veo telenovelas por la tarde.
4. Veo partidos de fútbol/ básquetbol/ tenis/ béisbol en la tele.
5. Hago ejercicio por la mañana.
6. Voy de compras los fines de semana.
7. Escucho música cuando estoy solo/a en mi cuarto.
8. Fumo.

If you and your partner have an answer in common, share it with the class:
Cristina y yo nunca manejamos después de tomar bebidas alcohólicas.

---

* **conducir = manejar** in Spain. Present tense: **conduzco, conduces, conduce, conducimos, conducís, conducen.**

4-5. **Mis pasatiempos favoritos.** Make a list of your favorite pastimes and share it with a classmate. Select the most interesting pastime from your list and from your classmate's. Be prepared to report back to the class.

Modelo: A mí me gusta... A Teresa le gusta...

Escenas

Un deportista muy serio

Pepita   Esteban

El sábado por la mañana en el parque cerca de la universidad. Esteban duerme en la hierba°. Llega Pepita.

grass

PEPITA: Esteban, ¿qué haces? ¿Durmiendo° tan temprano?

sleeping

ESTEBAN: Uhmm, Pepita... ¿Qué tal? Estoy... tomando el sol.

PEPITA: ¿Con suéter y jeans?

ESTEBAN: Bueno, estoy descansando antes de° tomar el sol. ¿Qué haces aquí?

antes... before

PEPITA: Estoy buscando a Octavio. Vamos a jugar al vólibol. ¿Quieres jugar con nosotros?

ESTEBAN: Mi deporte favorito es ver la televisión.

PEPITA: (*Riéndose°.*) ¡Eres incorregible! ¿Nunca haces ejercicio?

Laughing

ESTEBAN: ¡Claro que sí! A veces juego al baloncesto o al fútbol con Manuel y Javier.

PEPITA: ¡Qué bien!

ESTEBAN: Pero con esos partidos me canso mucho.

PEPITA: ¡Ah! Ahora comprendo. Por eso estás descansando hoy.

ESTEBAN: Bueno... sí. Necesito recuperar energía para el próximo° partido.

next

PEPITA: Tienes razón°. Más tarde Octavio y yo vamos a la heladería°. ¿Quieres acompañarnos?

Tienes... *You are right. / ice cream parlor*

ESTEBAN: ¿A la heladería? Sí, voy con ustedes. Comer helados es otro de mis deportes favoritos... ¡y soy un deportista muy dedicado!

¿Qué pasa?

1. ¿Dónde está Esteban? ¿Qué hace? **Está...**

2. ¿A qué van a jugar Pepita y Octavio en el parque?

3. ¿Cuál es el deporte favorito de Esteban?

4. ¿Piensa usted que Esteban hace suficiente ejercicio?

5. ¿Por qué está descansando?

6. ¿Cuál es el otro deporte favorito de Esteban?

Estructuras

1 Talking about activities in the present: Additional *yo*-irregular verbs

> Conozco a María, el amor de mi vida, pero ella ni sabe mi nombre. ¡Ay, ay ay!

A. *Saber* and *conocer*

These verbs both mean *to know*, but have very different uses. Observe the irregular **yo** form in their conjugations.

> **saber:** **sé**, sabes, sabe, sabemos, sabéis, saben
>
> **conocer:** **conozco**, conoces, conoce, conocemos, conocéis, conocen

- **Saber** means *to know* (*facts, information*) and *to know how to* (*skills*). It describes the kind of knowledge that one learns (a piece of information) and skills that can be demonstrated.

    Sé dónde vive Inés. Ella **sabe** tocar el piano.

- **Conocer** means *to know, be acquainted* or *familiar with persons, places,* or *things*. It also means *to meet* (*for the first time*).

    Conozco a Carmen. Ella **conoce** bien la ciudad de Ponce.

    Quiero **conocer** a Marta Uribe. Creo que es dominicana.

    ¿**Conoce** usted la poesía de Nicolás Guillén?

Práctica y comunicación

4-6. ¿Qué sabemos hacer?

Moving about the classroom, find out who knows how to do each of the following things. Jot down the name of the person by the activity. You have seven minutes. Be prepared to report back to the class.

1. esquiar ¿Sabes...? Sí, sé... *o* No, no sé...
2. nadar bien
3. bailar y/o cantar bien
4. cocinar bien
5. tocar el piano/ el violín/ la guitarra/ la trompeta/ el saxofón/ el clarinete
6. jugar al tenis/ vólibol/ béisbol/ fútbol/ fútbol americano/ golf/ baloncesto
7. hablar italiano/ francés/ ruso/ japonés/ alemán

4-7. Deportistas famosos.

Ask each other if you know who the following famous athletes are. Use the list of categories provided.

Categorías
basquetbolista
beisbolista
ciclista
futbolista
golfista
tenista

Modelo:

Mia Hamm

Estudiante 1: ¿Sabes quién es Mia Hamm?

Estudiante 2: Sí, sé quién es. Es una futbolista famosa. *o*
No, no sé quién es.

¿Sabes quién es/quiénes son?
1. Tiger Woods
2. Serena y Venus Williams
3. Sammy Sosa y Barry Bonds
4. Jason Kidd y Shaquille O'Neal
5. Claudio Reina
6. Lance Armstrong

The verb **conocer** is often used with direct object pronouns. **Lo** and **los** replace masculine nouns; **la** and **las** replace feminine nouns.

—¿Conoces a Ana?	—*Do you know Ana?*
—Sí, **la** conozco.	—*Yes, I know* **her.**
—¿Quieres conocer a sus padres?	—*Do you want to meet her parents?*
—Sí, **los** quiero conocer. *o* Quiero conocer**los**.	—*Yes, I want to meet* **them.**

Note the position of the pronoun: immediately in front of the main verb, or attached to the infinitive.

4-8. ¿Quieres conocerlo/la?
Say whether or not you want to meet/get acquainted with the following famous people.

Modelo: ¿Quiere usted conocer a Jennifer López?

Sí, quiero conocerla. *o* Sí, la quiero conocer. *o* No, no...

o No sé quién es.

¿Quiere usted conocer a...?

1. Antonio Banderas
2. Bill Gates
3. Enrique Iglesias
4. Ricky Martin
5. Whoopi Goldberg y Oprah Winfrey
6. El presidente Bush y su esposa
7. Jennifer Aniston

4-9. Lugares (*Places*) interesantes.
Tell the class what interesting places you are acquainted with in each of the categories listed.

Modelo: parques nacionales

Conozco el parque Yosemite en California,...

1. ciudades famosas
2. lugares para esquiar en la nieve o en el agua
3. playas extraordinarias para nadar, hacer *surf* o caminar por la playa

4-10. ¿Lo/La conoces bien?
Ask your partner for information about one of your other classmates. Student 1 completes the blanks in the questions with **sabes** or **conoces**, as appropriate. Student 2 answers the questions. Then reverse roles.

Estudiante 1

¿_____ a (*classmate's name*)?

¿_____ dónde vive?

¿_____ su número de teléfono o su dirección electrónica?

¿_____ cuántos años tiene?

¿_____ si tiene novio/a?

¿_____ a los amigos de él/ella?

Estudiante 2

Sí, lo/la _____.

...

...

...

...

...

¡Pienso que (no) lo/la _____ muy bien!

B. Additional verbs with an irregular *yo* form

In **Chapter 1** you learned two verbs with an irregular *yo* form: **salir** and **hacer**. Review them, and then observe the verbs that follow.

salir (de) *to leave, go out*	**salgo**, sales, sale, salimos, salís, salen
hacer *to do, make*	**hago**, haces, hace, hacemos, hacéis, hacen
traer *to bring*	**traigo**, traes, trae, traemos, traéis, traen
poner *to put, place*	**pongo**, pones, pone, ponemos, ponéis, ponen
oír *to hear*	**oigo, oyes, oye**, oímos, oís, **oyen** (*note the* **y**)
ver *to see*	**veo**, ves, ve, vemos, veis, ven (*no accent in* **veis**)
dar *to give*	**doy**, das, da, damos, dais, dan (*no accent in* **dais**)

- **Salir** is followed by **de** when the subject is leaving a stated place.
    Salen del gimnasio. *vs.* **Salen** con sus amigos.

- When the verb **hacer** is used in a question, it does not necessarily require a form of the verb **hacer** in the answer.
    —¿Qué **haces** normalmente por la tarde?
    —**Voy** a la biblioteca, **hago** la tarea y después, **trabajo** en la librería.

HINT Think of the following verbs as the "yo-go verbs"—verbs whose **yo** forms end in **go**: **salir, hacer, traer, poner, oír, tener, venir,** and **decir.**

Like **tener**, which you learned in **Chapter 2**, the verbs **venir** and **decir** have irregular **yo** forms in addition to stem-changes.

tener (ie) *to have*	**tengo, tienes, tiene,** tenemos, tenéis, **tienen**
venir (ie) *to come*	**vengo, vienes, viene,** venimos, venís, **vienen**
decir (i) *to say, tell*	**digo, dices, dice,** decimos, decís, **dicen**

Práctica y comunicación

4-11. **¿Lo hago o no?** Read each statement that follows. Your partner will guess whether it is true or not. If necessary, set the record straight. Then reverse roles.

> **Modelo:** Estudiante 1: **Traigo comida y bebidas a la clase de español.**
> Estudiante 2: **Es verdad./No es verdad.**
> Estudiante 1: **No es verdad. Traigo mi libro y mi cuaderno a la clase.**

1. Pongo (*I turn on*) el televisor inmediatamente al entrar en mi casa/cuarto.
2. Veo telenovelas con mucha frecuencia.
3. Oigo las noticias (*news*) en la tele casi todos los días.
4. Hago ejercicio todos los días.
5. Salgo con mis amigos casi todos los jueves por la noche.
6. Hago la tarea los sábados por la noche.
7. Digo «**Buenos días, profe**» al entrar en la clase de español.
8. Siempre vengo a clase con la tarea lista.
9. En clase, siempre doy respuestas correctas.
10. Traigo tacos y Coca-Cola a clase.
11. Cuando tengo dificultades en la clase, hablo con la profesora/el profesor.

Now tell the class something you learned about your partner: **Susana dice que ve telenovelas con mucha frecuencia.**

4-12. **¿Qué hace Pepita?** Tell what Pepita does and then what the two of you do.

> **Modelo:** **Pepita duerme bien. No oye la música del despertador (*alarm*).**
> **Nosotros (no) dormimos bien y (no) oímos la música del despertador.**

dormir… / no oír… / del despertador

1. hacer… / por la mañana

2. llegar a clase / a las… traer…

3. poner…

4. saber todas…

5. salir de… / a las…

4-13. Preguntas personales.

4-13. **Preguntas personales.** Formulate questions combining the interrogative words with the cues provided. Your partner will answer the questions. Then reverse roles.

> ¿Cuándo?   ¿A qué hora?   ¿Con quién?   ¿Qué?   ¿A quién?

Modelo: conocer muy bien / en la clase de español
> Estudiante 1: ¿A quién conoces muy bien en la clase de español?
> Estudiante 2: Conozco a...

1. conocer muy bien / en la clase de español
2. hacer / la tarea
3. programas de televisión / ver con frecuencia
4. salir / los fines de semana
5. volver a la residencia / los sábados por la noche
6. deportes / practicar
7. instrumento musical / tocar
8. tipo de música / preferir

DICHOS

Decir y hacer son dos cosas, y la segunda es la dificultosa.

¿Puede usted explicar este dicho?

4-14. **¿Qué haces los sábados?** Answer the question truthfully, giving as many activities as possible. Your instructor will set a time limit. The student with the longest list wins.

Modelo: ¿Qué haces los sábados? **Los sábados trabajo, ...**

Así se dice
Preferencias, obligaciones e intenciones

Read the conversation between the devil and the angel to find out about their preferences, obligations, and intentions. Then identify the expressions that fall into each category.

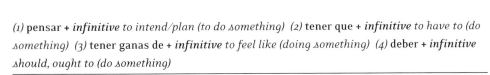

EL DIABLO:	¿Qué **piensas hacer**(1) esta noche?
EL ÁNGEL:	**Tengo que cantar**(2) en el coro celestial.
EL DIABLO:	¿No **tienes ganas de salir**(3) conmigo?
EL ÁNGEL:	Tú sabes que no quiero ni **debo salir**(4) contigo. ¡Tienes mala fama°!

mala... *a bad reputation*

(1) pensar + *infinitive to intend/plan (to do something)* *(2)* tener que + *infinitive to have to (do something)* *(3)* tener ganas de + *infinitive to feel like (doing something)* *(4)* deber + *infinitive should, ought to (do something)*

② **4-15.** **¿Preferencias u obligaciones?** Tell whether the characters *have to do* or *feel like doing* the activities depicted in the drawings.

Natalia

> **Modelo:** Natalia
> **Natalia tiene ganas de ver videos.**

1. Esteban

2. Inés

3. Javier

4. Camila

5. Rubén

6. Carmen

7. Pepita

8. Octavio

9. Linda

④ **4-16.** **Obligaciones, preferencias y planes.** Tell what you have to do, feel like doing, or plan/intend to do. Appoint a secretary to record the information and to read it to the class.

> tener que...   deber...   tener ganas de...   pensar...

> **Modelo:** Estamos muy preocupados/as hoy porque tenemos examen mañana.
> **Tenemos que estudiar mucho esta noche./ No debemos ver la tele,...**

1. Estamos muy ocupados/as esta semana.

2. Estamos aburridos/as con la vida social de la universidad.

3. Estamos un poco estresados/as hoy.

4. ¡Estamos muy contentos/as! ¡Tenemos un día sin obligaciones!

② **¡Qué dilema!** *Le dices a tu pareja que no puedes salir con él/ella esta noche porque tienes que estudiar. Más tarde decides ir al cine con otro/a "amigo/a" y, ¡qué sorpresa! ¡Ves a tu pareja allí! Él/Ella te pregunta:* **¿Qué haces aquí? ¿No tienes que estudiar esta noche? ¿Quién es tu amigo/a?**

Noticias culturales

El fútbol: rey° de los deportes

king

¡Los argentinos son muy aficionados al fútbol! (Buenos Aires)

Para gran parte del mundo hispano —y para la mayor parte de la gente del planeta— el fútbol es verdaderamente el rey de los deportes. Para los dominicanos, los puertorriqueños, los cubanos y los venezolanos, el béisbol es el deporte más importante; pero en los otros países hispanos muchos consideran que el fútbol es más que un deporte —¡es una forma de vida!

Los fanáticos hacen de este deporte casi una religión. Ver un partido importante, en el estadio o por televisión, es una obligación. El fútbol no respeta horarios° ni lugares: en muchos países los empleados ponen televisores en sus lugares de trabajo para ver jugar a sus equipos favoritos.

schedules

La pasión por el fútbol aumenta al máximo cada cuatro años con la celebración de la Copa Mundial°. Durante la Copa, los fanáticos no se pierden° ningún partido. Los futbolistas talentosos son auténticos héroes nacionales y mundiales.

World Cup

se... miss

¿Qué recuerda?

1. ¿Qué frases describen la importancia del fútbol para los hispanoamericanos?

2. ¿Por qué dicen que el fútbol no respeta horarios ni lugares?

3. ¿Qué pasa durante la Copa Mundial?

2 Conexiones y contrastes

1. ¿Sabe usted cuándo y dónde se celebró (*took place*) la última Copa Mundial?

2. ¿Es la afición al fútbol americano en los EE.UU. tan fuerte como (*as strong as*) la afición al fútbol en Latinoamérica?

3. ¿Qué eventos deportivos en su país tienen mucha importancia?

4. ¿Es usted fanático/a de algún deporte? ¿De qué deporte? ¿Cuál es su equipo favorito?

Muchos jóvenes aspiran a ser famosos futbolistas.

2 Making future plans: *Ir* + a + infinitive

Voy a impresionar a Pepita con mis músculos.

To talk about plans and actions yet to occur, use a form of the verb **ir** + **a** + *infinitive.*

Vamos a jugar al básquetbol mañana.	*We are going to play* basketball *tomorrow.*
Inés **va a practicar** el piano esta noche.	*Ines is going to practice* piano *tonight.*
Y tú, ¿qué **vas a hacer** mañana por la tarde?	*And you, what are you going to do tomorrow afternoon?*

The following expressions are useful to talk about the future.

En el futuro

la semana que viene	*next week*
la próxima semana	*next week*
el mes/ año/ verano que viene	*next month/year/summer*
el próximo mes/ año/ verano	*next month/year/summer*

Práctica y comunicación

4-17. **¿Qué voy a hacer?** Decide what you are going to do, given the following conditions or circumstances. You may be asked to report some of your responses to the class.

1. Estoy cansado/a. **Voy a...**
2. Estoy aburrido/a.
3. ¡Tengo mucha energía!
4. Tengo hambre.
5. Tengo sed.

4-18. **En el futuro.** Describe what you and your friends *are going to do* next weekend and next summer. Use your imagination! Write at least four sentences for each category. Then share your plans with a classmate.

1. El fin de semana que viene...

2. El próximo verano...

Así se dice

El clima y las estaciones (*The weather and the seasons*)

There are several ways to ask what the weather is like: ¿Qué tiempo hace? ¿Cómo está el clima? ¿Qué tal el clima?[1]

Hace sol[2]. **Hace (mucho) calor**[3]. Octavio **tiene calor**[4]. Es **verano**[5].

Hace frío[6]. Esteban **tiene frío**[7]. Es **invierno**[8].

Hace buen tiempo[9]. **Hace fresco**[10]. **Está nublado**[11]. Hay **nubes**[12]. Es **primavera**[13].

Llueve[14] todas las tardes. **Está lloviendo**[15] ahora. Dicen que después de la **lluvia**[16] sale el sol.

Hace mal tiempo[17]. **Hace viento**[18]. Es **otoño**[19].

Aquí, en el invierno, **nieva**[20] casi todos los días. **Está nevando**[21] ahora. ¡**Me encanta*** **la nieve**[22]!

(1) What's the weather like? (2) It's sunny. (3) It's (very) hot. (4) . . . is hot; **tener calor** *to be hot (5) summer (6) It's cold. (7) . . . is cold;* **tener frío** *to be cold (8) winter (9) It's nice weather. (10) It's cool. (11) It's cloudy. (12) clouds (f.) (13) spring (14) It rains;* **llover (ue)** *to rain (15) It's raining. (16) rain (17) It's bad weather. (18) It's windy;* **el viento** *the wind (19) fall, autumn (20) it snows;* **nevar (ie)** *to snow (21) It's snowing. (22) I love snow! (The snow delights me!)* **la nieve** *the snow*

---

* The verb **encantar** functions like **gustar** (see p.105): **Me encantan las rosas amarillas.**

Práctica y comunicación

4-19. **Por el mundo hispano.** Tell what the weather is like and identify the season of the year and the country.

Modelo: Hace frío y hay mucha nieve.
Es invierno[3].
Estamos en Argentina.

Parque Nacional Los Glaciares, Argentina

1. Playa Manuel Antonio, Costa Rica

3. Tres Piedras, Nuevo México

2. Huracán Luis, Puerto Rico

4. Refugio, Nevado de Ruiz, Colombia

5. Maestrazgo, España

---

[3] The seasons of the year are reversed in the northern and southern hemispheres; for example, when it is winter in Argentina, it is summer in the United States and Canada.

4-20. **El clima y las estaciones.** Take turns asking and answering the following questions.

1. ¿Cuáles son los meses de invierno en nuestro país? ¿De primavera? ¿De verano? ¿De otoño?

2. ¿Cuál es tu estación favorita? ¿Por qué?

3. ¿En qué estación estamos ahora? ¿En qué estación están en Argentina, Chile y Uruguay?

4. ¿Qué deportes asocias con la primavera? ¿El otoño? ¿El invierno?

5. ¿Cuáles son tus pasatiempos favoritos en el invierno? ¿Y en el verano?

6. ¿Cómo está el clima hoy?

7. ¿Qué tiempo hace (probablemente) en San Francisco, CA? ¿En Miami, FL? ¿En Fairbanks, AK? ¿En Portland, OR? ¿Y en Toronto, Canadá?

8. ¿Qué te gusta hacer cuando llueve?

9. Cuando tienes frío, ¿qué bebida prefieres tomar? ¿Y cuando tienes mucho calor?

DICHOS

A mal tiempo... buena cara°.
¿Qué significa el dicho?

face

El termómetro indica que la temperatura está a 50 grados Fahrenheit. ¿Cuál es la temperatura en centígrados? Si la temperatura está a 40 grados Celsius, ¿hace mucho frío o hace mucho calor?

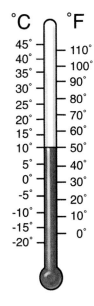

3 Emphasizing that an action is in progress: The present progressive

¿Qué estás pintando, Camila?

¿No es obvio?

To indicate that an action is in progress (present progressive), English uses the *to be* + *-ing* (present participle) form of the verb: *He is resting.*

Spanish uses the **estar** + **-ndo** (present participle) form of the verb.

Elena **está estudiando** para un examen.	*Ellen is studying for an exam.*
Ana **está comiendo** galletas.	*Ana is eating cookies.*

	stem	+ ending	= present participle
-ar *verbs*	**estudi**ar	**-ando**	**estudiando**
-er *verbs*	**com**er	**-iendo**	**comiendo**
-ir *verbs*	**escrib**ir	**-iendo**	**escribiendo**

Four frequently used irregular present participles are:

decir (i)	**diciendo**	dormir (u)	**durmiendo**
pedir (i)	**pidiendo**	leer	**leyendo**

The present progressive emphasizes that an *action* is *in progress at a particular time.* In Spanish, it is not used as frequently as the simple present tense.

Trabajo todos los días.	*I work (am working) every day.* (act not in progress)
Estoy trabajando ahora.	*I am working (right) now.* (act in progress)
Juana, ¿todavía **estás comiendo**[4]?	*Juana, are you still eating?* (act in progress)

---

[4] The present participle always ends in **-ndo**: it does not change to agree with the subject. **Estar**, however, always changes to agree with the subject.

Práctica y comunicación

4-21. **¿Qué están haciendo?** Indicate what each person is doing.

1. Javier **está** estudiando.

2. Inés

3. Linda y Manuel

4. Esteban

5. Alfonso

6. Octavio

7. Manuel

4-22. **Actores y actrices.** Eight volunteers dramatize each of the following activities in front of the class. The rest of the class indicates what each actor *is doing.* Close your textbooks!

Modelo: Profesor/a: ¿Qué está haciendo José?

Estudiante: **Está caminando por el aula.**

1. leer un libro muy interesante

2. hablar con sus amigos por teléfono

3. caminar por el aula

4. manejar su coche nuevo

5. comer espaguetis

6. tocar la guitarra

7. hacer ejercicio

8. dormir

4-23. **Probablemente.** Imagine what the following people are doing. Use the present progressive.

1. Linda y Manuel están en el restaurante Ritz el sábado por la noche.

2. Mis amigos están en la playa durante las vacaciones de primavera.

3. Mi padre está en casa frente a la computadora el viernes por la noche.

4. Mi madre está en casa el día antes de (*before*) una gran fiesta.

5. Mi compañero/a de cuarto está en su cuarto y son las diez de la noche.

4 Describing people, places, and things: *Ser* and *estar* (A summary)

HINT Before beginning this section, review the information and exercises on **ser/estar** in **Chapter 2**, pp. 78–81 and 85–90.

Imagine that you are contemplating going on a blind date. What questions might you ask about the person? Who is he/she (a student, a lawyer)? Where is he/she from? What is he/she like? These questions and their accompanying responses require the verb **ser**.

Use *ser*:

- to identify *who* or *what the subject is* (vocation, profession, religion, etc.)

    Alejandro **es estudiante** de la Universidad de Texas.
    Quiere **ser biólogo**.
    Es católico (*Catholic*).

- to indicate *origin* (where the subject is from) and *nationality*

    Es de Puerto Rico.
    Es puertorriqueño.

- to indicate *what the subject is like*—descriptive characteristics or qualities, physical or personality traits inherent to the person, place, or thing described

    Es alto, moreno, simpático y muy inteligente.
    Es un hombre muy bueno y un poco extrovertido.
    Puerto Rico, su país natal, **es una isla muy bella** (*beautiful*).

Use *estar*:

- to indicate the physical or emotional *condition* of the subject at a given time (how the subject feels, appears)—often indicates a change from the usual

    Ahora **está un poco estresado** a causa de (*because of*) su carro.
    El carro **está en malas condiciones** y necesita un motor nuevo.

- to tell *where the subject is* (indicate the physical location of the person, place, or thing)

    Ahora **está en Puerto Rico** para las vacaciones de primavera.

Note how the use of **ser** and **estar** with the same adjective can change or slightly alter the meaning of that adjective.

Roberto **es aburrido/ está aburrido**.	*Roberto **is boring/ is bored**.*
Carmen **es** muy **bonita/**	*Carmen **is** very **pretty/***
está muy **bonita** hoy.	***looks** very **pretty** today.*

Watch out for these nuances when speaking about your blind date or a friend!

Other uses of *ser/estar*:

- **Ser** + *day, date, season, time:*

  Es lunes. (*day*)   Es primavera. (*season*)
  Es el ocho de abril. (*date*)   Son las nueve de la mañana. (*time*)

- **Ser** to indicate possession:

  —¿**Es de Susana** la raqueta?
  —No, **es mi** raqueta.

- **Estar** + **-ando/-iendo** to indicate an action in progress:

  Está jugando al tenis **ahora**.

Práctica y comunicación

(2) 4-24. **¿Quieres salir con él/ella?** Your classmate wants to arrange a blind date for you. Find out all you can about the person before accepting. Use the correct form of **ser** or **estar** to complete the dialog.

ESTUDIANTE 1:	¿Cómo se llama?
ESTUDIANTE 2:	Juan/Juana González. _____ de la ciudad de Nueva York.
ESTUDIANTE 1:	¿_____ estudiante?
ESTUDIANTE 2:	Sí, de esta (*this*) universidad. Y también _____ atleta. Le gusta jugar al tenis y al básquetbol, montar en bicicleta, levantar pesas...
ESTUDIANTE 1:	Pues, ¿cómo _____? Descríbemelo/la.
ESTUDIANTE 2:	_____ una persona muy buena, muy amable.
ESTUDIANTE 1:	¿_____ guapo/a?
ESTUDIANTE 2:	Sí, _____ muy guapo/a, rubio/a y delgado/a. ¿Quieres conocerlo/la?
ESTUDIANTE 1:	Sí, ¡por supuesto (*of course*)! ¿Dónde _____ ahora?
ESTUDIANTE 2:	Pienso que _____ en el laboratorio de biología. Probablemente _____ trabajando ahora porque _____ asistente/asistenta del profesor.
ESTUDIANTE 1:	No importa. ¡Vamos al laboratorio!

Now your classmate wants to set you up with another friend of his/hers. Ask several questions about the prospective blind date. Then reverse roles.

② **4-25.** **¿Qué pasa?** Use the cues provided to tell what each person is *normally* like. Then select an adjective from the list to indicate a *change* in his/her disposition. Your partner will ask the reason for the change. Take turns.

aburrido/a
animado/a
cansado/a
enojado/a
estresado/a
nervioso/a
preocupado/a
triste
…

Modelo: Manuel / enérgico

Estudiante 1: Manuel *normalmente* es muy enérgico, pero *ahora* está cansado.

Estudiante 2: ¿Por qué?

Estudiante 1: Porque está en el equipo de fútbol y practica todos los días.

1. Rubén / tranquilo
2. Natalia / curiosa y animada
3. Pepita / alegre (*happy, cheerful*)
4. Alfonso / serio
5. Camila / tranquila
6. Mis amigos/as / …
7. (yo) / …

Así se pronuncia

The pronunciation of the consonants *ll* and *v*

ll Remember that double **l** approximates the English *y* sound as in *yes*.

llueve   **ll**oviendo   **ll**uvia   **ll**over

v/b Between vowels, **v** (like **b**) is pronounced with the lips barely touching. Repeat the same words, now concentrating on the **v** sound.

llue**v**e   llo**v**iendo   llu**v**ia   llo**v**er

v/b Initial **v/b** is pronounced like the English *b* in *boy*.

vólibol   **v**iento   **v**iolín   **v**iernes

Repeat the sentences to practice the pronunciation of **ll** and **v**.

ll En las noches de luna **ll**ena° las estre**ll**as° bri**ll**an°.

v El **v**iento mue**v**e la **v**ela° suavemente°.

luna... *full moon / stars / shine*
sail / softly

Dicho y hecho

Conversando

4 **Un día sin clases.** Imagine that it is early in the morning on a day with no classes. Plan your free day. Talk about:

- el clima (para determinar las actividades y posibles destinos)
- lo que tienen ganas de hacer y adónde tienen ganas de ir
- lo que pueden/ van a hacer hoy
- lo que piensan comer y dónde
- si (*if*) salen de la universidad, cuándo piensan volver

Share some of your plans with the class.

¡A escuchar!

¡Todo sobre el fútbol! Listen to the comments of the radio announcer and the commentator Andrés Mauricio. Then answer the first two questions.

1. ¿De dónde son los dos equipos rivales? ❏ de España ❏ de México
2. ¿Se decide el campeón de la liga hoy? ❏ sí ❏ no

Listen to the broadcast again and choose the correct answers to the following questions:

3. ¿Para qué equipo juega Sergio Flores? ❏ Madrid ❏ Barcelona
4. ¿Cuál es el número de Miguel? ❏ 9 ❏ 45
5. ¿Quién marca el gol? ❏ Miguel ❏ Sergio
6. ¿Quién gana? ❏ Barcelona ❏ Madrid

De mi escritorio

Una excursión. Write a paragraph to present to the class about a possible outing that you and your friends want to make.

- Pensamos ir a... Es un lugar... (*describe the place*)
- Queremos/Podemos... (*mention activities, pastimes, etc.*)
- Vamos a...
- De comer vamos a llevar (*take*)...
- Regresamos...

Panorama cultural

Las Antillas Mayores: Cuba, la República

Nacionalidades:
cubano(a)
dominicano(a)
puertorriqueño(a)

Preguntas sobre el mapa

1. ¿Cuál es la isla de las Antillas Mayores más cercana (*closest*) a la Florida?
2. ¿Cuál es la isla más grande? ¿Cuál es su capital? ¿Y la más pequeña? ¿Y su capital?
3. ¿Qué dos países ocupan una sola isla? ¿Cuál es la capital del país donde se habla español?

El joven de la foto toca con mucho sentimiento. Una banda en La Habana, Cuba.

Person@je del momento

¿Sabe usted quién es Roberto Clemente?
Busque información en el Internet y compártala con sus compañeros/as de clase.

Tres países de habla hispana

Las Antillas Mayores, situadas entre el océano Atlántico y el mar Caribe, incluyen tres países de habla hispana: Cuba, Puerto Rico y la República Dominicana. La República Dominicana ocupa gran parte de la isla «La Española», nombrada así por Cristóbal Colón en su primera visita a América. Las Antillas son territorios muy importantes por su posición como «puertas» al continente americano.

La caña de azúcar, el tabaco, las frutas tropicales y el ron[1] han sido[2] las principales industrias de estas islas durante siglos[3]. Hoy, por su clima y belleza natural, las Antillas Mayores atraen un gran número de turistas.

La música y las danzas de estas islas son la expresión cultural preferida de sus habitantes. Los bailes como la salsa, el mambo, el bolero y el merengue tienen influencia española en sus melodías pero en los ritmos es evidente la influencia africana.

El deporte nacional de Cuba, Puerto Rico y la República Dominicana es el béisbol. ¡Los beisbolistas talentosos de estos países son conocidos en todo el mundo! ¿Conoce usted al famoso jugador dominicano en la foto?

Dominicana, Puerto Rico

Cuba

¿Sabía usted que...?

- Cuba fue una colonia española hasta 1898.
- Después de la guerra entre los Estados Unidos y España, Cuba pasó a ser un «protectorado» de los EE.UU.
- Cuba se independizó en 1902, pero su economía continuó dependiendo de los EE.UU.
- La revolución de 1959 instituyó una dictadura marxista, y bajo[4] Fidel Castro, Cuba empezó a depender económicamente de la Unión Soviética.
- El embargo de los Estados Unidos (1963) y la disolución de la Unión Soviética (1992) contribuyeron a la crisis económica en Cuba.

Parte del plan económico de Castro consiste en la construcción y restauración de hoteles y lugares de veraneo[5] para atraer el turismo, industria principal de la isla. Varadero (vea la foto) es un ejemplo, ofreciendo playas magníficas y otras atracciones naturales. ¿Cuáles son las atracciones turísticas en el área donde usted vive?

La República Dominicana

¿Sabía usted que...?

- En 1496 los españoles fundaron Santo Domingo, la primera ciudad de origen europeo en América.
- Los franceses establecieron una colonia (Haití) al oeste de la colonia española.
- Después de años de guerra — ¡contra los españoles, los franceses y los haitianos!— la República Dominicana se independizó en 1865.
- En 1927, después de una ocupación estadounidense, el general Rafael Trujillo tomó el poder. Su dictadura fue totalitaria y terminó con su asesinato en 1965.
- Hoy la República Dominicana es una democracia.

¡A la universidad!

La primera universidad del continente americano se estableció en Santo Domingo en 1538.

[1]*rum* [2]*have been* [3]*centuries* [4]*under* [5]*lugares... summer beach resorts*

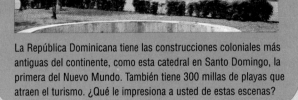

La República Dominicana tiene las construcciones coloniales más antiguas del continente, como esta catedral en Santo Domingo, la primera del Nuevo Mundo. También tiene 300 millas de playas que atraen el turismo. ¿Qué le impresiona a usted de estas escenas?

Puerto Rico

Además de la salsa y el merengue tradicionales, los jóvenes puertorriqueños están escuchando más y más la música «rapera», convirtiéndola en una de las formas musicales más populares de la isla. ¿A usted le gusta la música «rapera»?

¿Sabía usted que...?

- Los taínos son los habitantes originales de la isla.
- Cristóbal Colón descubrió Puerto Rico y el español Juan Ponce de León comenzó su colonización en 1508.
- En 1898, después de la guerra entre España y los Estados Unidos, Puerto Rico se convirtió en una colonia estadounidense, y en 1948 el nombre y la categoría oficial de Puerto Rico se convierten en «el Estado Libre Asociado de Puerto Rico».
- Los puertorriqueños son ciudadanos[6] estadounidenses, su moneda es el dólar y tienen las mismas leyes federales que el resto de los EE.UU.
- Tienen dos himnos nacionales, dos banderas[7] y fiestas nacionales estadounidenses y puertorriqueñas; pero el idioma oficial es el español.
- El 1 de mayo de 2003, Puerto Rico celebró el fin de las operaciones navales estadounidenses en la isla Vieques. Después de 60 años, los puertorriqueños van a poder disfrutar[8] de nuevo de las bellezas naturales de la isla. Los. EE.UU. está coordinando su restauración.

La fortaleza El Morro en San Juan, Puerto Rico, fue construida para defender a San Juan de los piratas, de los ingleses y de los franceses. ¿Quiénes la construyeron?

[6]*citizens*
[7]*flags* [8]*enjoy*
[9]*encourage*

¿Qué descubrimos?

To which country of the Greater Antilles does each of the following statements pertain: **Cuba**, **Puerto Rico**, or **la República Dominicana**?

1. Comparte «La Española» con otra nación.
2. Está relacionado políticamente con los EE.UU.
3. Es la isla más grande de las Antillas.
4. Su gobierno no es democrático.
5. La primera catedral del Nuevo Mundo está situada en su ciudad capital.
6. Tiene dos banderas y dos himnos nacionales.

La belleza de sus playas y la rica herencia colonial de Puerto Rico, principalmente en ciudades como San Juan y Ponce, fomentan[9] el turismo en la isla. Esta foto muestra la zona colonial de San Juan. ¿De qué color son los edificios? ¿Qué países representan las dos banderas que se ven a la distancia?

Coquí

El coquí es una rana (*frog*) muy famosa en Puerto Rico. Su nombre viene del sonido (*sound*) que hace, y es un símbolo importante de la lucha (*struggle*) para proteger el medio ambiente (*environment*).

2 Adivinanzas

Write an identification for each of the following references. Then call out your definitions to another pair of students, who will identify the person, place, etc. Take turns.

«La Española»	los taínos	Juan Ponce de León
El Morro	Fidel Castro	el general Rafael Trujillo
Santo Domingo	Cristóbal Colón	el coquí

Artes literarias

Nicolás Guillén

Nicolás Guillén (1902-1989), poeta cubano, es conocido por su poesía afrocubana. Su estilo es rítmico, con temas derivados de la mitología del pueblo afroantillano. La poesía de Guillén adopta un nuevo estilo literario que revela la magnitud de la contribución africana a la cultura cubana y latinoamericana.

*Sensemayá: a goddess represented by a snake in some Afrocuban religions.

**The Mayombé: an African (Yoruba) religious sect.

[1]Canto... *Incantation to kill a snake* [2]ojos... *eyes of glass* [3]se... *entwines itself* [4]*tree* [5]*Tú... Hit it with an ax* [6]se... *it dies* [7]*Hit it!* [8]No... *Don't kick it* [9]te... *it will bite you* [10]*to whistle* [11]*look, see* [12]*to bite* [13]no... *it doesn't move* [14]se... *died*

Sensemayá* (Canto para matar una culebra[1])
de Nicolás Guillén

¡Mayombe-bombe-mayombé!**
¡Mayombe-bombe-mayombé!
¡Mayombe-bombe-mayombé!
La culebra tiene los ojos de vidrio[2];
la culebra viene y se enreda[3] en un palo[4];
con sus ojos de vidrio, en un palo;
con sus ojos de vidrio.

[...]

¡Mayombe-bombe-mayombé!
Tú le das con el hacha[5] y se muere[6].
¡Dale[7] ya!
¡No le des con el pie[8], que te muerde[9];
no le des con el pie, que se va!

[...]

La culebra muerta no puede comer;
la culebra muerta no puede silbar[10];
no puede caminar,
no puede correr.
La culebra muerta no puede mirar[11];
la culebra muerta no puede beber;
no puede respirar,
no puede morder[12].
¡Mayombe-bombe-mayombé!
Sensemayá, la culebra...
¡Mayombe-bombe-mayombé!
Sensemayá, no se mueve[13]...
¡Mayombe-bombe-mayombé!
Sensemayá, la culebra...
¡Mayombe-bombe-mayombé!
¡Sensemayá, se murió[14]!

Preguntas

1. ¿Qué características interesantes tiene la culebra?

2. ¿Qué hace la culebra?

3. ¿Cómo es posible matar la culebra?

4. ¿Qué peligro (*danger*) representa la culebra para los humanos?

5. ¿Qué no puede hacer la culebra muerta?

6. En su opinión, ¿es el canto una de las causas de la muerte de la culebra?

READING STRATEGY

Using Title and Format to Understand Content

1. Pay attention to the poem's title: It will give you a clue about how it is meant to be read.

2. First, skim the poem, paying attention to the repetition of both verses and words.

3. On your second reading, focus on:
- the rhythm created by the stress on certain syllables and
- the description of the snake.

4. Read the lines straight through and, while reading, tap out the rhythm as if you were playing bongo drums.

Adjetivos

amarillo/a
anaranjado/a
azul
beige
blanco/a
gris
marrón
morado/a
negro/a
rojo/a
rosado/a
verde

Adverbios y expresiones adverbiales

(casi) siempre
a veces
nunca

la semana que viene
la próxima semana
el mes/ año/ verano que viene
el próximo mes/ año/ verano

Las estaciones

el invierno
el otoño
la primavera
el verano

El clima

¿Qué tiempo hace?/
  ¿Cómo está el clima?/
  ¿Qué tal el clima?
Hace buen/mal tiempo.
Hace (mucho) frío.
Hace (mucho) calor.
Hace fresco.
Hace sol.
Hace viento.
Llueve./ Está lloviendo.
  la lluvia

Nieva./ Está nevando.
  la nieve
Está (muy) nublado.
  las nubes

Sustantivos

Los deportes

el baloncesto/
  el básquetbol
el béisbol
el fútbol
el fútbol americano
el golf
el tenis
el vólibol
el ejercicio
el equipo
el partido
la pelota

En el parque

el árbol
la flor
la hoja
el lago

Verbos y expresiones verbales

bailar
caminar
cantar
conocer
correr
dar
  dar un paseo
deber + *infinitive*
decir (i)
descansar
esquiar
fumar
ganar
hacer
  hacer ejercicio
ir de compras

jugar (ue)
  jugar al + *sport*
limpiar
llover (ue)
manejar
nadar
nevar (ie)
oír
pensar (ie) + *infinitive*
perder (ie)
pintar
poner
practicar
saber
salir (de)
tocar
  tocar + *musical instrument*
traer
venir (ie)
ver
  ver la tele(visión)

levantar pesas
me encanta(n)
montar en bicicleta
tener calor
tener frío
tener ganas de + *infinitive*
tener que + *infinitive*
tomar el sol

I. *Saber* and *conocer*. Complete the dialog with the correct form of the appropriate verb.

MARTA: ¿_____ (tú) tocar la guitarra? Necesito encontrar un guitarrista para nuestra fiesta.

PABLO: No _____ tocar la guitarra, pero (yo) _____ a una persona que sabe tocarla muy bien.

MARTA: ¿_____ (tú) dónde vive?

PABLO: No _____. Pero podemos buscar su dirección (*address*) y número de teléfono en la guía telefónica y llamarlo/la. Podemos ir en mi coche a su casa. (Yo) _____ bien la ciudad y puedo acompañarte.

MARTA: ¡Gracias!

II. Additional *yo*-irregular verbs. What do perfect students do?

Modelo: tener interés en la clase (Juan, yo)
Juan tiene interés en la clase.
Yo tengo interés en la clase también.

1. venir a clase todos los días (tú, yo)
2. decir «hola» a los estudiantes al entrar en la clase (nosotros, yo)
3. traer la tarea a clase (ellas, yo)
4. poner la tarea en el escritorio del profesor (Ana, yo)
5. saber todo el vocabulario (nosotros, yo)
6. hacer preguntas en clase (ustedes, yo)
7. no salir de clase temprano (ella, yo)

III. *Ir* + *a* + infinitive. What is happening tomorrow?

Modelo: Lisa / estudiar
Lisa va a estudiar.

1. Marta / jugar al tenis
2. Luisa y Alberto / montar en bicicleta
3. (yo) / ver un partido de fútbol
4. (tú) / preparar la paella
5. nosotros / ir a la playa

IV. The present progressive. What is happening right now?

Modelo: Llueve.
Está lloviendo.

1. Nieva.
2. El niño duerme.
3. Leo una novela.
4. Vemos la tele.
5. Mis hermanos preparan la cena.

V. *Ser* and *estar*. Use the correct form of **ser** or **estar**.

Luisa Pereira _____ mexicana. _____ de la Ciudad de México pero ahora _____ en Guadalajara. _____ abogada y _____ una mujer inteligente y dinámica. Hoy _____ preocupada porque tiene un caso importante en la corte municipal.

VI. General review. Answer with complete sentences.

1. ¿Qué está haciendo usted en este momento?
2. ¿Qué va a hacer usted esta noche?
3. ¿Qué hace usted los fines de semana?
4. ¿Qué tiene que hacer usted mañana?
5. ¿Qué tiene ganas de hacer ahora?
6. ¿A quién conoce usted muy bien en la clase de español?
7. ¿Qué trae usted a la clase?
8. ¿Cuál es su estación favorita? ¿Por qué?
9. ¿Qué tiempo hace hoy?

Answers to the *Autoprueba y repaso* are found in **Apéndice 2**.

Capítulo 5

La rutina diaria

Goals for communication

- To talk about daily routines
- To talk about how actions take place
- To talk about actions in the past
- To talk about job-related issues

Así se dice

La rutina diaria

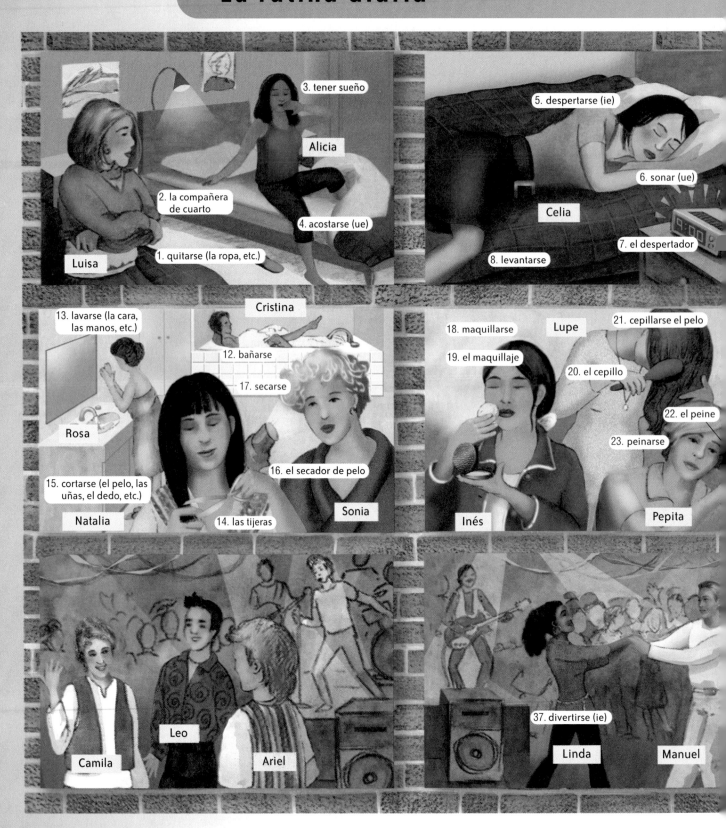

3. tener sueño

Alicia

2. la compañera de cuarto

4. acostarse (ue)

1. quitarse (la ropa, etc.)

Luisa

5. despertarse (ie)

6. soñar (ue)

Celia

7. el despertador

8. levantarse

13. lavarse (la cara, las manos, etc.)

Cristina

12. bañarse

17. secarse

Rosa

15. cortarse (el pelo, las uñas, el dedo, etc.)

16. el secador de pelo

Natalia

14. las tijeras

Sonia

18. maquillarse

Lupe

21. cepillarse el pelo

19. el maquillaje

20. el cepillo

22. el peine

23. peinarse

Inés

Pepita

Camila

Leo

Ariel

37. divertirse (ie)

Linda

Manuel

1. to take off (one's clothes, etc.)
2. roommate (f.) **compañero de cuarto** (m.)
3. to be sleepy
4. to go to bed
5. to wake up
6. to ring, sound
7. alarm clock
8. to get up, arise
9. to go to sleep, fall asleep
10. to put on (shoes, clothes, etc.)
11. to get dressed
12. to take a bath, bathe
13. to wash one's (face, hands, etc.)
14. scissors
15. to cut one's (hair, nails, finger, etc.)
16. hairdryer
17. to dry (oneself)
18. to put on makeup
19. makeup
20. brush
21. to brush one's hair
22. comb
23. to comb one's hair
24. deodorant
25. soap
26. toilet paper
27. to take a shower
28. shampoo
29. shaving cream
30. razor
31. electric shaver
32. to shave (oneself)
33. to brush one's teeth
34. toothbrush
35. toothpaste
36. towel
37. to have a good time

Práctica y comunicación

5-1. **En la residencia estudiantil.** It is 9:00 P.M. Indicate what the people in the dorm (pages 168–169) are doing by answering the following questions.

1. Luisa, la chica del suéter verde, tiene sueño y quiere dormir. ¿Se quita[1] o se pone el suéter? **Se...** Su compañera de cuarto, Alicia, también tiene sueño. ¿Va a acostarse o va a levantarse? **Va a...**

2. En el otro cuarto, Celia toma una siesta. ¿Suena el teléfono o suena el despertador? ¿Debe despertarse o debe dormirse? **Debe...** ¿Debe levantarse o debe acostarse?

3. ¡Qué sorpresa! Esta noche Esteban no sale con sus amigos. ¿Para qué clase está estudiando? Su compañero de cuarto, Pepe, ¿va a ver la tele, a estudiar o a dormirse?

4. En el otro cuarto, los chicos van a salir. ¿Alex se pone o se quita los zapatos? ¿Tomás se quita la ropa o se viste?

5. Cristina está en la bañera (*bathtub*). ¿Qué hace? **Se...** ¿Rosa se lava la cara o se lava las manos? ¿Qué usa Natalia para cortarse el pelo? ¿Qué usa Sonia para secarse el pelo?

6. Inés se maquilla. ¿Piensa usted que ella va a estudiar o va a salir esta noche? ¿Qué usa Lupe para cepillarse el pelo? ¿Qué usa Pepita para peinarse?

7. ¿Qué se pone Alfonso? ¿Qué se ve cerca de (*near*) Alfonso? **Se ve... y...** ¿Pedro se ducha o se baña? ¿Qué usa para lavarse el pelo?

8. ¿Qué usa Octavio para afeitarse? ¿Y Felipe? José va a cepillarse los dientes. ¿Qué le pone al cepillo de dientes?

9. Los estudiantes que están en la fiesta, ¿la están pasando mal o se divierten? ¿Qué está haciendo Camila? ¿Y Linda y Manuel?

10. Carmen visita la residencia estudiantil esta noche. ¿Quién más está allí? ¿Qué están haciendo?

11. ¿Qué está haciendo Rubén? ¿A quiénes les gusta la música?

---

[1] Most verbs presented thus far in this chapter use the third-person pronoun **se**. You will study these verbs in the first *Estructura* of this chapter; for now, just follow the verb forms in the questions.

5-2. **Nuestras actividades diarias.** With which activities in the drawings on pages 168–169 do you associate the following items?

> **Modelo:** el despertador
> despertarse, levantarse, sonar

1. la ropa
2. el champú
3. el pelo
4. las tijeras
5. el peine
6. la pasta de dientes
7. el maquillaje
8. el jabón
9. el desodorante
10. la navaja
11. la toalla
12. el cepillo

Protege tu boca aún cuando no te estás cepillando.

¡La nueva COLGATE TOTAL, con su avanzada fórmula de acción prolongada sigue trabajando después de cepillarte y te ayuda a proteger tu boca contra las caries, el sarro, la placa, la gingivitis y el mal aliento, hasta por doce horas! Colgate Total es una pasta tan avanzada que sigue trabajando entre cepilladas mientras te diviertes, mientras trabajas y hasta cuando duermes. ¡Hora tras hora tras hora!

Visite nuestro website http://www.colgate.com

La cepillada tan avanzada que trabaja entre cepilladas.

¿Contra qué protege Colgate? ¿Cuándo sigue (*does it continue*) trabajando? ¿Qué marca (*brand*) de pasta de dientes usa usted?

5-3. La rutina diaria.
Place the following activities in chronological order according to your personal daily routine. Number them 1–15. Then compare your list with that of a classmate.

___ acostarse

___ afeitarse

___ bañarse/ducharse

___ cenar

___ cepillarse los dientes

___ desayunar

___ despertarse

___ dormirse

___ estudiar/ver la tele

___ ir a clase

___ levantarse

___ peinarse

___ quitarse la ropa

___ secarse

___ vestirse/ponerse la ropa

Escenas
La guerra del baño

Javier   Clara

Javier está esperando para bañarse. Como casi todas las mañanas, su hermana Clara tarda mucho en salir del baño.

JAVIER: (*¡Pum!, ¡pum!, ¡pum!, dando con la mano en la puerta.*) ¿Qué estás haciendo, Clara? Necesito usar el baño. (*Silencio.*) ¿No me oyes? *Shouting* (*Gritando°.*) ¿Puedes salir del baño y escucharme, por favor?

CLARA: ¿Qué pasa? ¿Quieres ducharte?

JAVIER: No. Quiero peinarme.

mirror CLARA: ¡Peinarte! ¿No tienes espejo° en tu cuarto?

the right JAVIER: Sí, pero también vivo en esta casa y tengo derecho° a usar el baño.

CLARA: Voy a salir en un minuto. Solamente tengo que secarme el pelo, cepillarme los dientes, peinarme, maquillarme, ponerme la ropa...

Enough! JAVIER: Basta!° ¡Ya no puedo esperar más! Tengo que salir ahora para no llegar tarde a la universidad.

CLARA: Lo siento. Vas a tener que levantarte más temprano si quieres entrar al baño antes que yo.

¿Qué pasa?
1. ¿Por qué está enojado Javier?
2. ¿Qué necesita hacer Javier en el baño?
3. ¿Qué más tiene que hacer Clara?
4. ¿Puede Javier esperar? ¿Por qué?
5. ¿Qué tiene que hacer Javier para entrar al baño antes que Clara?

Estructuras

1 Talking about daily routines: Reflexive verbs

Some verbs use reflexive pronouns (**me, te, se, nos, os, se**) to show that the person is doing the action to her/himself. This *pronoun + verb* combination often describes daily routine or personal care. Study the following pairs of sentences and the change in meaning created by the addition of the reflexive pronoun.

Pero mamá, no quiero bañarme. Quiero jugar.

Carlos **baña** a su hermanito.	*Carlos bathes his little brother.* (nonreflexive)
Carlos **se baña**.	*Carlos bathes himself.* (reflexive)
Vamos a **vestir** a los niños.	*We're going to dress the children.* (nonreflexive)
Vamos a **vestirnos**.	*We're going to get dressed.* (reflexive)

Formation of reflexive verbs

In a reflexive construction (the combination of reflexive pronoun and verb), the reflexive pronoun and the subject of the verb refer to the same person.

(yo)	**me** visto	(nosotros/as)	**nos** vestimos
(tú)	**te** vistes	(vosotros/as)	**os** vestís
(Ud., él, ella)	**se** viste	(Uds., ellos, ellas)	**se** visten

- The reflexive pronoun is placed *immediately before a single conjugated verb.*

Me despierto a las seis.	*I wake up at six.*
No **nos** acostamos tarde.	*We don't go to bed late.*

- With verbs followed by an infinitive or a present participle (-**ando**/-**iendo**), the reflexive pronoun may be placed either *before the conjugated verb* or *attached to the infinitive* or *present participle.*

Me tengo que levantar temprano.	*I have to get up early.*
Tengo que **levantarme** temprano.	
Linda **se** está divirtiendo[2].	*Linda is having a good time.*
Linda está **divirtiéndose**.	

- With reflexive verbs, use the definite article, not a possessive adjective, to refer to parts of the body or articles of clothing.

Voy a cepillarme **los** dientes.	*I am going to brush **my** teeth.*
¿Vas a ponerte **el** suéter?	*Are you going to put on **your** sweater?*

---

[2] Some reflexive verbs have a stem-change in the present participle (e→i: v**e**stirse→v**i**stiéndose; div**e**rtirse→div**i**rtiéndose; o→u: d**o**rmirse→d**u**rmiéndose).

Práctica y comunicación

② **5-4.** **Nuestra rutina.** Complete the statements to indicate your daily routine. Make note of things you have in common.

> **Modelo:** Me levanto...
>
> Estudiante 1: **Me levanto a las siete de la mañana.**
>
> Estudiante 2: **Yo también me levanto a las siete.** *o* **Me levanto a las ocho y media.**

1. Me levanto...

2. Me ducho/baño... (¿Por la mañana/noche?)

3. Me lavo el pelo...

4. Me afeito...

5. Me cepillo los dientes... (¿Cuántas veces al día?)

6. Desayuno...

7. Salgo de la residencia/mi casa...

8. Vuelvo a la residencia/mi casa...

9. Me acuesto...

Now share with the class something you and your partner have in common.
Tina y yo (nos)...

5-5. **La rutina de Camila.** Talk about Camila's morning routine by describing what she's doing in each drawing.

> **Modelo:** **Camila se despierta a las ocho de la mañana.**

1.

2.

3.

4.

5.

5 **5-6.** **Todas las mañanas.** Student 1 starts the chain by saying *and acting out* one thing he/she does every morning; Student 2 repeats that and adds one more activity; Student 3 repeats the first two and adds one more, etc. Don't break the chain!

> **Modelo:** Estudiante 1: (*yawning*) **Me despierto a las 7:00.**
>
> Estudiante 2: (*yawning*) **Me despierto a las 7:00 y** (*pretending to shower*) **me ducho.**
>
> Estudiante 3: **Me despierto a las 7:00, me ducho y me lavo el pelo.**

5-7. **Actrices y actores.** In front of the class, each of eight students acts out one of the following activities. The class says what each student *is doing*. Then determine the chronological order of the activities.

> **Modelo:** bañarse
>
> **Tina está bañándose.** *o* **Tina se está bañando.**

1. bañarse
2. vestirse
3. despertarse
4. peinarse
5. afeitarse
6. cepillarse los dientes
7. secarse
8. lavarse el pelo

2 **5-8.** **Consejos (*Advice*).** One of you indicates a problem that you have; the other gives advice about what you should do. Take turns.

> **Modelo:** Estudiante 1: **Tengo sueño.**
>
> Estudiante 2: **Debes acostarte/tomar una siesta...**

1. Tengo el pelo muy desordenado (*messy*). **Debes...**
2. ¡Ay! Comí ensalada y ahora tengo lechuga entre los dientes.
3. Sudo (*I sweat*) mucho cuando hago ejercicio.
4. Tengo que salir en treinta minutos.
5. No puedo levantarme por la mañana.
6. ¡Son las dos de la mañana! Estoy muy cansado/a.

② 5-9. **Preguntas personales.** Take turns asking and answering the following questions.

1. ¿Tienes sueño ahora? ¿A qué hora te acuestas normalmente?
2. ¿A qué hora te levantas los días de clase?
3. ¿Cuántas veces al día te cepillas los dientes? ¿Qué marca de pasta de dientes prefieres? ¿Y de jabón o papel higiénico?
4. ¿Prefieres bañarte por la mañana o por la noche? ¿Prefieres bañarte o ducharte?
5. ¿Te lavas el pelo todos los días? ¿Qué marca de champú prefieres?
6. ¿Prefieres secarte el pelo con toalla o con secador de pelo?
7. ¿Prefieres afeitarte con navaja o con máquina de afeitar?
8. ¿Dónde te cortas el pelo? ¿Cuánto cuesta?
9. ¿Te diviertes mucho los fines de semana? (¿Cómo?)

Así se dice

¿Qué acabas de hacer? *(What have you just done?)*

acabar de + *infinitive*   *to have just (completed an action)*
Acabo de vestirme.   *I have just gotten dressed.*

② 5-10. **¡Estamos listos (*We're ready*)!** You and your friends are now looking your best and ready to go out. Say what each one of you *has just done* to get ready. Jot down your answers. You may be asked to share some of them with the class.

> **Modelo:** (yo)...
> **Acabo de cortarme el pelo y comprarme zapatos nuevos.**

1. (yo)...
2. mi amiga Elena y yo...
3. Alberto...
4. Dulce...
5. Aurora y Susana...
6. Octavio y Manuel...
7. (tú)...
8. (nosotros)...

2 Describing how actions take place: Adverbs

Tengo que estudiar constantemente si quiero mejorar mis notas.

An adverb tells *how, how much, how often, when, why,* or *where* an action takes place. Some adverbs you already know are: **ahora, hoy, mañana, tarde, bien, mal, muy, a veces, nunca,** and **siempre.**

| *How?* | Estoy **muy bien**, gracias. |
| *When?* | **A veces** desayuno en la cafetería. |

- Most adverbs are formed by adding **-mente** (equivalent to the English *-ly*) to an adjective. Add **-mente** to adjectives ending in **-e** or a consonant.

| posible | ➔ | **posiblemente** |
| personal | ➔ | **personalmente** |

- Add **-mente** to the feminine singular form of adjectives ending in **-o/-a.**

| rápido | ➔ | rápida | ➔ | **rápidamente** |
| tranquilo | ➔ | tranquila | ➔ | **tranquilamente** |

- Adjectives with written accents maintain the accent in the adverbial form.

| rápido | ➔ | **rápidamente** | fácil | ➔ | **fácilmente** |

Some common adverbs

constantemente	*constantly*	normalmente	*normally*
desafortunadamente	*unfortunately*	personalmente	*personally*
fácilmente	*easily*	posiblemente	*possibly*
frecuentemente	*frequently*	probablemente	*probably*
generalmente	*generally*	rápidamente	*rapidly*
inmediatamente	*immediately*	recientemente	*recently*
lentamente	*slowly*	tranquilamente	*peacefully*

Práctica y comunicación

5-11. **¿Cómo o cuándo?** Complete the sentences with appropriate activities. Be prepared to report back to the class.

> **Modelo:** Cuando vuelvo a casa,... inmediatamente.
>
> Cuando vuelvo a casa, **llamo a mis amigos** inmediatamente.

1. Cuando me levanto tarde, tengo que... rápidamente.
2. Cuando veo a mi pareja, lo/la... apasionadamente.
3. Cuando estoy muy cansado/a,... lentamente.
4. Cuando estoy con mis amigos/as,... constantemente.
5. Nosotros frecuentemente...
6. Esta noche, probablemente vamos a...
7. Antes de (*Before*) acostarme, generalmente...

5-12. **Lo que hacen normalmente.** Select persons from the following list and indicate what activities they do. Also choose appropriate adjectives and change them to adverbs to indicate how, when, how often, etc., they do these activities. Be prepared to report back to the class.

> **Modelo:** los profesores
>
> **Los profesores generalmente dan clases, hablan con los estudiantes, van a conferencias...**

Personas	Adjetivos
los profesores	constante
mi profe de español	desafortunado
mi madre/padre	fácil
mis padres	frecuente
mi hermano/a	general
mis hermanos/as	normal
mi compañero/a de cuarto	posible
mi mejor amigo/a	probable
mis amigos/as	rápido
mi novio/a	reciente
mi esposo/a	tranquilo

Así se dice

El trabajo

Read the following paragraph and accompanying art captions (in pairs) and familiarize yourselves with the new expressions.

El trabajo es otra de las rutinas en nuestra vida. A veces tenemos un **trabajo de tiempo completo**[1] y otras es **de tiempo parcial**[2]. A veces **ganamos**[3] mucho **dinero**[4] y otras veces poco. Algunos prefieren **trabajar para**[5] una **compañía**[6] grande y otros para **empresas**[7] pequeñas. Hay personas que trabajan en una oficina, otras en una escuela o universidad, en una **tienda**[8] o en las calles° de una ciudad como los policías. Otros son **empleados**[9] de una **fábrica**[10], de un restaurante o de un supermercado. ¿Qué tipo de trabajo prefiere usted?

streets

HINT | Review the professions in **Chapter 2**, p. 83.

Carmen es **secretaria**[11] y **recepcionista**[12]. ¿Para qué compañía trabaja?

Linda es **dependienta**[13] en una tienda de ropa. ¿Qué vende?

Alfonso es **mesero**[14] en un restaurante y Natalia es **cajera**[15]. ¿Qué tipo de restaurante es?

Esteban es **repartidor**[16] de pizzas. Reparte muchas pizzas a los estudiantes de la universidad. ¿Cómo se llama la pizzería?

(1) full-time job (2) part-time (3) we earn; **ganar** *to earn (money), to win (4) money (5) to work for (6) company (7) businesses, companies (8) store;* **tienda de ropa** *clothing store (9) employees (10) factory (11) secretary (f.);* **secretario** *(m.) (12) receptionist (m./f.* **el/la** *(13) salesclerk (f.);* **dependiente** *(m.) (14) waiter (m.);* **mesera** *waitress (15) cashier (f.);* **cajero** *(m.) (16) delivery person (m.);* **repartidora** *(f.)*

Práctica y comunicación

HINT | For additional professions see
Apéndice 3, pp. A–14.

5-13. Empleo, presente y futuro.
Walking about the classroom, question three or four of your classmates about their current job status and future job/professional aspirations. Take notes: you may be asked to report back to the class.

1. ¿Trabajas? ¿Es un trabajo de tiempo completo o de tiempo parcial? ¿Qué tipo de trabajo tienes?
2. Este (*This*) verano, ¿vas a buscar empleo? ¿Qué tipo de trabajo?
3. Después de graduarte, ¿qué tipo de trabajo vas a buscar? *o* ¿Qué quieres ser?
4. ¿Qué es más importante para ti (*for you*), ganar mucho dinero o tener el trabajo ideal?

Expresión útil

¿Cuánto paga por mes/año?
How much does it pay per month/year?

⑤ 5-14. Buscamos trabajo.
Role play: One of you works for an employment agency; the other four seek employment.

Modelo: Empleado/a: ¿Qué tipo de trabajo busca usted?

Estudiante: **Quiero trabajar para.../ ser empleado de.../ Quiero ser...**

5-15. La vida profesional.
Choose one profession and write five sentences about a day in the life of a person in that profession.

Modelo: (*Nombre de persona*) **es... Cada mañana se levanta a las...**

② ¡Qué dilema!
*Llamas a tu jefa (boss, f.) y le dices que no puedes trabajar hoy porque estás **muy** enfermo/a. Tres horas más tarde estás almorzando en un restaurante con un amigo. Tu jefa entra, se acerca a (she approaches) la mesa y te dice: **Buenas tardes,...***

3 Talking about actions in the past: The preterit of regular verbs and *ser* and *ir*

The preterit tense is used to talk about completed past actions with a specific beginning, an end, or both.

Me **levanté** a las ocho y **desayuné**.	*I **got up** at eight and **had breakfast.***
Trabajé en la biblioteca por dos horas.	*I **worked** in the library for two hours.*
—¿Cuándo **volviste**?	*When **did you return**?*
—**Volví** a la una.	*I **returned** at one.*
Comencé a estudiar a las tres.	*I **began** to study at three.*
Terminé a las seis.	*I **finished** at six.*

Regular verbs

	estudiar *to study*	volver *to return*	salir *to leave*
(yo)	estudi**é**	volv**í**	sal**í**
(tú)	estudi**aste**	volv**iste**	sal**iste**
(Ud., él, ella)	estudi**ó**	volv**ió**	sal**ió**
(nosotros/as)	estudi**amos**[3]	volv**imos**	sal**imos**[3]
(vosotros/as)	estudi**asteis**	volv**isteis**	sal**isteis**
(Uds., ellos, ellas)	estudi**aron**	volv**ieron**	sal**ieron**

- Note that **-er/-ir** preterit verb endings are identical.
- In the preterit tense, **-ar** and **-er** verbs never change their stems. (See **volver** above.)

---

[3] The **nosotros** foms of **-ar** and **-ir** verbs in the preterit are the same as their respective present tense forms.

Verbs with spelling changes in the preterit

Verbs ending in **-gar**, **-car**, and **-zar** change spelling only in the **yo** form of the preterit.

-gar	g → gu	jugar	yo **jugué**, tú jugaste,…
		llegar	yo **llegué**, tú llegaste,…
-car	c → qu	tocar	yo **toqué**, tú tocaste,…
		buscar	yo **busqué**, tú buscaste,…
		sacar	yo **saqué**, tú sacaste,…
-zar	z → c	abrazar	yo **abracé**, tú abrazaste,…
		almorzar	yo **almorcé**, tú almorzaste,…

The verbs **leer** (*to read*) and **oír** (*to hear*) change the **i** of the third-person singular and plural endings to **y** (-ió → -yo; -ieron → -yeron).

leer	leí, leíste, **leyó**, leímos, leísteis, **leyeron**
oír	oí, oíste, **oyó**, oímos, oísteis, **oyeron**

The verbs *ser* and *ir*

Ser and **ir** have identical but irregular preterit endings; context clarifies which verb is used.

ser/ir	**fui, fuiste, fue, fuimos, fuisteis, fueron**

(ir)	**Fueron** a la playa ayer.	*They went to the beach yesterday.*
(ser)	**Fue** un día extraordinario.	*It was an extraordinary day.*

Así se dice
¿Qué pasó?

Read about Pepita's activities and learn the new expressions.

Anteayer[1] fue un desastre (así son algunos días de mi vida), pero **ayer**[2] fue un día bastante ordinario. **Primero**[3] me levanté temprano y corrí tres millas. **Luego**[4], me bañé. Desayuné a eso de las siete de la mañana, y **después**[5] asistí a mis clases. Llegué temprano a mi primera clase porque nunca me gusta llegar tarde. A las doce almorcé y **entonces**[6] fui al Centro Estudiantil para encontrarme

(1) The day before yesterday (2) yesterday (3) First (4) Then, Later (5) afterwards (6) then

con mis amigos. Más tarde mandé unos mensajes por correo electrónico, oí las noticias en la radio, y regresé al restaurante de la U. para cenar. **Anoche**(7) estudié antes de acostarme. Ustedes **ya**(8) saben que soy una magnífica estudiante. Bueno, muy estudiosa al menos. ¿Quieren saber lo que me pasó **el fin de semana pasado**(9)? ¿Y **la semana pasada**(10)? Eso° es para otro episodio.

that

(7) *Last night* (8) *already* (9) *last weekend;* **el año/ mes/ verano pasado** *last year/month/ summer* (10) *last week*

Práctica y comunicación

② **5-16. El día de Pepita.** Based on the description of Pepita's activities, take turns telling each other what she did yesterday.

> **Modelo:** Primero, **se levantó** temprano.

② **5-17. Mi día «bastante ordinario».** Assume that yesterday was a class day. Tell your partner what you did, following the same format as in Pepita's account. Then switch roles.

5-18. El sábado pasado. Tell what Javier and his younger brother, Samuel, did last Saturday. Refer to the drawings.

> **Modelo:** Primero, Javier y Samuel comieron pizza.

comer…

1. tomar…

3. ir…

4. cenar…

5. volver…

2. jugar…

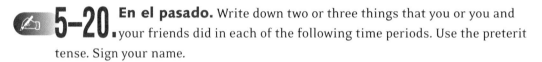

5-19. Preguntas personales. Take turns asking and answering the following questions. Note the number of any questions to which you both respond affirmatively.

1. ¿Te levantaste temprano esta mañana? ¿A qué hora te levantaste?
2. ¿Desayunaste en el restaurante universitario? (¿Qué comiste?)
3. ¿Viste la tele anoche? (¿Qué programas viste?)
4. ¿Te acostaste tarde? ¿A qué hora te acostaste?
5. ¿Fuiste a todas tus clases ayer?
6. ¿Hablaste con uno de tus profesores ayer o anteayer? (¿Con qué profe hablaste?)
7. ¿Fuiste al supermercado ayer o anteayer? (¿Qué compraste?)
8. ¿Visitaste a tu familia el fin de semana pasado? ¿Dónde vive tu familia?
9. ¿Cenaste en un restaurante el fin de semana pasado? (¿En qué restaurante?)
10. ¿Fuiste a la biblioteca la semana pasada?
11. ¿Saliste con tus amigos el sábado pasado? (¿Adónde fueron?)
12. ¿Viste una película (*movie*) o DVD? (¿Cuál?)

Now exchange information with another group, telling them what the two of you did: **Nosotros...**

5-20. En el pasado. Write down two or three things that you or you and your friends did in each of the following time periods. Use the preterit tense. Sign your name.

- El verano pasado...
- La semana pasada...
- El fin de semana pasado...
- Anoche...

Turn in your list to the instructor. She/He will give it to another student for correction. In pairs, tell each other what the person whose list you now have did during those time periods. Then share interesting information with the class.

5-21. Lo que pasó. Tell each other what the following person or persons did in the circumstances described.

1. Antes de acostarme anoche:
   Primero,... Entonces,... Y después,...
2. Después de levantarme esta mañana:
   Primero,... Entonces,... Y más tarde,...
3. Cuando mis padres fueron a... el verano pasado.
   Primero,... Luego,... También,...
4. Cuando mis amigos y yo fuimos a una fiesta el fin de semana pasado:
   Primero,... También,... Y luego,...
5. Cuando mi mejor amigo/a ganó (*won*) la lotería:
   Primero,... Luego,... También,...

Noticias culturales

Los días festivos

Los días festivos marcan un cambio en la rutina diaria hispana. Son de dos tipos: religiosos o cívicos. Las fiestas religiosas celebran las tradiciones de la religión católica, y las cívicas, los hechos° históricos. Cada país tiene sus propias° fiestas, pero hay muchas que todos los hispanos conmemoran.

*events, facts / * **sus...** *their own*

La fiesta religiosa hispana más popular es la Semana Santa. Muchos participan en procesiones por las calles, llevando imágenes de Cristo o de la Virgen María. Hay música y representaciones de escenas bíblicas. La celebración termina con bailes y fuegos artificiales°. Semana Santa en Sevilla, España.

fuegos... *fireworks*

Otras festividades religiosas honran al santo patrón de una ciudad o de un país. Durante la fiesta de San Fermín en Pamplona (España) ¡sueltan° toros por las calles°! Los habitantes de la ciudad y enorme cantidad de turistas se visten de blanco con pañuelos° y cinturones° rojos y corren detrás° o delante° de los toros. La fiesta atrae 1.5 millones de turistas cada año.

set free / streets neck scarves / sashes / behind / in front

parades

Las festividades cívicas son especialmente populares en Latinoamérica. El Día de la Independencia es una de las fechas más importantes. Generalmente, esta celebración consiste en grandes desfiles°. En algunas comunidades participan la armada nacional y los estudiantes de las escuelas. Numerosas banderas decoran las ciudades, y la gente se divierte hasta muy tarde en las ferias y bailes.

¿Qué recuerda? Indique la fiesta (Semana Santa, San Fermín, Día de la Independencia) que corresponde a cada descripción.

1. Los toros y la gente corren por las calles.

2. Hay desfiles con estudiantes y militares.

3. Las procesiones llevan figuras de Cristo.

4. Las ciudades están decoradas con banderas; hay ferias y bailes.

5. Se celebra al santo patrón de la ciudad.

6. Es la fiesta religiosa más popular de los países hispanos.

Conexiones y contrastes

1. ¿Cuáles son algunas festividades famosas en su país o en la región donde usted vive?

2. ¿Cómo se celebran?

4 **Referring to persons and things: Direct object pronouns**

Felipe, mi amiga Rosa quiere conocerte.

¿Rosa? La vi ayer en la cafetería.

La conozco. ¡Es muy simpática!

In **Chapter 4** you studied some direct object pronouns (**lo, la, los, las**). A direct object identifies the person or thing that directly receives the action of the verb and answers the question *Who/Whom?* or *What?* It can be a noun or a pronoun.

(*Who/Whom?*)	Vi[4] **a Laurie.**	*I saw **Laurie**.*
	La vi en el gimnasio.	*I saw **her** in the gym.*

Laurie is the direct object noun; *her* is the direct object pronoun.

(*What?*)	Laurie compró **el champú.**	*Laurie bought **the shampoo**.*
	Lo compró ayer.	*She bought **it** yesterday.*

Shampoo is the direct object noun; *it* is the direct object pronoun.

The following are direct object pronouns. Study their usage in the example sentences.

Pronombres de complemento directo		
me	*me*	Carlos no **me** llamó.
te	*you*	¿**Te** llamó a ti?
lo	*him, you (m.), it (m.)*	**Lo** conozco bien.
la	*her, you (f.), it (f.)*	Lola es su novia. ¿**La** conoces?
nos	*us*	Laurie **nos** visitó anoche.
os	*you*	¿**Os** visitó?
los	*them (m.), you (m.)*	¿Vas a preparar los tacos para la fiesta?
		Sí, voy a preparar**los.**
las	*them (f.), you (f.)*	¿Y las bebidas?
		También **las** voy a preparar.

---

[4] The words **vi** and **vio** do not have a written accent mark because a one-syllable Spanish word needs a stress mark only if there is another word like it with a different meaning. For example: **si** (*if*) / **sí** (*yes*); **el** (*the*) / **él** (*he*).

- Direct object pronouns must agree with the nouns they replace or refer to.

—¿Compraste **la pasta de dientes**?	*Did you buy **the toothpaste**?*
—Sí, **la** compré.	*Yes, I bought **it**.*
—¿Usaste **el nuevo jabón**?	*Did you use **the new soap**?*
—Sí, **lo** usé.	*Yes, I used **it**.*

- As with reflexive object pronouns, the direct object pronoun is normally placed immediately before a conjugated verb.

Lo compré.	*I bought **it**.*

- Direct object pronouns may, however, be attached to infinitives and present participles (**-ndo** form), or be placed before the conjugated verb.

Voy a invitar**la**. *o* **La** voy a invitar.	*I am going to invite **her**.*
Estoy llamándo**la**[5]. *o* **La** estoy llamando.	*I am calling **her**.*

Práctica y comunicación

② **5-22.** **Los preparativos para una fiesta.** Your friend asks you many questions about plans for a party. Answer **si** or **no** as indicated, using the appropriate direct object pronoun. Then switch roles.

Estudiante 1	**Estudiante 2**
—¿Conoces *a Ana?*	—Sí, la...
—¿Sabes *su número de teléfono?*	—Sí,...
—¿La llamaste?	—Sí,...
—¿La invitaste a la fiesta?	—Sí,...
—¿Ya compraste *la comida y las bebidas* para la fiesta?	—No, no..., pero voy a...
—¿Vas a preparar *el pastel?*	—Sí, estoy... ahora mismo.
—¿Vas a limpiar *el apartamento* antes de la fiesta?	—No, no... ¡Pienso que tú debes...!
—¿Por qué?	—¡Porque haces demasiadas preguntas!

---

[5] When a pronoun is attached to the present participle (**-ndo** form), a written accent mark is added to preserve the original stress pattern of the participle.

2 **5-23.** **¿Quién tiene mis tijeras?** Students tend to freely borrow each other's things. Imagine that you live in the dorm on pages 168–169, and ask who has each of your "missing" items. A friend (your partner) identifies *who has each item* and *for what it is being used*. Take turns being the friend.

> **Modelo:** tijeras
> Estudiante 1: **¿Quién tiene mis tijeras?**
> Estudiante 2: **Natalia las tiene. Está usándolas para cortarse el pelo.**

1. secador de pelo
2. peine
3. cepillo
4. maquillaje
5. champú

6. máquina de afeitar
7. pasta de dientes
8. despertador
9. desodorante
10. guitarra

3 **5-24.** **Cosas (*Things*) para vender.** Has anyone ever tried to sell you a used item? Take turns trying to sell each other the following things. You determine the price. Keep track of the money you make.

> **Modelo:** un refrigerador pequeño (en buenas condiciones)
> Estudiante 1: **Tengo un refrigerador pequeño para vender. Está en buenas condiciones.**
> Estudiante 2: **¿Cuánto cuesta?**
> Estudiante 1: **Cuesta $25.00. ¿Quieres comprar*lo*?**
> Estudiante 2: **Sí, *lo* compro.** *o* **No gracias. Ya tengo uno.**

1. una máquina de afeitar (casi nueva)
2. un radio-despertador (un poco usado)
3. un teléfono celular (casi nuevo)
4. un libro de psicología (casi nuevo)
5. una impresora a color (casi nueva)
6. un sofá (muy usado)
7. un televisor muy grande (casi nuevo)
8. una computadora IBM (usada por tres años)
9. unos discos compactos de música clásica (en buenas condiciones)

Now add up your earnings. What student earned the most money? **Gané...**

5-25. **La telenovela «Un día de la vida».** You are auditioning for the roles of Aurora and Anselmo, famous characters from the soap opera «Un día de la vida». First, complete the dialog filling in the blanks with the direct object pronouns **me, te,** or **lo.** Then read it dramatically. You really want the parts!

ANSELMO: Mi amor, estás muy triste. ¿Qué pasa?... _____ amas, ¿verdad?

AURORA: _____ amo con todo mi corazón, pero tengo que ser muy franca. También adoro a Rafael, y sé que él _____ adora a mí.

ANSELMO: Pero yo también _____ adoro. Eres el amor de mi vida. _____ necesitas, ¿verdad?

AURORA: Claro que _____ necesito, pero no puedo imaginar mi vida sin Rafael. También _____ necesito a él. _____ extraño° mucho.

miss

ANSELMO: Mi cielo, tú sabes muy bien que no va a volver, y tú sabes que yo estoy aquí y que _____ quiero.

sobs

AURORA: (*Ella solloza°.*) Pero él es único. Yo no _____ quiero a ti como _____ quiero a él.

admit

ANSELMO: (*También solloza.*) Tengo que reconocer° que también _____ quiero. Yo también _____ extraño.

AURORA: Nunca vamos a encontrar otro perro como él.

Así se pronuncia

The pronunciation of *r* and *rr*

r If not used at the beginning of a word, the single **r** approximates the sound of *tt* as in *Betty likes butter better* or *dd* as in *Eddy.*

desodo**r**ante queda**r**se tije**r**as

rr The double **r** has a trilled sound as in mimicking a motorcycle; initial single **r** has the same sound.

ce**rr**ar **r**ápidamente **r**estaurante

Read the following verse:

Erre con erre cigarro,
Erre con erre barril.
Rápido corren los carros,
Carros del ferrocarril°.

railroad

Dicho y hecho

⊡⊟ Conversando

2   **Mi rutina ideal.** Assume that your life is a bit boring. Share ideas on what you consider to be the ideal routine for a perfect day, from the time you get up until you go to bed.

- Me levanto a las...
- Luego,...

🎧 ¡A escuchar!

¿La hora del examen ya pasó? Esteban's phone has been ringing for a long time. Finally he answers. It is his friend Manuel calling. Listen to the conversation; then answer the first three questions.

1. ¿Qué está haciendo Esteban cuando   ❒ Está   ❒ Está
     el teléfono suena?   estudiando.   durmiendo.

2. ¿Se canceló el examen de sociología?   ❒ sí   ❒ no

3. ¿Estudió Esteban mucho para el examen?   ❒ sí   ❒ no

Now listen to the conversation again; then answer the following questions.

4. ¿A qué hora se acostó Esteban? **A las...**

5. ¿A qué hora llamó Manuel?

6. ¿Cómo fue el examen?

✍ De mi escritorio

Un día muy interesante en mi vida. Write a description of an interesting day in your life that occurred some time *in the past*. Write about yourself or pretend that you are another university student, a university professor, or a housewife/mother who also happens to be a businesswoman.

Your instructor will ask several students to read their compositions aloud, and the class will decide who had the most interesting day.

Panorama cultural

España contemporánea: Herencia° y modernidad

¿Coincidencia?

Miguel de Cervantes (autor de *Don Quijote*) y William Shakespeare, los escritores más importantes de España e Inglaterra, murieron exactamente el mismo día: el 23 de abril de 1616.

Person@je del momento

Para saber más de Pedro Almodóvar, busque información en el Internet. Luego, compártala con sus compañeros/as de clase.

Preguntas sobre el mapa

1. ¿Cuál es la capital de España?
2. ¿Cuáles son dos ciudades importantes en la costa este?
3. ¿Cuáles son tres ciudades importantes en el sur de España (no en la costa)?
4. ¿Cómo se llaman las montañas que están entre España y Francia?
5. ¿Cómo se llaman las islas que están en el mar Mediterráneo?
6. ¿Qué otro país forma parte de la península ibérica?
7. ¿Cómo se llama el estrecho que separa España de Marruecos?

¿Sabía usted que...?

- Los idiomas oficiales de España son: el castellano (variedad del español, hablado en el centro de la península ibérica), el catalán, el gallego y el vascuence.
- Las playas, montañas y los numerosos lugares históricos hacen de España uno de los destinos turísticos más populares de Europa.
- Las aceitunas, el aceite de oliva y las naranjas de Valencia son famosos en todo el mundo.

[1]*grouping*
[2]*among*
[3]*currency*
[4]*ceramic tiles*

Herencia y modernidad

En España podemos visitar el pasado y al mismo tiempo vivir las innovaciones del presente.

España es parte de la Unión Europea, un conjunto[1] de organizaciones creadas entre[2] la mayoría de los países de la Europa Occidental. La unión tiene el fin de articular cooperación económica, política y social entre los países participantes. Según el mapa, ¿cuáles son?

En el año 2002 entró en circulación en España el euro, sustituyendo la moneda[3] nacional, la peseta.

Por toda España se refleja la herencia de varias culturas y civilizaciones, una de las cuales es la herencia árabe (711–1492). La Alhambra, gran palacio y fortaleza situada en Granada, es exquisito ejemplo de la belleza arquitectónica de esta cultura. Una de las múltiples atracciones de su decoración interior es el uso de diseños geométricos y también azulejos[4] de colores vivos. ¿Qué contraste ve usted entre el interior y el exterior de la Alhambra? Vea las fotos.

La influencia del arquitecto Antonio Gaudí y de los artistas Pablo Picasso, Joan Miró y Salvador Dalí son evidentes en la vida diaria de los españoles. La pintura, la arquitectura y el diseño contemporáneos reflejan sus contribuciones. En este cuadro, *Still Life* de Salvador Dalí, ¿qué cosas puede usted identificar? ¿Le gusta a usted el arte contemporáneo?

En la España contemporánea se crea una vigorosa cultura que combina la herencia de un pasado brillante con las nuevas posibilidades del futuro. La arquitectura futurista del Museo Guggenheim en Bilbao, refleja la vitalidad de la vida cultural de España. ¿Le gusta este tipo de arquitectura o prefiere la tradicional?

Las películas[5] de Pedro Almodóvar, ganador de un *Oscar*, y otros directores españoles de fama mundial continúan atrayendo al público. Considere esta escena de la película *Hable con ella* de Almodóvar. ¿Qué hace la pareja?

Las varias regiones de España constituyen diferentes zonas culturales con sus propios bailes, comidas, vestidos[6] típicos y formas de hablar. El baile flamenco es típico de Andalucía, región en el sur de España. ¿Hay bailes típicos en la región donde usted vive?

Un superescritor

Lope de Vega, un escritor español del siglo XVII, escribió más de 1.500 obras de teatro.

¿Qué descubrimos?

1. ¿Cuáles son algunos ejemplos de la variedad lingüística de España?
2. ¿Qué productos de España son famosos en todo el mundo?
3. ¿Qué moneda usa España hoy?
4. ¿Cuál es un ejemplo exquisito de la herencia árabe de España?
5. ¿Cuál es un ejemplo arquitectónico de la España contemporánea?
6. ¿Cuál es un baile regional típico de España?
7. ¿Cuáles son algunos ejemplos contemporáneos de la rica cultura de España?

[5]*films*
[6]*attire*

Encuentro cultural

Artes ornamentales

Los azulejos[1] de España

Desde hace muchos siglos los azulejos de cerámica adornan los castillos y palacios de España. La palabra *azulejo* viene de *al zuleiq*, que en árabe quiere decir «pequeña piedra pulida»[2]. Con la presencia musulmana[3] (de origen árabe) comenzó la tradición de los azulejos en España.

[1]*ceramic tiles* [2]*polished*
[3]*Muslim* [4]*Ya... Since*
[5]*Mosque* [6]*tapestries*
[7]*even*

Ya que[4] la religión musulmana no permite la representación de figuras humanas o de animales, los azulejos árabes utilizan sólo formas geométricas. El palacio de la Alhambra en Granada y la Gran Mezquita[5] en Córdoba contienen los ejemplos más espectaculares de este arte decorativo. Los diseños más recientes también contienen imágenes religiosas, describen una historia o imitan tapices[6] y pinturas.

Plaza de España. Sevilla, España

Los azulejos tienen colores vivos y se utilizan para decorar exteriores e interiores de iglesias, restaurantes y hasta[7] estaciones de metro. España produce azulejos para uso doméstico y para exportación. Hoy todavía existen muchos artesanos que hacen azulejos tradicionales a mano, pero gran parte de la producción de azulejos en España utiliza técnicas industriales.

Azulejo decorativo en el palacio de la Alhambra. Granada, España

Preguntas

1. ¿Cuál de los azulejos representa la tradición árabe? ¿Por qué? ¿Dónde se encuentra este azulejo?
2. ¿Cuál representa un diseño más reciente? ¿Por qué?
3. ¿Cómo se llama la plaza? ¿Piensa usted que los azulejos son artesanales o industriales?
4. ¿Hay azulejos en su casa/apartamento? ¿En dónde? ¿Son decorativos o simplemente prácticos?
5. ¿Existen edificios o lugares públicos decorados con azulejos en su ciudad o pueblo? Describa uno.

Adverbios y expresiones adverbiales

constantemente
desafortunadamente
fácilmente
frecuentemente
generalmente
inmediatamente
lentamente
normalmente
personalmente
posiblemente
probablemente
rápidamente
recientemente
tranquilamente

anoche
anteayer
ayer
el fin de semana pasado
el… pasado (año/ mes/ verano, etc.)
la semana pasada
ya

entonces
después
luego
más tarde
primero

Sustantivos

La rutina diaria

el cepillo
  el cepillo de dientes
el champú
la crema de afeitar
el desodorante
el despertador
el jabón
el maquillaje
la máquina de afeitar
la navaja
el papel higiénico
la pasta de dientes
el peine
el secador de pelo
las tijeras
la toalla

El trabajo

la compañía
el dinero
la empresa
la fábrica
la tienda
  de ropa
el trabajo
  de tiempo
  completo/ parcial

Más personas y profesiones

la cajera
el cajero
la compañera de cuarto
el compañero de cuarto
la dependienta
el dependiente
la empleada
el empleado
la mesera
el mesero
la recepcionista
el recepcionista
el repartidor
la repartidora
la secretaria
el secretario

Verbos y expresiones verbales

acostarse (ue)
afeitarse
bañarse
cepillarse los dientes/ el pelo
cortarse el pelo/ las uñas/ el dedo
despertarse (ie)
divertirse (ie)
dormirse (ue)
ducharse

ganar
lavarse las manos/ la cara, etc.
levantarse
maquillarse
peinarse
ponerse los zapatos/ la ropa, etc.
quitarse
  la ropa
secarse
sonar (ue)
vestirse (i)

acabar de + *infinitivo*
tener sueño
trabajar para…

I. Reflexive verbs. It is 8:00 A.M. in the dorm. Indicate what happens.

> **Modelo:** Alfonso / levantarse
> **Alfonso se levanta.**

1. mi compañero/a de cuarto / despertarse
2. yo / levantarse
3. tú / bañarse
4. Pepita / cepillarse los dientes
5. nosotros / ponerse suéteres porque hace frío
6. Octavio y Manuel / vestirse

II. Adverbs. Express each idea in a different way by using an appropriate adverb.

> **Modelo:** Mi abuela no camina muy rápido.
> Camina… **lentamente.**

1. Carmen llama a sus abuelos con mucha frecuencia.
   Los llama…
2. Sofía habla español con facilidad. Lo habla…
3. Tomás acaba de llegar. Llegó…
4. Felipe responde a mis mensajes electrónicos el momento en que los recibe. Me responde…

III. The preterit of regular verbs and *ser/ir*.
A. Indicate what happened this morning before work.

> **Modelo:** yo / levantarse temprano
> **Me levanté temprano.**

1. yo / ducharse
2. Pepita / peinarse
3. tú / lavarse la cara
4. nosotros / afeitarse
5. ellos / cepillarse los dientes

B. Indicate what happened during the workday.

> **Modelo:** yo / desayunar en Starbucks
> **Desayuné en Starbucks.**

1. yo / llegar al trabajo a las nueve
2. dos colegas / leer las noticias (*news*) del día
3. mi colega y yo / mandar un mensaje electrónico al presidente de la compañía
4. tú / escribir un memo muy importante
5. nosotros / ir a un restaurante chino para almorzar
6. en la tarde, mi colega / llamar a varios de nuestros clientes
7. ella / resolver un problema serio
8. nosotros / salir del trabajo a las cinco de la tarde

IV. Direct object pronouns.
A. Camila is going to invite to her party everyone who wants to come.

> **Modelo:** Elena quiere ir a la fiesta.
> **Pues, Camila va a invitarla.**

1. Yo quiero ir.
2. Nosotros queremos ir.
3. Ustedes quieren ir.
4. Mis hermanas quieren ir.
5. Mis hermanos quieren ir.
6. Pepita quiere ir.
7. Tú quieres ir.

B. Answer the questions with the appropriate direct object pronoun.

> **Modelo:** ¿Quiere usted conocer al presidente de la universidad?
> **Sí, quiero conocerlo/Sí, lo quiero conocer.**
> *o* **No, no quiero conocerlo/No, no lo quiero conocer.**

1. ¿Quiere usted ver a sus amigos/as hoy?
2. ¿Va a llamar a sus padres esta noche?
3. ¿Está haciendo la tarea para la clase de español ahora?
4. ¿Completó usted todos los ejercicios del Capítulo 5?
5. ¿Va a estudiar todo el vocabulario?

V. General review. Answer each question with as many activities as possible.

1. ¿Qué hace usted por la mañana después de levantarse?
2. ¿Qué hace usted antes de acostarse?
3. ¿Adónde fue usted ayer? ¿Qué más ocurrió ayer?
4. ¿Qué pasó el fin de semana pasado?
5. ¿Llamó usted a su mejor amigo/a la semana pasada? ¿De qué hablaron?

Answers to the *Autoprueba y repaso* are found in **Apéndice 2**.

Capítulo 6

Por la ciudad

Goals for communication

- To talk about places and things in the city
- To carry out transactions at the post office and the bank
- To point out persons and things
- To talk about actions in the past
- To express negation

Así se dice

Por la ciudad

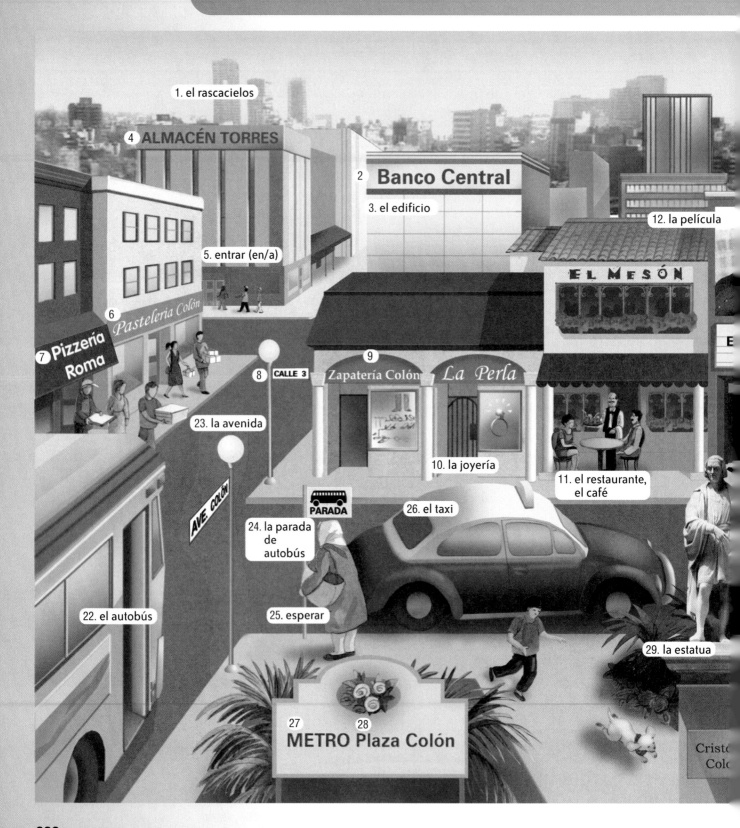

1. el rascacielos
4. ALMACÉN TORRES
2. Banco Central
3. el edificio
12. la película
5. entrar (en/a)
EL MESÓN
6. Pastelería Colón
7. Pizzería Roma
8. CALLE 3
9. Zapatería Colón
La Perla
23. la avenida
AVE. COLÓN
10. la joyería
11. el restaurante, el café
PARADA
26. el taxi
24. la parada de autobús
22. el autobús
25. esperar
29. la estatua
27 28 METRO Plaza Colón
Cristó Colo

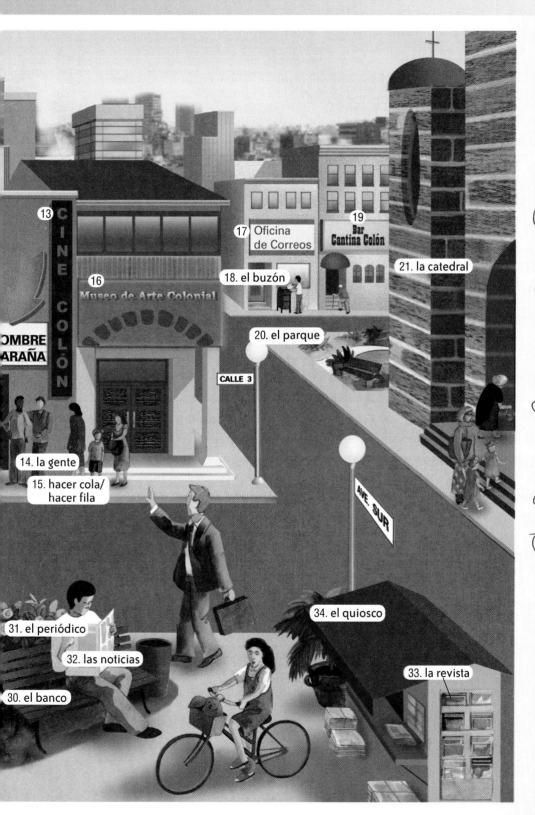

The illustration contains the following labels:

13. CINE COLÓN
17. Oficina de Correos
19. Bar Cantina Colón
16. Museo de Arte Colonial
18. el buzón
21. la catedral
20. el parque
CALLE 3
OMBRE ARAÑA
14. la gente
15. hacer cola/ hacer fila
AVE SUR
34. el quiosco
31. el periódico
32. las noticias
33. la revista
30. el banco

1. skyscraper
2. bank
3. building
4. department store (m.)
5. to enter, go into
6. pastry shop
7. pizzeria
0. street (f.)
9. shoe store
10. jewelry shop
11. restaurant, cafe
12. film, movie
13. movie theater, cinema (m.)
14. people
15. to get (stand) in line
16. museum
17. post office
18. mailbox
19. bar (m.)
20. park
21. cathedral; **la iglesia** church
22. bus
23. avenue
24. bus stop
25. to wait for
26. taxi
27. metro, subway
28. plaza, town square
29. statue
30. bench
31. newspaper
32. news
33. magazine
34. newsstand

Práctica y comunicación

Note: beginning with this chapter, direction lines for all exercises and activities will be in Spanish. Review *Así se dice*, page 38.

6-1. En la ciudad. Conteste según el dibujo (*according to the drawing*) de las páginas 200–201.

1. ¿En qué avenida están el Banco Central y el Almacén Torres? ¿Cuántas personas van a entrar en[1] el almacén?
2. ¿Qué piensa usted que compraron las dos personas que salen de la Pastelería Colón?
3. ¿Cuántas personas salen de la Pizzería Roma?
4. ¿Qué tipo de tiendas hay en la calle 3?
5. ¿Qué están haciendo las personas que están en el restaurante/café El Mesón? ¿Quién trae las bebidas?
6. ¿Para qué hace cola la gente frente al cine?
7. ¿Qué tipo de arte podemos ver en el museo?
8. ¿Qué hay enfrente de la oficina de correos?
9. ¿Quién entra en el bar?
10. ¿Hay árboles en el parque? ¿Y gente?
11. ¿En qué avenida está la catedral? ¿Quiénes entran?
12. ¿Quién está esperando el autobús en la parada?
13. ¿Cómo se llama la parada del metro?
14. ¿Qué hay en el centro de la plaza?
15. ¿Qué busca el hombre que lleva un maletín (*briefcase*)?
16. Andrés está sentado (*seated*) en el banco del parque. ¿Qué está haciendo?
17. ¿Qué venden en el quiosco?
18. ¿Quién persigue (*chases*) al perro por la plaza? ¿Y qué hace Elena?
19. ¿Qué tipo de edificios son los edificios muy, muy altos que se ven a la distancia?

6-2. De memoria. Observen el dibujo de las páginas 200–201. Luego cierren los libros. Escriban lo que hay y lo que ocurre en la ciudad. ¿Qué grupo tiene la descripción más completa?

---

[1] **Entrar a** is more common in Latin America, **entrar en** is more common in Spain.

En el centro de la ciudad

En el centro encontramos los **lugares**(1) más interesantes de la ciudad. Vamos a **pasar**(2) el día allí pero primero necesitamos **averiguar**(3)* a qué hora **se abren**(4) las tiendas y los museos, y a qué hora **se cierran**(5). También queremos saber dónde comprar **entradas**(6) para una **obra de teatro**(7), y a qué hora **empieza**(8) el *show*. En la mañana queremos ir de compras en las tiendas pequeñas y también en el **centro comercial**(9). Podemos visitar los museos, tomar algo y luego pasar la tarde en un parque o dar un paseo en un jardín botánico o zoológico. En el centro siempre encontramos los **mejores**(10) restaurantes, donde podemos **invitar**(11)** a un buen amigo a cenar. ¿Y para regresar a casa? Después de ir al **teatro**(12) y **terminar**(13) las actividades de un largo día, podemos tomar el metro.

*(1) places (2) to spend (time); to happen, pass (3) to find out, inquire (4) open; **abrir** to open (5) close; **cerrar (ie)** to close (6) (admission) tickets (7) play (8) begins; **empezar (ie)** to begin (9) mall, shopping center (10) best; **el/la mejor** (11) to invite (12) theater (13) finishing; **terminar** to finish*

Se + *a verb in the third-person singular or plural often indicates that the subject (doer of the action) is unknown or unimportant. The emphasis is on the action.*

El banco **se abre** a las nueve.   *The bank opens at nine.*

Las tiendas **se abren** a las diez.   *The stores open at ten.*

(The persons who open the bank/stores are not mentioned.)

6-3.
¿Adónde vamos? ¿A qué lugares vamos para...?

1. encontrar una gran variedad de tiendas y almacenes
2. tomar un refresco
3. descansar en el centro de la ciudad
4. ver una película
5. participar en ceremonias religiosas
6. ver el arte de pintores famosos
7. ver una obra de Shakespeare
8. comprar revistas y periódicos
9. comprar estampillas/ zapatos/ joyas
10. comer pizza/ pasteles
11. depositar dinero
12. esperar el autobús

---

* Preterit: **averigüé, averiguaste, averiguó, averiguamos, averiguasteis, averiguaron**. The sounds [gwe] and [gwi] are written **güe**, **güi**.

** **Invitar** requires the preposition **a** when followed by the infinitive: **Me invitó a** *cenar*.

6-4. **Nuestros lugares favoritos.** Piensen en varios lugares en la ciudad que ustedes visitan con frecuencia. Determinen para qué (*for what purpose*) van a estos lugares. Usen los dibujos como punto de partida (*points of departure*).

Modelo: 1. Voy al cine con frecuencia para ver películas de ciencia ficción.

1.

2.

3.

4.

5.

6.

6-5. **Preguntas personales.** Háganse las siguientes preguntas (*Ask each other the following questions*).

1. ¿Piensas cenar en un restaurante este fin de semana? ¿Qué más piensas hacer?
2. Si quieres cenar en un restaurante, ¿a quién invitas?
3. ¿Cuáles son los mejores restaurantes de tu ciudad? ¿Y los peores (*the worst ones*)?
4. Cuando estás en una ciudad grande, ¿qué lugares te gusta visitar?
5. ¿Prefieres visitar un museo de arte moderno o un museo de arte clásico?
6. ¿Te gusta ir de compras a los centros comerciales? ¿A qué centro comercial vas con más frecuencia? ¿Sabes a qué hora se abre? ¿Y a qué hora se cierra?
7. ¿Prefieres ir de compras a los almacenes o a las tiendas?
8. De noche, ¿prefieres ir a un concierto de *rock* o a un concierto de música clásica? ¿A qué hora empiezan los conciertos normalmente? ¿Y a qué hora terminan? ¿Cuánto cuestan las entradas?
9. ¿Prefieres ir al cine o ver un DVD en casa?
10. ¿Qué tipo de películas prefieres? ¿De ciencia ficción? ¿Románticas? ¿Cómicas? ¿De terror? ¿Cuáles son tus películas favoritas?

3 *Inés, Manuel y Linda van a un café en la plaza después de ir al cine. Inés habla con sus amigos de sus vacaciones en Nueva York.*

MANUEL: Chicas, ¿les gustó la película?

LINDA: ¡A mí me gustó mucho! Las películas filmadas en Nueva York siempre me impresionan.

INÉS: Tienes razón. Nueva York es una ciudad única.

MANUEL: Inés, tú visitaste Nueva York el verano pasado, ¿verdad? ¿Te gustó?

INÉS: Es una ciudad fascinante, pero muy diferente.

LINDA: ¿Por qué?

INÉS: Bueno, en Nueva York no hay plazas como ésta, pero hay parques enormes. También hay barrios° étnicos como el chino, el italiano, el ruso y El Barrio°, donde viven muchos puertorriqueños. ¡Es como estar en pequeñas ciudades dentro de una gran ciudad! Y hay excelentes restaurantes de todas las nacionalidades.   *neighborhoods* / *East/Spanish Harlem*

LINDA: ¿Cómo es el centro de la ciudad?

INÉS: En Manhattan las calles van de este a oeste y las avenidas de norte a sur. Es muy fácil encontrar cualquier lugar; además° el metro es muy accesible.   *besides*

MANUEL: ¿Fuiste al teatro o a algún museo?

INÉS: ¡Claro! Vi una obra en Broadway y visité el Museo Metropolitano. Su colección de arte es realmente impresionante. Tienen hasta° una réplica de un templo egipcio. También visité la Estatua de la Libertad, el edificio Empire State y la Zona Cero.   *even*

LINDA: ¿Y las tiendas? ¿Fuiste al famoso almacén Macy's en la calle 34?

MANUEL: ¿Fuiste a alguna discoteca?

INÉS: No pude° ir de compras porque se me terminó el dinero°. Pero sí fui a una discoteca...   *I couldn't / se... I ran out of money*

LINDA: ¿Te divertiste? ¿Conociste a alguien interesante?

INÉS: Conocí a muchas personas interesantes, ¡pero la gente más interesante la vi en el metro de regreso a mi hotel!

¿Qué pasa?

1. ¿Por qué dice Inés que visitar Nueva York es como visitar varias ciudades en una?

2. ¿Qué lugares famosos visitó Inés?

3. ¿Fue de compras a Macy's?

4. ¿En dónde vio Inés la gente más interesante?

Estructuras

① **Indicating relationships between persons and things: Prepositions; pronouns with prepositions**

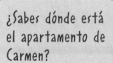

¿Sabes dónde está el apartamento de Carmen?

Sí. Está en la avenida Sur, cerca del museo y frente al parque.

A. Prepositions of location and other useful prepositions

Prepositions are words that express a relationship between nouns or pronouns and other words in a sentence. You have already learned some prepositions such as: **a** (*to, at*), **en** (*in, on, at*), **de** (*from, of, about*), **con** (*with*), and **sin** (*without*). Below are some additional prepositions that will help you describe location and movement through a place.

Preposiciones de lugar	
cerca de/ lejos de	*near/far from*
dentro de/ fuera de	*inside/outside*
debajo de/ encima de	*beneath, under/on top of, above*
detrás de/ delante de	*behind/in front of*
enfrente de	*in front of, opposite*
frente a	*in front of, opposite, facing*
al lado de	*beside*
sobre, en	*on*
entre	*between, among*
por	*by, through, alongside, around*

Otras preposiciones útiles	
antes de/ después de	*before/after*
en vez de	*instead of*
para + *infinitive*	*in order to (do something)*
al + *infinitive*	*upon + (doing something)*

In Spanish a verb following a preposition is always in the infinitive (**-ar, -er, -ir**) form. In contrast, English uses the *-ing* form. Some prepositions commonly used with infinitives are:

> al   antes de   después de   en vez de   para   sin

Antes de ir al teatro, vamos a cenar.

Before going to the theatre, we're going to have dinner.

	UNA RIMA		
left	A la izquierda°	Abajo°	*Down*
right	a la derecha°	arriba°	*up*
	delante	enfrente	
	detrás	encima,	
	cerca	y ahora muchachos	
	lejos	se acaba°	*se... ends*
	y algo más.	la rima.	

¿Qué preposiciones pueden encontrar en la rima?
Repitan y dramatícenla (*act it out*).

Práctica y comunicación

② **6-6.** **¿Cierto o falso?** Según la ilustración de las páginas 200–201, determinen si las oraciones siguientes son ciertas o falsas. Si son falsas, corríjanlas (*correct them*).

> **Modelo:** La pizzería está al lado de la joyería.
> **Falso. Está al lado de la pastelería.**

1. El buzón está detrás de la oficina de correos.

2. La calle 3 está entre la avenida Colón y la avenida Sur.

3. Juanito corre por la calle.

4. El Museo de Arte Colonial está cerca del Almacén Torres.

5. El Banco Central está delante de la zapatería y de la joyería.

6. Los periódicos están al lado del quiosco.

7. Vemos a la gente que está dentro del Cine Colón.

8. Hay un parque enfrente de la catedral.

9. Hay un bar al lado del museo.

④ **6-7.** **La invasión de los gatos.** Mientras (*While*) la profesora Falcón está en la universidad, sus diecisiete gatos juegan en la sala (*living room*). Identifiquen dónde están los gatos, usando las preposiciones apropiadas. Un/a secretario/a apunta la información. ¿Qué grupo puede identificar dónde está el mayor (*largest*) número de gatos? Tienen cinco minutos.

> **Modelo:** Un gato está encima del sofá. Otro está…

la planta
el estante
el televisor
la lámpara
el sofá
la papelera
Ofelia Sofía Maya

6-8. **Nuestros lugares interesantes.** Un/a estudiante de un país hispano acaba de llegar a la universidad. Escríbale una lista de cinco lugares interesantes en la ciudad donde está su universidad. Indique dónde están (**cerca de…, lejos de…, al lado de…, en la calle…,** etc.). Compare su lista con la de otro/a compañero/a. Guarde (*Save*) la información para usarla más tarde en el proyecto del **Capítulo 6.**

② **6-9.** **Expresión personal.** Completen las ideas, indicando actividades que son apropiadas para ustedes.

> **Modelo:** A veces vemos la tele **en vez de…**
> **A veces vemos la tele en vez de estudiar.**

1. Los sábados vamos al centro **para**…
2. Al… al centro, siempre buscamos estacionamiento (*parking*).
3. A veces vamos al parque **para**…
4. Es difícil entrar en nuestra pastelería favorita **sin**…
5. Nos gusta cenar en un restaurante **antes de**…
6. A veces buscamos un taxi **en vez de**…
7. Nunca, nunca manejamos **después de**…

Ahora, dígale a su compañero/a lo que usted hace **en vez de…, antes de…** y **para**…

B. Pronouns with prepositions

Object pronouns that follow prepositions are the same as subject pronouns, with the exception of **yo** and **tú**, which become **mí** and **ti**.

—¿Es este cuadro para mí? *Is this painting for **me**?*
—Sí, es para **ti**. *Yes, it's for **you**.*

Pronombres objetos de la preposición			
mí[2]	*me*	**nosotros/as**	*us*
ti	*you* (informal)	**vosotros/as**	*you* (informal pl.)
usted	*you* (formal)	**ustedes**	*you* (formal pl.)
él	*him*	**ellos**	*them*
ella	*her*	**ellas**	*them*

The combination of **con** + **mí** or **ti** becomes **conmigo** (*with me*) or **contigo** (*with you*).

—¿Quieres ir **conmigo**? *Do you want to go **with me**?*
—¡Sí! Voy **contigo**. *Yes! I'll go **with you**.*

HINT Remember that with verbs like **gustar**, **a** + *prepositional pronoun* is sometimes used for emphasis or clarification.
A él no **le** gustó la película.
He didn't like the movie.
A mí tampoco **me** gustó.
I didn't like it either.

Práctica y comunicación

② **6-10.** **Información personal.** Háganse las preguntas.

1. ¿Quieres ir al cine conmigo esta noche? ¿Quieres ir a un concierto de música clásica conmigo este fin de semana? ¿Quieres estudiar conmigo para el próximo examen de español?

2. ¿Estudió tu novio/a o tu mejor amigo/a contigo anoche? ¿Comió en la cafetería contigo? ¿Pasó mucho tiempo contigo el fin de semana pasado? ¿Cómo lo pasaron?

3. ¿Quién se sienta (*is seated*) detrás de ti en la clase de español? ¿Y delante de ti? ¿Y a la izquierda/derecha? ¿A quién conoces mejor?

4. A mí me gustan los ejercicios que hacemos en parejas. ¿Te gustan a ti?

---

[2] Note the accent on **mí** (*me*) *vs.* **mi** (*my*).

6-11. **Linda y Manuel.** Lean la conversación dramáticamente, completándola con los pronombres apropiados.

Linda está sentada en un sillón grande en la sala de su casa. Habla por teléfono con su amor, Manuel.

MANUEL: Linda, ¿quieres salir con_____ esta noche? Me muero por verte.

LINDA: Sí, mi amor. Voy cont_____ adonde quieras.

MANUEL: Pues, te voy a llevar a un lugar muy especial, y... ¡tengo una sorpresa maravillosa para ____!

LINDA: ¿Para ____? ¡Eres un ángel, Manuel! A ____ me encantan las sorpresas. Yo también tengo una sorpresa para _____.

MANUEL: ¿Ah, sí? ¿Cuál es?

LINDA: Pues, no vamos a estar solos esta noche porque mi hermanito menor tiene que venir con _____.

stay MANUEL: ¿Con _____? ¿No pueden tus padres quedarse° con ____?

be LINDA: Manuelito, sé° flexible. ¿No quieres hacerlo por ____?

It seems MANUEL: Bueno. Parece° que los tres vamos a salir.

LINDA: ¡Gracias, mi amor!

Estructuras

2 **Pointing out things and persons: Demonstrative adjectives and pronouns**

Demonstrative adjectives

Demonstrative adjectives point out specific objects or persons. Like all adjectives, demonstratives agree in gender and number with the noun they describe. The demonstrative adjective you use depends upon how close you are to the item you are pointing out.

Me gusta **este** parque.		*I like **this** park.*
¿Te gusta **esa** pizzería?		*Do you like **that** pizzeria?*
Vamos a visitar **esos** museos.		*We are going to visit **those** museums.*
Aquella tienda tiene lo que buscamos.		*That store (over there) has what we are looking for.*

Los demostrativos					
close to speaker		*at a short distance*		*at a great distance*	
this (m.) **este** bar	*that*	**ese** bar	*that*	**aquel** bar
(f.) **esta** calle		**esa** calle		**aquella** calle
these (m.) **estos** bares	*those*	**esos** bares	*those*	**aquellos** bares
(f.) **estas** calles		**esas** calles		**aquellas** calles

Demonstrative pronouns

Demonstrative adjectives become demonstrative pronouns (*this one, that one, those, etc.*) with the addition of a written accent on the stressed vowel. There is no difference in pronunciation.

A demonstrative pronoun is used *instead of a noun*, usually to avoid repetition and redundancy, while the demonstrative adjective is used *with the noun*. Compare the demonstrative adjectives and pronouns in the following sentences.

Voy a visitar **esta** tienda y **aquélla**.
      adjective   *pronoun*

*I am going to visit **this** store and **that one**.*

¿Te gustan **estos** zapatos?
      adjective

*Do you like **these** shoes?*

No. Prefiero **ésos**.
      pronoun

*No. I prefer **those**.*

The demonstratives **esto** (*this*) and **eso** (*that*) are neuter (neither masculine nor feminine), because they refer to an idea, situation, or statement, or to an object that has not yet been identified. Since they cannot be confused with demonstrative adjectives, no written accent is needed.

    ¿Qué es **esto**? ¡No sé!   *What is this? I don't know!*

    ¿Qué quiere? ¡**Eso** es ridículo!   *What does he want? That's ridiculous!*

Práctica y comunicación

6-12. **Soy guía turístico.** Imagine que usted trabaja para una agencia de turismo y le muestra (*show*) la ciudad a un grupo de visitantes. Use adjetivos demostrativos.

> **Modelo:** la catedral es del período colonial (un poco lejos)
>
> **Esa catedral es del período colonial.**

1. el rascacielos es el más moderno de la ciudad (muy lejos)
2. la estatua es del presidente (un poco lejos)
3. la estación del metro está cerrada (muy lejos)
4. el parque es muy famoso (un poco lejos)
5. las flores que están en el parque son muy bonitas (un poco lejos)
6. los almacenes venden de todo (cerca)
7. el restaurante sirve comida argentina (cerca)

② **6-13.** **¡Tengo hambre! ¿Cuánto cuestan?** Usted entra en la Pastelería Colón y le pregunta los precios a la dependienta. Ella le contesta según la lista de precios. Usen los demostrativos.

> **Modelo:** Cliente: ¿Cuánto cuesta este pastel de limón?
>
> Dependienta: **Ése cuesta dos dólares, cincuenta y cinco centavos.**

Palabras Útiles

medialuna *croissant*

empanada *turnover/pie*

Precios de hoy:

galletas de chocolate $2.75 la docena
de azúcar $2.00 la docena

pastel de manzana $2.50
de limón $2.55

torta de chocolate $3.80
de fresa $4.25

pan de queso $1.25
de aceitunas $1.60

empanadas de carne $1.00 cada una
vegetarianas $.75 cada una

medialunas de jamón y queso $.90 cada una
de chocolate $.80 cada una

Al final, dígale a la dependienta lo que va a comprar. **Voy a comprar este/ese...**

Así se dice

En la oficina de correos

Quiero mandarle/ **enviar**le[1] esta **tarjeta postal**[2] a mi amigo.

Recibí[3] una **carta**[4] de mi amiga.

Quiero **contestar**le[5] inmediatamente. Escribo la **dirección**[6] en el **sobre**[7].

Necesito comprar una **estampilla**/ un **sello**[8].

¿Para quién es este **paquete**[9]?

(1) to send (2) postcard (3) I received; **recibir** *to receive (4) letter (5) to answer (6) address*
(7) envelope (8) stamp (9) package

Práctica y comunicación

6-14. **La historia de una carta.** Determinen el orden cronológico de estos eventos. ¿Qué pasó primero? ¿Y después?

___ buscar el buzón

___ comprar un sello de 80 centavos

___ enviar la carta

___ escribir la dirección en el sobre

___ ir a la oficina de correos

___ mi amigo / abrirla y leerla

___ mi amigo / contestarme inmediatamente

___ mi amigo / recibir la carta

_1_ escribir la carta

Ahora narren la historia cronológicamente, cambiando los verbos al pretérito.

Modelo: _1_   **Primero, escribí la carta.**

6-15. **En la oficina de correos.** Imagine que usted está en la oficina de correos en Buenos Aires. Hable con el empleado para hacer lo siguiente (*the following*). Túrnense (*Take turns*).

- comprar estampillas para mandar una tarjeta postal a...
- comprar estampillas para mandar una carta a...
- recoger (*to pick up*) un paquete de su familia que acaba de llegar a la oficina de correos
- mandarle un paquete a su familia en...

Noticias culturales

La plaza

heart

La plaza es el corazón° de las ciudades y los pueblos hispanos. Normalmente ocupa la parte más vieja de la ciudad o del pueblo, y es el centro político, religioso, social y comercial de una población. En ella se instalan° mercados al aire libre y se celebran festivales y ceremonias importantes.

se... are set up

surrounding it

Una plaza típica tiene a su alrededor° una iglesia, edificios públicos, cafés, tiendas y bares. Generalmente en el centro hay una estatua o un monumento, y en muchas ocasiones también hay fuentes° y jardines. Las plazas aún° tienen mucha importancia para los habitantes de una comunidad. Durante el día la gente camina, conversa, toma refrescos, lee o juega cartas° o dominó. En las noches los jóvenes se reúnen para charlar y para hacer planes para ir al cine o a bailar.

fountains / still

cards

city (town) hall

La Plaza de Mayo en Buenos Aires es sitio de reunión y protesta para los argentinos. Está rodeada por la catedral, el cabildo° y la Casa Rosada, el equivalente de la Casa Blanca en Washington, D. C. Otras plazas famosas son la Plaza Mayor en Madrid, la Plaza del Zócalo en México, D.F. y la Plaza de Armas en Chile.

Plaza de Mayo, Buenos Aires, Argentina

¿Qué recuerda?

1. Generalmente, la plaza principal se encuentra en...
2. En una plaza típica es común encontrar...
3. En el centro de las plazas podemos ver...
4. Durante el día la gente utiliza las plazas para...
5. Los jóvenes visitan la plaza para...
6. Una de las plazas más famosas es...

Plaza de Armas, Santiago, Chile

② Conexiones y contrastes

1. ¿Cuál es el lugar público más importante de su ciudad o pueblo? ¿Qué pasa allí?
2. ¿Es la función social de las plazas comparable a la de los centros comerciales en los EE.UU.? Mencione similitudes y diferencias.

3 Talking about actions in the past: The preterit of *hacer* and stem-changing verbs

A. *Hacer*

The verb **hacer** is irregular in the preterit. Note that the stem (**hic-**) is constant and that **c → z** before **o**. Also observe the special preterit endings **-e** and **-o**.

> **hic**e, **hic**iste, **hiz**o, **hic**imos, **hic**isteis, **hic**ieron

—¿Qué **hiciste** anoche?   *What **did you do** last night?*
—Fui al gimnasio e **hice ejercicio**.   *I went to the gym and **worked out**.*

Remember that you do not always use **hacer** to answer **hacer** questions.

—¿Qué *hicieron* ustedes ayer?   *What **did you do** yesterday?*
—*Fuimos* al centro y *vimos*   *We **went** downtown and **saw**
   una película.   a movie.*

Práctica y comunicación

6-16. Los sábados de Javier.
Javier describe sus sábados rutinarios. Lea el párrafo. Luego, cambie (*change*) la narración de Javier para describir *el sábado pasado*. Cambie los verbos en negrilla (*boldface*) al pretérito.

HINT | Before doing Exercise 6–16, review the preterit of regular verbs and of **ser** and **ir** (pp. 181–182).

¿Que **hago** los sábados? Pues, **me levanto** un poco tarde y **desayuno** en casa. A las diez de la mañana **juego** al tenis con mi hermanito Samuel y luego **voy** al laboratorio de química para trabajar. Después, mi amiga Marlena y yo **hacemos** algunas compras en el centro. Por la noche **salimos** con nuestros amigos; **cenamos** en algún restaurante y **vamos** al cine. **Volvemos** a casa bastante tarde. ¿Y mi hermana Clara? Ella es muy perezosa y no **hace** nada. Mis padres, por el contrario, **hacen** miles de cosas. ¡Pobrecitos!

Modelo: Javier: ¿Qué **hice** el sábado pasado?...

6-17. **Ayer, en el centro.** Imaginen que ustedes fueron a los lugares indicados. ¿Qué hicieron ustedes allí? Háganse preguntas.

> **Modelo:** en el centro comercial
> Estudiante 1: ¿Qué hiciste en el centro comercial?
> Estudiante 2: **Fui de compras.**

¿Qué hiciste...?

1. en el parque
2. en la plaza
3. en el gimnasio
4. en el restaurante
5. en el museo
6. en el teatro
7. en la oficina de correos

Estructuras

B. Stem-changing verbs

Note that **-ir** verbs with a stem change in the present tense (o ➔ ue, e ➔ ie, e ➔ i) also change in the preterit.[3] The change in the preterit (o ➔ u and e ➔ i) occurs only in the third-person singular (**usted/ él/ ella**) and third-person plural (**ustedes/ ellos/ ellas**) forms.

HINT First, review the present tense stem-changing verbs on p. 108. Then practice the preterit tense of the verbs presented in this section.

---

[3] Note that **-ar** and **-er** stem-changing verbs in the present tense never change their stems in the preterit.

This same change also occurs in the present participle (-**ando**/-**iendo** form). Note the pattern of change in the following model verbs.

dormir (o → u)		pedir (e → i)	
dormí	dormimos	pedí	pedimos
dormiste	dormisteis	pediste	pedisteis
d**u**rmió	d**u**rmieron	p**i**dió	p**i**dieron

d**o**rmir(se) (ue, u)	*to sleep, to go to sleep, fall asleep*	Sandra d**u**rmió en la casa de su amiga. Las dos chicas se d**u**rmieron inmediatamente.
m**o**rir (ue, u)	*to die*	El perro de Mónica y Ana m**u**rió en un accidente.
pref**e**rir (ie, i)	*to prefer*	Las chicas pref**i**rieron no hablar del incidente.
div**e**rtirse (ie, i)	*to have a good time*	¿Se div**i**rtieron ustedes en el restaurante anoche?
p**e**dir (i, i)	*to ask for, request*	Tina p**i**dió una paella de mariscos.
s**e**rvir (i, i)	*to serve*	¿Qué más s**i**rvieron?
rep**e**tir (i, i)	*to repeat*	El mesero rep**i**tió la lista de postres dos veces.
v**e**stirse (i, i)	*to get dressed*	Más tarde se v**i**stieron y fueron a un baile.

When a verb shows two stem changes in parentheses, (**ue, u**) for example, the first (**ue**) refers to a stem change in the present tense; the second (**u**) refers to a stem change in the preterit tense and in the -**ndo** form.

dormir (ue, u)	
present:	d**ue**rmo, d**ue**rmes, d**ue**rme, dormimos, dormís, d**ue**rmen
preterit:	dormí, dormiste, d**u**rmió, dormimos, dormisteis, d**u**rmieron
-**ndo** *form*:	d**u**rmiendo

Práctica y comunicación

6-18. **Las actividades de Alicia.** Relacione las actividades de la columna A con las actividades correspondientes de la columna B. Lea las oraciones relacionadas.

A

____ **1.** Para prepararse para el examen, Alicia escuchó el CD del Capítulo 6.

____ **2.** Estudió casi toda la noche.

____ **3.** Después del examen, compró un periódico para leer las noticias.

____ **4.** Por la noche, ella y dos de sus amigas cenaron en un restaurante.

____ **5.** El mesero les sirvió tres postres diferentes.

B

a. Leyó que tres personas murieron en un accidente.

b. Todas pidieron pasta con camarones y ensalada.

c. Repitió las palabras del vocabulario.

d. Las chicas prefirieron la torta de chocolate.

e. No durmió mucho.

6-19. **¿Qué pasó?** Describan los dibujos usando las palabras indicadas. Cambien los verbos al pretérito.

> **Modelo:** Ayer Carmen y Natalia fueron al laboratorio. Escucharon un CD y repitieron los poemas.

1. Ayer Carmen y Natalia / ir… / Escuchar… repetir…

2. Esteban y Camila / ir… / Él/Ella / pedir…

3. Juanito y Elena / ir… / Pedir…

4. Octavio y Pepita / ir… / Él/Ella / preferir…

5. Anoche Alfonso / no dormir… / Sus amigos / …

6. Durante las vacaciones la planta del profesor / morir / Las plantas de la profesora / …

6-20. El día de Fulano[4]. Primero, determinen el orden cronológico de las actividades de Fulano. Luego, escriban lo que hizo, usando el pretérito.

Modelo: Se levantó a las 7:00. Luego,...

___ irse al trabajo

___ bañarse

___ desayunar en un café

___ salir con sus amigos

_1_ levantarse a las 7:00

___ vestirse

___ pedir café con leche y pan

___ acostarse a medianoche

___ dormirse

___ cenar en casa

___ divertirse mucho

Ahora, usando el día de Fulano como modelo, describan lo que ocurrió en un día típico de la vida de usted. **Me desperté...**

6-21. Sondeo de la clase. Camine por la clase haciéndoles preguntas a sus compañeros/as. Apunte el nombre de cada estudiante que responde afirmativamente a una pregunta. ¿Cuántas respuestas afirmativas puede usted descubrir en cinco minutos?

Modelo: leer el periódico ayer
Usted: *¿Leíste el periódico ayer?*
Juan: **Sí, leí el periódico.** *o* **Sí, lo leí.**
(*Usted apunta el nombre de Juan.*)

SONDEO DE LA CLASE

_____ 1. estudiar mucho anoche

_____ 2. dormir menos de cinco horas anoche

_____ 3. dormir más de ocho horas anoche

_____ 4. leer el periódico ayer

_____ 5. oír las noticias en la radio o en la tele ayer

_____ 6. pedir pizza o comida china el fin de semana pasado

_____ 7. divertirse el fin de semana pasado

_____ 8. ir al laboratorio la semana pasada (repetir el vocabulario)

_____ 9. invitar a tus amigos/as a tu casa/apartamento la semana pasada (servir una comida muy buena) (¿Qué comida?)

Ahora escriba una lista de lo que hicieron cuatro de sus compañeros/as de clase: **Juan leyó el periódico ayer.** Algunos/as estudiantes van a compartir (*share*) su lista con la clase.

---

[4] **Fulano/a** is the Spanish equivalent of *So and so* or *John/Jane Doe.*

Así se dice

El dinero y los bancos

¿Qué podemos hacer con el dinero?

ganar/ gastar	*to earn/to spend (money)*
depositar/ retirar	*to deposit/to take out, withdraw*
perder (ie)/ encontrar (ue)	*to lose/to find*
ahorrar	*to save (money)*
cambiar	*to change, exchange*
contar (ue)	*to count*
invertir (ie, i)	*to invest*
pagar (la cuenta)	*to pay (for) (the bill, check)*
abrir/ cerrar una cuenta	*to open/to close an account*

¿Cómo pagamos? ¿Cómo recibimos dinero?

el cheque	*check*
el cheque de viajero	*traveler's check*
firmar (un cheque)	*to sign (a check)*
cobrar	*to cash, to charge*
endosar	*to endorse (a check)*
la tarjeta de crédito	*credit card*
el efectivo	*cash*
el cambio	*change, small change, exchange*
la moneda	*currency, money, coin*
el cajero automático	*ATM machine*

Práctica y comunicación

6-22. **Preguntas sobre las finanzas.** ¿Cómo controlan ustedes sus finanzas? Primero contesten la pregunta; luego digan (*say*) ¿Y tú?

1. ¿Trabajaste el verano pasado? (¿Dónde?)
2. ¿Ganaste mucho o poco dinero?
3. ¿Ahorraste un poco para este año académico?
4. ¿Gastas mucho dinero cada mes? (¿En qué?)
5. ¿Pagaste tu cuenta de teléfono el mes pasado? (¿Cuánto fue?)
6. ¿Cuántas veces por mes retiras dinero del banco? ¿Usas el cajero automático?
7. ¿Recibes cheques o dinero en efectivo de tus padres?
8. ¿Tienes tarjetas de crédito? (¿Qué tipo?)
9. Cuando vas de compras, ¿pagas con tarjeta de crédito, con cheque o en efectivo?
10. ¿Inviertes dinero? (¿En qué compañías?)

2 **6-23.** **Hay que ser organizado.** Imaginen que están de vacaciones en Santiago, Chile. Háganse las preguntas para saber si (*if*) ya hicieron ciertas cosas. Usen pronombres en sus respuestas.

> **Modelo:** ¿Encontraste el cajero automático?
> **Sí, ya lo encontré.** *o* **No, no lo encontré.**

1. ¿Contaste el dinero que retiraste del cajero automático?
2. ¿Cambiaste los cheques de viajero?
3. ¿Pagaste la cuenta del hotel?
4. ¿Usaste la tarjeta de crédito?
5. ¿Encontraste la oficina de correos?
6. ¿Enviaste las tarjetas postales?
7. ¿Compraste las entradas para el concierto?
8. ¿Hiciste las reservaciones en el restaurante?

4 **6-24.** **Una visita al banco.** Tienen cinco minutos para describir la escena según el dibujo. Mencionen lo que está pasando, lo que pasó y/o lo que va a pasar. Un/a estudiante sirve de secretario/a y apunta las ideas. ¡Usen la imaginación! ¿Qué grupo puede escribir la descripción más completa?

Palabras útiles	
se escapa	*escapes*
recoger	*to pick up*
suelo	*floor*

3 **¡Qué dilema!**

Estás en el aeropuerto y decides tomar un taxi con una persona a quien no conoces. Los dos deciden pagar el viaje para llegar al centro. Cuando llegas a tu destino ¡descubres que no tienes tu billetera (wallet)! ¿Qué le dices al taxista? **¡Ay! Señor...** *¿Qué le dices a tu compañero/a?* **Puedes...** *¿Cómo reacciona él/ella?*

4 Expressing negation: Indefinite and negative words

¿Hay alguien en ese taxi?

No, no hay nadie. ¿Te lo llamo?

You have previously used some indefinite and negative Spanish words, such as **siempre**, **a veces**, and **nunca**. Here are some additional indefinite and negative words.

Palabras indefinidas y negativas				
algo	something	→	**nada**	nothing, not anything
alguien	someone, somebody	→	**nadie**	no one, nobody
también	also	→	**tampoco**	neither, not either

To express a negative idea in Spanish with the expressions above, a "double negative" construction is often used.

> **no + verb + negative word**

—¿Compraste **algo** en la tienda?   *Did you buy **something** at the store?*
—Hoy **no** compré **nada**.   *I didn't buy **anything** today.*

—¿Hay **alguien** en el taxi?   *Is there **someone** in the taxi?*
—No, **no** hay **nadie**.   *No, there is **no one**.*

However, negative words may precede the verb, thereby eliminating the use of **no**.

> **negative word + verb**

—**Nunca** uso el metro.   *I **never** use the metro.*
—**Tampoco** yo.   *Me **neither**.*

Alguien and **nadie**, when they are objects of the verb, are preceded by the "personal **a**."

> —¿Viste **a alguien** corriendo por el parque?
> —No, no vi **a nadie**.

Práctica y comunicación

6-25. **¿Cierto o falso?** Refiéranse al dibujo de la ciudad, páginas 200–201. ¿Son las siguientes declaraciones ciertas o falsas? Si son falsas, corríjanlas, usando palabras indefinidas y negativas.

> **Modelo:** En este momento, nadie espera el autobús.
> **Falso. Alguien espera el autobús— una mujer.**

1. Alguien está entrando en la zapatería.
2. Hay algo en la mesa que está frente al restaurante.
3. Nadie entra en el teatro.
4. El hombre que está enfrente de la oficina de correos pone algo en el buzón.
5. El hombre en el quiosco no vende periódicos. Tampoco vende revistas.
6. El autobús nunca para (*stops*) en la avenida Colón.
7. Hay alguien en el parque.

6-26. **¡Un ladrón (*thief*) en el banco!** Conteste las preguntas según los dibujos.

1. ¿Ve el ladrón a alguien en el banco?
2. ¿Alguien entró en el banco con el ladrón?
3. ¿Alguien lo vio entrar?
4. ¿Busca el ladrón algo en el banco?
5. ¿Lleva (*Does he carry*) algo en la mano?
6. ¿Hay algo en su bolsa (*bag*)?

7. ¿Alguien oyó la alarma?
8. ¿Alguien llamó a la policía?
9. ¿Hay algo en la bolsa del ladrón?
10. ¿Tiene el ladrón algo en la mano?
11. ¿Qué dice el policía? ¿Y el ladrón?

6-27. Buscando información. Háganse las preguntas y contéstenlas en oraciones completas.

1. ¿Estudiaste con alguien anoche? (¿Con quién?)
2. ¿Hablaste con alguien por teléfono anoche? (¿Con quién?)
3. ¿Viste algo divertido en la tele anoche? (¿Qué?)
4. ¿Oíste algo interesante en la radio anoche o esta mañana? (¿Qué?)
5. ¿Leíste algo interesante en el periódico ayer? (¿Qué?)
6. ¿Saliste con alguien interesante el fin de semana pasado? (¿Con quién?)

Ahora cuéntele (*tell*) a la clase una actividad de su compañero/a: **Andrés salió con alguien interesante el fin de semana pasado...**

Así se pronuncia

The pronunciation of the consonants *g* and *z*

g Remember that before **e** or **i**, **g** has the English *h* sound as in *help*.

gente   **ge**neralmente   **gi**mnasio   pá**gi**na

z In Spanish America, **z** is pronounced the same as **s**. (In Spain it is commonly pronounced with a *th* sound.) The English *z* sound is never used in Spanish.

bu**z**ón   pi**z**arra   pla**z**a   **z**apatería

Repeat the poem line by line.

Zapatero°, zapatero, zapatero remendón°
Cuando haces los zapatos pones vida y corazón°...
Analizas tu trabajo, su pureza y perfección,
zapatillas° o sandalias, zapatito° o zapatón°.

Shoemaker / cobbler / pones... you put your heart and soul into it
slippers / little shoe / big shoe

Dicho y hecho

Conversando

3 **Un día en el centro.** Decidan qué ciudad van a visitar. Formulen un plan de actividades para la mañana, la tarde y la noche. Ustedes pueden visitar el centro, las tiendas, los parques, monumentos, etc. Digan adónde van y por qué seleccionaron esos lugares. Su profesor/a puede pedirles que presenten su plan al resto de la clase. Un/a secretario/a toma apuntes.

¡A escuchar!

Unas vacaciones fabulosas en Buenos Aires, Argentina. Marta habla con su amiga Inés. Es la primera visita de Inés a Buenos Aires. Las dos se sientan en un café en la calle Corrientes. Escuche la conversación. Luego, conteste las dos primeras preguntas.

1. ¿Cómo fue el día de Inés?   ❑ muy activo   ❑ muy tranquilo
2. ¿Visita ella la ciudad de Buenos Aires con su amiga Marta?   ❑ sí   ❑ no

Ahora, escuche la conversación otra vez y complete las oraciones.

3. La calle Florida y la calle Corrientes están en _____.
4. Una atracción del barrio (*neighborhood*) La Boca es _____.
5. En el barrio La Recoleta ellas pueden visitar _____.
6. En Buenos Aires el subte es el _____.
7. La sorpresa (*surprise*) de Marta es que Inés _____ dos _____ para la ópera en el Teatro Colón.
8. Además de las entradas, ¿qué quiere Inés? _____.

De mi escritorio

4 **Un folleto (*brochure*) turístico.** Para el proyecto del **Capítulo 6**, escriban un folleto turístico de la ciudad donde está su universidad. Es para los estudiantes hispanohablantes que acaban de llegar.

Describan:

- la ciudad (incluso la población)
- cuatro atracciones interesantes de la ciudad y dónde están (refiéranse al Ejercicio 6-8)
- los mejores restaurantes, cines, museos, etc.
- los mejores lugares para ir de compras (almacenes, tiendas, centros comerciales)

Si quieren mejorar su folleto, incluyan fotos.

Por la ciudad   doscientos veinticinco **225**

Panorama cultural

Argentina y Chile

Preguntas sobre el mapa

1. ¿Cuál es la capital de Argentina?
2. ¿Con qué países tiene frontera[1] Argentina?
3. ¿Cuál es la capital de Chile?
4. ¿Cómo se llama el desierto que está en el norte de Chile?
5. ¿Cómo se llama la cordillera que pasa por Chile y Argentina?

Dos colosos del Cono Sur

La cordillera de los Andes es la frontera natural entre Chile y Argentina—los dos países con mayor influencia europea en Latinoamérica. Esta influencia es aparente en su cultura y también en su población.

[1]boundary, border

Argentina

Argentina es el país hispano más grande del mundo. Tiene varias regiones distintas. Al norte encontramos las planicies[2] del río Paraná (vea el mapa), donde está la jungla; al sur está La Patagonia, una llanura[3] rica en petróleo. A pesar de la gran extensión de su territorio, la vida argentina se centra en su capital, Buenos Aires, llamada «el París de las Américas».

[2]*flatlands*
[3]*plain*
[4]*wide*
[5]*lanes*
[6]*tiers*

La avenida 9 de Julio, una de las más anchas[4] del mundo, y el obelisco, que conmemora la fundación de la ciudad, son símbolos famosos de Buenos Aires. ¿Cuántos carriles[5] tiene esta avenida?

¡Evita, Evita!

¿Conoce usted la obra musical *Evita* y la canción «No llores por mí, Argentina»? Pues, el tema de este musical es Eva Perón, esposa del dictador Juan Perón (1895–1974).

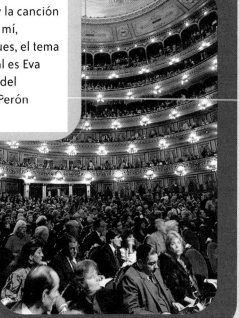

El espectacular Teatro Colón de la capital presenta conciertos, óperas, recitales y *shows*. Atrae músicos y artistas del mundo entero. ¿Cuántas gradas[6] hay en el teatro?

En esta fascinante ciudad de elegantes tiendas, restaurantes y una intensa vida nocturna, las artes son muy importantes. En Buenos Aires nació el tango, el sofisticado baile que todo el mundo asocia con Argentina. ¿Sabe usted bailar tango?

Los Andes están al oeste del país y es aquí donde está el pico más alto de Sudamérica, el Aconcagua, de 22.835 pies de altura[7]. ¿Le gustaría a usted (*Would you like*) escalar[8] esta montaña?

[7]**pies...** *feet high*
[8]*to climb*
[9]*cattle-raising*
[10]*cowboy*
[11]*tie himself*
[12]*horse*

La pampa ocupa la zona central del país, una vasta llanura dedicada en gran parte a la ganadería[9]. La pampa es la tierra del gaucho[10] argentino— el prototipo del hombre valiente y solitario que no quiere atarse[11] a nadie ni a nada y que prácticamente vive sobre su caballo[12]. ¿Cuál es el equivalente al gaucho en la historia norteamericana?

Un escritor excepcional

Jorge Luis Borges (1899–1986), autor argentino y gigante de la literatura latinoamericana, terminó sus días ciego (*blind*), dictando sus creaciones a una secretaria.

Person@je del momento

¿Sabe usted quién es Manu Ginóbili? Busque información en el Internet y compártala con sus compañeros/as de clase.

¿Sabía usted que...?

- Los primeros exploradores españoles llegaron a Argentina en el siglo XVI.
- En 1536 Pedro de Mendoza fundó Buenos Aires, pero los colonos abandonaron la ciudad a causa de los ataques persistentes de los indios. Se fundó otra vez en 1580.
- Los héroes nacionales José de San Martín y Manuel Belgrano comandaron la guerra que hizo de Argentina un país independiente en 1816.
- En la primera parte del siglo XX se alternaron gobiernos civiles y militares hasta 1946, cuando Juan Perón asumió la presidencia.
- Perón fue presidente hasta 1955, cuando los militares lo obligaron a abandonar el poder.
- Después de una serie de dictaduras militares, Argentina volvió a un sistema democrático.

Chile

Chile tiene una configuración geográfica única: es una larga faja[13] de tierra que va desde los Andes en el este hasta el océano Pacífico en el oeste. El país tiene 2.880 millas de largo y solamente 265 millas de ancho. En Chile, es posible esquiar en el mar por la mañana y esquiar en la nieve por la tarde.

[13]*strip* [14]*copper*
[15]*hot-water springs*
[16]*fishing* [17]*elected*
[18]*coup d'etat*

¡A esquiar!

La superficie esquiable más grande del hemisferio sur está al este de Santiago. «Los Tres Valles de los Andes» tiene un total de 10.000 hectáreas y montañas que sobrepasan los 5.000 metros (16.400 pies) de altura.

Al norte de Chile está el desierto de Atacama, ¡el lugar más seco del mundo! En esta región hay muchas minas de cobre[14], un metal que Chile exporta a varias partes del mundo. ¿Le gustaría a usted pasar unos días explorando este desierto? ¿Por qué?

Los 1.100 km de la Carretera Austral cruzan los lugares más atractivos del sur de Chile, con sus montañas, parques nacionales, fiordos, termas[15], ríos y lagos, ideales para la pesca[16] deportiva. El Parque Nacional Torres del Paine (vea la foto) es uno de los más espectaculares del país. ¿Le gustaría visitar esta región? ¿Hay glaciares en alguna región de su país? ¿Dónde?

¿Sabía usted que...?

- Los mapuches (araucanos) y otros grupos de indios vivieron en lo que hoy es Chile antes de la llegada de los españoles.
- Pedro de Valdivia estableció la primera colonia española en Santiago en 1541.
- Chile se independizó de España en 1818 gracias a los famosos generales José de San Martín y Bernardo O'Higgins.
- En 1970 los chilenos eligieron[17] al primer presidente socialista del continente, Salvador Allende; pero en 1973 Augusto Pinochet dio un golpe de estado[18] y estableció una dictadura militar.
- En 1989 Chile tuvo elecciones libres; hoy en día continúa siendo un país democrático.

El centro de Chile es una zona fértil de clima moderado donde vive la mayoría de la población, y en la que se producen muchas frutas y legumbres. En esta zona está la capital, Santiago, una ciudad cosmopolita, moderna y con aspecto europeo. Describa la foto de la capital.

¡Primer Premio Nobel!

En 1945, la poeta chilena Gabriela Mistral (1889-1957) ganó el primer Premio Nobel de Literatura en toda Hispanoamérica.

¿Qué descubrimos?

¿A qué país se refiere cada una de las siguientes oraciones?

1. Su capital se llama «el París de las Américas».
2. Se puede esquiar en el mar y en las montañas el mismo día.
3. En este país está la pampa, la tierra del legendario gaucho.
4. La zona central de este país es muy fértil y allí está situada la capital.
5. En este país podemos visitar el Aconcagua, el pico más alto de Sudamérica.

¡Qué uvas!

¿Sabía usted que muchas de las uvas que compramos son importadas de Chile? Los vinos chilenos también son famosos.

2 Adivinanzas

Identifiquen cada una de las siguientes referencias:

Santiago	José de San Martín	Evita Perón	Jorge Luis Borges
Buenos Aires	Salvador Allende	Gabriela Mistral	los mapuches
la Patagonia	Juan Perón	el Atacama	los gauchos

Luego, su profesor/a le va a asignar a cada pareja una de las referencias. Escriban una descripción de la referencia y entréguensela (*turn it in*) al profesor/a la profesora.

Ahora la clase se divide en dos equipos. El/La profe le presenta a cada equipo, por turnos, una descripción, y el equipo indica la referencia que le corresponde. Cada respuesta correcta vale dos puntos. El equipo con más puntos gana la competencia.

Encuentro cultural

Artes literarias

Pablo Neruda

Pablo Neruda acepta el Premio Nobel del Presidente de Suecia.

READING STRATEGY

Anticipating Content Through Illustration

1. Examine the illustration. What does it tell you about the content of the **pregunta** that follows?
2. On the basis of the illustration, can you guess the meaning of the words **vuela** and **pájaro**?

Pablo Neruda (1904-1973) es de origen chileno, pero pasó gran parte de su vida adulta en varios países de Asia y Europa. Es una de las figuras más distinguidas de la poesía latinoamericana del siglo XX. Su producción literaria es extensa y excepcional, y le ganó el Premio Nobel de Literatura en 1971. Dejó[1] al morir ocho libros inéditos[2]. Las siguientes selecciones vienen de una de esas obras: *Libro de las preguntas.*

¿Cómo se llama una flor que vuela de pájaro en pájaro?

¿Y por qué el sol es tan mal amigo del caminante en el desierto?

¿Y por qué el sol es tan simpático en el jardín del hospital?

¿Qué cuentan[3] de nuevo las hojas de la reciente primavera?

¿Hay algo más triste en el mundo que un tren inmóvil en la lluvia?

¿Dónde está el niño que yo fui, sigue adentro de mí o se fue?

¿Conversa el humo[4] con las nubes?

[1] *He left behind*
[2] *unpublished*
[3] *tell*
[4] *smoke*

2 Actividades

1. Hagan dibujos (*drawings*) de tres de las preguntas. Luego, compártanlas con otra pareja. ¿Pueden sus compañeros/as identificar las preguntas que corresponden a las ilustraciones? Cambien de papel (*Change roles*).
2. Hablen de sus preguntas favoritas y por qué las prefieren.
3. Escriban dos preguntas originales al estilo de Pablo Neruda. Luego, compártanlas con la clase.

Adjetivo

el mejor

Palabras indefinidas y negativas

algo
alguien
nada
nadie
tampoco

Preposiciones

al + *infinitivo*
al lado de
antes de
cerca de
debajo de
delante de
dentro de
después de
detrás de
en
encima de
enfrente de
entre
en vez de
frente a
fuera de
lejos de
para + *infinitivo*
por
sobre

Sustantivos

En la ciudad

el almacén
el autobús
la avenida
el banco
el bar
el café

la calle
la catedral
el centro comercial
el cine
el edificio
la entrada
la estatua
la gente
la iglesia
la joyería
el lugar
el metro
el museo
las noticias
la obra de teatro
la parada de autobús
el parque
la pastelería
la película
el periódico
la pizzería
la plaza
el quiosco
el rascacielos
la revista
el taxi
el teatro
la zapatería

En el banco

el cajero automático
el cambio
el cheque
el cheque de viajero
la cuenta
el efectivo
la moneda
la tarjeta de crédito

En la oficina de correos

el buzón
la carta
la dirección
la estampilla/ el sello
el paquete
el sobre
la tarjeta postal

Verbos y expresiones verbales

abrir
ahorrar
averiguar
cambiar
cerrar (ie)
cobrar
contar (ue)
contestar
depositar
empezar (ie) (a)
encontrar (ue)
endosar
entrar (en/a)
enviar
esperar
firmar
gastar
invertir (ie, i)
invitar (a)
morir (ue, u)
pagar
pasar
recibir
repetir (i, i)
retirar
terminar

hacer cola/fila

Autoprueba y repaso

I. Prepositions of location. Todas las siguientes oraciones son falsas. Para corregirlas, cambie las preposiciones.

> **Modelo:** El buzón está detrás de la oficina de correos.
> **El buzón está *frente a* la oficina de correos.**

1. La gente está fuera del cine.
2. La catedral está enfrente del banco.
3. La estatua está lejos del centro de la ciudad.
4. En el quiosco, las revistas están debajo de los periódicos.

II. Pronouns with prepositions. Termine las oraciones con los pronombres de preposición correctos.

1. ¿Quieres ir con _____ (*me*)?
2. Lo siento; no puedo ir con _____ (*you, fam., s.*).
3. El pastel es para _____ (*them*).
4. Y, ¿qué tienes para _____ (*us*)?

III. Demonstrative adjectives and pronouns.

A. Indique qué lugares va a visitar usted. Use adjetivos demostrativos según las indicaciones.

> **Modelo:** Voy a visitar el museo. (cerca)
> **Voy a visitar este museo.**

1. Voy a visitar la catedral. (un poco lejos)
2. Voy a visitar el museo. (cerca)
3. Quiero ver las obras de arte. (cerca)
4. Queremos ver los rascacielos. (muy lejos)

B. Conteste con un pronombre demostrativo.

> **Modelo:** ¿Te gusta este almacén?
> **No, prefiero ése.**

1. ¿Te gustan estas tiendas?
2. ¿Te gustan estos zapatos?
3. ¿Te gusta este restaurante?
4. ¿Te gusta esta pizzería?

IV. The preterit of *hacer* and stem-changing verbs. Hoy usted es el/la profe. Usando el pretérito, hágales preguntas a las personas indicadas. Imagine que ellos responden. Escriba las preguntas y las respuestas.

> **Modelo:** repetir las direcciones / Ana
> Profesor/a: **Ana, ¿repitió usted las direcciones?**
> Ana: **Sí, las repetí.**

1. pedir las entradas / Carlos y Felipe
2. preferir la ópera o el ballet / Susana
3. hacer algo interesante en el centro / Linda y Celia
4. divertirse / Linda y Celia
5. dormir bien después de volver del centro / Alberto

V. Indefinite and negative words. Conteste con oraciones negativas.

> **Modelo:** ¿Compró usted algo en el almacén ayer?
> **No, no compré nada.**

1. ¿Alguien fue con usted a Nueva York?
2. ¿Hizo usted algo interesante en el centro?
3. Yo no visité la Zona Cero. ¿Y usted?

VI. General review. Conteste con oraciones completas.
1. ¿A qué hora se abren los bancos en su ciudad? ¿Y los almacenes?
2. ¿Gastó usted mucho dinero en restaurantes el mes pasado? (¿Qué pidió?)
3. Ayer usted fue a un café con sus amigos. ¿Qué pidieron ustedes?
4. ¿Fueron usted y sus amigos al centro el sábado por la noche? (¿Para qué?)
5. ¿Cuántas horas durmió usted anoche?
6. ¿Duerme usted ocho horas casi siempre o casi nunca? (¿Por qué?)
7. ¿Qué hizo usted anoche?
8. ¿Qué hicieron usted y sus amigos el fin de semana pasado?

Answers to the *Autoprueba y repaso* are found in **Apéndice 2.**

De compras

Goals for communication

- To talk about and purchase clothing
- To indicate and emphasize possession
- To talk about actions in the past
- To indicate to or for whom something is done

Así se dice

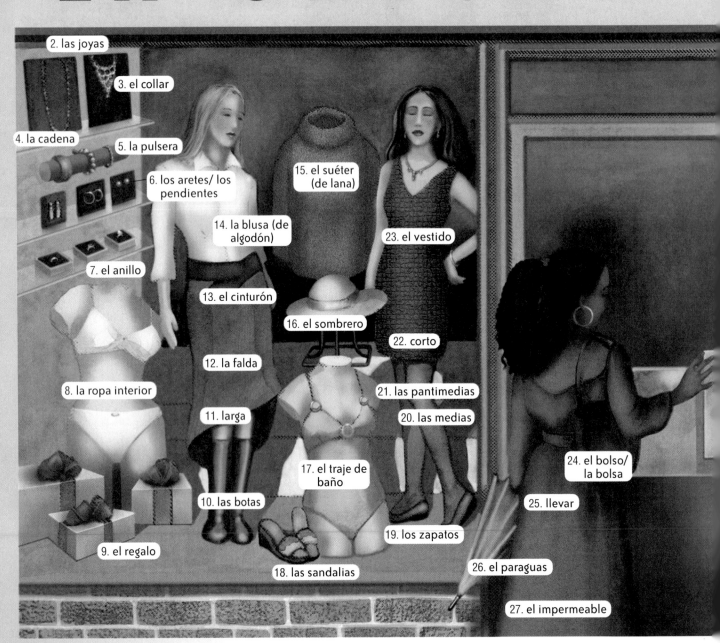

LA ÚNICA ①ROPA

2. las joyas

3. el collar

4. la cadena

5. la pulsera

6. los aretes/ los pendientes

7. el anillo

8. la ropa interior

9. el regalo

10. las botas

11. larga

12. la falda

13. el cinturón

14. la blusa (de algodón)

15. el suéter (de lana)

16. el sombrero

17. el traje de baño

18. las sandalias

19. los zapatos

20. las medias

21. las pantimedias

22. corto

23. el vestido

24. el bolso/ la bolsa

25. llevar

26. el paraguas

27. el impermeable

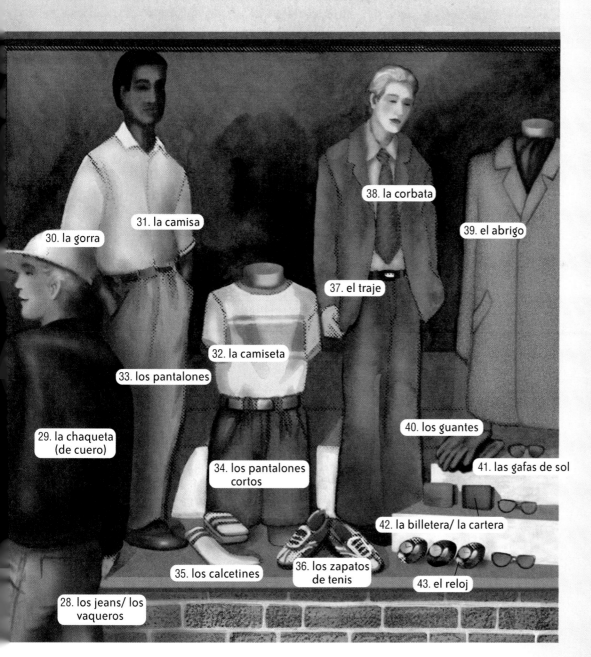

PARA DAMAS Y CABALLEROS

30. la gorra
31. la camisa
38. la corbata
39. el abrigo
37. el traje
32. la camiseta
33. los pantalones
29. la chaqueta (de cuero)
40. los guantes
34. los pantalones cortos
41. las gafas de sol
42. la billetera/ la cartera
35. los calcetines
36. los zapatos de tenis
43. el reloj
28. los jeans/ los vaqueros

1. clothing, clothes
2. jewelry
3. necklace
4. chain
5. bracelet
6. earrings
7. ring
8. underwear
9. gift
10. boots
11. long
12. skirt
13. belt
14. blouse (cotton)
15. sweater (wool)
16. hat
17. bathing suit
18. sandals
19. shoes
20. stockings, hose, socks
21. panty hose
22. short
23. dress
24. purse, bag
25. to wear, carry, take
26. umbrella
27. raincoat
28. jeans
29. jacket (leather)
30. cap
31. shirt
32. T-shirt, undershirt
33. pants
34. shorts
35. socks
36. tennis shoes
37. suit
38. tie
39. coat
40. gloves
41. sunglasses
42. wallet
43. watch

Práctica y comunicación

7-1. **En la tienda de ropa.** Linda y Manuel van de compras a la tienda La Única. Contesten las preguntas según el dibujo de las páginas 236–237.

1. Está lloviendo. ¿Qué tipo de abrigo lleva Linda? ¿Qué más lleva?
2. ¿Qué tipo de joyas se venden en la tienda?
3. ¿Qué lleva el maniquí (*mannequin*) de pelo rubio?
4. ¿Qué ropa lleva el otro maniquí? ¿Qué joyas lleva?
5. ¿Le gusta a usted el suéter de lana de la tienda?
6. Si Linda quiere ir a la playa, ¿qué puede comprar en la tienda?
7. ¿Qué más hay en el escaparate (*shop window*)?
8. ¿Qué tipo de pantalones lleva Manuel? ¿Qué más lleva?
9. ¿Qué lleva el maniquí de pelo negro?
10. ¿Qué ropa lleva el otro maniquí?
11. Manuel se va a la Florida para las vacaciones de primavera. ¿Qué debe comprar?
12. El padre de Manuel se va a Buenos Aires donde ahora están en invierno. ¿Qué debe comprar Manuel para su padre?
13. ¿Qué puede comprar Manuel en la tienda para guardar (*keep*) el dinero? ¿Y para saber la hora?

7-2. **¿Te gusta?** Pregúntele a su compañero/a si (*if*) le gusta alguna de la ropa en el escaparate. Usen los demostrativos y los colores.

> **Modelo:** Estudiante 1: ¿Te gusta *esa/esta* blusa *blanca*?
> Estudiante 2: Sí, me gusta. *o* No, no me gusta.

7-3. **El color perfecto para cada ocasión.** Lean las descripciones que están en la página 239. Luego, contesten las siguientes preguntas.

1. ¿Qué color representa mejor tu personalidad?
2. ¿Qué color representa energía? ¿Calma? ¿Misterio?
3. ¿Qué colores se[1] llevan con frecuencia cuando hace mucho calor? ¿Y cuando hace frío?
4. ¿Qué colores asocias con una persona que frecuentemente está contenta? ¿Y con una persona que está triste?

---
[1] The word **se** placed before the verb slightly alters the meaning of the verb. Here, **se llevan** = *are worn*; **llevan** = *they, you (pl.) wear.*

el color perfecto para cada ocasión

- ROJO. Ideal para buscar trabajo. Se relaciona con el éxito; refleja energía, excitación y pasión.
- NARANJA. Para comunicar mensajes. Te dota de vibras positivas, vitalidad y buen humor.
- AMARILLO. Para un evento alegre (una boda). Es el color del sol y sugiere calidez y optimismo.
- VERDE. Es el color del dinero, llévalo cuando estés en una campaña para reunir fondos.
- AZUL. Ideal para viajar en auto con los niños porque transmite serenidad y calma.
- MORADO. Para fiestas: sugiere que eres misteriosa y creativa.

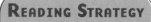

Así se dice

La transformación de Carmen

Carmen nos habla de su pequeña transformación.

Para empezar, fui a visitar al oculista° y como resultado de la visita abandoné mis **gafas**⁽¹⁾ por **lentes de contacto**⁽²⁾, un hecho° que cambió mi vida radicalmente. Ahora me siento° más joven, más **a la moda**⁽³⁾. Luego, organicé mi **ropero**⁽⁴⁾; lavé toda la ropa **sucia**⁽⁵⁾, colgué° toda la **limpia**⁽⁶⁾ y eliminé varias prendas°. Por supuesto, mi amiga Irene y yo vamos a tener que ir de compras. Primero, voy a pensar en las **cosas**⁽⁷⁾ que necesito: unos aretes, un collar y tal vez unos anillos de fantasía° porque de **oro**⁽⁸⁾ o **plata**⁽⁹⁾ son muy **caros**⁽¹⁰⁾. ¡El **precio**⁽¹¹⁾ para una madre de gemelas es siempre importante! También necesito pantalones negros, dos faldas, una blusa **de manga corta**⁽¹²⁾ y otra **de manga larga**⁽¹³⁾. No sé cuánto va a **costar**⁽¹⁴⁾ todo esto, pero Irene me asegura° que hay lugares donde se vende bueno y **barato**⁽¹⁵⁾ y que primero vamos a **mirar**⁽¹⁶⁾ la ropa en todas las tiendas y a comparar precios. ¡Ah! y en cuanto a° la **talla**⁽¹⁷⁾, debo olvidarme° de ese problemita; me voy a poner a dieta y todo va a estar perfecto.

eye doctor (m./f.)

act

me... I feel

hung up / articles of clothing

costume

me... assures me

en... as for, concerning / forget about

(1) *eyeglasses* (2) *contact lenses;* **lente** *(m/f)* (3) *in style* (4) *closet; also* **el clóset** (5) *dirty* (6) *clean* (7) *things* (8) *gold* (9) *silver* (10) *expensive* (11) *price* (12) *short-sleeved* (13) *long-sleeved* (14) *to cost* (**ue**) (15) *inexpensive* (16) *to look at* (17) *size*

② **7-4.** **¡Qué caro es!** Indiquen los precios de los siguientes artículos. Según ustedes, ¿son caros o baratos?

> **Modelo:** Estudiante 1: **El reloj de oro cuesta** $3.450.
>
> Estudiante 2: **¡Es (muy) caro!**

$3.450

1. $25

2. $2.500

3. $6

4. $370

5. $65

6. $36

7. $175

8. $125

② **7-5.** **Un gran contraste.** Describan la ropa que lleva Esteban, comparándola con la ropa que lleva Octavio. Usen las palabras indicadas. (*Watch out for adjective agreement and the correct use of ser and estar.*)

Esteban   Octavio

> sucio / limpio
> nuevo / viejo
> largo / corto
> caro / barato
> ordenado / desordenado

2 **7-6.** **Tú y yo.** Pregúntele a su compañero/a de clase lo siguiente. Túrnense.

> **Modelo:** Pregúntele si... prefiere ropa de algodón o de poliéster
> Estudiante 1: **¿Prefieres ropa de algodón o de poliéster?**
> Estudiante 2: **Prefiero ropa de algodón. ¿Y tú?**

Pregúntele si...

1. prefiere suéteres de lana o de algodón
2. prefiere faldas largas o faldas cortas
3. prefiere llevar camisas de manga larga o de manga corta
4. prefiere llevar zapatos, sandalias o botas
5. lleva impermeable cuando llueve ¿Y paraguas?
6. lleva botas cuando nieva
7. lleva gafas de sol cuando maneja
8. lleva lentes de contacto o gafas
9. va de compras frecuentemente (¿Adónde?)
10. compra regalos con frecuencia (¿Para quién?) (¿Qué tipo de regalos?)
11. compra camisetas de talla pequeña, mediana, grande o extra grande
12. compra ropa interior en la tienda *Victoria's Secret*

3 **7-7.** **¿Qué vamos a llevar?** ¿Qué ropa y accesorios quieren llevar ustedes a los tres lugares indicados? Escriban tres listas.

1. Vamos a **la Patagonia** en el sur de Argentina (cerca de la Antártida) en el invierno. Hace mucho frío.
2. Vamos a visitar las bellas playas de **la República Dominicana** en el verano. Hace mucho calor.
3. Somos representantes de los Estados Unidos y tenemos una invitación oficial para visitar **Las Cortes del gobierno** (*Congress*) en Madrid, España. Es otoño.

Ahora su profesor/a les va a pedir a tres estudiantes que escriban sus listas en la pizarra, una lista cada uno. La clase añade (*adds*) ropa/accesorios.

> The prepositions **por** and **para** each have several meanings in different contexts. You have already studied some. Additional usages are:
> **Para** + *the reference to a person = for + the recipient*
> Esta blusa es **para** mi novia.   *This blouse is **for** my girlfriend.*
> **Por** + *an amount = for, in exchange for*
> Pagué $200 **por** el collar.   *I paid $200 **for** the necklace.*

② **7-8.** **¿Y cuánto gastaste?** Dígale a su amigo/a para quién compró cada regalo y cuánto dinero gastó. Túrnense.

> **Modelo:** Estos guantes son para mi hermana.
> Los compré por $15.

1.
2.
3.
4.
5.
6.
7.
8.

7-9. **Un gran desfile de modas (*A great fashion show*).** Preparen un gran desfile de modas. Varios voluntarios/as desfilan enfrente de la clase mientras que otros/as describen la ropa que llevan. Al final, la clase determina quiénes están más a la moda.

While shopping, one usually looks for, looks at, and sees various items. Observe the differences between the verbs **buscar** (*to look for*), **mirar** (*to look at*), and **ver** (*to see*).

Natalia y Camila…	Natalia and Camila . . .
buscan un regalo para Rubén,	***are looking for*** a gift for Ruben,
miran varias gafas de sol	***look at*** various sunglasses (attentively),
y **ven** las que quieren comprar.	and ***see*** the ones they want to buy.

Escenas

En la tienda de ropa

Camila   Natalia

3 *Natalia y Camila van de compras. Están buscando un regalo para Rubén.*

CAMILA: ¡Mira, Natalia, un almacén nuevo! ¿Por qué no entramos? Allí podemos comprar el regalo de cumpleaños para Rubén.

NATALIA: Está bien, vamos. Pero yo no sé qué comprar. ¿Tienes alguna idea?

CAMILA: No sé... ¿qué tal un suéter y una gorra de lana?

NATALIA: No, a Rubén no le gustan los suéteres; prefiere las camisetas negras. Además él nunca lleva gorras. Dice que dan mucho calor. ¿Sabes que ni siquiera° en invierno lleva calcetines?   *ni... not even*

CAMILA: Es verdad, él adora sus sandalias. ¡Ya sé! Podemos comprarle una camisa de algodón y una corbata.

NATALIA: ¡Camila, por favor! No me puedo imaginar a Rubén con corbata. Él siempre lleva camisetas y dice que detesta las corbatas porque no tienen ninguna función práctica.

CAMILA: Esto es difícil. Vamos a ver... Necesitamos algo práctico, algo que corresponda a la personalidad de Rubén... ¡Ya! ¡Tengo la solución!

NATALIA: A ver°, ¿qué?   *A... Let's see*

CAMILA: Pues, ¡unas gafas de sol! ¿Qué te parece?°   *¿Qué... What do you think?*

NATALIA: Es una excelente idea. Rubén perdió sus gafas favoritas en la playa la semana pasada.

CAMILA: Sí, vamos al departamento de ropa para caballeros.

(Van hasta la sección de «Caballeros».)

DEPENDIENTE: Buenos días. ¿En qué puedo servirles?

CAMILA: Buenos días. Necesitamos unas gafas de sol de buena calidad.

DEPENDIENTE: Tienen suerte°. Tenemos una gran selección y a muy buen precio.   *luck*

(Van hasta un mostrador° lleno de gafas.)   *display case*

NATALIA: Mira, Camila. Esas gafas son muy similares a las de Rubén. *(Al dependiente.)* Señor, ¿están en oferta° esas gafas?   *en... on sale*

DEPENDIENTE: Sí. *(Saca las gafas del mostrador.)* Estas gafas están hechas de plástico reciclado y el precio es excelente. ¡Ah!, y además traen esta camiseta de regalo.

CAMILA: A ver, ¿y qué dice la camiseta?

DEPENDIENTE: «Plasti-gafas: reciclamos para ver mejor el futuro».

CAMILA Y NATALIA: ¡Es el regalo perfecto! ¿Dónde pagamos?

¿Qué pasa?

1. ¿Qué hacen Natalia y Camila?

2. ¿Cuál es la primera idea de Camila para el regalo de Rubén?

3. ¿Por qué no es buena idea comprarle una corbata a Rubén?

4. ¿Qué piensa Natalia acerca de la idea de comprar las gafas de sol?

5. ¿Por qué dice el dependiente que las chicas tienen suerte?

6. ¿Piensa usted que Natalia y Camila están contentas con su compra? ¿Por qué?

Estructuras

① **Emphasizing possession: Possessive adjectives and pronouns**

You have already learned one form of possessive adjectives (**mi, tu, su, nuestro, vuestro, su**). These possessive adjectives have a corresponding form that is used for emphasis.

Es **mi** bolsa.	*It's **my** purse.*
Esa bolsa es **mía**.	*That purse is **mine**.*

The emphatic possessive forms are adjectives that agree in gender (masculine and feminine) and number (singular and plural) with the thing possessed. They follow either a form of the verb **ser** to indicate *mine, yours, . . .* or a noun to indicate *of mine, of yours*, etc.

Esas botas son **mías**.	*Those boots are **mine**.*
Pero un amigo **mío** dice que son **suyas**.	*But a friend **of mine** says that they are **his**.*

Los posesivos enfáticos

mío/a, míos/as	*mine*	Esa chaqueta es **mía**.
tuyo/a, tuyos/as	*yours*	¿Los guantes azules son **tuyos**?
suyo/a, suyos/as	*his*	Pepe dice que esa gorra es **suya**.
	hers	Ana dice que esas botas son **suyas**.
	yours	¿El bolso de cuero es **suyo**?
nuestro/a, nuestros/as	*ours*	Esa casa es **nuestra**
		Esos dos gatos son **nuestros**.
vuestro/a, vuestros/as	*yours*	¿Es **vuestro** ese carro?
		¿Son **vuestras** las bicicletas?
suyo/a, suyos/as	*theirs*	Ana y Tere dicen que esas cosas son **suyas**.

- As with **su/sus** (see p. 74), if the ownership referred to by **suyo/a/os/as** is not clear from the context, you may use an alternate form for clarity.

  Es **su** ropa. *o*   Es la ropa **de**... $\left\{\begin{array}{l}\text{él/ ella/ usted.}\\ \text{ellos/ ellas /ustedes.}\end{array}\right.$

  Esa ropa es **suya**. *o*   Esa ropa es **de**...

- With the addition of the definite articles **el**, **la**, **los**, or **las**, the emphatic possessives become pronouns.

  —Tengo mi suéter. ¿Tienes **el tuyo**?   *I have my sweater. Do you have **yours**?*

  —Sí, tengo **el mío**.   *Yes, I have **mine**.*

Práctica y comunicación

7–10. **En la lavandería (*laundromat*).** Alfonso y Rubén están en la lavandería y usan la misma (*same*) secadora. Ahora cada uno busca su ropa. Conteste las siguientes preguntas según el dibujo.

¿Quién lo dice? ¿Alfonso o Rubén?

1. Esta chaqueta es mía.
2. Este suéter es mío.
3. Estos calcetines son míos.
4. Estas camisetas son mías.

¿De quién es...?

5. Rubén dice que la **chaqueta es**...
6. Rubén dice que las...
7. Alfonso dice que el...
8. Alfonso dice que los...

Alfonso   Rubén

suyo
suya
suyos
suyas

7–11. **¡Un ladrón o una ladrona (*thief*) en la clase!** ¡Cierren los ojos! (El profesor/La profesora camina por la clase «robando» algunos de los artículos de los estudiantes. Los pone sobre su escritorio.) Ahora, abran los ojos y contesten las preguntas del profesor/de la profesora.

Modelo: Profesor/a: Señor/Señorita, ¿es suyo este reloj?

Estudiante: **No, no es mío.**

Profesor/a a la clase: Pues, ¿de quién es?

Un/a estudiante indica: **Es suyo.** *o* **Es de Lisa.**

Noticias culturales

La ropa tradicional

parades

La ropa tradicional de España y de Hispanoamérica es muy variada. En las ciudades, sólo se usa los días de fiesta nacional. En los desfiles° cívicos los niños, jóvenes y adultos se visten con la ropa típica de las diversas regiones de su país y bailan música tradicional. Las compañías nacionales de danza también usan ropa típica. Todo el mundo conoce los trajes típicos del sur de España, gracias a los bailarines de flamenco.

Los indígenas de las zonas rurales de muchos países, por ejemplo, Bolivia, Ecuador, Guatemala y México, usan ropa típica todos los días. En la península de Yucatán en México, las mujeres usan el **huipil**², un vestido blanco de origen maya con un bordado° de flores de colores vivos°. Se distingue la región donde vive la mujer por el diseño del huipil.

embroidery
bright

lace

beads / golden

rope-soled sandals

En el pueblo de Otavalo, en la región andina de Ecuador, las mujeres llevan una falda negra con bordados de colores, una blusa blanca bordada de encajes°, muchos collares y pulseras de cuentas° rojas y doradas° y un turbante en la cabeza. Generalmente, los hombres de esta región llevan un poncho de lana sobre una camisa y pantalones blancos con alpargatas° blancas y un sombrero negro.

---

² The **huipil** can also designate a brightly colored, embroidered blouse.

Las **polleras** de las panameñas son verdaderos tesoros: estos vestidos están decorados con finos encajes y bordados con hilos° de oro. En las regiones costeras, sobre todo en el Caribe, es común ver hombres con **guayaberas**: camisas de telas livianas° y bordadas de colores claros que son perfectas para el clima caliente de la zona.

threads

telas*... light fabrics*

¿Qué recuerda?

1. ¿Cuándo es común ver gente vestida de ropa típica en las ciudades?

2. ¿Por qué conoce todo el mundo los trajes del sur de España?

3. ¿Cómo es el huipil que llevan las mujeres indígenas de Yucatán?

4. ¿Cómo es la ropa de la mujer andina de Otavalo? ¿Y la del hombre?

5. ¿Qué tienen de especial las polleras?

6. ¿Por qué son tan cómodas (*comfortable*) las guayaberas?

¿Según las fotos, puede usted identificar la ropa de la región andina? ¿La pollera panameña? ¿El huipil? Describa cada foto.

Conexiones y contrastes

1. ¿Se lleva ropa tradicional hoy en algunas regiones de su país? ¿Dónde?

2. ¿Puede usted describir un ejemplo de la ropa típica de su país?

 Expressing actions in the past: The preterit of irregular verbs

In **Chapter 6**, you learned the irregular preterit forms of the verb **hacer**. The following verbs also have one consistent preterit stem and the same endings as **hacer**.

Verbos irregulares en el pretérito		
infinitive	*stem +*	*irregular endings*
estar	**estuv-**	estuv**e**, estu**viste**, estuv**o**, estu**vimos**, estu**visteis**, estu**vieron**
tener	tuv-	tuve, tuviste, tuvo, tuvimos, ~~tuvisteis~~, tuvieron
poder	pud-	pude, pudiste, pudo, pudimos, pudisteis, pudieron
poner	pus-	puse, pusiste, puso, pusimos, pusisteis, pusieron
saber	sup-	supe, supiste, supo, supimos, supisteis, supieron
hacer	hic-	hice, hiciste, hizo, hicimos, hicisteis, hicieron
venir	vin-	vine, viniste, vino, vinimos, vinisteis, vinieron
querer	quis-	quise, quisiste, quiso, quisimos, quisisteis, quisieron
traer	**traj-**	traj**e**, traj**iste**, traj**o**, traj**imos**, traj**isteis**, traj**eron**
decir	dij-	dije, dijiste, dijo, dijimos, dijisteis, dijeron

- Notice the difference in the **ellos, ellas, ustedes** endings (**-ieron** and **-eron**) between the two groups of verbs above. Verbs whose stems end in **j** add **-eron** instead of **-ieron**.

- Observe the use of the irregular preterit forms in the sample sentences.

No **tuve** que trabajar anoche.	*I didn't **have** to work last night.*
Algunos amigos **vinieron** a visitarme.	*Some friends **came** to visit me.*
Rubén **trajo** su guitarra.	*Rubén **brought** his guitar.*

- In the preterit, the verbs **saber, querer,** and **poder** convey a slightly different meaning than in the present.

saber	**Supe** hacerlo.	*I **found out**/ **figured out** how to do it.*
querer	**Quise** hablar con ella.	*I **tried** to speak with her.*
no querer	Ella **no quiso** hablar conmigo.	*She **refused** to speak with me.*
poder	**Pude** terminar el proyecto.	*I **succeeded** (after much effort) in finishing the project.*
no poder	**No pude** encontrar al profesor.	*I **failed** (after trying) to find the professor.*

Práctica y comunicación

7-12. **Muchas actividades.** ¿Quiénes participaron en las siguientes actividades? Levanten la mano (*Raise your hand*) y luego contesten la pregunta.

> **Modelo:** Profesor/a: Anoche, ¿quiénes hicieron la tarea para la clase de español? (*Varios estudiantes levantan la mano.*)
> Un/a estudiante responde: **Yo hice la tarea...**/ **Marta y yo hicimos la tarea...**

1. Ayer o anteayer, ¿quiénes hicieron ejercicio en el gimnasio? ¿Por cuánto tiempo?
2. Ayer o anteayer, ¿quiénes fueron de compras? ¿Qué compraron?
3. Anoche, ¿quiénes tuvieron que estudiar mucho? ¿Para qué clases?
4. Anoche, ¿quiénes pudieron salir con sus amigos? ¿Adónde fueron?
5. Esta mañana, ¿quiénes estuvieron en el centro estudiantil? ¿Para qué?
6. ¿Quiénes trajeron comida y/o una bebida a clase hoy? ¿Qué trajeron?

7-13. **Dos amigos conversan.** Completen la conversación entre Ana y Juan. Prepárense para leérsela a la clase.

JUAN: ¿Qué hiciste anoche?

ANA: Tuve que... y... ¿Y tú?

JUAN: ¡Estuve en... cuatro horas!

ANA: Pues, yo quise... anoche, pero no pude... porque... vinieron aquí a las nueve de la noche. Trajeron... y... ¡Lo pasamos muy bien! Esta noche voy a tener que... ¡Ay de mí!

7-14. **Preguntas personales.** Háganse las preguntas.

1. ¿Que hiciste el fin de semana pasado? ¿Te divertiste?
2. ¿Tuviste que estudiar durante el fin de semana? (¿Para qué clases?)
3. ¿Qué cosas quisiste hacer pero no pudiste?
4. ¿Vinieron algunos amigos a visitarte? (¿De dónde?)
5. ¿Dónde estuviste anoche a la medianoche?
6. ¿A qué hora te levantaste esta mañana?
7. ¿Te pusiste calcetines limpios/ropa limpia hoy?
8. ¿A qué hora llegaste a clase? ¿Qué cosas trajiste a la clase?

7–15. Una fiesta para el cumpleaños de Carmen. Según los dibujos, describa lo que pasó antes de y durante la fiesta.

Modelo: Primero, Inés y Camila compraron algunos regalos para Carmen.

1. Inés y Camila / comprar…

2. Inés y Camila / hacer…

3. Ellas poner… / llevarlos…

4. Manuel / traer…

5. En la fiesta, Carmen / abrir… /
Todos le decir… / y comer…

6. A medianoche, Camila e Inés / tener que…

7–16. Un crimen. Un crimen ocurrió en la universidad ayer. Usted es el/la detective e interroga a una de las personas acusadas (su compañero/a de clase). Formule preguntas según el modelo.

Modelo: tener clases / ayer por la tarde

Detective: **¿Tuvo usted clases ayer por la tarde?**

Acusado/a: **Sí, tuve clases.** o **No, no tuve clases.**

1. dónde / estar / ayer entre las cuatro y las seis de la tarde

2. qué / hacer / entre esas horas

3. saber / algo del crimen

4. querer / salir de la universidad al oír la noticia

5. poder / salir de la universidad

6. hablar / con el policía

7. qué / le decir

Ahora, algunos van a defender o a incriminar a la persona que interrogaron:

El señor/La señorita… probablemente cometió/no cometió el crimen porque…

7-17. Mi aventura. Escriba cinco oraciones describiendo una aventura (real o imaginaria). ¿Adónde fue? ¿Cuánto tiempo estuvo allí? ¿Tuvo alguna experiencia interesante? ¿Qué hizo? ¿Hay algo que quiso hacer pero no pudo?

3 Indicating to whom or for whom something is done: Indirect object pronouns

An indirect object identifies the person *to whom* or *for whom* something is done. Thus, this person receives the action of the verb *indirectly*. In English, the *to* or *for* may be stated or implied.

¿Quién te regaló ese suéter tan bonito?

To whom?	*I gave the ring **to her**. / I gave **her** the ring.*
For whom?	*I bought a necklace **for her**. / I bought **her** a necklace.*

In contrast, remember that the direct object indicates *who* or *what* directly receives the action of the verb.

Who(m)?	*I saw **her** yesterday.*
What?	*Did you see **her** ring? She bought **it** at Tiffany's.*

> **HINT** Review the direct object pronouns in **Chapter 5**, p. 187. Remember to ask the questions *Who(m)?* or *What?* to identify the direct object.

The indirect object pronouns are the same forms that you used with the verb **gustar** to indicate *to whom* something is pleasing.

A Carlos **le** gustó mucho el regalo. *Carlos liked the gift very much.*

Formation and use of indirect object pronouns

Pronombres de complemento indirecto		
me	*me (to/for me)*	José **me** dio un reloj.
		Joe gave me a watch (gave a watch to me).
te	*you*	¿**Te** dio un anillo?
le	*you*	Él quiere dar**le** un regalo a usted.
	him	Yo quiero dar**le** un regalo a él.
	her	Quiero dar**le** un regalo a ella también.
nos	*us*	Nuestros amigos **nos** compraron chocolates.
os	*you*	¿**Os** trajeron algo?
les	*you/them*	¿Ellos **les** mandaron tarjetas postales **a ustedes**?

- The indirect object pronoun, like the direct object pronoun and reflexive pronoun, is placed immediately before a conjugated verb, but may be attached to the infinitive and to the present participle.

    Me dijeron que esa tienda es muy buena. ¿Quieres entrar?

    ¿Vas a comprar**me** esa cartera? / ¿**Me** vas a comprar esa cartera?

    Estoy preguntándo**le** el precio. / **Le** estoy preguntando el precio.

- It is common to use an indirect object *noun in conjunction with* the third-person pronouns **le** and **les**.

    Les escribí a mis primos.   *I wrote to my cousins.*

    También **le** escribí a Mónica.   *I wrote to Monica too.*

- **Le** and **les** are often clarified with the preposition **a** + *pronoun*.

    Le escribí a ella anoche.   *I wrote to her last night.*

- For emphasis, it is common to use the forms **a mí, a ti, a usted, a él, a ella, a nosotros/as, a vosotros/as, a ustedes, a ellos, a ellas** with the indirect object pronoun.

    Sancho **me** mandó el paquete **a mí**.   *Sancho sent the package to me.*
                                           (not to someone else)

Verbs that frequently require indirect object pronouns

The verb **dar** is almost always used with indirect objects. Review its present tense conjugation and study the preterit. Note that in the preterit **dar** uses **-er/-ir** endings but with no written accent.

dar *to give*	
Presente	**Pretérito**
doy	di
das	diste
da	dio
damos	dimos
dais	disteis
dan	dieron

Indirect objects are also frequently used with the following verbs, as one generally sends, shows, lends, etc. things *to someone.*

contar (ue) *to tell, narrate*   **mandar, enviar** *to send*
  (a story or incident)   **mostrar (ue)** *to show*
decir (i) *to say, tell*   **pedir (i, i)** *to ask for, request*
devolver (ue) *to return (something)*   **preguntar/ contestar** *to ask/answer*
escribir *to write*   **prestar** *to lend*
explicar *to explain*   **regalar** *to give (as a gift)*

Práctica y comunicación

7-18. ¿Qué hice yo o qué voy a hacer? Relacione las declaraciones de la columna A con las actividades correspondientes de la columna B. Lea las oraciones relacionadas.

A

___ **1.** Mi abuela siempre quiere saber lo que estoy haciendo en la universidad.

___ **2.** Es el cumpleaños de mi madre.

___ **3.** Fui de compras ayer y me compré unos pantalones, una chaqueta y zapatos.

___ **4.** Mi amiga Natalia no tiene transporte y necesita ir al centro.

___ **5.** Quiero ir al restaurante Cuba-Cuba esta noche, pero no sé dónde está.

___ **6.** Mi compañero/a de cuarto quiso saber lo que pasó anoche.

___ **7.** Alicia no entendió el *Panorama cultural*.

___ **8.** Camila siempre tiene problemas con las matemáticas.

___ **9.** Rubén va a tocar en un concierto este fin de semana.

B

a. Voy a prestarle mi carro.

b. Le di una de mis calculadoras.

c. Le voy a pedir la dirección a la profesora.

d. Le conté toda la historia (*story*).

e. Le mostré las cosas nuevas a mi amigo.

f. Voy a escribirle una carta larga.

g. Le mandé un regalo.

h. Voy a devolverle la guitarra que me prestó.

i. Le expliqué algunas de las ideas más importantes.

7-19. El regalo de cumpleaños de Linda. Completen las oraciones. Usen el pronombre **lo** (directo) o **le** (indirecto) según la situación.

1. Manuel _____ dio un regalo a Linda para su cumpleaños.

2. _____ compró un suéter muy bonito. Me dijo que _____ compró en una tienda muy elegante.

3. Linda _____ abrió inmediatamente y _____ dio las gracias a Manuel. ¡Es evidente que _____ gustó mucho el suéter!

¡Qué dilema! *Tu novio/a te da un regalo. Lo abres y descubres que es... ¡una camisa/blusa rosada que detestas! ¿Qué le dices?* **Mi amor,...**

② **7-20.** **Preguntas personales.** Háganse las preguntas.

> **Modelo:** ¿Les mandas tarjetas de cumpleaños a tus padres?
>
> **Sí, les mando tarjetas de cumpleaños.** *o* No, no les mando tarjetas de cumpleaños.

Generalmente...

1. ¿Le pides dinero a tu padre/ madre/ tío/ tía?
2. ¿Les muestras tus notas a tus padres/ amigos?
3. ¿Les mandas mensajes electónicos a tus amigos? (Cuando ellos te mandan mensajes, ¿respondes inmediatamente?)
4. ¿Le prestas ropa a tu compañero/a de cuarto o a tu mejor amigo/a? ¿Por qué sí o por qué no?
5. ¿Le cuentas todos los detalles de tu vida personal a tu mejor amigo/a ? ¿Por qué sí o por qué no?

En el pasado...

6. ¿Les enviaste tarjetas postales a tus amigos y amigas el verano pasado? (¿De dónde?)
7. ¿Le regalaste algo a tu novio/a o mejor amigo/a para su cumpleaños? (¿Qué le regalaste?)
8. Al entrar en el aula hoy, ¿le dijiste «Buenos días» o «Buenas tardes» a la profesora/al profesor?
9. ¿Le preguntaste a la profesora/al profesor si hay tarea para mañana? (¿Qué dijo?)

② **7-21.** **Mis personas favoritas.** Dígale a un/a compañero/a de clase lo que hace su mejor amigo/a o lo que hacen algunos de sus parientes favoritos. Combinen la información presentada en las columnas A, B y C. Usen el tiempo presente.

> **Modelo:** **Mi mejor amigo/a con frecuencia me manda mensajes electrónicos.**

A	B	C	
¿quién?	¿cuándo?	¿qué?	
mi mejor amigo/a	a veces	darme...	hablarme de...
mi madre/padre	con frecuencia	regalarme...	prestarme...
mi hermano/a	(casi) siempre	enviarme...	
mi tío/a	(casi) nunca	mandarme...	
mi abuelo/a		escribirme...	
mi primo/a		preguntarme si (*if*)...	

Luego, algunos estudiantes presentan ejemplos a la clase.

Estructuras

4 **Answering *Who?*, *What?*, and *To/For whom?*: Direct and indirect object pronouns combined**

¿Quién nos mandó las flores?

¡Manuel me las mandó!

¿Pepe? ¿Octavio? ¿Ruben?

Review the direct and indirect object pronouns listed below.

Pronombres de complemento	
directo	**indirecto**
me	me
te	te
lo	le
la	
nos	nos
os	os
los	les
las	

- When a verb takes both an indirect and a direct object pronoun, the indirect object pronoun always comes first: indirect + direct.

    La profesora **me lo** prestó.   *The professor lent **it to me**.*

- Direct and indirect object pronouns used in combination follow the same rules for placement as single object pronouns: before conjugated verbs or attached to infinitives and the **-ndo** form. In a negative statement, **no** precedes both objects.

    Pedro no **me lo** explicó.   *Pedro did not explain **it to me**.*

    Carlos va a explicár**melo**³. *o*   *Charles is going to explain **it to me**.*
    Carlos **me lo** va a explicar.

    Carlos está explicándo**melo**. *o*   *Charles is explaining **it to me**.*
    Carlos **me lo** está explicando.

---

³ Note that when two pronouns are added to the infinitive or present participle, a written accent is added to preserve the original stress pattern: **Va a mostrármelo. Está mostrándoselo.**

De compras   doscientos cincuenta y cinco   **255**

- When both the indirect and direct object pronouns refer to the third person and they are used together, the indirect object pronoun **le** or **les** changes to **se**.

$$
\text{le } (or) \text{ les } + \begin{cases} \text{lo} \\ \text{la} \\ \text{los} \\ \text{las} \end{cases} = \begin{array}{l} \text{se lo} \\ \text{se la} \\ \text{se los} \\ \text{se las} \end{array}
$$

—¿Le diste **la foto** a Linda?   *Did you give the photo to Linda?*

—Sí, **se la** di.   *Yes, I gave it to her.*

Práctica y comunicación

7-22. **¡Nos encantan los regalos!** Octavio fue a Ecuador y les trajo varios regalos a sus amigas. Estudien los dibujos para ver qué regalos trajo y para quién.

1. Natalia / la camiseta   **2.** Pepita / el póster   **3.** Carmen e Inés / las toallas para la playa   **4.** Camila y Linda / los collares y los pendientes

Según los dibujos, ¿quién dice lo siguiente? ¿Y de qué habla? Preste atención a los pronombres de complemento directo e indirecto.

1. ¡Impresionante! Octavio me lo regaló. **Pepita lo dice. Habla del...**
2. ¡Nos encantan! Octavio nos las regaló. ... e ... lo dicen. Hablan de...
3. ¡Qué bonitos son! Octavio nos los regaló.
4. ¡Me encanta! Octavio me la regaló.

Ahora, digan qué regalo le dio Octavio a cada persona. Luego repitan la oración sustituyendo el objeto por un pronombre.

Modelo: Octavio le dio la camiseta a Natalia.

Octavio *se la* dio a Natalia.

7-23. **¿Son generosos o no?** Háganse preguntas.

> **Modelo:** prestarme... tu chaqueta
>
> **¿Me prestas tu chaqueta?**
>
> **Sí, te la presto.** *o* **No, prefiero no prestártela.**

1. prestarme...
tu tarjeta de crédito
tu bicicleta
tu paraguas
tu coche
cincuenta dólares

2. explicarme...
la tarea
los verbos irregulares
la gramática
el ejercicio del cuaderno
las palabras que no entiendo

3. darme...
ese reloj/ ese anillo
esa cadena
ese suéter
tu tarjeta de crédito
diez dólares

4. mostrarme...
tu tarea
tu reloj
tu anillo
las fotos de tu cartera
la revista que compraste

7-24. **Estudiantes generosos.** Cada estudiante le da a un/a compañero/a de clase un artículo (reloj, tarjeta de crédito, gorra, bolígrafo, etc.). Luego, la persona que recibe «el regalo» lo pone encima de su pupitre. Conteste las preguntas de la profesora/del profesor.

> **Modelo:** Susana, ¿quién le dio a usted esa chaqueta?
>
> **Carlos me la dio.**

Ahora, usando los mismos artículos, los estudiantes caminan por la clase, haciéndoles preguntas a cinco o seis estudiantes diferentes.

> **Modelo:** Estudiante 1: **Melvin, ¿quién te dio ese reloj?**
>
> Estudiante 2: **Carla me lo dio.**

Al final, devuélvale el artículo a su compañero/a de clase, por favor.

7-25. **Un/a estudiante desafortunado/a.** Un/a estudiante se sienta (*sits*) frente a la clase y pretende que perdió todas sus cosas en un robo. Ustedes, como son generosos, quieren darle algunas cosas. ¿Hay voluntarios?

> **Modelo:** Profesor/a: ¿Quién quiere darle algo?
>
> Estudiante generoso/a: **Quiero darle mi libro de español.**

Ahora, ya que (*Nombre de estudiante*) tiene tantas cosas, contesten las preguntas para indicar quiénes se las dieron. Respondan según el modelo.

> **Modelo:** ¿Quién le dio este libro de español a...?
>
> Estudiante generoso/a: **Yo se lo di.**
>
> Profesor/a: ¿Verdad, clase?
>
> Clase: **Sí, ... se lo dio.**

Dicho y hecho

Conversando

El equipaje perdido (*Lost luggage*). Imaginen que están en el aeropuerto Mariscal Sucre en Quito, Ecuador. Los oficiales de la línea aérea les dicen que el equipaje del grupo no llegó, y que probablemente ¡está perdido! Ustedes van a estar en Ecuador por una semana, visitando las zonas montañosas y la costa. Ahora ustedes necesitan ir de compras para poder continuar su viaje (*trip*). La línea aérea es muy generosa y les da $175 a cada uno/a. (El dólar es la moneda de Ecuador.)

Vayan de compras a las siguientes tiendas. Cada tienda tiene dos dependientes/ dependientas (estudiantes de la clase).

- Mi Comisariato (venden productos de higiene personal)
- Zapatería Cotopaxi
- Beatriz (ropa para mujeres)
- El Ecuatoriano (ropa para hombres)
- La Esmeralda (tienda unisex)

Hagan una lista de sus compras y lo que pagan. No deben gastar más de $175. ¡Es buena idea regatear (*bargain*)! Al final, compartan su lista con un/a compañero/a de clase. ¿Quién tuvo más éxito (*success*) en sus compras?

¡A escuchar!

Desfile de modas: Temporada otoño-invierno. Escuche la descripción del desfile de modas. Preste atención a los tres tipos de ropa que se presentan y a los colores que predominan. Luego, conteste las tres primeras preguntas.

1. ¿Qué tipo de ropa presentan primero?
   - ❐ ropa para la mujer profesional
   - ❐ ropa informal
   - ❐ ropa para reuniones de cóctel

2. ¿Qué tipo de colores son populares en la ropa de Ana Sastre? (Hay más de una opción.)
   - ❐ blanco, negro y gris
   - ❐ rojo, amarillo y azul
   - ❐ verde pistacho

3. ¿Llevan las modelos muchas joyas?

❐ sí

❐ no

Escuche otra vez. Apunte el nombre de la prenda o accesorio que combine bien con la ropa o los accesorios indicados.

4. Los pantalones de cuero negro combinan con _____.

5. Las chaquetas de lana de cachemir combinan con _____.

6. Los zapatos de la colección Sastre combinan con _____.

7. Los vestidos cortos de seda (*silk*) combinan con _____.

De mi escritorio

Mi ropero. Escriba una descripción de su ropa.

Incluya:

- cuál es su ropa favorita y cómo expresa su personalidad
- dónde compra usted generalmente su ropa
- sus accesorios favoritos y por qué le gustan
- la ropa o los accesorios que alguien le regaló a usted

Panorama cultural

COLOMBIA
VENEZUELA
GUYANA
SURINAM

80°

0° ECUADOR
Quito
ECUADOR
▲ Pico Chimborazo
Guayaquil

5°

BRASIL

PERÚ

10°

Callao• •Lima

▲ Machu Picchu
•Cuzco

15°

OCÉANO

PACÍFICO

Lago
Titicaca
✪ La Paz   BOLIVIA

20°

✪ Sucre

Nacionalidades:
peruano(a)
boliviano(a)
ecuatoriano(a)

| 0 | 150 | 300 Millas |

| 0 | 150 | 300 Kilómetros |

80°   75°

CHILE   ARGENTINA   PARAGUAY

ISLAS GALÁPAGOS

Dictaduras generosas.
Los emperadores incas fueron benevolentes. Bajo su gobierno nadie tuvo hambre o estuvo sin ropa.

Preguntas sobre el mapa

1. ¿Cuál es la capital de Ecuador? ¿Dónde está situada?
2. ¿Cuál es una ciudad importante en la costa de Ecuador?
3. ¿Cuál es la capital de Perú? ¿Dónde está situada? ¿Cuál es un puerto importante que está muy cerca de la capital?
4. ¿Cómo se llaman las ruinas incas cerca de Cuzco, Perú?
5. ¿Cuál es el lago que está en la frontera entre Perú y Bolivia?
6. ¿Con qué países tiene frontera Bolivia? ¿Cuáles son las capitales de Bolivia?

El gran imperio inca

Ecuador, Perú y Bolivia, situados en el corazón[1] de los Andes, formaron el imperio inca. Este imperio se llamó Tahuantinsuyo. Con una extensión de 3.000 millas de norte a sur, la zona contiene espectaculares picos nevados, impresionantes volcanes y el inmenso lago Titicaca.

¿Peines de oro?

La nobleza (*nobility*) incaica con frecuencia usó utensilios e instrumentos de oro, como los peines y los cuchillos (*knives*).

[1]*heart*
[2]*cattail plant*
[3]*advances* [4]*livestock*
[5]**bultos**... *bundles of cloth*
[6]*weigh* [7]*bodies* [8]*dead*

En la frontera entre Bolivia y Perú, a 12.506 pies de altura, está el lago Titicaca. En la parte boliviana del lago está la Isla del Sol. Una leyenda dice que el primer inca salió de esta isla para fundar Cuzco, la capital del imperio. El Titicaca es el lago más grande de Sudamérica (122 millas cuadradas) y el lago navegable más alto del mundo. ¿Le gustaría a usted cruzar el lago en una canoa de totora[2]?

En 1999, en las afueras de Lima, Perú, se descubrió un cementerio inca con una extensión aproximada de 20 acres. Esta zona se conoce con el nombre de Puruchuco-Huaquerones. Hasta el momento más de 2.200 momias en bultos de tela[5] han sido exhumadas de este sitio arqueológico. Dichos bultos pueden llegar a pesar[6] hasta 500 libras y contienen cuerpos[7] más los artefactos que los difuntos[8] usaron en vida. ¿Le gustaría a usted explorar un sitio arqueológico como éste? ¿Por qué?

Además de sus adelantos[3] en la arquitectura, la ingeniería y la medicina, los incas perfeccionaron el cultivo de la patata y el cuidado del ganado[4] de los Andes, como las llamas, alpacas y vicuñas. Muchos indígenas continúan llevando el traje típico de los indios andinos: sarapes, ponchos y sombreros hechos de lana de vicuña o alpaca. ¿Puede usted identificar este animal de la región andina de Perú?

Perú

Perú es el tercer país más grande de Sudamérica y tiene tres zonas geográficas distintas. La costa árida del Pacífico (donde están Lima y el puerto principal, El Callao) es la región más dinámica del país. El área andina, con montañas muy elevadas, domina la geografía del país. La influencia indígena en Perú es muy marcada. Las lenguas oficiales son el español y el quechua, idioma inca.

Cerca de Cuzco, Perú, a más de 8.000 pies de altura, los incas construyeron la ciudad de Machu Picchu. Esta ciudad, perdida por siglos, refleja el alto nivel de tecnología del imperio inca. Tuvo más de 10 millones de habitantes antes de la conquista. ¿Qué le impresiona a usted de esta vista de Machu Picchu?

Al este del país está la fascinante selva amazónica. ¿Qué colores predominan en la escena?

Esta calle en Cuzco muestra la fusión de la cultura indígena y la española. ¿Quiénes construyeron el muro de piedra[9]? ¿Y la parte superior del edificio?

¿Qué le impresiona a usted de esta escena de la Cordillera Blanca, en Perú?

Person@je del momento

¿Sabe usted quién es Mario Vargas Llosa? Busque información en el Internet y compártala con sus compañeros/as de clase.

¿Sabía usted que...?

- En 1532 Francisco Pizarro y sus soldados llegaron a Perú en busca de oro.
- Con caballos y armas de fuego, que los incas nunca habían visto[10], los españoles capturaron al último emperador inca, Atahualpa, y conquistaron la región.
- En este período se estableció el virreinato, y Lima se convirtió en el centro colonial más importante de Sudamérica.
- Después de su independencia en 1824, Perú tuvo numerosos conflictos internos y con países vecinos.
- Hoy Perú es un país democrático que lucha por resolver sus problemas económicos.

[9]muro... *stone wall*   [10]habían... *had seen*

Ecuador

Ecuador es un país pequeño de grandes contrastes geográficos. En sus costas cálidas y secas existen excelentes playas. En la región oriental está la zona amazónica, donde el clima es caliente y húmedo y existe una gran variedad de vegetación y fauna. El área andina, con impresionantes volcanes, tiene un clima frío y seco.

¿Tiene usted interés en visitar el Chimborazo, el volcán más alto de Ecuador? ¿Por qué?

Una rosa para ti.

Muchas de las flores y plantas que se venden en las florerías en los EE.UU. y en Europa vienen de Ecuador.

En las Islas Galápagos, un verdadero tesoro ecológico a 600 millas de la costa ecuatoriana, coexisten especies de reptiles, aves[11] y plantas únicas en el mundo. Las tortugas[12] de las Galápagos, Ecuador, pueden vivir un año sin comer y pueden pesar 500 libras y vivir por 100 años.

Quito, la capital de Ecuador, tiene una zona antigua de gran belleza con numerosos ejemplos de arte y de arquitectura coloniales. Por eso muchos la llaman «la cara de Dios». Situada en un valle andino, contempla desde su altura horizontes increíblemente bellos. Describa la foto de la Plaza de la Independencia en Quito.

¿Sabía usted que...?

- La línea ecuatorial que pasa por el norte de Quito le dio su nombre al país.
- En 1535 se descubrieron las Islas Galápagos.
- El 10 de agosto de 1809 se dio en Quito el primer grito[13] de independencia de América Latina.
- En 1822, después de la batalla de Pichincha, Ecuador se independizó de España y se incorporó a la Gran Colombia. En 1830 se convirtió en república independiente.
- En 1997 Ecuador firmó una serie de tratados con Perú para poner fin a los conflictos fronterizos que empezaron durante la época de la independencia.

[11]*birds*   [12]*turtles*   [13]*call, cry*

Bolivia

¿Sabía usted que...?

- El nombre de este país es un homenaje a Simón Bolívar, el héroe sudamericano de las guerras de independencia.
- Bolivia fue parte de Perú durante casi toda la época colonial.
- Las minas de plata de Potosí fueron la atracción principal para los españoles. ¡En tiempos coloniales Potosí fue la ciudad más poblada de América!
- Bolivia se independizó en 1825, pero poco después tuvo varias guerras con países vecinos. En una guerra con Chile perdió su única salida al mar.

Sucre es la capital constitucional de Bolivia. La Paz, la capital congresional, es el verdadero centro administrativo del gobierno y, a 12.725 pies de altura, es famosa por ser la ciudad más alta del mundo. Mencione algunos aspectos interesantes de esta fotografía de La Paz.

Bomberos (firemen) aburridos.
La Paz, Bolivia es una ciudad donde hay muy pocos incendios (fires). Debido a la altura y al poco oxígeno, es muy difícil encender (start) y mantener un fuego.

¿Qué descubrimos?

1. ¿Cuál es el único país andino sin un puerto marítimo?
2. ¿Dónde es posible encontrar especies de animales y plantas únicas en el mundo?
3. ¿Dónde se encuentra el lago Titicaca?
4. ¿A qué país llegaron primero Francisco Pizarro y sus soldados?
5. ¿Cuál es el país andino con dos capitales? ¿Cuáles son?
6. ¿Cuáles son dos ejemplos del ganado de los Andes?
7. ¿En qué país está Machu Picchu? ¿Quiénes la construyeron?
8. ¿Qué línea pasa por el norte de la capital de Ecuador?

② Adivinanzas

Escriban una breve descripción de cada una de las siguientes referencias:

el imperio inca	Cuzco	Quito
el lago Titicaca	Francisco Pizarro	Islas Galápagos
Puruchuco-Huaquerones	Atahualpa	La Paz
Machu Picchu	Lima	Simón Bolívar

Ahora, la clase se divide en dos equipos. El/La profe le presenta a cada equipo, por turnos, una referencia, y el equipo la describe. ¡No se permite usar las descripciones escritas! Cada respuesta correcta vale dos puntos. El equipo con más puntos gana la competencia.

Encuentro cultural

Artes ornamentales

El oro de la cultura lambayeque

La cultura lambayeque se desarrolló[1] en la costa norte de Perú entre los años 900 y 1100-1200 d. C. Se cree[2] que los lambayeque convivieron[3] con los chimús e incas. Hacia los años 1940[4] se encontraron los grandes entierros[5] de esta cultura en Batán Grande, su capital.

Los lambayeque creían en otra vida después de la muerte[6]. Por eso, enterraban a los caciques[7], máxima autoridad de esa época, con todas sus posesiones para llevarlas a la otra vida. En los entierros de los caciques se encontraron grandes piezas[8] de oro y ornamentos que cubrían[9] al muerto. Las piezas fotografiadas son de esos entierros.

[1]*se... developed* [2]*Se... It is believed* [3]*coexisted* [4]**Hacia...** *around the 1940s* [5]*burial sites* [6]*death* [7]*chiefs* [8]*pieces* [9]*covered* [10]*copper* [11]**con...** *sharp edge*

Los collares de oro y crisocola (turquesa peruana) del monarca lo acompañaban también en su entierro. Créditos: Museo Oro del Perú, Fundación Miguel Mujica Gallo. Lima, Perú.

La máscara funeraria fue utilizada en ritos ceremoniales y también cubría la cara del muerto en los entierros. Créditos: Museo Oro del Perú, Fundación Miguel Mujica Gallo. Lima, Perú.

El tumi o cuchillo ceremonial de oro y crisocola fue utilizado en ritos ceremoniales. Los tumis de cobre[10] con filo[11] se utilizaron para cortar o para hacer sacrificios rituales. Créditos: Museo Oro del Perú, Fundación Miguel Mujica Gallo. Lima, Perú.

Preguntas

1. ¿Dónde se encuentran las ruinas de la ciudad precolombina Batán Grande?
2. ¿Qué objetos se encuentran en las tumbas de los caciques?
3. En su opinión, ¿cuál es el uso más interesante de la máscara funeraria? ¿Y del tumi?

Adjetivos

barato/a
caro/a
corto/a
largo/a
limpio/a
sucio/a

Sustantivos

La ropa

a la moda
el abrigo
la blusa
de manga corta/larga
las botas
los calcetines
la camisa
la camiseta
la chaqueta
el cinturón
la corbata
la falda
la gorra
los guantes
el impermeable
los jeans/ los vaqueros
las medias
las pantimedias
los pantalones
los pantalones cortos
la ropa interior
las sandalias
el sombrero
el suéter
el traje
el traje de baño
el vestido
los zapatos
los zapatos de tenis

el algodón
el cuero
la lana

Las joyas

de oro/ plata
el anillo
los aretes/ los pendientes
la cadena
el collar
la pulsera
el reloj

Otras palabras útiles

la billetera/ la cartera
el bolso/ la bolsa
la cosa
las gafas
las gafas de sol
los/las lentes de contacto
el paraguas
el precio
el regalo
el ropero/ el clóset
la talla

Verbos

contar (ue)
dar
devolver (ue)
explicar
llevar
mirar
mostrar (ue)
preguntar
prestar
regalar

I. Possessive adjectives and pronouns.

A. Usted y sus amigos tienen su ropa en la residencia estudiantil. Indique de quién es la ropa.

> **Modelo:** yo: calcetines, impermeable, chaqueta
> **Los calcetines son míos. El impermeable es mío.**
> **La chaqueta es mía.**

1. yo: abrigo, botas, guantes, gorra
2. nosotros: ropa interior, jeans, corbatas
3. tú: blusa, vestido, camiseta, medias
4. Ana y Elena: ropa de verano, faldas, trajes de baño

B. Indique con quiénes van las personas a la fiesta. Siga el modelo.

> **Modelo:** yo / un amigo
> **Voy con un amigo mío.**

1. mi primo / unos amigos
2. Viviana / un amigo
3. mi hermana y yo / un amigo
4. yo / unos amigos

II. The preterit of irregular verbs. Diga quién hizo las siguientes cosas.

> **Modelo:** hacer la torta para la fiesta (yo)
> **Hice la torta para la fiesta.**

1. traer las decoraciones (Natalia y Linda)
2. poner las flores en la mesa (nosotros)
3. querer venir pero no poder (Javier)
4. venir (casi todos los estudiantes)
5. estar en la fiesta por cuatro horas (tú)
6. tener que salir temprano (yo)

III. Indirect object pronouns. ¿Qué hizo el generoso tío Pedro?

> **Modelo:** a mí / comprar / una chaqueta nueva
> **Me compró una chaqueta nueva.**

1. a mí / dar / su reloj
2. a mi hermana / regalar / un bolso de cuero
3. a mis hermanos / comprar / una computadora nueva
4. a nosotros / mandar / tarjetas postales del Perú
5. a ti / prestar / su cámara

IV. Direct and indirect object pronouns combined.
Forme oraciones en el pasado usando el verbo **regalar** y pronombres de complemento directo e indirecto.

> **Modelo:** yo / unas gafas de sol / a Luisa
> **Se las regalé.**

1. nosotros / un televisor pequeño / a los abuelos
2. mi hermano / una mochila nueva / a su prima
3. mis hermanas / joyas / a mamá
4. yo / una chaqueta de cuero / a mi hermano
5. mi madre / un perrito / a nosotras

V. General review. Conteste con oraciones completas.

1. ¿Qué ropa llevan las mujeres a un restaurante elegante? ¿Y los hombres?
2. ¿Qué ropa debe usted llevar a Alaska? ¿Y a la Florida?
3. ¿Fue usted de compras el fin de semana pasado? (¿Adónde?) (¿Qué compró?)
4. ¿Dónde estuvo usted anoche? ¿Y qué hizo? (Mencione varias cosas.)
5. ¿Qué trajo usted a clase hoy/ ayer/ anteayer?
6. ¿Le dio usted la tarea para hoy a la profesora/al profesor?

Answers to the *Autoprueba y repaso* are found in **Apéndice 2**.

Capítulo 8

La salud

Goals for communication

- To talk about health and related ailments
- To identify parts of the body
- To use commands in formal situations
- To talk about and describe persons, places, and actions in the past
- To indicate how long an action has been going on or how long ago it happened

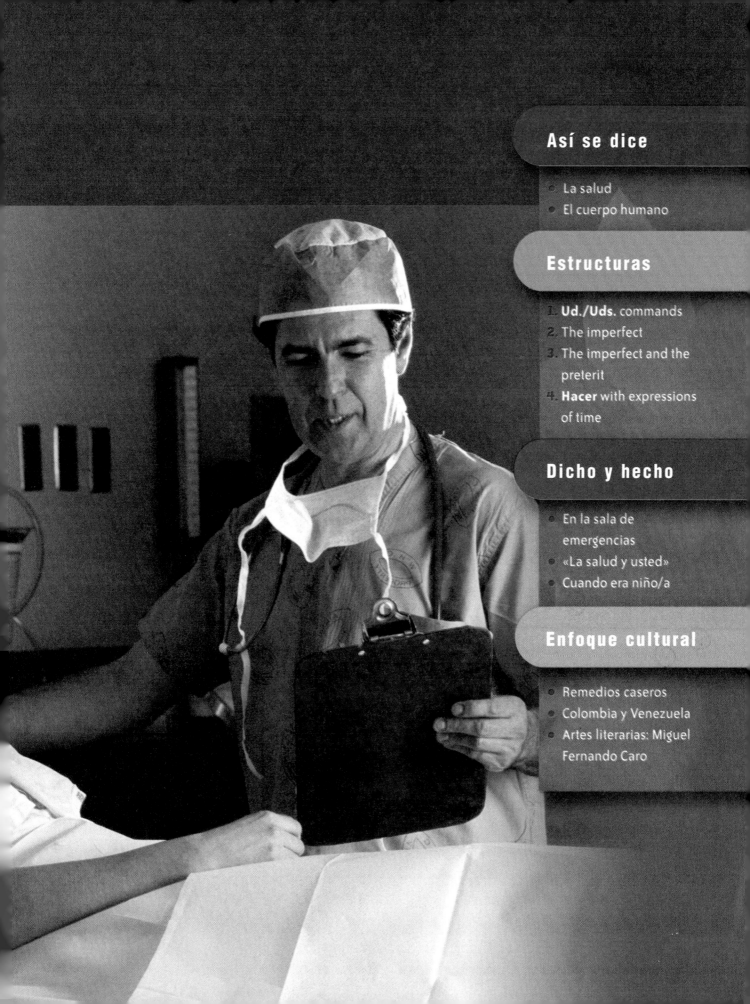

Así se dice

La salud

13. el pulmón
12. el corazón
11. el estómago

2

14. tomar la temperatura
15. el termómetro
16. tomar la presión arterial/ el pulso
10. poner una inyección/ una vacuna

18. ¿Te duele?

3

HORAS DE VISITA
10:00 A.M.–12:00 P.M.
4:00 P.M.–7:00 P.M.

17. sacar sangre/ hacer un análisis de sangre

19. la habitación
20. quedarse

Cuatro días más.

21. preocuparse (por)
26. estar de pie
25. enfermarse
22. sentarse
24. la cama
23. estar sentado/a

1

1. la sala de espera
7. examinar
8. el hueso
9. sacar una radiografía
6. lastimarse (el brazo)
5. el consultorio de la médica

← **Radiología**

2. la recepción
3. hacer una cita
4. estar embarazada

Hospital San Rafael

Emergencias

37

36 AMBULANCIA

35. los paramédicos

34. el/la paciente

una herida grave (en la cabeza)

28. la venda

9. el yeso

30. fracturarse el brazo/ la pierna

31. la silla de ruedas

32. las muletas

33. torcerse el tobillo

1. waiting room
2. reception, front desk
3. to make an appointment
4. to be pregnant
5. doctor's office
6. to hurt oneself (one's arm)
7. to examine
8. bone
9. to x-ray
10. to give a shot/vaccination
11. stomach
12. heart
13. lung
14. to take one's temperature
15. thermometer
16. to take one's blood pressure/pulse
17. to draw blood/do a blood test
18. Does it hurt?; **doler (ue)** to hurt
19. room
20. to stay
21. to worry (about)
22. to sit down
23. to be seated
24. bed
25. to get/become sick
26. to be standing
27. a serious wound (in the head)
28. bandage
29. cast
30. to break one's arm/leg
31. wheelchair
32. crutches
33. to sprain one's ankle
34. patient
35. paramedics
36. ambulance
37. emergency

Práctica y comunicación

8-1. **En el hospital.** Contesten las preguntas según los dibujos de las páginas 270–271. Túrnense.

1. ¿Cómo se llama el hospital?
2. ¿Cuántas personas están en la sala de espera?
3. Nancy y el profesor Marín-Vivar están en la recepción. ¿En qué condición está ella? ¿Qué hace?
4. En el consultorio nº 1, ¿qué problema tiene el paciente? ¿Qué hace la doctora?
5. ¿Por qué hay una radiografía en el consultorio nº 1? Según la radiografía, ¿hay una fractura en el hueso?
6. ¿Qué hace el enfermero en el consultorio nº 2? ¿Qué usa para tomarle la temperatura a la paciente?
7. ¿Cree usted que el enfermero le va a poner una inyección a la paciente?
8. ¿Qué muestra el cuadro anatómico en la pared?
9. En el consultorio nº 3, ¿qué le hace la enfermera a la niña? ¿Le duele?
10. Si usted quiere visitar a un/a paciente en este hospital por la tarde, ¿entre qué horas puede hacerlo?
11. En la habitación nº 4, ¿quién se enfermó? ¿Se sienta la hija cerca o lejos de su padre? ¿Se preocupa ella por él? ¿Está sentado o está de pie el médico? Según él, ¿cuántos días más tiene que quedarse el padre en el hospital?
12. ¿Qué le pasó al hombre que sale del hospital? Descríbanlo.
13. También sale del hospital una mujer. ¿Qué le pasó? ¿Qué usa para caminar?
14. ¿Dónde está la ambulancia? Qué hacen los paramédicos?

8-2. **Pobre Octavio.** Primero, determinen el orden cronológico de lo que le pasó a Octavio.

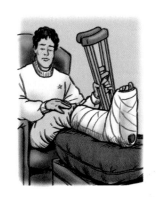

____ la doctora / ponerle un yeso
____ salir del hospital en una silla de ruedas
____ ir a emergencias
_1_ fracturarse la pierna esquiando
____ empezar a caminar con muletas
____ la doctora / examinarle la pierna
____ varias semanas más tarde, la doctora / quitarle el yeso
____ la doctora / sacarle una radiografía
____ empezar un programa de fisioterapia
____ la doctora / darle medicamentos para el dolor (*pain*)

Luego lean la narración en orden cronológico, cambiando los verbos al pretérito.

Modelo: _1_ Octavio se fracturó la pierna esquiando.

1. la cabeza

2. el pelo

3. el ojo

5. la cara

6. la nariz

7. la boca

8. el diente

9. la lengua

10. el labio

4. la oreja/ el oído

(1) head   (2) hair   (3) eye   (4) ear (outer)/ ear (inner)   (5) face   (6) nose   (7) mouth (8) tooth   (9) tongue   (10) lip

1. el cuerpo

2. el cuello

3. el hombro

11. la mano

10. el dedo

9. la uña

4. el pecho

5. el brazo

8. la espalda

6. la pierna

7. el pie

(1) body   (2) neck   (3) shoulder   (4) chest, breast   (5) arm   (6) leg   (7) foot   (8) back (9) fingernail   (10) finger   (11) hand

8-3.

¿Qué partes del cuerpo se usan? Indiquen qué partes del cuerpo se usan para cada una de las siguientes actividades. Un/a secretario/a apunta las partes del cuerpo en la pizarra.

Modelo: esquiar

Para esquiar se usan los brazos, los hombros y las piernas.

1. manejar

2. leer

3. escuchar música

4. nadar

5. comer

6. besar

7. tocar el piano

8. ...

8-4.

¡Soy artista! Un/a estudiante artístico/a va a la pizarra. Los otros estudiantes le indican las partes del cuerpo que él/ella debe dibujar para crear un hombre *muy* interesante.

Modelo: **Tiene pies grandes. No tiene pelo. Tiene una cabeza grande. Tiene veinte dedos.**

Pues, ¿cómo se llama?

Escenas

Octavio va a la clínica

Octavio

2 *Hace ya tres días que Octavio está enfermo y hoy está en la clínica de la universidad. La enfermera ya le tomó la temperatura, la presión arterial y el pulso. Entra la doctora Ruiz con el expediente médico° en mano.*

expediente... *medical record*

DOCTORA: Buenas tardes. A ver, ¿qué le pasa, Sr. Bermúdez? Según veo en su expediente usted tiene una fiebre de 39[1] grados.

OCTAVIO: Buenas, doctora. Todo comenzó hace tres días°. Al principio me dolía° un poco la cabeza, bueno, todo el cuerpo. Tenía escalofríos°. Me tomé la temperatura y descubrí que tenía una fiebre de 38 grados.

hace... *three days ago*
ached / *chills*

DOCTORA: ¿Le duele la garganta° también?

Le... *Do you have a sore throat?* / *cough*

OCTAVIO: Bastante. Además, tengo tos° y congestión nasal.

DOCTORA: Bien, permítame examinarlo. Respire profundamente por favor. ... Otra vez ... Abra la boca y diga ¡ah!, por favor. (*Lo examina.*) Bueno, usted tiene gripe°. Por esta época del año es muy común.

flu

OCTAVIO: Necesito sentirme bien pronto. Tengo un examen en mi clase de ciencias políticas mañana. Por favor recéteme° un antibiótico que me quite esta gripe.

prescribe for me

DOCTORA: Lo siento, los antibióticos no resultan efectivos contra las infecciones virales. Para recuperarse se requiere más que nada descanso y tomar muchos líquidos. Y no se preocupe por los exámenes en este momento; el estrés contribuye a debilitar las defensas inmunológicas.

OCTAVIO: Entonces, ¿no me va a recetar nada?

DOCTORA: Sí, un expectorante para la congestión nasal y la tos. ¿Es usted alérgico a la aspirina?

OCTAVIO: No, doctora.

DOCTORA: Muy bien. La aspirina le puede ayudar a bajar la fiebre.

OCTAVIO: Muchas gracias, doctora. Me voy a quedar en la cama descansando y viendo televisión. A veces, como dice el dicho, «No hay mal que por bien no venga.»

¿Qué pasa?

1. ¿Cuál es la temperatura de Octavio?
2. ¿Hace cuánto tiempo (*How long ago*) empezó a sentirse mal Octavio?
3. ¿Qué le dolía? ¿Qué otros síntomas tenía?
4. Según la doctora, ¿es bueno tomar antibióticos para una gripe?
5. ¿Qué le recomienda la doctora a Octavio? ¿Qué le receta?
6. ¿Qué va a hacer Octavio?
7. ¿Cómo interpreta usted el dicho «No hay mal que por bien no venga»? ¿Cuál es el equivalente en ingles?

---

[1] 39 Celcius = 102.2 Fahrenheit

Estructuras

1 Giving direct orders and instructions to others: *Ud./Uds.* Commands

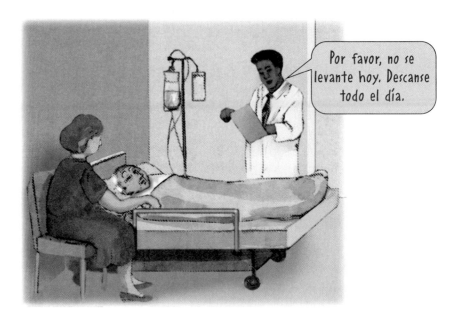

> Por favor, no se levante hoy. Descanse todo el día.

Spanish has both formal and informal command forms. You have seen and used **usted** commands since the beginning of the text (**cierre el libro, lean la oración**). These commands are used with people you address as **usted** or **ustedes**.

Regular forms

All **Ud./Uds.** regular **-ar** verb commands end in **-e(n)**; all regular **-er/ir** verb commands end in **-a(n)**. The appropriate ending is attached to the verb stem.

	esperar	**beb**er	**escrib**ir
Ud.	Esper**e**./ No esper**e**.	Beb**a**./ No beb**a**.	Escrib**a**./ No escrib**a**.
Uds.	Esper**en**./ No esper**en**.	Beb**an**./ No beb**an**.	Escrib**an**./ No escrib**an**.

- Object and reflexive pronouns *are attached* to the end of all *affirmative* **usted** commands. A written accent is necessary on the syllable that is normally stressed.

Béba**lo**.	*Drink it.*
Tóme**se** la pastilla.	*Take the pill.*
Tóme**sela** antes del desayuno.	*Take it before breakfast.*

- Object and reflexive pronouns *precede* the verb in all *negative* **usted** commands.

No lo beba.	*Don't drink it.*
No se tome la pastilla.	*Do not take the pill.*
No se la tome antes de comer.	*Do not take it before eating.*

Stem-changing and irregular forms

Most stem-changing and irregular verbs delete the final **-o** from the **yo** form of the present tense and add the indicated endings. Observe the following commands:

Infinitivo	Presente, forma de *yo*	Mandato (*command*)
decir	digø	**diga/ digan**
hacer	hagø	**haga/ hagan**
repetir	repitø	**repita/ repitan**
encontrar	encuentrø	**encuentre/ encuentren**
dormir	duermø	**duerma/ duerman**

One important exception is the verb **ir**, whose command form is **vaya/ vayan**.

Así se dice
Lo que nos dice el/la doctor/a en el consultorio

Abra la boca.	*Open your mouth.*
Saque la lengua.	*Stick out your tongue.*
Diga «¡Ah!»	*Say "Ah!"*
Respire profundamente.	*Breathe deeply.*
Tome líquidos.	*Drink liquids.*
Descanse.	*Rest.*
Vaya a la farmacia.	*Go to the pharmacy.*
Lleve la receta a la farmacia.	*Take the prescription to the pharmacy.*
Tome aspirinas/ la pastilla/ las cápsulas.	*Take aspirin/the pill/the capsules.*

Práctica y comunicación

(2) **8-5.** **¿Qué le dice el doctor/la doctora?** Uno/a hace el papel del doctor/de la doctora; el otro/la otra pretende obedecer las órdenes.

> **Modelo:** respirar profundamente
> **Respire profundamente, por favor.**

1. abrir la boca
2. sacar la lengua
3. decir «¡Ah!»
4. cerrar la boca

5. tomar la pastilla
6. beberse todo el jugo
7. hacer gárgaras (*gargle*) con sal
8. descansar

8-6. **¡Sigan (*Follow*) las instrucciones!** Sigan las instrucciones del profesor/de la profesora. Dramaticen las acciones.

1. Levántense.
2. Abran la boca.
3. Saquen la lengua.
4. Respiren profundamente.
5. Díganle algo en español a la persona que está al lado de usted.
6. Quítense los zapatos.

7. Lávense la cara.
8. Péinense.
9. Cepíllense los dientes.
10. Es la hora de la siesta. Duérmanse.
11. ¡Despiértense!
12. Pónganse los zapatos.

(4) **8-7.** **¡Un concurso!** Escojan uno o varios de los siguientes temas e inventen mandatos de **usted** o **ustedes** (afirmativos y negativos), según la situación. Tienen ocho minutos. Un/a secretario/a escribe los mandatos y al final los comparte con la clase. ¿Qué grupo tiene el mayor número de mandatos?

1. la enfermera hablándole al paciente antes de su examen médico (Ud.)
2. el médico hablándole al paciente después de examinarlo (Ud.)
3. los padres hablándoles a los hijos (Uds.)
4. la profesora/el profesor hablándoles a los estudiantes (Uds.)

> *Para regular el colesterol*
>
> EVITE alimentos con mucha grasa y colesterol.
> NO FUME.
> BAJE de peso (si lo necesita).
> HAGA ejercicio con regularidad.
> COMA más frutas y vegetales.
> COMA más pan integral, cereales, frijoles y arroz.
> SIGA las instrucciones de su médico.

¿Qué instrucciones nos dan para regular el colesterol? En su opinión, ¿cuáles son las más importantes?

8-8. **¿Puede pedirlo?** Usted es dietista y está en el restaurante Larios con su paciente y amigo, el señor Fulano, que tiene problemas con el colesterol. El señor Fulano estudia el menú y le pregunta si él puede pedir ciertas cosas. Usted le responde según el contenido de colesterol de cada plato. Túrnense.

Modelo: El señor Fulano: **Para empezar, ¿puedo pedir la sopa de pollo?**

Usted: **Sí, pídala.**

El señor Fulano: **¿Y los plátanos fritos?**

Usted: **No los pida.**

SOPAS
SOUPS

SOPA DEL DÍA	$3.75
SOUP OF THE DAY	
SOPA DE POLLO	$3.50
CHICKEN SOUP	
SOPA DE FRIJOLES NEGROS	$3.50
BLACK BEAN SOUP	

TORTILLAS
OMELETTES

TORTILLA ESPAÑOLA	$6.75
CON ARROZ Y PLÁTANOS	
SPANISH OMELETTE, RICE & PLANTAINS	
TORTILLA DE PLÁTANO	$5.95
CON ARROZ Y FRIJOLES NEGROS	
PLANTAIN OMELETTE WITH RICE & BEANS	

ENSALADAS
SALADS

ENSALADA MIXTA	$4.75
HOUSE SALAD	
ENSALADA DE SARDINAS	$6.95
SARDINE SALAD	
ENSALADA DE TOMATE	$3.50
TOMATO SALAD	
SERRUCHO EN ESCABECHE	$8.25
PICKLED KINGFISH	
PLATO DE FRUTAS	$4.95
FRUIT PLATTER	

AVES
CHICKEN

PECHUGA DE POLLO A LA PLANCHA	$8.25
BONELESS GRILLED CHICKEN BREAST	
POLLO ASADO	$7.95
ROASTED CHICKEN	
CHICHARRONES DE POLLO	$7.95
DEEP FRIED CHICKEN CHUNKS	
ARROZ CON POLLO	$6.95
CHICKEN AND YELLOW RICE	
PECHUGA DE POLLO RELLENA *CON CAMARONES*	$8.95
CHICKEN BREAST STUFFED WITH SHRIMP	

PESCADOS
FISH

PESCADO EMPANIZADO	$9.95
BREADED FISH	
PESCADO A LA PLANCHA	$9.75
GRILLED FISH	
BROCHETA DE CAMARONES	$11.75
SHRIMP KABOB	
CAMARONES EMPANIZADOS	$12.25
BREADED SHRIMP	
CAMARONES AL AJILLO	$12.25
SHRIMP IN GARLIC	
LANGOSTA ENCHILADA	$20.50
LOBSTER CREOLE	

TODOS ESTOS PLATOS SE SIRVEN CON ARROZ Y PLÁTANOS FRITOS

CARNES
MEATS

BISTEC DE PALOMILLA	$8.95
CUBAN STEAK	
LOMO DE PUERCO	$9.75
ROAST PORK LOIN-CUBAN STYLE	
MASAS DE PUERCO	$9.25
FRIED PORK CHUNKS	
CHULETAS DE PUERCO	$8.50
PORK CHOPS	
CARNE AL PINCHO	$12.95
SHISH KABOB	
PICADILLO A LA CUBANA	$6.25
CUBAN GROUND BEEF CREOLE	

POSTRES
DESSERTS

PUDÍN DE PAN	$3.75
BREAD PUDDING	
FLAN DE LECHE	$3.75
CUSTARD	
ARROZ CON LECHE	$3.75
RICE PUDDING	
COCO RALLADO	$3.25
SHREDDED COCONUT	

HELADOS
ICE CREAM

COCO	$2.95
MANGO	$2.95
GUANÁBANA SORBET	$2.95
CHOCOLATE	$2.95
VAINILLA	$2.95

DICHOS

Ajo, cebolla y limón, y déjate de° inyección.
¿Qué significa el dicho? ¿Es verdad?

°stop having

> To express aches, pains, and how you feel, use the following verbs and expressions:
>
> **doler** (like **gustar**): *indirect object* + **doler (ue)** + **el/la/los/las** + *body part*
> Me duelen las piernas.   ¿Te duele el estómago?
>
> **tener dolor de** + *body part*   Tengo dolor de espalda.
>
> **sentirse (ie, i)** + *adjective*   Se sintió/ Se siente bien, mal, enfermo/a, triste,
>   cansado/a, etc.

Así se dice
Su salud[1]

Usted está *muy* enfermo/a. Antes de ver al médico usted necesita completar el siguiente cuestionario.

Su salud

	Sí	No
1. **¿Le duele la cabeza**[2] con frecuencia?	Sí	No
2. **¿Tiene dolor de estómago**[3]?	Sí	No
3. ¿Tiene mucha **tos/ Tose**[4] mucho?	Sí	No
4. ¿Tiene **fiebre**[5]?	Sí	No
5. ¿Tiene **diarrea**[6]?	Sí	No
6. ¿Tiene **resfriados**[7] o **gripe**[8] con frecuencia?	Sí	No
7. ¿Tiene **alergias**[9]?	Sí	No
8. ¿Tiene **congestión nasal**[10]? **¿Estornuda**[11] mucho?	Sí	No
9. **¿Le duele la garganta**[12] con frecuencia?	Sí	No
10. ¿Tiene **vómitos/ Vomita**[13]?	Sí	No
11. ¿Tiene **náuseas**[14]?	Sí	No
12. ¿Tiene **escalofríos**[15]?	Sí	No
13. **¿Se cansa**[16] con frecuencia?	Sí	No
14. ¿Duerme bien?	Sí	No
15. **¿Se siente deprimido/a**[17]?	Sí	No

Otros síntomas: _____

(1) health (2) Do you have a headache? (3) Do you have a stomachache? (4) cough/Do you cough; **toser** *to cough (5) fever (6) diarrhea (7) colds (8) flu (f.) (9) allergies (10) nasal congestion (11) Do you sneeze?;* **estornudar** *to sneeze (12) Do you have a sore throat? (13) Are you vomiting? (14) nausea (15) chills (16) Do you feel tired?;* **cansarse** *to get/feel tired (17) Do you feel depressed?;* **sentirse** *(ie, i) to feel . . .*

② **8-9.** **¿Cuál es el diagnóstico y el medicamento?** Usando las respuestas en su cuestionario, dígale al doctor o a la doctora los síntomas que usted tiene. Él/Ella va a diagnosticar el caso y recomendarle el medicamento, según el cuadro (*chart*). Túrnense.

> **Modelo:** Paciente: **Buenas tardes, doctor/a... Tengo muchos problemas hoy....**
>
> Doctor/a: **A ver... Tome...**

Diagnóstico	Medicamento
gripe	tomar aspirinas, líquidos, descansar
alergia	tomar Alegra dos veces al día
problemas estomacales	tomar Pepto Bismol dos veces al día
infección en el oído	tomar antibióticos
resfriado	tomar muchos líquidos, descansar
bronquitis	tomar jarabe para la tos y un expectorante
depresión	ir a ver al psicólogo

② **8-10.** **En el consultorio de la Dra. Socorro.** Tomen los papeles (*roles*) de la doctora y de un/a paciente. Completen la conversación de una manera original.

DRA.: Buenos días,... ¿cómo se siente usted hoy?

USTED: Buenos días, Dra. Socorro. Me siento.../ Estoy.../ Tengo.../ Me duele...

DRA.: ¿Tiene usted...?

USTED: ... y no puedo/ no tengo ganas de...

(*Después del examen físico.*)

DRA.: Bueno, tengo varias recomendaciones. Primero, ..., ..., ... y no... Llame por teléfono si tiene más problemas.

USTED: Muchas gracias, Dra. Socorro. Hasta luego.

⑤ **¡Qué dilema!**
Eres paciente en el hospital. Después de las horas oficiales de visita, tres de tus amigos llegan a tu habitación con comida, bebidas y música. La jefa de enfermeras, una mujer muy seria y mandona (bossy), entra en la habitación y dice: **¿Qué están haciendo ustedes aquí a estas horas de la noche?**

2 Describing in the past: The imperfect

> Era medianoche y hacía mucho viento. Los niños caminaban por la calle desierta...

Spanish has two simple past tenses: the preterit and the imperfect. You have already learned to use the preterit to talk about completed past actions and past actions within a specific time frame (*yesterday, last night,* etc.).

The imperfect tense is used primarily:

- to describe in the past (background, weather, ongoing conditions, persons, places, things).

Hacía sol.	*It **was** sunny.*
La playa **era** hermosa.	*The beach **was** beautiful.*
El mar **estaba** muy tranquilo.	*The sea **was** very tranquil.*
Los niños **llevaban** trajes de baño y camisetas.	*The children **were wearing** bathing suits and T-shirts.*
Estaban muy contentos.	*They **were** very happy.*

- to indicate that past actions were in progress, ongoing, or habitual.

Un niño **jugaba** en el agua.	*One child **was playing** in the water.*
Otro **construía** un castillo.	*Another **was building** a castle.*
A otros siempre **les gustaba** jugar a pelota.	*Others always **liked** to play ball.*

Regular verbs

Delete the -**ar**, -**er**, or -**ir** from the infinitive and add the endings indicated below. Note that the imperfect -**er**/-**ir** endings are identical.

	examinar *to examine*	**toser** *to cough*	**salir** *to leave, go out*
(yo)	examin**aba**	tos**ía**	sal**ía**
(tú)	examin**abas**	tos**ías**	sal**ías**
(Ud., él, ella)	examin**aba**	tos**ía**	sal**ía**
(nosotros/as)	examin**ábamos**	tos**íamos**	sal**íamos**
(vosotros/as)	examin**abais**	tos**íais**	sal**íais**
(Uds., ellos, ellas)	examin**aban**	tos**ían**	sal**ían**

The imperfect tense corresponds to four past forms in English:

Mientras **esperaba** al médico, leyó un artículo en una revista.

*While she **was waiting/waited** for the doctor, she read an article in a magazine.*

El doctor le **examinaba** el colesterol una vez al año.

*The doctor **used to/would check** her cholesterol once a year.*

Irregular verbs

Only three verbs are irregular in the imperfect:

ser *to be*		**ir** *to go*		**ver** *to see*	
era	éramos	iba	íbamos	veía	veíamos
eras	erais	ibas	ibais	veías	veíais
era	eran	iba	iban	veía	veían

Era un médico muy bueno.

*He **was** a very good doctor.*

Íbamos a su consultorio cada semana.

*We **would go** to his office every six months.*

Siempre lo **veíamos** cuando teníamos problemas.

*We **would** always **see** him when we had problems.*

Práctica y comunicación

8-11. **En la época de nuestros abuelos.** ¿Cómo era el mundo cuando nuestros abuelos eran jóvenes? ¿La gente hacía o no hacía lo siguiente? Hagan un contraste entre *antes* y *ahora*.

> **Modelo:** Se usaban mucho las computadoras.
>
> **Antes no se usaban mucho las computadoras. Ahora sí se usan.**
>
> Los jóvenes respetaban a los adultos.
>
> **Antes los jóvenes respetaban a los adultos. Ahora también los respetan/ no los respetan.**

1. Los doctores examinaban el colesterol de los pacientes.
2. Las personas consumían comida rápida.
3. Las personas consumían comida muy saludable (*healthy*).
4. Se hablaba mucho del SIDA (*AIDS*).
5. El correo electrónico era muy popular.
6. Las personas no tenían mucho estrés.
7. Los jóvenes salían los fines de semana.
8. Había[2] muchos problemas con las drogas.

8-12. **¡Para mejorar la salud!** Al volver de un viaje (*trip*), ustedes descubren muchos cambios. Primero, digan lo que hacían las personas antes. Luego, indiquen lo que ya no hacen.

> **Modelo:** **Antes el ogro comía muchas papas fritas.**
> **Ya no las come.**

el ogro / papas fritas

1. Esteban / cerveza   **2.** Carmen / postres   **3.** Héctor / fumar

Ahora, indiquen algo que cada uno de ustedes hacía antes, pero que ya no hace.

> **Modelo:** **Antes yo tomaba mucho café, pero ya no lo tomo.**

---

[2] **Había**, like **hay**, denotes existence, but in the past: **Había** tres pacientes en la sala de espera. *There were* three patients in the waiting room.

4 **8-13.** **El Hospital San Rafael.** Describan el hospital y lo que hacían algunas personas en el hospital. Refiéranse a los dibujos de las páginas 270–271. Usen el imperfecto.

> **Modelo:** Había una ambulancia al lado de la entrada de emergencias.
> Un hombre salía del hospital en silla de ruedas.

2 **8-14.** **Cuando estábamos en la escuela secundaria...** Háganse preguntas.

> **Modelo:** estudiar mucho
> Estudiante 1: ¿Estudiabas mucho?
> Estudiante 2: Sí, estudiaba mucho. *o* No, no estudiaba mucho.

En la escuela secundaria...

1. ser tímido(a)/ perezoso(a)/ trabajador(a)
2. salir mucho con tus amigos (¿Adónde iban cuando salían?)
3. fumar
4. tener novio/a (¿Cómo se llamaba?)
5. ir de compras con frecuencia (¿Adónde?)
6. hablar mucho por teléfono (¿Con quién?)
7. ver mucho la televisión (¿Qué programas?)
8. leer muchas revistas (¿Cuáles?)
9. escuchar la radio (¿Qué tipo de música o programas?)
10. jugar a algún deporte (¿Cuál?)
11. tocar un instrumento musical (¿Cuál?)
12. trabajar (¿Dónde?)

Ahora, dígale a la clase algo de su compañero/a: **En la escuela secundaria, Juanita jugaba al tenis.**

4 **8-15.** **Las etapas (*stages*) de la vida.** Describan algunas actividades que ustedes hacían en las siguientes etapas de la vida. También incluyan lo que les gustaba/ no les gustaba. Un/a secretario/a apunta las ideas del grupo. No pasen más de tres minutos en cada categoría.

> **Modelo:** Cuando éramos bebés, nosotros... **dormíamos mucho, tomábamos mucha leche, nos gustaba jugar con nuestros juguetes (*toys*)...**

1. Cuando teníamos de cuatro a seis años...
2. Cuando teníamos de diez a doce años...
3. Cuando teníamos de quince a diecisiete años...

Luego, algunos grupos van a presentar sus ideas a la clase.

Noticias culturales

Remedios... *Home remedies*

Remedios caseros° del mundo hispano

Los azahares, la flor del naranjo.

Un té de tilo es bueno para calmar el estrés.

Desde... *Since* / se... *realized* / *pains* / *herbs*

cures

Desde que° el ser humano se dio cuenta° de que podía aliviar sus padecimientos° con la ayuda de hierbas° y plantas medicinales, hay toda una tradición de secretos que se transmite de generación a generación. Cada cultura, cada país, cada región tiene sus propias curas°. A continuación usted va a encontrar algunas de las tradiciones médicas populares del mundo hispano. Recuerde que no debe tomar remedios caseros ni farmacéuticos sin consultar con su médico/a.

Resfriados/ gripe

se... *are added* / *honey*

rum

Todos los remedios comienzan con una limonada caliente. Lo que cambia de receta a receta son los ingredientes que se agregan°. Algunos ponen miel° en la limonada, otros ron° o «whisky».

Hiccup

Hipo°

sips / *to scare*
a piece of thread / *forehead*
to stop

Otra vez los consejos son múltiples. Se recomienda poner jugo de limón en la lengua o tomar sorbos° de agua. Otros piensan que se debe asustar° al paciente. En México, las abuelitas les ponen un hilo° rojo en la frente° a los bebés para detener° el hipo.

Orzuelos°

Se recomienda hervir° unos clavos de olor° en agua y cuando está tibia° aplicarla al orzuelo. Según los costarricenses es un remedio seguro. Otros afirman que lo mejor es aplicar miel. En realidad los orzuelos son infecciones y si persisten deben ser tratadas con antibióticos.

Sties

to boil / clavos... *cloves* / *lukewarm*

Dolor de oído

Se recomienda dorar° un ajo al fuego, ponerlo en un algodón y colocarlo a la entrada del oído.

to brown

Dolor de pies

Para relajar los pies y aliviar el cansancio no hay como ponerlos en agua de sal tibia. También un masaje con una crema hidratante hace maravillas°.

hace... *works wonders*

Nerviosismo/ estrés

Las flores del naranjo, los azahares, hervidas en agua tienen propiedades sedantes. Tambien un té de tilo, otra hierba medicinal, ayuda a calmar la ansiedad.

Dientes blancos

Según viejas tradiciones, el jugo de limón es excelente como blanqueador° de dientes.

whitener

La próxima vez que usted le pregunte a un hispanoparlante sobre remedios caseros, prepárese; va a recibir muchos consejos° y respuestas.

advice

¿Qué recuerda?
1. ¿Qué puede hacer usted si tiene un orzuelo?
2. ¿Qué puede tomar si sufre de mucha tensión o estrés?
3. ¿Cómo se puede blanquear los dientes?
4. ¿Qué puede hacer después de mucho caminar?
5. ¿Qué le puede recomendar a un amigo que tiene gripe?
6. ¿Qué puede hacer si tiene hipo?

Conexiones y contrastes
1. ¿Usan remedios caseros en su familia? ¿Cuáles? ¿Son efectivos?
2. ¿ Prefiere usted usar remedios caseros o farmacéuticos?

3 **Talking about and describing persons, things, and actions in the past: The imperfect and the preterit**

> Los niños caminaban por la calle desierta cuando de repente ¡vieron un fantasma!...

HINT | Review the preterit tense of regular, stem-changing, and irregular verbs in **Chapters 5**, **6**, and **7**.

Although both the preterit and the imperfect tenses refer to the past, they convey different meanings. Study the contrasts in the following chart.

The preterit . . .	*The imperfect . . .*
1. focuses on a past action or condition with an evident *beginning, end,* or *time frame.*	**1.** describes the *middle* of a past action, state, or condition; indicates that it was *in progress*, with no emphasis on the beginning or end.

Anita **se enfermó el sábado**.
    Estuvo enferma toda la semana.
    Salió del hospital **ayer**.
    Pasó tres días allí.
    Se recuperó completamente.
	Juan **estaba enfermo**.
	    No **quería** comer.
	    Sólo **dormía** y **veía** la tele.

2. indicates a *single past action*, generally quickly completed, or a *series of actions* in the past.	**2.** describes a past action that was *repeated* or *habitual* over an indefinite period of time.

El paciente **entró** en el consultorio.
    El enfermero le **tomó** la temperatura, le **explicó** el problema y le **puso** una inyección.
	La enfermera **visitaba** a sus pacientes **todas las noches**.
	    Siempre les **llevaba** jugo de naranja.

When narrating an incident or telling a story:

the imperfect ...

1. sets the stage, giving background information.

the date, the season	**Era** el 12 de diciembre. **Era** invierno.
what time it was	**Era** medianoche.
the weather	**Hacía** frío y **nevaba**.
a description of the setting	La casa **era** muy vieja y **tenía** un árbol muy grande en frente.

2. describes people.

physical and personality traits	La abuela **era** bonita y muy amable.
age	**Tenía** ochenta años.
mental or emotional condition	**Estaba** tranquila y contenta.

3. describes ongoing actions. Ella **leía** un libro.

the preterit ...

1. often interrupts an ongoing (imperfect) action.

Mientras ella leía el libro, **sonó** el teléfono.

2. moves the story forward, telling what happened.

Se levantó, **contestó** el teléfono y **salió** de la casa inmediatamente.

A time reference often helps to determine which past tense to use. The following words or expressions serve as a general guideline.

Imperfecto		Pretérito	
muchas veces	*many times, often*	una vez	*once, one time*
todos los días	*every day*	ayer	*yesterday*
cada	*each, every*	el verano pasado	*last summer*
con frecuencia	*frequently*	anoche	*last night*
siempre/	*always/*	hace diez años	*ten years ago*
generalmente	*generally*	de repente	*suddenly*
mientras	*while*	por fin	*finally*

Todos los veranos **íbamos** a la playa, pero el verano pasado **fuimos** a las montañas.

*Every summer we **would go** to the beach, but last summer we **went** to the mountains.*

Práctica y comunicación

③ 8-16. Nuestro gato Rodolfo. Lean lo que le pasó. Presten atención a los usos del pretérito y del imperfecto.

Ayer, nuestro gato Rodolfo **se enfermó.** No **quería** comer y **tenía** diarrea. ¡Pobrecito! Por supuesto, todos **nos preocupamos** mucho. Elena y yo lo **llevamos** al veterinario y **nos sentamos** en la sala de espera, donde **había** muchos animales. Rodolfo **estaba** en una caja de cartón° y, por supuesto, no **estaba** nada contento. ¡**Tuvimos que** esperar por una hora! Por fin, el veterinario lo **examinó, descubrió** que el pobre Rodolfo **tenía** una infección intestinal y le **recetó** un antibiótico. **Volvimos** a casa e inmediatamente le **dimos** su medicamento. En poco tiempo, **se recuperó.** ¡Qué suerte°!

caja... cardboard box

¡Qué... What luck!

Ahora identifiquen:

1. lo que le pasó a Rodolfo ayer y sus síntomas
2. lo que hicieron el padre y Elena
3. el tiempo que esperaron en la sala de espera y lo que había allí
4. la condición emocional de Rodolfo
5. el diagnóstico del veterinario y lo que hizo
6. lo que le pasó a Rodolfo al final

8-17. ¡Siempre hay interrupciones! Según los dibujos, indique lo que hacían los estudiantes cuando algo o alguien los interrumpió.

| **Modelo:** | El profesor Marín-Vivar navegaba por la red cuando Carmen entró en el laboratorio. |

El profesor Marín-Vivar /
navegar… / Carmen / entrar…

1. Pepita / limpiar…
Camila / llamarla

2. Esteban / dormir…
el teléfono / sonar

3. Inés / tocar…
Rubén / entrar…

4. Alfonso / tocar… cantar…
Inés / salir…

8-18. **La abuelita cambió de rutina.** Diga lo que la abuelita hacía *casi todos los días* y lo que hizo *un día* para cambiar su rutina.

> **Modelo:** caminar por el parque
>
> Casi todos los días **caminaba por el parque.**
>
> Pero un día, **caminó por la avenida principal de la ciudad.**

Casi todos los días...   **pero un día, ...**

1. manejar su viejo Ford   ...
2. leer su revista favorita, *Buenhogar*   ...
3. ver episodios de *Amigos*   ...
4. comer en casa   ...
5. preparar una ensalada de frutas   ...
6. llamar a sus nietos   ...

8-19. **Más sobre Rodolfo.** Describan al gato Rodolfo y algunas de sus aventuras juveniles. Usen el pretérito o el imperfecto según el caso.

Es verdad que Rodolfo es un gato único°. Cuando _____ (tener) dos años y _____ (llegar) a nuestra casa, _____ (ser) gordo y bonito. _____ (poder) correr muy rápido y aun subir a° los árboles, donde le _____ (encantar) «mirar» los pájaros°. Año tras° año nos _____ (dar) sorpresas. Por ejemplo, normalmente _____ (tomar) agua de su bol, pero un día la _____ (tomar) ¡del inodoro°! Casi siempre _____ (dormir) en el sótano, en el sofá, pero una noche _____ (dormir) afuera, en el jardín. _____ (ser) allí donde conoció a Gitana°, su gata favorita. Unos días más tarde, nos _____ (dar) otra sorpresa: ¡Se _____ (comer) el jamón de mi sándwich! Cuando yo _____ (entrar) en la cocina y lo _____ (descubrir), el «delincuente» ¡_____ (salir) corriendo de la casa! Allí _____ (ver) a Gitana, y los dos se _____ (escaparse). _____ (regresar) a casa ¡tres días más tarde! Ahora tenemos una pareja gatuna durmiendo junto a la chimenea y probablemente una familia por venir.

unique

climb

birds / after

toilet

Gypsy

8-20. **El accidente de Martín un martes trece.** Narren la historia en el pasado. Cambien los verbos al pretérito o al imperfecto.

Martín **maneja** muy contento. No **ve** el alto° y **choca**° con otro coche que **viene** en la dirección opuesta. Al otro conductor no le **pasa** nada, pero el pobre de Martín **se lastima.** **Llega** la policía y una ambulancia que lo **lleva** al hospital. La pierna le **duele** mucho. El médico lo **examina** y lo **manda** a radiología. **Es** un mal día para Martín. **Se fractura** la pierna y **sale** del hospital en muletas. **Es** un martes trece[3] y ya lo dice bien el dicho: «Martes, ni te cases ni te embarques, ni de tu casa te apartes»[4].

stop sign / collides

---

[3] In the Hispanic world the bad luck day is Tuesday the thirteenth, not Friday.
[4] On Tuesday (the 13th) neither marry, nor set sail, nor leave your home.

(4) **8-21.** **Una aventura fantástica.** Revivan (*Relive*) o inventen una aventura fantástica o extraordinaria. Piensen en por qué usan el pretérito o el imperfecto. Un/a secretario/a escribe la aventura para luego leérsela a la clase.

Temas posibles

1. una noche en la ciudad de Nueva York (u otra ciudad)

2. una noche en la sala de emergencias de un hospital

3. un sábado por la noche en una fiesta en la universidad

4. un día durante las vacaciones de primavera en una playa de Cancún (u otro lugar)

5. un viaje a un país sudamericano

6. un día en la vida de los Simpsons

Incluyan

- referencia a la fecha, el día, la hora y el lugar donde estaban
- descripción del tiempo, del lugar, de las personas
- descripción de lo que pasaba en ese lugar (acciones en progreso, etc.)
- lo que pasó
- final de la historia

(3) **8-22.** **Un evento memorable en mi vida.** Cada estudiante del grupo tiene tres minutos para pensar en un evento (verdadero o ficticio) del pasado. Luego tiene un minuto para narrárselo al grupo. El grupo decide si es verdadero.

4 **Indicating how long an action has been going on or how long ago it happened: *Hacer* with expressions of time**

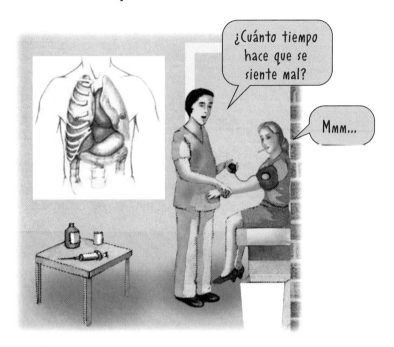

¿Cuánto tiempo hace que se siente mal?

Mmm...

A. *Hacer* to express how long an action has been going on

Spanish uses a special construction to indicate that an action or condition has been going on for a period of time and still is.

> **hace** + *time* + **que** + *present tense*

- In this construction, **hace** never changes.

  Hace dos días **que está** enfermo.   *He has been sick for two days.*

  Hace veinte minutos **que**   *We have been here for twenty minutes.*
  estamos aquí.

- To ask how long an action or condition has been going on, use the question ¿Cuánto tiempo hace que...?

  —¿**Cuánto tiempo hace que**   *How long has Carmen been waiting*
    Carmen espera a la doctora?   *for the doctor?*

  —Hace diez minutos que la espera.   *She has been waiting for her for ten*
                                        minutes.

Práctica y comunicación

8-23. **¿Cuánto tiempo hace?** ¿Cuánto tiempo hace que cada persona en los dibujos participa en la actividad?

Javier / dos horas

> **Modelo:** Hace dos horas que Javier trabaja en su proyecto de química.

1. Inés / quince minutos

2. Linda y Manuel / media hora

3. Esteban / dos horas

4. Alfonso / una hora

5. Octavio / cuarenta minutos

6. Manuel / veinte minutos

 8-24. **¿Días, semanas, meses o años?** Háganse las siguientes preguntas. Luego, dígale a la clase algo acerca de su compañero/a.

1. ¿Cuánto tiempo hace que estudias en la universidad? Hace... que... ¿Y tú?
2. ¿Cuánto tiempo hace que estudias español?
3. ¿Dónde vives ahora? ¿Cuánto tiempo hace que vives allí?
4. ¿Tienes novio/a? ¿Cuánto tiempo hace que lo/la conoces?
5. ¿Quién es tu mejor amigo/a? ¿Cuánto tiempo hace que lo/la conoces?
6. ¿Practicas algún deporte? ¿Cuánto tiempo hace que lo practicas?
7. ¿Tocas un instrumento musical? ¿Cuánto tiempo hace que lo tocas?

B. *Hacer* to express *ago*

To indicate how long ago an action took place, use the *preterit tense* of the verb + **hace** + *the amount of time* (hours, days, weeks, months, years).

Salió **hace diez minutos**.	*He left **ten minutes ago**.*
Estuvo aquí **hace dos semanas**.	*He was here **two weeks ago**.*

- The *ago* construction is most commonly used to answer two types of questions:

  (specific) **¿Cuánto (tiempo) hace que te hiciste un examen médico?**
  How long ago did you have a physical examination?

  (general) **¿Cuándo te hiciste un examen médico?**
  When did you last have a physical examination?

- When answering a question with the *ago* construction, the verb is often omitted.

  Hace dos meses. *Two months ago.*

- Statements about how long ago something took place have two possible word orders.

  > *Preterit* + **hace** + *time*   or   **Hace** + *time* + **que** + *preterit*

Lo **vi** hace una hora.	*I saw him an hour ago.*
Hace una hora que lo **vi**.	*I saw him an hour ago.*

Práctica y comunicación

8-25. **¿Cuánto tiempo hace?** Háganse las preguntas y contéstenlas para indicar cuánto tiempo hace (**horas, días, semanas, meses, años**) que ustedes participaron en la actividad.

> **Modelo:** ¿Cuándo fue la última vez (*the last time*) que fuiste al dentista?
>
> **Hace seis meses.** *o* **Hace seis meses que fui al dentista.** *o* **Fui al dentista hace seis meses.**

1. ¿Cuándo aprendiste a manejar?
2. ¿Cuándo llegaste a la universidad?
3. ¿Cuándo conociste a tu mejor amigo/a o novio/a? (¿Cómo se llama?)
4. ¿Cuándo fue la última vez que visitaste a tus abuelos/ padres/ tíos?
5. ¿Cuándo fue la última vez que limpiaste tu cuarto?
6. ¿Cuándo fue la última vez que fuiste de compras? (¿Qué compraste?)
7. ¿Cuándo fue la última vez que tuviste gripe/ un resfriado?
8. ¿Cuándo fue la última vez que fuiste al médico/a la médica?
9. ¿Alguna vez en el pasado te fracturaste una pierna/ un brazo? ¿ Te torciste un tobillo? (¿Hace cuánto tiempo?)

Ahora, díganle a la clase algo acerca de su compañero/a de clase: **Paco limpió su cuarto hace tres meses.** *o* **Hace tres meses que Paco limpió su cuarto.**

8-26. **Actividades memorables.** Primero, cada uno de ustedes prepara una lista de tres cosas interesantes que hicieron hace un tiempo (*some time ago*). Luego háganse preguntas para averiguar cuánto tiempo hace que hicieron las actividades de la lista.

Actividades memorables
1. Visité Alaska.
2. Fui a un concierto de...
3. Esquié en las montañas de Colorado.

> **Modelo:** Estudiante 1: **¿Cuándo visitaste Alaska?**
>
> Estudiante 2: **Hace cinco años.** *o* **Visité Alaska hace cinco años.**

Dígale a la clase cuánto tiempo hace que su compañero/a hizo la actividad más interesante de la lista: **José visitó Alaska hace cinco años.** *o* **Hace cinco años que José visitó Alaska.**

8-27. **Guía para la comunidad médica.** La clase va a dividirse en tres grupos. Cada grupo, con un/a secretario/a, prepara una lista de preguntas, expresiones y mandatos útiles. Incluyan preguntas y expresiones con **hacer**. Al final, compartan sus listas con la clase.

Grupo 1: el/la recepcionista al hablar con un/a paciente
Grupo 2: el enfermero/la enfermera al hablar con un/a paciente
Grupo 3: el doctor/la doctora al hablar con un/a paciente

Dicho y hecho

Conversando

4 **En emergencias.** Imaginen que tres de ustedes ahora están en la sala de emergencias de la clínica de la universidad. Cada uno/a le explica al/a la recepcionista por qué necesita ver a la doctora. El/La recepcionista les hace preguntas para determinar quién va primero.

Posibilidades

- Ud. estaba corriendo, se cayó (*fell*) y ahora...
- Ud. se comió unos mariscos y ahora...
- Ud. cree tener la gripe.
- Ud. tiene bronquitis.

¡A escuchar!

«La salud y usted.» Escuche lo que les dice la doctora Alvarado a los estudiantes. Luego, complete las dos primeras oraciones.

1. La doctora va a hablar sobre _____.

2. Muchos tienen interés en el tema porque ahora son los meses de _____, cuando se presenta la enfermedad.

Escuche otra vez y complete las siguientes oraciones.

3. Aún cuando una persona contrae la gripe después de la vacuna, los síntomas son _____.

4. La vacuna es necesaria para personas mayores de _____ y para personas con enfermedades del _____ o del _____.

5. Para los que vivimos en el hemisferio norte, la vacuna generalmente se aplica entre los meses de _____.

6. Algunas personas son alérgicas a la vacuna porque también son alérgicas a _____.

De mi escritorio

Cuando era niño/a... Escriba una descripción de algo que le ocurrió cuando era niño/a. Use el imperfecto y el pretérito.

Incluya:

- cuándo (hace cuánto tiempo) ocurrió
- cuántos años tenía usted cuando ocurrió
- dónde estaba usted y una descripción del lugar
- lo que pasó y si usted estaba triste/ contento(a)/ enojado(a), etc. al final

Panorama cultural

Colombia y Venezuela

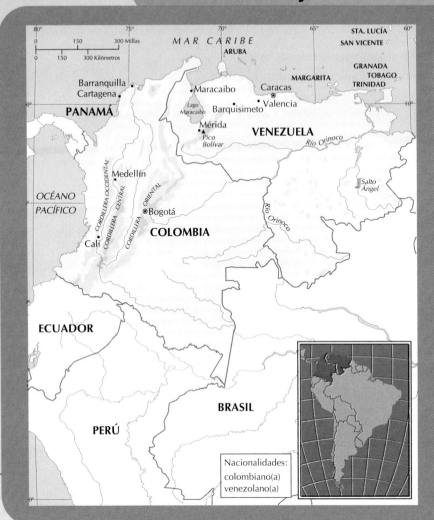

Nacionalidades:
colombiano(a)
venezolano(a)

¡Esmeraldas y oro!

Colombia es el principal productor de esmeraldas en el mundo y el primer productor de oro en Sudamérica.

Person@je del momento

¿Sabe usted quién es Shakira? Busque información en el Internet y compártala con sus compañeros/as de clase.

UNA IGLESIA SALADA

En Colombia hay una catedral de sal construida debajo de la tierra en una antigua mina de sal.

Preguntas sobre el mapa

1. ¿En qué país es posible visitar las playas del Pacífico y también las del mar Caribe?
2. ¿Con qué países tiene frontera Colombia?
3. ¿Cuál es la capital de Colombia? ¿Cuáles son dos ciudades importantes en la costa?
4. ¿Cómo se llaman las tres cordilleras que cruzan el país?
5. ¿Cuál es el río principal que pasa por Venezuela y Colombia?
6. ¿Cuál es la capital de Venezuela? ¿Cuál es la ciudad que está cerca del famoso pico Bolívar en los Andes de Venezuela? ¿Y la ciudad que está a orillas (*on the banks*) de un lago?

Colombia

¿Sabía usted que...?

- Los españoles llegaron a Colombia en 1500, en busca de El Dorado. Esta leyenda indicaba que en esta región existía muchísimo oro.

- En la época colonial, Colombia era parte de la Nueva Granada, que también incluía los territorios actuales de Panamá, Ecuador y Venezuela.

- Cuando la Nueva Granada se independizó de España (1810), Simón Bolívar, el líder de la independencia, creó la Federación de la Gran Colombia.

- Primero, Ecuador y Venezuela abandonaron la Federación y más tarde, con la ayuda de los EE.UU., Panamá también se independizó.

- Actualmente, Colombia ha incrementado su lucha contra la guerrilla y los narcotraficantes.

El espíritu del pueblo colombiano se ve en su música, sus bailes y en sus diversiones populares. La cumbia y el vallenato son ritmos bailables de origen colombiano muy famosos en todo el mundo. ¿Conoce usted los ritmos caribeños? ¿Le gusta a usted bailar?

Bogotá, la capital, está en un valle central. Tiene más de 6 millones de habitantes y es una ciudad moderna, llena de rascacielos, tiendas de moda y grandes avenidas. Pero en esta ciudad también existen barrios muy pobres que contrastan con el lujo de muchas áreas. ¿Qué elementos interesantes hay en esta vista de Bogotá?

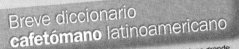

Breve diccionario cafetómano latinoamericano

- **AMERICANO (México, Miami):** café aguado, en taza grande.
- **CAFÉ (todos los países):** cualquier cosa, pida más información.
- **CAFÉ-CAFÉ (Chile):** café de grano, normalmente en taza chica.
- **CAFÉ COMÚN (Argentina):** café aguado, en taza grande.
- **CAFÉ CON LECHE (todos los países):** autoexplicativo, pero la proporción leche/café es variable.
- **CAFÉ DOBLE (Argentina):** café cargado, en taza grande.
- **CAPUCHINO (todos los países):** un tercio de café, un tercio de leche, un tercio de espuma de leche. En Chile lleva además crema batida.
- **CAPUCCINO (Argentina, Colombia):** capuchino.
- **CARIOCA (Brasil):** café aguado, en taza chica.
- **CORTADO (Chile, Argentina):** café cargado con un toque de leche.
- **CORTADITO (Miami):** ídem.
- **CUBANO (Miami):** café muy cargado, muy dulce y muy "tacaño": menos de la mitad de una taza chica.
- **CURTO (Brasil):** café cargado en taza chica.
- **EXPRESO (varios países):** café concentrado especial en taza chica.
- **ESPRESSO (Miami):** expreso.
- **EXPRESS (Chile):** expreso.
- **GRANIZADO (Colombia):** café helado, con hielo picado, en vaso.
- **GUAYOYO (Venezuela):** café negro suave, hecho en colador de tela.
- **MARRÓN (Venezuela):** café cargado con un toque de leche.
- **NEGRITO (Venezuela):** café sin leche en taza chica.
- **NEGRO (varios países):** café sin leche ni azúcar.
- **PERICO (Colombia):** café cargado con un toque de leche.
- **PINGADO (Brasil):** café con leche en taza grande.
- **TETERO (Venezuela):** leche caliente con un poco de café.
- **TINTO (Colombia):** café relativamente suave, en taza chica.

Colombia es el segundo productor de café del mundo, después de Brasil. Según el diccionario cafetómano, ¿qué tipos de café son populares en Colombia? ¿Cuál es su café favorito?

Venezuela

¿Sabía usted que...?

- El nombre de este país significa «pequeña Venecia».
- Alonso de Ojeda, el primer explorador español de la zona, llamó así al país en 1500 porque los habitantes —los indios guajiros— vivían en chozas[1] suspendidas sobre isletas en el lago Maracaibo.
- En Venezuela los españoles encontraron fabulosas riquezas en oro, plata y perlas, y establecieron prósperas colonias.

En Venezuela está el Salto Ángel, ¡la cascada más alta del mundo (3.281 pies/979 metros)! Describa usted la foto del famoso Salto Ángel.

Caracas está cerca de la costa y es una de las ciudades más cosmopolitas del continente. Los caraqueños son amantes del arte y tienen un admirable Museo de Bellas Artes y una magnífica Orquesta Sinfónica. Caracas también cuenta con uno de los servicios de metro más sofisticados del mundo. Describa la foto.

El teleférico de Mérida es un sistema de cuatro teleféricos en serie que cubre una distancia de 12.5km./7.75 millas entre la ciudad de Mérida y Pico Espejo. Es considerado el más alto y largo del mundo. ¿Le gustaría a usted subir al Pico Espejo en este teleférico?

[1] huts [2] plains
[3] a third
[4] cattle-raising

¿Qué descubrimos?

¿Se refieren a **Colombia** o a **Venezuela**?

1. el primer productor de esmeraldas del mundo
2. los indios guajiros
3. el petróleo
4. ciudad capital situada en un valle
5. la cumbia y el vallenato
6. ciudad capital situada cerca de la costa

El «oro negro» o petróleo es la mayor riqueza del país. La explotación de los grandes depósitos petrolíferos en el lago Maracaibo comenzó a principios del siglo XX. La industria petrolera generó mucha prosperidad en el país y su población se cuadruplicó. Considere la foto y el mapa. ¿Es grande o pequeño el lago Maracaibo?

② Adivinanzas

Primero, escriban una breve descripción de cada una de las siguientes referencias. Luego, lean las descripciones, una a la vez, a otra pareja. Ellos/Ellas identifican la referencia. Túrnense.

Bogotá	Simón Bolívar	el pico Bolívar
Caracas	«pequeña Venecia»	tepuyes
El Dorado	«oro negro»	el Salto Ángel
la Nueva Granada	el río Orinoco	el lago Maracaibo

El río Orinoco cruza los extensos llanos[2] venezolanos que ocupan un tercio[3] del país y son una importante zona ganadera[4]. En los llanos del sur están los tepuyes, misteriosas elevaciones en forma de mesa. Describa usted estos tepuyes de Venezuela.

Encuentro cultural
Artes literarias

Miguel Fernando Caro

La siguiente narración del escritor colombiano Miguel Fernando Caro es un ejemplo del minicuento o minificción, un género literario entre el cuento y el poema. El objetivo del minicuento es establecer una historia interesante y revelar una sorpresa con muy pocas palabras. Por eso, su composición es difícil y algunas personas dicen que es similar al *haikú* japonés. El minicuento es muy popular, especialmente en Colombia y Venezuela, en donde existen revistas especializadas y se han publicado varias colecciones.

El amigo

Todas las mañanas, cumpliendo[1] con la rutina de mi trabajo, paso por una casa en cuyo[2] balcón hay un viejo sentado en su silla de ruedas. Siempre, al pasar junto a la casa, el viejo y yo nos saludamos batiendo[3] nuestras manos.

No sé cómo se llama ni él sabe mi nombre. Tal vez el vernos todos los días casi obligatoriamente nos haya hecho amigos.

Hoy no nos vimos y al pasar por su balcón me he sentido muy triste al pensar en lo que pudo haberle ocurrido; ya a su edad, y con la mala salud que aparentaba[4], despertar a un nuevo día era una sorpresa.

Esta mañana me he sentido muy alegre pues el viejo ha sido el primero en traer flores a mi tumba[5].

Preguntas

1. ¿Por dónde pasa el narrador cada día? ¿Quién está allí?
2. ¿Cómo se saludan los personajes de la historia?
3. ¿Qué relación existe entre los personajes de la historia? ¿Cree usted que se hablan? Explique.
4. ¿Por qué se siente triste el narrador? ¿Qué piensa el narrador que ha pasado? Y después, ¿por qué se siente alegre (contento)?
5. Según la información de la última línea, ¿quién muere primero?
6. ¿Qué demuestra la acción del viejo?
7. ¿Tiene usted una amistad como la de esta historia? ¿Qué sabe usted de esa persona?
8. En su experiencia, ¿es necesario saber mucho de una persona para establecer una buena amistad? Explique.

> ### READING STRATEGY
>
> **Noticing verb tenses**
> Focus on the verb endings and note the variety of verb tenses that the author uses throughout the story.
> • How many different tenses can you identify?
> • Are similar verb tenses grouped together? Interwoven?
> • Is the tense at the beginning and the end of the story the same?

[1]*fulfilling* [2]*whose* [3]*waving* [4]*appeared to have* [5]*grave*

Adjetivos

deprimido/a
embarazada

Adverbios

cada
de repente
mientras
por fin
una vez/ muchas veces

Expresiones sobre la salud

dolerle + el/la/los/las/…
hacer un análisis de sangre/ sacar
  sangre
hacer una cita
poner una inyección/ una vacuna
sacar una radiografía
tener dolor de…
tener náuseas/ escalofríos/ vómitos
tomar la temperatura/ la presión
  arterial/ el pulso

Órdenes que nos da un doctor/una doctora

Abra la boca.
Descanse.
Diga «¡Ah!»
Lleve la receta a la farmacia.
Respire profundamente.
Saque la lengua.
Tome aspirinas/ la pastilla/ las
  cápsulas/ líquidos.
Vaya a la farmacia.

Sustantivos

En el hospital

la ambulancia
la cama
el consultorio del médico/de la
  médica
emergencias
la habitación
la inyección
las muletas
el/la paciente

el/la paramédico/a
la recepción
la receta
la sala de espera
la silla de ruedas
el termómetro
la vacuna
la venda
el yeso

Algunos problemas de salud

la alergia
la congestión nasal
la diarrea
la fiebre
la gripe
la herida (grave)
el resfriado
la tos

El cuerpo humano

la boca
el brazo
la cabeza
la cara
el corazón
el cuello
el dedo
el diente
la espalda
el estómago
la garganta
el hombro
el hueso
el labio
la lengua
la mano
la nariz
el oído
el ojo
la oreja
el pecho
el pelo
el pie
la pierna
el pulmón
el tobillo
la uña

Verbos

cansarse
enfermarse
estornudar
examinar
fracturar(se)
lastimarse
preocuparse (por)
quedarse
sentarse (ie)
  estar sentado(a)/de pie
sentirse (ie, i)
torcer(se)
toser
vomitar

Autoprueba y repaso

I. Ud./Uds. commands. Dé mandatos afirmativos y negativos.

Modelo: traerlo
Tráigalo./ No lo traiga.

1. decírmelo
2. venir
3. sentarse
4. leerlo
5. explicárselo

II. The imperfect. Diga cómo las personas eran y lo que hacían cuando eran niños/as.

Modelo: yo / ser muy obediente
Era muy obediente.

1. mis hermanos y yo / ser niños muy buenos
2. nosotros / ir a una escuela pequeña
3. yo / escuchar a mis maestras
4. José / jugar al vólibol durante el recreo
5. Ana y Tere / ver la tele por la tarde
6. tú / comer galletas todos los días

III. The imperfect and the preterit. Lea la historia y luego decida si los verbos en paréntesis deben estar en el imperfecto o el pretérito.

Modelo: Roberto no ___se sentía___ (sentirse) nada bien.

1. Por eso _____ (llamar) al consultorio de su doctor y _____ (hablar) con la recepcionista.
2. Roberto le _____ (explicar) que _____ (estar) enfermo.
3. La recepcionista le _____ (preguntar) qué _____ (tener).
4. Él le _____ (explicar) que le _____ (doler) todo el cuerpo y que _____ (tener) fiebre, dolor de cabeza y escalofríos.
5. Ella también _____ (querer) saber si _____ (estar) muy congestionado.
6. Roberto _____ (contestar) afirmativamente.
7. La recepcionista le _____ (decir) que le _____ (poder) dar una cita para las dos de la tarde.
8. Roberto _____ (aceptar) y le _____ (dar) las gracias.
9. Como era temprano y _____ (sentirse) mal, _____ (dormirse) otra vez.

IV. Hacer with expressions of time.

A. Diga cuánto tiempo hace que usted…

Modelo: estudiar en esta universidad
Hace un año que estudio en esta universidad.

1. estar en clase
2. estudiar español
3. conocer al/a la profesor/a de español
4. vivir en la misma casa o apartamento
5. tener licencia de conducir un auto

B. Diga cuánto tiempo hace que pasó lo siguiente.

1. hablar con su familia
2. comprar un regalo para alguien
3. hacerse un examen médico
4. visitar un museo
5. llegar a la universidad

V. General review. Conteste con oraciones completas.

1. ¿Qué síntomas tenía usted la última vez que fue al médico?
2. ¿Cuánto tiempo hace que usted estudia en la universidad?
3. ¿Cuánto tiempo hace que usted conoció a su mejor amigo/a?
4. ¿Quién y cómo era su maestro/a preferido/a en la escuela primaria?
5. ¿Dónde estaba usted cuando ocurrió el ataque terrorista del 11 de septiembre?
6. ¿Cómo se sintió usted al oír las noticias? ¿Qué hizo usted después?

Answers to the *Autoprueba y repaso* are found in **Apéndice 2**.

Así es mi casa

Goals for communication

- To talk about a house or an apartment and its contents
- To talk about household chores
- To use commands in informal situations
- To talk about what has or had happened
- To make comparisons

Así se dice

Así es mi casa

1. el techo
2. el dormitorio/ la recámara
   La habitación
3. la pared
4. las cortinas
5. la lámpara
6. el espejo
7. la cómoda
8. guardar
9. el segundo piso
10. la escalera
11. el baño
12. el lavabo
13. el suelo/ el piso
20. la sala
21. el sofá
22. la alfombra
23. el estéreo
24. la chimenea
25. el sillón
26. subir
27. bajar
28. el primer piso
37. el comedor

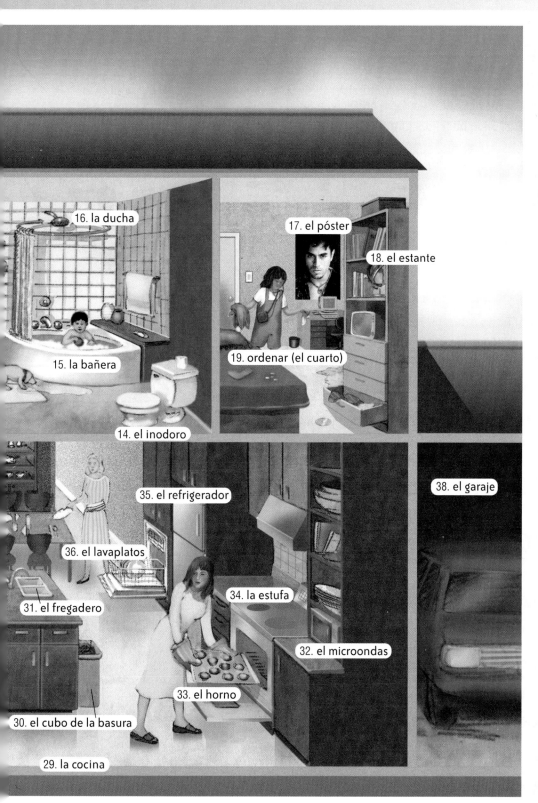

16. la ducha
17. el póster
18. el estante
15. la bañera
19. ordenar (el cuarto)
14. el inodoro
35. el refrigerador
38. el garaje
36. el lavaplatos
34. la estufa
31. el fregadero
32. el microondas
33. el horno
30. el cubo de la basura
29. la cocina

1. roof
2. bedroom
3. wall
4. curtains
5. lamp
6. mirror
7. chest of drawers
8. to keep, put away
9. second floor
10. stairs
11. bathroom
12. bathroom sink
13. floor
14. toilet
15. bathtub
16. shower
17. poster
18. bookshelf, shelf
19. to tidy (the room)
20. living room
21. sofa
22. rug, carpet
23. stereo
24. fireplace, chimney
25. easy chair
26. to go up
27. to go down
28. first floor
29. kitchen
30. trash can
31. kitchen sink
32. microwave
33. oven
34. stove
35. refrigerator
36. dishwasher
37. dining room
38. garage

Práctica y comunicación

2 **9-1.** **En casa.** Conteste según los dibujos de las páginas 306–307.

Los abuelos, tíos y primos visitan a la familia. Estamos en el segundo piso.

1. La abuela Lucía está en el dormitorio[1] principal. ¿Dónde está sentada?
2. ¿Qué está aprendiendo a[2] hacer Ana?
3. ¿Qué artículos de ropa, etc. se ven en el ropero/clóset?
4. ¿Dónde podemos guardar la ropa interior y los calcetines?
5. ¿Qué hay en la pared? ¿Y en la ventana? ¿Y al lado de la cama?
6. ¿Dónde está Juanito? ¿Cuál es el problema? ¿Qué hace el perro Teo?
7. ¿Qué cosas se ven en el baño?
8. ¿Qué cosas guarda Elena en su estante? ¿Qué hay en la pared? ¿Qué está haciendo ella?
9. Para bajar al primer piso, ¿qué usamos?

Ahora estamos en el primer piso.

10. ¿Dónde está sentado el abuelo Noé? ¿Qué está haciendo?
11. El tío Antonio, Tere y Ricardo están haciendo un rompecabezas (*puzzle*). ¿Dónde están sentados Antonio y Tere?
12. ¿Dónde duermen Rodolfo, Gitana y sus gatitos? ¿Por qué les gusta dormir allí?
13. ¿Qué más hay en la sala? ¿Le gusta a usted el cuadro en la pared?
14. ¿Qué electrodomésticos hay en la cocina?
15. Julia, la madre, preparó las empanadas. ¿Dónde las pone?
16. ¿Dónde ponen la basura?
17. La tía Elisa está en el comedor. ¿Dónde pone los platos? ¿Cuántas personas van a cenar?

3 **9-2.** **¿Dónde están?** Según los dibujos de las páginas 306–307, ¿dónde están situadas algunas de las cosas que se ven en la casa?

> **Modelo:** entre
>
> **La escalera está entre la sala y la cocina.**

1. al lado de
2. encima de
3. frente a
4. cerca de

5. lejos de
6. fuera de
7. dentro de
8. delante de

---

[1] Remember that **dormitorio** = *bedroom* and **residencia estudiantil** = *dorm.*
[2] **Aprender** requires the preposition **a** when followed by an infinitive.

9-3. ¿Para qué sirve?

Primero, escriban una breve definición indicando para qué sirve cada objeto en la mesa. Luego, lean sus definiciones a otra pareja. Ellos/Ellas identifican la palabra. Túrnense.

Modelo: 1. el vaso
Sirve para beber agua, ...

1. vaso
2. copa
3. taza
4. cuchara
5. cucharita
6. cuchillo
7. tenedor
8. plato
9. servilleta

Y ahora, indiquen para qué sirven otras cosas de la casa: **la cómoda, el estante, el espejo, el lavabo, el fregadero** y **la escalera.**

Así se dice
En el hogar[1]

Pues, ¿por qué es diferente mi casa? Lea con cuidado y lo va a descubrir.

Vivo en una casa grande de dos pisos. Mi familia es **dueña**[2] de la casa; no tenemos que **alquilar**la[3]. Me encanta esta casa y no tengo deseos de **mudarme**[4]. Los **vecinos**[5] son buenos y simpáticos. Mi cuarto preferido en el invierno es la **sala familiar**[6]. ¿Saben por qué? Pues muy sencillo: cuando hace frío, me acuesto junto a la chimenea y no quiero **moverme**[7] de allí. No me molesta cuando los otros miembros de la familia **prenden**[8] o **apagan**[9] la **luz**[10], el radio o el televisor. Si suena el teléfono, lo ignoro. En el verano prefiero el **sótano**[11] porque es más fresco. Mi **mueble**[12] favorito, un viejo sofá, está allí, y los **ruidos**[13] de la **lavadora**[14] y de la **secadora**[15] me **ayudan**[16] a* dormirme. No crean que soy perezoso. Guardo mis energías para los paseos de noche por el **jardín**[17]. También ayudo a mantener la casa libre de ratones°. Soy un buen gato. Me llaman Rodolfo.

libre... *free of mice*

(1) home (2) owner (f.) (3) to rent (4) move; **mudarse** *to move (from house to house)*
(5) neighbors (6) family room (7) move (myself); **mover (ue)** *to move (8) turn on;* **prender** *to turn on (lights, etc.) (9) turn off;* **apagar** *to turn off (10) light (11) basement (12) piece of furniture (13) noises (14) washer (15) dryer (16) help me;* **ayudar** *to help (17) garden*

---

* **Ayudar** requires the preposition **a** when followed by an infinitive.

9-4. **Preguntas personales.** Háganse las preguntas.

1. ¿Dónde vive tu familia ahora? ¿Cuánto tiempo hace que viven allí? ¿Cuándo se mudaron allí?
2. ¿Tiene tu casa/apartamento chimenea? ¿Sala familiar? ¿Garaje? ¿Sótano? ¿Jardín?
3. ¿Cuántas recámaras tiene? ¿Cuántos baños? ¿Cuántos pisos?
4. ¿Cuál es tu cuarto preferido? ¿Por qué?
5. ¿Te gustan los vecinos? ¿Quién es tu vecino/a favorito/a? ¿Por qué?
6. ¿Vives ahora con tu familia? Si no, ¿dónde vives?
7. ¿Qué muebles hay en tu recámara? ¿Tienes pósteres o fotos en las paredes? (¿De quién/qué?)
8. En tu cuarto, ¿tienes un lugar especial para guardar tus cosas «secretas»? (¿Dónde las guardas?) (¿Qué tipo de cosas guardas?)
9. Al salir, ¿apagas la luz? ¿Y la computadora?
10. Después de terminar tus estudios universitarios, ¿piensas alquilar un apartamento o comprar una casa? (¿Dónde?)

Así se dice

Los quehaceres domésticos° *Housekeeping chores*

Otros quehaceres

darle comida al perro/
  al gato
hacer las compras
lavar el carro
lavar la ropa
limpiar los baños
ordenar el cuarto
preparar la comida

1. hacer la cama /
pasar la aspiradora

2. poner la mesa /
quitar la mesa

3. lavar los platos /
secar los platos

4. sacar la basura /
cortar el césped

 9-5. **Las rutinas.** Usen los quehaceres presentados en el *Así se dice* para contestar las siguientes preguntas.

1. Según los dibujos, ¿qué hacían los estudiantes habitualmente en la casa que alquilaron por el verano? **Alfonso...**
2. ¿Qué hacían ustedes para ayudar a la familia cuando eran niños?
3. ¿Quiénes en su familia normalmente hacen los quehaceres indicados?
4. ¿En cuáles deben participar más los hombres/las mujeres? ¿Con cuáles deben ayudar los niños?

Manuel   Linda   Inés

3 *Inés y Linda van a compartir un apartamento el próximo año académico. Después de buscar apartamento todo el día, las chicas se encuentran con Manuel en un café.*

MANUEL: ¿Qué tal? ¿Encontraron un apartamento apropiado?

LINDA: Bueno, vimos muchos apartamentos, pero no encontramos exactamente lo que buscábamos.

MANUEL: ¿Y cómo eran los apartamentos que vieron?

INÉS: Uno tenía dos dormitorios, pero sólo un baño; otro tenía una cocina muy pequeña...

LINDA: Y no encontramos nada cerca de la universidad.

INÉS: Uno que vimos cerca del parque tenía sala y comedor, pero tenía muy pocas ventanas; no había suficiente luz.

LINDA: ¡Ay, Manuel! ¡Nunca vamos a encontrar nuestro apartamento ideal!

MANUEL: Pues, ¿qué es lo que buscan?

INÉS: El apartamento que queremos debe tener dos recámaras grandes, dos baños completos, una sala y un comedor alfombrados, ¡y muchas ventanas!

LINDA: Sí, y también una cocina equipada con microondas y lavaplatos. Y una piscina°.   *swimming pool*

INÉS: ¡Ah! Y el alquiler debe ser barato. Sólo queremos pagar 700 dólares mensuales.

MANUEL: Supongo° que también quieren aire acondicionado, ¿no?   *I suppose*

INÉS Y
LINDA: ¡Claro que sí!

MANUEL: Pues... ¡buena suerte°! Van a necesitarla.   **buena...** *good luck!*

¿Qué pasa?

1. ¿Qué hicieron Inés y Linda hoy?

2. ¿Por qué no les gustaron los apartamentos que vieron?

3. ¿Cómo es el apartamento que quieren?

4. ¿Cuánto quieren pagar Inés y Linda?

5. ¿Por qué les desea Manuel «buena suerte» a las chicas?

6. ¿Cómo es el lugar donde vive usted? ¿Es el lugar ideal? Explique.

¿Cómo va a ser la casa de sus sueños? Dígaselo a un/a compañero/a de clase.

Estructuras

1 **Giving orders and advice to family and friends:** *Tú* **commands**

> Ven, mi amor. No te desanimes. Camina hacia tu abuelita.

Informal **tú** commands are used to give orders or advice to persons whom you address informally as **tú** (friends, children, etc.). Affirmative and negative **tú** command forms differ from each other.

A. Affirmative *tú* commands

Regular affirmative **tú** command forms are identical to the third-person singular (**él, ella, usted**) forms of the present tense.

Present tense	**Affirmative *tú* command**	
Él mira.	¡Mira!	*Look!*
Ella espera.	¡Espera!	*Wait!*
Usted vuelve.	¡Vuelve!	*Come back!*
Él lo abre.	¡Ábrelo!	*Open it!*
Ella me lo muestra.	¡Muéstramelo!	*Show it to me!*

Some affirmative **tú** command forms are irregular:

decir	**di**	**Di**me la verdad.
hacer	**haz**	**Haz** la cama, por favor.
ir	**ve**	**Ve** al garaje para buscar los refrescos.
poner	**pon**	**Pon** la ropa en el ropero.
salir	**sal**	**Sal** de mi cuarto, por favor.
ser	**sé**	**Sé** bueno, por favor.
tener	**ten**	**Ten** paciencia. Vamos a cenar muy pronto.
venir	**ven**	**Ven** a la cocina para ayudarme.

Object and reflexive pronouns are *always* attached to the end of affirmative **tú** commands. A written accent is added in combinations of more than two syllables.

Cómpralo.	*Buy it.*
Póntelo.	*Put it on.*
Hazlo.	*Do it.*

Práctica y comunicación

9-6. **Los quehaceres domésticos.** Según los dibujos, díganle a las personas lo que deben hacer. Use el mandato de **tú**.

1. sacar la basura

2. sacudir los muebles

3. pasar la aspiradora

4. ordenar el cuarto

5. hacer la cama

6. lavar y secar los platos

7. poner la mesa

8. darle comida al gato

9. sacar a pasear al perro

10. regar (ie) las plantas

11. cortar el césped

12. barrer el patio

¿Cuáles de estos quehaceres haces o hacías tú?

9-7. **¡Hazlo, por favor!** Uno/a de ustedes es el hermano/ la hermana mayor y le da instrucciones a su hermano/a menor que tiene siete años. Use mandatos de **tú** afirmativos. Túrnense.

> **Modelo:** salir...
> **Sal del clóset, por favor. ¡No debes jugar allí!**

1. lavar...

2. poner la ropa...

3. ayudarme a...

4. traerme...

5. apagar...

6. venir...

7. sentarte en...

8. quitarte...

9. ponerte...

10. decirme que...

11. ir a...

12. ¡ser bueno!

B. Negative *tú* commands

To make a negative **tú** command, simply add **-s** to the **Ud.** command.

Ud. command	Negative *tú* command	
Espere en la sala.	No **esperes** en la sala.	*Don't wait in the living room.*
Ponga los libros allí.	No **pongas** los libros allí.	*Don't put the books there.*
Cierre la ventana.	No **cierres** la ventana.	*Don't close the window.*

Object pronouns are placed before the verb in all negative commands. Observe the placement of the pronouns in the following negative and affirmative commands.

Negative	Affirmative
¡No **lo** comas!	Cómelo!
¡No **los** compres!	¡Cómpralos!
¡No **lo** hagas!	¡Hazlo!
¡No **te** vayas!	¡Vete!

DICHOS

No digas en secreto lo que no quieres oír en público.

¿Qué puede pasar si usted le dice algo en secreto a otra persona?

Práctica y comunicación

9-8. **¡No, no, no!** ¿Qué le dice la madre al niño?

> **Modelo:** prender el televisor ahora
> **No prendas el televisor ahora.**

1. tocar el horno
2. jugar con esas tijeras
3. correr por la casa
4. ponerte esos calcetines sucios
5. comerte todas las galletas
6. hablar con comida en la boca
7. molestar al gato
8. dormirte ahora ¡Vamos a cenar!

9-9. **Dos amigos mandones.** Imaginen que ustedes son dos amigos/as mandones/as que constantemente le dan órdenes contradictorias a otra persona que vive con ustedes. Combinen las opciones presentadas para completar cada orden. Túrnense.

> **Modelo:** Lava...
> **Amigo/a 1:** Lava la ropa ahora, por favor.
> **Amigo/a 2:** No la laves ahora. Lávala más tarde.

1. Lava...	la luz	hoy
2. Seca...	el estéreo	mañana
3. Limpia...	la cama	ahora

4. Saca...	la aspiradora	más tarde
5. Haz...	la ropa	el lunes
6. Pasa...	los discos compactos	en la mañana
7. Apaga...	los platos	esta tarde
8. Prende...	la basura	este fin de semana
9. Devuelve...	el baño	pronto

9–10. **El diablo y el ángel.** Hay un conflicto en su conciencia entre lo que dice el diablo y lo que dice el ángel. Primero, escriban un mandato afirmativo. Luego, cámbienlo a la forma negativa.

> **Modelo:** fumar...
> El diablo: **¡Fuma cigarrillos! Son buenos para la salud.**
> El ángel: **¡No fumes!**

1. beber...   **6.** salir...

2. comer...   **7.** ir...

3. comprar...   **8.** manejar...

4. gastar...   **9.** dormir...

5. ver...

¡Hazlo!
¡No lo hogas!

Ahora, presenten algunos de sus mandatos a la clase.

9–11. **Nuestro amigo Esteban.** Esteban es «un poco» desordenado. Estudien el dibujo y díganle lo que debe o no debe hacer. Usen mandatos de **tú** afirmativos y negativos. Un/a secretario/a escribe los mandatos y luego se los presenta a la clase.

Palabras útiles	
cajón	*drawer (bureau)*
recoger	*to gather, pick up*

¡Mira! ¡Por fin he aprendido a esquiar!

2 Saying what has happened: The present perfect

The present perfect describes actions that began in the past and whose consequences are still felt in the present. The time period that frames the action is not over yet. When the action is completed in a period of time that is over, *the preterit*, not the present perfect, is used.

> **He estudiado** mucho hoy y ahora voy a jugar al tenis.
> *I have studied a lot today and now I am going to play tennis.*

> El semestre pasado **estudié** mucho.
> *Last semester I studied very hard.*

The present perfect combines the present tense of **haber** (*to have*) and the past participle of a verb. It corresponds to the English *have/has* + past participle (verb + *-ed/-en*).

> Esteban **ha prendido** el televisor.   *Esteban has turned on the TV.*
> Se **ha comido** toda la pizza.   *He has eaten all the pizza.*

el presente de *haber* + el participio pasado					
(yo)	**he**		*I have*		
(tú)	**has**		*you have*		
(Ud., él, ella)	**ha**	**+ llamado**	*you have, he/she has*	**+ called**	
(nosotros/as)	**hemos**	**+ salido**	*we have*	**+ left**	
(vosotros/as)	**habéis**		*you have*		
(Uds., ellos, ellas)	**han**		*you/they have*		

To form the past participle of most Spanish verbs, add **-ado** to the stem of **-ar** verbs and **-ido** to the stem of **-er** and **-ir** verbs. When used with **haber**, the past participle does not change; it always ends in **-o**.

llamar	llam	+	**-ado**	=	**llamado**
comer	com	+	**-ido**	=	**comido**
vivir	viv	+	**-ido**	=	**vivido**

The following **-er** and **-ir** verbs have irregular past participles.

abrir	**abierto**	*opened, open*
decir	**dicho**	*said, told*
escribir	**escrito**	*written*
hacer	**hecho**	*done*
morir	**muerto**	*died, dead*
romper (*to break*)	**roto**	*broken*
poner	**puesto**	*put, placed*
ver	**visto**	*seen*
volver	**vuelto**	*returned*
devolver	**devuelto**	*returned*
resolver (*to resolve*)	**resuelto**	*resolved*

Direct objects, indirect objects, and reflexive pronouns immediately precede the conjugated form of **haber**.

Todavía no **lo** he terminado.   *I haven't finished **it** yet.*

Le he escrito varias veces.   *I have written **(to) him** several times.*

Nos hemos preocupado por él.   *We have worried about him.*

> The past participle may also be used as an adjective with **estar** and with nouns to show a condition. As an adjective, it agrees in gender and number with the noun it describes. You have used this construction in previous chapters.
>
> La puerta está **cerrada**.   *The door is **closed**.*
> Duermo con las ventanas **abiertas**.   *I sleep with the windows **open**.*
> Mis amigos están **sentados** en el sofá.   *My friends are **seated** on the sofa.*

Práctica y comunicación

9-12. Los amigos llegan.
Usted y su compañero/a de apartamento esperan la visita de unos amigos muy especiales. Han trabajado mucho. ¿Qué han hecho para prepararse para la visita?

Modelo: lavar la ropa
Hemos lavado la ropa.

1. ordenar la casa
2. hacer las camas
3. pasar la aspiradora
4. lavar los platos
5. sacar la basura
6. ir al supermercado
7. empezar a preparar la comida
8. poner la mesa
9. bañarse
10. vestirse

9-13. ¿Qué hay de nuevo?

Imagine que usted estudió en España el semestre pasado y al volver a la universidad descubre que han ocurrido muchas cosas.

Octavio / fracturarse

Modelo: Octavio se ha fracturado una pierna.

1. Esteban / sacar   **2.** Rubén / cortarse   **3.** el profesor Marín-Vivar / afeitarse la barba   **4.** Javier / ganar   **5.** Linda / aprender a   **6.** Camila / pintar

9-14. ¿Qué ha pasado?

Caminando por la clase, hágales preguntas a sus compañeros/as para averiguar lo que han hecho recientemente. Apunte el nombre de cada estudiante que responde *afirmativamente* a una pregunta.

Modelo:

ir a la biblioteca

Estudiante 1: **¿Has ido a la biblioteca recientemente?**

Estudiante 2: **Sí, he ido a la biblioteca recientemente.**

Recientemente...

HINT | * = irregular past participle

_____ **1.** ayudar a un/a amigo/a (¿A quién?)

_____ **2.** limpiar tu recámara/apartamento (¿Cuándo?)

_____ **3.** salir con alguien interesante/especial (¿Con quién?)

_____ **4.** ver* una película buena (¿Cuál?)

_____ **5.** ir a un concierto de *rock* (¿Cuál?)

_____ **6.** sacar una «A» en un examen (¿En qué clase?)

_____ **7.** escribir* un trabajo (¿Para qué clase?)

_____ **8.** decirle* una mentira (*lie*) a alguien

_____ **9.** viajar (*to travel*) fuera del país (¿Adónde?)

_____ **10.** mudarte (¿De dónde a dónde?)

_____ **11.** hacer* ejercicio en el gimnasio (¿Cuándo?)

_____ **12.** divertirte mucho (¿Dónde?)

Ahora, según los nombres que tiene, dígale a la clase algo que un/a estudiante ha hecho. ¿Quién tiene el mayor número de compañeros en la lista?

9–15. **Aventuras interesantes.** Escriba tres cosas interesantes que usted ha hecho recientemente—lugares adonde ha ido, cosas que ha visto, etc. Luego, compare sus aventuras con las de un compañero/a. Finalmente, cuéntele a la clase la aventura más interesante de su compañero/a.

---

④ **¡Qué dilema!**

Sus padres salieron de fin de semana y los dejaron a ustedes encargados (in charge) de la casa. Ustedes decidieron tener una pequeña fiesta. Sus padres regresan un día antes, y la casa está hecha un desastre. Preguntan enojados: **¿Qué ha pasado aquí?**

Estructuras

③ **Saying what had happened: The past perfect**

...pero Juanito, me dijiste que ya habías ordenado tu cuarto.

The past perfect describes an action that had already occurred prior to another event in the past.

> Cuando llegaron los abuelos, ya **habíamos limpiado** la casa.
> *When our grandparents arrived, we **had** already **cleaned** the house.*

The past perfect is formed with the imperfect tense of **haber** and the past participle of the verb. It corresponds to the English *had eaten, had spoken,* etc.

el imperfecto de *haber* + el participio pasado				
(yo)	**había**		I had	
(tú)	**habías**		you had	
(Ud., él, ella)	**había**	+ **llamado**	you/he/she had	+ *called*
(nosotros/as)	**habíamos**	+ **salido**	we had	+ *left*
(vosotros/as)	**habíais**		you had	
(Uds., ellos, ellas)	**habían**		you/they had	

Así es mi casa

Práctica y comunicación

9-16. **¡Qué hijos tan malos!** Los padres salieron de casa. ¿Qué descubrieron al regresar? ¿Qué habían y no habían hecho los hijos?

Modelo: ordenar la sala familiar

Probablemente habían/no habían ordenado la sala familiar.

1. pasar la aspiradora
2. hacer las camas
3. invitar a amigos a la casa
4. comerse toda la comida en el refrigerador
5. sacar la basura
6. lavar los platos
7. ver muchas películas
8. romper una ventana

9-17. **¡Los abuelos llegan!** Antes de la llegada de los abuelos, ¿qué habían hecho los miembros de la familia? Mencionen varias actividades y usen la imaginación. Tienen cuatro minutos.

Cuando llegaron los abuelos...

1. Mi madre ya había...
2. Mi padre...
3. Mis hermanos/as...
4. Yo...

¿Qué grupo tiene el mayor número de actividades? Léanselas a la clase.

DICHOS

Sobre gustos no hay nada escrito.

distance   **Del dicho al hecho hay largo trecho°.**

Dicho y hecho.

¿Cuál de estos refranes es el título de su libro de español?

¿Cuál se refiere a las personas que hablan mucho pero no hacen nada?

¿Cuál se refiere a las preferencias individuales?

Noticias culturales

El patio de las casas hispanas: Un parque privado

Uno de los elementos más representativos de muchas viviendas hispanas es el patio. Casi todas las casas —aun las más pequeñas— tienen algún tipo de patio. El diseño tradicional del patio hispano, rodeado de° paredes altas, es una mezcla° de influencias romanas y árabes. En estas dos culturas la vida privada era muy importante y las casas estaban separadas de la calle por paredes y muros. La luz y el aire entraban en los cuartos por las ventanas, puertas y los balcones que rodeaban el patio central.

rodeado... surrounded by / mixture

Hoy, las casas hispanas de estilo colonial tienen este tipo de patio central, con una fuente° y plantas; pero en las casas más modernas, el patio generalmente está detrás de la casa. A diferencia de los «decks» tan populares en los EE.UU., los patios hispanos no tienen pisos de madera°; frecuentemente el suelo está cubierto de cerámica o piedra°.

fountain

wood

stone

El patio, un lugar privado al aire libre°, es un espacio fundamental en la vivienda hispana porque tiene varias funciones importantes. Es un sitio cómodo° para tomar un poco de sol, recibir visitas o dar una pequeña fiesta.

al... open air

comfortable

¿Qué recuerda?

1. ¿Por qué es el patio un elemento representativo de las viviendas hispanas?
2. ¿Qué influencias culturales se manifiestan en el diseño de los patios tradicionales hispanos?
3. ¿Cómo es el patio de una vivienda hispana tradicional?
4. ¿Dónde está el patio en las casas más modernas?
5. ¿Qué diferencia existe entre un «deck» y un patio?
6. ¿Cómo utilizan los hispanos el patio? Dé dos ejemplos.

Conexiones y contrastes

1. ¿Tiene su casa un patio o un «deck»? ¿Qué hace usted allí?
2. ¿Piensa usted que el patio o el «deck» de su casa es un área suficientemente privada? Descríbalo.

Un patio tradicional hispano. Colombia. Describa este patio. ¿Qué actividades son posibles en esta parte de la casa?

4 Making comparisons: Comparisons of equality and inequality

A. Comparisons of equality

Es tan guapo como Antonio Banderas, ¿no?

- Use **tan... como** (*as . . . as*) to make an equal comparison with adjectives and adverbs.

Esta torta es **tan** rica **como** la otra.	*This cake is **as** delicious **as** the other one.*
Yo cocino **tan** bien **como** tú.	*I cook **as** well **as** you.*

- Use **tanto/a/os/as... como** (*as much/many . . . as*) with nouns to compare equal quantities.

Tengo **tanto** trabajo **como** tú.	*I have **as much** work **as** you.*
Hay **tantos** libros **como** videos en el estante.	*There are **as many** books **as** videos on the shelf.*
Hay **tantas** revistas **como** periódicos aquí.	*There are **as many** magazines **as** newspapers here.*

- Use **tanto como** (*as much as*) with verbs to compare equal actions.

Estudio **tanto como** tú.	*I study **as much as** you do.*

Práctica y comunicación

(2) **9-18.** **Son muy parecidos (*They're a lot alike*).** Hagan comparaciones de igualdad refiriéndose a los dibujos.

> **Modelo:** 1. Octavio es tan inteligente como Javier.

1. Octavio / Javier
ser / tan… como…

2. Javier / su amigo
ser / tan… como…

3. Camila / su hermana
ser / tan… como…

4. el ogro / su amigo
ser / tan… como…

5. Alfonso/ el profesor
tener / tanto… como…

6. Linda / Inés
tener / tantas… como…

7. Natalia / Rubén
… tanto como…

8. Pepita / Esteban
… tanto como…

9-19. **Otras personas y yo.** Escriba comparaciones de igualdad entre otras personas (compañeros de clase, amigos, parientes, etc.) y usted. Tiene cinco minutos. Algunos estudiantes van a leer sus comparaciones a la clase. Incluya:

1. características personales

2. cosas que tienen

3. actividades en que participan

Soy tan… como…

Tengo tanto/a/os/as… como

…tanto como…

B. Comparisons of inequality and the superlative

Comparisons of inequality

Teo, ¡corres más rápido que yo! ¡No te escapes!

- Use **más/menos... que** (*more/fewer, less . . . than*) with adjectives, adverbs, or nouns to compare *persons or things that are not equal.*

  Este apartamento es **más/menos** caro **que** el otro.
  *This apartment is **more/less** expensive **than** the other one.*

  Ella limpia su apartamento **más/menos** frecuentemente **que** yo.
  *She cleans her apartment **more/less** frequently **than** I.*

  Esta casa tiene **más/menos** ventanas **que** la otra.
  *This house has **more/fewer** windows **than** the other one.*

- Use **más/menos que** (*more/less than*) with verbs to compare *unequal actions.*
  Ella paga **más/menos que** tú.
  *She pays **more/less than** you.*

- Use **de** instead of **que** before a number.
  El sillón costó **más/menos de** $625.
  *The armchair cost **more/less than** $625.*

Some Spanish adjectives and adverbs have irregular comparative forms. These forms do not use **más** or **menos**.

Adjetivo		Adverbio		Comparativo	
bueno/a	*good*	bien	*well*	mejor	*better*
malo/a	*bad*	mal	*badly*	peor	*worse*
joven	*young*			menor	*younger*
viejo/a	*old*			mayor	*older (referring to age of a person)*

Esta película es **buena.**	*This movie is **good.***
Ésa es **mejor que** ésta.	*That one is **better than** this one.*
Ese restaurante es **malo.**	*That restaurant is **bad.***
Aquél es aún **peor.**	*That one is even **worse.***

The superlative

The superlative form of the adjective is used when persons or things are singled out as being *the most . . . , least . . . , best . . . , worst . . . , tallest . . . , etc.*

To form the superlative use:

> **el/la/los/las... más/menos... de (in)...**

La cocina es **el** cuarto **más** popular **de** nuestra casa.

The kitchen is the most popular room in our house.

> **el/la/los/las + mejor(es)/peor(es)... de...**

Los mejores restaurantes **de** la ciudad están en el centro.

The best restaurants in the city are downtown.

Según la tienda, ¿cuáles son los mejores productos de Argentina? Mencione tres. Mendoza, Argentina.

Práctica y comunicación

② **9-20.** **¿De acuerdo (*Do you agree*)?** Digan si ustedes están de acuerdo con las siguientes generalizaciones. Si no están de acuerdo, indiquen su opinión. Túrnense.

> **Modelo:** El español es más difícil que el inglés.
>
> **Sí, el español es...** *o* No, el español no es... Es más fácil. *o*
>
> **El español es tan difícil/fácil como el inglés.**

1. La clase de español es más divertida que la clase de matemáticas.
2. Las mujeres de esta clase son más inteligentes que los hombres.
3. Los hombres de esta clase trabajan más que las mujeres.
4. Las mujeres, en general, gastan menos dinero que los hombres.
5. Los hombres hispanos bailan mejor que los hombres estadounidenses.
6. Los coches estadounidenses son mejores que los japoneses.
7. El dinero es más importante que el amor.
8. Vivir en la ciudad es mejor que vivir en el campo.
9. El alcohol es peor que los cigarrillos.

③ **9-21.** **Entre nosotros.** Primero, todos escriben los nombres de las personas de su grupo en el cuadro. Luego, háganse preguntas para completar el cuadro y apunten la cantidad (*quantity*). Después, hagan comparaciones usando la información del cuadro.

Modelo: Tengo más/menos hermanos que Juan. *o*
Tengo tantos hermanos como Juan.

Número de...	_____	_____	_____
1. hermanos que tiene			
2. clases que tiene este semestre			
3. discos compactos de música que tiene			
4. mensajes electrónicos que recibe cada semana			
5. horas que estudia por semana			
6. horas que trabaja por semana			

Ahora, presenten algunas de sus comparaciones a la clase.

② **9-22.** **Las fotos de mi amiga.** Comparen las siguientes fotos. Hagan varias comparaciones en cada caso.

La familia de Raúl y Adelina. México D.F., México

Casa en la ciudad. Mérida, Yucatán, México

Desayuno en la casa de Raúl y de Adelina. México D.F., México

La familia de Gustavo y Elvira. San Juan, Puerto Rico

Casa (*choza*) en el campo. Yucatán, México

Desayuno en un restaurante. Madrid, España

9-23. **Necesito alquilar un apartamento.** Usted decide alquilar un apartamento en la República Dominicana. Lea los tres anuncios. Luego, escriba cuatro oraciones comparando los tres apartamentos. ¿Cuál prefiere y por qué?

1.

Encantador Penthouse en Serrallés, RD$21,000, 3 habs., 3 baños con terraza, jacuzzi, bar. BUENA VISTA 565-2132

2.

Estudio amueblado. E. Morales RD$7,000. Bello, 1 Hab., baño, sala comedor, cocina. Totalmente equipado. Muebles nuevos. Inversor. NUEVOS HORIZONTES 592-2100

3.

Penthouse amueblado. 4 habs., 4.5 baños, 3 balcones, 2 terrazas techadas, amplias áreas de servicio. Vista panorámica, 2 parqueos techados, planta full, ascensor. RD$39,500. Lucía. 541-1987

9-24. **Los más o los menos.** Usen el superlativo de los adjetivos para comparar las palabras en cada serie.

> **Modelo:** caro: el sillón, la computadora, los discos compactos
> **La computadora es la más cara de los tres.** *o*
> **Los discos compactos son los menos caros.**

1. necesario: el teléfono   las cortinas   el lavaplatos

2. barato: el refrigerador   la estufa   el radio

3. útil: la cómoda   el espejo   el cuadro

4. indispensable: el estante   el inodoro   la alfombra

5. importante: la secadora   la lavadora   el microondas

9-25. **¿Cuál es el mejor?** Primero, escojan (*choose*) cuatro de las siguientes categorías. Luego, en cada categoría, comparen varias opciones y decidan cuál es el/la mejor... de todos.

> **Modelo:** coches: el Ford, el Honda, el Mercedes
> **El... es el mejor de los tres.**

1. coches

2. revistas

3. películas recientes

4. programas de televisión

5. actores/actrices

6. cantantes/grupos musicales

7. restaurantes en la ciudad

8. equipos de...

Ahora, algunos grupos presentan sus conclusiones a la clase. ¿Están los otros estudiantes de acuerdo?

9-26. **Un anuncio comercial.** Escriban un anuncio comercial de treinta segundos para la televisión. Comparen tres productos similares (hamburguesas de Wendy's, MacDonald's, y Burger King, por ejemplo). Usen los comparativos y los superlativos. Presenten sus anuncios a la clase. ¿Quién presentó el mejor?

Dicho y hecho

Conversando

3. Bienes raíces (*Real estate*). Uno/a de ustedes es agente de bienes raíces con propiedades en Latinoamérica. Dos de ustedes quieren comprar propiedad en Costa Rica, Ecuador o Uruguay. Comparen las opciones presentadas.

Hablen de:

- ubicación (*location*)
- precio
- tipo de vivienda

- ventajas (*advantages*) y desventajas de cada una
- su decisión

80% vendido Primera Etapa ¡LLAME YA!

Entrega Inmediata

CONDOMINIO BALCONES DE SANTA ANA

BALCONES DE SANTA ANA está compuesto por 16 condominios independientes de 248 a 293 mts² cada uno.
Situado en Santa Ana, la zona de más plusvalía en San José, cuenta con piscina, casa club, zona de juegos, generosos jardines y hermosas vistas sobre los cerros de Escazú. Localizado a sólo 5 minutos de Multiplaza, 700 mts. de Santa Ana y fácil acceso a la pista San José – Caldera.

Una nueva forma de vivir...

Envueltos por la verde naturaleza

$215.000 a $225.000US

Cada casa cuenta con:

- Habitación principal con balcón, walk-in closet, baño y jacuzzi
- 2 y 3 habitaciones con closet
- 3 ½ – 4 ½ baños
- Amplio ático para múltiples usos*
- Sala de T.V.
- Sala con prevista para bar
- Comedor
- Cuarto de servicio o estudio
- Cocina de Euromobilia
- Lavandería y pilas
- Amplio jardín privado
- Terraza techada
- Cochera cubierta para dos carros

San José, Costa Rica

En la bella playa de Atacames, Ecuador.

Suites Playa Atacames

Usted merece un espacio propio para disfrutar de sus vacaciones.

- Frente al mar
- Departamentos de dos dormitorios, sala, cocina, comedor y balcón
- Pisos de cerámica
- Áreas comunales
- Tres piscinas
- Micromercado
- Áreas de estacionamiento

TODO ESTO POR: $36.000US

Playa de Atacames, Ecuador

En la más exclusiva ciudad vacacional de Latinoamérica, Punta del Este, Uruguay.

Condominios Península

Propiedades en venta. Amplios y luminosos ambientes, frente al mar y próximo a todo.

- Living-Comedor
- Terraza
- Dos dormitorios, dos baños
- Cocina

- Lavadero
- Dormitorio y baño de servicio
- Garage
- Muebles

$98.000US

Punta del Este, Uruguay

🎧 ¡A escuchar!

El nuevo apartamento de Susana. Su amiga Susana alquiló un apartamento y ahora ella necesita su ayuda para poner los muebles y otras cosas en un buen lugar. Escuche las instrucciones de ella y escriba el número de cada cosa en el lugar correspondiente. Opcional: Dibuje las cosas en el lugar correspondiente.

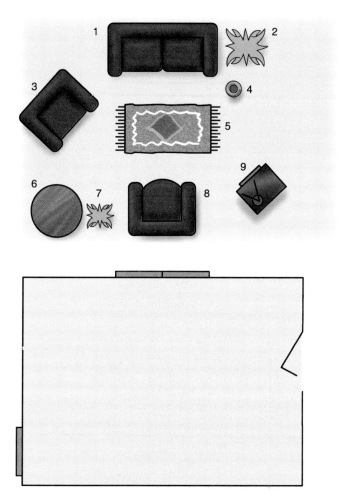

> **Palabra útil**
>
> el rincón   *corner*

✍️ De mi escritorio

Una casa muy especial. Escriba una descripción de la casa en la que usted vivía cuando era niño/a. Use formas del imperfecto y del pretérito.

Mencione:

- cuántos pisos tenía
- los colores
- las diferentes habitaciones
- los muebles de la casa
- si tenía jardín
- recuerdos especiales vividos allí

Así es mi casa

trescientos veintinueve **329**

Panorama cultural

Paraguay y Uruguay

Nacionalidades:
paraguayo(a)
uruguayo(a)

Person@je del momento

¿Sabe usted quién es José Luis Chilavert?
Busque información en el Internet y compártala con sus compañeros/as de clase.

Preguntas sobre el mapa

1. ¿Cuáles son los tres países vecinos de Paraguay?
2. ¿Cuál es la capital de Paraguay?
3. ¿Dónde está situada la capital de Uruguay?

Durante el período colonial estos países tuvieron una historia muy similar. Sin embargo, su situación geográfica y su destino político generaron diferencias regionales que resultaron en dos naciones con identidades muy distintas. Por ejemplo, en Uruguay la población es uniforme —casi todos descienden de inmigrantes. En Paraguay hay mucha diversidad. La población incluye inmigrantes europeos y aproximadamente veinticinco tribus indígenas.

Uruguay y Paraguay, junto con Brasil y Argentina, crearon en 1991 El Mercosur, una zona económica que corresponde a una área cuatro veces más grande que la de la Unión Europea.

Paraguay

Como Bolivia, Paraguay está en el corazón de Sudamérica y no tiene salida al océano. Paraguay deriva su nombre del río que lo cruza de norte a sur. Casi el 95% de la población vive al este del río. La zona del oeste es una extensa planicie llamada el Gran Chaco, que significa «lugar de caza[1]» en quechua.

Hoy en día Paraguay produce abundante energía eléctrica. La represa[4] de Itaipú puede generar hasta 12.600.000 kilovatios. Paraguay exporta la mayor parte de esta enorme producción eléctrica a Brasil. ¿Hay una represa en su estado?

La capital, Asunción, está a orillas[2] del río Paraguay. Es la ciudad más moderna del país y es el puerto más importante. La ciudad conserva muchos ejemplos de arquitectura colonial. Los tranvías[3] amarillos de Asunción se consideran una antigüedad. ¿Qué otras ciudades famosas también tienen tranvías?

Las espectaculares cataratas del Iguazú están en la frontera entre Argentina, Brasil y Paraguay. ¿Prefiere usted visitarlas en helicóptero o en bote?

[1]*hunting* [2]*a... on the banks* [3]*trolleys* [4]*dam* [5]*slaves*

A partir de 1609 los jesuitas establecieron comunidades autosuficientes que agrupaban a cientos de indígenas guaraníes y los protegían de los traficantes de esclavos[5] portugueses y españoles. Vea la foto de las ruinas de las misiones en Trinidad, Paraguay. ¿Conoce usted unas misiones como éstas? ¿Dónde están?

¿Sabía usted que...?

- Hoy, existen en Paraguay dos lenguas principales, el español y el guaraní. Los paraguayos cantan, escriben y expresan sus emociones en las dos lenguas.
- Paraguay es el único país de Latinoamérica en el cual la biosfera no está contaminada.

Uruguay

Uruguay es la república sudamericana más pequeña. El nombre del país viene de un río, el río Uruguay, que lo separa de Argentina. La geografía uruguaya es uniforme: al norte están las llanuras[6] y al sur está la Banda Oriental, una región muy plana donde está situada la capital.

La agricultura y la ganadería son la base de la economía del país. La industria pesquera y la manufactura de productos derivados del ganado (lana, cuero, carne) son otra parte importante del sector comercial. El turismo también genera muchos beneficios y representa casi el 30% de la actividad económica.

¿Sabía usted que...?

- La legislación social de Uruguay es una de las más innovadoras de Hispanoamérica. Todas las personas que han trabajado treinta años tienen derecho a jubilarse[9] con pensión.
- La vida cultural de Uruguay es muy intensa y el país tiene el índice de alfabetismo[10] más alto de Hispanoamérica (96%).

¿Qué descubrimos?

Existen varios contrastes importantes entre Paraguay y Uruguay. ¿A qué país hace referencia cada oración?

1. No tiene costas.
2. Su capital tiene costas sobre el Atlántico.
3. El español es la única lengua oficial.
4. Se hablan dos idiomas principales.
5. Su población es diversa; existe una gran variedad de tribus indígenas.
6. Su población es uniforme; casi todos descienden de inmigrantes.

(2) Adivinanzas

Escriban una breve descripción de cada una de las siguientes referencias. Luego otra pareja identifica cada una. Túrnense.

Mercosur	jesuitas	legislación social
Asunción	guaraní	Punta del Este
Itaipú	Montevideo	fútbol
Iguazú	economía de Uruguay	alfabetismo

Montevideo, la bella capital, está situada a orillas del Río de la Plata y el Atlántico; posee el mejor puerto natural de Sudamérica. En esta ciudad vive la mitad[7] de la población del país. Inicialmente Montevideo era un fuerte militar; por eso, no existen grandes edificios ni monumentos coloniales como en otras capitales. El aspecto de la ciudad es moderno. ¿Le gustaría a usted vivir en Montevideo?

Los uruguayos son fanáticos del fútbol. Han conquistado dos títulos olímpicos, dos campeonatos mundiales, catorce americanos y la Copa de Oro en 1980. El estadio Centenario en Montevideo es monumento histórico del fútbol mundial y sitio del primer mundial de fútbol en 1930. Capacidad: 80.000 personas. ¿Es usted fanático/a del fútbol?

Punta del Este, centro vacacional de fama mundial, es sinónimo de playas. Ofrece kilómetros de variada costa, desde las tranquilas aguas de sus bahías hasta el mar abierto y las olas[8] fuertes del lado del Atlántico.

[6]*flatlands* [7]*half* [8]*waves* [9]*to retire* [10]*literacy*

Encuentro cultural
Artes pictóricas

Pedro Figari

El pintor uruguayo Pedro Figari nació en Montevideo, Uruguay, en 1861 y murió en 1938. Pasó gran parte de su infancia en una granja[1] y allí vivió la cultura uruguaya que luego pintó en sus cuadros. Además de pintor fue un distinguido abogado, educador, periodista, político, filósofo y escritor.

En la pintura[2] *Baile criollo*, nos presenta una escena de danzas típicas. Figari pensaba que las culturas europeas habían alterado[3] la armonía de la vida en el Nuevo Mundo y que le correspondía al latinoamericano reestablecer ese orden o armonía. Le interesaban los temas nativos como este baile con gauchos. Observe atentamente la pintura antes de continuar.

Pedro Figari, *Baile Criollo*; 61x82 cm, óleo sobre lienzo. Photo courtesy Museo Virtual de Artes El País. ©1997 País.

Preguntas

1. ¿Cuáles son los colores del cuadro?
2. ¿Cómo son los trajes de los gauchos?
3. ¿Qué instrumento musical hay en la pintura?
4. ¿Qué hacen las diferentes personas?
5. ¿Por qué se viste de manera diferente la mujer del vestido rojo?
6. ¿Están afuera o dentro de la casa ¿Cómo lo sabe?
7. ¿Por qué tienen ventanas con rejas (*railings*)? ¿Tienen rejas las ventanas en su ciudad?

[1]*farm* [2]*painting*
[3]habían... *had altered*

Adverbio

peor

Sustantivos

Las partes de la casa

el baño
la chimenea
la cocina
el comedor
el dormitorio/ la recámara
la escalera
el garaje
el jardín
la pared
el primer piso
la sala
la sala familiar
el segundo piso
el sótano
el suelo/ el piso
el techo

Las cosas en la casa/ el apartamento

la alfombra
la cómoda
las cortinas
el cubo de la basura
el estante
el estéreo
la lámpara
la lavadora
la luz
los muebles
el póster
la secadora
el sillón
el sofá

En el baño

la bañera
la ducha
el espejo
el inodoro
el lavabo

En la cocina

la estufa
el fregadero
el horno
el lavaplatos
el microondas
el refrigerador

En la mesa

la copa
la cuchara
la cucharita
el cuchillo
el plato
la servilleta
la taza
el tenedor
el vaso

Otras palabras útiles

la dueña
el dueño
el hogar
el ruido
la vecina
el vecino

Verbos y expresiones verbales

alquilar
apagar
ayudar
bajar
guardar
mover(se)
mudarse
prender
romper
resolver
subir

cortar el césped
hacer la cama
lavar/ secar los platos
ordenar el cuarto
pasar la aspiradora
poner/ quitar la mesa
sacar la basura

I. Affirmative *tú* commands. ¿Qué le dice la mamá a los diferentes miembros de la familia?

Modelo: Irma / ir al mercado
Irma, ¡ve al mercado!

1. Beatriz / hacer la cama
2. María / pasar la aspiradora
3. Luis / devolver los libros al estante
4. Laila / poner la mesa
5. Miguel / limpiar el baño
6. Juanito / sacar la basura

II. Negative *tú* commands. ¿Qué le dice el hermano mayor al menor?

Modelo: no ponerte mi ropa
No te pongas mi ropa, por favor.

1. no prender el estéreo
2. no usar mi computadora
3. no tocar mis cosas
4. no salir ahora
5. no decirme mentiras (*lies*)
6. no preocuparte

III. The present perfect. ¿Qué han hecho las siguientes personas esta semana?

Modelo: yo / dormir mucho
He dormido mucho.

1. la abuela / trabajar en el jardín
2. todos nosotros / lavar y secar la ropa
3. papá / limpiar el garaje
4. mi hermana / salir dos veces a bailar
5. tú / no hacer nada

IV. The past perfect. Una noche hubo una tormenta y un apagón (*blackout*). ¿Qué habíamos hecho antes del incidente?

Modelo: nosotros / terminar nuestro proyecto
Habíamos terminado nuestro proyecto.

1. yo / apagar la computadora
2. tú / imprimir tu trabajo escrito
3. mi compañero/a de cuarto / cerrar las ventanas
4. nosotros / hacer la tarea para la clase de español
5. Linda y Teresa / leer la novela para la clase de inglés

V. Equal comparisons. Haga comparaciones de igualdad.

Modelo: Teresa tiene dos clases por la tarde. Yo tengo dos clases también.
Tengo tantas clases por la tarde como Teresa. *o*
Teresa tiene tantas clases por la tarde como yo.

1. Los estudiantes son simpáticos. Los profesores también son simpáticos.
2. El francés es difícil. El tailandés también es difícil.
3. Ana tiene mucha paciencia. Susana también tiene mucha paciencia.
4. Alberto compró dos libros. Su hermano también compró dos.

VI. Unequal comparisons and the superlative.

A. Diga cuál elemento de la serie es más grande, mejor, etc. que el otro.

Modelo: grande: Nueva York, Toronto
Nueva York es más grande que Toronto.

1. caro: el reloj Rolex, el reloj Timex
2. económico: comprar una casa, alquilar un apartamento
3. mejor: ir de vacaciones a la playa, ir de vacaciones a las montañas
4. divertido: limpiar la casa, ver la tele

B. Diga cuál elemento de la serie es el mejor, el más interesante, etc. de los tres.

Modelo: vieja: Roma, Boston, Calgary
Roma es la más vieja de las tres.

1. fría: Duluth, Minnesota; Santa Fe, New Mexico; Atlanta, Georgia
2. rico: Bill Gates, su profe, George W. Bush
3. mejor: el Ford, el Subaru, el Honda
4. interesante: las revistas *National Geographic, Newsweek, Movie Line*

VII. General review. Conteste con oraciones completas.

1. ¿Es usted tan generoso/a como su mejor amigo/a?
2. ¿Tiene usted tantos amigos como él/ella?
3. ¿Estudia usted más o menos que él/ella?
4. ¿Cuál es la clase más interesante de la universidad? ¿Por qué?
5. ¿Quién es el/la mejor profesor/a de esta universidad? ¿Por qué?
6. Usted vio el apartamento perfecto ayer. ¿Cómo era? (Use la imaginación.)
7. ¿Qué cosas importantes ha hecho usted este año?
8. ¿Qué cosas interesantes había hecho usted antes de empezar su carrera universitaria?

Answers to the *Autoprueba y repaso* are found in **Apéndice 2**.

Capítulo

10

Amigos y algo más

Goals for communication

- To talk about human relationships and the stages of life
- To express wishes and requests related to other people's actions
- To express emotional reactions and feelings about other people's actions

Así se dice

Amigos y algo más

1. la amistad
2. llevarse bien

Pepita Natalia

3. encontrarse (ue) con

Carmen Alfonso

Javier
Marlena
Esteban

4. reunirse (con)
Rubén

5. salir (con)
6. la cita

Inés Octavio

7. llorar
8. pensar (ie) en

Camila

9. extrañar
10. romper (con)

20. ¡Felicidades!

24. las etapas de la vida
25. el nacimiento
26. nacer
27. la infancia
28. la niñez
29. los niños
30. la juventud/ la adolescencia
31. los jóvenes/ los adolescentes

11. el amor

12. enamorarse (de)

13. estar enamorado/a (de)

14. comprometerse (con)

Manuel

Linda

15. estar comprometido/a

16. la boda

Juan

17. casarse (con)

la profesora Falcón

18. estar casado/a (con)

19. la pareja

21. los recién casados

HOSPITAL

23. dar a luz

Nancy

el profesor Marín-Vivar

irse de luna de miel

33. los adultos

34. la vejez

35. los ancianos

36. la muerte

2. la madurez

1. friendship *la amistad*
2. to get along well; **llevarse mal** to get along badly *llavarse bien*
3. to meet up (with) (by chance) *encontrarse con*
4. to meet, get together (with) *reunirse con*
5. to go out (with), date *salir (con)*
6. date, appointment *la cita*
7. to cry *llorar*
8. to think about (someone or something) *pensar*
9. to miss *extrañar*
10. to break up (with) *romper (con)*
11. love *el amor*
12. to fall in love (with) *enamorarse*
13. to be in love (with) *estar enamorado del*
14. to get engaged (to) *comprometerse*
15. to be engaged *estar comprometerse*
16. wedding *la boda*
17. to get married (to) *casarse*
18. to be married (to) *estar casado*
19. couple, husband and wife *la pareja*
20. congratulations, best wishes
21. newlyweds
22. **irse** to leave, depart, go away; **la luna de miel** honeymoon
23. to give birth
24. stages of life
25. birth
26. to be born
27. infancy
28. childhood
29. children
30. youth/adolescence
31. young people/adolescents
32. adulthood, maturity
33. adults
34. old age
35. the elderly; **el/la anciano/a** old man/woman
36. death

Práctica y comunicación

10-1. ② **Las amistades y algo más.** Contesten las preguntas o completen las oraciones según los dibujos de las páginas 338–339.

1. Hace mucho tiempo que Pepita y Natalia son amigas. ¿Se llevan bien o mal?
2. Carmen está caminando por el parque. ¿Con quién se encuentra?
3. ¿Con qué amigos se reúne Javier? ¿Qué están haciendo?
4. Esta noche Octavio tiene una cita. ¿Con quién sale? ¿Dónde están?
5. ¿Piensa Camila mucho en su ex-novio? ¿Lo extraña? Al mirar la foto de él, ¿cómo reacciona ella? ¿Piensa usted que él rompió con ella?
6. La primera vez que Manuel salió con Linda, se enamoró de ella. Es muy obvio que los dos están...
7. Linda y Manuel miran el anillo. Acaban de... Ahora, están...
8. La profesora Falcón y Juan hacen buena pareja. Decidieron casarse. Es el día de su...
9. El viaje que hacen los recién casados es su... ¿Juan y la profesora se fueron a las montañas o a una isla tropical? ¿Qué les dice el portero del hotel?
10. Nancy está embarazada. ¿Para qué va al hospital?
11. Entre el nacimiento y la muerte, ¿cuáles son cinco etapas importantes de la vida? **la infancia**...
12. Cuando tenemos ocho años, somos... A los quince años somos... y a los treinta,... Cuando llegamos a los ochenta, noventa y más, ya somos...

10-2. ② **Preguntas personales.** Háganse las preguntas.

HINT | **Pienso en...** *I think about something or someone.* ¿**Qué piensas de...?** *What do you think about...?* (opinion) **Pienso/Creo que...** *I think/believe that...*

1. ¿En qué piensas cuando estás completamente solo/a? **Pienso en...**
2. ¿Tienes amigos/as fuera de la universidad? ¿Los/Las extrañas?
3. ¿Siempre te llevas bien con todos tus amigos? ¿Te llevas bien o mal con tu compañero/a de cuarto (compañero/a de apartamento/ pareja)?
4. ¿Con quiénes te reúnes[1] cuando vas al centro estudiantil?
5. ¿Sales con alguien ahora? (¿Cuánto tiempo hace que lo/la conoces?) (¿Estás enamorado/a?)
6. En la escuela secundaria, ¿estabas enamorado/a de alguien? (¿De quién?)
7. ¿Tienes amigos que están comprometidos? ¿Cuándo piensas comprometerte tú, o es que ya estás comprometido/a?
8. ¿Qué piensas del matrimonio? ¿Piensas casarte, o es que ya estás casado/a?
9. ¿Cuál es la edad ideal para casarse? ¿Es buena o mala idea casarse inmediatamente después de graduarse? ¿Por qué sí o no?
10. ¿Quieres tener hijos, o es que ya los tienes? (¿Cuántos?)
11. ¿Cuál es un lugar ideal para un viaje (*trip*) de luna de miel?

---

[1] The present tense of **reunirse** is: **me reúno, te reúnes, se reúne, nos reunimos, os reunís, se reúnen.** Note the accents.

Así se dice

Es difícil definir el amor, esa química misteriosa que nos transforma. Sin embargo, todos lo sentimos tarde o temprano; y cuando llega ese «alguien especial» hay una magnífica explosión interna y la vida cambia de color. Lea los siguientes anuncios personales y aprenda las nuevas expresiones para poder hablar del amor y las relaciones.

ELLAS

Liliana Matamoros. Viuda[1], 50 años, **sincera**[2], **cariñosa**[3]; con mucha personalidad e independencia. Me encanta leer buenos libros y viajar. **Mi media naranja**[4] puede ser **soltero**[5], viudo o **divorciado**[6]. Mi único requisito es que pueda **comunicarse**[7] bien. Busco solamente un compañero. ¡No me quiero casar! Si usted **está listo**[8] para una relación como la que deseo, escríbame al Apartado Postal 555, San Jacinto, Honduras.

Irma Murillo. Soltera, 20 años, secretaria. Busco un príncipe de buen carácter, divertido y **comprensivo**[9]. **Creo**[10] en el **amor a primera vista**[11]; no creo en el **divorcio**[12] ni en la separación. Soy optimista y romántica de pies a cabeza. Nos vamos a cuidar y **estar juntos**[13] para toda la vida. Dirección: Apartamentos Los Pinos, Apto. C, 125 metros oeste Catedral. Moravia, Costa Rica.

Genoveva Vásquez. Maestra, casada, 35 años. Mi signo es Sagitario, soy amistosa, expresiva, atractiva e inteligente. Estoy atrapada en un matrimonio sin amor y necesito **separarme**[14] o **divorciarme**[15]. **He tratado de**[16] **resolver**[17] nuestros problemas, pero ¡mi marido es imposible! ¡Busco un caballero valiente que me libere de esta prisión! Dirección: 18 Av. A, 119, Zona 1, Guatemala, Guatemala.

ELLOS

Arturo Flores. Estoy divorciado, tengo 45 años y soy administrador de negocios y estudiante de artes plásticas. Creo que **me he olvidado**[18] un poco del amor: no **recuerdo**[19] cuándo fue la última vez que salí a divertirme. Nací en Perú, pero ahora soy ciudadano de EE.UU. Signo Leo, romántico y deportista. Serio, responsable, católico. No bebo ni fumo. Busco amistades. Enviar foto. Dirección: 375 Forest Ave., Des Plaines, Illinois, EE.UU.

Roberto R. Mendoza. Soltero, 23 años, dibujante comercial. Apasionado y romántico. Busco la compañera de mi vida. Mi única condición es: «Ud. no debe ser **celosa**[20].» Mi experiencia es que los celos **matan**[21] el amor. Dirección: Barrio Sta. Marta, Calle Atlántica No. 1180, San Salvador, El Salvador.

Gregorio José Ramírez. Soltero, 29 años, profesor. Me gustaría recibir correo de chicas de 20 a 26 años con fines matrimoniales. Soy responsable, sin vicios, delgado y simpático. Siempre **me acuerdo de**[22] los cumpleaños y otras fechas especiales. **Nunca tengo celos**[23], **no me quejo de**[24] nada y raramente **me enojo**[25]. Busco a alguien que pueda **reírse de**[26]* los problemas de la vida, alguien optimista y **fiel**[27]. Dirección: Cerrado del Cóndor, 175 Bis. Acayucán, México, D.F.

(1) widow; **viudo** *widower (2) honest, sincere (3) affectionate (4) my soul mate, other half (5) single (6) divorced (7) to communicate (8) are ready;* **estar listo/a** *to be ready (9) understanding (10) I believe;* **creer** *to believe (11) love at first sight (12) divorce (13) to be together (14) to separate (15) to get divorced (16) I have tried to;* **tratar de** *+ infinitive to try to (do something) (17) to resolve* **resolver (ue)** *(18) I have forgotten;* **olvidarse de/ olvidar** *to forget (19) I don't remember;* **recordar (ue)** *to remember (20) jealous (21) kill;* **matar** *to kill (22) I remember;* **acordarse (ue) de...** *to remember... (23) I am never jealous;* **tener celos** *to be jealous (24) I don't complain;* **quejarse de** *to complain about (25) I get angry;* **enojarse** *to get, become angry (26) to laugh at (27) faithful*

---

* The present tense of **reírse** is: **me río, te ríes, se ríe, nos reímos, os reís, se ríen.**

④ 10-3. Anuncios personales. Lean otra vez los anuncios personales (p. 341) y luego contesten las preguntas.

1. ¿Cuál es el más interesante de los tres en la categoría **ellas**? ¿Por qué? ¿Y en la categoría **ellos**? ¿Por qué?
2. Según los anuncios, ¿quién es (posiblemente) la mujer ideal para Roberto? ¿Por qué?
3. ¿Quién va a tener la mayor dificultad en encontar pareja? ¿Por qué?
4. ¿Creen ustedes que los celos matan el amor?

10-4. Mi respuesta. Ahora, escríbale una nota a una de las personas de los anuncios. Preséntese brevemente, dígale lo que usted cree sobre las relaciones e indique su interés en él/ella.

> Remember that past participles used as adjectives agree with the noun they describe. (See p. 317) This form is used throughout this chapter.
>
> Linda y Manuel están **enamorados**.   Mi hermana está **casada**.

② 10-5. ¿Qué dicen? Busquen la declaración que mejor corresponda a cada circunstancia.

Circunstancias	Declaraciones
1. Es muy cariñoso.	**a.** «Te amo con todo mi corazón.»
2. Tiene celos.	**b.** «Quiero verte. Hace mucho tiempo que no te veo.»
3. Extraña a su novia.	**c.** «¡Hola, Paco! ¿Qué hay de nuevo?»
4. Rompió con su novio.	**d.** «¡Estoy furioso! ¡Mi novia bailó con otro chico en la fiesta!»
5. Se encuentra con su amigo.	**e.** «Lo siento, pero ya no te amo y no puedo salir más contigo.»
6. Está enamorado.	**f.** «Me gustan los abrazos.»
7. ¡Dio a luz ayer!	**g.** «La vi y en ese momento supe que era la persona perfecta para mí.»
8. Se olvidó del cumpleaños de su amiga.	**h.** «¡Ay! Lo siento. Estaba tan ocupado que ni pensé en la fecha.»
9. Es muy comprensiva.	**i.** «Mira al bebito. ¡Qué precioso es!»
10. Fue amor a primera vista.	**j.** «Entiendo exáctamente cómo te sientes.»

10–6. Nuestras relaciones. Hablen de los siguientes temas. Un/a secretario/a apunta información interesante para luego compartirla con la clase.

Temas

- el amor a primera vista
- si existe sólo una «media naranja» para cada persona o si existen varias
- ventajas (*advantages*) o desventajas de ser soltero/a
- ventajas o desventajas de casarse joven
- la idea de vivir juntos antes de casarse ¿Por qué sí/no?

②

10–7. Pensamientos sobre el amor. Lean los pensamientos y decidan cuáles son sus favoritos. Luego, inventen su propio (*own*) «pensamiento» y compártanlo con sus compañeros/as de clase.

1. «El amor es el único tesoro° que se multiplica al dividirlo.» (Anónimo)   *treasure*
2. «La raíz° de todas las pasiones es el amor. De él nace la tristeza, el gozo°, la   *root / pleasure*
   alegría y la desesperación.» (Lope de Vega, España)
3. «Ama como puedas, ama a quien puedas, ama todo lo que puedas, pero ama
   siempre.» (Amado Nervo, México)
4. «No hacemos el amor. El amor nos hace.» (Mario Benedetti, Uruguay)
5. «Hombre invisible busca mujer transparente para hacer lo nunca visto.»
   (Pintado en el metro de Madrid)

Luis Felipe Cabezas y de San Simón   *Raymond Ernest Ruf*
M.ᵃ Teresa Gutiérrez Maturana   *Carolyn Dale Wingfield Ruf*

Participan en el próximo enlace de sus hijos

Mónica y Edward

*y tienen el gusto de invitarle(s) a la ceremonia religiosa que se
celebrará (D.m.) el jueves 31 de agosto, a las 7 de la tarde,
en la Real e Insigne Colegiata, La Granja de
San Ildefonso (Segovia) y a la cena que se servirá a
continuación en el
Rancho de la Aldegüela, Torrecaballeros (Segovia)*

Luis de Salazar, 3   *Se ruega confirmación*   *401 Kersey Lane*
28002 Madrid   *Julio 31, 2003*   *Rockville, MD 20854*
Tel. 415 60 96   *Tel. 301 800 7159*

¿Puede usted identificar: el nombre de la novia y del novio, los nombres de los padres de la novia (M.ᵃ = María), la fecha de la boda, el país en que se celebra, la probable nacionalidad de la pareja?

Escenas

Fin del amor

Rubén

Natalia

2 *Natalia y Rubén tienen una cita en el parque, cerca de la universidad. Natalia está sentada en un banco. Rubén llega.*

RUBÉN:	Hola, Natalia, tengo algo para ti. (*Le da una flor.*)
NATALIA:	Gracias. Rubén, tenemos que hablar.
RUBÉN:	¿Qué pasa? Te veo muy preocupada. (*Se sienta a su lado.*)
NATALIA:	Rubén... lo siento, pero tenemos que romper nuestra relación. Nuestra amistad es maravillosa, pero tenemos ideologías un poco diferentes...

barely

RUBÉN:	Pero, Natalia, yo te quiero... nos llevamos muy bien, y ¡hace apenas° una semana que estamos juntos!

No... It's no use

NATALIA:	No tiene caso° que digas nada. En este momento de mi vida prefiero estar sola.
RUBÉN:	Está bien. Como tú quieras, Natalia.
NATALIA:	Perdóname.
RUBÉN:	(*Con un tono híper-dramático.*) Te prometo que no te voy a molestar nunca más. Me voy a ir de voluntario a las junglas de Guatemala y

never

	jamás° volveré. Adiós, Natalia. (*Se levanta y comienza a irse.*)
NATALIA:	¡Rubén!... ¿Me vas a escribir con frecuencia?

hope

RUBÉN:	¿Cómo? ¿Es que aún tengo alguna esperanza°? (*Vuelve.*)
NATALIA:	No... pero estoy coleccionando sellos. (*Sonríe.*)
RUBÉN:	(*Sonríe también.*) Siempre has tenido un excelente sentido del humor. ¿Amigos?
NATALIA:	¡Amigos! (*Se dan la mano.*)

¿Qué pasa?

1. ¿Por qué está preocupada Natalia?
2. ¿Cuánto tiempo hace que Natalia y Rubén salen juntos?
3. ¿Qué prefiere Natalia en este momento de su vida?
4. ¿Qué va a hacer Rubén?
5. ¿Por qué quiere Natalia recibir cartas de Rubén?
6. ¿Cuál es la relación de Natalia y Rubén al final de la conversación?

Estructuras

1 Talking about each other: Reciprocal constructions

English uses the phrases *each other* and *one another* to express reciprocal actions: *They love each other/one another.* Spanish uses the pronouns **nos** and **se**, accompanied by the corresponding verb forms, to express reciprocal or mutual actions.

Linda y yo nos entendemos y nos queremos mucho. Vamos a estar juntos para toda la vida.

> Ana y yo **nos** queremos mucho.
> *Ana and I love **each other** very much.*

> Claudia, Juana y Bill **se** conocen muy bien.
> *Claudia, Juana, and Bill know **one another** very well.*

Práctica y comunicación

2 **10-8.** **Una historia de amor triste.** Determinen la cronología de la «historia de amor» de él y ella, dándole un número a cada actividad.

_____ encontrarse / en el parque / la siguiente noche

_____ una semana más tarde / comprometerse

__1__ conocerse en una fiesta

_____ besarse

_____ enamorarse

_____ abrazarse

_____ finalmente, desafortunadamente / divorciarse

_____ dos meses más tarde / casarse

_____ hablarse

_____ ¡Cómo es la vida! Cuatro meses más tarde / separarse

Ahora, narren la historia para indicar lo que ocurrió: **Se conocieron en una fiesta. ...**

10-9. **Su propia historia de amor.** Describa su historia (verdadera o imaginaria) en cinco oraciones. ¿Qué cosas ocurrieron entre usted y su pareja? Algunos voluntarios van a leer sus historias.

> **Modelo:** Nos vimos por primera vez en...

10-10.
¿Un buen matrimonio o el divorcio? Las mujeres de la clase forman grupos y también los hombres. Cada grupo escribe dos listas que incluyen:

1. las características de un matrimonio feliz: **Se comunican bien...**

2. las razones principales de los divorcios: **No tratan de resolver sus problemas...**

Luego, presenten sus ideas a la clase. Noten las diferencias entre las opiniones de las mujeres y las de los hombres.

3 **¡Qué dilema!**

En una fiesta tu novio te presenta a su mejor amigo, Ariel. Tú y Ariel se miran y sienten una atracción muy fuerte; es obvio que es amor a primera vista. Ustedes quieren conocerse más y tratan de comunicarse discretamente.
NOVIO: **Te presento a mi amigo Ariel.**
TÚ: **¡Qué gusto en conocerte!**
ARIEL: ...

Así se dice
Para estar en contacto: las llamadas telefónicas[1]

2 Pepita y Natalia visitan la ciudad de Nueva York y desean comunicarse con amigos y familiares. Lean la conversación y aprendan las nuevas expresiones.

NATALIA: Pepita, quiero usar el teléfono público para llamar a mi viejo amigo Karl. Creo que vive en Brooklyn.

PEPITA: ¿Sabes su número de teléfono?

NATALIA: No. A ver si lo encuentro en esta **guía telefónica**[2]. Necesito su **código de área**[3] para ver si es llamada **de larga distancia**[4].

PEPITA: ¿Quieres usar mi **teléfono celular**[5]?

NATALIA: Gracias, pero tengo una **tarjeta telefónica**[6]. (*Natalia encuentra el número y llama a su amigo.*)

NATALIA: ... No contesta. ... Le voy a **dejar un mensaje**[7].

PEPITA: A propósito°, necesito hacer una llamada a mi familia, para decirles que estamos aquí. (*Pepita marca° el número.*) ¡Ay! **¡La línea está ocupada**[8]!

NATALIA: Podemos hacer las llamadas más tarde. Ahora tengo hambre. ¿Quieres almorzar en ese restaurante mexicano?

Expresiones útiles

¿Cómo se contesta el teléfono?

¡Hola! *Argentina*
¡Sí!, ¡Diga!, ¡Dígame!
España
¡Bueno! *México*
¡Aló! *otros países*

A... *By the way*
dials

---

(1) *telephone calls* (2) *phone book* (3) *area code* (4) *long distance* (5) *cell phone* (6) *calling card* (7) *to leave a message* (8) *The line is busy!*

Práctica y comunicación

2 **10-11.** **Preguntas personales.** Háganse las siguientes preguntas.

1. ¿Cuál es tu número de teléfono, empezando con el código de área?
2. ¿A quién llamas con mucha frecuencia?
3. ¿Haces muchas llamadas de larga distancia? (¿A quién?)
4. ¿Tu cuenta del teléfono es muy alta? ¿Aproximadamente cuánto pagas cada mes?
5. ¿Recibes muchos mensajes telefónicos? (¿De quién?)
6. ¿Tienes tarjeta telefónica? (¿De qué compañía?) (¿Cuándo la usas?)
7. ¿Tienes un teléfono celular? (¿Cuándo lo usas?)
8. ¿Por qué son prácticos los teléfonos celulares?
9. ¿Ves a muchas personas usando sus teléfonos celulares y a la vez haciendo otras cosas? (¿Qué cosas?) ¿Es buena o mala idea? ¿Por qué?

2 **10-12.** **Por teléfono.** Dramatice cada una de las siguientes conversaciones telefónicas con un/a compañero/a de clase diferente.

- quiere hacer planes con su amigo/a para el fin de semana
- conversa con... una persona famosa con quien quiere salir
- se le olvidó la cita con su profe de español y le explica lo que pasó
- marca 911 porque hay una emergencia

> **Expresión útil**
>
> Se me olvidó.
> *I forgot.*

Estructuras

2 **Expressing subjective reactions to the actions of others: The subjunctive mood—an introduction; the present subjunctive**

Most verb forms that you have studied (such as the present, the preterit, and the imperfect) are part of what is called the indicative mood. The indicative is used for stating facts, communicating specific knowledge, or asking questions.

Quiero conocer a Jaime.	*I want to meet Jaime.*
¿Sabes dónde vive?	*Do you know where he lives?*

The subjunctive, in contrast, is a more subjective mood. It is used to convey a speaker's wishes, attitudes, hopes, fears, doubts, uncertainties, and other personal reactions to events and to the actions of others.

Quiero que *conozcas* a Jaime.	*I want you to meet Jaime.*
Espero que *esté* en casa.	*I hope that he is at home.*

The present subjunctive is usually translated like the present indicative, although it can also mean *may* or *will*.

In this and subsequent chapters you will be introduced to various uses of the subjunctive and to its four forms (present, present perfect, imperfect, and past perfect). You have already used forms of the subjunctive in **Ud/s.** commands and in negative **tú** commands.

A. Regular and stem-changing verbs

The present subjunctive of regular -**ar**, -**er**, and -**ir** verbs is formed by deleting the final -**o** from the **yo** form of the present indicative and adding the endings indicated. Note that -**er** and -**ir** verbs have the same endings.

> Quiero que aprendan el subjuntivo.

> ¡¿El qué?!

HINT | To form the present subjunctive, always think "opposite endings:" -**ar** verbs have an **e** in every ending; -**er** and -**ir** verbs have an **a**.

	bailar → bail**ø**	comer → com**ø**	vivir → viv**ø**
(yo)	bail**e**	com**a**	viv**a**
(tú)	bail**es**	com**as**	viv**as**
(Ud., él, ella)	bail**e**	com**a**	viv**a**
(nosotros/as)	bail**emos**	com**amos**	viv**amos**
(vosotros/as)	bail**éis**	com**áis**	viv**áis**
(Uds., ellos, ellas)	bail**en**	com**an**	viv**an**

More examples:

conocer	→	conozc**ø**	→	**conozca, conozcas,…**
decir		dig**ø**		**diga, digas,…**
hacer		hag**ø**		**haga, hagas,…**
poner		pong**ø**		**ponga, pongas,…**
salir		salg**ø**		**salga, salgas,…**
tener		teng**ø**		**tenga, tengas,…**
traer		traig**ø**		**traiga, traigas,…**
venir		veng**ø**		**venga, vengas,…**

- Stem-changing -**ar** and -**er** verbs follow the same pattern in the present subjunctive as in the present indicative—stem changes occur in all forms except **nosotros** and **vosotros**.

pensar (e → ie)		volver (o → ue)	
piense	pensemos	vuelva	volvamos
pienses	penséis	vuelvas	volváis
piense	piensen	vuelva	vuelvan

- Stem-changing -ir verbs follow the pattern of the present indicative, but also have an additional stem change (e → i and o → u) in the **nosotros** and **vosotros** forms.

divertirse (e → ie, i)		pedir (e → i, i)		dormir (o → ue, u)	
me divierta	nos divirtamos	pida	pidamos	duerma	durmamos
te diviertas	os divirtáis	pidas	pidáis	duermas	durmáis
se divierta	se diviertan	pida	pidan	duerma	duerman

- Verbs ending in **-gar**, **-car**, and **-zar** have spelling changes in all persons in the present subjunctive. They are the same spelling changes that occur in the **yo** form of the preterit (see p. 182).

-gar (g → gu) llegar	→	llegue, llegues,...
-car (c → qu) tocar	→	toque, toques,...
-zar (z → c) almorzar	→	almuerce, almuerces,...

B. Irregular verbs in the present subjunctive

The following verbs have irregular forms in the present subjunctive.

dar	dé, des, dé, demos, deis, den
estar	esté, estés, esté, estemos, estéis, estén
ir	vaya, vayas, vaya, vayamos, vayáis, vayan
saber	sepa, sepas, sepa, sepamos, sepáis, sepan
ser	sea, seas, sea, seamos, seáis, sean
haber	haya, hayas, haya, hayamos, hayáis, hayan

Haya is the subjunctive form of **hay** (*there is, there are*).

Espero que **haya** otras soluciones.   *I hope that **there are** other solutions.*

Práctica y comunicación

10-13. Se busca compañero/a. Usted quiere encontrar una persona para compartir su apartamento. Diga si quiere o no quiere que la persona haga las siguientes cosas.

Modelo: hacer la cama todos los días
Quiero que haga la cama todos los días.

Quiero que.../ No quiero que...

1. poner los pies en los muebles
2. hablar en su teléfono celular día y noche
3. escucharme cuando yo hablo
4. fumar
5. beber mucha cerveza
6. prender la tele a las dos de la mañana
7. pagar las cuentas a tiempo
8. comerse toda la comida que yo compro
9. ayudarme a limpiar el apartamento
10. acostarse muy tarde
11. invitar a sus amigos/as al apartamento
12. tener intereses similares a los míos

10-14. Amigos perezosos. Usted tiene unos amigos con problemas académicos serios. ¿La causa? ¡Son muy perezosos! ¿Les recomienda usted que hagan o que no hagan las siguientes cosas?

Modelo: estudiar más
Les recomiendo que estudien más.

Les recomiendo que.../ Les recomiendo que *no*...

1. asistir a todas sus clases
2. llegar a las clases a tiempo
3. salir con sus amigos todas las noches
4. hacer la tarea todos los días
5. dormirse durante las clases
6. desayunar antes de ir a clase
7. jugar al Nintendo cada noche
8. ver la tele todas las noches
9. pensar en su futuro
10. empezar a² estudiar inmediatamente

② 10-15. Mi media naranja. Digan si es importante o no es importante que su media naranja tenga los siguientes atributos.

Modelo: ser rico/a
(No) Es importante que sea rico/a.

Es importante que.../ No es importante que...

1. ser fiel
2. ser comprensivo(a)/ sincero(a)/ cariñoso(a)
3. darme regalos
4. saber cocinar/ bailar
5. tener sentido del humor
6. estar conmigo día y noche
7. estar muy enamorado/a de mí
8. ser atlético/a
9. acordarse de mi cumpleaños
10. ir conmigo a la iglesia/ a partidos de...

---

² **Empezar**, like **aprender**, **invitar**, and **ayudar**, requires the preposition **a** when followed by an infinitive.

3 **Expressing wishes and requests related to other people's actions: The subjuntive with expressions of influence**

Juanito, quiero que ordenes tu cuarto ahora mismo.

You have learned how to express what you want or prefer to do by using verbs such as **querer/ preferir/ desear** + *infinitive.*

    Quiero ir a la fiesta.   *I want to go to the party.*

However, when you want to express a desire, preference, recommendation, request, or suggestion that *someone else* do something, use *a verb of preference* + **que** + *subjunctive form.*

    Quiero que vayas a la fiesta.   *I want you to go to the party.*

Notice that the verb in the first clause (**Quiero...**) is in the indicative; the verb in the second clause, which expresses what the speaker wishes (**que vayas...**), is in the subjunctive. There are *two* subjects involved: the person influencing and the person influenced. If there is only *one* subject, the subjunctive is not used. (**Quiero ir.** *vs.* **Quiero que vayas.**)

Subject 1		Subject 2
expression of wish to influence + **que** +		*action influenced*
indicative		*subjunctive*

Some verbs that express the wish to influence include:

querer (ie)	*to want*	**Quiero** que me **ayudes.**
preferir (ie, i)	*to prefer*	**Prefieren** que **salgamos** ahora.
insistir (en)	*to insist (on)*	**Insisten** en que **lleguemos** a tiempo.
recomendar (ie)	*to recommend*	Te **recomiendo** que lo **llames.**
sugerir (ie, i)	*to suggest*	Te **sugiero** que lo **invites** a la fiesta.
pedir (i, i)	*to request*	Le **pedimos** que **traiga** pan.
decir (i)	*to say*	Te **digo** que no **esperes** más.

- The verbs **recomendar**, **sugerir**, **pedir**, and **decir** are commonly used with indirect object pronouns (**me, te, le, nos, os, les**), as one recommends, suggests, etc. something *to someone else*. Place the indirect object immediately before the verb.

    Te sugiero que vayas.   *I suggest that you go.*

- When clarification is needed, the clarifying noun or pronoun is usually placed after the verb.

    Le recomiendo **a mi amiga Leticia**   *I recommend that my friend Leticia*
    que hable con el profesor.   *speak with the professor.*

Práctica y comunicación

10-16. **La agencia *Mi Media Naranja*.** En este momento, usted no tiene novio/a y por eso decide ir a la agencia *Mi Media Naranja* para encontrar la persona de sus sueños. Complete el formulario.

Nombre: _____
Edad: _____
Soltero/a _____   Divorciado/a _____
Fuma _____   No fuma _____
Intereses y pasatiempos _____
Prefiero que mi media naranja…
         sea mayor ❏   menor ❏   de la misma edad que yo ❏
         sea más alto/a ❏   más bajo/a ❏   de la misma altura que yo ❏
         sea…, …, …
         viva en…
         tenga…
         pueda…
         quiera…
Y prefiero que a él/ella le guste/n…, …, …

2 Ahora, uno/a de ustedes es el/la empleado/a de la agencia. El/La otro/a le dice sus preferencias según el cuestionario. Quizás (*Perhaps*) él/ella conozca la persona perfecta para usted. Cambien de papel.

10-17. **La influencia de mamá.** Las madres siempre influyen en la vida de los hijos. Indique lo que tiene que hacer Juanito (y el perro) según los deseos de la madre.

Modelo: La madre quiere que Juanito se acueste.

La madre quiere que…

1. La madre quiere que…

2. La madre le pide que…

3. La madre le pide que…

4. La madre le sugiere que…

5. La madre insiste en que…

6. La madre le dice al perro que…

(4) **10–18.** **Todos tienen algo que decir.** Indiquen las recomendaciones, deseos y sugerencias de las siguientes personas. Completen cada oración con varias actividades. Un/a secretario/a escribe las oraciones y al concluir puede compartirlas con la clase.

1. La profesora/El profesor de español nos recomienda que…

2. Le sugerimos a la profesora/al profesor que…

3. Quiero que mis amigos…

4. Mi compañero/a de cuarto insiste en que yo…

5. Prefiero que mi pareja…

6. Les pido a mis hermanos/as menores que…

10–19. **Para olvidar a mi novio/a.** Imagine que su novio/a rompió con usted hace una semana y usted está deprimido/a. Todos le dan consejos (*advice*) para que lo/la olvide. Escriba cinco consejos, usando los verbos de la lista.

| recomendarme | sugerirme | decirme | pedirme | insistir en | querer |

Modelo: Mi mejor amiga… **me sugiere que conozca a otras personas.**

1. Mi mejor amigo/a…

2. Mi compañero/a de cuarto…

3. Mi madre/padre…

4. Mis hermanos/as…

5. Todos mis amigos/as…

Noticias culturales

Los cibercafés: otro modo de consolidar amistades

¿Cómo hacen nuevas amistades los jóvenes hispanos? Los métodos son múltiples
y las viejas tradiciones siguen en vigor. Es a menudo° por medio de otros amigos,
en la universidad, en el trabajo, a la salida de la iglesia o en fiestas que comienzan
la gran mayoría de las amistades. En los pueblos, las plazas también sirven de
lugar de encuentro. Tampoco hay que excluir las discotecas y los cines donde los
jóvenes acuden° en grupos para pasar un buen rato.

often

go

Ahora, sin embargo, los hispanos tienen otro medio de conocer y estar en
contacto con personas del mundo entero: el ciberespacio. Con tan sólo oprimir°
unas teclas, están conectados. Nadie se escapa de ese fenómeno de la
globalización.

pressing

¿Sabe usted lo que son los *cibercafés*? Si su respuesta fue «café espacial» casi
acertó°. Son sitios que además de ser acogedores° ofrecen una extensa lista de
bebidas y comidas. Sin embargo, el verdadero atractivo es ofrecerle a la clientela
un lugar donde poder ponerse en contacto con familiares y amigos vía la red.
En cómodas° estaciones semiprivadas con computadoras, los cibernautas o
internautas pasan el rato «chateando», estudiando o comprando en línea.
Los españoles fueron pioneros del concepto y los han estado disfrutando° desde
el año 1994.

were right / inviting

comfortable

enjoying

Los cibercafés, o los cafés Internet, se han puesto de moda en todo el mundo
hispano. No es raro encontrarlos aun en los más remotos pueblecitos. La próxima
vez que usted salga de viaje a Latinoamérica o a España y sienta la necesidad de
ponerse en contacto con algún ser querido, pregunte por el cibercafé más cercano.
¡Y no se olvide de usar la lengua del ciberespacio y de las emociones, los
Emoticones! Para ver una lista completa de Emoticones, vaya a:

http://humor.ciudadfutura.com/emoticones/

Emoticones

:0) sonriendo
:0(triste
>:0(enojado
:0* un besito

Un cibercafé en Guatemala.

¿Qué recuerda?

1. En el mundo hispano, ¿qué lugares sirven para hacer nuevas amistades?
2. ¿Qué ofrecen los cibercafés?
3. ¿Cómo pasan el tiempo los cibernautas?
4. ¿Dónde se originaron los cibercafés? ¿Dónde se encuentran ahora?
5. ¿Qué son *Emoticones*? ¿Los usa usted?

2 Conexiones y contrastes

1. ¿Cuáles son las similitudes y diferencias entre su modo de hacer amistades y el hispano?
2. ¿Hay cibercafés en su país?
3. ¿Es usted internauta? ¿Dónde «se conecta» usted?
4. ¿Manda usted tarjetas por medio de la red? ¿Le gusta recibirlas? ¿Prefiere un método tradicional?
5. ¿Encuentra usted verdaderos amigos en la red o solamente conexiones de corta duración?

Estructuras

4 Expressing emotional reactions and feelings about other people's actions: The subjuntive with expressions of emotion

Espero que me llame...

The subjunctive is used when a speaker expresses emotional reactions and feelings (joy, hope, sorrow, etc.) about the actions or condition of another subject (whether person or thing).

Me alegro de que mi amigo me **visite.**
I'm glad that my friend is visiting me.

Esperamos que pueda quedarse unos días.
We hope that he can stay a few days.

The first clause (**Me alegro de...**), expressing the speaker's emotions/feelings, is in the indicative; the second clause (**que mi amigo me visite**), which expresses the actions or condition of another person or thing, is in the subjunctive.

> expression of emotion + **que** + action or condition of another subject
> indicative   subjunctive

Some verbs and expressions of emotion are:

alegrarse (de)	*to be glad (about)*	**Me alegro de que estén** comprometidos.
esperar	*to hope, expect*	**Espero que se casen** este verano.
sentir (ie, i)	*to be sorry, regret*	**Siento que vivan** tan lejos.
temer	*to fear, be afraid*	**Tememos que no puedan** visitarnos.
¡Ojalá que[3]...!	*I hope*	**¡Ojalá que me inviten** a la boda!

If there is no change of subject after the expression of emotion, the infinitive is used, not **que** + *subjunctive.*

One subject	**Change of subject**
Siento no **poder** ir a la reunión.	Siento que ellos no **puedan** ir a la reunión.
I regret not being able to go to the meeting.	*I regret that they cannot go to the meeting.*

Práctica y comunicación

10-20. **Reacciones.** Oigan lo que dice su profe y reaccionen a las situaciones. Usen **Me alegro de que...** *o* **Siento que...**

> **Modelo:** No hay examen mañana.
> **Me alegro de que no haya examen mañana.**

1. No hay clase el viernes.

2. El examen final es difícil.

3. Mi familia viene de visita este fin de semana.

4. Estoy muy cansado/a hoy.

5. Tengo mucho dolor de cabeza.

6. Pueden usar sus teléfonos celulares durante la clase.

7. ¡Voy a... para las vacaciones de primavera!

---

[3] This expression comes from Arabic and it means literally "God grant" or "Would to God." In modern Spanish it is synonymous with *I hope.* It is always followed by a verb in the subjunctive.

2 **10–21.** **Mis deseos.** Combinen cada declaración de la columna A con la expresión de la columna B que le corresponde. Luego hagan una oración usando **Ojalá que...** para expresar sus deseos. Túrnense.

> **Modelo:** Jaime no estudió mucho para el examen. → pasar el examen
> **Ojalá que pase el examen.**

A

1. Mi hermana se queja de que no tiene novio.
2. Inés va a dar una fiesta para celebrar el compromiso de Linda y Manuel.
3. No me acordé del cumpleaños de mi amiga.
4. Mañana cumplo veintiún años.
5. Pepita y su amiga quieren ir a Costa Rica.
6. Esteban estudió mucho, pero la clase es difícil.

B

a. pasar el examen
b. encontrar por fin su media naranja
c. nadie olvidarse de mi cumpleaños
d. invitarme
e. no enojarse conmigo
f. poder ir este verano

2 **10–22.** **Reacciones y emociones.** Describan las reacciones o emociones de las personas según las situaciones.

> **Modelo:** Juanito, Elena y el perro sienten que... **llueva.**

1. Juanito, Elena y el perro se alegran de que…

2. Nancy y su marido sienten que…

3. Esteban se alegra de que…

4. Linda y Manuel esperan que Javier…

5. Pepita siente que Natalia…

6. Camila espera que su ex-novio… pero teme que…

(4) **10-23.** **Generaciones.** Piensen en las diferentes etapas de la vida y completen las oraciones. ¡Ojo! En la primera oración de cada serie no se usa el subjuntivo. En la segunda, sí.

> **Modelo:** Los bebés necesitan... **dormir mucho y tomar mucha leche.**
>
> Los bebés necesitan que sus padres... **los bañen.**

1. Los niños quieren...

Los niños quieren que sus padres...

2. Los jóvenes prefieren...

Los jóvenes prefieren que los adultos...

3. Los adultos esperan...

Los adultos esperan que los jóvenes...

4. Los ancianos temen...

Los ancianos temen que los jóvenes...

Ahora, presenten algunas de sus ideas a la clase.

(2) **10-24.** **El valor de la amistad.** Lean el párrafo acerca de la amistad y miren la foto. Luego, contesten las preguntas.

Palabras útiles	
vínculo	*bond*
apoyo	*support*

POR DORIS TORRES
La amistad es una de las relaciones más importantes y hermosas en la vida. Somos afortunados cuando contamos con amigos verdaderos. Este vínculo nos brinda confianza, solidaridad y apoyo, tanto en los momentos buenos como en los malos, y nos hace sentir entendidos y aceptados incondicionalmente. Todos queremos tener y ser amigos excepcionales.

el valor de la AMISTAD

1. ¿Qué dice el artículo acerca de la amistad?

2. ¿Qué nos brindan (dan) nuestras amistades?

3. ¿Qué queremos todos?

Ahora, díganse lo que ustedes aprecian (*appreciate*) de sus amigos/as. Usen las siguientes expresiones.

> Me alegro de que… Aprecio mucho que… Estoy contento/a que… Es fenomenal que…

> **Modelo:** Aprecio mucho que mi amiga Alicia sea tan sincera.

2 **10-25.** **Soy muy comprensivo/a.** Su amiga Teresa lo/la llama por teléfono y le dice que está deprimida a causa de una serie de incidentes. Usted la escucha, la consuela y le da consejos. Use las siguientes expresiones.

> Siento que…   Me preocupo de que…   Es muy triste que…   Espero que…   Ojalá que…

AMIGO/A 1: ¡Ay! Estoy deprimido/a.

AMIGO/A 2: Cuéntame. ¿Qué pasa?

AMIGO/A 1: Pues,…

AMIGO/A 2: Siento mucho que…

AMIGO/A 1: Y además…

…

DICHOS

Amigo en la adversidad, amigo de verdad.
En largos caminos° se conocen los amigos.   *roads*
¿Cómo explica usted estos dichos?

2 **10-26.** **Pensamientos sobre la amistad.** Lean los pensamientos y luego indiquen la idea central de cada uno. Apunten sus ideas para luego compartirlas con la clase.

Modelo: «La amistad supone sacrificios y sólo el que está dispuesto a hacerlos sin molestia comprende la amistad». (Noel Clarasó, escritor español)
Es necesario hacer sacrificios por los amigos.

1. «Al amigo no le busques perfecto. Búscalo amigo». (José Narosky, escritor argentino)

2. «Un buen amigo es un hombre para el cual no tenemos secretos y que, a pesar de° todo, nos aprecia». (León Daudí, escritor español)   *a… in spite of*

3. «La amistad no se compra, aunque muchos la venden, que los amigos comprados no lo son y valen° poco». (Baltasar Gracián, jesuita y escritor español)   *are worth*

4. «A los amigos, como a los dientes, los vamos perdiendo con los años, no siempre sin dolor». (Santiago Ramón y Cajal, médico español)

Ahora hablen de sus mejores amigos: quiénes son y por qué son buenos amigos.

Dicho y hecho

Conversando

3 **Problemas matrimoniales.** Dos de ustedes visitan a un/a consejero/a matrimonial (*marriage counselor*) porque tienen problemas serios.

Ustedes hablan con el/la consejero/a acerca de:
- los problemas en su matrimonio
- por qué quieren separarse
- la custodia compartida (*joint*) de sus niños

Él/Ella habla con ustedes acerca de:
- lo que deben tratar de hacer para resolver los problemas
- lo que deben tratar de hacer para mantener la familia unida
- las decisiones que deben tomar

¡A escuchar!

La radionovela «Amalia». En este episodio de la radionovela «Amalia, el corazón nunca se olvida», Luisa Fernanda habla con José Ricardo, su marido. Escuche el episodio para determinar qué problema tienen. Luego, conteste las tres primeras preguntas.

1. ¿José Ricardo estaba en la oficina cuando su esposa lo buscó? ❏ sí ❏ no

2. ¿Es Amalia cliente de José Ricardo? ❏ sí ❏ no

3. ¿José Ricardo conocía a Amalia antes de casarse con Luisa Fernanda? ❏ sí ❏ no

Ahora escuche el episodio otra vez y conteste las tres preguntas siguientes.

4. ¿Dónde vio Luisa Fernanda a Amalia?

5. ¿Qué noticia tiene Luisa Fernanda para su marido?

6. Imagine que usted es escritor/a del próximo episodio. ¿Qué va a pasar?

De mi escritorio

Cartas a los «desesperados». Imagine que usted es Victoria, periodista del periódico *El Investigador* y la responsable de la columna «Problemas personales». Escríbales una carta breve a dos de las siguientes tres personas, indicando sus reacciones y recomendaciones. Use las siguientes expresiones.

> Le recomiendo que...   Le sugiero que...   Espero que...   ...

Querida Victoria:

Tengo un novio magnífico. Se llama Luis y es el hombre más simpático y cariñoso del mundo. ¡Siempre me trae flores y chocolates! Hace dos años que salimos juntos. El problema es Ronaldo, un chico que conocí el fin de semana pasado. ¡Es tan guapo! ¡Y qué ojos! Salimos a cenar, pero todavía no le he dicho nada a Luis. ¿Qué debo hacer?

«Confundida en Caracas»

Querida Victoria:

A mí me cae bien° Leonardo, el nuevo amigo de nuestra hija Elsa, pero a mi esposo no le gusta para nada. Critica el tatuaje de serpiente que tiene en el brazo, los aretes que lleva en la nariz y en la oreja, su pelo largo ¡y su motocicleta! Leonardo se siente muy incómodo en nuestra casa a causa de mi marido, y Elsa se siente desesperada. ¿Cómo puedo resolver esta situación?

«Madre preocupada en Valencia»

A... *I like*

Querida Victoria:

Hace dos semanas me comprometí con mi novia y decidimos casarnos este verano. La semana pasada mi novia me dijo que su mejor amigo le había declarado amor eterno y rompió nuestro compromiso. Anteayer mi novia me llamó para pedirme que la perdone: quiere continuar con nuestra relación y los planes de matrimonio. Yo la quiero mucho pero no quiero más sorpresas. ¿Debo darle otra oportunidad?

«Un indeciso en Maracaibo»

Panorama cultural

Guatemala, Honduras, Nicaragua y El Salvador

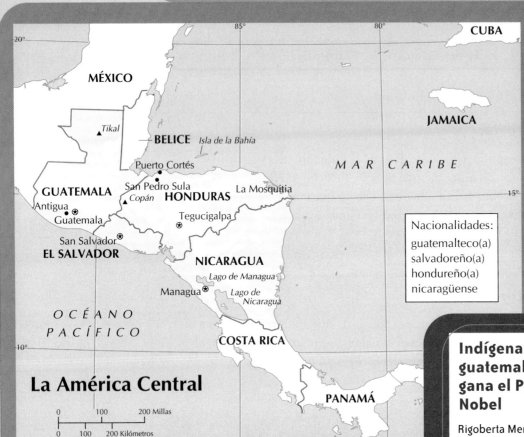

La América Central

Nacionalidades:
guatemalteco(a)
salvadoreño(a)
hondureño(a)
nicaragüense

Indígena guatemalteca gana el Premio Nobel

Rigoberta Menchú ganó el Premio Nobel de la Paz por sus contribuciones al ponerle fin a 30 años de guerra civil en Guatemala.

El señor presidente

Miguel Ángel Asturias, escritor guatemalteco, ganó el Premio Nobel de Literatura (1967) por su controversial novela *El señor presidente*.

Preguntas sobre el mapa

1. ¿Cuáles son los cuatro países vecinos de Guatemala?
2. ¿Qué país tiene una capital con el mismo nombre del país?
3. ¿Cuál es el país más pequeño de América Central? ¿Cuál es su capital?
4. ¿Cuál es la capital de Honduras? ¿Qué ciudad importante se encuentra en el noroeste del país?
5. En Nicaragua, ¿qué lago grande se encuentra cerca de la capital? ¿Y hacia el sur?
6. ¿En qué país se encuentra Tikal, la famosa ciudad de los mayas? ¿Y los templos y pirámides de Copán?

Guatemala, Honduras, Nicaragua y El Salvador

Guatemala, Honduras, Nicaragua y El Salvador forman la parte norte de Centroamérica. Estos países tienen un clima y una geografía similares. Sus tierras son muy fértiles y fáciles de cultivar; y con la excepción de Honduras, todos tienen volcanes. El clima de la región es agradable, pero los huracanes y las tormentas son comunes. En 1998, el huracán Mitch causó grandes daños[1] en toda el área, sobre todo en Honduras.

[1]*damages* [2]*earthquakes* [3]*landscape*

Guatemala

La mitad de la población guatemalteca es de origen maya. Por eso, Guatemala tiene la cultura indígena más dinámica de todos los países centroamericanos. Las ruinas mayas más impresionantes están en Tikal, en la selva guatemalteca.
¿Ha visto usted alguna vez unas ruinas?

Originalmente, la capital del país era la ciudad de Antigua. Después de varios terremotos[2] catastróficos, la capital se transfirió a la ciudad de Guatemala. Hoy Antigua es un importante destino turístico por la belleza de su paisaje[3] y la arquitectura colonial. Mire la foto del inmenso y bello Volcán de Agua, que ocupa un lugar muy importante en la vida del pueblo. ¿Le preocuparía a usted vivir cerca de un volcán?

¿Sabía usted que...?

- Guatemala fue el centro de la civilización maya.
- A partir de 1960 ciertos grupos guerrilleros comenzaron una lucha contra el gobierno.
- En 1996 esta nación centroamericana puso en marcha un plan para la reconciliación y finalmente la paz.

Honduras

Las dos ciudades más importantes de Honduras son San Pedro Sula, el centro industrial del país, y Tegucigalpa, la capital. Tegucigalpa está situada en la montañosa zona central. Observe la pintoresca Iglesia de Nuestra Señora de los Dolores en el centro de Tegucigalpa. ¿Le gustaría visitar este mercado al aire libre?

Person@je del momento

¿Sabe usted quién es América Ferrera? Busque información en el Internet y compártala con sus compañeros/as de clase.

En Honduras predominan varios grupos étnicos. El área más aislada y remota del país es la Mosquitia, donde viven 50.000 indios miskitos. (Vea el mapa.) En la costa caribeña viven los garífuna, quienes llegaron a Honduras en el siglo XVIII, escapándose de la esclavitud[4] bajo las colonias inglesas del Caribe. Vea la foto de una familia garífuna. Describa a la familia y la escena.

¿Sabía usted que...?

- Los habitantes indígenas de Honduras eran los mayas y los lencas.
- Para el año 800 d. C., los mayas habían abandonado inexplicablemente sus ciudades.
- Cuando llegaron los españoles en 1523, sólo encontraron las ruinas de Copán, una gran ciudad de palacios y pirámides.

[4]*slavery*

Nicaragua, el país más grande de Centroamérica, se caracteriza por sus hermosos lagos y volcanes. Managua, la capital del país desde 1858, está al lado del lago del mismo nombre. Vea esta perspectiva de Managua. Describa la escena. ¿Qué se ve a la distancia?

El gran Lago de Nicaragua tiene más de 8.000 km^2 y es el más grande de Centroamérica. Ometepe, en el gran Lago de Nicaragua, es la isla más grande del mundo situada en un lago. Describa la escena. ¿Se están divirtiendo los niños?

¿Sabía usted que...?

- La dictadura de Anastasio Somoza causó la revolución sandinista (de orientación marxista) en 1979.
- Los Sandinistas tomaron posesión del gobierno, pero los Contras, apoyados[5] por el gobierno de los EE.UU., lucharon contra los Sandinistas.
- Esta guerra civil continuó hasta finales de los años ochenta. Las elecciones de 1990 establecieron finalmente la democracia en Nicaragua.

[5]*supported*

El Salvador

¿Sabía usted que...?

■ Los pipiles y los mayas fueron los únicos habitantes de El Salvador hasta 1524, cuando los españoles colonizaron la zona.

El Salvador tiene casi seis millones de habitantes. Es el país más poblado y más pequeño de Centroamérica y tiene impresionantes volcanes. Vea la foto del volcán Izalco. Permaneció activo desde 1770 hasta 1966. ¿Le gustaría a usted visitar este volcán? ¿Por qué?

¿Qué descubrimos?

Complete la información con el país que le corresponde: Guatemala, Honduras, Nicaragua, El Salvador.

1. En _____ el 50% del país es de origen maya.

2. El lago más grande de Centroamérica está en _____ .

3. Las ruinas de la ciudad maya de Copán están en _____ .

4. Las ruinas de la ciudad maya de Tikal están en _____.

5. _____ es el país más pequeño y más poblado de Centroamérica.

6. Anastasio Somoza y la revolución sandinista son parte de la historia de _____ .

② Adivinanzas

Identifiquen cada una de las siguientes referencias:

Tegucigalpa	Tikal	los garífuna
San Pedro Sula	Antigua	los miskitos
Managua	Copán	los Contras
San Salvador		

Luego, su profesor/a le va a asignar a cada pareja una de las referencias. Escriban una descripción de la referencia y entréguensela al profesor/a la profesora.

Ahora, la clase se divide en dos equipos. El/La profe le presenta a cada equipo, por turnos, una descripción, y el equipo indica la referencia que le corresponde. Cada respuesta correcta vale dos puntos. El equipo con más puntos gana la competencia.

Encuentro cultural
Artes populares

Textiles de Guatemala

Las telas[1] guatemaltecas son famosas en todo el mundo por sus colores brillantes y sobre todo por sus diseños, que indican la región de origen del textil. Esto ocurre porque hasta hace poco tiempo, la población guatemalteca vivía en regiones bastante aisladas[2] entre sí. La falta de comunicación contribuyó a la conservación de las tradiciones de origen maya, que han cambiado poco desde la época prehispánica.

Los textiles tradicionales de Guatemala utilizan materiales, colores y técnicas que forman parte de la herencia cultural maya. La fibra favorita en esta zona desde tiempos prehispánicos es el algodón, y los guatemaltecos usan tintas y colorantes naturales hechos a base de plantas, insectos y minerales. Cientos de símbolos diferentes aparecen en los textiles mayas. Cada persona que fabrica una tela selecciona una combinación de símbolos para representar una historia o un episodio mitológico; por eso, es casi imposible encontrar dos piezas idénticas. Los siguientes símbolos son ejemplos de los más comunes:

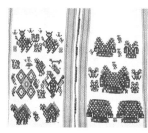

Una interesante combinación de figuras y motivos tradicionales decoran este tzute (manto para la cabeza).

Detalle de los coloridos bordados de un huipil.

1   2   3   4   5

Los diamantes ① representan el universo y el movimiento diario del sol: los diamantes más pequeños que están arriba y abajo representan el este y el oeste. El diamante en el centro representa el sol al mediodía. La segunda figura ② representa una deidad[3] suprema: el dios de la tierra. El siguiente símbolo ③ representa la cola[4] de un escorpión y a su lado ④ está la representación de una rana[5]. El último símbolo ⑤ representa un buitre[6]. Observe los ejemplos de textiles.

Preguntas

1. ¿Qué caracteriza los textiles guatemaltecos?
2. ¿Qué elementos tradicionales de la cultura maya persisten en la fabricación de los textiles?
3. ¿Cuáles son los símbolos que usted reconoce en los tejidos que aparecen en las fotos?
4. ¿Puede usted encontrar un diseño nuevo en estas fotos? ¿Puede describirlo?
5. En su país, ¿se utilizan símbolos en la ropa? Dé ejemplos.
6. ¿Qué tipo de textiles prefiere usted ponerse? ¿Algodón? ¿Lana? ¿Lino?

[1]*fabrics* [2]*isolated* [3]*deity* [4]*tail* [5]*frog* [6]*vulture*

Adjetivos

cariñoso/a
celoso/a
comprensivo/a
divorciado/a
fiel
sincero/a
soltero/a
viudo/a

Expresiones útiles

el amor a primera vista
felicidades
mi media naranja
Ojalá que…

Sustantivos

Las relaciones y algo más

los adultos
la amistad
el amor
los ancianos
  la anciana
  el anciano
la boda
la cita
el divorcio
las etapas de la vida
la infancia
los jóvenes/ los adolescentes
la juventud/ la adolescencia
la luna de miel
la madurez
el marido
la muerte
el nacimiento
la niñez
los niños
la pareja
los recién casados
la vejez
la vida

Las llamadas telefónicas

el código de área
la guía telefónica
la línea está ocupada
la llamada
  de larga distancia
la tarjeta telefónica
el teléfono celular

Verbos reflexivos

acordarse de (ue)
alegrarse (de)
casarse (con)
comprometerse (con)
comunicarse
divorciarse
enamorarse (de)
encontrarse (ue) (con)
enojarse
irse
olvidarse de
quejarse (de)
reírse (de)
reunirse (con)
separarse (de)

Otros verbos y expresiones verbales

creer
esperar
extrañar
insistir (en)
llorar
matar
nacer
olvidar
pensar (ie) (en)
recomendar (ie)
recordar (ue)
resolver (ue)
romper (con)
salir (con)
sentir (ie, i)
sugerir (ie, i)
temer

dar a luz
dejar un mensaje
estar casado/a (con)
estar comprometido/a
estar enamorado/a (de)
estar juntos/as
estar listo/a
llevarse bien/mal
tener celos
tratar de + *infinitivo*

I. Reciprocal constructions. Imagine que usted está contándoles a sus amigos anécdotas de sus padres. Use el pretérito o el presente según la situación.

> **Modelo:** mis padres / conocerse en la universidad
> **Se conocieron en la universidad.**

1. enamorarse inmediatamente
2. comprometerse seis meses más tarde
3. casarse en secreto dos meses más tarde
4. aún hoy, después de veinticinco años, amarse mucho

II. The present subjuntive (formation). Indique lo que la profesora quiere. Complete las oraciones con la forma correcta del verbo. Use el presente del subjuntivo.

> **Modelo:** traer la tarea a clase (yo, nosotros)
> **Quiere que traiga la tarea a clase.**
> **Quiere que traigamos la tarea a clase.**

1. estudiar más (nosotros, Ana y Linda)
2. hacer la tarea (Esteban, nosotros)
3. volver pronto (Juan, nosotros)
4. divertirse en clase (yo, nosotros)
5. ser puntual/es (los estudiantes, tú)
6. ir a la biblioteca (yo, todos los estudiantes)

III. The subjunctive with expressions of influence. Sus amigos se van a Puerto Rico. Indique lo que usted desea o recomienda que ellos hagan.

> **Modelo:** querer / que irse de vacaciones a Puerto Rico
> **Quiero que se vayan de vacaciones a Puerto Rico.**

1. sugerirles / que irse durante el invierno
2. preferir / que explorar las playas remotas
3. querer / que divertirse mucho durante su visita a San Juan
4. querer / que visitar el bosque lluvioso (*rain forest*)
5. recomendarles a mis amigos / que hablar en español todo el tiempo
6. pedirles a todos / que comprarme un regalo

IV. The subjunctive with expressions of emotion. Es su primera cita con una persona muy especial. Exprese sus sentimientos.

> **Modelo:** esperar / que (él/ella) ser muy sincero/a conmigo
> **Espero que sea muy sincero/a conmigo.**

1. alegrarse de / que (nosotros) tener una cita esta noche
2. Ojalá / que (él/ella) llevarme a un buen restaurante
3. temer / que (él/ella) llegar un poco tarde
4. esperar / que (él/ella) no olvidarse de la cita
5. Ojalá / que (nosotros) poder comunicarnos bien

V. General review. Conteste con oraciones completas.

1. Cuando usted sale con sus amigos/as, ¿adónde van? ¿Qué hacen ustedes normalmente?
2. ¿Con quién/es se lleva usted muy bien?
3. ¿Hace usted muchas llamadas de larga distancia? ¿A quién? ¿De qué hablan?
4. Imagine que usted fue a una fiesta y conoció a una persona muy interesante. ¿Qué pasó? **Nos conocimos, nos...**
5. Es el lunes por la noche. ¿Qué quiere usted que hagan o no hagan sus amigos/as?
6. ¿Qué prefiere usted que haga o no haga la persona con quien vive?
7. ¿Qué espera usted que haga su profesor/a de español?

Answers to the *Autoprueba y repaso* are found in **Apéndice 2**.

Aventuras al aire libre

Goals for communication

- To talk about outdoor adventures and the environment
- To express likes, dislikes, and interests
- To express destination, purpose, and motive
- To express doubt and disbelief
- To react to recent events

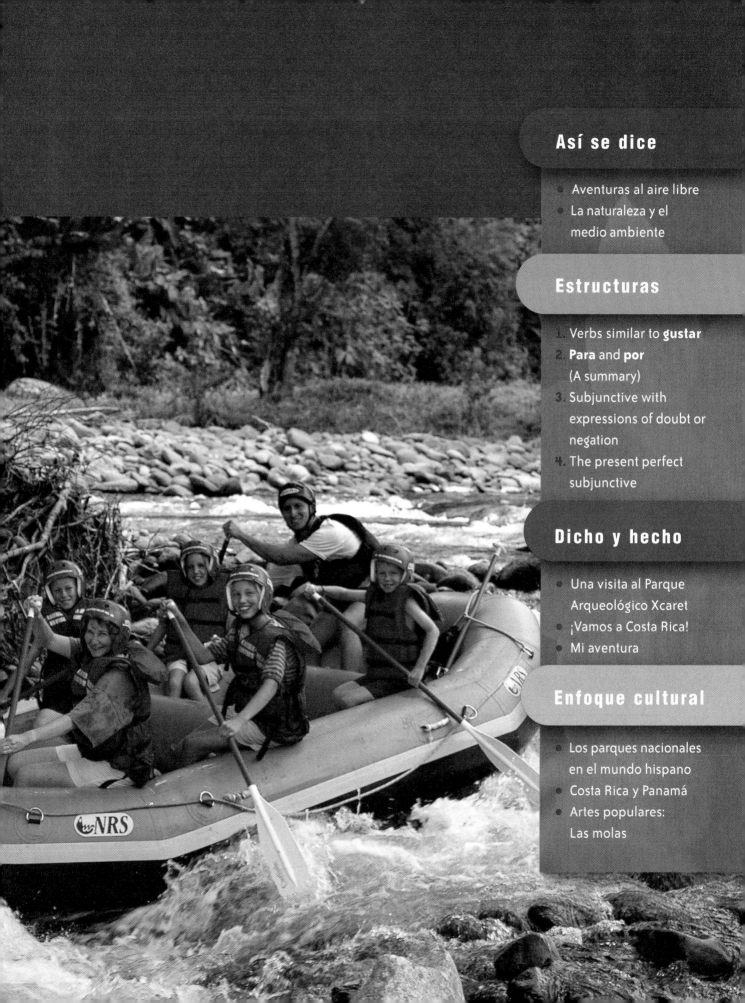

Así se dice

40. Me fascinan las nuevas aventuras.

35. el andinismo/ el alpinismo

36. escalar (la montaña)

37. dar una caminata

38. viajar de mochila

21. la naturaleza

39. el ciclismo de montaña

26. el cielo

22. el valle

25. montar a caballo

27. la luna

24. el caballo

28. las estrellas

29. la tienda de campaña

32. el campamento

31. acampar

33. la fogata   34. el fuego   30. el saco de dormir

1. waterfall
2. dangerous
3. river
4. kayak
5. to go white-water rafting
6. raft
7. to row
8. to go on a cruise, take a trip on a cruise ship/boat
9. to go parasailing
10. ocean
11. sea
12. wave
13. to surf
14. sand
15. to fish
16. boat (small)
17. island
18. to go snorkeling
19. to scuba dive, skin-dive
20. fish
21. nature
22. valley
23. forest
24. horse
25. to ride horseback
26. sky
27. moon
28. stars
29. tent
30. sleeping bag
31. to camp
32. camp
33. campfire
34. fire
35. mountain climbing (ref. to the Andes/Alps)
36. to climb (the mountain)
37. to take a hike
38. to backpack
39. mountain biking
40. I'm fascinated by . . . , . . . fascinate me
41. we are going on vacation; **ir(se) de vacaciones** to go on vacation

Aventuras al aire libre

Práctica y comunicación

(2) **11-1.** **¡Aventuras!** Primero describan las escenas de las páginas 372–373 y digan lo que están haciendo las personas. Luego, contesten las preguntas.

1. ¿Cuáles son las actividades acuáticas? ¿Han practicado algunas? ¿Cuáles? ¿Dónde?
2. ¿Cuáles son las actividades terrestres? ¿Han practicado algunas? ¿Cuáles? ¿Dónde?
3. ¿Qué actividades pueden ser peligrosas? ¿Por qué?
4. Según el dibujo, ¿a quién le encanta viajar? ¿A quién le fascinan las aventuras? ¿Cuándo se van de vacaciones?

(2) **11-2.** **¿Te acuerdas de las palabras?** Lean cada definición y luego den la palabra correspondiente.

> **Modelo:** tierra rodeada por agua, como Cuba
> la/una isla

La naturaleza

1. agua cae desde lo alto de un río, como el Niágara
2. terreno plano (*flat*) entre montañas, como San Fernando en California
3. gran extensión de agua, como el Pacífico
4. muchos árboles y plantas en un lugar
5. donde están el sol, la luna y las estrellas
6. hacemos esto en los campamentos para poder cocinar
7. cuando acampamos, lo usamos para dormir

Aventuras y actividades

8. practicamos este deporte en los ríos con una balsa
9. hacemos esto para capturar peces
10. en vacaciones tomamos un barco grande para visitar el Caribe
11. practicamos esta actividad en las olas
12. subir montañas
13. caminar por el campo, un bosque, etc.
14. lo practicamos con equipo especial para admirar la fauna marina

Gustos y preferencias. Pregúntense si les gusta/ les gustaría (*would like*) hacer las siguientes actividades.

¿Te gusta...?

1. pescar
2. nadar en los ríos/ en los lagos/ en el mar
3. jugar en las olas
4. construir castillos de arena
5. montar a caballo
6. contemplar la naturaleza
7. acampar
8. dar caminatas en las montañas

¿Y cuál de estas ocho actividades te gusta más que las otras?

¿Te gustaría...?

9. hacer *surf* en Costa Rica
10. hacer un viaje en crucero por las islas del Caribe
11. practicar el descenso de ríos en Panamá
12. escalar el Aconcagua en Argentina/Chile
13. bucear en Belice
14. practicar el *parasail* en Cancún
15. ver las cataratas del Iguazú (Argentina/Paraguay)

Ahora, dígale a la clase algo sobre los gustos de su compañero/a:

A Julia le gusta/le gustaría...

¿Te gustaría saltar de un avión (*airplane*) en un paracaídas?

③ **11-4.** **El descenso de ríos.** Imagine que usted y sus amigos buscan una aventura en el descenso de ríos. Lean la información y luego contesten las preguntas.

EQUIPO

los remos

el casco

el chaleco

Clasificación de ríos

Clase 1: Corriente moderada, sin rápidos.
Clase 2: Rápidos suaves y algo de oleaje, apto para toda la familia.
Clase 3: Rápidos más fuertes, olas grandes y algunas pendientes escalonadas. Es apto para todas las edades, pero se debe tener más precaución.
Clase 4: Rápidos fuertes, olas grandes, rocas en el camino y, en algunas partes, pendientes muy pronunciadas. Sólo para mayores de 16 años.
Clase 5: Rápidos muy fuertes, sólo para personas experimentadas.
Clase 6: Río peligroso y no explorado. Cuando alguien logra navegar un río de clase 6, éste se convierte en categoría 5.

LA COMPAÑÍA DE *RAFTING* DEBE TENER:

- Equipo en buen estado
- Guías experimentados
- Guías capacitados con cursos de rescate° y primeros auxilios°
- Seguro° contra accidentes

rescue
first aid
insurance

El *rafting* en Latinoamérica le permite explorar y conocer remotos y fascinantes santuarios de la naturaleza. Unos ejemplos:

El río Savegre, en Costa Rica: un paraíso con aguas cristalinas, abundante fauna y bella selva° tropical.

El río Usumacinta, en México: revela remotos templos y pirámides mayas, densa selva e impresionantes cascadas.

El río Futaleufu, en Chile: pasa por bosques de la Patagonia y por espectaculares paisajes° de roca, nieve y hielo.

El río Colca, en Perú: pasa por dramáticos cañones con altas cataratas y vistas de volcanes activos.

landscapes

jungle

1. ¿Qué equipo se necesita para practicar el descenso de ríos?
2. ¿Cuáles son las cosas más importantes que debe ofrecerle la compañía de *rafting*?
3. ¿Qué clasificación de ríos prefieren? ¿Por qué?
4. ¿Qué ríos prefieren navegar? ¿Por qué?

Es primavera y los estudiantes **están de vacaciones**[1]. Acompañan a sus amigos/as a lugares muy diferentes.

la granja[2]

la vaca[3]

la tierra[7]

la hierba[4]

la gallina[5]

el cerdo[6]

Linda e Inés dan un paseo por el campo, donde viven los abuelos de Linda.

la tormenta[18]

el relámpago[19]

la colina[20]

la cámara[22]

sacar/ tomar fotos[23]

la serpiente[21]

tener miedo[11]

el pájaro[12]

la araña[10]

el animal[13]

la mariposa[14]

los insectos[15]

la mosca[9]

el mosquito[16]

Esteban, con su clase de biología, está explorando la **selva**[8] panameña.

Natalia y Pepita dan una caminata por el **desierto**[17] de Nuevo México. La familia de Natalia vive cerca de allí.

(1) are on vacation; **estar de vacaciones** *to be on vacation (2) farm (3) cow (4) grass (5) chicken (6) pig (7) earth, land (8) jungle (9) fly (10) spider (11) to be afraid (12) bird (13) animal (14) butterfly (15) insects (16) mosquito (17) desert (18) storm (19) lightning (20) hill (21) snake (22) camera (23) to take photos*

11-5.

Unas vacaciones un poco diferentes. Observen los dibujos de la página 377 y contesten las preguntas.

Un paseo por el campo

1. ¿Qué cosas ven Linda e Inés en su paseo?

2. ¿Qué comen los animales?

3. ¿Qué se cultiva en la granja?

Explorando la selva

4. ¿De qué puede tener miedo Esteban?

5. ¿Qué insectos probablemente no le gustan?

6. ¿Cuál posiblemente le fascina más?

Una caminata por el desierto

7. ¿Cómo está el clima? **Hay/Hace...**

8. ¿De qué está sacando Pepita una foto?

9. ¿Natalia y Pepita tienen miedo de la serpiente?

10. ¿Qué llevan probablemente en sus mochilas?

11-6.

Aventureros/as. Caminando por la clase, hágales preguntas a sus compañeros/as. Siga el modelo.

Modelo: bucear

Estudiante 1: **¿Has buceado?**

Estudiante 2: **Sí, he buceado.**

Estudiante 1: **¿Dónde? ¿Cuándo?**

Estudiante 2: **En Cancún. El verano pasado/Hace dos años, etc.** (*Apunte el nombre del estudiante y la información.*)

Nombres

HINT | * = irregular past participle

_____ **1.** hacer* el *esnórquel*

_____ **2.** practicar el *parasail*

_____ **3.** viajar por un desierto

_____ **4.** dar una caminata por una selva

_____ **5.** vivir en o visitar una granja con muchos animales

_____ **6.** descender un río en balsa, kayak o canoa

_____ **7.** ver* una catarata grande

_____ **8.** ver una serpiente muy grande

_____ **9.** hacer un viaje en crucero

_____ **10.** hacer *surf*

_____ **11.** escalar una montaña muy alta

_____ **12.** acampar

Ahora, dígale a la clase algo de las aventuras de sus compañeros/as.

11-7. **¿Sabía usted que...?** Lean las descripciones e identifiquen el país o la región que le corresponde a cada una.

> Bolivia/Perú   Venezuela   Himalayas: Tibet/Nepal
>
> Michigan, EE.UU.   El norte de África   África: Tanganyika/Ruanda → el Mediterráneo

1. El Everest es la montaña más alta del mundo (29.028 pies/8.848 metros de altura).
2. El Sahara es el desierto más grande del mundo (área: 3.500.000 millas cuadradas/9.065.000 kilómetros cuadrados/km²).
3. El Nilo es el río más largo del mundo (4.180 millas/6.690 kilómetros).
4. El Salto Ángel es la cascada más alta del mundo (3.281 pies/979 metros).
5. El Titicaca es el lago navegable más alto del mundo (12.506 pies de altura/3.751 metros).
6. El lago Superior es el lago de agua dulce más grande del mundo (área: 31.820 millas cuadradas/82.414 km²).

DICHOS

Más vale pájaro en mano que cien volando.

En boca cerrada no entran moscas.

¿Conoce usted el equivalente en inglés de cada uno de estos dichos?

El Salto Ángel en Venezuela es la cascada más alta del mundo.

Natalia

Pepita

Escenas
Aventuras en el parque ecológico

Octavio

Javier
Rubén

 5 Nuestros amigos están acampando en el parque ecológico del Arenal en Costa Rica. Es de noche y Pepita y Natalia se están preparando para visitar el volcán.

	PEPITA: Este parque ecológico debe de ser el lugar más espectacular del planeta. Aquí no hay basura ni contaminación, sólo bosques y animales…
	NATALIA: (*Interrumpiéndola*)… y qué maravilloso es respirar aire puro. (*Llegan Octavio y Javier.*)
	PEPITA: ¡Hola, chicos! ¿Dónde está Rubén?
	OCTAVIO: Está en el pueblo organizando la manifestación contra la deforestación.
trails	PEPITA: …y se le olvidó que Natalia y yo vamos a caminar por los senderos° cerca del volcán. ¿Ustedes quieren ir con nosotras?
darkness	JAVIER: ¿Ahora? ¿En la oscuridad?° ¡No!
	NATALIA: ¿Por qué no? La actividad volcánica es más impresionante de noche.
	JAVIER: El año pasado Octavio y yo tuvimos una experiencia nocturna muy extraña…
	PEPITA: ¿De verdad? ¿Qué pasó?
flashlights	OCTAVIO: Una noche nosotros decidimos usar las linternas° y explorar los alrededores del campamento. De repente, comenzó a llover
en… on the way	fuertemente. Decidimos regresar y en camino° oímos un ruido muy
followed	extraño. Empezamos a correr y un animal muy grande nos siguió°.
bear	NATALIA: ¿Qué era? ¿Un puma? ¿Un oso°?
	JAVIER: No, una vaca.
	PEPITA: ¿Una vaca? ¡Qué miedosos!
	OCTAVIO: Bueno, entonces si ustedes no tienen miedo y quieren dar una caminata cerca del volcán a estas horas, pueden ir solas.
	NATALIA: Pues nosotras somos muy valientes, no le tenemos miedo a nada.
	PEPITA: ¡Vámonos! (*Se escucha un ruido…*) ¿Qué fue eso?
mud	(*Aparece Rubén, totalmente cubierto de lodo°.*)
the Abominable Snowman,	TODOS: (*Se van corriendo, con miedo.*) ¡Es el Yeti°! ¡Qué horror! ¡Socorro°!
Big Foot, Sasquatch / Help!	RUBÉN: ¿Adónde van? Soy yo, Rubén. Tuve un pequeño accidente. Me caí° en
Me… I fell / strange	el lodo… ¡Qué amigos tan extraños° tengo!

¿Qué pasa?

1. ¿Qué piensa Pepita del parque ecológico?

2. ¿Dónde está Rubén? ¿Qué se le olvidó?

3. ¿Por qué no quieren Octavio y Javier acompañar a las chicas?

4. ¿Qué tipo de animal siguió a los muchachos?

5. ¿Por qué son Pepita y Natalia más valientes que los chicos?

6. ¿Quién es el «animal»? ¿Por qué piensa Rubén que sus amigos son extraños?

Estructuras

1 **Expressing likes, dislikes, and interests: Verbs similar to *gustar***

In **Chapter 3** you learned to use **gustar** to express likes and dislikes.

HINT Review **gustar** on p. 105.

gusta + *verb*	Me gusta nadar.
gusta + *singular noun*	Me gusta el agua verde-azul del Caribe.
gustan + *plural noun*	Me gustan las playas de Costa Rica.

The following verbs express additional and varying degrees of likes, dislikes, and interests.

encantar	*to love, to delight, to enchant*	**Me encanta** esquiar en el lago.
fascinar	*to be fascinating to, to fascinate*	**¿Te fascinan** las tormentas?
molestar	*to be annoying to, to bother*	**Le molesta** el calor.
interesar	*to be interesting to, to interest*	**Nos interesan** los reptiles.
importar	*to be important to, to matter*	No **les importa** si llueve.

These verbs function like **gustar**; they are used with indirect object pronouns (**me, te, le, nos, os, les**) and with the third-person singular or plural form of the verb.

Práctica y comunicación

11-8. **¿Qué me encanta, fascina o molesta?** Escriba tres cosas/actividades en cada una de las tres categorías a continuación. Luego, lea algunas de sus oraciones a la clase.

> **Modelo:** Me encanta nadar en el mar.
> Me encantan los gatos.

1. Me encanta/n...   **2.** Me fascina/n...   **3.** Me molesta/n...

11-9. **Unas vacaciones llenas de (*full of*) aventuras.** En la agencia de viajes Aventuras Sin Límites, el agente le pregunta a usted si le interesan o no las actividades de la lista. Según sus respuestas, él/ella le recomienda lugares de vacaciones. Cambien de papel.

> **Modelo:** Agente: ¿Le interesa el andinismo?
> Cliente: Sí, me interesa mucho.
> Agente: **En ese caso, le recomiendo que vaya a las montañas de Colorado o a los Andes en Argentina.**

1. el andinismo/alpinismo   **6.** el ciclismo de montaña
2. visitar una selva tropical   **7.** la pesca
3. bucear   **8.** el *esnórquel*
4. hacer *surf*   **9.** tomar el sol o nadar en el mar
5. el *rafting*   **10.** el *parasail*

11-10. **¿Le importa?** Completen el siguiente sondeo individualmente y luego comparen sus respuestas.

¿Te importa o no te importa...?	Sí	No
1. sacar buenas notas	❐	❐
2. tener un coche caro	❐	❐
3. ganar mucho dinero	❐	❐
4. tener ropa de moda	❐	❐
5. tener pareja adinerada (con mucho dinero)	❐	❐
6. conocer otras partes del mundo	❐	❐
7. preservar la naturaleza	❐	❐

SONDEO

Ahora, presenten algunas de sus conclusiones a la clase. **A Beth le importa...**
A Beth y a Lee les importa... A nosotros nos importa...

11-11. Mis reacciones. Escriba una oración que describa cada uno de los siguientes tópicos.

- las clases que **le interesan/fascinan** más a usted
- los aspectos de la vida universitaria que **le encantan/gustan** o **no le gustan**
- lo que **les molesta** a sus profesores
- lo que **les importa** a los estudiantes en la universidad

Estructuras

② Stating purpose, destination, and motive: *Para* and *por* (A summary)

¡Qué divertido! Tenemos que pasar por estos rápidos para llegar al campamento.

You have been using **para** and **por** since **Chapter 1**. Both prepositions often translate as *for* in English, but convey very different meanings in Spanish. The following charts review some of their more frequent uses and meanings.

Para *indicates:*		
1. Purpose or goal	*in order to + infinitive*	Sonia fue a Costa Rica **para** ver los bosques tropicales.
2. Recipient	*for*	Sacó unas fotos del bosque **para** su madre.
3. Destination	*for*	Sonia sale **para** Panamá el viernes.
4. Deadline	*by, for*	Tiene que estar allí **para** el lunes.
5. Employment	*for*	Ella trabaja **para** una compañía hotelera.

Por *indicates:*		
1. Cause, reason, motive	*because of*	Esteban no completó su trabajo escrito **por** estar un poco enfermo.
	on behalf of, for	Pepita, su amiga, habló con el profesor **por** él.
2. Duration of time	*for, during*	Más tarde, Esteban habló con el profesor **por** más de media hora.
	in, at	Decidió trabajar en el proyecto **por** la tarde y **por** la noche.
3. Exchange, price	*for*	Pepita le compró un diccionario **por** diez dólares.
	for, in exchange for	Él le dio las gracias[1] **por** el diccionario.
4. General physical movement in and around a given place	*down, by, along, through*	Ahora camina **por** el campus con sus libros y su diccionario.

Práctica y comunicación

② 11–12. **El viaje de Carmen.** Carmen hizo un viaje de negocios a Panamá. Refiriéndose a los dibujos, completen las oraciones para indicar dónde trabaja y lo que hizo durante su viaje. Piensen en los usos de **para** y **por**.

1. 2. 3. 4. 5. 6.

1. Carmen trabaja **para** la compañía _____. Hizo un pequeño viaje de negocios y de vacaciones a Panamá.

2. Salió **para** _____ en el vuelo (*flight*) número _____ a las _____ de la mañana.

3. Fue a Panamá **para** _____ el famoso _____ y **para** trabajar un poco. Quiere pasar mucho tiempo caminando **por** _____ y observándolo. Siempre le ha fascinado.

4. A una de las vendedoras le compró una _____ **para** su amiga Natalia. _____ mil pesos **por** la camiseta.

5. Natalia le dio las gracias **por** _____.

6. Carmen tuvo que volver a la oficina **para** _____ de julio.

---

[1] To thank someone for something, always use **gracias por…**

2 **11–13.** **¡A las montañas!** Usted y unos amigos van a las montañas para escalar y acampar en el monte Chirripó en Talamanca, Costa Rica. Usted y otro/a amigo/a conversan del viaje. Completen la conversación con **por** o **para**.

USTED:	Salimos _para_ el Chirripó el sábado a las 6:00 de la mañana.
AMIGO/A:	¿_Por_ cuántos días van?
USTED:	_Por_ tres o cuatro días. Vamos _para_ acampar y escalar el pico más alto de la región.
AMIGO/A:	¿Van a tomar la ruta que va _por_ el río?
USTED:	Sí, y luego vamos a dar una caminata _por_ el bosque hasta encontrar un buen lugar _para_ acampar.
AMIGO/A:	¿Saben tus amigos armar la tienda de campaña?
USTED:	Creo que no. Pero yo puedo hacerlo mientras ellos buscan leña° _para_ la fogata.
AMIGO/A:	¿Están ellos en buenas condiciones físicas para subir el monte?
USTED:	Pues, espero que sí. Vamos a salir muy temprano _por_ la mañana y llegar a la cumbre° _para_ el mediodía, antes de que empiece a llover.
AMIGO/A:	Es un buen plan. A propósito°, tu saco de dormir se ve muy nuevo. ¿Dónde lo compraste?
USTED:	Lo compré en una tienda de descuento _por_ $38.00.
AMIGO/A:	Buen precio... y antes de que se me olvide, tengo algo _para_ ustedes: un mapa topográfico de la región para que no se pierdan.
USTED:	Muchas gracias _por_ el mapa. ¡Nos va a ser muy útil!
AMIGO/A:	Pues, ¡buen viaje!

firewood

summit

A... *By the way*

4 **11–14.** **Nuestra aventura.** Imaginen que tienen una semana libre (*free*) y deciden organizar una aventura a un país/lugar interesante. Usen las preguntas que siguen para formular su plan. Un/a secretario/a escribe el plan.

1. ¿Cuándo salen para...?
2. ¿Por cuánto tiempo van a estar allí?
3. ¿Para qué van?
4. ¿Qué piensan hacer por la mañana/ tarde/ noche?
5. ¿Para qué fecha tienen que volver?
6. ¿Cuánto piensan pagar por el viaje?

Algunos grupos presentan su plan a la clase.

Así se dice

La naturaleza y el medio ambiente[1]

A causa de[2] los **problemas**[3] ambientales que existen en todo el **mundo**[4], muchos científicos creen que nuestro **planeta**[5] está en peligro.

¿Qué se puede hacer para **conservar**[6] el planeta tierra?

Podemos: controlar la **contaminación**[7] producida por las fábricas…

… y por los vehículos;

reducir la contaminación que **destruye**[8]* la **capa de ozono**[9];

controlar la **deforestación**[10] y plantar más árboles;

prevenir[11] los **incendios forestales**[12];

evitar[13] el uso excesivo de pesticidas;

proteger[14]** los animales que están en peligro de extinción;

prevenir la contaminación de ríos y mares;

no **desperdiciar**[15] los **recursos naturales**[16];

comprar coches eficientes que no desperdicien la gasolina;

y **recoger**[17] y **reciclar**[18] basura.

HINT | Note that **el problema** and **el planeta** end in **-a** but are masculine.

*(1) environment (2) because of (3) problems (m.) (4) world (5) planet (m.) (6) to save, conserve (7) pollution (8) destroys; **destruir** to destroy (9) ozone layer (10) deforestation (11) to prevent (12) forest fires (13) to avoid (14) to protect (15) to waste (16) natural resources (17) to pick up, gather (18) to recycle*

---

* **Destruir** changes the **i** to **y** in all forms of the present tense except **nosotros** and **vosotros**: destruyo, destruyes, destruye, destruimos, destruís, destruyen.

** **Proteger** changes the **g** to **j** in the yo form of the present tense: protejo, proteges,…

Práctica y comunicación

2 **11-15.** **El medio ambiente.** Contesten las preguntas según los dibujos de la página 386.

1. ¿Cuáles son algunas de las causas de la contaminación del aire?
2. ¿Qué problemas afectan los bosques, las selvas y la tierra?
3. ¿Cuáles afectan los animales?
4. ¿Cuáles afectan la salud de las personas?
5. ¿Qué recursos naturales desperdicias: el agua, la electricidad o la gasolina?
6. ¿Qué podemos hacer para proteger y conservar el medio ambiente?

2 **11-16.** **Serios problemas ecológicos.** Piensen en varios resultados negativos de cada uno de los siguientes problemas. Apunten sus ideas para luego presentárselas a la clase.

A causa de...

1. la deforestación ...
2. la contaminación del aire ...
3. los derrames de crudo (*oil spills*) ...
4. la destrucción de la capa de ozono ...
5. la lluvia ácida ...

> **Palabras útiles**
>
> el aire puro
> la erosión
> la sequía   *drought*
> contaminar
> derretirse (i, i)   *to melt*
> respirar

4 **11-17.** **Un mundo ideal.** Describan su imagen de un mundo ideal. Un/a secretario/a apunta la información. ¿Qué grupo tiene la descripción más completa?

Vista aérea de un derrame de crudo en la costa.

Un mundo ideal.

Noticias culturales

Los parques nacionales en el mundo hispano

La protección del medio ambiente no es una idea nueva en el mundo hispano: la creación de muchos parques nacionales y reservas en estos países ocurrió en la *half* primera mitad° del siglo XX. España tiene muchos parques de notable belleza, pero los parques y reservas más conocidos están en Costa Rica: los «bosques *sacred* nubosos» en la reserva de Monteverde protegen a los quetzales (pájaros sagrados° *turtles* para los mayas), y cada verano miles de tortugas° ponen sus huevos en las playas del parque nacional Tortuguero.

Otros países también tienen parques espectaculares. México combina las reservas naturales con monumentos arqueológicos: un ejemplo es Xcaret en Yucatán. Allí es posible admirar ruinas mayas entre la flora y fauna de la región. *high plateaus* En las selvas del interior de Venezuela están los tepuyes, altas mesetas° rodeadas de nubes y vegetación tropical. En las Islas Galápagos en el Ecuador podemos ver de cerca las aves y reptiles que inspiraron la teoría de la evolución de Darwin. Torres del Paine en el sur de Chile es famoso por sus montañas de granito, impresionantes costas y gigantescos glaciares. Este parque de 450.000 acres protege a los guanacos *ostrich* (animales parecidos a las llamas) y los ñandús (similares al avestruz°).

Hoy, los países hispanos continúan creando parques y reservas para reflejar el aumento de la conciencia ecológica y el interés por el ecoturismo de sus habitantes.

¿Qué recuerda?

1. ¿Es la protección del medio ambiente una preocupación nueva en el mundo hispano?
2. ¿Cuándo fueron creados algunos de los parques y reservas en territorios hispanos?
3. ¿Puede usted nombrar un parque o reserva costarricense? ¿Qué animal podemos encontrar allí?
4. ¿Cuál es una de las atracciones especiales de las Islas Galápagos? ¿Y de Xcaret en Yucatán?

Conexiones y contrastes

1. ¿Existe un parque nacional o reserva en el estado/país donde vive usted o su familia? ¿Hay alguna especie protegida en este parque o reserva?
2. ¿Cuál es el parque o reserva natural más conocido de su país? ¿Puede usted mencionar algunas de sus atracciones?
3. ¿Qué efectos negativos tiene el turismo en los parques nacionales? ¿Existen soluciones para este tipo de problemas?

3 The subjunctive with expressions of doubt or negation

Creo que podemos escalar este pico.

Dudo que podamos escalarlo hoy.

When a speaker expresses doubt, uncertainty, or disbelief relevant to an action or condition, the subjunctive is used.

Dudo que el guía **llegue** a tiempo.   *I doubt that the guide will arrive on time.*

No puedo creer que las balsas no **estén** aquí.   *I can't believe that the rafts aren't here.*

The verb of the first clause, which indicates the speaker's doubt, uncertainty, or disbelief, is in the indicative (**Dudo...**/ **No puedo creer...**); the second clause is in the subjunctive.

> *expression indicating doubt/uncertainty/disbelief (indicative)*
> **+ que +**
> *action or condition that is doubted, uncertain, etc. (subjunctive)*

Some verbs and expressions of doubt, uncertainty, or disbelief are:

dudar	*to doubt*	**Dudo** que **haya** rápidos de clase 5 en este río.
no estar seguro/a (de)	*not to be sure*	**No estamos seguros de** que la compañía **tenga** guías experimentados.
no creer	*not to believe*	**No creen** que **podamos** descender el río hoy.

● When **creer** and **estar seguro** ask a question that expresses the speaker's doubt or uncertainty, they are followed by the subjunctive.

¿Estás seguro que **puedan** encontrar los remos?   *Are you sure that they can find the oars?*

¿Crees que el río **sea** peligroso?   *Do you think that the river is dangerous?*

● However, when **creer** and **estar seguro** express certainty, they are followed by the indicative.

El guía **está seguro de/ cree** que **podemos** navegar los rápidos.   *The guide is sure/believes that we can run the rapids.*

Práctica y comunicación

11-18. ¿Lo cree o lo duda? Indique si usted cree en las siguientes declaraciones o duda de ellas.

Modelo: El ciclismo de montaña requiere mucha experiencia.

Dudo que *requiera* mucha experiencia. *o*

Creo que *requiere* mucha experiencia.

1. Escalar rocas (*Rock climbing*) requiere equipo especial.
2. Es peligroso navegar en un lago en canoa.
3. El buceo en aguas profundas requiere instrucción.
4. Es peligroso descender ríos de clase 1.
5. Es difícil viajar de mochila en las montañas por tres días.
6. El casco protege la cabeza en el descenso de ríos.
7. La balsa tiene más flexibilidad en el agua que el kayak.

② 11-19. La compañía de *rafting*. Usted y su amigo/a van a descender ríos y tienen opiniones muy diferentes en cuanto a la compañía que van a usar. Indiquen sus reacciones.

Modelo: el equipo / estar en buen estado

Estudiante 1: **Dudo que/No estoy seguro(a) de que el equipo *esté* en buen estado.**

Estudiante 2: **Estoy seguro(a)/Creo que el equipo *está* en buen estado.**

1. la compañía / tener balsas nuevas
2. los guías / ser experimentados
3. los guías / saber qué hacer en caso de emergencia
4. la compañía / llevar a niños en los rápidos de clase 4
5. la compañía / evitar / los rápidos de clase 5

③ ¡Qué dilema!

Estás en Costa Rica con tus amigos y ustedes deciden practicar el rafting. Piensan que van a descender un río de clase 3 pero al llegar al punto de partida, descubren que en realidad es ¡un río de clase 5! Como no sabes nadar, tienes miedo. Tus amigos son muy aventureros e insisten en descender el río. Ustedes hablan:
Tú: **¡Ay! ¿Un río de clase 5? ¡Ni pensarlo! ¡No sé nadar!**
Amigo/a 1: ...
Amigo/a 2: ...

4 **11-20.** **Las Cabañas Bataburo.** Ustedes piensan hacer un viaje a estas cabañas en la selva del Ecuador. Para llegar, van a navegar por el río Tinguino en canoas con motor. Lean la siguiente información.

Cabañas Bataburo

¿Desean más información? Visiten:
www.ecuadorexplorer.com/kempery/home.html

En el corazón místico y salvaje de la selva primaria del territorio Huaorani, se han construido las Cabañas Bataburo. El diseño de construcción está totalmente en armonía con la selva. Les ofrecemos confort sin perder el sentimiento de aventura de este paraíso lleno de misterio.

Tenemos alojamiento en habitaciones dobles o matrimoniales con baños privados o compartidos, mosquiteros, luz eléctrica y torre de observación de aproximadamente 40 mts. El comedor sirve excelente comida típica.

Actividades:

- Caminatas de 5 a 6 horas en las que el guía habla sobre la flora y fauna de la zona.
- Tour nocturno de observación de insectos (tierra) y caimanes (río).
- Pesca de pirañas; observación de anacondas en su hábitat.

Ahora comenten y den sus reacciones respecto a:

1. la localización de las cabañas
2. su diseño (*design*)
3. el alojamiento (*lodging*)
4. la comida
5. las actividades

Posibles reacciones:

¡Qué bueno que...!
Dudamos que…
Nos fascina que…
Nos encanta que…
Estamos seguros/as que…
Esperamos poder…, etc.

4 Expressing reactions to recent events: The present perfect subjuntive

The present perfect subjunctive is used to express reactions to events that have occurred in the past but are closely tied to the present.

Espero que **hayan visto** las cataratas.   *I hope that they have seen the waterfalls.*
Dudo que **hayan cruzado** el río.   *I doubt that they have crossed the river.*

It is formed with the present subjunctive of **haber** + *past participle*.

el presente del subjuntivo de *haber* + el participio pasado

El guía duda que...   *The guide doubts that . . .*

    (yo) **haya perdido** el remo.   *I have lost the oar.*
    (tú) lo **hayas perdido**.   *you have lost it.*
    (Ud./él/ella) lo **haya perdido**.   *you have/he, she has lost it.*
    (nosotros/as) lo **hayamos perdido**.   *we have lost it.*
    (vosotros/as) lo **hayáis perdido**.   *you have lost it.*
    (Uds./ellos/ellas) lo **hayan perdido**. *you/they have lost it.*

HINT | Review the present perfect indicative in **Chapter 9**, pp. 316–317. Focus on the irregular past participles.

Práctica y comunicación

11-21. **Alberto se va a Costa Rica.** Su amigo Alberto le informa que va a pasar un semestre estudiando en San José, Costa Rica. Le menciona a usted algunos detalles del viaje. Responda apropiadamente a cada detalle.

Alberto le dice:

1. No debo llevar dinero en efectivo.

2. Me gusta sacar fotos.

3. Voy a vivir con una familia costarricense.

4. La familia costarricense no habla inglés.

5. Mis abuelos siempre se preocupan cuando viajo a otro país.

6. Siempre espero hasta el último momento para organizarme.

Usted responde:

a. Me alegro de que hayas aceptado su invitación.

b. Espero que hayas conseguido una tarjeta de ATM.

c. Espero que te hayas comprado una cámara digital.

d. ¡Ojalá que hayas solicitado tu pasaporte!

e. ¡Ojalá que no les hayas dicho que te vas por un semestre!

f. Me alegro de que hayas estudiado español.

11-22. ¿Cómo reaccionan ustedes?

Según los dibujos, indiquen su reacción positiva o negativa a lo que ha ocurrido recientemente. Usen: **Nos alegramos de que...** o **Sentimos que...**

Modelo:	...Octavio...
	el campeonato de esquí.
	Nos alegramos de que Octavio haya ganado el campeonato de esquí.

1. ...Inés...
en un concierto.

2. ...Camila...
en su trabajo escrito.

3. ...Esteban...
en su trabajo escrito.

4. ...Javier...
para su cumpleaños.

5. ...Alfonso...
para nosotros.

6. ...el abuelo de Carmen...

11-23. ¿Qué ha hecho?

Piense en algo interesante que usted ha hecho recientemente. Puede ser real o imaginario. Preséntaselo a su grupo. Luego, cada uno de sus compañeros reacciona, usando una de las siguientes expresiones.

> Dudo que... No creo que... Creo que... Me alegro que... Siento que...

Modelo:	He ganado la lotería tres veces.
	Compañero/a: **Dudo que/No creo que hayas ganado la lotería.**

Luego presenten información interesante a la clase: **Andrés dice que ha ganado la lotería tres veces, pero nosotros dudamos que la haya ganado.**

Dicho y hecho

🔲 Conversando

4) **Una visita al Parque Arqueológico Xcaret.** Imaginen que van a pasar dos días en este fabuloso parque, situado en la Riviera Maya de México. Estudien las opciones presentadas y decidan qué atracciones les interesan más a ustedes. Luego formulen un plan de lo que van a hacer cada día. Un/a secretario/a apunta la información. Al final, algunos grupos presentan su plan a la clase.

PRINCIPALES ATRACTIVOS DEL INCREÍBLE PARQUE ECOARQUEOLÓGICO XCARET **(VER MAPA DESPLEGABLE)**

B-2 / C-1 DELFINES I y II. Lo invitamos a retozar, nadar y convivir con estas inteligentes criaturas. Haga su reservación en el Museo; existe gran demanda y cupo limitado (actividad no incluida en su boleto de entrada).

B-2 LOS RIOS SUBTERRANEOS. Lo culminante de XCARET, son una maravilla natural única en el mundo. Disfrute de una experiencia que jamás olvidará, flotando río abajo en cristalinas aguas de cenote, a través de canales y túneles naturalmente iluminados.

D-1 SALIDA DE LOS RIOS SUBTERRANEOS. Al concluir, devuelva el chaleco salvavidas y con su llave contraseña le entregarán su bolsa con sus pertenencias

D-1 TOUR DE BUCEO Y ESNORQUEL. Centro de reservaciones para la excursión y renta de equipo (no incluido en su boleto de entrada).

C-1 CAMINANDO BAJO EL MAR. Disfrute de la fascinante experiencia de caminar bajo el mar de la manera más sencilla, segura y divertida. No se requiere saber nadar. (No incluido en su boleto de entrada).

C-1 LA CALETA. Ideal para aprender a esnorquelear yadmirar peces de mil colores. Esta pequeña entrada de agua es de donde el Parque toma su nombre (XCARET significa "pequeña caleta" en maya).

C-1 / D-1 LAS PLAYAS Y POZAS DE MAR. De finas arenas blancas, son ideales para asolearse y nadar. Aquí, puede rentar equipo para una estancia más placentera.

B-3 LAS CABALLERIZAS. Admire la gracia y habilidad de caballos y jinetes que hablan por sí mismos de México y sus tradiciones. Aventúrese a cabalgar entre la selva hasta llegar a la playa y sentir la brisa del Mar Caribe (actividad no incluida en su boleto de entrada).

C-2 PUEBLO MAYA. Aventúrese a recorrer un pasaje subterráneo que lo conducirá al sorprendente nacimiento de un pequeño pueblo maya.

D-2 MARIPOSARIO. Considerado uno de los más grandes del mundo y único en su género por su reproducción autosuficiente de mariposas. Le sugerimos visitarlo antes del mediodía.

D-2 CAPILLA SAN FRANCISCO DE ASIS. Muestra arquitectónica de la fusión de dos culturas con una fachada producto de la conquista española y la nave prehispánica de la cultura maya.

B-2 ACUARIO DE ARRECIFES DE CORAL. El más grande del mundo en su tipo, donde se puede admirar toda la belleza de este impresionante jardín submarino. Asómbrese con la riqueza de colores y formas de un hábitat natural con peces viviendo entre arrecifes.

C-2 TORTUGAS MARINAS. Conozca de cerca a estos legendarios y maravillosos animales en diferentes etapas de su desarrollo.

B-3 EL JARDIN BOTANICO Y VIVERO. Acceso junto al "Arbol Caído" (que se negó a morir en el huracán "Gilberto" en 1988). Gran variedad de plantas y árboles nativos en estado virgen, que se encuentran en una hondonada protegida, formando su propio microclima.

A-4 TORRE ESCENICA. La más bella vista del Caribe Mexicano y el punto más alto para disfrutar de Xcaret , la Riviera Maya y en el horizonte la isla de Cozumel.

A-3 ORQUIDEARIO. Aprecie nuestra colección de 52 especies nativas más 26 híbridos. La reproducción in-vitro nos permite rescatar las orquídeas en peligro de extinción repoblando y decorando Xcaret con sus sorprendentes flores.

A-3 CULTIVO DE HONGOS. La "Granja de Hongos" comestibles, donde estamos estudiando la posibilidad de desarrollo de una industria semicasera para las comunidades rurales de la región.

A-4 EL GRAN TLACHCO. (Lugar donde se juega la pelota). Majestuoso escenario en el que más de 250 artistas lo harán disfrutar de la inigualable aventura de Xcaret, Noche Espectacular.

C-3 JUEGO DE PELOTA. Es la representación en vivo del más importante evento religioso deportivo de la Cultura Maya.

B-2 VOLADORES DE PAPANTLA. Ceremonia dedicada al Dios del Sol, que representa una de las tradiciones prehispánicas que se conservan hasta nuestros días.

C-2 ISLAS DE FELINOS. Jaguares y pumas en un hábitat perfectamente integrado para lograr la reproducción en cautiverio de estas especies nativas en peligro de extinción.

C-3 EL MUSEO DE XCARET. Edificación proyectada para mimetizarse con el paisaje y el entorno natural que la rodea. Alberga escenificaciones en miniatura de los asentamientos mayas más importantes. Centro de información, cafetería, baños casilleros, tienda y centro fotográfico.

D-2 AVIARIO DE VUELO LIBRE. Localizado detrás del Museo y muestra un fantástico mundo de aves del sureste de México, muchas de ellas en peligro de extinción.

C-2 LAGUNA DE LOS MANATIES. Contemple a los fabulosos Manatíes en una laguna de agua cristalina, observe con que parsimonia se mueven estos también llamados elefantes marinos.

B-1 / B-2 / C-2 LAS ZONAS ARQUEOLOGICAS DE XCARET. Con más de mil años de historia, XCARET es uno de los sitios mayas más importantes de Quintana Roo, destacando principalmente en el postclásico tardío (1400 D.C.) hasta la llegada de los españoles en 1517.

B-3 PLAZA DEL VITRAL. Con un edificio de majestuosa arquitectura disfrute de un vitral dedicado a las mariposas de México así como al colorido de la vegetación.

RINCON MEXICANO. Imagine estar en en el antiguo México, un domingo en la tarde, con la banda en el quiosco, vendedores de caramelos, aguas frescas, frutas picadas con chile.

C-2 PASEO POR EL CIELO. Vuele entre las nubes y contemple el maravilloso paisaje de Xcaret y la Riviera Maya, una experiencia inolvidable.

C-1 / D-1 HAMACAS. Le ofrecemos la oportunidad de descansar frente a la laguna y también en los estanques, una serie de hamacas para reponer fuerzas y retornar a la exploración de Xcaret.

¡Ah...y no olvide traer su camará y esnorquel!

🎧 ¡A escuchar!

¡Vamos a Costa Rica! El Instituto Costarricense de Turismo lo/la invita a descubrir Costa Rica y a gozar de (*enjoy*) una experiencia fascinante. Escuche el anuncio. Luego, identifique los tres lugares siguientes.

> volcán   bosque nuboso   playa

1. Seleccione la descripción correcta para cada lugar.

   a. Manuel Antonio _____

   b. Monteverde _____

   c. Arenal _____

Escuche el anuncio otra vez y conteste las preguntas para indicar sus preferencias.

2. ¿Qué desea usted ver en Monteverde? _____

3. ¿Qué quiere usted hacer en Manuel Antonio? _____

4. ¿Qué puede usted hacer en Arenal? _____

✍ De mi escritorio

Mi aventura. Escriba una descripción de una aventura al aire libre que usted tuvo en el pasado. ¡Se puede usar la imaginación! ¡Ojo! Atención al pretérito y al imperfecto.

Incluya:

- cuántos años tenía cuando ocurrió
- adónde fue y con quién
- cómo era el lugar
- lo que hizo/hicieron

Panorama cultural

Costa Rica y Panamá

MÉXICO

BELICE *Isla de la Bahía*

JAMAICA

MAR CARIBE

GUATEMALA

HONDURAS

15°

EL SALVADOR

NICARAGUA

Nacionalidades:
costarricense
panameño(a)

*OCÉANO
PACÍFICO*

COSTA RICA

10°

Volcán Irazú

Golfo de Nicoya

San José

Puerto Limón
Canal de Panamá

Colón

Panamá

Golfo de San Blás
*Archipiélago
de San Blás*

La América Central

0   100   200 Millas

0   100   200 Kilómetros

PANAMÁ

COLOMBIA

90°

85°

80°

20°

Preguntas sobre el mapa

1. ¿Cuál es la capital de Costa Rica? ¿Cómo se llama uno de los volcanes que está cerca de la capital? ¿Y el puerto que está en el mar Caribe?

2. ¿Cuál es la capital de Panamá? ¿Con qué países tiene fronteras Panamá?

@

Person@je del momento

Busque información en el Internet sobre la presidenta de Panamá y compártala con sus compañeros/as de clase.

¡Nobel, Nobel! Óscar Arias Sánchez fue presidente de Costa Rica entre 1986 y1990 y ganó el Premio Nobel de la Paz en 1987. El título de su tesis doctoral (1974) fue: *Who rules Costa Rica?*

Costa Rica

La capital de Costa Rica, San José, está situada en la meseta central. Es una ciudad diversa, con hermosos parques y lugares históricos. Sin embargo, la verdadera atracción del país está en su geografía, su fauna y su flora. Costa Rica se distingue por sus playas, ríos, cascadas, volcanes y montañas con abundante vegetación.

Las playas de Costa Rica atraen a turistas de todo el mundo. Hay excelentes playas en la costa caribeña, en el Golfo de Nicoya y en el Pacífico. Esta foto presenta unas de las más famosas del Pacífico—las playas del Parque Nacional Manuel Antonio. ¿Le gustaría a usted practicar algún deporte en estas playas? ¿Cuál?

Los volcanes son característicos del país. A unos 30 kilómetros de San José y de Cartago (la capital original), hay cuatro volcanes. Dos de ellos, el Poás y el Irazú, a veces están activos. Desde el Irazú (con 3.432 m de altura) se pueden ver las costas del Caribe y el Pacífico al mismo tiempo. Considere la foto del Irazú. ¿Por qué es tan impresionante el cráter?

Costa Rica es uno de los países latinoamericanos con más conciencia ecológica; se protege más del 25% de su territorio. Existen más de 15 reservas y parques nacionales que contienen una biodiversidad sorprendente: 14.000 especies de plantas y árboles, 1.000 especies de mariposas y 850 especies de pájaros. Costa Rica tiene hoy una imagen turística única basada en intereses ecológicos. ¿Qué le impresiona más a usted de la foto de Monteverde, «Bosque Nuboso»?

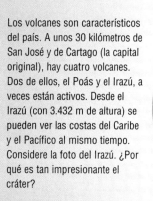

¿Sabía usted que...?

- Colón descubrió Costa Rica en 1502.
- En 1821 Costa Rica se independizó de España y se unió a la Federación Centroamericana.
- En 1848 se convirtió en una república independiente.
- Costa Rica es una democracia pacífica; el país no tiene ejército[1].
- El nivel de analfabetismo[2] es de los más bajos de Latinoamérica—sólo 5%.
- La economía y el nivel de vida están entre los mejores de América Central.
- La mayor parte de la población es descendiente de españoles y no existen grandes comunidades indígenas.

[1]army [2]illiteracy

Panamá

Por su clima tropical, en Panamá es posible jugar al golf y al tenis, y practicar deportes acuáticos todo el año. Panamá también tiene algunas de las más accesibles y espectaculares selvas tropicales del mundo. Al igual que su vecino Costa Rica, Panamá ha establecido varios parques nacionales para proteger su diversidad ecológica.

Panamá es un puente entre América del Norte y América del Sur. Gracias al tránsito de barcos por el canal (15.000 al año), este país es importante para el comercio mundial y la banca internacional. La Zona del Canal, libre de impuestos[3], es otro atractivo del país.

La capital, Panamá, está en la parte del canal que termina en el Pacífico. En su zona colonial se conservan edificios de arquitectura francesa, italiana y española que contrastan con los rascacielos, centros comerciales, hoteles y bancos de la zona moderna.

A 10 km de la capital moderna está la primera capital, Panamá la Vieja, fundada en 1516. En 1671 el pirata Henry Morgan la atacó y la destruyó. Hoy sólo quedan las ruinas de la catedral y de varios otros edificios.

La variada población de Panamá incluye comunidades indígenas, europeas, africanas y asiáticas. En Panamá existen cuatro grupos indígenas importantes que son famosos por sus artesanías[4]. Considere la foto de la niña kuna de las islas de San Blas, Panamá. Describa su vestido.

En la Zona del Canal se pueden ver cruzar barcos de todas partes del mundo. ¿Qué océanos une este canal?

[3]taxes [4]crafts [5]handed over

¿Sabía usted que...?

- Colón llegó a Panamá en 1502. En el siglo XVI llegaron otros españoles para explorar y abrir rutas comerciales entre el Viejo y el Nuevo Mundo. Todas las expediciones españolas a Sudamérica pasaron por Panamá.
- En 1902 los EE.UU. comenzó la construcción del Canal de Panamá—lo que sería el mayor canal navegable del continente, con 82.6 kilómetros de largo.
- El 31 de diciembre de 1999 los EE.UU. les entregó[5] el Canal a los panameños.
- En 1999, Mireya Moscoso, la primera mujer presidente de Panamá, fue elegida por el pueblo por su dedicación a combatir los enormes problemas del desempleo y de la pobreza.

¡Nadar es más barato!

El precio más alto pagado por cruzar el canal de Panamá fue de $141.244,97 por el crucero Crown Princess. El más bajo lo pagó Richard Haliburton, un hombre que cruzó el canal nadando en 1928 y sólo pagó 36 centavos.

¿Qué descubrimos?

1. ¿Cómo sabe usted que la paz y la educación son dos de las prioridades de los costarricenses?
2. ¿Qué hace Costa Rica para proteger su medio ambiente?
3. ¿Cuáles son algunas de las atracciones turísticas de Costa Rica?
4. ¿Qué hicieron los españoles al llegar a Panamá en el siglo XVI?
5. ¿Qué pasó con Panamá la Vieja?
6. ¿Por qué es la Zona del Canal muy atractiva para hacer compras?
7. ¿Qué diferencias existen entre la población de Costa Rica y la de Panamá?

Encuentro cultural

Artes populares

Las molas

Por lo general, todas las regiones de un país tienen artesanías típicas. Por ejemplo, las mujeres indígenas de la tribu kuna, que viven en las islas de San Blas, en Panamá, son famosas en todo el mundo por sus molas.

Las molas son una forma de arte textil[1]. Consisten en una base de tela[2] de algodón negro y varias capas[3] de tela de colores brillantes cosidas[4] una sobre la otra. Las capas de tela se cortan y se unen con puntadas[5] especiales para crear ilustraciones detalladas[6]. Hace muchos siglos los kunas pintaban diseños geométricos muy complejos en su piel[7], pero el comercio textil cambió la tradición: ahora el medio de expresión es la mola y no la piel.

Mola con la imagen de un dragón.

Los diseños geométricos todavía son los más populares. La flora y la fauna de la región también son elementos comunes tanto como las escenas que ilustran tradiciones, supersticiones y la vida diaria de la tribu. Las imágenes más abstractas tienen origen en los sueños y la fantasía de los kuna. Hoy, las imágenes en revistas y anuncios publicitarios inspiran nuevas ideas para las molas.

Mola con las banderas de Panamá y los EE.UU.

Lo interesante es que no hay dos molas idénticas; por eso, muchos museos a nivel mundial incluyen molas en sus colecciones de arte. Observe cuidadosamente las fotografías de las dos molas y conteste las siguientes preguntas.

[1]*textile* [2]*cloth* [3]*layers* [4]*sewn* [5]*stitches* [6]*detailed* [7]*skin*

Preguntas

1. ¿Qué figuras aparecen en estas molas?
2. ¿Cuál de estas molas puede representar mejor la superstición? ¿Y la política?
3. En su opinión, ¿por qué hay dos banderas en la mola? ¿Qué relación existía entre Panamá y los EE.UU.?
4. ¿Cuál de las molas es su favorita? ¿La prefiere usted por sus colores o por el tema?
5. ¿Tiene usted ropa que expresa su opinión o su personalidad?
6. ¿Tiene usted ropa o accesorios que puedan considerarse arte? ¿Cuáles son?

Adjetivo

peligroso/a

Palabras y expresiones útiles

a causa de
para
por

Sustantivos

La naturaleza

la arena
el bosque
la catarata/ la cascada
el cielo
la colina
el desierto
la estrella
la fogata
el fuego
la granja
la hierba
la isla
la luna
el mar
el medio ambiente
el océano
la ola
el relámpago
el río
la selva
la tierra
la tormenta
el valle

Los animales y los insectos

la araña
el caballo
el cerdo
la gallina
la mariposa
la mosca
el mosquito
el pájaro
el pez (los peces)
la serpiente
la vaca

Aventuras y otras palabras

el alpinismo/ el andinismo
la balsa
el barco
el bote
la cámara
el campamento
el ciclismo de montaña
el crucero
el kayak
el saco de dormir
la tienda de campaña

El medio ambiente

la capa de ozono
la contaminación
la deforestación
el incendio forestal
el mundo
el planeta
el problema
el recurso natural

Verbos y expresiones verbales

acampar
bucear
conservar
desperdiciar
destruir
dudar
encantar
evitar
fascinar
importar
interesar
molestar
pescar
prevenir
proteger
reciclar
recoger
remar
viajar

dar una caminata
escalar una montaña
estar de vacaciones
estar seguro/a (de)
hacer el *esnórquel*
hacer *surf*
hacer un viaje en barco/crucero
ir(se) de vacaciones
montar a caballo
practicar el descenso de ríos/el
   rafting
practicar el *parasail*
sacar/tomar fotos
tener miedo
viajar de mochila

I. Verbs similar to *gustar*. Primero, determine quién habla; luego, escriba una oración usando el verbo en paréntesis.

> **Modelo:** Veo el océano. (encantar)
> **Me encanta el océano.**

1. Vemos los relámpagos. (fascinar)
2. Juan y José oyen los mosquitos. (molestar)
3. Tina está leyendo un libro de biología. (interesar)
4. Voy a pescar. (encantar)
5. Para Pablo, la familia es su prioridad. (importar)

II. *Para and por*. Indique lo que hizo usted el verano pasado. Complete las oraciones con la forma **yo** del verbo en el pretérito y **por** o **para**. Siga el modelo.

> **Modelo:** trabajar / el Banco Nacional
> **Trabajé para el Banco Nacional.**

1. trabajar / poder ir a Costa Rica
2. salir / Costa Rica el 6 de agosto
3. estar allí / un mes
4. viajar / todo el país
5. comprar un libro sobre los bosques nubosos / mi madre
6. comprarlo / tres mil colones
7. mi madre decirme, «Gracias / el libro»

III. The subjunctive with expressions of doubt or negation.

A. Escriba sus reacciones.

> **Modelo:** dudar / que la balsa / pasar por ese cañón
> **Dudo que la balsa pase por ese cañón.**

1. no creer / que ustedes / encontrar el remo
2. no estar seguro(a) de / que el guía / saber hablar español
3. dudar / que los kayaks / llegar a tiempo
4. no estar seguro(a) de / que (nosotros) / estar remando bien
5. no creer / que (tú) / poder ir con nosotros

B. Conteste las preguntas. Use el subjuntivo sólo (*only*) para expresar duda.

> **Modelo:** ¿Tiene Roberto la tienda de campaña? (creer)
> **Creo que la tiene.**
> ¿Tiene el mapa? (no creer)
> **No creo que lo tenga.**

1. ¿Cuesta el viaje más de doscientos dólares? (creer)
2. ¿Hay un problema serio? (no creer)
3. ¿Es muy larga la caminata al río? (dudar)
4. ¿Son los guías buenos? (no estoy seguro/a de)
5. ¿Vienen con nosotros nuestros amigos? (estoy seguro/a de)

IV. The present perfect subjunctive. ¿Siente que o se alegra de que las siguientes cosas hayan ocurrido?

> **Modelo:** mi mejor amiga / irse de la universidad
> **Siento que mi mejor amiga se haya ido de la universidad.**

1. mis amigos / llegar recientemente
2. mi mejor amiga / comprarme un regalo
3. tú / perder tu cámara
4. mis amigos / llamarme
5. ellos / tener un accidente

V. General review. Conteste con oraciones completas.

1. ¿Qué animales/ insectos/ reptiles le fascinan o interesan a usted más? ¿Cuáles le molestan?
2. ¿Qué aspectos de la naturaleza le encantan a usted?
3. ¿Qué aventuras al aire libre le interesan más a usted?
4. ¿Cree usted que es muy bueno para la salud hacer ejercicio al aire libre?
5. ¿Duda usted que hayamos hecho todo lo posible para proteger el medio ambiente? ¿Qué debemos hacer para protegerlo más?
6. ¿Ha viajado usted mucho? ¿Se alegra de que haya viajado mucho? o ¿Siente que no haya viajado más?

Answers to the *Autoprueba y repaso* are found in **Apéndice 2**.

Capítulo 12

De viaje al extranjero°

abroad

Goals for communication

- To carry out simple travel transactions
- To state recommendations, emotional reactions, and doubts through impersonal expressions
- To make indefinite and negative references
- To refer to unspecified or nonexistent persons and things
- To talk about what will happen

Así se dice

De viaje al extranjero

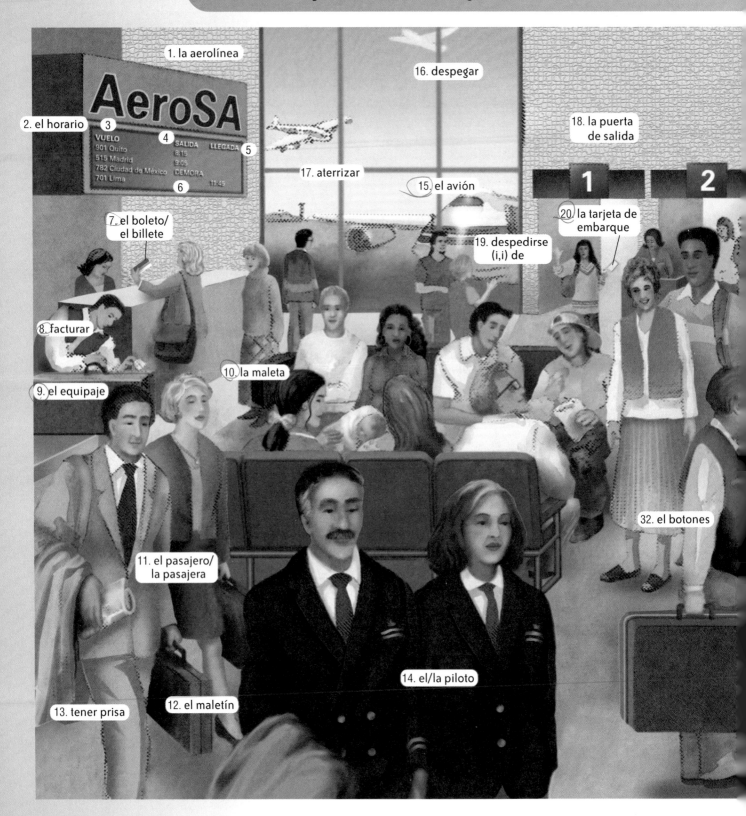

1. la aerolínea
2. el horario
3.
4.
5.
6.
7. el boleto/ el billete
8. facturar
9. el equipaje
10. la maleta
11. el pasajero/ la pasajera
12. el maletín
13. tener prisa
14. el/la piloto
15. el avión
16. despegar
17. aterrizar
18. la puerta de salida
19. despedirse (i,i) de
20. la tarjeta de embarque
32. el botones

AeroSA

VUELO · SALIDA · LLEGADA
901 Quito · 8:15 ·
515 Madrid · 9:05 ·
782 Ciudad de México · DEMORA ·
701 Lima · · 11:45

1. airline
2. schedule
3. flight
4. departure
5. arrival
6. delay
7. ticket
8. to check (baggage)
9. luggage
10. suitcase
11. passenger (m./f.)
12. briefcase, carry-on bag
13. to be in a hurry
14. pilot (m./f.)
15. airplane
16. to take off
17. to land
18. gate
19. to say good-bye
20. boarding pass
21. customs
22. baggage claim
23. hotel
24. airport
25. welcome
26. plant
27. main floor
28. elevator
29. laptop/notebook (computer)
30. to register
31. guest (m./f.)
32. bellhop

Práctica y comunicación

12-1. **En el aeropuerto.** Los estudiantes y sus profesores se van de viaje. Un grupo va a Madrid, otro a la Ciudad de México y Natalia se va sola a Ecuador. Conteste las preguntas según los dibujos de las páginas 404–405.

1. ¿Cómo se llama la aerolínea?
2. ¿Cuál es el número del vuelo a Madrid? ¿Qué vuelo tiene una demora? ¿Qué otra información hay en el horario?
3. La profesora Falcón está hablando con la empleada de la aerolínea AeroSA. ¿Qué tiene la profesora en la mano?
4. ¿Qué hace el empleado con el equipaje de la profesora?
5. Carmen está detrás de la profesora. ¿Cuántas maletas lleva ella?
6. ¿Qué llevan en la mano el pasajero y la pasajera? ¿Por qué tienen prisa?
7. ¿Quiénes son las personas que llevan uniforme?
8. Los estudiantes que se van a España y a México están en la sala de espera. ¿Cuántos están sentados? ¿Y de pie? ¿De qué hablan, probablemente?
9. El profesor Marín-Vivar está hablando con Javier y Camila. ¿Quién está a su lado? ¿A quién admira Inés?
10. Alfonso está mirando los aviones por la ventana. ¿Qué acaba de hacer el avión que está en el aire? ¿Y el que está en tierra?
11. Natalia sale para Ecuador, donde va a estudiar por un semestre. Está en la puerta nº 1. ¿Qué tiene en la mano? ¿De quién se despide?
12. ¿Qué hacen las dos mujeres frente a la entrada de la aduana?
13. Éste es un aeropuerto internacional. ¿Dónde revisan los oficiales el equipaje? ¿Dónde reclaman los pasajeros el equipaje?
14. El Hotel Aeropuerto tiene un letrero (*sign*) muy grande en la pared. ¿Qué dice?
15. En este hotel, ¿qué deben usar los huéspedes para subir de la planta baja[1] al segundo piso?
16. ¿Qué tipo de computadora usa la mujer que está sentada cerca del ascensor?
17. La mujer elegante que viaja con su perro Fifi va a quedarse en el hotel varios días. ¿Qué está haciendo? ¿Cuántas maletas tiene? ¿Quién va a llevar sus maletas a la habitación?
18. El tío Antonio y la tía Elisa también van a ser huéspedes en este hotel. ¿Qué le pide la tía Elisa al recepcionista?

---

[1] Generally, **la planta baja** is the equivalent of the first floor in the U.S. and Canada; **el primer piso** is then the second, and so on.

Antes del viaje, los estudiantes van a **sacar los pasaportes**(1),…

…**conseguir**(2) los boletos, **confirmar**(3) los vuelos,…

…**hacer las maletas/empacar**(4),…

…y llegar al aeropuerto **con** dos horas **de anticipación**(5).

la azafata(6)
el auxiliar de vuelo(7)

Camila, Pepita, y Rubén son parte del grupo que se va a España. Ahora van a **subirse al**(8) avión. ¿Quiénes los saludan?

la ventanilla(9)
el asiento(10)
el pasillo(11)

¿Prefiere Camila el asiento de la ventanilla o del pasillo? ¿Y Rubén? ¿Quién debe **abrocharse el cinturón**(12)? **Parece que**(13) les gusta **volar**(14).

Carmen y los otros **se bajan del**(15) avión. Van a **disfrutar de**(16) su viaje, ¿verdad? ¿A qué **países**(17) ha viajado usted?

(1) to get passports (2) to get, obtain; **conseguir (i, i)** *(3) to confirm (4) to pack (5) … ahead of time (6) flight attendant (f.) (7) flight attendant (m.) (8) to get on, board (9) window (airplane, train, car) (10) seat (11) aisle (12) to fasten one's seat belt (13) It seems that … (14) to fly;* **volar (ue)** *(15) get off …;* **bajarse de** *= to get off, get out of … (16) to enjoy (something) (17) countries;* **el país** *country*

12-2. **Preguntas para un/a compañero/a.** Háganse las siguientes preguntas.

1. ¿Disfrutas de tus viajes en avión? ¿Por qué? ¿Te da miedo volar?
2. ¿Qué aerolínea prefieres?
3. ¿Conoces varios aeropuertos? ¿Cuáles son? ¿Qué aeropuerto te gusta menos? ¿Por qué?
4. ¿Has volado mucho? (¿A qué ciudades?)
5. ¿Tienes pasaporte? ¿A cuántos países has viajado? ¿Cuál es tu país favorito? ¿Por qué?
6. ¿Prefieres un asiento de pasillo o de ventanilla en el avión?
7. ¿Te gusta la comida de los aviones? ¿Qué bebida tomas normalmente en los vuelos? ¿Quién sirve la comida y las bebidas durante el vuelo?
8. ¿Has tenido una demora en algún viaje? ¿Cuánto tiempo tuviste que esperar? ¿Te quejaste? ¿Qué hiciste?
9. ¿Qué países del mundo o qué continentes quieres visitar? ¿Japón o China? ¿África? ¿Europa? ¿Sudamérica?
10. ¿Te gustaría ser azafata o auxiliar de vuelo? ¿Piloto? ¿Agente de viajes?
11. ¿Te gusta sacar fotos cuando viajas? (¿De qué?) ¿Prefieres usar una cámara digital o una tradicional?
12. ¿Te gusta mandar tarjetas postales? ¿A quién se las mandas?

12-3. **Un viaje en avión a Madrid.** Imaginen que ustedes volaron de su ciudad al aeropuerto de Barajas en Madrid. Hagan una lista cronológica de lo que hicieron desde que sacaron sus pasaportes hasta que recogieron el equipaje en Madrid. Tienen cinco minutos. ¿Qué grupo tiene la lista más larga? Léansela a la clase.

1. Sacamos los pasaportes.
2. ...

¡Qué dilema!

Estás en un vuelo internacional y quieres dormir porque estás muy cansado/a. El/La pasajero/a a tu lado insiste en hablar contigo. Primero, él/ella se presenta:
Hola. Me llamo... ¿Y tú?... Mucho gusto. ... y... y... y...

Escenas

Carmen   Prof. Falcón   Esteban

A la llegada a Madrid

4 *La profesora Falcón viaja con sus estudiantes. Van a pasar el mes de julio en Madrid. Al llegar al aeropuerto de Barajas, recogen su equipaje y van al hotel.*

CARMEN: Bueno, por fin llegamos. Para un vuelo largo, no estuvo mal, ¿no le parece, profesora?

PROF. FALCÓN: Siempre me pongo nerviosa cuando el avión despega y cuando aterriza, pero los asientos eran relativamente cómodos° y las azafatas muy amables. Mira, allí llega nuestro equipaje.

comfortable

ESTEBAN: Parece que todo está aquí. ¿Vamos a inmigración?

PROF. FALCÓN: Sí. A ver si encuentro mi pasaporte.

ESTEBAN: Y a ver si encuentro el mío también. (*Busca en su mochila.*) Sí, aquí lo tengo. (*Se le cae° un papel al suelo.*)

falls/drops

PROF. FALCÓN: Mira, se te cayó° ese papel.

se... you dropped

ESTEBAN: ¡Ah! Es mi tarjeta de embarque. Ya no la necesito, ¿verdad? Voy a tirarla a la basura.

PROF. FALCÓN: Bueno, vámonos a la aduana.

(*Más tarde, en el Hotel Gran Vía frente a la Plaza de España, donde van a pasar dos días antes de mudarse a las residencias estudiantiles.*)

RECEPCIONISTA: Buenas tardes. ¡Bienvenidos!

PROF. FALCÓN: Buenas tardes. Tenemos reservaciones para seis habitaciones. Están a nombre de Ana María Falcón.

RECEPCIONISTA: Vamos a ver. Sí, aquí están: son todas habitaciones sencillas°, con baño privado.

single

PROF. FALCÓN: Correcto. Aquí tiene los pasaportes y mi tarjeta de crédito. También, si no es mucha molestia, ¿podría enviar nuestro equipaje a las habitaciones con el botones? Es que tenemos prisa. Nos esperan en la Complutense² en menos de una hora.

RECEPCIONISTA: Vale°. Primero les voy a dar las llaves° de las habitaciones. (*Les entrega las llaves y les devuelve los pasaportes y la tarjeta de crédito.*)

Fine, Very well, OK (Spain) / keys

CARMEN: ¿En qué piso está el restaurante?

RECEPCIONISTA: Tome el ascensor hasta el piso doce. Allí encontrará el restaurante y la cafetería. ¿Algo más?

PROF. FALCÓN: No, creo que es todo. Gracias.

¿Qué pasa?

1. ¿Adónde viajan la profesora Falcón y sus estudiantes?

2. ¿Cómo estuvo el vuelo? ¿Cuándo se puso nerviosa la profesora Falcón?

3. ¿Qué se le cae a Esteban?

4. ¿Cómo son las habitaciones que ha reservado la profesora Falcón?

5. ¿Por qué tienen prisa?

6. ¿Dónde está el restaurante del hotel?

---

² **La Universidad Complutense** was founded in 1293 in Complutum, today Alcalá de Henares. It was moved to Madrid in 1836 and renamed **Universidad Central**, but it recovered its original name in 1927.

Estructuras

1 **Expressing recommendations, emotion, and doubt: The subjunctive with impersonal expressions**

Es fenomenal que podamos quedarnos en España por un mes, ¿verdad?

Use the subjunctive with impersonal expressions such as *It's important . . .* , *It's necessary . . .* , etc. to express:

- the desire to influence the actions of someone else

  Es importante que **hagas** la reservación.

  It's important that *you make* the *reservation.*

- emotional reactions to the actions or conditions of another person or thing

  Es una lástima que **tengas** que irte tan temprano.

  It's a shame that *you have* to go *so early.*

- doubts and uncertainties

  Es posible que **perdamos** la conexión en Miami.

  It's possible that *we'll miss the connection in Miami.*

  impersonal expression + **que** + *subjunctive*

Impersonal expressions that frequently use the subjunctive include:

desire to influence	es bueno	*it's good*
	es mejor	*it's better*
	es necesario, es preciso	*it's necessary*
	es importante	*it's important*
	es urgente	*it's urgent*

emotional reactions	es una lástima	*it's a shame*
	es extraño	*it's strange*
	es fenomenal	*it's wonderful*
	es ridículo	*it's ridiculous*
	es horrible	*it's horrible*
	no es justo	*it's unfair*
doubt and uncertainty	es posible	*it's possible*
	es imposible	*it's impossible*
	es probable	*it's probable*
	es improbable	*it's improbable*

Index card- always subjunctive

Impersonal expressions that do not normally use the subjunctive include:

certainty	es verdad	*it's true*
	es cierto	*it's true, correct*
	es obvio	*it's obvious*

- If there is no change of subject after the impersonal expression, generally the infinitive is used, not **que** + *subjunctive*.

  Es necesario salir para el aeropuerto ahora.

  It's necessary to leave for the airport now.

  Es necesario **que salgamos** para el aeropuerto ahora.

  It's necessary for us to leave for the airport now.

- Expressions such as **es verdad, es cierto**, and **es obvio** when used affirmatively require the indicative, not the subjunctive, as they introduce factual *vs.* subjective statements.

  Es verdad/cierto que **hace** calor en Madrid en el verano.

  It's true that it is hot in Madrid in the summer.

  Es obvio que Carmen **necesita** un ventilador.

  It's obvious that Carmen needs a fan.

Práctica y comunicación

② **12-4.** **Un vuelo en la aerolínea «Buena Suerte».** Indiquen sus
reacciones a lo que pasa en el vuelo 13 con destino a la Isla Paraíso.
Usen expresiones impersonales.

Good Luck

> **Modelo:** No hay asientos reservados.
>
> **Es una lástima/Es extraño que no haya asientos reservados.**

1. La azafata no da <u>instrucciones</u>. *(flight attendant)* *(de)*
2. El auxiliar de vuelo sirve langosta.
3. Las películas son gratis (no cuestan nada). *(sean)*
4. Hay mucha turbulencia.
5. Frecuentemente se apagan las luces. *(que / que)*
6. Varios pasajeros duermen profundamente.
7. Una pasajera está fumando un cigarro.
8. Un bebé está llorando.
9. El piloto pide un cóctel. *(pida)*

12-5. **Los primeros días de Esteban en Madrid.**
Indique lo que debe hacer nuestro amigo.

> **Modelo:** **Es urgente que Esteban se despierte para asistir a su clase.**
>
> **Es obvio que está muy cansado.** Salió anoche con sus amigos.

Es urgente que… Es
obvio que…

1. Es urgente que… Es
obvio que…

2. Es importante que… Es
verdad que…

3. Es bueno que… Es
mejor que…

4. Es mejor que… Es
obvio que…

5. Es preciso que… Es
importante que…

6. Es buena idea que… Es
cierto que…

12-6. **¿Es posible?** Indique si, en su opinión, es **posible/imposible** o es **probable/improbable** que los estudiantes hayan hecho lo siguiente durante su primera semana en Madrid.

> **Modelo:** Esteban / sacar una «F» en la clase de historia.
>
> **Es imposible que Esteban haya sacado una «F» en la clase de historia.**

1. Carmen / perderse en el metro
2. Camila y Rubén / visitar el Museo del Prado
3. Pepita / ir a una discoteca
4. la profesora Falcón / bailar toda la noche en la discoteca
5. el grupo / aprender a bailar flamenco
6. todos / comer mucha tortilla española
7. Esteban / enamorarse de una española
8. nuestros amigos / comprar recuerdos para sus familias
9. los estudiantes / hacer una excursión a Toledo

12-7. **Situaciones.** Den varias reacciones a cada una de las siguientes situaciones. Usen las expresiones de la lista. Un/a estudiante sirve como secretario/a y luego presenta algunas de las reacciones a la clase.

> Es imposible que…   Es urgente que…   Es obvio que…
>
> Es una lástima que…   Es cierto/verdad que…   …

1. Me voy de viaje mañana, ¡y no puedo encontrar mi pasaporte!
   Es urgente que… Es obvio que…
2. Tengo que salir para el aeropuerto en veinte minutos, ¡y no estoy listo/a!
3. Estoy en el aeropuerto y anuncian que nuestro vuelo tiene una demora de cinco horas.
4. Estoy en el avión y el piloto anuncia que vamos a pasar por una zona de tormenta y que el avión tiene problemas mecánicos.
5. Estoy en la aduana y el inspector de aduanas sospecha que tengo algo ilegal en la maleta.
6. Estoy en un hotel y descubro que en el baño no hay agua caliente y que hay una araña en la cama.

12-8. **Lo positivo de mi vida.** Escriba cinco oraciones sobre su vida. Use la expresión **Es fenomenal que…** Léale su lista a un/a compañero/a de clase o a la clase.

[handwritten notes in top-left margin:]
1,3,7,10,12,13, 2
1, 7, 3, 13,

calefacción
que ac
la cama doble
la habitación

la piscina(14)
el aire acondicionado(13)
el baño privado(11)
dejar(8)
la calefacción(12)
la camarera(2)
las llaves(9)
la propina(10)
la cama doble(3)
el servicio de habitación(7)
la almohada(4)
la sábana(5)
la manta/ la cobija(6)
la habitación doble(1)

> **HINT** | Note the difference between **salir** (*to leave, go out*) and **dejar** (*to leave an object behind*): Camila **salió** de su habitación y **dejó** la chaqueta.

(1) double room; **la habitación sencilla** *single room (2) maid (hotel) (3) double bed;* **la cama sencilla** *single bed (4) pillow (5) sheet (6) blanket (7) room service (8) to leave (behind) (9) keys (10) tip (11) private bath (12) heating (13) air-conditioning (14) swimming pool*

Práctica y comunicación

12-9. **En el hotel.** Describa la escena anterior. Hable de:

- lo que hace la camarera
- lo que hay en la habitación
- lo que los huéspedes dejaron en el cuarto (cosas que se les olvidaron)
- lo que los huéspedes dejaron para la camarera

2 **12–10.** **¿Cómo se dice?** Imaginen que usted y un/a amigo/a llegan a un hotel y hablan con la recepcionista sobre los servicios que desean. El problema es que se han olvidado de algunas de las palabras. Túrnense para explicarle a la recepcionista lo que desean sin usar las palabras en paréntesis.

> **Modelo:** Deseamos una habitación (doble).
>
> **Deseamos una habitación para dos personas.**

1. una habitación (sencilla)   **5.** otra (toalla) _ para

2. un baño (privado)   **6.** otra (cobija) para el frío

3. (la llave)   **7.** el servicio (de habitación)

4. otra (almohada)   **8.** una (sábana) más para el frío

4 **12–11.** **¿★ o ★ ★ ★ ★ ★ ?** Describan las características de un hotel muy económico o un hotel de cinco estrellas. Un/a secretario/a escribe las características y luego se las presenta a la clase o a otro grupo de estudiantes.

3 **12–12.** **Buscamos habitación.** Los muy aventureros Aurora y Anselmo, de viaje de luna de miel, llegan al Hotel Mil Estrellas sin haber reservado una habitación. Hablan con el/la recepcionista para averiguar si tiene todo lo que desean. Hagan los papeles de Aurora, Anselmo y el/la recepcionista.

> **Modelo:** Recepcionista: **Buenas noches. ¿En qué puedo servirles?**
>
> Aurora: ...
>
> Recepcionista: ...
>
> Anselmo: ...

Así se dice
Los números ordinales

primer[3], primero/a	*first*	sexto/a	*sixth*
segundo/a	*second*	séptimo/a	*seventh*
tercer[3], tercero/a	*third*	octavo/a	*eighth*
cuarto/a	*fourth*	noveno/a	*ninth*
quinto/a	*fifth*	décimo/a	*tenth*

---

[3] **Primero** and **tercero** become **primer** and **tercer** when they immediately precede a masculine, singular noun: **El ascensor está en el** *tercer* piso.

12-13. **Suba al quinto piso.** Usted se está quedando en el Hotel Plaza de España y desea usar ciertos servicios que se ofrecen allí. Usted va a la recepción para averiguar dónde puede encontrar los lugares o los servicios que busca. El/La recepcionista le indica el piso según la «Guía para huéspedes».

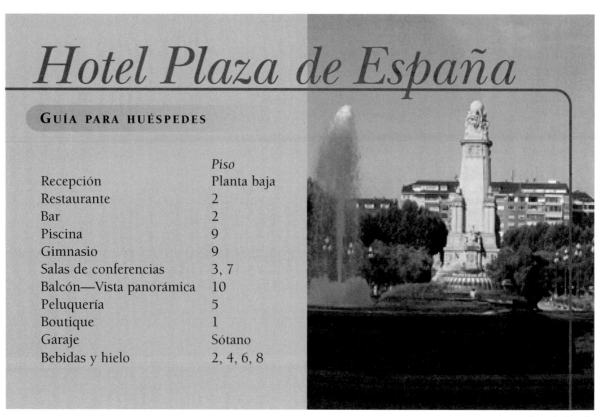

Hotel Plaza de España

GUÍA PARA HUÉSPEDES

	Piso
Recepción	Planta baja
Restaurante	2
Bar	2
Piscina	9
Gimnasio	9
Salas de conferencias	3, 7
Balcón—Vista panorámica	10
Peluquería	5
Boutique	1
Garaje	Sótano
Bebidas y hielo	2, 4, 6, 8

Plaza de España

Modelo: Usted quiere cortarse el pelo.

Huésped: **Perdón. ¿Dónde se encuentra la peluquería del hotel?**

Recepcionista: **Suba/Vaya al quinto piso. Allí está la peluquería.**

1. Desea tomar una bebida y cenar.
2. Quiere nadar y hacer ejercicio.
3. Quiere comprar un regalo para su novio/a.
4. Desea asistir a una conferencia en este hotel.
5. Desea unos refrescos y hielo para la habitación.
6. Quiere sacar fotos panorámicas de la Plaza de España.
7. Necesita buscar algo que está en el coche.

2 **Making indefinite and negative references: More indefinite and negative words**

¿No hay ninguna habitación con Jacuzzi?

In **Chapter 6** you studied some indefinite words and their negative counterparts: **algo/nada, alguien/nadie, también/tampoco**. Observe the additional words in the following chart.

Palabra indefinida		Palabra negativa	
alguno/a/os/as	any, some, someone	**ninguno/a**	no, none, no one
o	or	**ni**	nor, not even
o... o	either . . . or	**ni... ni**	neither . . . nor

- Just as **uno** shortens to **un**, the forms **alguno** and **ninguno** become **algún** and **ningún** before a masculine singular noun.

    ¿Vas a visitar Madrid **algún** día?   *Are you going to visit Madrid some day?*

- Notice that the words **ninguno/a** mean *not a single* and consequently do not have a plural form.

    –¿**Algunos** estudiantes van a Sevilla?   *¿Are some students going to Seville?*

    –No, **ningún** estudiante va a Sevilla.   *No, **no** students are going to Seville.*
    Not a single student is going to Seville.

    –Ninguno/a fue a Granada.   ***None** went to Granada.*

Palabras útiles

convivir *to live with*
brindar *to offer*
funcionar *to work, function*
usuarios *users*

HOSTAL EL ENCANTO

Le ofrecemos una atmósfera amigable donde descansar y convivir con otros viajeros como usted. Los baños, la cocina y la sala de televisión son de uso común. Tenemos dormitorios comunes de hasta seis personas y algunos cuartos privados con tres camas. La ropa de cama está incluida en el precio del hostal. Para su uso le brindamos lavadoras y secadoras que funcionan con monedas. Los usuarios tienen llave para los dormitorios; además el hostal cuenta con cajas de seguridad. La recepción está abierta de las 7:00 a las 22:30.

12-14. **Alojamiento estudiantil: el Hostal El Encanto.** Octavio sigue en México con sus amigos. Esta noche se van a quedar en el Hostal El Encanto y él quiere saber si tiene ciertas comodidades (*comforts*). Usted tiene la descripción del hostal y le contesta. Lea la descripción.

> **Modelo:** ¿Hay habitaciones con televisor?
>
> **No, no hay ninguna habitación con televisor.** *o*
> **No, no hay ninguna.**
>
> ¿Hay cajas de seguridad (*safety deposit boxes*)?
>
> **Sí, hay algunas.**

1. ¿Hay baños privados en el hostal?
2. ¿Hay lavadoras y secadoras?
3. ¿Hay cuartos privados?
4. ¿Hay cuartos dobles con aire acondicionado?
5. ¿Hay restaurante en el hostal?
6. ¿Hay viajeros amigables?

12-15. **Una nueva experiencia para Inés.** Inés nunca se ha quedado en un hostal y tiene muchas preguntas para el recepcionista. Completen la conversación, usando palabras de la siguiente lista. Al final, lean el diálogo.

alguna	algunos/as	ningún	ninguna	ni...ni

(handwritten annotations: Something / Something / none / nothing / neither nor)

INÉS: Perdón, señor. ¿Hay __alguna__ habitación que tenga televisor?

RECEPCIONISTA: Lo siento mucho, señorita. Aquí __ninguna__ habitación tiene televisor, pero sí hay una sala de televisión de uso común.

INÉS: Bueno... ¿y tienen __algunos__ cuartos con baño privado?

RECEPCIONISTA: Lo siento pero en este hostal no hay __ningún__ cuarto con baño privado.

INÉS: Pues, ¿hay piscina o gimnasio en el hostal? Me gusta hacer ejercicio.

RECEPCIONISTA: No hay __ni__ piscina __ni__ gimnasio aquí, pero en el Hotel Continental en el centro sí hay. Señorita, ¿se ha quedado usted __alguna__ vez en un hostal?

INÉS: No señor, pero el lugar me gusta y como dice el refrán: «La curiosidad mató al gato».

12-16. Un día en la capital. Alfonso va a un Café Internet en la capital y le escribe un mensaje electrónico a usted. Léalo.

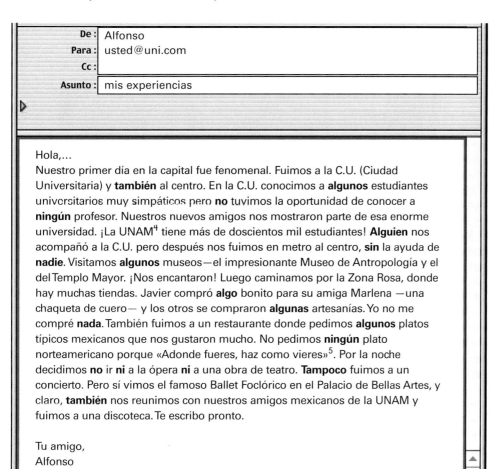

De: Alfonso
Para: usted@uni.com
Cc:
Asunto: mis experiencias

Hola,...
Nuestro primer día en la capital fue fenomenal. Fuimos a la C.U. (Ciudad Universitaria) y **también** al centro. En la C.U. conocimos a **algunos** estudiantes universitarios muy simpáticos pero **no** tuvimos la oportunidad de conocer a **ningún** profesor. Nuestros nuevos amigos nos mostraron parte de esa enorme universidad. ¡La UNAM[4] tiene más de doscientos mil estudiantes! **Alguien** nos acompañó a la C.U. pero después nos fuimos en metro al centro, **sin** la ayuda de **nadie**. Visitamos **algunos** museos—el impresionante Museo de Antropología y el del Templo Mayor. ¡Nos encantaron! Luego caminamos por la Zona Rosa, donde hay muchas tiendas. Javier compró **algo** bonito para su amiga Marlena —una chaqueta de cuero— y los otros se compraron **algunas** artesanías. Yo no me compré **nada**. También fuimos a un restaurante donde pedimos **algunos** platos típicos mexicanos que nos gustaron mucho. No pedimos **ningún** plato norteamericano porque «Adonde fueres, haz como vieres»[5]. Por la noche decidimos **no** ir **ni** a la ópera **ni** a una obra de teatro. **Tampoco** fuimos a un concierto. Pero sí vimos el famoso Ballet Foclórico en el Palacio de Bellas Artes, y claro, **también** nos reunimos con nuestros amigos mexicanos de la UNAM y fuimos a una discoteca. Te escribo pronto.

Tu amigo,
Alfonso

2 Ahora, cuéntele a un/a compañero/a algo de lo que le contó Alfonso a usted. Use las palabras de la siguiente lista y los verbos indicados a continuación. Túrnense.

algo	alguien	algunos/as	también	ni... ni
nada	nadie	ningún/ninguno/a	tampoco	

1. ir: Alfonso y sus amigos fueron... y también...

2. (no) conocer: Conocieron a... pero no conocieron a...

3. acompañar

4. visitar

5. (no) comprar

6. (no) pedir

7. decidir

8. ir

---

[4] **La Universidad Nacional Autónoma de México:** one of the largest and most important universities in the world. It opened its doors in 1910. **La Ciudad Universitaria**, a huge and magnificent architectural complex, was inaugurated in 1952.

[5] "When in Rome, do as the Romans do."

3 Talking about unknown or nonexistent persons or things: The subjunctive with indefinite entities

When a reference to a person or thing is either (1) *nonspecific* (*unidentified, hypothetical, unknown*) or (2) *nonexistent* in the mind of the speaker, Spanish uses the subjunctive in the clause following **que**.

¿**Hay alguien** aquí que **pueda** ayudarme con las maletas?	*Is there someone here who can help me with the suitcases?*
Preferimos una habitación que **tenga** aire acondicionado.	*We prefer a room that has air-conditioning.*
No queda ninguna habitación que **tenga** baño privado.	*There aren't any rooms left that have a private bath.*

However, if the person or thing is known, identified, or definitely exists in the mind of the speaker, the indicative is used in the clause following **que**.

Hay un botones que **puede** ayudarle.	*There is a bellhop who can help you.*
Encontramos un hotel que **tiene** aire acondicionado.	*We found a hotel that has air-conditioning.*

DICHOS

No hay mal que por bien no venga.
¿Puede usted explicar el significado de este dicho español?

Práctica y comunicación

12-17. **Un sondeo.** Escuche las preguntas del profesor/de la profesora. Levante la mano para contestar afirmativamente. La clase cuenta las respuestas afirmativas para cada pregunta y apunta el total.

En esta clase, ¿hay alguien...	Número
1. que hable chino?	_____
2. que sepa pilotear un avión?	_____
3. que sea vegetariano/a?	_____
4. que tenga ocho hermanos?	_____
5. que tenga su cumpleaños este mes?	_____
6. que piense ir a España pronto?	_____
7. que se haya quedado en un hostal?	_____
8. que se haya comprometido este año?	_____

2 Ahora, en parejas, repasen los resultados de cada pregunta. Hagan oraciones según el modelo.

Modelo: En esta clase, hay dos personas que hablan chino. *o*
No hay nadie (ninguna persona) que hable chino.

2 **12-18.** **Preguntas personales.** Háganse las siguientes preguntas.

Modelo: ¿Hay alguien en tu familia que... saber / hablar español?
¿Hay alguien en tu familia que *sepa* hablar español?
Sí, mi tía *sabe*... *o* No, no hay nadie en mi familia que *sepa*...

1. ¿Hay alguien en tu familia que...
tener / más de ochenta años? (¿Quién?)
saber / tocar el piano? (¿Quién?)
ser / famoso/a? (¿Quién?)
haberse / graduado de esta universidad? (¿Quién?)

2. ¿Conoces algún/alguna estudiante que...
haber / sacado una «A» en todas sus clases?
nunca haber / estado en la biblioteca?
tener / más de cuarenta años?
jugar / con uno de los equipos de la universidad?

4 **12–19.** **En un mundo ideal.** Cada grupo selecciona una oración y la completa con tres o cuatro posibilidades diferentes. En cada grupo, un/a secretario/a escribe las oraciones. Al concluir, él/ella las comparte con la clase.

1. Queremos un/a profesor/a que...
2. Necesitamos encontrar un/a compañero/a de cuarto o de apartamento que...
3. Nosotras (las mujeres de la clase) estamos buscando un hombre que...
4. Nosotros (los hombres de la clase) estamos buscando una mujer que...
5. Buscamos un lugar de vacaciones que...
6. Vamos a conseguir un trabajo o empleo que...
7. Queremos visitar un país donde...

Noticias culturales

lodging

El alojamiento° en el mundo hispano

globetrotter

¿Qué tipo de viajero es usted? ¿Un clásico turista de verano? ¿Un hombre o mujer de negocios? ¿Un trotamundos°? A todos los viajeros, el mundo hispano les ofrece el alojamiento ideal para hacer su visita memorable.

demanding

Para los empresarios o los turistas exigentes°, todas las ciudades importantes cuentan con hoteles de excepcional calibre y cadenas reconocidas mundialmente como los hoteles Meliá o Hilton. Para los trotamundos, los jóvenes con un presupuesto módico° o los viajeros menos exigentes, hay hostales y pensiones (hoteles modestos a veces en casas privadas) que son más «caseras» y

presupuesto... modest budget

económicas. Estos establecimientos no tienen las comodidades y lujos de los grandes hoteles, pero en cambio° brindan la oportunidad de conocer mejor a los nacionales y de hacer amigos en un ambiente° convivial.

en... on the other hand

atmosphere

Hostal Reyes Católicos, Santiago de Compostela, España

Entrada principal del *Hostal Reyes Católicos*

Entre los hospedajes más bellos y pintorescos del mundo hispano están los paradores[6] nacionales o históricos. En España, algunos son antiguos monasterios, castillos o palacios. En la opulencia de la Alhambra, con vista a los Jardines del Generalife[7], se halla uno de los más bellos paradores de España: El *Parador de Granada*. El sitio fue un antiguo convento franciscano donde reposaron los restos° de los Reyes Católicos hasta el año 1521, fecha en que fueron trasladados° a la catedral de Granada. El *Hostal Reyes Católicos* en Santiago de Compostela es otro ejemplo de este tipo de hospedaje.

remains

moved

Si dirigimos los ojos hacia Sudamérica, Venezuela nos ofrece *Los Frailes*, un parador de excepcional belleza enclavado en lo alto de los Andes. Se trata de un antiguo monasterio convertido en hospedaje para el viajero que exige lo mejor. En México, el *Hotel Parador San Javier* fue una hacienda en Guanajuato, hoy patrimonio cultural del país.

No importa cuáles sean sus intereses o gustos, el mundo hispano le espera con un lugar especial para satisfacer sus necesidades y exigencias.

¿Qué recuerda?

1. ¿Qué tipo de alojamiento prefiere un hombre o una mujer de negocios?
2. ¿Qué son las pensiones?
3. ¿Qué ofrecen los hostales que no tienen los grandes hoteles?
4. ¿Qué era anteriormente el *Parador de Granada*? ¿Y el *Hotel Parador San Javier*?
5. ¿Dónde se encuentra *Los Frailes*?
6. ¿Le gustaría pasar unos días en uno de estos paradores? ¿Cuál? ¿Por qué?

Conexiones y contrastes

1. ¿Tiene su país alojamientos similares a los paradores?
2. ¿Qué tipo de viajero es usted? ¿Qué tipo de alojamiento prefiere?

Parador *Los Frailes*, Venezuela

---

[6] Historical buildings transformed into luxurious hotels.
[7] The fourteenth century summer palace of the Moorish kings of Granada.

4 **Talking about what will happen: The future tense**

Viajarás por todo el mundo, te casarás con una persona fenomenal, encontrarás el trabajo de tus sueños,...

The future tense of all regular -**ar**, -**er**, or -**ir** verbs is formed by adding the same set of endings to the infinitive.

<table>
<tr><th colspan="4">El futuro: infinitivo + -é, -ás, -á, -emos, -éis, -án</th></tr>
<tr><td></td><td>llam**ar**</td><td>volv**er**</td><td>**ir**</td></tr>
<tr><td>(yo)</td><td>llamar**é**</td><td>volver**é**</td><td>ir**é**</td></tr>
<tr><td>(tú)</td><td>llamar**ás**</td><td>volver**ás**</td><td>ir**ás**</td></tr>
<tr><td>(Ud., él, ella)</td><td>llamar**á**</td><td>volver**á**</td><td>ir**á**</td></tr>
<tr><td>(nosotros/as)</td><td>llamar**emos**</td><td>volver**emos**</td><td>ir**emos**</td></tr>
<tr><td>(vosotros/as)</td><td>llamar**éis**</td><td>volver**éis**</td><td>ir**éis**</td></tr>
<tr><td>(Uds., ellos, ellas)</td><td>llamar**án**</td><td>volver**án**</td><td>ir**án**</td></tr>
</table>

HINT | Remember: Add the future endings to the *entire infinitive*, not the stem.

—¿**Irás** a España con la profesora Falcón? | *Will you go to Spain with professor Falcón?*

—**Iré** si trabajo bastante para conseguir el dinero. | *I'll go if I work hard enough to get the money.*

The following verbs add regular future endings to the irregular stems shown (not to the infinitive).

Infinitivo	Raíz	Formas del futuro
hacer	**har-**	har**é**, har**ás**, har**á**, har**emos**, har**éis**, har**án**
decir	**dir-**	diré, dirás,...
poder	**podr-**	podré, podrás,...
querer	**querr-**	querré, querrás,...
saber	**sabr-**	sabré, sabrás,...
poner	**pondr-**	pondré, pondrás,...
salir	**saldr-**	saldré, saldrás,...
tener	**tendr-**	tendré, tendrás,...
venir	**vendr-**	vendré, vendrás,...

Los estudiantes **harán** excursiones por España y México.	*The students **will take** tours throughout Spain and Mexico.*

Note that in Spanish, the future may be expressed three ways:

- the present tense

Ella **llega** esta noche. (*immediate future*)	*She **arrives/is arriving** tonight.*

- ir + a + *infinitive*

Voy a estudiar[8] en México este verano.	*I'm going to study in Mexico this summer.*

- the future tense

Estudiaré en México este verano.	*I **will study** in México this summer.*

The future of **hay** (*there is, there are*) is **habrá** (*there will be*).

Habrá varias conferencias en la universidad.	***There will be** several lectures at the university.*

The future tense may also be used to express conjecture or probability.

¿Quién **será**?	*I **wonder** who (Who do you **suppose**) it **is**?*
Será Ricardo.	*It's **probably** Richard.*

Práctica y comunicación

12-20. **En Quito, Ecuador.** Usted visita una agencia de viajes para reservar su vuelo de Quito a Guayaquil. Éste es el anuncio que usted lee sobre una de las aerolíneas del país. Encuentre las referencias al tiempo futuro. ¿Le parece una buena aerolínea?

En el aire...

Un mayor espacio entre asientos (35 pulgadas°) hará su viaje más confortable. Será mimado° con cócteles de cortesía, refrescos y bocaditos. Seleccione entre 3 platos fuertes, además de ensaladas frescas, una variedad de panes y la selección de un delicioso postre. Podrá seguir con café o algún licor para después disfrutar de una siesta o una película a bordo. También encontrará audífonos para disfrutar de la música o para ver una película, diarios locales y nuestra revista de cortesía *Aboard...* y la más amable tripulación°, dispuesta siempre a asistirlo.

inches / spoiled / crew

---

[8] In spoken Spanish, the **ir** + **a** + *infinitive* construction is used more frequently than the future tense.

4 **12-21. Dentro de cincuenta años.** Indiquen si ustedes están de acuerdo o no con los siguientes pronósticos. Algunos grupos van a compartir sus ideas con la clase.

> **Modelo:** El número de aeropuertos aumentará.
>
> **Creemos que el número de aeropuertos *aumentará*. o**
>
> **No creemos que el número de aeropuertos *aumente*.**

1. Los aviones tendrán capacidad para más de 700 pasajeros.
2. Habrá más contaminación del aire y de los ríos y mares.
3. En las ciudades grandes tendremos que llevar máscaras de oxígeno por la contaminación del aire.
4. Para disminuir la congestión en las ciudades, muchas personas se mudarán al campo.
5. Habrá más pobreza en el mundo.
6. El uso de la tecnología y de las computadoras aumentará.
7. En las universidades, las máquinas reemplazarán a muchos de los profesores.
8. Encontraremos una cura para el SIDA y el cáncer.
9. Podremos hacer viajes interplanetarios.
10. También, dentro de cincuenta años...

2 **12-22. Planes para el verano.** Háganse las preguntas sobre lo que piensan hacer durante el verano.

no me mudaré Sí volveré
1. ¿Te mudarás? ¿Volverás a casa?
2. ¿Buscarás trabajo?
3. ¿Tomarás cursos de verano?
4. ¿Tendrás que trabajar todo el verano?
5. ¿Qué más querrás hacer este verano? *Yo querré viajar o Yo viajaré*
6. ¿Qué cosas no podrás hacer?
7. ¿Saldrás con frecuencia con tus amigos? (¿Adónde irán ustedes?)
8. ¿Harás algún viaje? (¿Adónde?)

② **12-23.** *gypsy*

La gitana de la Puerta del Sol.[9] Imagine que usted es «la gitana» y puede pronosticar el futuro según las líneas de la mano. Examine la mano de su compañero/a de clase y dígale lo que le pasará en el futuro. Túrnense. Algunos van a compartir sus predicciones con la clase.

> graduarte en…   ser… (profesión)   vivir en…   hacer un viaje a…
>
> casarte con…   tener… (hijos/nietos)   ganar la lotería   …
>
> *tendré*

Modelo: Esta línea de tu mano me dice que… **tendrás cinco hijas.**

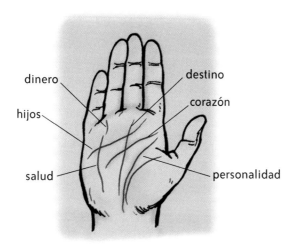

dinero

destino

hijos

corazón

salud

personalidad

✍ **12-24.** **¿Quién será?** Escriba dos oraciones representativas de sus aspiraciones para el futuro. Entregue su papel al/a la profe. Él/Ella se lo lee a la clase y pregunta: **¿Quién será?** La clase contesta: **Será** (*It's probably*)…

③ **12-25.** **Un día en Madrid.** Imaginen que van a estar en Madrid por un día con los estudiantes de la profesora Falcón. Estudien las opciones presentadas en la «Guía de la ciudad» (páginas 428–429) y formulen un plan.

Hablen de:

- lo que van a hacer en la mañana, tarde y noche
- por qué quieren/prefieren ir a esos lugares

Al final, algunos grupos presentan su plan a la clase.

---

[9] **La Puerta del Sol**, a famous plaza at the very heart of the business section of Madrid, dates back to 1478. Although the gate no longer exists, its name comes from the fact that it faced east.

Guía de la ciudad

MUSEO DEL PRADO Uno de los más famosos museos de arte del mundo. Presenta las pinturas más importantes de las escuelas italiana, flamenca, holandesa, veneciana, inglesa y española de los siglos XII al XIX. Si quiere ver arte contemporáneo y vanguardista, visite el **MUSEO NACIONAL CENTRO DE ARTE REINA SOFÍA**. Aquí se encuentra *Guernica*, el famoso cuadro de Picasso.

TERRAZA
Gta. de Atocha

BÁVARO: TERRAZA Situado al lado del Jardín Botánico; la terraza más veterana de Madrid; buena música, excelente coctelería.

TEATRO LOPE DE VEGA Esta noche: «El hombre de La Mancha», musical; ballet y orquesta de la Ópera de Kiev.

LUIS RAMIREZ para PIGMALION presenta

Del 6 de agosto al 13 de septiembre

BALLET Y ORQUESTA DE LA OPERA DE K

Programa
EL LAGO DE LOS CISNES
ROMEO Y JULIETA
LA BELLA DURMIENTE
CASCANUECES
CENICIENTA

TEATRO LOPE DE VEGA

VENTA DE ENTRADAS EN   VENTA TELEFONICA   INFORMA Y GRUP
ServiCaixa   y taquillas   902 33 22 11   902 484
"la Caixa"   del Teatro   902 400 222

Restaurante AL-AMAN II

Cocina Típica Marroquí

Delicatessen Arabes

C/ Leganitos, 27 Tel: 91-559 22 58 MADRID

RESTAURANTE AL-AMAN II
Auténtico restaurante marroquí; exquisito cus cus; también hay platos vegetarianos y deliciosos postres típicos.

Si desea una exquisita paella, cene en la **ARROCERÍA PUERTA DE ATOCHA.** ¡Sirve 14 clases de arroz!

El **RESTAURANTE REDONDELA** ofrece las mejores carnes y mariscos de la gastronomía gallega.

Casa de Campo, s/n. - Teléfono: 91 526 80 31 - Autobuses: Líneas 33 y 65 - Metro: Línea 10 (Estación Batán)
Dirección en Internet: http://www.ddnet.es/parque_de_atracciones

PARQUE DE ATRACCIONES Abierto todos los días desde las 12:00. Las mejores atracciones: Los Rápidos, Los Fiordos, el Flume Ride, el Top Spin, el Star Láser.

PLAZA MAYOR La antigua Plaza Mayor es el lugar ideal para comprar recuerdos, tomar un aperitivo en un bar o dar un paseo. Día y noche hay gente en la plaza.

PARQUE DEL RETIRO
Está situado en el centro de la ciudad, y es el más popular de los parques madrileños. Tiene 119 hectáreas y 15.000 árboles. Es muy divertido ir en barcas en el lago.

Dicho y hecho

⟨⟩ Conversando

3 **¡Problemas en el viaje!** Seleccionen una de las siguientes situaciones y resuelvan el problema. Al final, dos grupos pueden representar las situaciones frente a la clase.

1. En la aduana:

Personajes: Dos pasajeros y el inspector/la inspectora de aduanas.

Situación: Dos pasajeros jóvenes llegan a la aduana del aeropuerto. El inspector/La inspectora de aduanas sospecha que hay un problema.

> **Modelo:** Inspector/a: (*a los pasajeros*) **Abran las maletas, por favor... ¿Qué es esto?**
>
> Pasajero/a 1: ...
>
> Inspector/a: ...
>
> Pasajero/a 2: ...

2. En la recepción de un hotel:

Personajes: Usted, su amigo/a y el/la recepcionista

Situación: Ustedes están un poco desilusionados con el hotel porque su habitación, las condiciones del baño, etc. no son buenas. Hablan con el/la recepcionista para tratar de resolver los problemas.

> **Modelo:** Usted: **Perdón, señor/señorita, pero tenemos algunos problemas con nuestra habitación.**
>
> Recepcionista: **¿Sí? ¿Qué tipo de problemas?**
>
> Usted: ...
>
> Amigo/a: ...

¡A escuchar!

La inversión (*investment*) del siglo se perdió. Estamos en el vuelo 515 con destino a Caracas cuando de repente se oye un anuncio. Habla la azafata. Escuche lo que dice y también los comentarios de la pasajera del asiento 23F. Luego, conteste las dos primeras preguntas.

1. ¿Por qué enciende el capitán la señal (*signal*) de emergencia?

❑ Hay problemas mecánicos.   ❑ Hay turbulencia.

2. ¿La pasajera del asiento 23F coopera inmediatamente con la azafata?

❑ sí   ❑ no

Ahora, escuche la conversación otra vez y complete las oraciones para indicar las instrucciones de la azafata y el problema de la pasajera.

3. La azafata dice que es urgente que los pasajeros regresen a...

4. Ella les dice: «Abróchense..., pongan..., terminen... y apaguen...»

5. La pasajera estaba mandando mensajes por...

6. Ella dice que ha perdido...

De mi escritorio

Unas vacaciones maravillosas. Imagine que usted está organizando un viaje a una ciudad del mundo hispano. Escriba un anuncio promoviéndolo. Busque información sobre el lugar en el Internet. Incluya:

- preparaciones que se deben hacer antes del viaje (**Es importante que...**, **Es preciso que...**, etc.)
- información sobre el transporte (avión, autobús, tren, coche)
- una descripción del lugar
- alternativas para alojamiento (hoteles, paradores, hostales)
- sugerencias para actividades durante el día
- actividades para la noche (restaurantes, teatro, etc.)
- en conclusión, palabras que afirmen la idea de escoger este lugar para las vacaciones

Panorama cultural

España—un mosaico de culturas

¡SOL, SOL, SOL!

Refiriéndose a la España de Carlos I, se decía: «En el imperio español nunca se pone (*sets*) el sol». ¿Qué significa este dicho?

Muchas palabras del español reflejan las diferentes culturas que han existido en España. Por ejemplo, ¿sabe usted que la palabra *cerveza* es celta y la palabra *azul* viene del árabe? La lengua española refleja cada episodio importante de la historia de la península. Examine la cronología. ¿Puede usted nombrar[1] las civilizaciones o culturas que se establecieron en la Península Ibérica antes de 1492? ¿Cuántas hay? ¿Puede usted identificar dos períodos cuando España conquistó otros territorios?

[1] *name*
[2] *stood out*
[3] *samples*

1500 a.C.	500 a.C.	1 d.C.	500 d.C.	1000

1100 a.C.
Llegan los fenicios, los griegos y los cartaginenses.

Los primeros habitantes de la Península Ibérica pertenecen a tribus iberas y celtas.

218 a.C.
Llegan los romanos y rápidamente conquistan la península.

414 d.C.
Los visigodos, de origen germánico, invaden la península.

711
Los árabes del norte de África invaden la península e introducen su cultura.

Escultura prerromana: La Dama de Elche.

¡Oh, Roma! ¿En qué año llegaron los romanos? Conquistaron la península rápidamente y establecieron allí su forma de gobierno y sus leyes. Entre las contribuciones más importantes de los romanos está su lengua, el latín, que dio origen al español. Además, los romanos dejaron muchas obras de ingeniería y arquitectura, como acueductos y carreteras y, finalmente, introdujeron el cristianismo. En su opinión, ¿cuántos años hace que se construyó el acueducto romano de la foto? Las Ferrenas, España.

La España árabe Los árabes (moros) establecieron prósperas ciudades en la península y sobresalieron[2] por sus conocimientos en ciencias, filosofía, arte, literatura y agricultura. Hoy España conserva bellas muestras[3] de su arquitectura, como el palacio de la Alhambra en Granada. Considere la foto de una vista interior del palacio. ¿Son los diseños geométricos, o ve usted figuras de plantas o animales?

¡¿Hablamos árabe?!

¿Sabía usted que aproximadamente 4.000 palabras del español vienen del árabe? Muchas palabras que comienzan con **al** son de origen árabe, como **álgebra, alcalde** (*mayor*), **almanaque, almendra** (*almond*) y otras palabras como **naranja** y **albaricoque** (*apricot*).

¿Qué descubrimos?

Determine el orden cronológico de los siguientes eventos de la historia de España. ¿Qué pasó primero? ¿Y después?

_____ **a.** Comienza la construcción del palacio de la Alhambra.

_____ **b.** España tiene posesiones en Europa, África, Filipinas y América.

_____ **c.** España financia los viajes de exploración de Colón.

_____ **d.** La guerra civil en España.

_____ **e.** España ingresa en la Comunidad Europea.

_1_ **f.** Los habitantes de la península comienzan a hablar latín.

_____ **g.** Entra en circulación en España el euro.

_____ **h.** Se legalizan los partidos políticos y se establece la democracia.

| 1100 | 1300 | 1500 | 1700 | 1900 |

1492
Los reyes Fernando e Isabel conquistan el último reino moro, poniendo fin a la Reconquista de España. Colón llega a América y España comienza la exploración del Nuevo Mundo.

1519
El gran imperio español prospera bajo el reino de Carlos I, con posesiones en Europa, el mar Mediterráneo, África, las Filipinas y América.

1808
El emperador Napoleón I invade la Península Ibérica.

1810–25
España pierde la mayoría de sus colonias, excepto las Filipinas, Cuba y Puerto Rico.

1898
España pierde sus últimas colonias en Asia y América.

La Reconquista Durante casí ocho siglos de dominio árabe, los reinos cristianos del norte, como Castilla, Navarra y Aragón, comenzaron a expulsar a los árabes hacia el sur y a reconquistar los territorios. El Cid, héroe español por excelencia, ayudó a recobrar tierras árabes para el rey de Castilla. Como Castilla era el reino más poderoso durante la Reconquista, hoy hablamos español (castellano) y no aragonés u otra lengua del norte de la península. Describa la estatua del Cid, que se encuentra en Burgos, España (Palabras útiles: la espada *sword*; la capa *cape*).

La unificación y la era de la exploración
La España cristiana se unificó con el matrimonio de los reyes católicos Isabel de Castilla y Fernando de Aragón. En 1492 los Reyes Católicos conquistaron el último reino moro (Granada), poniendo fin al dominio árabe en España. En ese año España también comenzó la exploración del Nuevo Mundo, financiando el viaje de Cristóbal Colón. Vea el mosaico. ¿Puede usted identificar a Colón? ¿Y a Fernando e Isabel?

¡Endemoniado!

Un indio cubano le dio un cigarro a un español, Rodrigo de Xerez. Como en Europa no se conocía el tabaco, cuando vieron a Rodrigo echando humo (*blowing smoke*) por la boca, la Inquisición lo condenó a varios años de prisión «por estar endemoniado».

1936–39
La Guerra Civil española.

1939–75
La dictadura de Francisco Franco.

1978
Establecimiento de la monarquía; elecciones libres.

1986
España ingresa en la Comunidad Europea.

1992
Juegos Olímpicos en Barcelona, EXPO '92 en Sevilla. Madrid se declara Ciudad Cultural de Europa.

1996
José María Aznar es elegido Presidente de Gobierno por el Partido Popular.

2002
Entra en circulación el euro.

«Guernica», Pablo Picasso, 1937. ©Art Resource NYC/Artists' Rights Society, New York.

La Guerra Civil y el gobierno de Franco El evento más importante de la primera mitad[4] del siglo XX en España fue la Guerra Civil. La guerra entre los nacionalistas (conservadores) y los republicanos (liberales) comenzó en 1936 y terminó en 1939 cuando el general Francisco Franco venció[5] a los republicanos. Franco pronto se convirtió en dictador de España. Su dictadura militar duró hasta su muerte en 1975. La censura y la represión caracterizaron este período y obligaron a muchos intelectuales y artistas a abandonar el país. *Guernica*, de Pablo Picasso (1937), refleja los horrores de la Guerra Civil. ¿Qué colores predominan en el cuadro? ¿Y qué símbolos?

Democracia y progreso Cuando murió Franco, España se convirtió en una monarquía constitucional. El joven rey, Juan Carlos de Borbón, tomó posesión del gobierno y ayudó a legalizar los partidos políticos y a establecer la democracia y la libertad de expresión en la nación española. Hoy España es un ejemplo de tolerancia, democracia y progreso. Considere la foto de Felipe (el hijo mayor), Sofía (la reina) y Juan Carlos. ¿Le gustaría a usted ser rey o reina? ¿Por qué? Si quiere saber más de esta familia, busque información en el Internet: http://www.casareal.es/casareal/home.html

[4]*half* [5]*defeated*
[6]*500th anniversary*

Adivinanzas

 Escriban una breve descripción de cada una de las siguientes referencias:

La Dama de Elche	Juan Carlos y Sofía	1492
El Cid	José María Aznar	1898
Fernando e Isabel	los romanos	1978
Carlos I	la Alhambra	1992
Francisco Franco	711	2002

Ahora, la clase se divide en dos equipos. El/La profe le presenta a cada equipo, por turnos, una referencia, y el equipo la describe. ¡No se permite usar las descripciones escritas! Cada respuesta correcta vale dos puntos. El equipo con más puntos gana la competencia.

Durante la celebración en 1992 del quinto centenario[6] del primer viaje de Colón a América, España fue el centro de atención del mundo. Ese año los Juegos Olímpicos se celebraron en Barcelona y la Exposición Universal fue en Sevilla. Estos eventos generaron nuevas industrias y una nueva imagen nacional. Según la foto de las ceremonias de apertura de los Juegos Olímpicos en Barcelona, ¿cuántas personas piensa usted que hay en el estadio?

I. The subjunctive with impersonal expressions. Complete las oraciones combinando la información de las declaraciones con la expresión impersonal indicada.

> **Modelo:** No llevo mi computadora portátil. Es mejor que…
> **Es mejor que no lleve mi computadora portátil.**

1. El avión llega tarde. Es una lástima que…
2. Tengo todo el equipaje. Es bueno que…
3. Vamos a la aduana. Es urgente que…
4. No puedo encontrar el boleto. Es horrible que…
5. No hay azafatas. Es extraño que…
6. No me gusta volar. Es cierto que…

II. More indefinite and negative words. Cambie las siguientes oraciones a la forma negativa.

> **Modelo:** Conozco a algunos jugadores del equipo de baloncesto.
> **No conozco a ningún jugador del equipo de baloncesto.**

1. O Jorge o Miguel te pueden ayudar a limpiar la casa.
2. El hotel tiene aire acondicionado y calefacción.
3. Muchos hoteles tienen televisores con pantalla grande.
4. Algunos estudiantes van a ir a Barcelona.
5. Todos fueron a la discoteca.

III. The subjunctive with indefinite entities.

A. Usted está en un hotel y pide varias cosas. Escriba oraciones con las palabras indicadas.

> **Modelo:** necesitar una habitación / no costar mucho
> **Necesito una habitación que no cueste mucho.**

1. necesitar una habitación / estar en la planta baja
2. preferir un cuarto / tener camas sencillas
3. querer un baño / ser más grande
4. necesitar una llave / abrir el mini-bar

B. Usted está en un hotel y habla con el recepcionista. Complete la conversación usando el verbo entre paréntesis en el subjuntivo o en el indicativo según la situación.

1. USTED: Busco una habitación que _____ (tener) vista al mar.

   RECEPCIONISTA: Tenemos una habitación que _____ (tener) vista al mar. ¿Desea verla?

2. USTED: Prefiero una habitación que _____ (estar) cerca de la piscina.

   RECEPCIONISTA: Lo siento, pero no tenemos ninguna habitación que _____ (estar) cerca de la piscina.

3. USTED: Busco una habitación que_____ (ser) económica.

   RECEPCIONISTA: No hay habitaciones en este hotel que _____ (ser) económicas.

4. USTED: Prefiero cenar en un restaurante que _____ (servir) comida vegetariana.

   RECEPCIONISTA: Pues, en el hotel hay un restaurante que _____ (servir) comida vegetariana.

IV. The future tense. Forme oraciones para hablar de lo que las siguientes personas harán este verano.

> **Modelo:** yo / tomar clases
> **Tomaré clases este verano.**

1. mi mamá / poder ir a la Florida
2. Luis / tener que trabajar
3. Carmen y sus amigos / querer visitar la Alhambra
4. mis abuelitos / venir a visitarnos
5. el profesor Vivar-Marín y su familia / viajar por México
6. yo / pasar los fines de semana en la playa

V. General review. Conteste con oraciones completas.

1. En el aeropuerto, ¿qué información encontramos en el horario?
2. Al llegar al aeropuerto, ¿qué hacen los pasajeros?
3. ¿Qué tipo de hotel busca usted para sus próximas vacaciones?
4. ¿Conoce usted algún lugar para vacacionar que sea económico?
5. ¿Hará usted un viaje este verano? ¿Qué más hará?

Answers to the *Autoprueba y repaso* are found in **Apéndice 2**.

En el extranjero

Goals for communication

- To talk about travel by car, train, and bus
- To make suggestions
- To express condition or purpose
- To react to past actions or events
- To talk about activities with a general or unknown subject

En el extranjero

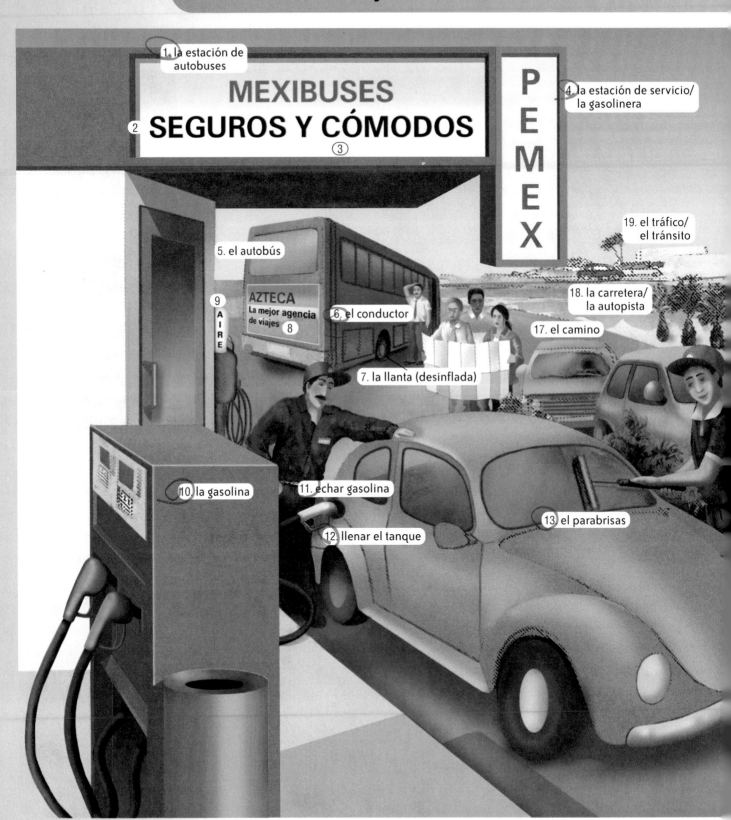

20. el semáforo
23. doblar
24. a la derecha
21. continuar/ seguir (i, i)
22. derecho/ recto
25. el puente
27. el camión
15. el kilómetro
26. cruzar
Señor, debe conducir más despacio.
80 KM MAX
16. la velocidad
¡Ay, no! ¡Otra multa!
29
Su licencia de conducir, por favor.
14. parar
36. la mujer policía
32. el policía
33. el accidente
34. el choque
35. chocar
...iba demasiado rápido. Hay que tener más cuidado.
39. la moto(cicleta)

1. bus station
2. safe
3. comfortable
4. service/gas station
5. bus
6. driver (m.); **la conductora** driver (f.)
7. (flat) tire
8. travel agency
9. air (m.)
10. gas
11. to put gas (in the tank)
12. to fill the tank
13. windshield
14. to stop
15. kilometer
16. speed
17. road
18. highway/freeway
19. traffic
20. traffic light
21. to continue, to follow
22. straight, straight ahead
23. to turn
24. to the right; **a la izquierda** to the left
25. bridge
26. to cross
27. truck
28. driver's licence
29. fine, ticket
30. to drive (**conduzco, conduces**...)
31. slow, slowly
32. policeman
33. accident
34. crash, collision
35. to crash, collide
36. policewoman
37. too, too much (adv.)
38. to be (more) careful
39. motorcycle

Práctica y comunicación

2 **13-1.** **Por el camino.** Conteste las preguntas según los dibujos de las páginas 440–441.

1. ¿Dónde está el autobús?
2. Según el anuncio, ¿cómo son los autobuses Mexibuses?
3. ¿En qué condición está una de las llantas del autobús? ¿Cómo se siente el conductor?
4. ¿Qué anuncio se ve en el autobús?
5. ¿Qué hacen el profesor Marín-Vivar y sus estudiantes?
6. ¿Dónde está el coche VW?
7. ¿Qué echa en el tanque uno de los empleados? ¿Qué está haciendo el otro empleado?
8. ¿A qué velocidad se puede manejar en el camino que está cerca de la estación de autobuses?
9. En la carretera que está a la distancia, ¿hay mucho tránsito? ¿Cuántos camiones hay?
10. ¿Ha cruzado el puente uno de los camiones?
11. Para ir a Querétaro por la carretera 57, ¿en qué dirección se debe doblar? ¿Y para ir a Taxco? Para ir a Puebla, ¿se debe doblar o seguir recto? ¿En qué carretera?
12. ¿Qué ha ocurrido en la intersección?
13. ¿Qué hace la mujer policía que está frente al tráfico? ¿Qué le pide a la conductora? ¿Qué piensa la conductora?
14. ¿Piensa usted que el carro rojo paró al llegar al semáforo?
15. ¿Qué le dice el policía al conductor del carro rojo?
16. ¿Puede el motociclista seguir o tiene que parar? ¿Por qué? ¿En qué está pensando?

4 **13-2.** **¿Qué pasa?** Describan lo que pasa/pasó en la escena de las páginas 440–441. Usen las siguientes palabras. Túrnense.

> **Modelo:** llanta
>
> **El autobús tiene una llanta desinflada. El conductor está preocupado a causa de la llanta.**

1. el autobús
2. los estudiantes y el profe
3. los empleados de la gasolinera
4. la velocidad
5. el semáforo
6. el puente

7. doblar
8. seguir/ continuar
9. parar
10. chocar
11. los policías
12. el motociclista

2 **13-3.** **¿Qué clase de conductor/a eres?** Háganse las siguientes preguntas para conocerse mejor. Túrnense.

1. ¿Tienes coche? ¿Qué tipo de coche manejas? ¿Es un coche seguro/ cómodo?
2. ¿Cuántos años tenías cuando sacaste tu licencia de conducir?
3. ¿Te gusta la idea de viajar por un país extranjero en auto? ¿Y en motocicleta?
4. ¿Has chocado alguna vez? (¿Dónde?) (¿Cuándo?) (¿Qué pasó?)
5. ¿Has recibido una multa recientemente? (¿Por qué?) (¿De cuánto?)
6. ¿Tienes cuidado al manejar?¿Manejas demasiado rápido/ despacio?
7. Cuando tu coche tiene una llanta desinflada, ¿tratas de inflarla? Si tienes que cambiarla, ¿puedes hacerlo tú mismo/a?
8. ¿A veces te olvidas de llenar el tanque?
9. ¿Te acuerdas siempre de abrocharte el cinturón? ¿Por qué es importante abrocharse el cinturón?
10. Al llegar a un semáforo, ¿te acuerdas de parar antes de doblar a la derecha?
11. Cuando estás manejando por la carretera y tienes prisa, ¿a qué velocidad manejas (millas[1]/kilómetros por hora)?

2 **13-4.** **Letreros (*Signs*) para los automovilistas.** Un/a compañero/a suyo/a está manejando por una ciudad latinoamericana y usted lo/la guía. Al ver cada letrero, dígale lo que debe hacer. Use mandatos de **tú**.

Modelo: No manejes/conduzcas a más de 90 km por hora.

Velocidad máxima 90 km.

 Prohibido doblar en U.	 Prohibido doblar a la izquierda.
 Prohibido seguir derecho.	 Prohibido estacionar o detenerse.

1. 2. 3. 4.

5. 6. 7. 8.

 Ceder el paso.	 No tocar la bocina.
 Parar.	 No cambiar de carril.

[1] One mile = 1.60 kilometers.

Los vehículos y los mecánicos

TALLER MECÁNICO⁽¹⁾ URIBE

Le **revisamos**⁽²⁾
la batería
y el aire de las llantas.

Le cambiamos
el aceite,
los filtros
y las llantas,
le **reparamos**⁽³⁾ los **frenos**⁽⁴⁾
y le **afinamos el motor**⁽⁵⁾.

Su auto **funcionará**⁽⁶⁾ como nuevo.

Estamos en la **esquina**⁽⁷⁾ de la calle 7 y la avenida 6
a tres **cuadras**⁽⁸⁾ de la estación de Mexibuses.

Consultas y café **gratis**⁽⁹⁾
No busque donde **estacionar**⁽¹⁰⁾. Tenemos amplio **estacionamiento**⁽¹¹⁾.
Tel 555-39-27

(1) auto repair shop (2) we check; **revisar** *to check (3) we repair;* **reparar** *to repair (4) brakes*
(5) we tune your motor; **afinar el motor** *to tune the motor (6) will run;* **funcionar** *to run, work,*
function (7) (street) corner (8) blocks (9) free (10) to park (11) parking

---

② **13–5.** **Se vende automóvil usado.** Usted vio un anuncio sobre un automóvil usado y decide llamar al vendedor del carro. Completen la conversación telefónica.

> VENDEDOR: Bueno.
>
> CLIENTE: Buenas tardes. Con el señor Benavides, por favor.
>
> VENDEDOR: Con él habla.
>
> CLIENTE: Señor Benavides, vi su anuncio en el periódico y me interesa saber más sobre su carro.
>
> VENDEDOR: Es un _____ del año _____. Acabo de traerlo del taller. Ahí le afinaron _____, le _____ la batería, le cambiaron _____ y_____ y le _____ los frenos. Ahora está como nuevo.

CLIENTE: ¿Me puede dar su dirección para ver y probar el coche?

VENDEDOR: Sí, es el número 2434 de la calle Esmeralda, a dos _____ de la estación de autobuses.

CLIENTE: ¿Cuándo puedo verlo?

VENDEDOR: Pues ahora mismo si quiere.

13-6. **Puebla, México.** Ustedes van a visitar varios lugares de interés en el centro histórico de Puebla. Lean la información y luego escojan los cuatro lugares que más les gustaría visitar.

Lugares interesantes en *Puebla*

1 La Catedral
Su construcción comenzó en 1575. Es una joya de la arquitectura colonial. Sus torres° son las más altas del país.

2 La Biblioteca Palafoxiana
Está clasificada como monumento histórico de México. Fue fundada en 1646.

3 Mercado El Parián
Es la antigua° plazuela de San Roque. Se construyó en 1801. Hoy es un mercado donde se pueden encontrar artesanías, dulces°, textiles, etc.

4 Iglesia de la Compañía de Jesús
Otra de las famosas iglesias de la ciudad; es de estilo barroco, tiene torres blancas y un bello altar.

5 La Casa del Alfeñique
Esta casa del siglo XVIII tiene mucha ornamentación blanca y por eso la llaman *alfeñique*, un dulce poblano°.

6 El Barrio del Artista
Es una plazuela con una hermosa fuente° y muchos talleres de artistas.

7 Museo Amparo
Una de sus exhibiciones más importantes es sobre las culturas mesoamericanas.

8 Capilla° del Rosario
Este ejemplo del arte barroco novohispano se considera una de las maravillas de México. El interior de la capilla es de estuco cubierto con lámina de oro de 22 quilates.

9 La Plazuela de los Sapos°
Rodeada de casas típicas y bazares de antigüedades, tiene una fuente muy linda en el centro. Aquí se pueden contratar mariachis y tríos.

towers

former

candy

from Puebla

fountain

Chapel

Toads

Catedral de Puebla, México

Lugar 1: _____   Lugar 3: _____

Lugar 2: _____   Lugar 4: _____

13-7. **Para ver un poco de Puebla.** Imagine que usted está en la ciudad de Puebla y alguien le da instrucciones para llegar a ciertos puntos de interés en la ciudad. Está en el estacionamiento del Hotel Colonial Puebla («E» en el mapa). Siga las instrucciones para ver adónde llega.

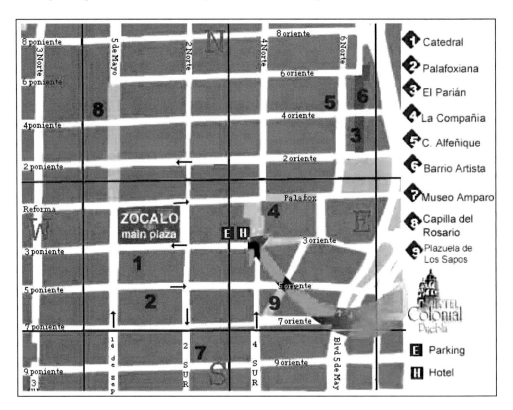

1. Abróchese el cinturón. Salga del estacionamiento y doble a la derecha (oeste) en la calle 3 Poniente.
2. Pase el Zócalo y doble a la derecha (norte) en la calle 16 de Septiembre.
3. Siga recto tres cuadras y doble a la derecha en la calle 4 Poniente.
4. Continúe recto tres cuadras, dirección este. La Casa del Alfeñique está en la esquina.
5. Siga media cuadra más. Estacione su carro. ¿Dónde está? ¿Qué se puede ver?

13-8. ② **¿Cómo se llega?** Ustedes se hospedan en el Hotel Colonial Puebla. Uno le pide direcciones al otro para llegar a los siguientes lugares. ¡Cuidado! Hay calles de una sola vía. Túrnense. Usen el mapa del Ejercicio 13-7.

Desde el hotel...

1. a la Catedral: **Salga del hotel y...**
2. a la Capilla del Rosario
3. a la Plazuela de los Sapos
4. al Museo Amparo
5. a la Biblioteca Palafoxiana
6. al Mercado El Parián

Escenas

Hacia Puerto Vallarta

Manuel

Linda

3 *Linda y Manuel alquilaron un carro y están en camino a Puerto Vallarta. Manuel conduce y Linda está a su lado. Desgraciadamente°, el carro no está en muy buenas condiciones.*

Unfortunately

LINDA: Manuel, vas muy rápido y casi no tenemos gasolina.

MANUEL: ¡Ay, Linda! Todo está bien. Tenemos prisa por llegar a Puerto Vallarta.

LINDA: ¿Qué es ese ruido? ¿No lo oyes? Hay un ruido en la llanta.

MANUEL: Es tu imaginación, Linda. Es mejor que te duermas.

LINDA: Por favor. Párate en esa estación de servicio para que revisen el coche. Si no, nunca vamos a llegar a la playa.

MANUEL: Bueno, bueno... está bien. Voy a parar.
(*Entran en la estación de servicio.*)

MANUEL: (*Al empleado.*) Buenas tardes, ¿puede llenar el tanque y revisar las llantas, por favor?

EMPLEADO: Sí, inmediatamente.
(*El empleado echa la gasolina y revisa las llantas.*)

EMPLEADO: ¿Quiere que le revise el motor y los frenos?

MANUEL: No, no es necesario.

LINDA: ¡Sí! ¡Sí, es necesario!

(*El empleado revisa el motor y los frenos.*)

EMPLEADO: (*A Manuel.*) Señor, la llanta delantera° derecha está en muy malas condiciones, el coche casi no tiene aceite, los frenos están gastados°... Necesito por lo menos cuatro horas para repararlo todo. Lo siento mucho.

front

worn out

LINDA: (*A Manuel.*) ¿Ves Manuel?

MANUEL: Es verdad, mi amor. Tenías razón°, como siempre. ¡Qué mala suerte hemos tenido con este carro!

Tenías... *You were right*

¿Qué pasa?

1. ¿Adónde van Linda y Manuel?

2. ¿Quién está conduciendo el coche?

3. ¿Por qué está nerviosa Linda?

4. ¿En dónde se paran?

5. ¿Qué revisa el empleado?

6. ¿Qué le pasa al coche?

¡Caramba!	*Oh, my gosh!*
¡Claro!/ ¡Por supuesto!	*Of course!*
¡Socorro!/ ¡Auxilio!	*Help!*
Lo siento mucho.	*I'm so sorry.*
¡Qué barbaridad!	*How awful!*
¡Qué lástima!	*What a shame!*
¡Qué lío!	*What a mess!*
¡Ay de mí!	*Poor me! (What am I going to do?)*
¡Qué suerte!	*What luck!/How lucky!*

13–9. **¡Caramba!** ¿Qué dice usted en las siguientes situaciones? Use todas las reacciones de la lista. Hay más de una respuesta posible.

¿Qué dice usted cuando...?

1. Un amigo de su compañero de cuarto ha tenido un accidente y está en el hospital.
2. Usted está en el centro de la Ciudad de México y ¡su coche tiene una llanta desinflada!
3. Llueve mucho y ¡los limpiaparabrisas no funcionan!
4. Usted está manejando muy rápidamente por las calles de San Francisco y descubre que ¡los frenos no funcionan!
5. Su mejor amiga le cuenta que anoche le robaron su coche nuevo.
6. Un policía lo para y le pide la licencia de conducir. Usted no la tiene.
7. Usted abre la puerta del coche de su amigo y ve que todo está muy sucio. Hay papeles, comida y ropa vieja por todas partes.
8. Su tía rica le pregunta si quiere un coche nuevo para su cumpleaños.

El airbag ya estaba inventado. Los plásticos de BASF lo han hecho más seguro.

El «Pez Globo» se llena de aire y aumenta de volumen para evitar los ataques de sus depredadores (*predators*). ¿Qué relación existe entre el «Pez Globo» y los *airbags*? ¿Tiene *airbags* su coche? ¿Se siente usted más seguro/a con *airbags*?

Estructuras

1 **Making suggestions: *Nosotros* (Let's) commands**

Sigamos la carretera 95 y tratemos de llegar a Taxco antes de las 5:00.

To express a *let's* command, Spanish uses the **nosotros** form of the present subjunctive.

Revisemos la batería.	***Let's check*** *the battery.*
No **esperemos** más.	***Let's*** *not* ***wait*** *any longer.*

- In **nosotros** commands, as in other command forms, object and reflexive pronouns are attached to an affirmative command but placed before a negative command.

    Hagámos**lo** mañana.

    No **lo** hagamos en este momento.

- To form the affirmative *let's* command of a reflexive verb, delete the final **-s** of the present subjunctive form before adding the pronoun **nos**. Note the written accent.

    levantemos̸ ➔ levantemo + **nos** = ¡**Levantémonos**!

- The verbs **ir** and **irse** have irregular affirmative *let's* commands;

    ¡**Vamos**! or ¡**Vámonos**!   *Let's go!*

    but the negative *let's* commands use the subjunctive form.

    ¡**No vayamos**!/ ¡**No nos vayamos**!   *Let's not go!*

- An alternative affirmative *let's* command form is **vamos a** + *infinitive*;

    ¡**Vamos a parar** aquí!   *Let's stop here!*

    however, its *negative* counterpart reverts to the subjunctive form.

    ¡**No paremos** aquí!   *Let's not stop here!*

Práctica y comunicación

④ 13-10. **Un fin de semana en Acapulco.** Ustedes viajan de la Ciudad de México hacia Acapulco. Una persona del grupo es un poco mandona y siempre insiste en organizarles a todos la vida. Determinen el orden cronológico de las instrucciones. Escriban el número al lado de cada oración.

_____ **a.** Desayunemos antes de salir.

_____ **b.** Mañana por la mañana, levantémonos a las seis.

_____ **c.** Durante el viaje, cambiemos de chofer cada dos horas.

_____ **d.** Salgamos a las siete en punto.

_____ **e.** Al llegar, estacionémonos en el Hotel Presidente.

_____ **f.** Almorcemos en el camino.

_1_ **g.** Hoy, llevemos el carro a la gasolinera para llenar el tanque y revisar las llantas.

_____ **h.** Bailemos toda la noche.

_____ **i.** Al atardecer, vamos a la Quebrada a ver los clavadistas (*cliff divers*).

_____ **j.** Acostémonos esta noche temprano para estar en forma para el viaje mañana.

_____ **k.** Busquemos un buen restaurante para cenar.

Un grupo lee la serie de acciones a la clase. ¿Hay diferencias de opinión?

④ 13-11. **Planeando un itinerario.** Usted y tres de sus amigos deciden hacer un viaje este verano. Usen los mandatos de **nosotros** para expresar sus deseos. Escriban su plan. Piensen en:

1. cuándo quieren salir y regresar: **Salgamos…**

2. adónde quieren ir

3. si van en moto, coche, autobús o tren

4. lo que quieren (o no quieren) hacer durante el viaje

5. lo que deben llevar (ropa, comida, etc.)

6. dónde van a dormir (acampar, hoteles, hostales)

7. cuánto dinero van a llevar para los gastos (*expenses*)

Lean su plan a otro grupo y/o a la clase.

Noticias culturales

La Carretera Panamericana

¿Ha pensado usted en recorrer Latinoamérica en carro? La Carretera Panamericana le ofrece una aventura inigualable°. Comienza en Fairbanks, Alaska, y continúa hasta Ushuaia, Tierra del Fuego, en Argentina. Esta gran vía conecta las culturas y los paisajes de las tres Américas, pasando por numerosas ciudades y pueblos, y cruzando las selvas y las montañas más importantes del continente. A veces es una autopista; otras es un camino de dos carriles°.

unequaled

lanes

El plan para su construcción comenzó en 1925 con un congreso celebrado en Buenos Aires. Los Estados Unidos cooperó con los países de Latinoamérica en la planificación y construcción de esta carretera, y actualmente sólo falta construir 160 km (casi 100 millas) en la densa selva del Darién, entre Panamá y Colombia. A causa de la importancia ecológica de la zona, es muy probable que nunca se termine de construir esta sección de la carretera. Al llegar a Darién, los viajeros transportan sus vehículos en barco hasta Venezuela o Colombia. Allí pueden retomar la Carretera Panamericana y continuar su viaje hacia el sur. ¡Un viaje promedio° a lo largo de toda la Carretera Panamericana puede durar hasta trece meses!

average

¿Qué recuerda?

1. ¿Dónde comienza la Carretera Panamericana? ¿Dónde termina?
2. ¿En dónde se interrumpe la carretera?
3. ¿Por qué es probable que nunca se termine la construcción de la carretera?
4. ¿Qué hay que hacer para continuar el viaje a Sudamérica?
5. ¿Aproximadamente cuánto tiempo es necesario para recorrer toda la Carretera Panamericana?

2 Conexiones y contrastes

1. En su país, ¿qué importancia tiene el coche?
2. ¿Qué tipo de coches son populares hoy en día? ¿Qué valores (*values*) reflejan esos gustos y preferencias?
3. ¿Le gusta a usted hacer viajes largos en coche? ¿Por qué?
4. ¿Recuerda usted su viaje más largo en coche? ¿Adónde iba?
5. ¿Cuál es la carretera más pintoresca de su país o su región? ¿Por qué?

Condorito es el protagonista de una tira cómica chilena. ¿Qué trabajo tiene Condorito? ¿En qué lugar de la Panamericana cree usted que está? ¿Por qué quiere suicidarse?

2 The subjunctive with expressions of condition or purpose

No podemos continuar el viaje a menos que encuentre el problema pronto.

The subjunctive is always used after the following conjunctions:

en caso de que *in case*   a menos (de) que *unless*
con tal (de) que *provided that* para que *so that, in order that*

- These conjunctions denote purpose (*so that*) and condition/contingency (*unless, provided that, in case*). They indicate that the outcome of the actions they introduce is dependent on other actions. Since the speaker considers the outcomes to be indefinite or pending, they may or may not take place.

Trae tu tarjeta de crédito **en caso de que** la **necesites**.	*Bring your credit card **in case you need** it.*
Puedes alquilar un coche **con tal de que tengas** una licencia válida.	*You can rent a car **provided you have** a valid license.*
No alquiles el auto **a menos que no encuentres** puesto en el tren.	*Don't rent the car **unless you cannot find** a seat on the train.*
Vamos a la agencia **para que preguntes** sobre las diferentes opciones.	*Let's go to the agency **so that you can ask** about the different options.*

- When there is no change of subject, the conjunction **para que** + *subjunctive* is usually replaced by the preposition **para** + *infinitive*.

Vamos a la estación de autobuses…	*We are going to the bus station …*
…**para que** ella **compre** los boletos.	*… **so that** she **can buy** the tickets.*
…**para comprar** los boletos.	*… **to (in order to) buy** the tickets.*

Práctica y comunicación

2 **13-12.** **Anticipando el viaje a Guadalajara, México.** Lean cada declaración de la columna A y complétenla con la frase apropiada de la columna B.

A

1. Vamos a la estación de autobuses...

2. Debemos llevar los pasaportes...

3. No podemos visitar todas las plazas y catedrales...

4. Al llegar, debemos comprarnos un mapa de la ciudad...

5. Carlos viene con nosotros...

6. Nos vamos a quedar en un hostal estudiantil...

7. Será difícil comprar las entradas al concierto de los mariachis...

B

a. en caso de que las autoridades quieran revisarlos.

b. con tal de que encontremos uno cerca del centro.

c. para buscar información acerca de los horarios.

d. a menos que lleguemos al teatro temprano.

e. a menos que nos quedemos varios días.

f. para que sea más fácil orientarnos.

g. con tal de que reciba el dinero que le mandó su tío.

2 **13-13.** **Por si acaso (*Just in case*).** Alfonso decide separarse del grupo para visitar Yucatán, México. Se prepara para su viaje. ¿Por qué lleva las siguientes cosas?

Modelo: 1. Alfonso lleva su paraguas en caso de que llueva.

1.

en caso de que

2.

3.

4.

5.

6.

7.

8.

② **13-14.** **Un viaje de negocios y placer.** Dos ejecutivos de Puebla, México, llegan a su universidad para asistir a una conferencia y conocer la ciudad. Ustedes son los guías. Expliquen para qué los llevan ustedes a los lugares indicados. Completen las oraciones.

> **Modelo:** Vamos a llevarlos a un restaurante de comida rápida **para que compren una hamburguesa.**

Vamos a llevarlos...

1. al centro comercial...

4. al centro estudiantil...

2. al banco...

5. a Kinko's...

3. a la oficina de correos...

6. a... (un sitio importante en su ciudad)

④ **13-15.** **Un viaje por México.** Imaginen que después de terminar sus estudios en la capital, ustedes deciden hacer un viaje en autobús por varias ciudades de México. Consulten el mapa y hagan una lista. Luego completen las oraciones. Un/a secretario/a escribe las respuestas para después leérselas a la clase.

1. Haremos un viaje por México. Visitaremos..., ... y ... con tal que...

2. Vamos a llevar... en caso de que...

3. Nos quedaremos en hostales a menos que...

4. Iremos a... para... y a... para...

Así se dice

En la estación del ferrocarril[1]

la taquilla[2]

los aseos/ el servicio[7]

Caballeros

el boleto/billete[3]

...de ida/sencillo[4]
...de ida y vuelta[5]
...de primera/segunda clase[6]

el tatuaje[12]

el maletero[8]

Damas

el andén[9]

el tren[10]

perder el tren[11]

(1) railroad station (2) ticket window (3) ticket (4) one way . . . (5) round-trip . . .
(6) first/second class . . . (7) restrooms (8) porter (9) platform (10) train (11) to miss the train
(12) tatoo

Práctica y comunicación

13-16. **En la estación del ferrocarril.** Describan la escena. Un/a estudiante de cada grupo sirve de secretario/a. Tienen cinco minutos.

2   **13-17.** **Un viaje a Sevilla en el AVE.** Ustedes están en España y ven .este anuncio en una agencia de viajes en Madrid. Primero lean el párrafo.

handicapped

Los trenes de alta velocidad AVE conectan Madrid con el sur de España. Hay tres clases: Club, Preferente y Turista. Un billete sencillo a Sevilla cuesta según la clase 110, 92 o 62 euros. Estos trenes ofrecen servicios tales como cafetería, venta de artículos a bordo, canales para escuchar música, videos, pasatiempos para niños, aseos y facilidades para los minusválidos°. La clase Club incluye aparcamiento, servicio de restaurante a la carta y hasta servicio de bar en el asiento. Usted puede viajar con su mascota (perros pequeños y gatos), transportar su bicicleta y llevar una maleta y un maletín. La RENFE[2] promete extrema puntualidad con demoras de sólo minutos.

Ahora un/a estudiante hace el papel del empleado de la RENFE y el otro/la otra es el/la pasajero/a. Hagan las siguientes transacciones

> **Modelo:**   Empleado: **Buenos días. ¿En qué puedo servirle?**
>
> Pasajero/a: **Deseo comprar...**
>
> Empleado: **Muy bien, señor/ita, aquí lo tiene. Cuesta...**

1. comprar un boleto para Sevilla en el AVE (clase y precio)
2. pedir información (sobre horario/ equipaje/ comida/ andenes/ aseos, etc.)
3. hablar de posibles demoras y tratar de resolver los problemas que puedan causar

2 **¡Qué dilema!** *Compraste un boleto de tren para viajar de Barcelona a Madrid. El revisor (conductor) te pide el boleto, y para tu horror te das cuenta que ¡lo has perdido! Ahora tendrás que comprar otro y pagar una multa—un gran inconveniente porque tienes poco dinero. Trata de explicarle tu situación:* **Señor, le aseguro que compré un billete en Barcelona. Lo tenía en mi mochila...**

---

[2] **Red Nacional de Ferrocarriles Españoles**, the Spanish National Railroad System.

3 Reacting to past actions or events: The imperfect subjunctive

Me recomendaron que llevara la cámara para sacar fotos de las ruinas mayas.

You have studied various uses of the subjunctive and practiced the present subjunctive (relating actions that take place in the present or in the future) and the present perfect subjunctive (relating actions and events that have taken place in the immediate past).

Present subjunctive

Espero que **se diviertan** en Acapulco.	*I hope that **they (will) have a good time** in Acapulco.*

Present perfect subjunctive

Me alegro que **se hayan divertido** en Acapulco.	*I am glad that **they have had a good time** in Acapulco.*

In the examples above, the verb of the *main clause* is in the present indicative, and the verb of the *secondary clause* is in the present subjunctive or present perfect subjunctive. In general, the imperfect (past) subjunctive is used in the same kinds of situations as the present subjunctive, but relates actions or events that took place in the past. When the verb of the *main clause* is in a past tense (usually preterit or imperfect), the imperfect subjunctive is used in the *secondary clause*.

Main clause	Secondary clause
present indicative	*present subjunctive*
Es bueno…	…que **hagas** las reservaciones.
	present perfect subjunctive
	…que **hayas hecho** las reservaciones.
past indicative	*imperfect subjunctive*
Les **recomendé**…	…que **hicieran** las reservaciones.
Siempre les **recomendaba**…	…que **viajaran** en tren.

Formation of the imperfect subjunctive

To form the imperfect subjunctive of all verbs, **-ar, -er,** and **-ir,** delete the **-ron** from the **ellos** form of the preterit indicative and add the following endings: **-ra, -ras, -ra, -ramos, -rais, -ran**[3]. The imperfect subjunctive thus automatically reflects all irregularities of the preterit.

	compr**ar**	volv**er**	sal**ir**
	compra~~ron~~	volvie~~ron~~	salie~~ron~~
(yo)	compra**ra**	volvie**ra**	salie**ra**
(tú)	compra**ras**	volvie**ras**	salie**ras**
(Ud., él, ella)	compra**ra**	volvie**ra**	salie**ra**
(nosotros/as)	comprá**ramos**	volvié**ramos**	salié**ramos**
(vosotros/as)	compra**rais**	volvie**rais**	salie**rais**
(Uds., ellos, ellas)	compra**ran**	volvie**ran**	salie**ran**

HINT | Remember to use the preterit tense, not the infinitive stem, to form the imperfect subjunctive. Review the regular, stem-changing, and irregular preterit tense verbs in **Chapters 5**, **6**, and **7**.

Other examples:

estar	estuvie~~ron~~	→	estuviera, estuvieras,...
leer	leye~~ron~~	→	leyera, leyeras,...
tener	tuvie~~ron~~	→	tuviera, tuvieras,...
dormir	durmie~~ron~~	→	durmiera, durmieras,...
ir/ser	fue~~ron~~	→	fuera, fueras,...
pedir	pidie~~ron~~	→	pidiera, pidieras,...

- **Hubiera** is the imperfect subjunctive form of **había** (*there was, there were*).

  Nos alegramos de que **hubiera** un vagón-restaurante en el tren.

  *We were happy that **there was** a dining car on the train.*

---

[3] In Spain and in certain dialects of Spanish, the imperfect subjunctive has an alternate set of endings: **-se, -ses, -se, -semos, -seis, -sen**. These forms are frequently found in writing.

Práctica y comunicación

13-18. Jefes, profes y padres. Según la situación, identifique quién esperaba o quiénes esperaban cada una de las siguientes cosas.

a. El jefe (*boss*) esperaba que los empleados…
b. Los padres esperaban que sus hijos…
c. El profe esperaba que los estudiantes…

Modelo: …los llamaran por teléfono
Los padres esperaban que sus hijos los llamaran por teléfono.

1. …llegaran a clase a tiempo
2. …trabajaran de 9 a 5
3. …limpiaran su cuarto
4. …no salieran del trabajo antes de tiempo
5. …comieran bien
6. …dijeran la verdad

7. …hablaran en español
8. …aprendieran el imperfecto del subjuntivo
9. …hicieran su trabajo eficientemente
10. …se acostaran temprano

13-19. Una visita a mi consejero/a (*adviser*). Usted fue a ver a su consejero/a académico. Diga lo que le recomendó.

Modelo: tomar menos clases
Me recomendó que tomara menos clases.

1. dejar la clase de química
2. organizar mis horas de estudio
3. trabajar menos horas en el supermercado
4. buscar un tutor para el curso de matemáticas
5. hablar con mi profesor de psicología
6. no ir a tantas fiestas
7. dormir más
8. estudiar más

2 **13-20.** **Natalia, de voluntaria en Ecuador.** Natalia trabajaba como voluntaria en una clínica. Decidió ir a Los Nevados, un pueblo remoto situado en los Andes, para llevar medicamentos. ¿Qué le recomendó su compañera de trabajo?

> **Modelo:** Le recomendó que...
>
> Le recomendó que llevara su mochila, los medicamentos y comida.

llevar...

Le recomendó que...

1. despertarse…

2. ponerse…

3. seguir la ruta…

4. escalar…despacio

5. cruzar…con cuidado

6. tomar mucha… comer…

7. darle los medicamentos…

8. despedirse de… regresar…

13-21. **¿Qué hicieron en la clase?** Un compañero de clase estuvo enfermo y lo/la llama a usted para saber lo que hicieron en la clase el viernes. Completen la conversación. ¡Atención! Algunos verbos están en el presente del subjuntivo y otros en el imperfecto del subjuntivo.

COMPAÑERO: Hola,... ¿qué tal? Te llamo para saber lo que la profe quiere que _____ (hacer) para el lunes.

USTED: Hola,... espero que _____ (sentirse) mejor. Pues, la profe dijo que quería que _____ (estudiar) los verbos en el imperfecto del subjuntivo y que _____ (escribir) una composición sobre los aztecas.

COMPAÑERO: ¿Explicó cuánto tenemos que escribir?

USTED: Sí, dijo que quería dos párrafos y que recomendaba que _____ (usar) al menos una fuente° de la red o de la biblioteca. Como siempre, insistió que _____ (tener) cuidado con los acentos y la ortografía. Ya conoces a la profe.   *source*

COMPAÑERO: ¿Ya encontraste tu fuente adicional?

USTED: No. Busqué en la red pero no encontré nada que me _____ (servir).

COMPAÑERO: Pues si tú no encontraste nada, dudo que yo _____ (tener) mejor suerte. Es mejor que (yo) _____ (ir) a la biblioteca.

USTED: Creo que tienes razón. ¡Ojalá que _____ (encontrar) algo. ¡Ah!, se me olvidaba. También dijo que _____ (hacer) los ejercicios del manual, y claro, que _____ (usar) un lápiz o bolígrafo de diferente color para hacer las correcciones. Tú sabes.

COMPAÑERO: Sí, por supuesto. Gracias otra vez. Te veo el lunes en clase.

13-22. **Hablando de la vida personal.** Complete las oraciones para indicar lo que pasaba durante los siguientes períodos.

1. Cuando tenía diez años,
  a. yo esperaba que mis padres...
  b. quería que mis hermanos/as...
  c. quería que mis amigos...
2. Cuando estaba en la escuela secundaria,
  a. buscaba un/a novio/a que...
  b. mis padres querían que yo...
  c. mis maestros recomendaban que yo...
3. Cuando salí para la universidad,
  a. temía que mi nuevo/a compañero/a de cuarto...
  b. esperaba que los profesores...
  c. esperaba que los otros estudiantes...

Al final, comparta algunos de sus deseos, temores y esperanzas con la clase.

4 **Talking about activities with a general or unknown subject: The impersonal *se***

When the subject is general, unknown, or not specific, English uses such words as *one, people, you, we, they,* or the passive voice[4]. In Spanish the following construction is commonly used:

> **se** + *third-person singular or plural verb*

Se **prohíbe** fumar.	Smoking *is prohibited.*
Se **venden** mapas.	*We sell* maps.
Se **debe** mostrar el pasaporte.	*You must* show your passport.
No se **debe** dejar el equipaje descuidado.	*One shouldn't* leave luggage unattended.
Se **practica** el clavadismo en Acapulco.	Cliff diving *is practiced* in Acapulco.
Se **construyó** el hotel sobre las rocas.	The hotel *was built* on the rocks.

Can you guess what the following signs say?

1.

2.

3.

4.

5.

---

[4] The English passive voice is formed with the verb *to be* + *the past participle*: The house *was built* in 1821.

Práctica y comunicación

13-23. **¿Dónde están los siguientes rótulos (*signs*)?** Asocie cada rótulo con el lugar o los lugares donde se ve.

Rótulo

1. Se prohibe fumar.

2. No se aceptan tarjetas de crédito.

3. Se necesita secretaria.

4. Se vende computadora como nueva.

5. Se arreglan llantas. *tires*

6. Se abre a las 9 A.M. y se cierra a las 6 P.M.

Lugar

a. en un hotel

b. en un periódico

c. en un restaurante

d. en un avión

e. en un taller mecánico

f. en un banco

13-24. **¿Qué nos ofrece Acapulco?** Lean el siguiente anuncio y luego preparen una lista de seis actividades interesantes que se pueden hacer en ese puerto mexicano. Algunos grupos van a leer su trabajo.

Modelo: Se ven muchos turistas, se puede...

Acapulco es el paraíso que nunca duerme. Usted siempre encontrará una actividad para pasar unas vacaciones inolvidables. Puede bucear en las aguas de la bahía°, pasear por la avenida Costera, pescar, ver a los clavadistas° de la Quebrada, explorar la ciudad en moto, alquilar un yate, disfrutar de magníficos restaurantes, jugar al golf o al tenis, nadar, practicar el esquí acuático, correr, descansar o bailar en una discoteca hasta el amanecer°.

bay
cliff divers

dawn

13-25. **Juguemos a «¿Cuál es la pregunta?»** ¡Atención! Lean con cuidado las respuestas (1–8) y luego piensen en preguntas lógicas asociadas a esas respuestas. Todas las preguntas deben incluir **se**. Un/a secretario/a escribe las preguntas. El grupo con más preguntas gana. ¡A jugar!

Modelo: en el estadio de los Yankees

¿Dónde se juega béisbol? ¿Dónde se venden perros calientes y cerveza?

1. en la biblioteca

2. en el cine

3. en la estación del tren

4. en el banco

5. en la oficina de correos

6. en el hotel

7. en la playa

8. en el centro de la ciudad

Dicho y hecho

🖳 Conversando

③ **Hablemos de viajes y de transportes.** La clase se divide en dos filas (fila A y fila B), una frente a la otra. Cada pareja habla por tres minutos acerca del tópico nº 1. Luego la primera persona de la fila A va al final de la fila, y esa fila se mueve hacia adelante (*forward*). Las nuevas parejas hablan del tópico nº 2, etc.

Tópicos

1. un viaje que hicieron en coche, tren o autobús
2. un viaje que quieren hacer en el futuro
3. la importancia de conocer lugares/personas diferentes
4. las ventajas de viajar en coche *vs.* en avión: **Se puede...**
5. las ventajas y desventajas de tener coche
6. los problemas con el estacionamiento en su ciudad o universidad

🎧 ¡A escuchar!

¡Venga aquí a comprar su coche! Tres vendedores de coches (A, B y C) presentan anuncios en televisión para promover (*promote*) sus modelos especiales. Aquí tenemos tres personas que desean comprar coches. Escuche los tres anuncios y decida a qué vendedor le va a comprar el coche cada una de las siguientes personas. Indique A, B o C según la letra del vendedor.

Personas

_____ **1.** Marcos: un ejecutivo de posición prestigiosa en su compañía
_____ **2.** Lidia: una persona joven, profesional, enérgica y aventurera
_____ **3.** Paco: un joven de dieciocho años que trabaja pero gana poco dinero

Ahora, escuche los anuncios otra vez. Decida cuál de los coches desea usted comprar y por qué. Mencione dos o tres razones.

4. Marca de coche que desea: ...
5. Por qué lo desea comprar: ...

De mi escritorio

Cartas a los «desesperados». Imagine que usted trabaja para el periódico *El Investigador*. Usted es Victoria y aconseja a los lectores. Escríbale una respuesta a una de las dos siguientes personas, indicando sus reacciones y recomendaciones. Use las expresiones indicadas como guía.

Te recomiendo que…	Debes… con tal que…	En caso de que…
Te sugiero que…	No debes… a menos que…	Mi recomendación final es…

Querida Victoria:

Salgo para la universidad en un mes. No te puedes imaginar cuántas ganas tengo de comprarme una motocicleta. ¡Me encanta volar por las autopistas y sentir el poder del motor en mi cuerpo! ¡Y he ahorrado suficiente dinero para comprármela! Pero mis padres quieren que compre un Volvo usado del año '98. ¡Qué aburrido! Pero dicen que es más seguro. ¿Qué debo hacer?

«El frustrado en Guadalajara»

Querida Victoria:

Me he enamorado de un coche. Es un convertible rojo, con un potente motor de 320 caballos de fuerza. Tiene una velocidad máxima de 250 kilómetros (155 millas) por hora. Mis amigos me recomiendan que no lo compre, porque cuesta 60.000 dólares. Yo tengo cinco tarjetas de crédito y hasta puedo pedir un préstamo° en el banco.

loan

«La soñadora° en Monterrey»

dreamer

Panorama cultural

México: Una historia milenaria[1]

El encanto de la civilización azteca

Durante los últimos años del imperio tolteca, los aztecas se instalaron en una isla del lago de Texcoco y allí fundaron su capital, Tenochtitlán. Comenzaron una expansión desde el valle central de México alrededor de 1325 d. C. En poco tiempo, por su habilidad militar y política, llegaron a ser la civilización más poderosa[2] de Mesoamérica.

Los aztecas eran buenos guerreros[4] y agricultores. La vida familiar era muy importante; adoraban a sus hijos. La educación también tenía mucha importancia; comenzaba en casa y continuaba en la escuela hasta los quince años. Después, los que debían ser sacerdotes[5] o jefes[6] asistían a instituciones especiales y los que debían servir las necesidades y tradiciones del pueblo asistían a otras.

Cuando llegaron los españoles en el siglo XVI, los aztecas, desde Tenochtitlán, controlaban 371 tribus en 33 provincias. Tenochtitlán era una ciudad flotante[3] de unos 250.000 habitantes. ¡Sus impresionantes templos, calles, jardines y palacios estaban construidos sobre un lago! Un complejo sistema de puentes unía la ciudad a tierra firme y los canales facilitaban su defensa. Hoy esta ciudad es la Ciudad de México, ¡la capital actual más antigua de Latinoamérica! Este modelo de la ciudad está en el famoso Museo de Antropología en México, D.F. ¿Cómo son los templos? ¿Dónde está situada la ciudad?

1000 a.C.	1 d.C.		1000 d.C.	1200	1500	1800

1000 a.C.
Durante esta época los olmecas, los toltecas y los mayas viven en el territorio mexicano. Se distinguen por sus avances en las ciencias, las matemáticas y la escritura.

1325 d.C.
El gran imperio azteca se establece en el centro y el sur de México.

1519
Hernán Cortés llega a tierras mexicanas.

1521
Los españoles conquistan el imperio azteca.

1535
Los españoles establecen en México el Virreinato de la Nueva España.

1810
El padre Hidalgo, héroe nacional de México, proclama el «Grito de Dolores», que inicia la rebelión contra España.

[1] *thousands of years old* [2] *powerful*
[3] *floating* [4] *warriors* [5] *priests* [6] *chiefs*

¡Fuego nuevo!

¿Sabía usted que cada 52 años, durante la ceremonia del fuego nuevo, los aztecas quemaban (*burned*) todos sus ídolos, muebles y ropas?

El pueblo azteca era muy religioso y sus ritos requerían sacrificios humanos para honrar a sus dioses[7] y para asegurar[8] la continuación del mundo. Las víctimas eran jóvenes prisioneros de guerra—fuertes y valientes. Los sacrificios eran públicos, con la presencia del emperador, de los músicos, bailarines y sacerdotes que ofrecían el corazón de las víctimas a los dioses. ¿Qué está pasando en la escena representada en este dibujo azteca del siglo XVI? Descríbala. (Palabra útil: sacar *to take out*)

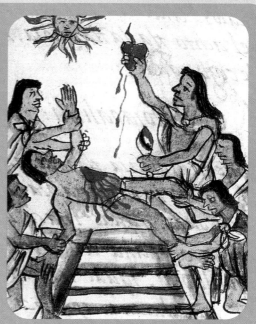

Cada sacrificio era programado de acuerdo con un elaborado sistema de fechas. Por eso, para los aztecas el concepto del tiempo era muy importante. Tenían un calendario ritual y otro solar, llamado la Piedra del Sol. Hoy, la Piedra del Sol está en el Museo de Antropología en México, D.F. ¿Ve usted el sol en este calendario? ¿Qué le impresiona a usted más de este calendario?

[7]*gods* [8]*to ensure*

¿Hablas náhuatl?

La lengua de los aztecas era el náhuall. Aún se habla en algunos estados de México.

1820 1840 1860 1880 1900

1821
México gana su independencia de España.

1848
Después de una guerra desastrosa con los EE.UU., México pierde los territorios del Río Grande (Nevada, California, Utah, Arizona, Nuevo México y parte de Colorado).

1864
Una invasión francesa da origen al imperio del hapsburgo Maximiliano, que dura tres años.

1876
Después de perder las elecciones del 1876, Porfirio Díaz derroca el gobierno y comienza una dictadura que dura 44 años.

1910
Empieza la Revolución Mexicana, que termina en 1917. Uno de los propósitos de la revolución es la redistribución de las tierras entre los pobres.

1917
Se firma la constitución mexicana.

1929
Nace el Partido Nacional Revolucionario, actualmente el Partido Revolucionario Institucional (PRI). Continuará en poder hasta el 2000.

1993
A causa de las malas condiciones en que viven, los Zapatistas (un grupo indígena guerrillero) se rebelan y toman el poder por la fuerza en Chiapas.

1994
Entra en vigor el Tratado de Libre Comercio (NAFTA) entre México, los EE.UU. y Canadá.

2000
La elección del Presidente Vicente Fox marca el fin de más de sesenta años de poder del PRI.

Papá, ¡No lo hago más!

Los niños aztecas rebeldes tenían que dormir en la tierra húmeda.

Cuando Hernán Cortés llegó a México en 1519, el imperio azteca era inmensamente extenso, sofisticado y rico. Sin embargo, en sólo dos años, los españoles conquistaron y controlaron sus territorios. Después de la conquista española, el imperio azteca desapareció, pero su influencia cultural es parte integral de la identidad mexicana moderna. Vea el dibujo del encuentro de dos civilizaciones. ¿Puede usted identificar a Hernán Cortés? ¿Y al emperador de los aztecas, Moctezuma?

¿Qué descubrimos?

1. ¿Cuáles son cuatro culturas importantes del México precolombino?
2. ¿Cuándo llegó Hernán Cortés a México?
3. ¿Qué pasó en 1521? ¿Y en 1821?
4. ¿Cuál fue el resultado de la guerra que ocurrió en 1848?
5. ¿Cómo era Tenochtitlán?
6. ¿Qué aspectos de la vida diaria eran importantes para los aztecas?
7. ¿Quiénes eran las víctimas de los sacrificios a los dioses aztecas?
8. ¿Qué idioma hablaban los aztecas?

Adivinanzas

2. Primero, escriban una breve descripción de cada una de las siguientes referencias. Luego, lean las descripciones, una a la vez, a otra pareja. Ellos/Ellas identifican la referencia. Túrnense.

Tenochtitlán	Moctezuma	PRI
la Piedra del Sol	el padre Hidalgo	NAFTA
el náhuatl	Porfirio Díaz	los Zapatistas
Hernán Cortés	1910	Vicente Fox

Encuentro cultural

Artes literarias

Octavio Paz

Octavio Paz (1914–1998), escritor mexicano y el ganador del Premio Nobel de Literatura en 1990, es conocido mundialmente por sus poemas y ensayos. Desde joven dividió su actividad intelectual entre la literatura y la historia. Sus poemas muestran la influencia de estas dos disciplinas. Con sus escritos, Paz intentó combatir la injusticia social y presentar una imagen de México que integraba la gloria del pasado azteca y maya. Sus temas preferidos eran la sociedad, la naturaleza, la historia, el amor, la vida y la muerte.

Serpiente[1] labrada[2] sobre un muro[3]

El muro al sol respira, vibra, ondula[4],

trozo[5] de cielo vivo y tatuado:

el hombre bebe sol, es agua, es tierra.

Y sobre tanta vida la serpiente

que lleva una cabeza entre las fauces[6]:

los dioses beben sangre, comen hombres.

Preguntas

1. ¿Qué similitudes hay entre el muro y la serpiente?
2. ¿Qué frases se refieren al sacrificio humano?
3. ¿Qué frases indican que «el hombre» es parte de la naturaleza?
4. ¿Quiénes construyeron el muro que describe Paz?
5. ¿Dónde piensa usted que está el muro?

READING STRATEGY

Interpreting Poetry

1. Quickly skim the poem. As you read, think about the words and phrases that can help you classify the poem as belonging to specific themes: nature, life and death, history.
2. Personification is a literary technique that gives human characteristics to inanimate objects. On your second, more detailed reading, try to find examples of personification in the poem.

[1] *Quetzalcoatl, the feathered serpent, one of the principal deities of the ancient peoples of Mexico* [2] *carved* [3] *wall* [4] *ondulates* [5] *piece* [6] *jaws*

Adjetivos

cómodo/a
desinflado/a
gratis
seguro/a

Adverbios y frases adverbiales

a la derecha
a la izquierda
demasiado
derecho/ recto
despacio

Conjunciones

a menos (de) que
con tal (de) que
en caso de que
para que

Expresiones útiles

¡Auxilio!
¡Ay de mí!
¡Caramba!
¡Claro!/ ¡Por supuesto!
Lo siento mucho.
¡Qué barbaridad!
¡Qué lástima!
¡Qué lío!
¡Qué suerte!
¡Socorro!

Sustantivos

En la carretera, en el camino

el accidente
el autobús
el camino
el camión
la carretera/ la autopista
el choque
la cuadra

la esquina
la estación de autobuses
la estación de servicio/ la gasolinera
el estacionamiento
el kilómetro
la moto(cicleta)
la mujer policía
la multa
el policía
el puente
el semáforo
el tráfico/ el tránsito
la velocidad

El automóvil

el conductor
la conductora
los frenos
la gasolina
la licencia de conducir
la llanta
el motor
el parabrisas
el taller mecánico
el tanque

En la estación del ferrocarril

el andén
los aseos/ el servicio
el boleto/ billete
  de ida/ sencillo
  de ida y vuelta
  de primera/ segunda clase
el maletero
la taquilla
el tren

Otras palabras útiles

la agencia de viajes
el aire
el tatuaje

Verbos y expresiones verbales

chocar
conducir
continuar
cruzar
doblar
estacionar
funcionar
llenar
parar
reparar
revisar
seguir (i, i)

afinar el motor
echar gasolina
hacer reservaciones/reservas
llenar el tanque
perder (ie) el tren
tener cuidado

Autoprueba y repaso

I. *Nosotros* **(Let's) commands.** ¿Hacerlo o no hacerlo? Dé la forma afirmativa y la negativa de los siguientes mandatos.

1. levantarnos a las diez
2. salir para el centro
3. ir por la ruta más directa
4. parar en el supermercado
5. cruzar el nuevo puente
6. seguir recto por cuatro cuadras
7. explorar el sector histórico de la ciudad

II. The subjunctive with expressions of condition or purpose. Termine las respuestas.

> **Modelo:** ¿Para qué llamas a tus padres tanto?
> Los llamo para que **no se preocupen por mí.**

1. ¿No ha llamado Marta todavía? No, voy a quedarme aquí en caso de que…
2. ¿José no sabe mi dirección? No, voy a mandársela para que (él)…
3. ¿Ya escribiste la carta? No, voy a escribirla en español con tal que (tú)…
4. ¿Puedo alquilar un coche? Por supuesto, con tal que…
5. ¿Vas a salir esta noche? Sí, pienso salir a menos que…

III. The imperfect subjunctive. Indique los deseos de las personas.

> **Modelo:** ¿Qué quería mamá que hiciera yo?
> sacar la basura
> **Quería que sacara la basura.**

1. ¿Qué quería Mamá que hiciera yo?
   a. limpiar mi cuarto
   b. ir al supermercado
   c. llamar a mis abuelos
   d. organizar mi clóset

2. ¿Qué nos sugirió la profesora de español?
   a. escribir los ejercicios del manual
   b. llegar a clase a tiempo
   c. hacer la tarea con cuidado
   d. participar en clase

3. ¿Qué esperaban los abuelos?
   a. llamarlos para Navidad
   b. escribirles un mensaje electrónico
   c. visitarlos en verano
   d. invitarlos para la graduación

IV. The impersonal *se*. Termine las siguientes oraciones.

> **Modelo:** En México _se habla_ español.

1. En Acapulco _____ el buceo submarino.
2. En un avión no _____ fumar.
3. En una biblioteca no _____ en voz alta.
4. Para el día de Acción de Gracias (*Thanksgiving*) _____ pavo (*turkey*).
5. Durante la semana de exámenes finales _____ mucho.

V. General review. Conteste con oraciones completas.

1. Cuando usted va a una gasolinera, ¿qué hace primero? ¿Y después?
2. ¿Qué dice usted cuando está en el centro de la ciudad de Nueva York y su coche no funciona? (¡…!)
3. ¿Ha hecho usted un viaje en tren o en autobús? (¿Cuándo?) (¿Adónde?)
4. ¿Le gusta a usted la idea de viajar en tren o en autobús? ¿Por qué?
5. ¿Qué cosas se pueden hacer durante un viaje en tren?
6. Cuando usted era niño/a, ¿hacía viajes en carro con su familia? (¿Adónde iban?)
7. Cuando usted era más joven, ¿qué quería que sus padres/maestros/amigos hicieran para mejorar su vida?

Answers to the *Autoprueba y repaso* are found in **Apéndice 2.**

El mundo en las noticias

Goals for communication

- To talk about major issues in today's global society
- To talk about pending actions
- To talk about what might or would happen
- To hypothesize
- To express hopes and wishes

NOTICIERO**60**

Así se dice

El mundo en las noticias

4. El empleo/ el desempleo
5. tener éxito
6. la jefa
7. la solicitud
8. solicitar
9. el gerente
10. la entrevista
23. El trabajo voluntario
PROYECTO HÁBITAT
24. el voluntario, la voluntaria
25. construir
11. La pobreza
12. los desamparados
1. el noticiero
13. sufrir
14. el hambre
2. la reportera
26. dar de comer
15. La sobrepoblación
27. el tutor
3. informar/ reportar
16. El crimen
21. La drogadicción
18. la víctima
17. el delincuente
19. robar
22. las drogas
20. la violencia

29. El terrorismo

48. La exploración del espacio

31. La guerra

32. la bomba

30. la explosión

49. la nave espacial

28. el reportero

46. Las curas

el cáncer 47. el SIDA el SARS

33. La política mundial

43. La igualdad

44. JUSTICIA

45. Libertad

34. los/las líderes

37. El gobierno

38. la candidata, el candidato

35. el acuerdo de paz

39. las elecciones

VOTE Murillo   VOTE Rojas

36. los derechos humanos

40. apoyar

42. votar (por)

41. los ciudadanos

1. newscast
2. reporter (f.)
3. to inform, to report
4. employment/unemployment
5. to be successful
6. boss (f.); **el jefe** (m.)
7. application
8. to apply (for a job)
9. manager (m.); **la gerente** (f.)
10. interview
11. poverty
12. the homeless
13. to suffer
14. hunger
15. overpopulation
16. crime
17. delinquent, offender, criminal
18. victim (m./f.)
19. to rob
20. violence
21. drug addiction
22. drugs
23. volunteerism
24. volunteer
25. to construct, to build
26. to feed
27. tutor (m.); **la tutora** (f.)
28. reporter (m.)
29. terrorism
30. explosion
31. war
32. bomb
33. world politics
34. leaders
35. peace accord; **la paz** peace
36. human rights
37. government
38. candidate
39. elections
40. to support (a candidate/cause)
41. citizens
42. to vote (for)
43. equality
44. justice
45. freedom (f.)
46. cures
47. AIDS
48. (outer) space exploration
49. spaceship

Práctica y comunicación

14-1 **Noticias actuales.** Según los dibujos de las páginas 474–475, describan lo que ocurre en cada pantalla. Usen las palabras del vocabulario.

14-2. **Preguntas para conversar.** Contesten las preguntas.

1. ¿Te gustaría ser reportero/a? ¿Por qué?
2. ¿Ves regularmente las noticias? ¿Estás al tanto (*Are you informed*) de lo que pasa en el mundo? ¿Qué noticiero ves?
3. Donde vives, ¿hay personas que sufren de hambre o de pobreza? Explica. ¿Y de desempleo? ¿Hay mucho crimen? Explica.
4. ¿En qué parte de este país hay muchos desamparados? En tu opinión, ¿por qué hay tantos desamparados en este país?
5. En la ciudad donde vive tu familia o en tu universidad, ¿hay un problema de drogas o de alcoholismo? Explica.
6. El terrorismo se ha convertido en un problema mundial. ¿Estamos haciendo lo suficiente para erradicarlo? ¿Qué más podemos hacer para mejorar la situación?
7. Cuando busques empleo en el futuro, ¿piensas que podrás encontrarlo fácilmente? ¿Qué tipo de empleo vas a buscar? ¿Cuánto quieres ganar?
8. ¿Has tenido entrevistas de empleo? ¿Para qué trabajo?
9. ¿Tienes fe (*faith*) en los líderes de este país? Explica. ¿Crees que haya justicia e igualdad para todos en este país? Explica. ¿Qué países, en tu opinión, no respetan (o antes, no respetaban) los derechos humanos?
10. ¿Has votado en alguna elección? (¿Por quién votaste?) ¿Crees que votar debe ser obligatorio para todos los ciudadanos?
11. ¿Haces o has hecho trabajo voluntario? (¿En qué tipo de proyecto participaste?)

¡Qué dilema!
Durante tu primer día en el pueblecito donde vas a trabajar como voluntario/a, el líder del grupo te muestra la choza (hut) en la que vas a vivir, el retrete (outhouse),… Acostumbrado/a a todo confort moderno, estás a punto de abandonar el proyecto.Un/a compañero/a trata de convencerte de que te debes quedar.
TÚ: **¡No hay ni baño!**
COMPAÑERO/A: **Sí, pero…**

cuatrocientos setenta y seis   **Capítulo 14**

Sus opiniones sobre los problemas mundiales

	Sí	No
¿Cree usted que sea posible...		
● evitar las guerras/ mantener la paz?	❏	❏
● **eliminar**[1] parte de la pobreza y el hambre del mundo?	❏	❏
● eliminar el **prejuicio**[2] y la **discriminación**[3]?	❏	❏
● prevenir el **narcotráfico**[4] y la drogadicción?	❏	❏
● controlar la sobrepoblación del mundo?	❏	❏
¿Está usted a favor de[5] **o en contra de**[6]...		
● el derecho a llevar armas?	❏	❏
● el derecho de la mujer a **escoger**[7]* el **aborto**[8]?	❏	❏
● la **pena de muerte**[9]?	❏	❏
● **legalizar**[10] la marijuana?	❏	❏
● darles amnistía a los inmigrantes indocumentados?	❏	❏
● expulsar a los que crucen la **frontera**[11] ilegalmente?	❏	❏
¿Cree usted que debemos...		
● eliminar las **leyes**[12] que **prohiben**[13] el consumo de alcohol para los menores de 21 años?	❏	❏
● gastar más para la exploración del espacio?	❏	❏
... para ayudar a los desamparados?	❏	❏
... para encontrar curas para el cáncer y el SIDA?	❏	❏
● **luchar por**[14] los derechos humanos y la libertad de todos?	❏	❏

(1) to eliminate (2) prejudice (3) discrimination (4) drug trafficking (5) Are you in favor of . . . ?;
Estar a favor de... *to be in favor of (6) against (7) to choose (8) abortion (9) death penalty*
(10) to legalize (11) border (12) laws (13) forbid; **prohibir** *to forbid (14) to fight for*

④ **14-3.** **Así pensamos.** Comparen sus respuestas a las preguntas del cuestionario anterior y defiendan sus opiniones. Un secretario/a debe tomar apuntes. Algunos grupos van a presentar sus ideas a la clase.

Modelo: Algunos/ La mayoría/ Todos estamos a favor de/ en contra de... porque...

---

* **Escoger** changes the **g** to **j** to maintain the same pronunciation in the **yo** form of the present indicative (**escojo**) and in all forms of the present subjunctive (**escoja, escojas, escoja, escojamos, escojáis, escojan**).

14-4. Organizaciones. ¿Qué causas apoyan las siguientes organizaciones? Combine la organización con la causa correspondiente.

Organización	Causa
1. Hábitat para la Humanidad	**a.** Lucha por los derechos humanos.
2. Asociación Americana contra el Cáncer	**b.** Protege los mares, los animales en peligro de extinción, el medio ambiente, etc.
3. Amnistía Internacional	**c.** Ayuda a los que sufren en catástrofes naturales, en guerras, etc.
4. ASPCA	**d.** Construye[1] viviendas para los pobres y los desamparados.
5. UNICEF	**e.** Ayuda a los pobres y a los desamparados.
6. Green Peace	**f.** Defiende los derechos de los animales.
7. El Ejército (*Army*) de Salvación	**g.** Busca curas para una enfermedad muy grave.
8. La Cruz Roja	**h.** Defiende los derechos de los niños por todo el mundo.

② 14-5. Los ataques terroristas del 11 de septiembre. Lean sobre el terrorismo y luego contesten las preguntas.

Los ataques terroristas del 11 de septiembre a las Torres Gemelas en Nueva York y al Pentágono en Washington, D.C., cambiaron el curso del mundo y nuestra forma de actuar y de vivir. Esos actos evidenciaron los rasgos° más crueles de la humanidad: el odio°, el uso de principios religiosos como una falsa excusa y la violación de los derechos humanos. También evidenciaron los sentimientos más altruistas y puros de los humanos. Hay incontables ejemplos de heroísmo: policías, bomberos°, ciudadanos y hasta perros que ofrecieron sus vidas intentando rescatar° las de otros.

traits

hatred

firemen
to rescue

1. ¿Dónde y cómo te enteraste de los ataques terroristas del 11 de septiembre?

2. ¿Cuál fue tu reacción inicial? ¿Duda, incredibilidad, miedo, tristeza?

3. ¿Conoces alguna historia de heroísmo asociada con este ataque o con otra catástrofe?

---

[1] The present indicative of **construir** is: construyo, construyes, construye, construimos, construís, construyen.

Escenas

Una entrevista

2 *Irene Piedras, reportera y presentadora° del noticiero «Verdad», entrevista al alcalde° de Buenavista unos días antes de las elecciones.*

    anchorwoman, host
    mayor

IRENE: Buenas tardes, Sr. Alcalde. Gracias por estar con nosotros hoy. Me gustaría que nos hablara de sus programas para luchar contra la drogadicción y el narcotráfico.

ALCALDE: Con mucho gusto. Bajo mi dirección hemos contratado° más policías y tenemos el apoyo de los ciudadanos de Buenavista para librar nuestra bella ciudad de tan grave problema.

    hemos... *we have hired*

IRENE: Sin embargo, Sr. Alcalde, ayer nuestro equipo filmó a traficantes de drogas frente a la alcaldía°. ¿Qué tiene que decir al respecto°?

    mayor's office / **al...** *about*

ALCALDE: Les aseguro° a los votantes que los responsables serán detenidos y castigados°.

    the matter / I assure
    punished

IRENE: Bueno, pasando a otro tema. Según las estadísticas que tengo, el crimen ha aumentado en los últimos años, la tasa° de desempleo ha subido, los desamparados sufren de hambre en nuestras calles y varias empresas y compañías han abandonado nuestra ciudad.

    rate

ALCALDE: Pues sí, es cierto. Buenavista está atravesando un momento difícil, pero la situación era peor antes de mi llegada a la alcaldía.

IRENE: ¿Hay algo más que quisiera decirles a los televidentes?

ALCALDE: Que voten mañana por mí, ¡el mejor de todos los candidatos!

IRENE: Bueno, ya lo oyeron de boca del Sr. Alcalde. Gracias por sus palabras y ¡buena suerte!

¿Qué pasa?

1. ¿Quién es Irene Piedras?
2. ¿A quién entrevista?
3. Según el alcalde, ¿que ha hecho para luchar contra la drogadicción?
4. ¿Qué le contesta la presentadora del noticiero?
5. ¿Qué problemas tiene Buenavista según las estadísticas?
6. ¿Cuál es la respuesta del alcalde?
7. Finalmente, ¿qué les pide el alcalde a los ciudadanos de Buenavista?

"Una Vida Sin Drogas Es Una Vida Feliz"

HISPANIC YELLOW PAGES™
a division of Vega & Associates

¿Sabías que nueve de cada diez drogadictos en centros de rehabilitación no se recuperan? ¿Conoces a personas que usen drogas? ¿Cómo y por qué comienzan a usarlas? ¿Es el alcohol también una droga? ¿Causa adicción?

Estructuras

1 **Talking about pending actions: The subjunctive with time expressions**

Cuando termines la lección, podemos jugar al tenis.

The subjunctive is used after the following conjunctions of time only when an action has not yet occurred. In contrast, if the action is completed or habitual, the indicative is used.

cuando	*when*	hasta que	*until*
antes de que²	*before*	tan pronto como	*as soon as*
después de que	*after*		

action pending, yet to occur ➜ subjunctive

Cuando llegue al orfanato, te llamaré.
When I arrive at the orphanage, I'll call you.

Compraré las medicinas **antes de que tú llegues.**
I will buy the medications before you arrive.

Los voluntarios saldrán **después de que terminen** el trabajo.
The volunteers will leave after they finish their work.

Me quedaré allí **hasta que** el director me **llame.**
I will stay there until the director calls me.

Tan pronto como reciba la llamada, recogeré a los niños.
As soon as I receive the call, I will pick up the children.

completed or habitual action ➜ indicative

Mi amigo me llamó **cuando llegó** al orfanato.
My friend called me when he arrived at the orphanage. (completed)

Mi amigo siempre me llama **cuando llega** a la ciudad.
My friend always calls me when he arrives in town. (habitual)

---

² The conjunction **antes de que**, because it signals an action that has not yet occurred, is always followed by the subjunctive.

When there is no change of subject, the conjunctions **antes de que**, **después de que**, and **hasta que** usually become **antes de** + *infinitive*, **después de** + *infinitive*, and **hasta** + *infinitive*.

> change of subject → subjunctive   no change of subject → infinitive

Lo terminaremos **antes de que salgas**.

Lo terminaremos **antes de salir**.

Tomaremos la decisión **después de que hagas** la llamada.

Tomaremos la decisión **después de hacer** la llamada.

Nos quedaremos aquí **hasta que lo termines**.

Nos quedaremos aquí **hasta terminar**lo.

Práctica y comunicación

14-6. **Proyecciones hacia el futuro.** Indique las opciones que mejor correspondan a sus planes. Luego, léaselas a un/a compañero/a de clase.

1. Antes de que termine este año escolar...
- ❒ hablaré con mis profesores de mis notas.
- ❒ estudiaré mucho y completaré mis trabajos escritos.
- ❒ saldré con todos mis amigos/as.
- ❒ iré a...
- ❒ ...

2. Después de que termine este año escolar...
- ❒ trabajaré.
- ❒ haré un viaje a...
- ❒ descansaré.
- ❒ volveré a casa.
- ❒ dejaré de fumar/ comer...
- ❒ me pondré a dieta.
- ❒ ...

3. Tan pronto como me gradúe...
- ❒ buscaré empleo.
- ❒ haré estudios de posgrado.
- ❒ me mudaré a...
- ❒ compraré un coche nuevo.
- ❒ ganaré mucho dinero
- ❒ ...

4. En el futuro, ...
- ❒ viajaré a Europa/ Sudamérica/...
- ❒ visitaré a todos mis parientes.
- ❒ seré voluntario/a.
- ❒ me casaré...
- ❒ ...

② **14-7.** **¿Cuándo saldrán?** Muy pronto, los universitarios se van de viaje en carro a hacer trabajo voluntario en Baja California. Indiquen cuándo saldrán. Sigan el modelo.

> **Modelo:** 1. Saldrán tan pronto como Javier termine el proyecto de química.

1. Javier / terminar el proyecto de…

2. Alfonso / devolver…

3. Esteban / reparar…

4. Rubén / llenar…

5. Carmen y Linda / comprar…

6. Pepita e Inés / hacer…

Ahora, imaginen que los estudiantes ya salieron. Cambien cada situación al tiempo pasado: **Salieron tan pronto como Javier terminó el proyecto de química.**

③ **14-8.** **¿Cuándo pasará?** Completen las oraciones con varias posibilidades según la situación.

1. Usted, un/a tutor/a, habla con los niños de una escuela primaria:
   Podemos salir a jugar después de que ustedes…
2. Usted habla con sus compañeros de apartamento, que son un poco irresponsables:
   No podemos ir a… antes de que ustedes…
3. El novio habla con la novia:
   Me casaré contigo cuando…
4. La madre habla con el hijo de siete años:
   Saldremos tan pronto como (tú)…
5. El mecánico del taller habla con el dueño del coche:
   No debe salir de viaje hasta que…

Noticias culturales

El servicio voluntario y el activismo estudiantil

En los países hispanos, los jóvenes forman organizaciones y participan activamente en éstas para servir al país en múltiples formas. Los universitarios, por ejemplo, encuentran en el trabajo voluntario y en el activismo excelentes oportunidades para educarse y contribuir al desarrollo° de la nación.

development

Algunos estudiantes voluntarios se dedican a la investigación y a la promoción del patrimonio cultural o al cuidado del medio ambiente. Otros se ocupan de gran parte de los programas de alfabetización en las zonas rurales. De igual importancia son los programas de salud y planificación familiar. Aunque los participantes son generalmente universitarios de las facultades de medicina o ciencias sociales, es común encontrar estudiantes de otras disciplinas y hasta° alumnos de escuelas secundarias.

even

La expresión política es también parte de la vida estudiantil. Los universitarios tienden a defender ideas más izquierdistas que las de los gobiernos y no dudan en expresarlas públicamente en manifestaciones callejeras. Es frecuente ver grupos protestando contra el gobierno, la contaminación ambiental, las condiciones educativas en las universidades o el aumento del costo de la matrícula. Las huelgas° asociadas con estas protestas estudiantiles frecuentemente interrumpen las clases.

strikes

¿Qué recuerda?

1. ¿Cuáles son algunos ejemplos de las actividades de los estudiantes voluntarios hispanos?
2. ¿Quiénes participan en los programas de salud y planificación familiar?
3. ¿Contra qué protestan los estudiantes en las universidades hispanas?

Conexiones y contrastes

1. ¿Participa usted en una organización de voluntarios? ¿A qué tipo de actividades se dedica su organización?
2. ¿Es importante el voluntarismo en su país? ¿Por qué sí o no?
3. ¿Ha participado usted en alguna manifestación estudiantil? ¿Contra qué protestaba?
4. ¿Contra qué protestarían típicamente los estudiantes en una universidad como la suya?

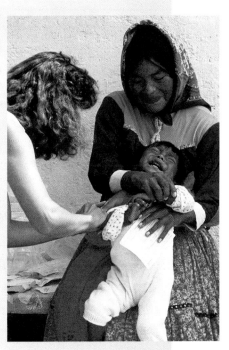

El voluntarismo en acción.

2 Talking about what would happen: The conditional tense

Mi candidata dice que apoyaría la educación.

Mi candidato dice que protegería el medio ambiente.

The conditional tells what *would* potentially happen in certain circumstances. Example: I *would*[3] go to South America (*if I had the money*). The conditional of all regular **-ar**, **-er**, and **-ir** verbs is formed by adding the following endings to the *entire infinitive.* Note that the conditional endings are identical to the imperfect tense endings of **-er** and **-ir** verbs.

	llam**ar**	volv**er**	**ir**
(yo)	llamar**ía**	volver**ía**	ir**ía**
(tú)	llamar**ías**	volver**ías**	ir**ías**
(Ud., él, ella)	llamar**ía**	volver**ía**	ir**ía**
(nosotros/as)	llamar**íamos**	volver**íamos**	ir**íamos**
(vosotros/as)	llamar**íais**	volver**íais**	ir**íais**
(Uds., ellos, ellas)	llamar**ían**	volver**ían**	ir**ían**

—¿**Solicitarías** empleo en esa compañía?
   ***Would** you **seek** a job with that company?*

—No, yo **buscaría** empleo en otra.
   *No, I **would look for** a job in another one.*

---

[3] When *would* implies *used to* (*habitual past action*), the imperfect is used: *Every summer, I would go to South America.* **Cada verano, iba a Sudamérica.**

The following verbs add regular conditional endings to irregular stems (not to the infinitive). The irregular stems for both the conditional and the future are identical.

Infinitivo	Raíz	Formas del condicional
hacer	har-	**haría, harías, haría, haríamos, haríais, harían**
poder	podr-	**podría, podrías,…**
poner	pondr-	**pondría, pondrías,…**
querer	querr-	**querría, querrías,…**
saber	sabr-	**sabría, sabrías,…**
tener	tendr-	**tendría, tendrías,…**
decir	dir-	**diría, dirías,…**
salir	saldr-	**saldría, saldrías,…**
venir	vendr-	**vendría, vendrías,…**

—¿**Podrías** ayudarnos?   *Would you be able to help us?*
—Ella dijo que lo **haría**.   *She said that she would do it.*

● The conditional of **hay** (*there is, there are*) is **habría** (*there would be*).
  Dijo que no **habría** ningún problema.   *He said that there would be no problem.*

Práctica y comunicación

 14-9. **¿Lo harías o no?** Háganse las siguientes preguntas. Luego, compartan información interesante con la clase.

1. ¿Votarías por una mujer para la presidencia del país?
2. ¿Eliminarías la pena de muerte?
3. ¿Lucharías por la legalización de la marijuana?
4. ¿Cambiarías la edad legal para consumir bebidas alcohólicas? ¿Y para obtener una licencia de conducir?
5. ¿Apoyarías la explotación del petróleo en los parques nacionales?
6. ¿Trabajarías como voluntario/a en un pueblo remoto sin electricidad y otros conforts?
7. ¿Adoptarías un/a bebé de otro país?
8. ¿Viajarías a otro planeta en una nave espacial?

Y ahora,… algunas locuras

9. ¿Saltarías en paracaídas (*parachute*) de un avión?
10. ¿Comerías insectos para no morirte de hambre?
11. ¿Nadarías en un río con pirañas?
12. ¿Harías un salto *bungee* de un puente?

14-10. ¿Qué tienen que decir sobre el récord?

(2) **14-10.** **¿Qué tienen que decir sobre el récord?** Lean la información de acuerdo con el *Guinness Book of World Records* y luego contesten las preguntas. Algunos estudiantes van a ofrecer sus predicciones a la clase.

1. Belinda Soszy de Australia subió los 1576 escalones (*steps*) del edificio Empire State en Nueva York en 12 minutos y 19 segundos en 1966. ¿Cuántos escalones subirían ustedes en el mismo tiempo? Den sus razones.

2. John Evans balanceó 96 cajones para leche (*milk crates*) sobre su cabeza el 6 de abril del año 2001. ¿Cuántos cajones podrían ustedes balancear?

3. Hossein Rezazadeh de Irán levantó 212.5 kilos (468.5 libras) en los Juegos Olímpicos de Sydney el 26 de septiembre del año 2000. ¿Cuántos kilos/libras levantarían ustedes? ¿Por qué creen eso?

4. Kimi Puntillo de los EE.UU. completó un maratón en cada uno de los continentes en 700 días, entre el 4 de noviembre de 1966 y el 4 de octubre de 1998. Comenzó en Nueva York y terminó en Argentina. ¿Participarían ustedes en un maratón? ¿Cuánto tiempo les tomaría a ustedes correr un maratón?

5. Fyona Campbell de Inglaterra caminó 30.231 kilómetros (18.840 millas) por 20 países y cuatro continentes, entre el 16 de agosto de 1983 y el 14 de octubre de 1994. Es decir, le tomó 11 años. ¿Cuánta distancia estarían ustedes dispuestos a caminar? ¿Por dónde y por cuánto tiempo?

6. ¿Qué podrían hacer ustedes para alcanzar un récord mundial?

(4) **14-11.** **Soluciones.** ¿Qué harían ustedes para empezar a resolver los problemas del mundo? Escriban una o dos soluciones que ustedes proponen para cada categoría. Un/a secretario/a escribe las ideas. Usen el *condicional*. Algunos grupos van a leer sus soluciones a la clase.

Categorías

1. el desempleo
2. el hambre y la pobreza
3. el crimen
4. la drogadicción
5. las enfermedades graves
6. la discriminación

3 Hypothesizing: *If* clauses

Si pudiera, eliminaría toda la pobreza del mundo.

The past subjunctive is used to express a situation that is hypothetical, i.e., contrary-to-fact or very unlikely to occur. The conditional is used to express the result, i.e., what *would occur* as a consequence. These elements can appear in either order (hypothetical situation first or last).

HINT | What you need to know about *if* clauses:

1. *Never* use the present subjunctive in a **si** (*if*) clause.

2. Use a past subjunctive in the **si** clause if the result clause says *would* (do something).

3. *Always* use a past subjunctive after **como si** (*as if*).

> **si** + *imperfect subjunctive* + *conditional*
> or
> *conditional* + **si** + *imperfect subjunctive*

Si **tuviera** el dinero, se lo **donaría** a los pobres.

*If I **had** the money, I **would donate** it to the poor.*

Hablaría con el presidente si él **estuviera** aquí.

*I **would speak** with the president if he **were** here.*

When an *if* clause poses a situation that is possible or likely to occur (not obviously contrary-to-fact or hypothetical), the *if* clause is in the present indicative and the result is in the present indicative or future tense.

> **si** + *present indicative* + *present/future*

Si **tengo** tiempo, **voy/iré**.

*If I **have** time, I go/I'll go.*

Práctica y comunicación

2 **14-12.** **¿Qué harías tú?** Háganse las preguntas y contéstenlas según su punto de vista.

1. Si hubiera una manifestación en Washington en contra del uso de las armas nucleares, ¿participarías o no? ¿Por qué?
2. Si hubiera una manifestación en la universidad que propusiera eliminar las «fraternidades» y «sororidades», ¿participarías o no? ¿Por qué?
3. Si un candidato político o una candidata política apoyara el derecho de la mujer a escoger el aborto, ¿votarías por él/ella o no? ¿Por qué?
4. Si un partido político decidiera apoyar a una compañía poderosa que destruye el medio ambiente pero que genera dinero, ¿lo apoyarías o no? ¿Por qué?
5. Si hubiera otra guerra ahora como la de Afganistán o la de Irak, ¿participarías o no? ¿Por qué?
6. Si el presidente de la universidad recomendara fines de semana de tres días, ¿estarías a favor o en contra de la idea? ¿Por qué?
7. Si tus amigos decidieran tomar bebidas alcohólicas ilegalmente y luego manejar, ¿irías con ellos o no? ¿Por qué?

4 **14-13.** **Aventuras por el mundo hispano.** Si ustedes pudieran ir a los lugares indicados, ¿qué cosas llevarían, según el clima, etc.? ¿Y qué harían ustedes allí? Al final, algunos grupos van a presentar sus ideas a la clase.

> **Modelo:** Si pudiéramos ir a Panamá, **llevaríamos ropa de verano, sandalias,..., visitaríamos el canal,...**

1. Si pudiéramos ir a Puerto Rico para las vacaciones de primavera,...
2. Si pudiéramos ir a la región andina de Chile o Argentina en el invierno,...
3. Si pudiéramos ir a Costa Rica por un semestre,...
4. Si pudiéramos pasar un año en España,...

14-14. **Emociones.** ¿Por qué se siente así? Escriba las razones.

> **Modelo:** Estaría muy triste **si mi perrita se muriera.**

1. Estaría muy preocupado/a si...
2. Estaría muy enojado/a si...
3. Estaría muy sorprendido/a (*surprised*) si...
4. Estaría muy contento/a si...

Lea algunas de sus conclusiones a la clase.

14-15. La imaginación. Observe los dibujos e indique lo que usted haría en esas circunstancias. Sea creativo/a.

Si / estar…

> **Modelo:** Si estuviera en la selva, observaría la naturaleza, me escaparía de las serpientes, exploraría el río,…

1. Si / ser…

2. Si / ser…

3. Si / vivir…

4. Si / vivir en una casa embrujada…

5. Si / estar en la prisión...

6. Si / ver un extraterrestre…

7. Si / ser…

8. Si / ser invisible…

14-16. Una cadena (*chain*) de posibilidades. Cada grupo escoge uno de los siguientes temas. En cinco minutos, escriban una cadena muy larga según el modelo. Después lean sus «creaciones» a la clase.

> **Modelo:** Si tuviera mil dólares, **haría un viaje.**
> **Si hiciera un viaje, iría a México.**
> **Si fuera a México, comería muchas tortillas.**
> **Si comiera muchas tortillas,...**

1. Si tuviera un coche nuevo,…

2. Si tuviera tiempo,…

3. Si tuviera novio/a,…

4. Si no estuviera aquí,…

5. Si me quedara sólo un año de vida,…

14-17. **En la Casa Blanca.** Escriba cinco oraciones indicando lo que usted haría si fuera presidente o presidenta de este país. Lea sus oraciones a un/a compañero/a de clase o a la clase.

④ 14-18. **Conversaciones.** Conversen acerca de los siguientes temas. Algunos estudiantes van a presentar sus ideas a la clase.

1. Si ganaras la lotería, ¿cómo cambiaría tu vida?
2. Si hubiera un incendio (*fire*) en tu casa y tuvieras cinco minutos para recoger cinco cosas, ¿qué recogerías? ¿Por qué?
3. Si pudieras vivir en cualquier país del mundo, ¿dónde vivirías? ¿Por qué?
4. Si pudieras conocer a cualquier personaje de la historia, ¿a quién te gustaría conocer? ¿Por qué?

② 14-19. **«Nuestros Pequeños Hermanos».** Lean sobre esta organización y luego completen las oraciones.

Elisabet, voluntaria del orfanato «NPH» en Honduras, es amiga de Nahum. ¿Participa usted en trabajo voluntario?

«Nuestros Pequeños Hermanos» es una organización que sirve a niños y jóvenes que viven en circunstancias difíciles en América Latina y el Caribe. Su misión es darles a los desamparados protección, comida, ropa, cuidados médicos y educación. Ofrece[4] a los huérfanos pobres una solución en un ambiente de familia y permite a las familias con gran número de hermanos permanecer juntos. Los voluntarios de NPH dan clases de inglés, ayudan a los niños con la tarea, les leen cuentos a los pequeños, juegan con los niños durante las horas de recreo, a veces ayudan a preparar la comida, y —lo más importante— les dan a los niños mucho cariño y amor. ¿Desea usted ser voluntario/a? Busque más información: www.nphhonduras.org y www.nphamigos.org

1. Me parece muy bueno que... y que...
2. Es fenomenal que... y que...
3. Si fuera voluntario/a en NPH, (yo)...., ..., ...

---

[4] The present indicative **yo** form of **ofrecer** (*to offer*) is **ofrezco**; consequently the present subjunctive is **ofrezca, ofrezcas, ofrezca, ofrezcamos, ofrezcáis, ofrezcan**.

4 Expressing hopes and wishes: The imperfect subjunctive with *ojalá*

¡Ojalá que pudiera viajar a la luna!

In **Chapter 10** you learned that **ojalá** or **ojalá que** is always followed by the subjunctive, since it expresses hope or desire.

- **Ojalá** and **ojalá que** followed by the present subjunctive indicate that there is a possibility the situation will occur.

Present subjunctive

Ojalá (que) mi candidato **gane** la elección.

I hope that my candidate wins the election.

- Followed by the imperfect subjunctive, they indicate that the situation is not likely to occur or is impossible.

Imperfect subjunctive

Ojalá (que) **pudiéramos** hacer el viaje a Washington.

I wish (If only) we could take the trip to Washington (but we can't).

Práctica y comunicación

14-20. **En un mundo ideal...** Ustedes desean que el mundo cambie, pero saben que es difícil. Indiquen sus deseos usando **Ojalá que (no) hubiera...**

> **Modelo:** desempleo
> **Ojalá que no hubiera desempleo en el mundo.**

1. pobreza

2. igualdad y justicia para todos

3. problemas económicos

4. políticos honestos

5. drogadicción

6. discriminación

7. epidemia del SIDA

8. paz entre las naciones

② **14-21 Sueños imposibles.** Completen cada oración con varias opciones. Luego compartan algunas de sus ideas con la clase.

1. Ojalá que en este mundo (no) tuviéramos...

2. Ojalá que en este mundo pudiéramos...

⑤ **14-22 Un noticiero.** Cada estudiante del grupo es reportero/a y presenta una de las cinco noticias en voz alta. Después de cada noticia, el grupo da sus reacciones. Usen las siguientes expresiones.

> Ojalá que...   Una solución para el problema de... sería...
>
> Es muy bueno que...   Es trágico que... porque...

Mortalidad infantil y juvenil

Cuenca, Ecuador—La Organización Mundial de Salud (OMS) declara que seis enfermedades infecciosas (SIDA, tuberculosis, malaria, rubeola, diarrea e infecciones de las vías respiratorias) son responsables del 90% de las muertes de los niños del mundo.

Niños trabajadores

Cuenca, Ecuador—La Organización Internacional de Trabajo (OIT) estima en 250 millones el número de niños menores de dieciocho años que trabajan en el mundo, de los cuales la mitad a tiempo completo.

warming
thawing
reached

El calentamiento° de la tierra

Buenos Aires, Argentina—El derretimiento° del hielo y los glaciares de Groenlandia y el polo ártico han alcanzado° niveles nunca vistos. Según los científicos, el hielo es mucho más delgado de lo habitual. Esto se debe al calentamiento provocado por las emisiones del dióxido de carbono que destruye el ozono del planeta.

Poco a poco se va lejos[5]

Buenos Aires, Argentina—El gobierno argentino ha modificado su plan de prevención contra el uso de las drogas. En las últimas décadas la lucha se basó fundamentalmente en explicar cuáles son los efectos que estas sustancias causan a quienes las consumen.

failure
cause, lead to

Debido al fracaso° del método, un nuevo modelo se está usando. Ahora, la idea es atacar las razones socio-culturales, familiares o individuales que provocan° el uso de las drogas.

¡«No» al terrorismo!

headed

Bilbao, España—Más de 120.000 personas participaron en Bilbao en una manifestación encabezada° por personalidades del mundo político. El sentimiento general fue demostrar que estaban en contra del terrorismo y de la violencia que éste produce. Todos los presentes buscaban paz y querían decirle a ETA[6] que no quieren una organización que

spreads

siembra° el terror y el sufrimiento en el pueblo.

---

[5] Spanish saying: *Taking it little by little* (*step by step*), *one goes far.*
[6] Euzkadi ta Azkatasuna—a militant terrorist organization that advocates the separation of the Basque region from the rest of Spain.

14-23. Último ejercicio. Lean el epílogo y luego contesten las preguntas.

EPÍLOGO

Usted ha llegado al final del libro. ¡Felicitaciones! Antes de la despedida, le ofrecemos a continuación el desenlace° de la historia.

outcome

El profesor **Marín-Vivar** y su colega, la profesora **Falcón**, están de regreso después de interesantes experiencias en México y España.

Carmen descubrió que tiene parientes en Málaga y piensa volver a España.

Esteban conoció a una española muy simpática y ahora vive escribiéndole mensajes electrónicos. Ha decidido continuar sus estudios de posgrado en Madrid.

Linda y **Manuel** encontraron trabajo y ya fijaron la fecha de la boda.

Natalia volvió de Ecuador satisfecha de su labor como voluntaria y ahora está contemplando la idea de servir en el Cuerpo de Paz.

Javier sigue con el tenis y quiere hacer trabajo voluntario en un hospital.

Alfonso se fue a Montreal a una escuela de arte culinario y va a combinar su gusto por la cocina con su interés en la informática.

Pepita se prepara para correr un maratón.

Inés sigue con sus conciertos de piano y piensa ir a Argentina a visitar a **Octavio**, que está en Mendoza trabajando con una compañía norteamericana.

Camila sigue estudios de arte en Nueva York. ¡Ah! Y por supuesto, **Rodolfo**, aunque ha usado ya varias de sus nueve vidas, sigue muy contento durmiendo junto a la chimenea con **Gitana** y sus tres gatitos.

1. ¿Cuáles son sus personajes favoritos y por qué? Inventen algunos detalles para agregarlos (*add them*) a la vida de sus personajes favoritos.

2. ¿Cuáles son sus planes profesionales para el futuro?

Dicho y hecho

Conversando

4 **Un noticiero.** Preparen un noticiero para luego presentárselo a la clase. Primero, inventen un nombre original para el programa. Luego, cada uno/a de ustedes estará a cargo de una noticia. Pueden consultar la red en español para ayudarse con las noticias del país y del mundo.

Esquema de la presentación

el nombre del noticiero

una noticia de la universidad — una noticia local — una noticia del país — una noticia mundial

¡A escuchar!

¡Manos a la obra (*Let's get to work*)! Escuche los siguientes anuncios de la estación de radio KZK 95FM que presenta oportunidades de trabajo voluntario en todas partes del mundo. Decida qué opción (A, B o C) mejor corresponde a cada uno de los tres estudiantes indicados.

Estudiantes

_____ **1.** Elena, estudiante de biología, adora los animales y le encanta viajar.

_____ **2.** Jaime, estudiante de matemáticas, tiene siete hermanos menores, es muy extrovertido y practica varios deportes.

_____ **3.** María, estudiante de español, vivió en México por un año, le interesa la sociología y le gusta mucho conocer gente de otros países.

Ahora, escuche los anuncios otra vez. Decida cuál de las tres opciones sería la mejor para usted y por qué.

Opciones

_____ **a.** El Paso (Centro de Auxilios Familiares)

_____ **b.** Los Ángeles (Programa de Verano)

_____ **c.** Galápagos (Centro Charles Darwin)

De mi escritorio

2 **Una entrevista.** Usted es reportero/a y su compañero/a es una persona famosa de la historia, de la literatura, o del mundo de la política, la música, el cine, etc. Juntos, escriban una entrevista para luego presentársela a la clase. Incluyan cinco preguntas imaginativas y sus respuestas.

Panorama cultural

Cinco exploradores españoles

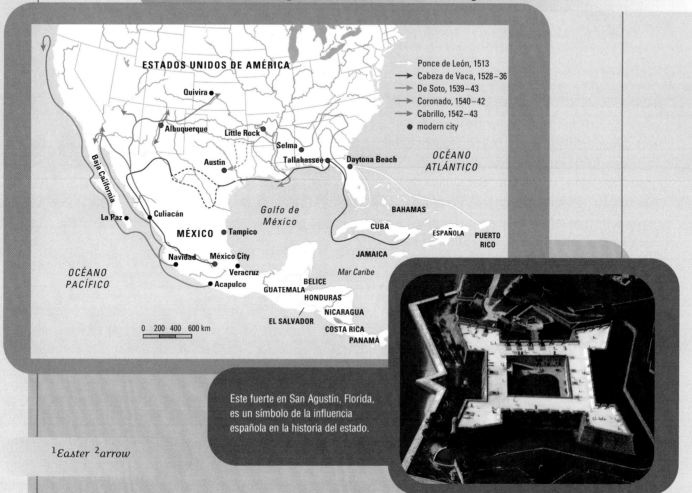

ESTADOS UNIDOS DE AMÉRICA

- Quivira
- Albuquerque
- Little Rock
- Selma
- Austin
- Tallahassee
- Daytona Beach

Baja California

La Paz · Culiacán

MÉXICO · Tampico

Navidad · México City · Veracruz · Acapulco

OCÉANO PACÍFICO

Golfo de México

GUATEMALA · BELICE · HONDURAS · EL SALVADOR · NICARAGUA · COSTA RICA · PANAMÁ

Mar Caribe

OCÉANO ATLÁNTICO

BAHAMAS · CUBA · ESPAÑOLA · PUERTO RICO · JAMAICA

→ Ponce de León, 1513
→ Cabeza de Vaca, 1528–36
→ De Soto, 1539–43
→ Coronado, 1540–42
→ Cabrillo, 1542–43
● modern city

0   200 400 600 km

Este fuerte en San Agustín, Florida, es un símbolo de la influencia española en la historia del estado.

[1]Easter [2]arrow

Preguntas sobre el mapa

1. ¿Quién exploró la costa de la Florida? ¿En qué año?
2. ¿Quién exploró la costa de California? ¿En qué años?
3. ¿Quién exploró el sureste de los Estados Unidos? ¿Y el suroeste?
4. ¿Cuál de los exploradores siguió la ruta más larga?

1. Juan Ponce de León

Buscando fama, oro, esclavos y la legendaria «fuente de la juventud», Juan Ponce de León llegó a las costas de la Florida cerca de lo que hoy es Daytona Beach. Creyó que había descubierto una isla y la llamó «Pascua Florida»[1], para conmemorar la fecha de su llegada. Continuó su viaje hacia el sur donde fue atacado por los nativos de la región no lejos del actual Cabo Cañaveral. Prosiguió hacia el sur y luego hacia el oeste con la mala fortuna de ser atacado otra vez. Entonces, decidió regresar a España y obtener un permiso para colonizar y conquistar la «Nueva Isla de la Florida». Arribó a las costas del Golfo procedente de España, pero ahí fue herido de flecha[2] y tuvo que regresar a Cuba, donde murió. Nunca supo que su «isla» era en realidad una península que hoy es el estado de la Florida.

2. Álvar Núñez Cabeza de Vaca

Historiador, pionero y explorador, Álvar Núñez Cabeza de Vaca fue de los primeros españoles en poner pie en territorio tejano. En 1528, acompañado por unos ochenta españoles y un africano llamado Estevanico, llegó a las costas de Tejas. Cabeza de Vaca sobrevivió increíbles infortunios[3] y pruebas en su marcha por Tejas y México. Ejecutó curas milagrosas[4] de enfermos y heridos nativos. Por sus habilidades médicas fue aceptado por los indígenas. Cuando por fin regresó a la «civilización» se desilusionó de sus compatriotas por el brutal trato que infligían a los indígenas.

[3]misfortunes [4]miraculous [5]priests [6]shores
[7]Viceroy [8]treasures [9]empty [10]anchored

Cabeza de Vaca ayuda a un indígena.
Ted DeGrazia, *Operation Arrowhead*, 1972. Oil on linen. Photograph provided courtesy of the DeGrazia Foundation, Gallery in the Sun, Tuscon, Arizona. Reproduced with permission.

Una procesión indígena como las que vio de Soto en sus exploraciones por el sureste de los Estados Unidos.

3. Hernando de Soto

Hernando de Soto fue el primer español en explorar el corazón del sureste de los Estados Unidos. Había llegado al Nuevo Mundo a la edad de catorce años y regresó rico a España después de haber participado en la conquista de Perú. Su ambición lo trajo a las costas de la Florida el 30 de mayo de 1539 con diez embarcaciones, seiscientos hombres, sacerdotes[5] y exploradores. Pasó varios años buscando oro y plata, explorando la región y maltratando a los nativos. En una confrontación con un jefe indio, de Soto proclamó que era el «hijo del sol». El astuto jefe le respondió que le creería cuando secase el gran río Misisipí. Murió desilusionado y fue enterrado en las riberas[6] del Misisipí en junio de 1542. Su expedición continuó y llegó al Golfo de México y posteriormente a México.

4. Francisco Vásquez de Coronado

Coronado nació en Salamanca en 1510. Era amigo del virrey[7] Antonio de Mendoza y éste lo nombró gobernador de Nueva Galicia. Muy pronto Coronado organizó una expedición en busca de los tesoros[8] de la fabulosa y mítica ciudad de Cíbola, que se creía estar en el actual suroeste de los Estados Unidos. Coronado y sus trescientos hombres por dos años investigaron ciudad por ciudad sin encontrar lo que tanto deseaban: oro. En 1542, regresó a la Ciudad de México con las manos vacías[9]. Continuó como gobernador de Nueva Galicia hasta que fue condenado por corrupción, negligencia y atrocidades cometidas contra los indígenas a su cargo. Murió en la Ciudad de México en 1544.

5. Juan Rodríguez Cabrillo

Juan Rodríguez Cabrillo fue el primer europeo en llegar a la actual costa del Pacífico de los Estados Unidos. En su juventud, había luchado en la conquista de Cuba, México y parte de Centroamérica. Cabrillo salió del puerto de Navidad (hoy Manzanillo, México) el 24 de junio de 1542. Llegó al puerto de San Diego y ahí ancló[10] sus naves en la bahía. Su expedición continuó hacia San Pedro, Santa Mónica, Santa Bárbara y Mendocino por la costa californiana. Sin embargo, su carrera terminó poco tiempo después el 3 de enero de 1543 en la isla de San Miguel. Murió de complicaciones asociadas con la fractura de una pierna.

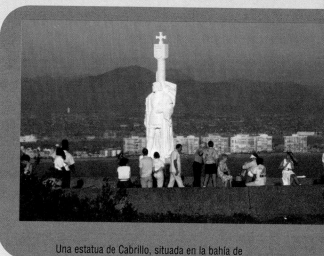

Una estatua de Cabrillo, situada en la bahía de San Diego.

② ¿Qué descubrimos?

Lean las siguientes oraciones y luego digan a cuál de los exploradores describe.

1. Murió en la Ciudad de México en 1544 después de haber sido condenado por corrupción.
2. Buscó la «fuente de la juventud» y creyó que la Florida era una isla.
3. Participó en la conquista de Perú y exploró el suroeste de los Estados Unidos.
4. Buscó oro y la mítica ciudad de Cíbola en el suroeste de los Estados Unidos.
5. Fue amigo de los indígenas; lo consideraban «médico».
6. Fue el primer español en explorar la costa del Pacífico.
7. Fue uno de los primeros españoles en llegar a Tejas.
8. Murió en Cuba a causa de una herida de flecha.
9. Fue enterrado en la ribera del río Misisipí.
10. Murió de complicaciones asociadas con la fractura de una pierna.

Encuentro cultural

Artes arquitectónicas

Las misiones de California

La llegada de los misioneros españoles, la construcción de El Camino Real[1] y la edificación de las veintiuna iglesias que forman la cadena de misiones californianas marcaron un cambio dramático en la historia de lo que actualmente es California.

Por medio de su sistema de misiones, los españoles pudieron introducir al Nuevo Mundo no sólo el cristianismo sino animales domésticos, frutos, flores, granos[2] e industria. Desgraciadamente, su arribo también marcó la destrucción de muchas de las culturas autóctonas, y en muchos casos la explotación de los indígenas.

Cada una de las misiones representa una página de la historia del estado. Todas han sido restauradas y pueden ser visitadas actualmente. En esta sección encontrará usted información sobre tres de esas misiones.

La cadena de misiones se extiende desde San Diego en el sur, hasta Sonoma (veinte millas al norte de San Francisco).

El Camino Real

Misión Santa Clara de Asís (1777)

Misión Santa Bárbara (1786)

Misión San Juan Capistrano (1776)

[1] *The Royal Road* [2] *grains*
[3] *swallows (birds)* [4] *chapel*

Misión San Juan Capistrano
- Las legendarias golondrinas[3] viajan desde Centroamérica y llegan a la misión cada año por el 19 de marzo.
- Se le ha llamado la «Joya de las Misiones» por su belleza y armonía arquitectónica.
- Ya que conserva la capilla[4] original, se le considera la iglesia más antigua de California.

Misión Santa Bárbara

- La única misión en manos de los Franciscanos desde su fundación.
- El sistema de canalización del agua de la misión es tan extraordinario que partes del mismo están aún en uso en la ciudad de Santa Bárbara.
- Al igual que muchas otras misiones californianas, ésta ha sido reconstruida debido a daños sufridos en movimientos sísmicos.

Misión Santa Clara de Asís

- Es la única misión situada en un campus universitario.
- Las campanas[5] de la misión han repicado[6] a las 8:30 P.M. por doscientos años.
- La Misión Santa Clara fue la primera en California en honrar a una mujer: Santa Clara—amiga de juventud de San Francisco.

Preguntas

1. ¿Cuántas misiones constituyen la cadena de misiones que sigue El Camino Real en California?
2. ¿Por qué piensa usted que los españoles construyeron sus misiones en las Américas?
3. ¿Qué tipo de animales y plantas introdujeron?
4. ¿Cuáles fueron otros resultados de la colonización española?
5. ¿Cuál es un aspecto excepcional de la Misión San Juan Capistrano? ¿Y Santa Bárbara? ¿Y Santa Clara?
6. ¿Cuál de las misiones le gustaría visitar a usted?

[5]*bells* [6]**han...** *have rung*

Conjunciones

antes de que
cuando
después de que
hasta que
tan pronto como

Sustantivos

Las noticias

el noticiero
la reportera
el reportero

Los problemas humanos

el aborto
la bomba
el crimen
el delincuente
los desamparados
el desempleo
la discriminación
la droga
la drogadicción
la explosión
la guerra
el hambre
el narcotráfico
la pobreza
el prejuicio
el SIDA
la sobrepoblación
el terrorismo
la víctima
la violencia

El empleo

la entrevista
el/la gerente
la jefa
el jefe
la solicitud

La política y la sociedad

el acuerdo de paz
la candidata
el candidato
la ciudadana
el ciudadano
la cura
los derechos humanos
la elección
la exploración del espacio
la frontera
el gobierno
la igualdad
la justicia
la ley
la libertad
el/la líder
la nave espacial
la paz
la pena de muerte
la política mundial
el trabajo voluntario
el tutor
la tutora
la voluntaria
el voluntario

Verbos y expresiones verbales

apoyar
construir
eliminar
escoger
informar/ reportar
legalizar
luchar (por)
prohibir
robar
solicitar
sufrir
votar (por)

dar de comer
estar a favor/ en contra de
tener éxito

I. The subjunctive with time expressions. Complete las oraciones con la frase entre paréntesis. Use el subjuntivo o el pretérito según las situaciones.

1. (yo / recibir el dinero)
   Te llamé tan pronto como…
   Te voy a llamar tan pronto como…

2. (tú / darme el número de teléfono del hotel)
   Haré las reservaciones cuando…
   Hice las reservaciones cuando…

3. (tú / llamarme)
   Fui a la agencia de viajes después de que…
   Iré a la agencia de viajes después de que…

4. (nosotros / regresar de la luna de miel)
   No anunciaré nuestro matrimonio hasta que…
   No anuncié nuestro matrimonio hasta que…

II. The conditional tense. Diga lo que harían las siguientes personas con un millón de dólares.

Modelo: Carlos / comprar una casa
Carlos compraría una casa.

1. yo / viajar a muchos países
2. Pepe / poner el dinero en el banco
3. tú / darles dinero a los pobres
4. ustedes / gastar todo el dinero
5. nosotros / hacer un viaje a la Patagonia
6. mis amigas / ir a Chile a esquiar

III. *If* clauses. Haga usted oraciones indicando la condición (**Si…**) y el resultado.

Modelo: encontrar un trabajo mejor / ganar más dinero
Si encontrara un trabajo mejor, ganaría más dinero.

1. ganar más dinero / ahorrarlo
2. ahorrarlo / tener mucho dinero
3. tener mucho dinero / comprar un coche
4. comprar un coche / hacer un viaje
5. hacer un viaje / ir a Puerto Vallarta
6. ir a Puerto Vallarta / quedarme allí dos meses
7. quedarme allí dos meses / perder mi trabajo
8. perder mi trabajo / no tener dinero

IV. The imperfect subjunctive with *ojalá*. Indique sus deseos en las siguientes situaciones. Siga el modelo.

Modelo: Mi padre es muy conservador.
Ojalá (que) mi padre no fuera tan conservador.

1. ¡El aire está tan contaminado!
2. Hay mucho desempleo en esta ciudad.
3. Muchas personas sufren del SIDA y del cáncer.
4. Tenemos muchos problemas que resolver.

V. General review. Conteste con oraciones completas.

1. ¿Cuáles son algunos de los problemas más serios de nuestra nación hoy en día?
2. Si usted pudiera cambiar una cosa de nuestro mundo, ¿qué cambiaría? ¿Por qué?
3. Cuando usted estaba en la escuela secundaria, ¿se preocupaba por algunos de los problemas del mundo? (¿Cuáles?) ¿Se preocupaba por otros problemas? (¿Cuáles?)
4. ¿Qué hará usted cuando se gradúe?

Answers to the *Autoprueba y repaso* are found in **Apéndice 2**.

Apéndice 1: *Verbos*

A. REGULAR VERBS

INFINITIVE

-ar	-er	-ir
hablar, *to speak*	comer, *to eat*	vivir, *to live*

PRESENT PARTICIPLE

hablando, *speaking*	comiendo, *eating*	viviendo, *living*

PAST PARTICIPLE

hablado, *spoken*	comido, *eaten*	vivido, *lived*

INDICATIVE MOOD

Present

I speak, do speak, am speaking, etc. | | *I eat, do eat, am eating, etc.* | | *I live, do live, am living, etc.* |

hablo	hablamos	como	comemos	vivo	vivimos
hablas	habláis	comes	coméis	vives	vivís
habla	hablan	come	comen	vive	viven

Preterit

I spoke, did speak, etc. | | *I ate, did eat, etc.* | | *I lived, did live, etc.* |

hablé	hablamos	comí	comimos	viví	vivimos
hablaste	hablasteis	comiste	comisteis	viviste	vivisteis
habló	hablaron	comió	comieron	vivió	vivieron

Imperfect

I was speaking, used to speak, spoke, etc. | | *I was eating, used to eat, ate, etc.* | | *I was living, used to live, lived, etc.* |

hablaba	hablábamos	comía	comíamos	vivía	vivíamos
hablabas	hablabais	comías	comíais	vivías	vivíais
hablaba	hablaban	comía	comían	vivía	vivían

Future

I will speak, etc. | | *I will eat, etc.* | | *I will live, etc.* |

hablaré	hablaremos	comeré	comeremos	viviré	viviremos
hablarás	hablaréis	comerás	comeréis	vivirás	viviréis
hablará	hablarán	comerá	comerán	vivirá	vivirán

Conditional

I would speak, etc. | | *I would eat, etc.* | | *I would live, etc.* |

hablaría	hablaríamos	comería	comeríamos	viviría	viviríamos
hablarías	hablaríais	comerías	comeríais	vivirías	viviríais
hablaría	hablarían	comería	comerían	viviría	vivirían

Present Perfect

I have, etc., ... | | | *... spoken* | *... eaten* | *... lived* |

he	hemos				
has	habéis	hablado	comido	vivido	
ha	han				

Past Perfect (Pluperfect)

I had, etc., ... | | | *... spoken* | *... eaten* | *... lived* |

había	habíamos				
habías	habíais	hablado	comido	vivido	
había	habían				

Future Perfect

I will have, etc., ...   *... spoken*   *... eaten*   *... lived*

habré	habremos			
habrás	habréis	hablado	comido	vivido
habrá	habrán			

Conditional Perfect

I would have, etc., ...   *... spoken*   *... eaten*   *... lived*

habría	habríamos			
habrías	habríais	hablado	comido	vivido
habría	habrían			

SUBJUNCTIVE MOOD

Present Subjunctive

(that) I (may) speak, etc.   *(that) I (may) eat, etc.*   *(that) I (may) live, etc.*

hable	hablemos	coma	comamos	viva	vivamos
hables	habléis	comas	comáis	vivas	viváis
hable	hablen	coma	coman	viva	vivan

Imperfect Subjunctive

(that) I might speak, etc.   *(that) I might eat, etc.*   *(that) I might live, etc.*

hablara	habláramos	comiera	comiéramos	viviera	viviéramos
hablaras	hablarais	comieras	comierais	vivieras	vivierais
hablara	hablaran	comiera	comieran	viviera	vivieran

Present Perfect Subjunctive

(that) I (may) have, etc., ...   *... spoken*   *... eaten*   *... lived*

haya	hayamos			
hayas	hayáis	hablado	comido	vivido
haya	hayan			

Past Perfect (Pluperfect) Subjunctive

(that) I might have, etc., ...   *... spoken*   *... eaten*   *... lived*

hubiera	hubiéramos			
hubieras	hubierais	hablado	comido	vivido
hubiera	hubieran			

Command Forms

usted	hable	coma	viva
	no hable	no coma	no viva
ustedes	hablen	coman	vivan
	no hablen	no coman	no vivan
nosotros	hablemos	comamos	vivamos
	no hablemos	no comamos	no vivamos
tú	habla	come	vive
	no hables	no comas	no vivas
(vosotros)	[hablad]	[comed]	[vivid]
	[no habléis]	[no comáis]	[no viváis]

B. STEM-CHANGING VERBS

Only the tenses with stem changes are given.

1. -ar and -er stem-changing verbs: e → ie and o → ue

pensar (ie) *to think*
Present Indicative: **pienso, piensas, piensa, pensamos, pensáis, piensan**
Present Subjunctive: **piense, pienses, piense, pensemos, penséis, piensen**

Commands:	piense (usted), piensen (ustedes), pensemos (nosotros), piensa (tú), no pienses (tú), [pensad (vosotros), no penséis (vosotros)]

volver (ue) *to return*

Present Indicative:	vuelvo, vuelves, vuelve, volvemos, volvéis, vuelven
Present Subjunctive:	vuelva, vuelvas, vuelva, volvamos, volváis, vuelvan
Commands:	vuelva (usted), vuelvan (ustedes), volvamos (nosotros), vuelve (tú), no vuelvas (tú), [volved (vosotros), no volváis (vosotros)]

Other verbs of this type are:

cerrar (ie)	*to close*	acostarse (ue)	*to go to bed*
despertarse (ie)	*to wake up*	almorzar (ue)	*to have lunch*
empezar (ie)	*to begin*	contar (ue)	*to count, tell*
entender (ie)	*to understand*	costar (ue)	*to cost*
nevar (ie)	*to snow*	encontrar (ue)	*to find*
perder (ie)	*to lose*	jugar (ue)	*to play*
querer (ie)	*to wish, want, love*	mostrar (ue)	*to show*
recomendar (ie)	*to recommend*	poder (ue)	*to be able, can*
sentarse (ie)	*to sit down*	recordar (ue)	*to remember*
		resolver (ue)	*to resolve*
		sonar (ue)	*to sound, ring*

2. -ir stem-changing verbs: e → ie, i and o → ue, u

sugerir (ie, i) *to suggest*

Present Participle:	sugiriendo
Present Indicative:	sugiero, sugieres, sugiere, sugerimos, sugerís, sugieren
Preterit:	sugerí, sugeriste, sugirió, sugerimos, sugeristeis, sugirieron
Present Subjunctive:	sugiera, sugieras, sugiera, sugiramos, sugiráis, sugieran
Imperfect Subjunctive:	sugiriera, sugirieras, sugiriera, sugiriéramos, sugirierais, sugirieran
Commands:	sugiera (usted), sugieran (ustedes), sugiramos (nosotros), sugiere (tú), no sugieras (tú), [sugerid (vosotros), no sugiráis (vosotros)]

dormir (ue, u) *to sleep*

Present Participle:	durmiendo
Present Indicative:	duermo, duermes, duerme, dormimos, dormís, duermen
Preterit:	dormí, dormiste, durmió, dormimos, dormisteis, durmieron
Present Subjunctive:	duerma, duermas, duerma, durmamos, durmáis, duerman
Imperfect Subjunctive:	durmiera, durmieras, durmiera, durmiéramos, durmierais, durmieran
Commands:	duerma (usted), duerman (ustedes), durmamos (nosotros), duerme (tú), no duermas (tú), [dormid (vosotros), no durmáis (vosotros)]

Other verbs of this type are:

divertirse (ie, i)	*to have a good time*
morir (ue, u)	*to die*
sentir (ie, i)	*to be sorry, regret*
sentirse (ie, i)	*to feel*

3. -ir stem-changing verbs: e → i, i

pedir (i, i) *to ask for*

Present Participle:	pidiendo
Present Indicative:	pido, pides, pide, pedimos, pedís, piden
Preterit:	pedí, pediste, pidió, pedimos, pedisteis, pidieron
Present Subjunctive:	pida, pidas, pida, pidamos, pidáis, pidan
Imperfect Subjunctive:	pidiera, pidieras, pidiera, pidiéramos, pidierais, pidieran

| Commands: | pida (usted), pidan (ustedes), pidamos (nosotros), pide (tú), no pidas (tú), [pedid (vosotros), no pidáis (vosotros)] |

Other verbs of this type are:

consequir (i, i)	to get, obtain
despedirse de (i, i)	to say good-bye
reírse (i, i)	to laugh
repetir (i, i)	to repeat
seguir (i, i)	to follow
servir (i, i)	to serve
vestirse (i, i)	to get dressed

C. VERBS WITH ORTHOGRAPHIC CHANGES

Only the tenses with orthographic changes are given.

1. c → qu

tocar *to play (instrument)*

Preterit:	**toqué**, tocaste, tocó, tocamos, tocasteis, tocaron
Present Subjunctive:	**toque, toques, toque, toquemos, toquéis, toquen**
Commands:	**toque** (usted), **toquen** (ustedes), **toquemos** (nosotros), toca (tú), **no toques** (tú), [tocad (vosotros), **no toquéis** (vosotros)]

Like **tocar** are **buscar**, *to look for*; **explicar**, *to explain*; **pescar**, *to fish*; and **sacar**, *to take out.*

2. z → c

empezar (ie) *to begin*

Preterit:	**empecé**, empezaste, empezó, empezamos, empezasteis, empezaron
Present Subjunctive:	**empiece, empieces, empiece, empecemos, empecéis, empiecen**
Commands:	**empiece** (usted), **empiecen** (ustedes), **empecemos** (nosotros), empieza (tú), **no empieces** (tú) [empezad (vosotros), **no empecéis** (vosotros)]

Like **empezar** are **abrazar**, *to hug*; **almorzar** (ue), *to have lunch*; and **cruzar**, *to cross.*

3. g → gu

pagar *to pay (for)*

Preterit:	**pagué**, pagaste, pagó, pagamos, pagasteis, pagaron
Present Subjunctive:	**pague, pagues, pague, paguemos, paguéis, paguen**
Commands:	**pague** (usted), **paguen** (ustedes), **paguemos** (nosotros), paga (tú), **no pagues** (tú), [pagad (vosotros), **no paguéis** (vosotros)]

Like **pagar** are **apagar**, *to turn off;* **jugar** (ue), *to play;* and **llegar**, *to arrive.*

4. gu → g

seguir (i, i) *to follow, continue*

Present Indicative:	sigo, sigues, sigue, seguimos, seguís, siguen
Present Subjunctive:	siga, sigas, siga, sigamos, sigáis, sigan
Commands:	siga (usted), sigan (ustedes), sigamos (nosotros), sigue (tú), no sigas (tú), [seguid (vosotros), **no sigáis** (vosotros)]

5. g → j

recoger *to pick up*
Present Indicative: recojo, recoges, recoge, recogemos, recogéis, recogen
Present Subjunctive: recoja, recojas, recoja, recojamos, recojáis, recojan
Commands: recoja (usted), recojan (ustedes), recojamos (nosotros), recoge (tú), no
recojas (tú), [recoged (vosotros), no recojáis (vosotros)]

Like **recoger** is **escoger**, *to choose*, and **proteger**, *to protect*.

6. i → y
leer *to read*
Present Participle: leyendo
Preterit: leí, leíste, leyó, leímos, leísteis, leyeron
Imperfect Subjunctive: leyera, leyeras, leyera, leyéramos, leyerais, leyeran

Like **leer** is **oír**, *to hear*; and in the present participle **traer**, *to bring*: **trayendo**; and **ir**, *to go*: **yendo**.

construir *to construct*
Present Participle: construyendo
Present Indicative: construyo, construyes, construye, construimos, construís, construyen
Preterit: construí, construiste, construyó, construimos, construisteis, construyeron
Present Subjunctive: construya, construyas, construya, construyamos, construyáis,
construyan
Imperfect Subjunctive: construyera, construyeras, construyera, construyéramos,
construyerais, construyeran
Commands: construya (usted), construyan (ustedes), construyamos (nosotros),
construye (tú), no construyas (tú), [construid (vosotros), no construyáis
(vosotros)]

Like **construir** is **destruir**, *to destroy*.

D. IRREGULAR VERBS

Only the tenses and commands that have irregular forms are given.

conocer *to know, be acquainted with*
Present Indicative: conozco, conoces, conoce, conocemos, conocéis, conocen
Present Subjunctive: conozca, conozcas, conozca, conozcamos, conozcáis, conozcan

dar *to give*
Present Indicative: doy, das, da, damos, dais, dan
Preterit: di, diste, dio, dimos, disteis, dieron
Present Subjunctive: dé, des, dé, demos, deis, den
Imperfect Subjunctive: diera, dieras, diera, diéramos, dierais, dieran

decir *to say, tell*
Present Participle: diciendo
Past Participle: dicho
Present Indicative: digo, dices, dice, decimos, decís, dicen
Preterit: dije, dijiste, dijo, dijimos, dijisteis, dijeron
Present Subjunctive: diga, digas, diga, digamos, digáis, digan
Imperfect Subjunctive: dijera, dijeras, dijera, dijéramos, dijerais, dijeran
Future: diré, dirás, dirá, diremos, diréis, dirán
Conditional: diría, dirías, diría, diríamos, diríais, dirían
Affirmative **tú** command: di

estar *to be*
Present Indicative: estoy, estás, está, estamos, estáis, están
Preterit: estuve, estuviste, estuvo, estuvimos, estuvisteis, estuvieron
Present Subjunctive: esté, estés, esté, estemos, estéis, estén
Imperfect Subjunctive: estuviera, estuvieras, estuviera, estuviéramos, estuvierais, estuvieran

haber *to have*
Present Indicative: he, has, ha, hemos, habéis, han
Preterit: hube, hubiste, hubo, hubimos, hubisteis, hubieron
Present Subjunctive: haya, hayas, haya, hayamos, hayáis, hayan
Imperfect Subjunctive: hubiera, hubieras, hubiera, hubiéramos, hubierais, hubieran
Future: habré, habrás, habrá, habremos, habréis, habrán
Conditional: habría, habrías, habría, habríamos, habríais, habrían

hacer *to do, make*
Past Participle: hecho
Present Indicative: hago, haces, hace, hacemos, hacéis, hacen
Preterit: hice, hiciste, hizo, hicimos, hicisteis, hicieron
Present Subjunctive: haga, hagas, haga, hagamos, hagáis, hagan
Imperfect Subjunctive: hiciera, hicieras, hiciera, hiciéramos, hicierais, hicieran
Future: haré, harás, hará, haremos, haréis, harán
Conditional: haría, harías, haría, haríamos, haríais, harían
Affirmative **tú** command: haz

ir *to go*
Present Participle: yendo
Past Participle: ido
Present Indicative: voy, vas, va, vamos, vais, van
Preterit: fui, fuiste, fue, fuimos, fuisteis, fueron
Imperfect: iba, ibas, iba, íbamos, ibais, iban
Present Subjunctive: vaya, vayas, vaya, vayamos, vayáis, vayan
Imperfect Subjunctive: fuera, fueras, fuera, fuéramos, fuerais, fueran
Affirmative **tú** command: ve
Affirmative **nosotros** command: vamos

oír *to hear*
Present Participle: oyendo
Past Participle: oído
Present Indicative: oigo, oyes, oye, oímos, oís, oyen
Preterit: oí, oíste, oyó, oímos, oísteis, oyeron
Present Subjunctive: oiga, oigas, oiga, oigamos, oigáis, oigan
Imperfect Subjunctive: oyera, oyeras, oyera, oyéramos, oyerais, oyeran

poder *to be able, can*
Present Participle: pudiendo
Present Indicative: puedo, puedes, puede, podemos, podéis, pueden
Preterit: pude, pudiste, pudo, pudimos, pudisteis, pudieron
Present Subjunctive: pueda, puedas, pueda, podamos, podáis, puedan
Imperfect Subjunctive: pudiera, pudieras, pudiera, pudiéramos, pudierais, pudieran
Future: podré, podrás, podrá, podremos, podréis, podrán
Conditional: podría, podrías, podría, podríamos, podríais, podrían

poner *to put, place*
Past Participle: puesto
Present Indicative: pongo, pones, pone, ponemos, ponéis, ponen
Preterit: puse, pusiste, puso, pusimos, pusisteis, pusieron
Present Subjunctive: ponga, pongas, ponga, pongamos, pongáis, pongan
Imperfect Subjunctive: pusiera, pusieras, pusiera, pusiéramos, pusierais, pusieran
Future: pondré, pondrás, pondrá, pondremos, pondréis, pondrán
Conditional: pondría, pondrías, pondría, pondríamos, pondríais, pondrían
Affirmative **tú** command: pon

querer *to wish, want*
Present Indicative: quiero, quieres, quiere, queremos, queréis, quieren
Preterit: quise, quisiste, quiso, quisimos, quisisteis, quisieron
Present Subjunctive: quiera, quieras, quiera, queramos, queráis, quieran
Imperfect Subjunctive: quisiera, quisieras, quisiera, quisiéramos, quisierais, quisieran
Future: querré, querrás, querrá, querremos, querréis, querrán
Conditional: querría, querrías, querría, querríamos, querríais, querrían

saber *to know*
Present Indicative: sé, sabes, sabe, sabemos, sabéis, saben
Preterit: supe, supiste, supo, supimos, supisteis, supieron
Present Subjunctive: sepa, sepas, sepa, sepamos, sepáis, sepan
Imperfect Subjunctive: supiera, supieras, supiera, supiéramos, supierais, supieran
Future: sabré, sabrás, sabrá, sabremos, sabréis, sabrán
Conditional: sabría, sabrías, sabría, sabríamos, sabríais, sabrían

salir *to go out, leave*
Present Indicative: salgo, sales, sale, salimos, salís, salen
Present Subjunctive: salga, salgas, salga, salgamos, salgáis, salgan
Future: saldré, saldrás, saldrá, saldremos, saldréis, saldrán
Conditional: saldría, saldrías, saldría, saldríamos, saldríais, saldrían
Affirmative **tú** command: sal

ser *to be*
Present Indicative: soy, eres, es, somos, sois, son
Preterit: fui, fuiste, fue, fuimos, fuisteis, fueron
Imperfect: era, eras, era, éramos, erais, eran
Present Subjunctive: sea, seas, sea, seamos, seáis, sean
Imperfect Subjunctive: fuera, fueras, fuera, fuéramos, fuerais, fueran
Affirmative **tú** command: sé

tener *to have*
Present Indicative: tengo, tienes, tiene, tenemos, tenéis, tienen
Preterit: tuve, tuviste, tuvo, tuvimos, tuvisteis, tuvieron
Present Subjunctive: tenga, tengas, tenga, tengamos, tengáis, tengan
Imperfect Subjunctive: tuviera, tuvieras, tuviera, tuviéramos, tuvierais, tuvieran
Future: tendré, tendrás, tendrá, tendremos, tendréis, tendrán
Conditional: tendría, tendrías, tendría, tendríamos, tendríais, tendrían
Affirmative **tú** command: ten

traducir *to translate*

Present Indicative:	**traduzco**, traduces, traduce, traducimos, traducís, traducen
Preterit:	**traduje, tradujiste, tradujo, tradujimos, tradujisteis, tradujeron**
Present Subjunctive:	**traduzca, traduzcas, traduzca, traduzcamos, traduzcáis, traduzcan**
Imperfect Subjunctive:	**tradujera, tradujeras, tradujera, tradujéramos, tradujerais, tradujeran**

Like **traducir** is **conducir**, *to drive.*

traer *to bring*

Present Participle:	**trayendo**
Past Participle:	**traído**
Present Indicative:	**traigo**, traes, trae, traemos, traéis, traen
Preterit:	**traje, trajiste, trajo, trajimos, trajisteis, trajeron**
Present Subjunctive:	**traiga, traigas, traiga, traigamos, traigáis, traigan**
Imperfect Subjunctive:	**trajera, trajeras, trajera, trajéramos, trajerais, trajeran**

venir *to come*

Present Participle:	**viniendo**
Present Indicative:	**vengo, vienes, viene,** venimos, venís, **vienen**
Preterit:	**vine, viniste, vino, vinimos, vinisteis, vinieron**
Present Subjunctive:	**venga, vengas, venga, vengamos, vengáis, vengan**
Imperfect Subjunctive:	**viniera, vinieras, viniera, viniéramos, vinierais, vinieran**
Future:	**vendré, vendrás, vendrá, vendremos, vendréis, vendrán**
Conditional:	**vendría, vendrías, vendría, vendríamos, vendríais, vendrían**
*Affirmative **tú** command:*	**ven**

Like **venir** is **prevenir**, *to prevent.*

ver *to see*

Past Participle:	**visto**
Present Indicative:	**veo**, ves, ve, vemos, veis, ven
Preterit:	**vi**, viste, **vio**, vimos, visteis, vieron
Imperfect:	**veía, veías, veía, veíamos, veíais, veían**
Present Subjunctive:	**vea, veas, vea, veamos, veáis, vean**

Autoprueba
Para empezar: Nuevos encuentros

I. 1. PEPITA: (Muy) Bien, gracias.
   PROFESORA: (Muy) Bien, gracias.
   2. PROFESORA: ¿Cómo te llamas?
   3. CARMEN: ¿Cómo estás? (¿Qué tal?)
      CARMEN: Muy bien, gracias. (Regular.)
   4. PROFESORA: Mucho gusto. (Encantada.)
      CARMEN: El gusto es mío. (Igualmente.)
   5. MANUEL: Me llamo Manuel.
      PEPITA: Me llamo Pepita.
      PEPITA: Igualmente.
   6. CARMEN: ¿Qué hora es?
      PEPITA: Hasta luego. (Hasta pronto.
                  Chao. Adiós.)

II. 1. Ellos son de Chile pero nosotras somos de México.
   2. Tú eres de Colombia pero ustedes son de España.
   3. Luis es de El Salvador pero Juan y Elena son de Honduras.

III. 1. (Los jeans cuestan) treinta y cinco dólares.
   2. (El suéter cuesta) cincuenta y siete dólares.
   3. (La chaqueta cuesta) setenta y dos dólares.
   4. (El sombrero cuesta) veintiséis dólares.
   5. (El video cuesta) quince dólares.
   6. (El CD cuesta) nueve dólares.

IV. 1. los lunes, los miércoles, los viernes (los martes, los jueves)...
   2. los sábados, los domingos (los viernes, los sábados)

V. 1. Es el catorce de febrero.
   2. Es el primero de abril.
   3. Es el cuatro de julio.
   4. Es el veintitrés de noviembre.
   5. Es el veinticinco de diciembre.

VI. 1. Es la una y cuarto (la una y quince) de la tarde.
   2. Son las nueve y media (las nueve y treinta) de la noche.
   3. Son las seis menos diez (las cinco y cincuenta) de la mañana.
   4. Son las doce menos veinte (las once y cuarenta) de la noche.
   5. Es (el) mediodía.

VII. 1. Es española.
   2. Es estadounidense.
   3. Es cubana.
   4. Es argentina.
   5. Es salvadoreño.

VIII. 1. Me llamo...
   2. Sí, (No, no) soy inflexible y arrogante.
      Sí, (No, no) soy responsable y generoso/a.
   3. Muy bien, gracias. (Regular.)
   4. Soy de...
   5. Soy...
   6. Es el... de...
   7. Es lunes, etc.
   8. Son las... (Es la...)

Autoprueba 1

I. A. 1. el, los ejercicios
   2. la, las lecciones
   3. la, las páginas
   4. el, los Capítulos
   B. un, una, un, una, unas, una, unos

II. 1. Voy a la cafetería (al centro estudiantil).
   2. Vamos al laboratorio (a la residencia estudiantil/al cuarto).
   3. Vamos al gimnasio.
   4. Van a la oficina del profesor.
   5. Vas a la librería.
   6. Va al cuarto (a la residencia estudiantil/a casa/al apartamento).

III. 1. Compro...
   2. Llegan...
   3. ¿Estudias...?
   4. ¿Trabaja...?
   5. Usamos...
   6. Escucha...

IV. 1. Asistimos... aprendemos...
   2. Vivo... estudio...
   3. Comen... toman...
   4. Leemos... escribimos...
   5. Imprimes... usas...
   6. Hago... salgo...

V. 1. Sí, (No, no voy) a clases todos los días.
   2. Mi primera clase es a la (las)...
   3. Hay... estudiantes en la clase de español.
   4. Sí, (No, no) hay (mucha) tarea todas las noches.
   5. Sí, (No, no) escribimos en el *Cuaderno de ejercicios* todas las noches.
   6. Voy a la librería. Voy al laboratorio (al centro de computadoras).
   7. Voy a...
   8. Ceno a las...
   9. Como en casa (en la cafetería/en mi apartamento/en un restaurante).

Autoprueba 2

I. 1. tengo
   2. tiene
   3. tienen
   4. tenemos
   5. tienes

II. 1. Tengo mis fotos.
   2. ¿Tienes tus libros?
   3. Tiene su diccionario.
   4. Tenemos nuestro televisor.
   5. ¿Tienen sus calculadoras?

III. 1. Es la foto de Marta.
   2. Son los cuadernos de José.
   3. Son los exámenes de los estudiantes.

IV. 1. soy, son perezosos
   2. son, es bajo
   3. somos, somos...simpáticos
   4. es, son difíciles

V. 1. Están en la librería.
   2. Estamos en el gimnasio.
   3. Estoy en la cafetería (en el centro estudiantil).
   4. Está en la oficina de la profesora Falcón.

VI. 1. Estoy nervioso/a (preocupado/a).
   2. Están (muy) ocupados.
   3. Está (muy) enfermo.
   4. Estamos contentos/as.

VII. 1. Tengo... años.
   2. Mi madre es simpática, etc. *o* Mi padre es alto, etc.
   3. Mis amigos/as son simpáticos/as, etc.
   4. Mis amigos/as están bien (contentos/as), etc.
   5. Sí, estamos preocupados/as por nuestras notas en la clase de... *o* No, no estamos preocupados/as por nuestras notas.
   6. Tenemos clases los lunes, etc.
   7. Mis (Nuestras) clases son difíciles, etc.

Autoprueba 3

I. 1. ¿A sus padres les gusta tomar café? Sí, (No, no) les gusta tomar café.
   2. ¿A ustedes les gusta la comida italiana? Sí, (No, no) nos gusta la comida italiana.
   3. ¿A ustedes les gusta desayunar temprano? Sí, (No, no) nos gusta desayunar temprano.
   4. ¿A su abuela le gustan los postres? Sí, (No, no) le gustan los postres.
   5. ¿A usted le gustan los frijoles negros? Sí, (No, no) me gustan los frijoles negros.

II. 1. ¿Pueden cocinar? Sí, (No, no) podemos cocinar.
   2. ¿Quieren ir al supermercado? Sí, (No, no) queremos ir al supermercado.
   3. ¿Almuerzan a las doce todos los días? Sí, (No, no) almorzamos a las doce todos los días.
   4. ¿Prefieren cenar en un restaurante o en la cafetería? Preferimos cenar en un restaurante (en la cafetería).
   5. ¿Normalmente piden postres en los restaurantes? Sí, normalmente pedimos postres en los restaurantes. *o* No, normalmente no pedimos...

III.A. 1. Dos cuestan doscientos cincuenta dólares.
   2. Dos cuestan trescientos cuarenta dólares.
   3. Dos cuestan novecientos dólares.
   4. Dos cuestan dos mil ochocientos dólares.
   5. Dos cuestan mil quinientos dólares.
   6. Dos cuestan cincuenta mil dólares.

B. 1. mil cuatrocientos noventa y dos
   2. mil quinientos ochenta y ocho
   3. mil setecientos setenta y seis
   4. mil novecientos ochenta y nueve
   5. dos mil uno

IV. 1. ¿Qué bebe? *o* ¿Por qué no bebe vino?
   2. ¿Cuál es su fruta favorita?
   3. ¿Cuándo trabaja? *o* ¿Qué hace por la mañana?
   4. ¿De dónde es?
   5. ¿Cuántos años tiene?
   6. ¿Dónde vive?
   7. ¿Adónde va? *o* ¿Cuándo va?
   8. ¿Cómo está?

V. 1. Como huevos, etc.
   2. Mi postre favorito es el helado, etc.
   3. Me gustan más las manzanas, etc.
   4. Quiero cenar en...
   5. Generalmente duermo... horas.
   6. Sí, (No, no) podemos estudiar toda la noche sin dormir.

Autoprueba 4

I. MARTA: Sabes
   PABLO: sé, conozco
   MARTA: Sabes
   PABLO: sé, conozco

II. 1. Tú vienes a clase todos los días. Yo vengo...
   2. Nosotros decimos «hola» a los estudiantes al entrar en la clase. Yo digo «hola»...
   3. Ellas traen la tarea a clase. Yo traigo...

   4. Ana pone la tarea en el escritorio del profesor. Yo pongo...
   5. Nosotros sabemos todo el vocabulario. Yo sé...
   6. Ustedes hacen preguntas en clase. Yo hago...
   7. Ella no sale de clase temprano. Yo no salgo...

III. 1. Marta va a jugar al tenis.
   2. Luisa y Alberto van a montar en bicicleta.
   3. Voy a ver un partido de fútbol.
   4. Vas a preparar la paella.
   5. Vamos a ir a la playa.

IV. 1. Está nevando.
   2. El niño está durmiendo.
   3. Estoy leyendo una novela.
   4. Estamos viendo la tele.
   5. Mis hermanos están preparando la cena.

V. es, Es, está, Es, es, está

VI. 1. Estoy escribiendo los ejercicios de la *Autoprueba.*
   2. Voy a estudiar, etc.
   3. Hago la tarea para la clase de..., etc.
   4. Tengo que estudiar, etc.
   5. Tengo ganas de dormir, etc.
   6. Conozco muy bien a...
   7. Traigo mis libros, etc.
   8. Mi estación favorita es la primavera (el verano, etc.) porque...
   9. Hace calor (buen tiempo/frío/viento/etc.)

Autoprueba 5

I. 1. Mi compañero/a de cuarto se despierta.
   2. Me levanto.
   3. Te bañas.
   4. Pepita se cepilla los dientes.
   5. Nos ponemos suéteres porque hace frío.
   6. Octavio y Manual se visten.

II. 1. ...frecuentemente.
   2. ...fácilmente.
   3. ...recientemente.
   4. ...inmediatamente.

III.A. 1. Me duché.
   2. Pepita se peinó.
   3. Te lavaste la cara.
   4. Nos afeitamos.
   5. Ellos se cepillaron los dientes.

B. 1. Llegué al trabajo a las nueve.
   2. Dos colegas leyeron las noticias del día.
   3. Mi colega y yo mandamos un mensaje...
   4. Escribiste un memo muy importante.
   5. Fuimos a un restaurante chino para almorzar.
   6. En la tarde, mi colega llamó a varios de nuestros clientes.
   7. Ella resolvió un problema serio.
   8. Salimos del trabajo a las cinco de la tarde.

IV.A. 1. Pues, Camila va a invitarme. *o* Camila me va a invitar.
   2. Pues, Camila va a invitarnos. *o* Camila nos va a invitar.
   3. Pues, Camila va a invitarlos/las. *o* Camila los/las va a invitar.
   4. Pues, Camila va a invitarlas. *o* Camila las va a invitar.
   5. Pues, Camila va a invitarlos. *o* Camila los va a invitar.
   6. Pues, Camila va a invitarla. *o* Camila la va a invitar.
   7. Pues, Camila va a invitarte. *o* Camila te va a invitar.

B. 1. Sí, (No, no) quiero verlos/las. *o* Sí, (No, no) los/las quiero ver.
   2. Sí, (No, no) voy a llamarlos. *o* Sí, (No, no) los voy a llamar.
   3. Sí, (No, no) estoy haciéndola ahora. *o* Sí, (No, no) la estoy haciendo ahora.
   4. Sí, (No, no) los completé.
   5. Sí, (No, no) voy a estudiarlo. *o* Sí, (No, no) lo voy a estudiar.

V.
1. Por la mañana después de levantarme, me ducho, etc.
2. Antes de acostarme, me cepillo los dientes, etc.
3. Ayer fui a... También...
4. El fin de semana pasado...
5. Sí, lo/la llamé. Hablamos de... o No, no lo/la llamé.

Autoprueba 6

I.
1. La gente está dentro del cine (en el cine).
2. La catedral está detrás del banco.
3. La estatua está cerca del centro de la ciudad.
4. En el quiosco, las revistas están encima de los periódicos.

II.
1. conmigo
2. contigo
3. ellos/ellas
4. nosotros

III.A.
1. Voy a visitar esa catedral.
2. Voy a visitar este museo.
3. Quiero ver estas obras de arte.
4. Queremos ver aquellos rascacielos.

B.
1. No, me gustan ésas (aquéllas).
2. No, me gustan ésos (aquéllos).
3. No, me gusta ése (aquél).
4. No, me gusta ésa (aquélla).

IV.
1. Carlos y Felipe, ¿pidieron ustedes las entradas? Sí, (No, no) las pedimos.
2. Susana, ¿prefirió usted la ópera o el ballet? Preferí la ópera (el ballet).
3. Linda y Celia, ¿hicieron ustedes algo interesante en el centro? Sí, hicimos algo interesante. o No, no hicimos nada interesante.
4. Linda y Celia, ¿se divirtieron ustedes? Sí, (No, no) nos divertimos.
5. Alberto, ¿durmió usted bien después de volver del centro? Sí, (No, no) dormí bien después de volver del centro.

V.
1. No, nadie fue conmigo.
2. No, no hice nada interesante (en el centro).
3. Tampoco la visité./ Yo no la visité tampoco.

VI.
1. Se abren los bancos a las... de la mañana. Se abren los almacenes a las...
2. Sí, gasté mucho dinero en restaurantes el mes pasado. Pedí... o No, no gasté...
3. Pedimos...
4. Sí, fuimos al centro para... o No, no fuimos al centro...
5. Dormí... horas.
6. Casi nunca (Casi siempre) duermo ocho horas porque...
7. Anoche estudié, etc. o No hice nada anoche.
8. El fin de semana pasado fuimos..., etc. o No hicimos nada.

Autoprueba 7

I. A.
1. El abrigo es mío. Las botas son mías. Los guantes son míos. La gorra es mía.
2. La ropa interior es nuestra. Los jeans son nuestros. Las corbatas son nuestras.
3. La blusa es tuya. El vestido es tuyo. La camiseta es tuya. Las medias son tuyas.
4. La ropa de verano es suya. Las faldas son suyas. Los trajes de baño son suyos.

B.
1. Mi primo va con unos amigos suyos.
2. Viviana va con un amigo suyo.
3. Mi hermana y yo vamos con un amigo nuestro.
4. Voy con unos amigos míos.

II.
1. Natalia y Linda trajeron las decoraciones.
2. Pusimos las flores en la mesa.
3. Javier quiso venir pero no pudo.
4. Casi todos los estudiantes vinieron.

5. Estuviste en la fiesta por cuatro horas.
6. Tuve que salir temprano.

III.
1. Me dio su reloj.
2. Le regaló un bolso de cuero.
3. Les compró una computadora nueva.
4. Nos mandó tarjetas postales del Perú.
5. Te prestó su cámara.

IV.
1. Se lo regalamos.
2. Se la regaló.
3. Se las regalaron.
4. Se la regaló.
5. Nos lo regaló.

V.
1. Las mujeres llevan vestido, etc. Los hombres llevan chaqueta y corbata, etc.
2. Debo llevar mi abrigo, mis suéteres, etc. a Alaska. Debo llevar mi traje de baño, mis pantalones cortos, etc. a la Florida.
3. Sí, fui de compras el fin de semana pasado a Sears. Compré zapatos de tenis, etc. o No, no fui de compras.
4. Estuve en casa (en una fiesta, etc.) Estudié, etc.
5. Traje mis libros, etc.
6. Sí, le di la tarea para hoy (se la di) a la profesora/al profesor. o No, no le di...

Autoprueba 8

I.
1. Dígamelo. / No me lo diga.
2. Venga. / No venga.
3. Siéntese. / No se siente.
4. Léalo. / No lo lea.
5. Explíqueselo. / No se lo explique.

II.
1. Mis hermanos y yo éramos niños muy buenos.
2. Íbamos a una escuela pequeña.
3. (Yo) Escuchaba a mis maestras.
4. José jugaba al vólibol durante el recreo.
5. Ana y Tere veían la tele por la tarde.
6. Comías galletas todos los días.

III.
1. llamó, habló
2. explicó, estaba
3. preguntó, tenía
4. explicó, dolía, tenía
5. quería, estaba
6. contestó
7. dijo, podía
8. aceptó, dio
9. se sentía, se durmió

IV.A.
1. Hace (*minutos/horas*) que estoy en clase.
2. Hace (*años/semanas/etc.*) que estudio español.
3. Hace (*semanas/meses/años/etc.*) que conozco al/a la profesor/a de español.
4. Hace (*semanas/meses/años/etc.*) que vivo en la misma casa (el mismo apartamento).
5. Hace (*meses/años/etc.*) que tengo licencia de conducir un auto.

B.
1. Hablé con mi familia hace (*días/semanas/ etc.*). o Hace (*días/semanas/etc.*) que hablé...
2. Compré un regalo para alguien hace (*días/semanas/etc.*). o Hace (*días/semanas/etc.*) que compré...
3. Me hice un examen médico hace (*semanas/meses/años/etc.*). o Hace (*semanas/meses/años/ etc.*) que me hice...
4. Visité un museo hace (*semanas/meses/años/etc.*). o Hace (*semanas/meses/años/etc.*) que visité...
5. Llegué a la universidad hace (*semanas/meses/años/etc.*). o Hace (*semanas/meses/años/etc.*) que llegué...

V.
1. La última vez que fui al médico tenía fiebre (dolor de cabeza, etc.).
2. Hace (*semanas/meses/años, etc.*) que estudio en la universidad.
3. Conocí a mi mejor amigo/a hace...años (meses, etc.). o Hace...años (meses, etc.) que conocí...

4. En la escuela primaria mi maestro/a preferido/a era (*nombre*). Era muy simpatíco/a, inteligente, etc.
5. Cuando ocurrió el ataque terrorista del 11 de septiembre (yo) estaba (en casa, en la escuela/el trabajo/etc.).
6. Al oír las noticias me sentí (deprimido/a, enojado/a, etc.). Después (yo) (llamé a.../fui a casa/etc.).

7. Este año he (viajado a.../estudiado en.../ comprado../etc.).
8. Antes de empezar mi carrera universitaria había (ido a.../conocido a.../estudiado.../etc.).

Autoprueba 9

I.
1. Beatriz, ¡haz la cama!
2. María, ¡pasa la aspiradora!
3. Luis, ¡devuelve los libros al estante!
4. Abuela ¡pon la mesa!
5. Miguel, ¡limpia el baño!
6. Juanito, ¡saca la basura!

II.
1. No prendas el estéreo, por favor.
2. No uses mi computadora, por favor.
3. No toques mis cosas, por favor.
4. No salgas ahora, por favor.
5. No me digas mentiras, por favor.
6. No te preocupes, por favor.

III.
1. La abuela ha trabajado en el jardín.
2. Todos hemos lavado y secado la ropa.
3. Papá ha limpiado el garaje.
4. Mi hermana ha salido dos veces a bailar.
5. No has hecho nada.

IV.
1. Había apagado la computadora.
2. Habías imprimido tu trabajo escrito.
3. Mi compañero/a de cuarto había cerrado las ventanas.
4. Habíamos hecho la tarea para la clase de español.
5. Linda y Teresa habían leído la novela para la clase de inglés.

V.
1. Los profesores son tan simpáticos como los estudiantes. *o* Los estudiantes son tan simpáticos como los profesores.
2. El tailandés es tan difícil como el francés. *o* El francés es tan difícil como el tailandés.
3. Susana tiene tanta paciencia como Ana. *o* Ana tiene tanta paciencia como Susana.
4. Su hermano compró tantos libros como Alberto. *o* Alberto compró tantos libros como su hermano.

VI.A.
1. El reloj Rolex es más caro que el reloj Timex. *o* El reloj Timex es menos caro que el reloj Rolex.
2. Comprar una casa es menos económico que alquilar un apartamento. *o* Alquilar un apartamento es más económico que comprar una casa.
3. Ir de vacaciones a la playa es mejor que ir de vacaciones a las montañas. *o* Ir de vacaciones a las montañas es mejor que ir de vacaciones a la playa.
4. Limpiar la casa es menos divertido que ver la tele. *o* Ver la tele es más divertido que limpiar la casa.

B.
1. La ciudad de Duluth es la más fría de las tres. *o* Duluth es la ciudad más fría de las tres.
2. Bill Gates es el hombre más rico de los tres.
3. El Honda (el Ford/el Subaru) es el mejor coche de los tres.
4. La revista *National Geographic* (*Newsweek/Movie Line*) es la más interesante de las tres. *o National Geographic* (*Newsweek/Movie Line*) es la revista más interesante de las tres.

VII.
1. Sí, soy tan generoso/a como (más generoso/a que) (menos generoso/a que) mi mejor amigo/a. *o* No, no soy más generoso/a que mi mejor amigo/a.
2. Sí, tengo tantos amigos como (más amigos que) (menos amigos que) él/ella. *o* No, no tengo tantos amigos como él/ella.
3. Estudio más que (menos que) (tanto como) él/ella.
4. La clase de... es la (clase) más interesante de la universidad porque...
5. (*Nombre*) es el/la mejor profesor/a de esta universidad porque...
6. El apartamento era...

Autoprueba 10

I.
1. Se enamoraron inmediatamente.
2. Se comprometieron seis meses más tarde.
3. Se casaron en secreto dos meses más tarde.
4. Aún hoy, después de veinticinco años, se aman mucho.

II.
1. Quiere que estudiemos más. Quiere que Ana y Linda estudien más.
2. Quiere que Esteban haga la tarea. Quiere que hagamos la tarea.
3. Quiere que Juan vuelva pronto. Quiere que volvamos pronto.
4. Quiere que me divierta en clase. Quiere que nos divirtamos en clase.
5. Quiere que los estudiantes sean puntuales. Quiere que seas puntual.
6. Quiere que (yo) vaya a la biblioteca. Quiere que todos los estudiantes vayan a la biblioteca.

III.
1. Les sugiero que se vayan durante el invierno.
2. Prefiero que exploren las playas remotas.
3. Quiero que se diviertan mucho durante su visita a San Juan.
4. Quiero que visiten el bosque lluvioso.
5. Les recomiendo a mis amigos que hablen en español todo el tiempo.
6. Les pido a todos que me compren un regalo.

IV.
1. Me alegro de que tengamos una cita esta noche.
2. Ojalá que me lleve a un buen restaurante.
3. Temo que llegue un poco tarde.
4. Espero que no se olvide de esta cita.
5. Ojalá que podamos comunicarnos bien.

V.
1. Vamos al cine (nos reunimos en.../etc.). Normalmente cenamos en un restaurante (escuchamos música/bailamos/etc.).
2. Me llevo muy bien con (*nombre de persona*).
3. Sí, hago muchas llamadas a larga distancia. Llamo a... Hablamos de... *o* No, no hago muchas llamadas a larga distancia.
4. ...nos hablamos, bailamos, nos abrazamos, nos besamos, etc.
5. Quiero que mis amigos estudien, que no vean la tele, etc.
6. Prefiero que limpie el cuarto (prepare la comida, etc.). Prefiero que no fume, (no hable por teléfono toda la noche/no lleve mi ropa/etc.).
7. Espero que me dé una «A» en el curso (que me escriba una carta de recomendación, etc.).

Autoprueba 11

I.
1. Nos fascinan los relámpagos.
2. Les molestan los mosquitos.
3. Le interesa la biología. *o* Le interesan los libros de biología.
4. Me encanta pescar.
5. (A Pablo) Le importa la familia.

II.
1. Trabajé para poder ir a Costa Rica.
2. Salí para Costa Rica el 6 de agosto.
3. Estuve allí por un mes.
4. Viajé por todo el país.
5. Compré un libro sobre los bosques de nubes para mi madre.
6. Lo compré por tres mil colones.
7. Mi madre me dijo, «Gracias por el libro».

III.A.
1. No creo que ustedes encuentren el remo.
2. No estoy seguro/a de que el guía sepa hablar español.
3. Dudo que los kayaks lleguen a tiempo.
4. No estoy seguro/a de que estemos remando bien.
5. No creo que puedas ir con nosotros.

B.
1. Creo que cuesta más de doscientos dólares.
2. No creo que haya un problema serio.

3. Dudo que sea muy larga.
4. No estoy seguro/a de que sean buenos.
5. Estoy seguro/a de que vienen con nosotros.

IV.
1. Me alegro de que mis amigos hayan llegado recientemente.
2. Me alegro de que mi mejor amiga me haya comprado un regalo.
3. Siento que hayas perdido tu cámara.
4. Me alegro de que mis amigos me hayan llamado.
5. Siento que hayan tenido un accidente.

V.
1. Me fascinan (interesan) más las arañas, etc. Me molestan los mosquitos, etc.
2. Me encantan...
3. Me interesan más...
4. Sí, creo que es muy bueno para la salud hacer ejercicio al aire libre. o No, no creo que sea muy bueno...
5. Sí, dudo que hayamos hecho todo lo posible para proteger el medio ambiente. Para protegerlo más debemos... o No, no dudo que hemos hecho...
6. Sí, he viajado mucho. Me alegro (No me alegro) de que haya viajado mucho. o No, no he viajado mucho. Siento (No siento) que no haya viajado más.

Autoprueba 12

I.
1. Es una lástima que el avión llegue tarde.
2. Es bueno que tenga todo el equipaje.
3. Es urgente que vayamos a la aduana.
4. Es horrible que no pueda encontrar el boleto.
5. Es extraño que no haya azafatas.
6. Es cierto que no me gusta volar.

II.
1. Ni Jorge ni Miguel te pueden ayudar a limpiar la casa.
2. El hotel no tiene aire acondicionado y (ni) calefacción. o El hotel no tiene ni aire acondicionado ni calefacción. o El hotel ni tiene aire acondicionado ni calefacción.
3. Ningún hotel tiene televisor(es) con pantalla grande.
4. Ningún estudiante va a ir a Barcelona. o Ninguno va...
5. Nadie fue a la discoteca. o Ninguno fue...

III. A.
1. Necesito una habitación que esté en la planta baja.
2. Prefiero un cuarto que tenga dos camas sencillas.
3. Quiero un baño que sea más grande.
4. Necesito una llave que abra el mini-bar.

B.
1. tenga, tiene
2. esté, esté
3. sea, sean
4. sirva, sirve

IV.
1. Mi mamá podrá ir a la Florida.
2. Luis tendrá que trabajar.
3. Carmen y sus amigos querrán visitar la Alhambra.
4. Mis abuelitos vendrán a visitarnos.
5. El profesor Vivar-Marín y su familia viajarán por México.
6. (Yo) Pasaré los fines de semana en la playa.

V.
1. Encontramos las horas de las salidas y llegadas de los vuelos.
2. Muestran sus pasaportes, facturan su equipaje, consiguen sus tarjetas de embarque, etc.
3. Busco un hotel que tenga... o Busco un hotel que sea...
4. Sí, conozco algún lugar que es económico. o No, no conozco ningún lugar que sea económico.
5. Sí, haré un viaje este verano. También... o No, no haré un viaje este verano.

Autoprueba 13

I.
1. Levantémonos a las diez. No nos levantemos...
2. Salgamos para el centro. No salgamos...
3. Vamos por la ruta más directa. No vayamos...
4. Paremos en el supermercado. No paremos...

5. Crucemos el nuevo puente. No crucemos...
6. Sigamos recto por cuatro cuadras. No sigamos recto...
7. Exploremos el sector histórico de la ciudad. No exploremos...

II.
1. me ...llame.
2. ...la sepa (la tenga).
3. ...me ayudes (me des papel, etc.).
4. ...tenga(s) veintiún años, licencia de conducir y tarjeta de crédito. o ...haya uno disponible.
5. ...tenga que trabajar (estudiar, etc.). o ...llueva, etc. o ...mi(s) padre(s) (esposo/a) insista(n) que yo...

III.
1. Quería que limpiara mi cuarto/ fuera al supermercado/ llamara a mis abuelos/ organizara mi clóset.
2. Nos sugirió que escribiéramos los ejercicios del manual/ llegáramos a clase a tiempo/ hiciéramos la tarea con cuidado/ participáramos en clase.
3. Esperaban que los llamara (llamáramos) para Navidad/ les escribiera (escribiéramos) un mensaje electrónico/ los visitara (visitáramos) en verano/ los invitara (invitáramos) para la graduación.

IV.
1. se practica (se puede practicar)
2. se permite (se puede)
3. se habla (se permite hablar/se debe hablar)
4. se come (se sirve)
5. se estudia (se debe estudiar)

V.
1. Primero reviso el aceite; después...
2. Digo ¡Ay de mí!, etc.
3. Sí, he hecho un viaje en tren/autobús a... o No, no he hecho...
4. Sí, me gusta la idea porque... o No, no me gusta la idea porque...
5. Se puede dormir (leer, comer, descansar, ver el paisaje, etc.).
6. Sí, hacía viajes en carro con mi familia. Íbamos a... o No, no hacía viajes en carro.
7. Quería que mis padres/maestros/amigos (*verbo: imperfecto del subjuntivo*)...

Autoprueba 14

I.
1. ...recibí el dinero., ...reciba el dinero.
2. ...me des el número de teléfono del hotel., ... me diste el número de teléfono del hotel.
3. ...me llamaste., ...me llames.
4. ...regresemos de la luna de miel., ... regresamos de la luna de miel.

II.
1. (Yo) Viajaría a muchos países.
2. Pepe pondría el dinero en el banco.
3. Les darías dinero a los pobres.
4. Ustedes gastarían todo el dinero.
5. Haríamos un viaje a la Patagonia.
6. Mis amigas irían a Chile a esquiar.

III.
1. Si ganara más dinero, lo ahorraría.
2. Si lo ahorrara, tendría mucho dinero.
3. Si tuviera mucho dinero, compraría un coche.
4. Si comprara un coche, haría un viaje.
5. Si hiciera un viaje, iría a Puerto Vallarta.
6. Si fuera a Puerto Vallarta, me quedaría allí dos meses.
7. Si me quedara allí dos meses, perdería mi trabajo.
8. Si perdiera mi trabajo, no tendría dinero.

IV.
1. Ojalá (que) el aire no estuviera tan contaminado.
2. Ojalá (que) no hubiera mucho desempleo en esta ciudad.
3. Ojalá (que) muchas personas no sufrieran del SIDA y del cáncer.
4. Ojalá (que) no tuviéramos muchos problemas que resolver.

V.
1. (En mi opinión,) Algunos de los problemas más serios son...
2. Cambiaría... porque...
3. Sí, me preocupaba por... o No, no me preocupaba por los problemas del mundo/otros problemas.
4. (Cuando me gradúe,) Trabajaré, haré un viaje, etc.

Afganistán afgano/a
Albania albanés
Alemania alemán, alemana
Andorra andorrano
Angola angoleño/a
Arabia Saudita árabe
Argelia argelino/a
Argentina (la) argentino/a
Armenia armenio
Australia australiano/a
Austria austriaco/a
Azerbaiyán azerbaiyano/a

Bahamas (las) bahamés
Bahrein Bahrení
Bangladesh bengalí
Barbados barbadense
Bélgica belga
Belice beliceño/a
Benin beninés
Bielorrusia bielorruso
Bolivia boliviano/a
Botswana botswanés
Brasil (el) brasileño/a
Bulgaria búlgaro/a
Burkina Faso burkineses
Burundi burundiano/a
Bután butanés, butanesa

Cabo Verde caboverdiano
Camboya camboyano/a
Camerún camerunés
Canadá (el) canadiense
Chad chadiano/a
Chile chileno/a
China chino/a
Chipre chipriota
Colombia colombiano/a
Comoras comorano
Congo (el) congoleño
Costa Rica costarricense
Croacia croata
Cuba cubano/a

Dinamarca danés, danesa

Ecuador ecuatoriano/a
Egipto egipcio/a
El Salvador salvadoreño/a
Emiratos Árabes Unidos amirí
Eritrea eritreo
Eslovaquia eslovaco/a
Eslovenia esloveno/a
España español/a
Estados Unidos estadounidense
Estonia estonio
Etiopía etíope

Fiji fijiano
Filipinas filipino/a
Finlandia finlandés, finlandesa
Francia francés, francesa

Gabón gabonés
Gambia gambiano
Georgia georgiano/a
Ghana ghanés
Granada granadino
Grecia griego/a
Guatemala guatemalteco/a
Guinea guineano/a
Guinea-Bissau guineano/a
Guinea Ecuatorial guineano/a
Guyana guyanés

Haití haitiano/a
Honduras hondureño/a
Hungría húngaro/a

India (la) indio/a
Indonesia indonesio
Irán iraní
Iraq iraquí
Irlanda irlandés, irlandesa
Islandia islandés, islandesa
Israel israelí
Italia italiano/a

Jamaica jamaicano/a
Japón (el) japonés, japonesa
Jordania jordano

Kazajstán kazako
Kenya keniano
Kirguistán kirguís
Kiribati kiribatiano/a
Kuwait kuwaití

Letonia letón, letona
Líbano (el) libanés
Liberia liberiano/a
Libia libio
Lituania lituano/a
Luxemburgo luxemburgués,
   luxemburguesa

Macedonia macedonio/a
Madagascar malgache
Malasia malayo/a
Malawi malawiano/a
Maldivas maldivo/a
Malí maliense
Malta maltés, maltesa
Marruecos marroquí
Mauricio mauriciano

Mauritania mauritano
México mexicano/a
Moldova moldovo
Mónaco monegasco/a
Mongolia mongol
Mozambique mozambiqueño/a

Namibia namibiano/a
Nauru nauruano
Nepal nepalés
Nicaragua nicaragüense
Níger nigerino
Nigeria nigeriano/a
Noruega noruego/a
Nueva Zelanda neozelandés

Omán omaní

Países Bajos neerlandés, neerlandesa
Pakistán pakistaní
Panamá panameño/a
Paraguay (el) paraguayo/a
Perú (el) peruano/a
Polonia polaco/a
Portugal portugués, portuguesa
Puerto Rico puertorriqueño/a

Reino Unido británico/a
Rep. Centroafricana centroafricano/a
República Checa (la) checo/a
República Dem. del Congo
   congolense/a
República Dem. Pop. Lao laosiano/a
República Dominicana (la)
   dominicano/a
Rumania rumano/a
Rusia ruso/a
Rwanda rwandés

Samoa samoano/a
San Marino sanmarinense
Santa Lucía santalucense
Senegal senegalés
Singapúr singapurense
Sierra Leona sierraleonés
Singapur singapurense
Siria sirio/a
Somalia somalí
Sudáfrica sudafricano/a
Sudán (el) sudanés
Suecia sueco/a
Suiza suizo/a
Swazilandia swazi

Tailandia tailandés, tailandesa
Taiwán chino/a
Tanzania tanzaniano/a
Tayikistán tayik
Togo togolés
Tonga tongano
Túnez tunesino
Turkmenistán turcomano/a
Turquía turco/a

Ucrania ucraniano/a

Uganda ugandés
Uruguay (el) uruguayo/a
Uzbekistán uzbeco

Venezuela venezolano/a
Vietnam vietnamita
Yemen yemenita
Yugoslavia yugoslavo/a
Zambia zambiano
Zimbabwe zimbabwense

Materias académicas

anatomy anatomía
anthropology antropología
architecture arquitectura
astronomy astronomía
biochemistry bioquímica
botany botánica
business administration administración
   de empresas
civil engineering ingeniería civil
creative writing composición,
   redacción
dramatic arts teatro, artes
   dramáticas
drawing dibujo
electrical engineering ingeniería
   eléctrica
film cine
finance finanzas
genetics genética
geography geografía
geology geología
geometry geometría
gymnastics gimástica
industrial engineering ingeniería
   industrial
journalism periodismo
jurisprudence derecho
linguistics lingüística
mechanical engineering ingeniería
   mecánica
microbiology microbiología
nursing enfermería
nutrition nutrición
obstetrics obstetricia
painting pintura
pharmacology farmacología
philology filología
physical education educación física
physiology fisiología
sculpture escultura
social work trabajo social
statistics estadística
swimming natación
theology teología
zoology zoología

Las profesiones

accountant contador/a
actor actor
actress actriz
administrator administrador/a
ambassador embajador/a
anchorperson presentador/a (de radio y televisión)
artist artista m/f
astrologer astrólogo/a
astronaut astronauta m/f
astronomer astrónomo/a
baker panadero/a
barber barbero m
bodyguard guardaespaldas m/f
bricklayer albañil m
businessman hombre de negocios
businesswoman mujer de negocios
butler mayordomo m
captain capitán/a
carpenter carpintero/a
cartographer cartógrafo/a
cashier cajero/a (en tienda)
chauffeur chofer
comedian, actor comediante
comedienne, actress comedianta
computer programmer programador/a
consultant, advisor consejero/a (en asuntos técnicos)
cook cocinero/a
counselor consejero/a
dancer bailarín m / bailarina f
dentist dentista m/f
designer diseñador/a
diplomat diplomático/a
dishwasher lavaplatos
doctor doctor/a, médico/a
electrician electricista m/f
engineer ingeniero/a
farmer agricultor/a
firefighter bombero/a
fisherman/fisherwoman pescador/a
flight attendant azafata f / auxiliar de vuelo m
florist florista m/f
flower grower floricultor/a
foreman/forewoman capataz/a
forest ranger guardabosque m/f
gardener jardinero/a
geographer geógrafo/a
geologist geólogo/a
governor gobernador/a
hairdresser peluquero/a
historian historiador/a
househusband amo m de casa
housewife ama f de casa
janitor conserje
jeweler joyero/a
journalist periodista m/f
judge juez m/f
laborer, worker obrero/a
lawyer abogado/a

librarian bibliotecario/a
maid, servant sirvienta f / criado/a
make-up artist maquillador/a
manager gerente m/f
manufacturer fabricante m
masseur/masseuse masajista m/f
mathematician matemático/a
mayor/mayoress alcalde/sa
mechanic mecánico/a
miner minero/a
musician músico/a
notary (public) notario/a
novelist novelista m/f
nurse enfermero/a
office worker oficinista m/f
painter pintor/a
parking attendant guardacoches m/f
pastor, clergyman pastor
pastry cook pastelero/a
philosopher filósofo/a
photographer fotógrafo/a
pianist pianista m/f
pilot piloto m/f
playwright, dramatist dramaturgo/a
plumber plomero m
poet, poeta
poetess poetisa
policeman, policewoman policía
police superintendent comisario/a
politician político/a
priest sacerdote
programmer programador/a
psychiatrist psiquiatra m/f
psychologist psicólogo/a
radio announcer locutor/a
real estate agent agente de bienes raíces
sailor marinero/a
sales clerk dependiente m / dependienta f
salesperson vendedor/a
sculptor, sculptress escultor/a
secretary secretario/a
shopkeeper tendero, comerciante
singer cantante m/f
social worker trabajador/a social
soldier soldado m / mujer soldado f
tailor sastre/a
teacher maestro/a
technician técnico/a
teller cajero/a (en banco)
tour guide guía m/f turístico
tradesman/tradeswoman comerciante m/f
translator traductor/a
truck driver camionero/a
veterinarian veterinario/a
waiter mesero, camarero (de restaurante)
waitress mesera, camarera (de restaurante)
warder, jailer carcelero/a
wrestler luchador/a
writer escritor/a

Vocabulario: *English-Spanish*

A

a un/uno/una 1
A.M. de la mañana P
able: to be ... poder (ue) 3
abortion aborto *m* 14
above encima de 6
accident accidente *m* 13
account cuenta *f* 6
accountant contador/a *m/f* 2
accounting contabilidad *f* 1
acquainted: to be ... with conocer 4
address dirección *f* 6; e-mail address dirección *f* electrónica 1
adolescence adolescencia *f* 10
adolescents adolescentes 10
adulthood madurez *f* 10
adults adultos *m, pl.* 10
affectionate cariñoso/a 10
afraid (to be ...) temer 10; tener miedo 11
after (class) después de (clase) 1; después de *prep.* 6; después de que *conj.* 14
afternoon tarde *f* P; every afternoon todas las tardes 1; good afternoon buenas tardes P; in the afternoon por/en la tarde 1
afterwards después 5
against (to be ...) estar en contra de 14
AIDS SIDA *m* 14
air aire *m* 13; air conditioning aire acondicionado 12
airline aerolínea *f* 12
airplane avión *m* 12
airport aeropuerto *m* 12
aisle pasillo *m* (between two rows of seats) 12
alarm clock despertador *m* 5
algebra álgebra *f* 1
all todo/a/os/as *adj.* 1; all afternoon/ morning/night toda la tarde/mañana /noche 1
allergy alergia *f* 8
(almost) always (casi) siempre 4
along por 6; to get along badly llevarse mal 10; to get along well llevarse bien 10;
along side por 6
already ya 5
also también 3
ambulance ambulancia *f* 8
American (from the United States) estadounidense *m/f, n., adj.* P
among entre 6

amusing divertido/a 2
and y 2
angry enojado/a 2
animal animal *m* 11
ankle tobillo *m* 8
annoy (to be annoying to) molestar 11
another otro/a 3
answer respuesta *f* 1; contestar 6
any algún (alguno/a/os/as) 12
apartment apartamento *m* 1
apple manzana *f* 3
application solicitud *f* 14
apply (job) solicitar 14
appointment cita *f* 10
April abril P
area code código *m* de área 10
Argentinian argentino/a *m/f, n., adj.* P
arise levantarse 5
arm brazo *m* 8
around por 6
arrival llegada *f* 12
arrive llegar 1
art arte *m* (*but las* artes) 1
as: as ... as tan ... como 9; as much as tanto como 9; as soon as tan pronto como 14
ask preguntar 7; to ask for pedir (i, i) 3
assignment tarea *f* 1
at a 1; en 2
attend asistir a 1
August agosto P
aunt tía *f* 2
autumn otoño *m* 4
avenue avenida *f* 6
avoid evitar 11
awful (How ... !) ¡Qué barbaridad! 13

B

baby bebé *m/f* 2
back espalda *f* 8
backpack: mochila *f* 1; to ... viajar de mochila 11
bacon tocineta *f*, tocino *m* 3
bad mal 2; malo/a 2
badly mal 2
bag bolsa *f* 7
baggage claim reclamo de equipajes *m, pl.* 12
baked al horno *m* 3
ball pelota *f* 4
ballpoint pen bolígrafo 1
banana banana *f*, plátano *m* 3
bandage venda *f* 8
bank banco *m* 6

bar bar *m* 6
basement sótano *m* 9
baseball béisbol *m* 4
basketball baloncesto *m*, básquetbol *m* 4
bath: private ... baño *m* privado 12
bathe bañar(se) 5
bathing suit traje *m* de baño 7
bathroom baño *m* 9
bathtub bañera *f* 9
be ser 1; estar 2
beach playa *f* 2
bean (green) judía *f* verde 3
beans frijoles *m, pl.* 3
beautiful hermoso/a 2
because porque 3; because of a causa de 11
become: to ... angry enojarse 10; to ... sick enfermarse 8
bed cama *f* 8; double bed cama doble 12; single bed cama sencilla 12; to go to bed acostarse (ue) 5
bedroom dormitorio *m*, recámara *f* 9
beef carne *f* 3
beer cerveza *f* 3
before antes de *prep.* 6; antes de que *conj.* 14
begin empezar (ie) (a) 6
behind detrás de 6
beige beige 4
believe creer 10
bellhop botones *m* 12
belt cinturón *m* 7
bench banco *m* 6
beneath debajo de 6
beside al lado de 6
best mejor 6; best wishes felicidades 10
better: it's ... es mejor 12
between entre 6
beverage bebida *f* 3
bicycle bicicleta *f* 4; to ride a bicycle ir en bicicleta 4
bill cuenta *f* 6
biology biología *f* 1
bird pájaro *m* 11
birth nacimento *m* 10
birthday cumpleaños *m* P
bit: a ... un poco 2
black negro/a 4
blanket cobija *f*, manta *f* 12
block (city) cuadra *f* 13
blond(e) rubio/a 2
blouse blusa *f* 7
blue azul 4

board subirse a 12
boarding pass tarjeta *f* de embarque 12
boat (small) bote *m* 11; by boat en barco 11
body cuerpo *m* 8
Bolivian boliviano/a *m/f*, *n.*, *adj.* P
bomb bomba *f* 14
bone hueso *m* 8
book libro *m* 1
bookshelf estante *m* 9
bookstore librería *f* 1
boots botas *f*, *pl.* 7
border frontera *f* 14
bored aburrido/a 2
boring aburrido/a 2
born (to be ...) nacer 10
boss jefe *m*, jefa *f* 14
bother molestar 11
boy chico *m*, muchacho *m* 2
boyfriend novio *m* 2
bracelet pulsera *f* 7
brakes frenos *m*, *pl.* 13
bread pan *m* 3; bread (toast) pan (tostado) 3
break: to ... romper 9; to ... one's (arm/leg) fracturar(se) (el brazo/ la pierna) 8; to ... up (with) romper (con) 10
breakfast desayuno *m* 3; to have breakfast desayunar 1
bridge puente *m* 13
briefcase maletín *m* 12
bring traer 4
broccoli brócoli *m* 3
brother hermano *m* 2
brother-in-law cuñado *m* 2
brown marrón 4
brunet(te) moreno/a 2
brush cepillo *m* 5; to brush one's hair cepillarse el pelo 5; to brush one's teeth cepillarse los dientes 5; toothbrush cepillo *m* de dientes 5
building edificio *m* 6
bureau cómoda *f* 9
bus autobús *m* 6; bus stop parada *f* de autobús 6
business empresa *f* 5
businessman hombre *m* de negocios 2
businesswoman mujer *f* de negocios 2
busy ocupado/a 2
but pero 2
butter mantequilla *f* 3
butterfly mariposa *f* 11
buy comprar 1
by por 6
bye chao P

C

cafe café *m* 6
cafeteria cafetería *f* 1
cake torta *f* 3

calculator calculadora *f* 1
calculus cálculo *m* 1
call llamar 2; telephone call llamada *f* telefónica 10
camera cámara *f* 11
camp: to ... acampar 11; campamento *m* 11
campfire fogata *f* 11
can poder (ue) 3
candidate candidato/a *m/f* 14
cap gorra *f* 7
car auto *m*, carro *m*, coche *m* 2
card tarjeta *f* 6; calling card tarjeta telefónica 10; credit card tarjeta de crédito 6
care: to take ... of cuidar 2
careful: to be (more) ... tener más cuidado *m* 13
carpet alfombra *f* 9
carrot zanahoria *f* 3
carry llevar 7
carry-on bag maletín *m* 12
cash cobrar 6; efectivo *m* 6
cashier cajero/a *m/f* 5
cast yeso *m* 8
cat gato *m* 2
cathedral catedral *f* 6
CD CD *m*; disco *m* compacto 2
center centro *m* 1; student center centro estudiantil 1
cereal cereal *m* 3
chain cadena *f* 7
chair silla *f* 1; easy chair sillón *m* 9; wheelchair silla de ruedas 8
chalk tiza *f* 1
chalkboard pizarra *f* 1
change cambiar 6; cambio *m* 6
chapter capítulo *m* 1
charge cobrar 6
check cheque *m*, cuenta *f* 6; traveler's check cheque de viajero 6; revisar 13; to check (baggage) facturar 12
cheese queso *m* 3
chemistry química *f* 1
cherry cereza *f* 3
chest pecho *m* 8
chicken pollo *m* 3; gallina *f* 11
child niño/a *m/f* 2
childhood niñez 10
children niños *m*, *pl.* 10
Chilean chileno/a *m/f*, *n.*, *adj.* P
chill escalofrío *m* 8
chimney chimenea *f* 9
choose escoger 14
church iglesia *f* 6
cinema cine *m* 6
citizen ciudadano/a *m/f* 14
city ciudad *f* 2
class clase *f* 1
classroom aula *f* (but *el* aula) 1
clean limpiar 4; limpio/a 7

clear: to ... the table quitar la mesa 9
clerk (store) dependiente *m/f* 5
climb: to ... (the mountain) escalar (la montaña) 11
clock reloj *m* 1
close cerrar (ie) 6
closed cerrado/a 2
closet ropero *m*, clóset *m* 7
clothes *f* ropa 7
clothing *f* ropa 7; clothing store tienda *f* de ropa 5
cloud nube *f* 4
cloudy: it's (very) ... está (muy) nublado 4
coat abrigo *m* 7
coffee café *m* 3
coin moneda *f* 6
cold resfriado *m* 8; frío/a 3; it's (very) cold hace (mucho) frío 4; to be cold tener frío 4
college universidad *f* 1
collide: to ... chocar 13
Colombian colombiano/a *m/f*, *n.*, *adj.* P
comb peine *m* 5; to comb one's hair peinar(se) 5
come venir 4
comfortable cómodo/a 13
communicate comunicarse 10
compact disk CD *m* 1; disco *m* compacto 1
company compañía *f*, empresa *f* 5
complain about quejarse de 10
computer computadora *f* 1; laptop (computer) computadora portátil 12; computer programmer programador/a *m/f* 2;
computer science computación *f*, informática *f* 1
confirm confirmar 12
congratulations felicidades *f*, *pl.* 10
conserve conservar 11
constantly constantemente 5
construct construir 14
contact lenses lentes *m* de contacto 7
contamination contaminación *f* 13
continue continuar, seguir (i, i) 13
cook cocinar 3
cookie galleta *f* 3
cool fresco/a 4; it's cool hace fresco 4
correct: it's ... es cierto 12
corn maíz *m* 3
corner esquina *f* 13
cost costar (ue) 7
Costa Rican costarricense *m/f*, *n.*, *adj.* P
cotton algodón *m* 7
cough tos *f* 8; to cough toser 8
count contar (ue) 6
country campo 2; país *m* 12
couple pareja *f* 10
course plato *m* 3; Of course! ¡Claro!, ¡Por supuesto! 13

cousin primo/a *m/f* 2
cow vaca *f* 11
crash choque *m* 13; **to ...** chocar 13
cream crema *f* 3
crime crimen *m* 14
criminal delincuente, criminal *m* 14
cross cruzar 13
cruise ship crucero *m* 11
crutches muletas *f, pl.* 8
cry llorar 10
Cuban cubano/a *m/f, n., adj.* P
cup taza *f* 9
cure cura *f* 14
currency moneda *f* 6
curtain cortina *f* 9
customs aduana *f* 12
cut: **to ... the lawn** cortar el césped 9; **to ... oneself** cortarse 5

D

dance bailar 4
dangerous peligroso/a 11
dark-skinned moreno/a 2
date cita *f* 10; fecha *f* P; salir (con) 10
daughter hija *f* 2
day día *m* P; **day before yesterday** anteayer 5; **all day** todo el día 1; **every day** todos los días 1
death muerte *f* 10, **death penalty** pena de muerte 14
December diciembre P
deforestation desforestación *f* 11
delay demora *f* 12
delight encantar 11
delighted: **... (to meet you)** encantado/a P
delinquent delincuente 14
delivery person repartidor/a *m/f* 5
deodorant desodorante *m* 5
depart irse 10
departure salida *f* 12
deposit depositar 6
depressed deprimido/a 8
descrimination descriminación 14
desert desierto *m* 11
desire desear 3
desk escritorio *m* 1; **student classroom desk** pupitre *m* 1; **front desk** recepción *f* 8
dessert postre *m* 3
destruir destroy 11
diarrhea diarrea *f* 8
dictionary diccionario *m* 1
die morir (ue, u) 6
difficult difícil 2
dining room comedor *m* 9
dinner cena *f* 3; **to have dinner** cenar 1
dirty sucio/a 7
disagreeable (person) antipático/a 2
discrimination discriminación *f* 14
dish plato *m* 9

dishwasher lavaplatos *m* 9
divorce divorcio *m* 10
   divorced divorciado/a 10; **to get divorced** divorciarse 10
do hacer 2; **do a blood test** hacer un análisis de sangre 8
doctor médico/a *m/f*; doctor/a *m/f* 2
doctor's office consultorio *m* del médico/de la médica 8
dog perro *m* 2
Dominican dominicano/a *m/f, n., adj.* P
door puerta *f* 1
dormitory residencia *f* estudiantil 1
doubt dudar 11
down: **to go ...** bajar 9
downtown centro *m* 1
draw: **to ... blood** sacar sangre 8
dress vestido *m* 7
dressed: **to get ...** vestirse (i) 5
drink beber, tomar 3; bebida *f* 3; **soft drink** refresco *m* 3
drive manejar 4; conducir 13
driver conductor/a 13
drug addiction drogadicción *f* 14
drug trafficking narcotráfico *m* 14
drugs drogas *f, pl.* 14
dry: **to ... the dishes** secar los platos 9; **to ... oneself** secarse 5
dryer: **hair ...** secador *m* 5; **clothes ...** secadora *f* 9

E

each cada 8
early temprano 1
earn ganar 5
ear (outer) oreja *f* 8; **ear (inner)** oído *m* 8
earrings aretes *m, pl*, pendientes *m, pl.* 7
earth tierra *f* 11
easily fácilmente 5
easy fácil 2
eat comer 2
economics economía *f* 2
Ecuadorian ecuatoriano/a *m/f, n., adj.* P
egg huevo *m* 3; **fried eggs** huevos fritos 3; **scrambled eggs** huevos *m, pl.* revueltos 3
eighth octavo/a 12
either: **either ... or** o... o 12
elderly ancianos *m, pl.* 10
election elección *f* 14
elevator ascensor *m* 12
eliminate eliminar 14
e-mail correo *m* electrónico 1; **e-mail message** mensaje *m* electrónico 1
emergencias emergency *f, pl* 8
employee empleado/a *m/f* 5
employment empleo *m* 14
enchant encantar 11
endorse (a check) endosar 6
engaged: **(to be ...)** estar comprometido/

a 10
English (language) inglés *m* 1
enjoy (something) disfrutar de 12
enter entrar (en/a) 6
envelope sobre *m* 6
environment medio *m* ambiente 11
equality igualdad *f* 14
eraser borrador *m* 1
evening noche *f* P; **every evening** todas las noches 1; **good evening** buenas noches P; **in the evening** por/en la noche 1
every cada 8
exam examen *m* 1
examine examinar 8
exchange cambiar 6; cambio *m* 6
excuse me con permiso, perdón P
exercise ejercicio *m* 1; hacer ejercicio 4
expect esperar 10
expensive caro/a 7
explain explicar 7
explosion explosión 14
explore (the web) navegar por la red 1
eye ojo *m* 8
eyeglasses gafas *f, pl.* 7

F

face cara *f* 8
facing frente a 9
factory fábrica *f* 5
fair justo 12
faithful fiel 10
fall otoño *m* 4; **to fall asleep** dormirse (ue) 5; **to fall in love (with)** enamorarse (de) 10
family familia *f* 2
family room sala *f* familiar 9
far (from) lejos (de) 6
farm granja *f* 11
fascinate fascinar 11
fascinating: **to be ...** fascinar 11
fashion *f* moda; **a la moda** in style 7
fasten: **to ... one's seat belt** abrocharse el cinturón 12
fat gordo/a 2
father padre *m* 2
father-in-law suegro *m* 2
favor: **to be in ... of** estar a favor de 14
fear temer 10
February febrero P
feed dar de comer 14
feel: **to ...** sentirse (ie, i) 8; **to ... like (doing something)** tener ganas de + *infinitivo* 4
fever fiebre *f* 8
few pocos/ as *m/f, adj.* 3
fifth quinto/a 12
fight (for) luchar (por) 14
fill: **to ... (the tank)** llenar (el tanque) 13
film película *f* 6
finally por fin 8

find encontrar (ue) 6; **to ... out** averiguar 6

fine bien P; multa *f* 13

finger dedo *m* 8

fingernail uña *f* 8

finish terminar 6

fire fuego *m* 11

fireplace chimenea *f* 9

first primero *adv* 5; **first class** de primera clase 13

fish pescado *m* 3; **to fish** pescar 11; **(live)** pez *m* (los peces) 11

fix reparar 13

flat (tire) llanta *f* desinflada 13

flight vuelo *m* 12; **flight attendant** *m* auxiliar *m* de vuelo 12; *f* azafata 12

floor suelo *m* 9; piso *m* (of a building) 9; **main floor** planta *f* baja 12; **first floor** primer piso 9; **second floor** segundo piso 9

flowers flores *f, pl.* 4

flu gripe *f* 8

fly mosca *f* 11; volar (ue) 12

follow continuar, seguir (i, i) 13

food comida *f* 3

foolish tonto/a 2

foot pie *m* 8

football fútbol *m* americano 4

for por, para 11

forbid prohibir 14

forest bosque *m* 11; **forest fires** incendios *m, pl.* forestales 11

forget olvidar 10; **to forget** olvidarse de 10

fork tenedor *m* 9

fourth cuarto/a 12

free gratis 13

freedom libertad *f* 14

French (language) francés *m* 1

french fries papas *f, pl.* fritas 3

frequently frecuentemente 5

Friday viernes *m* P

fried frito/a 3

friend amigo/a *m/f* 2; **best friend** mejor amigo/a *m/f* 2

friendship amistad *f* 10

from de *prep.* P

front: **in ... of** delante de 6; enfrente de 6; frente a 6

fruit fruta *f* 3

function funcionar 13

full-time job trabajo *m* de tiempo completo 5

funny divertido/a 2

furniture muebles *m, pl.* 9

G

game partido *m* 4

garage garaje *m* 9

garden jardín *m* 9

garlic ajo *m* 3

gas gasolina *f* 13; **to put gas (in tank)**

echar gasolina 13

gas station gasolinera *f* 13

gate puerta *f* de salida 12

gather recoger 11

generally generalmente 5

German (language) alemán *m* 1

get conseguir (i, i) 12; **to get along well** llevarse bien 10; **to get along badly** llevarse mal 10; **to get angry** enojarse 10; **to get dressed** vestirse (i) 5; **to get engaged (to)** comprometerse (con) 10; **to get a grade** sacar una nota 1; **to get married (to)** casarse (con) 10; **to get on** subirse a 12; **to get off** bajarse de 12; **to get out of** bajarse de 12; **to get sick** enfermarse 8; **to get (stand) in line** hacer cola 6; **to get tired** cansarse 8; **to get together** reunirse (con) 10; **to get up** levantarse 5

gift regalo *m* 7

girl chica *f*, muchacha *f* 2

girlfriend novia *f* 2

give dar 7; **to give a shot/vaccination** poner una inyección/una vacuna 8; **to give (as a gift)** regalar 7; **to give birth** dar a luz 10

glad: **to be ... about** alegrarse (de) 10

glass (drinking) vaso *m* 9

gloves guantes *m, pl.* 7

go ir 1; **to go away** irse 10; **to go into** entrar (en/a) 6; **to go to bed** acostarse (ue) 5; **to go down** bajar 9; **to go on a cruise** hacer un viaje en crucero/en barco 11; **to go out (with)** salir (con) 10; **to go parasailing** practicar el *parasail* 11; **to go shopping** ir de compras 4; **to go to sleep** dormirse (ue, u) 5; **to go up** subir 9; **to go white-water rafting** practicar el descenso de los ríos 11

goblet copa *f* 9

gold oro *m* 7

golf golf *m* 4

good bueno/a 2; **it's good** es bueno 12

good-bye adiós P; **to say good-bye** despedirse (i, i) 12

good-looking guapo/a 2

gosh (Oh, my ... !) ¡Caramba! 13

government gobierno *m* 14

grade nota *f* 1

granddaughter nieta *f* 2

grandfather abuelo *m* 2; **great grandfather** bisabuelo *m* 2

grandmother abuela *f* 2; **great grandmother** bisabuela *f* 2

grandparents abuelos *m, pl.* 2

grandson nieto *m* 2

grape uva *f* 3

grass hierba *f* 11

gray gris 4

green verde 4

green bean judía *f* verde 3

grilled a la parilla 3

Guatemalan guatemalteco/a *m/f, n., adj.* P

guest huésped/a *m/f* 12

guitar guitarra *f* 4

gym(nasium) gimnasio *m* 1

H

hair pelo *m* 8; **hair dryer** secador *m* de pelo 5

half media *f* P; **my other half** mi media naranja 10

half-brother medio hermano *m* 2

half-sister media hermana *f* 2

ham jamón *m* 3

hamburger hamburguesa *f* 3

hand mano *f* 8

handsome guapo/a 2

happen pasar 6

happening (What's ... ?) ¿Qué pasa? (*formal*) P

happy contento/a 2

hard difícil 2

hardworking trabajador/a 2

hat sombrero *m* 7

have tener 2; **to have a good time** divertirse (ie) 5; **to have dinner** cenar 1; **to have just** (completed an action) acabar de + *infinitivo* 5; **to have lunch** almorzar (ue) 3; **to have to** (do something) tener que + *infinitivo* 4

he él *m, subj.* P

head cabeza *f* 8; **headache** dolor *m* de cabeza 8

headphones audífonos *m, pl.* 1

health salud *f* 8

hear oír 4

heart corazón *m* 8

heating calefacción *f* 12

help ayudar (a) 9

Help! ¡Socorro!, ¡Auxilio! 13

her su/sus 2; ella *obj. prep.* 6; la *dir. obj.* 5; **(to, for her)** le *ind. obj.* 7

hers suyo/a/os/as 7

here aquí 2

herself se *refl. pron.* 5

hi ¡hola! P

highway autopista *f* 13; carretera *f* 13

hike: **to take a ...** dar una caminata 11

hill colina *f* 11

him él *obj. prep., pron.* 6; **to/for him** le *ind. obj.* 7; lo *dir. obj.* 5

himself se *refl. pron.* 5

his su/sus 3; suyo/a/os/as 7

history historia *f* 1

home casa *f* 2; hogar *m* 9; **at home** en casa 2

homeless desamparados *m, pl.* 14

homemaker amo/a *m/f* de casa 2

homework tarea *f* 1

Honduran hondureño/a *m/f, n., adj.* P

honest sincero/a 10
honeymoon luna *f* de miel 10
hope esperar 10; **I hope** ojalá que... 10
horrible: **it's ...** es horrible 12
horse caballo *m* 11
horseback: **to ride ...** montar a caballo *m* 11
hose medias *f, pl.* 7
hot (temperature) caliente 3; **it's (very) hot** hace (mucho) calor 4; **to be hot** tener calor 4
hotel hotel *m* 12
house casa *f* 1
how? ¿cómo? 3; **How are you?** ¿Cómo está usted? (*formal*), ¿Cómo estás? (*informal*); ¿Qué tal? (*informal*) P; **How many?** ¿cuantos/as? 2; **How much?** ¿cuanto/a? 3;
hug abrazar 2
hunger hambre *m* 14
hungry: **to be ...** tener hambre 3
hurry: **to be in a ...** tener prisa 12
hurt: **Does it ...?** ¿Te duele? 8; **to ... oneself** lastimarse 8
husband esposo *m*, marido *m* 2

I

I yo *subj.* P
ice hielo *m* 3; **ice cream** helado *m* 3
immediately inmediatamente 5
important: **to be ...** to importar 11; **it's ...** es importante 12
impossible: **it's ...** es imposible 12
improbable: **it's ...** es improbale 12
in en 2; **in case** en caso de que 13; **in love (with)** enamorado/a (de) 10
inexpensive barato/a 7
infancy infancia *f* 10
inform informar 14
inquire averiguar 6
insects insectos *m, pl.* 11
inside dentro de 6
insist (on) insistir (en) 10
instead of en vez de 6
intelligent inteligente 2
intend: **(to do something)** pensar (ie) + *infinitivo* 4
interest interesar 11; **to be interesting to** interesar 11
interview entrevista *f* 14
introduce presentar P
invest invertir (ie, i) 6
invite invitar (a) 6
injection inyección *f* 8
island isla *f* 11
it la *f, dir. obj.*, 5; lo *dir. obj.* 5; **it seems that...** parece que 12
Italian (language) italiano *m* P
its su/sus 2

J

jacket chaqueta *f* 7

jam mermelada *f* 3
January enero P
Japanese (language) japonés *m* 1
jealous celoso/a 10; **to be jealous** tener celos *m, pl.* 10
jeans jeans *m, pl.*; vaqueros *m, pl.* 7
jewelry joyas *f, pl.* 7; **jewelry shop** joyería *f* 6
juice jugo *m*, zumo *m* 3
July julio P
June junio P
jungle selva *f* 11
just: **to have ...** acabar de + *infinitivo* 5
justice justicia *f* 14

K

kayak kayak *m* 11
keep guardar 9
key llave *f* 12
keyboard teclado *m* 1
kill matar 10
kilometer kilómetro *m* 13
kind amable 2
kiss besar 2
kitchen cocina *f* 9
knife cuchillo *m* 9
know conocer, saber 4; **to know how to** saber 4

L

laboratory laboratorio *m* 1
lake lago *m* 4
lamp lámpara *f* 9
land aterrizar 12; tierra *f* 11
last: **... year/ month/ summer** el año/ mes/ verano pasado... 5
large grande 2
later más tarde 1
laugh: **to ... at** reírse (de) 10
law ley *f* 14
lawyer abogado/a *m/f* 2
lazy perezoso/a 2
leader líder *m/f* 14
learn aprender 1
leather cuero *m* 7
leave: salir 1; irse 10; **to ... (behind)** dejar 12; **to ... a message** dejar un mensaje 10
leaves hojas *f, pl.* 4
left: **to the ...** a la izquierda *f* 13
leg pierna *f* 8
legalize legalizar 14
lemon limón *m* 3
lend prestar 7
less menos P
lesson lección *f* 1
letter carta *f* 6
lettuce lechuga *f* 3
library biblioteca *f* 1
license: **driver's ...** licencia *f* de conducir 13
life vida *f* 10; **stages of life** etapas *f, pl.* de la vida 10

lift weights levantar pesas *f* 4
light luz *f* 9
lightning relámpago *m* 11
like gustar 3; **I would like** quisiera ... 3; **to like a lot** encantar 4
likeable simpático/a 2
line (of people or things) cola *f*, fila *f* 6
lip labio *m* 8
listen (to) escuchar 1
literature literatura *f* 1
little pequeño/a *adj.* 2; poco *adv.* 3; **(quantity)** poco/a *adj.* 3
live vivir 1
living room sala *f* 9
lobster langosta *f* 3
long largo/a 7; **long distance call** llamada *f* de larga distancia 10; **long-sleeved** de manga *f* larga 7
look: **to ... at** mirar 7; **to ... for** buscar 1
lose perder (ie) 4
lot: **a ...** mucho 3; mucho/a/os/as *adj.* 3
love querer (ie) 3; amar 2; encantar 4; amor *m* 10; **love at first sight** amor *m* a primera vista 10; **to fall in love (with)** enamorarse (de) 10; **to be in love (with)** estar enamorado/a (de) 10
luck (**What ...** !) ¡Qué suerte! 13
lucky (**How ...** !) ¡Qué suerte! 13
luggage equipaje *m* 12
lunch almuerzo *m* 3; **to have lunch** almorzar (ue) 3
lung pulmón *m* 8

M

machine: **ATM ...** cajero *m* automático 6
magazine revista *f* 6
maid (hotel) camarera *f* 12
mailbox buzón *m* 6
make: **to ... the bed** hacer la cama 9
makeup maquillaje *m* 5; **to put on makeup** maquillarse 5
mall (shopping) centro *m* comercial 6
man hombre *m* 2
manager gerente/a *m/f* 14
many mucho/a/os/as *adj.* 3; **as much/many...as** tanto/a/os/as... como 9
many times muchas veces *f, pl.* 8
map mapa *m* 1
March marzo P
market mercado *m* 3
married: **to be ... (to)** estar casado/a (con) 10; **to get ... (to)** casarse (con) 10
match partido *m* 4
mathematics matemáticas *f, pl.* 1
matter importar 11
maturity madurez *f* 10
May mayo P
me me *dir. obj.* 5; **to/for me** me *ind. obj.* 7; mí *obj. prep.* 6; **Poor me!** ¡Ay de mí! 13
meal (main) comida *f* 3
meat carne *f* 3

meet reunirse (con) 10; **to meet up (with) (by chance)** encontrarse (ue) (con) 10

mess **(What a ... !)** ¡Qué lío! 13

metro metro *m* 6

Mexican mexicano/a *m/f, n., adj.* P

microwave microondas *m* 9

midnight medianoche *f* P

milk leche *f* 3

mine mío/a/os/as 7

mirror espejo *m* 9

miss extrañar 10; **to miss the train** perder (ie) el tren 13

Monday lunes *m* P

money dinero *m* 5; moneda *f* 6

month mes *m* P

moon luna *f* 11

more más 3

morning: **every ...** todas la mañanas 1; **good ...** buenos días P; **in the ...** por/en la mañana 1

mosquito mosquito *m* 11

mother madre *f* 2

mother-in-law suegra *f* 2

motor motor *m* 13; **to tune the motor** afinar el motor 13

motorcycle motocicleta *f* 13

mountain biking ciclismo de montaña 11

mountain climbing andinismo *m*, alpinismo *m* 11

mountains montañas *f, pl.* 2

mouse ratón *m* 1

mouth boca *f* 8

move **(from house to house)** mudarse 9

movie película *f* 6; **movie theater** cine *m* 6

much mucho 3; mucho/a/os/as *adj.* 3; **too much** demasiado *adv.* 13

museum museo *m* 6

music música *f* 1

my mi/mis 2

myself me *refl. pro.* 5

N

napkin servilleta *f* 9

narrate **(a story or incident)** contar (ue) 7

nasal congestion congestión *f* nasal 8

natural resources recursos naturales *m, pl.* 11

nature naturaleza *f* 11

nausea náuseas *f, pl.* 8

near cerca de 6

necessary: **it's ...** es necesario; es preciso 12

neck cuello *m* 8

necklace collar *m* 7

need necesitar 3

neighbor vecino/a *m/f* 9

not, either, neither tampoco 6;

neither... nor ni... ni 12

nephew sobrino *m* 2

nervous nervioso/a 2

never nunca 4

new nuevo/a 2; **What's new?** ¿Qué hay de nuevo? *(formal)* P

newlyweds recién casados *m, pl.* 10

news noticias *f, pl.* 6

newscast noticiero *m* 14

newspaper periódico *m* 6

newsstand quiosco *m* 6

next próximo/a 4; **next week** semana *f* que viene 4

Nicaraguan nicaragüense *m/f, n., adj.* P

nice simpático/a 2; **nice meeting you too** igualmente P

niece sobrina *f* 2

night noche *f* P; **at night** por/en la noche 1; **every night** todas las noches 1; **last night** anoche 5

ninth noveno/a 12

no ningún (ninguno/a) 12

no one nadie 6

nobody nadie 6

noise ruido *m* 9

none ningún (ninguno/a) 12

nose nariz *f* 8

noon mediodía *m* P

normally normalmente 5

notebook cuaderno *m* 1

notes apuntes *m, pl.* 1; **to take notes** tomar apuntes 1

nothing nada 6

November noviembre P

now ahora 1

nurse enfermero/a *m/f* 2

O

obtain conseguir (i, i) 12

obvious: **it's ...** es obvio 12

ocean océano *m* 11

October octubre P

of de *prep.* P

offender delincuente 14

off: **to turn ...** apagar 9; **to get ...** bajarse (de) 12

office oficina *f* 1

often muchas veces *f, pl.* 8

oil aceite *m* 3

okay regular P

old viejo/a, anciano/a 2; **old age** vejez *f* 10; **to be ... years old** tener ... años 2

older mayor 2

olive aceituna *f* 3

on en, sobre 6

once una vez *f* 8

one un/uno/una 1; **one time** una vez *f* 8

onion cebolla *f* 3

open abierto/a 2

open abrir 6

opposite enfrente de 6; frente a 6

or o 2

orange anaranjado/a 4; naranja *f* 3

order pedir (i) 3; **in order that** para que 13; **in order to (do something)** para + *infinitivo* 6

other otros/as 3

ought to **(do something)** deber + *infinitive* 4

our nuestro/a/os/as 2

ours nuestro/a/os/as 7

ourselves nos *refl. pron.* 5

outside fuera de 6

oven horno *m* 9

overpopulation sobrepoblación *f* 14

owner dueño/a 8

ozone layer capa *f* de ozono *m* 11

P

P.M. de la tarde, de la noche P

pack empacar, hacer las maletas 12

package paquete *m* 6

page página *f* 1; **Web page** página web *f* 1

paint pintar 4

painting cuadro *m* 4

Panamanian panameño/a *m/f, n., adj.* P

pants pantalones *m, pl.* 7

panty hose pantimedias *f, pl.* 7

paper papel *m* 1; **(academic)** trabajo *m* escrito 1

Paraguayan paraguayo/a *m/f, n., adj.* P

paramedics paramédicos *m, pl.* 8

parasailing: **to go ...** practicar el *parasail* 11

pardon me con permiso; perdón P

parents padres *m, pl.* 2

park parque *m* 6; **to park** estacionar 13

parking estacionamiento *m* 13

part-time job trabajo *m* de tiempo parcial 5

partner pareja *f* 2

party fiesta *f* 1

pass: **... (time)** pasar 6; **boarding ...** tarjeta *f* de embarque 12

passenger pasajero/a *m/f* 12

pastry pastel *m* 3; **pastry shop** pastelería *f* 6

patient *m/f* paciente 8

pay **(for)** pagar 6

pea guisante *m* 3

peace paz *f* 14; **peace accord** acuerdo *m* de paz 14

peacefully tranquilamente 5

peach durazno *m*, melocotón *m* 3

pear pera *f* 3

pen **(ballpoint ...)** bolígrafo *m* 1

pencil lápiz *m* 1

people gente *f* 6; **young people** jóvenes *m, pl.* 10

pepper pimienta *f* 3

personally personalmente 5

Peruvian peruano/a *m/f*, *n.*, *adj.* P
pharmacy farmacia *f* 8
philosophy filosofía *f* 1
phone book guía *f* telefónica 10
photos (to take ...) sacar/tomar fotos *f*, *pl.* 11
physics física *f* 1
pick up recoger 11
picture cuadro *m* 4
pie pastel *m* 3
pig cerdo *m* 11; puerco *m* 3
pillow almohada *f* 12
pilot piloto/a *m/f* 12
pineapple piña *f* 3
pink rosado/a 4
pizzeria pizzería *f* 6
place lugar *m* 6; to place poner 4
plan (to do something) pensar (ie) + *infinitivo* 4
planet planeta *m* 11
plant planta *f* 12
plate plato *m* 9
platform andén *m* 13
play jugar (ue) 4; (instruments) tocar 4; (sports) jugar (ue) al (deporte) 4; play obra *f* de teatro 6
plaza plaza *f* 6
please por favor P
pleased: ... to meet you mucho gusto P
pleasure: the ... is mine el gusto es mío P
policeman policía *m* 13
policewoman mujer *f* policía 13
pollution contaminación *f* 11
pool (swimming) piscina *f* 12
poor pobre 2
pork carne *f* de cerdo/puerco 3; pork chop chuleta *f* de cerdo 3
porter maletero *m* 13
possible: it's ... es posible 12
possibly posiblemente 5
postcard tarjeta *f* 6
post office oficina *f* de correos 6
poster póster *m* 9
potato papa *f*, patata *f* 3
poverty pobreza *f* 14
practice praticar 1
prefer preferir (ie) 3
pregnant embarazada 8
prejudice prejuicio *m* 14
prepare preparar 1
prescription receta *f* 8
pretty bonito/a 2
prevent prevenir 11
price precio *m* 7
print imprimir 1
printer impresora *f* 1
probable: it's ... es probable 12
probably probablemente 5
problem problema *m* 11
professor profesor/a *m/f* 1

programmer (computer) programador/a *m/f* 2
protect proteger 11
provided that con tal (de) que 13
psychology psicología *f* 1
Puerto Rican puertorriqueño/a *m/f*, *n.*, *adj.* P
purple morado/a 4
purse bolso *m* 7
put poner 4; to put away guardar 9; to put gas (in the tank) echar gasolina 13; to put on (shoes, clothes, etc.) ponerse (los zapatos, la ropa, etc.) 5

Q

quarter cuarto P
question pregunta *f* 1
quiz prueba *f* 1

R

raft balsa *f* 11
rafting: to go white-water ... practicar el descenso de ríos/el *rafting* 11
rain llover (ue) 4
rain lluvia *f* 4
raincoat impermeable *m* 7
raining: it's ... está lloviendo 4; llueve 4
rapidly rápidamente 5
razor navaja *f* 5
read leer 1
ready: to be ... estar listo/a 10
receive recibir 6
recently recientemente 5
reception recepción *f* 8
receptionist recepcionista *m/f* 5
recommend recomendar (ie) 10
recycle reciclar 11
red rojo/a 4
refrigerator refrigerador *m* 9
register registrarse 12
regret sentir (ie, i) 10
relative pariente *m* 2
religion religión *f* 1
remember acordarse (ue) de 10; recordar (ue) 10
rent alquilar 9
repair reparar 13
repeat repetir (i, i) 6
report reportar 14
reporter reportero/a *m/f* 14
responsible responsable 3
request pedir (i, i) 3
resolve resolver (ue) 9
rest descansar 4
restaurant restaurante *m* 1
restroom aseos *m*, *pl.*, servicio *m* 13
return volver (ue) 3; regresar 1; to return (something) devolver (ue) 7
rice arroz *m* 3
rich rico/a 2
ride: to ... a bicycle ir en bicicleta 4; to ...

horseback montar a caballo 11
ridiculous: it's ... es ridículo 12
right (to the) a la derecha 13
human rights derechos *m*, *pl.* humanos 14
ring sonar (ue) 5; anillo *m* 7
river río *m* 11
road camino *m* 13
rob robar 14
roof techo *m* 9
room cuarto *m* 2; habitación *f* 8; double room habitación *f* doble 12; room service servicio *m* de habitación 12; single room habitación *f* sencilla 12
roommate compañero/a *m/f* de cuarto 5
round-trip viaje *m* de ida y vuelta 13
row remar 11
rug alfombra *f* 9
run correr 4; to run funcionar 13
Russian (language) ruso *m* 1

S

sad triste 2
safe seguro/a 13
salad ensalada *f* 3
salt sal *f* 3
Salvadorean salvadoreño/a *m/f*, *n.*, *adj.* P
sand arena *f* 11
sandals sandalias *f*, *pl.* 7
sandwich bocadillo *m*, sándwich *m* 3
Saturday sábado *m* P
sausage chorizo *m*, salchicha *f* 3
save: conservar 11; to ... (money) ahorrar 6
say decir (i) 4
schedule horario *m* 12
school: elementary ... escuela *f* 2; high ... colegio *m* 2
science ciencia *f* 1; computer science computación *f*, informática *f* 1; political science ciencias *f* políticas 1
scissors tijeras *f*, *pl.* 5
score nota *f* 1
scuba dive bucear 11
screen pantalla *f* 1
sea mar *m* 11
seafood marisco *m* 3
season estación *f* 4
seat asiento *m* 12
seat belt cinturón *m* 12
seated: to be ... estar sentado/a 8
second segundo/a 12; second class de segunda clase 13
secretary secretario/a *m/f* 5
see ver 4
sell vender 3
send mandar 1; enviar 6
sentence oración *f* 1
separate separarse (de) 10
September septiembre P

serious serio/a 2

serve servir (i) 3

service: ... station estación f de servicio 13; room ... servicio m de habitación 12

set: to ... the table poner la mesa 9

seventh séptimo/a 12

shame: it's a ... es una lástima 12; What a ...! ¡Qué lástima! 13

shampoo champú m 5

shave (oneself) afeitarse 5

shaver (electric ...) máquina f de afeitar 5

she ella f, subj. P

sheet sábana f 12; sheet of paper hoja f de papel 1

shelf estante m 9

shirt camisa f 7

shoes zapatos m, pl. 7; tennis shoes zapatos m, pl. de tenis 7

shop taller m mecánico 13

shopping: to go ... ir de compras 4; ... center centro m comercial 6

short bajo/a 2; corto/a 7; short-sleeved de manga f corta 7

shorts pantalones m, pl. cortos 7

should (do something) deber + infinitive 4

shoulder hombro m 8

show mostrar (ue) 7

shower ducha f 9; to take a shower ducharse 5

shrimp camarón m 3

sick enfermo/a 2; to get sick enfermarse 8

sign firmar 6

significant other pareja f 2

silver plata f 7

sincere sincero/a 10

sing cantar 4

single soltero/a 10

sink: kitchen ... fregadero m 9; bathroom ... lavabo m 9

sister hermana f 2

sister-in-law cuñada f 2

sit: to ... down sentarse (ie, i) 8

sixth sexto/a 12

size (clothing) talla f 7

ski esquiar 4

skin dive bucear 11

skinny flaco/a 2

skirt falda f 7

sky cielo m 11

skyscraper rascacielos m 6

sleep dormir (ue) 3; to go to sleep dormirse (ue) 5

sleepy: to be ... tener sueño 5

sleeping bag saco m de dormir 11

sleeve manga f 7; long-/short-sleeved de manga larga/corta 7

slender delgado/a 2

slow despacio 13

slowly lentamente 5; despacio 13

small pequeño/a 2; small change cambio m 6

smoke fumar 4

snack merienda f 3

snake serpiente f 11

sneeze estornudar 8

snow nieve f 4; to snow nevar (ie) 4

snowing (it's ...) está nevando 4; nieva 4

so: ... long chao P; ... that para que 13

soap jabón m 5

soccer fútbol m 4

sociology sociología f 1

socks calcetines m, pl., medias f, pl. 7

sofa sofá m 9

soft drink refresco m 3

some algún (alguno/a/os/as) 12; unos/unas 1

somebody alguien 6

someone alguien 6; algún (alguno/a/os/as) 12

something algo 6

sometimes a veces 4

somewhat un poco 2

son hijo m 2

soon: as ... as tan pronto como 14; see you ... hasta pronto P

sorry: I'm so ... Lo siento mucho. P; to be ... sentir (ie, i) 10

so-so regular P

soul mate, my mi media naranja 10

sound sonar (ue) 5

soup sopa f 3

space (outer) exploration exploración f del espacio 14

space ship nave f espacial 14

Spanish español/española m/f, n., adj. P; (language) español m 1

speak hablar 1

speed velocidad f 13

spend gastar 6

spider araña f 11

spoon cuchara f 9

sport deporte m 4; to play a sport jugar (ue) al (deporte) 4

sprain: to ... one's ankle torcerse el tobillo m 8

spring primavera f 4

square (town) plaza f 6

stairs escalera f 9

stamp estampilla f, sello m 6

stand: to ... in line hacer cola f, hacer fila f 6

standing: to be ... estar de pie 8

star estrella f 11

station: bus ... estación f de autobuses 13; gas ... gasolinera f 13; service ... estación de servicio 13; railroad ... estación del ferrocarril 13

statue estatua f 6

stay quedarse 8

steak bistec m 3

stepbrother hermanastro m 2

stepfather padrastro m 2

stepmother madrastra f 2

stepsister hermanastra f 2

stereo estéreo m 9

still todavía 3

stockings medias f, pl. 7

stomach estómago m 8; stomach ache dolor m de estómago 8

stop: to ... (movement) parar 13; bus ... parada f de autobus 6

store tienda f 5; clothing store tienda f de ropa 5; department store almacén m 6; shoe store zapatería f 6

storm tormenta f 11

stove estufa f 9

straight: ... ahead derecho, recto 13

strange: it's ... es extraño 12

strawberry fresa f 3

street calle f 6

stressed estresado 2

strong fuerte 2

student estudiante m/f 1; alumno/a m/f 1; student center centro m estudiantil 1

study estudiar 1

subway metro m 6

successful: to be ... tener éxito 14

suddenly de repente 8

suffer sufrir 14

sugar azúcar m 3

suggest sugerir (ie, i) 10

suit traje m 7; bathing suit traje de baño 7

suitcase maleta f 12

summer verano m 4

sun sol m 4

sunbathe tomar el sol 4

Sunday domingo m P

sunglasses gafas f, pl. de sol 7

sunny: it is ... hace sol 4

supper cena f 3

support (a candidate/cause) apoyar 14

sure seguro/a 13

surf hacer surf 11; to surf the web navegar por la red 1

sweater suéter m 7

swim nadar 4

swimming pool piscina f 12

T

table mesa f 1

take tomar 3; llevar 7; to take a bath bañarse 5; to take a hike dar una caminata 11; to take care of cuidar 2; to take off (clothes, etc.) quitarse (la ropa, etc.) 5; (plane) despegar 12; to take out (money) retirar 6; to take out the garbage sacar la basura 9; to take

photos sacar/tomar fotos *f, pl.* 11; **to take a shower** ducharse 5; **to take a trip on a cruise ship/boat/cruise ship** hacer un viaje en crucero/en barco 11; **to take a walk/stroll** dar un paseo 4

tall alto/a 2

tank tanque *m* 13

task tarea *f* 2

tattoo tatuaje *m* 13

taxi taxi *m* 6

tea té *m* 3

teaspoon cucharita *f* 9

teacher maestro/a *m/f* 2

team equipo *m* 4

telephone teléfono *m*: **telephone book** guía *f* telefónica 10; **telephone call** llamada *f* (telefónica) 10; **cell phone** teléfono celular 10

television set televisor *m* 1

tell contar (ue) 7; decir (i) 4

tennis tenis *m* 4; **tennis shoes** zapatos *m, pl.* de tenis 7

tent tienda *f* de campaña 11

tenth décimo/a 12

terrific fenomenal P

test examen *m* 1

terrorism terrorismo *m* 14

thank you gracias P

that aquel/aquella 6; ese/a 6; que 3

the el *m. def. art.* 1; la *f. def. art.* 1; las *f, pl. def. art.* 1; los *m, pl. def. art.* 1

theater teatro *m* 6

their su/sus 2

theirs suyo/a/os/as 7

them las *f. dir. obj.* 5; **to, for them** les *ind. obj.* 7; los *m, dir. obj.* 5; ellas/ellos *obj. prep.* 6

themselves se *refl. pron.* 5

then luego, entonces 5

there allí 2; **there is/are** hay 1

thermometer termómetro *m* 8

these estos/as 6

they ellas *f subj.*, ellos *m, subj.* P

thing cosa *f* 7

think creer 10; pensar (ie) 3; **to think about (someone or something)** pensar (ie) (en) 10

third tercer 12; tercero/a/os/as 12

thirsty: to be ... tener sed 3

this este/esta *adj.* 6; éste/ésta *pron.* 6

those alquellos/as *adj.* 6; aquéllos/as *pron.* 6

those esos/as 6

throat garganta *f* 8; **sore throat** dolor *m* de garganta *f* 8

through por 6

Thursday jueves *m* P

ticket billete *m* 12; boleto *m* 12; multa *f* 13; **(movie, theater)** entrada *f* 6; **ticket window** taquilla *f* 13

tidy: to ... a room ordenar (el cuarto) 9

tie corbata *f* 7

time hora *f* P; **on time** a tiempo 1; **one time** una vez *f* 8

tip propina *f* 12

tire llanta *f* 13; **flat tire** llanta desinflada 13

tired cansado/a 2

to a 1

toast pan *m* tostado 3

today hoy P

together juntos/as; **to be together** estar juntos/as 10

toilet inodoro *m* 9; **toilet paper** papel *m* higiénico 5

tomato tomate *m* 3

tomorrow mañana P; **see you tomorrow** hasta mañana P

tongue lengua *f* 8

tonight esta noche 1

too demasiado *adv.* 13

tooth diente *m* 8

toothpaste pasta *f* de dientes 5

top: on ... of encima de 6

towel toalla *f* 5

town square plaza *f* 6

traffic tráfico *m*, tránsito *m* 13; **traffic light** semáforo *m* 13

train tren *m* 13

trash can cubo *m* de la basura 9

travel viajar 11; **travel agency** agencia *f* de viajes 13

tree árbol *m* 4

trip viaje *m* 13

truck camión *m* 13

true: it's ... es verdad, es cierto 12

try: to ... to (do something) tratar de + *infinitivo* 10

T-shirt camiseta *f* 7

Tuesday martes *m* P

turn doblar 13; **to turn off** apagar 9

tutor tutor/a *m/f* 14

U

ugly feo/a 2

umbrella paraguas *m* 7

uncle tío *m* 2

under debajo de 6

undershirt camiseta *f* 7

understand entender (ie) 3

understanding comprensivo/a 10

underwear ropa *f* interior 7

unemployment desempleo *m* 14

unfair: it's ... no es justo 12

unfortunately desafortunadamente 5

university universidad *f* 1

unless a menos (de) que 13

unpleasant (persons) antipático/a 2

until hasta que 14

up: to go ... subir 9

upon (doing something) al + *infinitivo* 6

urgent: it's ... es urgente 12

Uruguayan uruguayo/a *m/f, n., adj.* P

us: to/for us nos *ind. obj.* 7; *dir. obj.* 5; nosotros/as *obj. prep.* 6

use usar 1

V

vacation vacaciones *f, pl.* 11; **to be on vacation** estar de vacaciones 11; **to go on vacation** ir(se) de vacaciones 11

vacuum: to ... pasar la aspiradora 9

valley valle *m* 11

vaccination vacuna *f* 8

VCR VCR *m* 1; videograbadora *f* 1

vegetable legumbre *f*, verdura *f* 3

Venezuelan venezolano/a *m/f, n., adj.* P

very muy 2

victim víctima *f* 14

vinegar vinagre *m* 3

violence violencia *f* 14

visit visitar 2

volar (ue) to fly 12

volleyball vólibol *m* 4

volunteer voluntario/a *m/f* 14

volunteerism trabajo voluntario *m* 14

vomit: to ... vomitar 8

vómito *m* vomit 8

vote (for) votar (por) 14

W

wait (for) esperar 6

waiter mesero *m* 5

waiting room sala *f* de espera 8

waitress mesera *f* 5

wake up despertarse (ie) 5

walk caminar 4; **to take a walk** dar un paseo 4

wall pared *f* 9

wallet billetera *f* 7; cartera *f* 7

want querer (ie); desear 3

war guerra *f* 14

wash: to ... the dishes lavar los platos 9; **to ... oneself** lavarse 5

washer lavadora *f* 9

waste desperdiciar 11; **waste basket** papelera 1

watch reloj *m* 7; **to watch TV** ver la tele(visión) 4

water agua *f* (*but el* agua) 3

waterfall cascada *f*, catarata *f* 11

watermelon sandía *f* 3

wave ola *f* 11

we nosotros/as *m/f, subj. pron.* P

weak débil 2

wear llevar 7

weather clima *m*, tiempo *m* 4; **it's good/bad weather** hace buen/mal tiempo 4

Web site sitio web *m* 1

wedding boda *f* 10

Wednesday miércoles P

week semana *f* P; **last week** semana *f*

pasada 5
weekend fin *m* de semana P; **last weekend** fin de semana pasado 5; **on weekends** los fines *m, pl.* de semana 1
weights pesas *f, pl.* 4; **to lift weights** levantar pesas *f, pl.* 4
welcome bienvenido/a 12; **you're welcome** de nada P
well bien 2; pues P
what lo que 3
what? ¿qué? 3; **What's your name?** ¿Cómo se llama usted? (*formal*), ¿Cómo te llamas? (*informal*) P
wheel chair silla *f* de ruedas 8
when cuando 3
when? ¿cuándo? 1
where? ¿dónde? 3; **(to) where?** ¿adónde? 1; **from where?** ¿de dónde? 3
which que 3; **that which** lo que 3 **which?** ¿qué? 3; **which one?** ¿cuál? 3; **which ones?** ¿cuáles? 3
while mientras 8
white blanco/a 4
who que 3
who? ¿quién/quiénes? 2
whose? ¿de quién? 3
why? ¿por qué? 3
widow viuda *f* 10
widower viudo *m* 10
wife esposa *f*, mujer *f* 2
win ganar 4
window ventana *f* 1; (airplane, train, car) ventanilla *f* 12; **ticket window** taquilla *f* 13
windshield parabrisas *m* 13
windy: it's ... hace viento 4
wine vino *m* 3
winter invierno *m* 4
with con 3
withdraw retirar 6
without sin 3
woman mujer *f* 2
wonderful: it's ... es fenomenal 12
wool lana *f* 7
word palabra *f* 1
world mundo *m* 11
work trabajar 1; trabajo *m* 5; **to work (machine)** funcionar 13; **to work out** hacer ejercicio 4; **at work** en el trabajo *m* 2; **to work for ...** trabajar para... 5
world politics política mundial 14
worried preocupado/a 2
worry (about) preocuparse (por) 8
worse peor 9
wound: serious ... herida seria 8
write escribir 1

X

x-ray: to ... sacar una radiografía 8

Y

year año *m* 4; **to be ... years old** tener ... años 2
yellow amarillo/a 4
yesterday ayer 5; **day before yesterday** anteayer 5
yet todavía 3
you la *f, ⅃., dir. obj.* 5; las *f, pl., dir. obj.* 5; **to/for you** le *⅃., ind. obj.* 7; **to/for you** les *pl., ind. obj.* 7; lo *m, dir. obj.* 5; los *m, dir. obj.* 5; os *dir. obj.* 5; **to/for you** os *ind. obj.* 7; te *dir. obj.* 5; **to/for you** te *ind. obj.* 7; ti *obj. prep.* (*informal*) 6; tú *subj.* (*informal*) P; vosotros/as (*pl, informal*); vosotros/as *m/f* (*formal*) P
young joven 2; **young people** jóvenes *m, pl.* 10
younger menor 2
your su/sus (*formal*) 2; tu/tus (*informal*) 2; vuestro/a/os/as (*formal*) 2
yours suyo/a/os/as (*formal*) 7; tuyo/a/os/as (*informal*) 7; vuestro/a/os/as (*informal*) 7
yourself se *refl. pron.* 5; te *refl. pron.* 5
yourselves os *refl. pron.* 5
youth juventud *f* 10

A

a at, to 1; a veces sometimes 4
abierto/a open 2
abogado/a *m/f* lawyer 2
aborto *m* abortion 14
abrazar to hug 2
abrigo *m* coat 7
abril April P
abrir to open 6
abrocharse el cinturón to fasten one's seat belt 12
abuela *f* grandmother 2
abuelo *m* grandfather 2
abuelos *m, pl.* grandparents 2
aburrido/a bored 2; boring 2
acabar de + *infinitivo* to have just (completed an action) 5
acampar to camp 11
accidente *m* accident 13
aceite *m* oil 3
aceituna *f* olive 3
acordarse (ue) de to remember 10
acostarse (ue) to go to bed 5
acuerdo *m* de paz *f* peace accord 14
adiós good-bye P
adolescencia adolescence 10
adolescentes *m, pl.* adolescents 10
¿adónde? (to) where? 1
aduana *f* customs 12
adultos *m, pl.* adults 10
aerolínea *f* airline 12
aeropuerto *m* airport 12
afeitarse to shave (oneself) 5
afinar el motor tune the motor 13
agencia *f* de viajes travel agency 13
agosto August P
agua *f* (*but el* agua) water 3
ahora now 1
ahorrar to save (money) 6
aire *m* air 13; aire acondicionado air conditioning 12
ajo *m* garlic 3
al + *infinitivo* upon (doing something) 6
al lado de beside 6
alegrarse (de) to be glad (about) 10
alemán *m* German (language) 1
alergia *f* allergy 8
alfombra *f* rug, carpet 9
algo something 6
algodón *m* cotton 7

alguien someone, somebody 6
algún (alguno/a/os/as) any, some, someone 12
allí there 2
almacén *m* department store 6
almohada *f* pillow 12
almorzar (ue) to have lunch 3
almuerzo *m* lunch 3
alquilar to rent 9
alto/a tall 2
alumno/a *m/f* student 1
amo/a *m/f* de casa homemaker 2
amable kind, nice 2
amar to love 2
amarillo/a yellow 4
ambulancia *f* ambulance 8
amigo/a *m/f* friend 2
amistad *f* friendship 10
amor *m* love 10; amor a primera vista love at first sight 10
anaranjado/a orange 4
ancianos *m, pl.* elderly 10
andén *m* platform 13
andinismo *m*, alpinismo *m* mountain climbing 11
anillo *m* ring 7
animal *m* animal 11
año *m* year 4; tener... años to be ... years old 2
anoche last night 5
anteayer day before yesterday 5
antes de *prep.* before 6; antes de que *conj.* before 14
antipático/a disagreeable, unpleasant (persons) 2
apagar to turn off 9
apartamento *m* apartment 1
apoyar to support (a candidate/cause) 14
aprender to learn 1
apuntes *m, pl.* notes 1
aquel/aquella *adj.* that 6;
aquél/aquélla *pron.* that one 6
aquellos/as *adj.* those 6; aquéllos/as *pron.* those 6
aquí here 2
araña *f* spider 11
árbol *m* tree 4
arena *f* sand 11
aretes *m, pl.* earrings 7
argentino/a *m/f, n., adj.* Argentinian P

arroz *m* rice 3
arte *m* (*but las* artes) art 1
ascensor *m* elevator 12
aseos *m, pl.* restroom 13
asiento *m* seat 12
asistir (a) to attend 1
aterrizar to land 12
audífonos *m, pl.* headphones 1
aula *f* (*but el* aula) classroom 1
auto *m* car 2
autobús *m* bus 6; parada *f* de autobús bus stop 6
autopista *f* highway 13
auxiliar *m* de vuelo flight attendant (*m*) 12
¡Auxilio! ¡Help! 13
avenida *f* avenue 6
averiguar to find out, inquire 6
avión *m* airplane 12
ayer yesterday 5
ayudar (a) to help 9
azafata *f* flight attendant (*f*) 12
azúcar *m* sugar 3
azul blue 4

B

bailar to dance 4
bajar to go down 9; bajarse de to get off, to get out of ... 12
bajo/a short 2
baloncesto *m* basketball 4
balsa *f* raft 11
banana *f* banana 3
bañarse to take a bath, bathe 5
banco *m* bank 6; bench 6
bañera *f* bathtub 9
baño *m* bathroom 9; baño privado private bath 12
bar *m* bar 6
barato/a inexpensive 7
barco *m* boat 11
básquetbol *m* basketball 4
bebé *m/f* baby 2
beber to drink 1
bebida *f* drink 3
beige beige 4
béisbol *m* baseball 4
besar to kiss 2
biblioteca *f* library 1
bicicleta *f* bicycle 4
bien fine P; well 2
bienvenido/a welcome 12

billete *m* ticket 12; **billete de ida y vuelta** round trip ticket 12

billetera *f* wallet 7

biología *f* biology 1

bisabuela *f* great-grandmother 2

bisabuelo *m* great-grandfather 2

bistec *m* steak 3

blanco/a white 4

blusa *f* blouse 7

boca *f* mouth 8

bocadillo *m* sandwich 3

boda *f* wedding 10

boleto *m* ticket 12; **boleto de ida y vuelta** round trip ticket 12

bolígrafo *m* ballpoint pen 1

boliviano/a *m/f, n., adj.* Bolivian P

bolso/a *m* purse, bag 7

bomba bomb 14

bonito/a pretty 2

borrador *m* eraser 1

bosque *m* forest 11

botas *f, pl.* boots 7

bote *m* boat (small) 11

botones *m* bellhop 12

brazo *m* arm 8

brócoli *m* broccoli 3

bucear to scuba dive, skin dive 11

bueno/a good 2; **es bueno** it's good 12

buscar to look for 1

buzón *m* mailbox 6

C

caballo *m* horse 11

cabeza *f* head 8; **dolor *m* de cabeza** headache 8

cada each, every 8

cadena *f* chain 7

café *m* coffee 3; cafe 6

cafetería *f* cafeteria 1

cajero *m* automático ATM machine 6

cajero/a *m/f* cashier 5

calcetines *m, pl.* socks 7

calculadora *f* calculator 1

cálculo *m* calculus 1

calefacción *f* heating 12

caliente hot (temperature, not spiciness) 3

calle *f* street 6

cama *f* bed 8; **cama doble** double bed 12; **cama sencilla** single bed 12

cámara *f* camera 11

camarera *f* maid (hotel) 12

camarón *m* shrimp 3

cambiar to change, exchange 6

cambio *m* change, small change, exchange 6

caminar to walk 4

camino *m* road 13

camión *m* truck 13

camisa *f* shirt 7

camiseta *f* T-shirt, undershirt 7

campamento *m* camp 11

campo *m* country 2

candidato/a *m/f* candidate 14

cansado/a tired 2

cansarse to get tired 8

cantar to sing 4

capa *f* de ozono ozone layer 11

capítulo *m* chapter 1

cara *f* face 8

¡Caramba! Oh my gosh! 13

cariñoso/a affectionate 10

carne *f* meat, beef 3; **carne de cerdo/puerco** pork 3; **carne de res** beef 3

caro/a expensive 7

carretera *f* highway 13

carro *m* car 2

carta *f* letter 6

cartera *f* wallet 7

casa *f* home, house 2; **amo/a *m/f* de casa** homemaker 2; **en casa** at home 2

casado/a married 10; **recién casados *m, pl.*** newlyweds 10

casarse (con) to get married (to) 10

cascada *f* waterfall 11

(casi) siempre (almost) always 4

catarata *f* waterfall 11

catedral *f* cathedral 6

causa (a causa de) because of 11

CD *m* CD, compact disk 1

cebolla *f* onion 3

celoso/a jealous 10

cena *f* supper, dinner 3

cenar to have dinner 1

centro *m* downtown 1; **centro comercial** mall, shopping center 6; **centro estudiantil** student center 1

cepillarse el pelo to brush one's hair 5; **cepillarse los dientes** to brush one's teeth 5

cepillo *m* brush 5; **cepillo de dientes** toothbrush 5

cerca de near 6

cerdo *m* pig 11; **chuleta *f* de cerdo** pork chop 3; **carne *f* de cerdo** pork 3

cereal *m* cereal 3

cereza *f* cherry 3

cerrado/a closed 2

cerrar (ie) to close 6

cerveza *f* beer 3

champú *m* shampoo 5

chao bye (so long) P

chaqueta *f* jacket 7

cheque *m* check 6; **cheque de viajero** traveler's check 6

chica *f* girl 2

chico *m* boy 2

chileno/a *m/f, n., adj.* Chilean P

chimenea *f* fireplace, chimney 9

chocar to crash, collide 13

choque *m* crash 13

chorizo *m* sausage 3

chuleta *f* de cerdo/puerco pork chop 3

ciclismo *m* de montaña mountain biking 11

cielo *m* sky 11

ciencias *f, pl.* políticas political science 1

cierto: es ... it's true, correct 12

cine *m* movie theater, cinema 6

cinturón *m* belt 7; **abrocharse el cinturón** to fasten one's seat belt 12

cita *f* date, appointment 10

ciudad *f* city 2

ciudadano/a *m/f* citizen 14

¡Claro! Of course! 13

clase *f* class 1

clima *m* weather 4

clóset *m* closet 7

cobija *f* blanket 12

cobrar to cash, to charge 6

coche *m* car 2

cocina *f* kitchen 9

cocinar to cook 3

código *m* de área area code 10

cola *f* line (of people or things) 6

colegio *m* high school 2

colina *f* hill 11

collar *m* necklace 7

colombiano/a *m/f, n., adj.* Colombian P

comedor *m* dining room 9

comer to eat 1

comida *f* food, main meal 3

¿cómo? how? 3; **¿Cómo está usted?** How are you? (*formal*) P; **¿Cómo estás?** How are you? (*informal*) P; **¿Cómo se llama usted?** What's your name (*formal*)? P; **¿Cómo te llamas?** What's your name? (*informal*) P

cómoda *f* bureau 9

cómodo/a comfortable 13

compañero/a *m/f* de cuarto roommate 5

compañía *f* company 5

comprar to buy 1

comprensivo/a understanding 10

comprometerse (con) to get engaged (to) 10

computación *f* computer science 1

computadora *f* computer 1; **computadora portátil**

laptop/notebook (computer) 12

comunicarse to communicate 10

con with 3; **Con permiso** Pardon me, excuse me P; **con tal (de) que** provided that 13

conducir to drive 13

conductor/a driver 13

confirmar to confirm 12

congestión *f* **nasal** nasal congestion 8

conocer to know, be acquainted with 4

conseguir (i, i) to get, obtain 12

conservar to save, conserve 11

constantemente constantly 5

construir construct 14

contabilidad *f* accounting 1

contador/a *m/f* accountant 2

contaminación *f* pollution 11

contar (ue) to count 6, tell, narrate (a story or incident) 7

contento/a happy 2

contestar to answer 6

consultorio *m* **del médico/de la médica** doctor's office 8

copa *f* goblet 9

corazón *m* heart 8

corbata *f* tie 7

correo *m* **electrónico** e-mail 1

correr to run 4

cortar: ... el césped to cut the lawn 9; **cortarse** to cut oneself 5

cortina *f* curtain 9

corto/a short 7; **de manga corta** short-sleeved 7

cosa *f* thing 7

costar (ue) to cost 7

costarricense *m/f*, *n.*, *adj.* Costa Rican P

creer to believe 10

crema *f* cream 3; **crema de afeitar** shaving cream 5

crimen *m* crime 14

crucero *m* cruise ship 11

cruzar to cross 13

cuaderno *m* notebook 1

cuadra *f* (city) block 13

cuadro *m* picture, painting 4

¿cuál? which (one)? 3

¿cuáles? which (ones)? 3

cuando when 3; **¿cuándo?** when? 1

¿cuánto/a? how much? 3

¿cuántos/as? how many? 2

cuarto a quarter P

cuarto *m* room 1

cuarto/a fourth 12

cubano/a *m/f*, *n.*, *adj.* Cuban P

cubo *m* **de la basura** trash can 9

cuchara *f* spoon 9

cucharita *f* teaspoon 9

cuchillo *m* knife 9

cuello *m* neck 8

cuenta *f* bill, check 6; account 6

cuero *m* leather 7

cuerpo *m* body 8

cuidar to take care of 2

cumpleaños *m* birthday P

cuñada *f* sister-in-law 2

cuñado *m* brother-in-law 2

cura *f* cure 14

D

dar to give 7; **dar a luz** to give birth 10; **dar de comer** to feed 14; **dar un paseo** to take a walk/stroll 4; **dar una caminata** to take a hike 11

de *prep.* of, from P; **de repente** suddenly 8

debajo de beneath, under 6

deber + *infinitive* ought to, should (do something) 4

débil weak 2

décimo/a tenth 12

decir (i) to say, tell 4

dedo *m* finger 8

desforestación *f* deforestation 11

dejar to leave (behind); 12; **dejar un mensaje** to leave a message 10

delante de in front of 6

delgado/a slender 2

delincuente *m* delinquent, offender, criminal 14

demasiado *adv.* too much 13

demora *f* delay 12

dentro de inside 6

dependiente/a *m/f* store clerk 5

deporte *m* sport 4

depositar to deposit 6

deprimido/a depressed 8

derecha: a la ... to the right 13

derecho straight, straight ahead 13

derechos *m*, *pl.* **humanos** human rights 14

desafortunadamente unfortunately 5

desamparados *m*, *pl.* homeless 14

desayunar to have breakfast 1

desayuno *m* breakfast 3

descansar to rest 4

descriminación *f* descrimination 14

desear to desire, want 3

desempleo *m* unemployment 14

desierto *m* desert 11

desodorante *m* deodorant 5

despacio slow, slowly 13

despedirse (i, i) to say good-bye 12

despegar to take off 12

desperdiciar to waste 11

despertador *m* alarm clock 5

despertarse (ie) to wake up 5

después de (clase) after (class) 1; afterwards 5; **después de** *prep.* after 6; **después de que** *conj.* after 14

destruir destroy 11

detrás de behind 6

devolver (ue) to return (something) 7

día *m* day P; **buenos días** good morning P

diarrea *f* diarrhea 8

diccionario *m* dictionary 1

diciembre December P

diente *m* tooth 8

difícil difficult, hard 2

dinero *m* money 5

dirección address 6; **dirección** *f* **electrónica** E-mail address 1

disco compacto *m* CD, compact disk 1

discriminación *f* discrimination 14

Disculpe. I am sorry. P

disfrutar de to enjoy (something) 12

divertido/a *m/f* amusing, funny 2

divertirse (ie) to have a good time 5

divorciado/a divorced 10

divorciarse to get divorced 10

divorcio divorce 10

doblar to turn 13

doctor/a *m/f* doctor 2

dolor *m* **de cabeza** *f* headache 8; **dolor de estómago** *m* stomach ache 8; **dolor de garganta** *f* sore throat 8

domingo *m* Sunday P

dominicano/a *m/f n.*, *adj.* Dominican P

¿dónde? where 2; **¿adónde?** (to) where? 3; **¿de dónde...?** from where? 3

dormir (ue) to sleep 3; **dormirse (ue)** to go to sleep, to fall asleep 5

dormitorio *m* bedroom 9

drogadicción *f* drug addiction 14

drogas *f*, *pl.* drugs 14

ducha *f* shower 9

ducharse to take a shower 5

dudar to doubt 11

dueño/a owner *m/f* 8

durazno *m* peach 3

E

echar gasolina to put gas (in the tank) 13

economía *f* economics 1

ecuatoriano/a *m/f*, *n.*, *adj.* Ecuadorian P

edificio *m* building 6

efectivo *m* cash 6

ejercicio *m* exercise 1; **hacer ejercicio** to exercise, to do exercises 4

el *m*, *definite article* the 1

él *m, subj.* he P; *obj. prep. pron.* him 6
elección *f* election 14
eliminar to eliminate 14
ella *f, subj.* she P; *obj. of prep.* her 6
ellas *f, subj.* they P; *obj. of prep.* them 6
ellos *m, subj.* they P; *obj. of prep.* them 6
embarazada pregnant 8
emergencias emergency *f, pl.* 8
empacar to pack 12
empezar (ie) (a) to begin 6
empleado/a *m/f* employee 5
empleo *m* employment 14
empresa *f* business 5
en in, at 2; on 6; **en caso de que** in case 13; **en vez de** instead of 6
enamorarse (de) to fall in love (with) 10
encantado/a delighted (to meet you) P
encantar to like a lot, love 4; to delight, to enchant 11
encima de on top of, above 6
encontrar (ue) to find 6; **encontrarse (ue) (con)** to meet up (with) (by chance) 10
endosar to endorse (check) 6
enero January P
enfermarse to get/become sick 8
enfermero/a *m/f* nurse 2
enfermo/a sick 2
enfrente de in front of, opposite 6
enojado/a angry 2
enojarse to get angry 10
ensalada *f* salad 3
entender (ie) to understand 3
entonces then 5
entrada *f* (admission) ticket 6
entrar (en/a) to enter, go into 6
entre between, among 6
entrevista *f* interview 14
enviar to send 6
equipaje *m* luggage 12
equipo *m* team 4
escalar (la montaña) to climb (the mountain) 11
escalera *f* stairs 9
escalofrío *m* chill 8
escoger to choose 14
escribir to write 1
escritorio *m* (teacher's) desk 1
escuchar to listen to 1
escuela *f* elementary school 2
ese/a *adj.* that 6; **ése/a** *pron.* that one 6
esos/as *adj.* those 6; **ésos/as** *pron.* those 6
espalda *f* back 8

español *m* Spanish (language) 1
español/española *m/f, n., adj.* Spanish P
espejo *m* mirror 9
esperar to wait (for) 6; to hope, expect 10
esposa *f* wife 2
esposo *m* husband 2
esquiar to ski 4
esquina *f* (street) corner 13
esta this, that 6; **esta mañana** this morning 1; **esta noche** tonight 1; **esta tarde** this afternoon 1
estación *f* season 4; **estación de autobuses** bus station 13; **estación de servicio** service station 13; **estación de ferrocarril** railroad station 13
estacionamiento *m* parking 13
estacionar to park 13
estadounidense *m/f, n., adj.* American (from the United States) P
estampilla *f* stamp 6
estante *m* bookshelf, shelf 9
estar to be 2; **estar a favor de** to be in favor of 14; **estar comprometido/a** to be engaged 10; **estar de pie** to be standing 8; **estar de vacaciones** *f, pl.* to be on vacation 11; **estar enamorado/a de** to be in love (with) 10; **estar en contra de** to be against 14; **estar sentado/a** to be seated 8
estatua *f* statue 6
este/a *adj.* this 6; **éste/a** *pron.* this one 6
estéreo *m* stereo 9
estómago *m* stomach 8; **dolor** *m* **de estómago** stomachache 8
estornudar to sneeze 8
estos/as *adj.* these 6; **estos/as** *pron.* these 6
estrella *f* star 11
estresado/a stressed 2
estudiante *m/f* student 1
estudiar to study 1
estufa *f* stove 9
etapas *f, pl.* **de la vida** stages of life 10
evitar to avoid 11
examen *m* exam 1
examinar to examine 8
explicar to explain 7
exploración *f* **del espacio** (outer) space exploration 14
explosión *f* explosion 14
extrañar to miss 10
extraño: **es** ... it's strange 12

F

fábrica *f* factory 5
fácil easy 2
fácilmente easily 5
facturar to check (baggage) 12
falda *f* skirt 7
familia *f* family 2
farmacia *f* pharmacy 8
fascinar to be fascinating to, to fascinate 11
favor (por favor) please P
febrero February P
fecha *f* date P
felicidades *f* congratulations 10
fenomenal terrific P; **es fenomenal** it's wonderful 12
feo/a ugly 2
fiebre *f* fever 8
fiel faithful 10
fiesta *f* party 1
fila *f* line (of people or things) 6
filosofía *f* philosophy 1
fin *m* **de semana** weekend 1; **fin de semana pasado** last weekend 5; **por fin** finally 8
firmar to sign 6
física *f* physics 1
flaco/a skinny 2
flores *f, pl.* flowers 4
fly volar (ue) 12
fogata *f* campfire 11
fracturar(se) (el brazo/ la pierna) to break one's (arm/leg) 8
francés *m* French (language) 1
frecuentemente frequently 5
fregadero *m* sink (kitchen) 9
frenos *m, pl.* brakes 13
frente a in front of, opposite, facing 6
fresa *f* strawberry 3
frijoles *m, pl.* beans 3
frío/a cold 3; **hace (mucho) frío** it's (very) cold 4
frito/a fried 3
frontera *f* border 14
fruta *f* fruit 3
fuego *m* fire 11
fuera de outside 6
fuerte strong 2
fumar to smoke 4
funcionar to run, work, function (machine) 13
fútbol *m* soccer 4; **fútbol americano** football 4

G

gafas *f, pl.* eyeglasses 7; **gafas de sol** sunglasses 7
galleta *f* cookie 3

gallina *f* chicken 11
ganar to win 4; to earn 5
garaje *m* garage 9
garganta *f* throat 8; dolor *m* de garganta sore throat 8
gasolina *f* gas 13
gasolinera *f* gas station 13
gastar to spend 6
gato *m* cat 2
generalmente generally 5
gente *f* people 6
gerente/a *m/f* manager 14
gimnasio *m* gym, gymnasium 1
gobierno *m* government 14
golf *m* golf 4
gordo/a fat 2
gorra *f* cap 7
gracias thank you P
grande large 2
granja *f* farm 11
gratis free 13
gripe *f* flu 8
gris gray 4
guantes *m, pl.* gloves 7
guapo/a good-looking, handsome 2
guardar to keep 9
guatemalteco/a *m/f, n., adj.* Guatemalan P
guerra *f* war 14
guía *f* telefónica phone book 10
guisante *m* pea 3
guitarra *f* guitar 4
gustar to like 3; el gusto es mío the pleasure is mine P

H

habitación *f* room 8; habitación doble double room 12; habitación sencilla single room 12
hablar to speak 1
hace buen/mal tiempo it's good/bad weather 4; hace (mucho) calor/fresco/frío/sol/ viento it's (very) hot/cool/cold/sunny/ windy 4; hace sol it's sunny 4
hacer to do, make 1; hacer un análisis de sangre do a blood test 8; hacer la cama to make the bed 9; hacer cola to get (stand) in line 6; hacer ejercicio to exercise, work out, do exercises 4; hacer el *esnórquel* to go snorkeling 11; hacer fila to get (stand) in line 6; hacer las maletas to pack 12; hacer *surf* to surf 11; hacer un viaje en crucero/en barco to go on a cruise, take a trip on a ship/boat/cruise ship 11

hambre *f* (*but el* hambre) hunger 14
hamburguesa *f* hamburger 3
hasta: Hasta mañana. See you tomorrow. P; hasta pronto see you soon P; hasta que until 14
hay there is/are 1
helado *m* ice cream 3
herida *f* seria serious wound 8
hermana *f* sister 2
hermanastra *f* stepsister 2
hermanastro *m* stepbrother 2
hermano *m* brother 2
hermoso/a beautiful 2
hielo *m* ice 3
hierba *f* grass 11
hija *f* daughter 2
hijo *m* son 2
historia *f* history 1
hogar *m* home 9
hoja *f* de papel sheet of paper 1;
hojas *f, pl.* leaves 4
hola hi P
hombre *m* man 2; hombre de negocios businessman 2
hombro *m* shoulder 8
hondureño/a *m/f, n., adj.* Honduran P
hora *f* time P
horario *m* schedule 12
horno *m* oven 9; al horno baked 3
horrible: es ... it's horrible 12
hotel *m* hotel 12
hoy today P
hueso *m* bone 8
huésped/a *m/f* guest 12
huevo *m* egg 3; huevos fritos fried eggs 3; huevos revueltos scrambled eggs 3

I

iglesia *f* church 6
igualdad *f* equality 14
igualmente nice meeting you too P
impermeable *m* raincoat 7
importante: es ... it's important 12
importar to be important to, to matter 11
imposible: es ... it's impossible 12
impresora *f* printer 1
imprimir to print 1
improbable: es ... it's improbable 12
incendios *m, pl.* forestales forest fires 11
infancia infancy 10
informar to inform 14
informática *f* computer science 1
inglés *m* English (language) 1
inmediatamente immediately 5
inodoro *m* toilet 9

improbable: es ... it's improbable 12
insectos *m, pl.* insects 11
insistir (en) to insist (on) 10
inteligente intelligent 2
interesar to be interesting to, to interest 11
invertir (ie, i) to invest 6
invierno *m* winter 4
invitar (a) to invite 6
inyección *f* injection 8
ir to go 1; ir de compras to go shopping 4; ir(se) de vacaciones to go on vacation 11; ir en bicicleta to ride a bicycle 4; irse leave, depart, to go away 10
isla *f* island 11
italiano *m* Italian (language) 1
izquierda *f*: a la... to the left 13

J

jabón *m* soap 5
jamón *m* ham 3
japonés *m* Japanese (language) 1
jardín *m* garden 9
jeans *m, pl.* jeans 7
jefa *f* boss 14
jefe *m* boss 14
joven young 2
jóvenes *m, pl.* young people 10
joyas *f, pl.* jewelry 7
joyería *f* jewelry shop 6
judía *f* verde green bean 3
jueves *m* Thursday P
jugar (ue) to play 4; jugar al (deporte) to play (sport) 4
jugo *m* juice 3
julio July P
junio June P
juntos/as: estar ... to be together 10
justicia *f* justice 14
justo fair 12; no es ... it's unfair 12
juventud youth 10

K

kayak *m* kayak 11
kilómetro *m* kilometer 13

L

la *f, definite article* the 1; *dir. obj.* her, you (f), it (f) 5
labio *m* lip 8
laboratorio *m* laboratory 1
lado: al...de beside 6
lago *m* lake 4
lámpara *f* lamp 9
lana *f* wool 7
langosta *f* lobster 3
lápiz *m* pencil 1

largo/a long 7; 10; **de manga larga**
  long-sleeved 7

las *dir. obj.* them (f), you (f, pl.) 5
  las *f, pl. definite article* the 1

lástima: es una ... it's a shame 12

lastimarse to hurt oneself 8

lavabo *m* sink (bathroom) 9

lavadora *f* washer 9

lavaplatos *m* dishwasher 9

lavar: ... los platos to wash the dishes
  9; **lavarse** to wash oneself 5

le *ind. obj.* you, him, her (to/for ...) 7

lección *f* lesson 1

leche *f* milk 3

lechuga *f* lettuce 3

leer to read 1

legalizar to legalize 14

legumbre *f* vegetable 3

lejos de far from 6

lengua *f* tongue 8

lentamente slowly 5

lentes *m* **de contacto** contact lenses 7

les *ind. obj.* you, them (to/for you,
  them) 7

levantar pesas to lift weights 4

levantarse to get up 5

ley *f* law 14

libertad *f* freedom 14

librería *f* bookstore 1

libro *m* book 1

licencia *f* **de conducir** driver's license
  13

líder *m/f* leader 14

limón *m* lemon 3

limpiar to clean 4

limpio/a clean 7

listo/a: estar ... to be ready 10

literatura *f* literature 1

llamada *f* **telefónica** telephone call 10;
  llamada de larga distancia long
  distance call 10

llamar to call 2

llanta *f* tire 13; **llanta desinflada** flat
  tire 13

llave *f* key 12

llegada *f* arrival 12

llegar to arrive 1

llenar (el tanque) to fill (the tank) 13

llevar to wear 7; **llevarse bien/mal** to
  get along well/badly 10

llorar to cry 10

llover (ue) to rain 4; **está lloviendo** it's
  raining 4;

llueve it's raining, it rains 4

lluvia *f* rain 4

lo *dir. obj. m*, him, you, it 5; **lo que**
  what, that which 3; **lo siento**
  (**mucho**) I'm (so) sorry P

los *m, dir. obj.* them, you 6; *m, pl.,
  definite article* the 1

luchar por to fight for 14

luego then 5

lugar *m* place 6

luna *f* moon 11; **luna de miel**
  honeymoon 10

lunes *m* Monday P

luz *f* light 9

M

madrastra *f* stepmother 2

madre *f* mother 2

madurez *f* adulthood, maturity 10

maestro/a *m/f* teacher 2

maíz *m* corn 3

mal bad, badly 2

maleta *f* suitcase 12

maletero *m* porter 13

maletín *m* briefcase, carry-on bag 12

malo/a *m/f* bad 2

mañana tomorrow, morning *f* P; **de la
  mañana** A.M. (in the morning) P;
  hasta mañana see you tomorrow P;
  por/en la mañana in the morning 1

mandar to send 1

manejar to drive 4

manga *f* sleeve 7; **de manga
  larga/corta** long-/short-sleeved 7

mano *f* hand 8

manta *f* blanket 12

mantequilla *f* butter 3

manzana *f* apple 3

mapa *m* map 1

maquillaje *m* makeup 5

maquillarse to put on makeup 5

máquina *m* **de afeitar** electric shaver
  5

mar *m* sea 11

marido *m* husband 2

mariposa *f* butterfly 11

marisco *m* seafood 3

marrón brown 4

martes *m* Tuesday P

marzo March P

más more 3; **más tarde** later 1

matar to kill 10

matemáticas *f, pl.* mathematics 1

mayo May P

mayor older 2

me *dir. obj.* me 5; *ind. obj.* me (to/for
  me) 7; *refl. pron.* myself 5; **me
  llamo...** my
  name is... P

media *f* half P; **media hermana** half-
  sister 2; **mi media naranja** my soul
  mate, other half 10

medias *f, pl.* stockings, hose, socks 7

medianoche *f* midnight P

médico/a *m/f* doctor 2

medio hermano *m* half-brother 2

medio *m* **ambiente** environment 11

mediodía *m* noon P

mejor best 6; **mejor amigo/a** *m/f* best
  friend 2; **es mejor** it's better 12

melocotón *m* peach 3

menor younger 2

menos less P; **a menos (de) que** unless
  13

mensaje *m* **electrónico** e-mail message
  1

mercado *m* market 3

merienda *f* snack 3

mermelada *f* jam 3

mes *m* month P

mesa *f* table 1

mesero/a *m/f* waiter/waitress 5

metro *m* metro, subway 6

mexicano/a *m/f, n., adj.* Mexican P

mí *obj. prep. pron.* me 6; **¡Ay de mí!**
  Poor me! (What am I going to do?) 13

mi/mis my 2

microondas *m* microwave 9

mientras while 8

miércoles *m* Wednesday P

mío/a/os/as (of) mine 7; **el gusto es
  mío** the pleasure is mine P

mirar to look at 7

mochila *f* backpack 1

moda *f* fashion; **a la moda** in style 7

molestar to be annoying to, to bother
  11

moneda *f* currency, money, coin 6

montañas *f, pl.* mountains 2

montar a caballo to ride horseback 11

morado/a purple 4

moreno/a brunet(te), dark-skinned 2

morir (ue, u) to die 6

mosca *f* fly 11

mosquito *m* mosquito 11

mostrar (ue) to show 7

motocicleta *f* motorcycle 13

motor *m* motor 13; **afinar el motor** to
  tune the motor 13

muchacha *f* girl 2

muchacho *m* boy 2

mucho *adv.* much, a lot 3;

mucho/a/os/as *m/f adj.* much, a lot 3;
  (muchas) gracias
  thank you (very much) P; **muchas
  veces** *f pl.* many times, often 8;
  mucho gusto pleased to meet you P

mudarse to move (from house to
  house) 9

muebles *m, pl.* furniture 9

muerte *f* death 10; **pena de muerte**

death penalty 14

mujer *f* woman, wife 2; **mujer de negocios** businesswoman 2; **mujer policía** policewoman 13

muletas *f., pl.* crutches 8

multa *f* fine, ticket 13

mundo *m* world 11

museo *m* museum 6

música *f* music 1

muy very 2; **muy bien** very well P

N

nacer to be born 10

nacimento *m* birth 10

nada nothing 6; **de nada** you're welcome P

nadar to swim 4

nadie no one, nobody 6

naranja *f* orange 3

narcotráfico *m* drug trafficking 14

nariz *f* nose 8

naturaleza *f* nature 11

náuseas *f., pl.* nausea 8

navaja *f* razor 5

nave *f* **espacial** space ship 14

navegar por la red to explore (surf) the web 1

necesario: es ... it's necessary 12

necesitar to need 3

negro/a black 4

nervioso/a nervous 2

nevar (ie) to snow 4; **está nevando** it's snowing 4

ni... ni neither ... nor 12

nicaragüense *m/f, n., adj.* Nicaraguan P

nieta *f* granddaughter 2

nieto *m* grandson 2

nieva it's snowing 4

nieve *f* snow 4

ningún (ninguno/a) no, none, no one 12

niña *f* child 2

niñez childhood 10

niño *m* child 2

niños *m., pl.* children 10

noche *f* night P; **buenas noches** good evening/night P; **de la noche** P.M. (in the evening, at night) P; **por/en la noche** in the evening, at night 1

normalmente normally 5

nos *dir. obj.* us 5; *ind. obj.* us (to/for us) 7; *refl. pron.* ourselves 5

nosotros/as *m/f, subj.* we P; *obj. prep.* us 6

nota *f* grade, score 1

noticias *f., pl.* news 6

noticiero *m* newscast 14

noveno/a ninth 12

novia *f* girlfriend 2

noviembre November P

novio *m* boyfriend 2

nube *f* cloud 4

nublado cloudy 4; **está (muy) nublado** it's (very) cloudy 4

nuestro/a/os/as our 2; (of) ours 7

nuevo/a new 2

nunca never 4

O

o or 2; **o... o** either ... or 12

obra *f* **de teatro** play 6

obvio: es ... it's obvious 12

océano *m* ocean 11

octavo/a eighth 12

octubre October P

ocupado/a busy 2

oficina *f* office 1; **oficina de correos** post office 6

ojo *m* eye 8

oído *m* ear (inner) 8

oír to hear 4

ojalá que... I hope 10

ola *f* wave 11

olvidar to forget 10; **olvidarse de** to forget 10

oración *f* sentence 1

ordenar (el cuarto) to tidy (the room) 9

oreja *f* ear (outer) 8

oro *m* gold 7

os *dir. obj.* you (pl.) 5; *ind. obj.* you (to/for you) 7; *refl. pron.* yourselves 5

otoño *m* autumn, fall 4

otro/a another 3

otros/as other 3

P

paciente *m/f* patient 8

padrastro *m* stepfather 2

padre *m* father 2

padres *m, pl.* parents 2

pagar to pay (for) 6

página *f* page 1; **página web** web page 1

país *m* country 12

pájaro *m* bird 11

palabra *f* word 1

pan *m* **(tostado)** bread (toast) 3

panameño/a *m/f, n., adj.* Panamanian P

pantalla *f* screen 1

pantalones *m., pl.* pants 7; **pantalones cortos** shorts 7

pantimedias *f., pl.* panty hose 7

papa *f* potato 3; **papas fritas** french fries 3

papel *m* paper 1; **papel higiénico** toilet paper 5

papelera *f* waste basket 1

paquete *m* package 6

para que so that, in order that 13; **para + infinitivo** in order to (do something) 6

parabrisas *m* windshield 13

parada *f* **de autobús** bus stop 6

paraguas *m* umbrella 7

paraguayo/a *m/f, n., adj.* Paraguayan P

paramédicos *m, pl.* paramedics 8

parar to stop (movement) 13

parece que it seems that... 12

pared *f* wall 9

pareja *f* partner, significant other 2; couple 10

pariente *m* relative 2

parque *m* park 6

parrilla (a la parrilla) grilled 3

partido *m* game, match 4

pasado: el año/ mes/ verano ... last year/ month/ summer 5

pasajero/a *m/f* passenger 12

pasar to spend (time), to happen, pass, 6; **pasar la aspiradora** to vacuum 9

pasillo *m* aisle (between rows of seats) 12

pasta *f* **de dientes** toothpaste 5

pastel *m* pie, pastry 3

pastelería *f* pastry shop 6

patata *f* potato 3

paz *f* peace 14

pedir (i, i) to ask for, request, order 3

pecho *m* chest, breast 8

peinarse to comb one's hair 5

peine *m* comb 5

película *f* film, movie 6

peligroso/a dangerous 11

pelo *m* hair 8; **secador** *m* **de pelo** hairdryer 5

pelota *f* ball 4

pendientes *m, pl.* earrings 7

pensar (ie) to think 3; **pensar (ie) + infinitivo** to intend/plan (to do something) 5; **pensar (ie) en** to think about (someone or something) 10

peor worse 9

pequeño/a small, little 2

pera *f* pear 3

perder (ie) to lose 4; **perder el tren** to miss the train 13

perdón pardon me, excuse me P

perezoso/a lazy 2

periódico *m* newspaper 6

pero but 2

perro *m* dog 2

personalmente personally 5

peruano/a *m/f, n., adj.* Peruvian P

pescado *m* fish 3

pescar to fish 11

pez *m* (**los peces**) fish 11

pie *m* foot 8; **estar de pie** to be standing 8

pierna *f* leg 8

piloto/a *m/f* pilot 12

pimienta *f* pepper 3

piña *f* pineapple 3

pintar to paint 4

piscina *f* swimming pool 12

piso *m* floor (of a building) 9

pizarra *f* chalkboard 1

pizzería *f* pizzeria 6

planeta *m* planet 11

planta *f* plant 12; **planta baja** main floor 12

plata *f* silver 7

plátano *m* banana 3

plato *m* dish, course 3; plate 9

playa *f* beach 2

plaza *f* plaza, town square 6

pobre poor 2

pobreza *f* poverty 14

poco *adv.* little 3; **un poco** a bit, somewhat 2

poco/a *m/f, adj.* little (quantity) 3; **pocos/ as** *m/f, adj.* few 3

poder (ue) to be able, can 3

policía *m* policeman 13

política *f* **mundial** world politics 14

pollo *m* chicken 3

poner to put, place 4; **poner la mesa** to set the table 9; **poner una inyección/una vacuna** to give a shot/vaccination 8; **ponerse (los zapatos, la ropa, etc.)** to put on (shoes, clothes, etc.) 5

por for, down, by, along, through 6; **por favor** please P; **por fin** finally 8; **por la mañana** in the morning 1; **por la noche** in the evening, at night 1; **por la tarde** in the afternoon 1; **¿por qué?** why? 3; **¡Por supuesto!** Of course! 13

porque because 3

posible: es ... it's possible 12

posiblemente possibly 5

póster *m* poster 9

postre *m* dessert 3

practicar to practice 1; **practicar el descenso de ríos** to go white-water rafting 11; **practicar el *parasail*** to go parasailing 11

precio *m* price 7

preciso: es ... it's necessary 12

preferir (ie, i) to prefer 3

pregunta *f* question 1

preguntar to ask 7

prejuicio *m* prejudice 14

prender to turn on 9

preocupado/a *m/f* worried 2

preocuparse (por) to worry (about) 8

preparar to prepare 1

prestar to lend 7

prevenir to prevent 11

primavera *f* spring 4

primer first 12; **primer piso** *m* first floor, 9

primero *adv.* first 5; **primero/a** first 12; **de primera clase** first class 13

primo/a *m/f* cousin 2

probable: es ... it's probable 12

probablemente probably 5

problema *m* problem 11

profesor/a *m/f* professor 1

programador/a *m/f* computer programmer 2

prohibir to forbid 14

propina *f* tip 12

proteger to protect 11

próximo/a next 4; **próxima semana** next week 4

prueba *f* quiz 1

psicología *f* psychology 1

puente *m* bridge 13

puerta *f* door 1; **puerta de salida** gate 12

puertorriqueño/a *m/f, n., adj.* Puerto Rican P

pues well P

pulmón *m* lung 8

pulsera *f* bracelet 7

pupitre *m* (student) desk 1

Q

que that 3; **lo que** what, that which 3

¿qué? what?, which? 3; **¿qué hay de nuevo?** what's new? (*informal*) P; **¿qué pasa?** what's happening? (*informal*) P; **¿qué tal?** how are you? (*informal*) P

¡Qué barbaridad! How awful! 13; **¡Qué lástima!** What a shame! 13; **¡Qué lío!** What a mess! 13; **¡Qué suerte!** What luck!/ How lucky! 13

quedarse to stay 8

quejarse de to complain about 10

querer (ie) to want, love 3

queso *m* cheese 3

¿quién/quiénes? who? 2; **¿de quién?** whose? 3

química *f* chemistry 1

quinto/a fifth 12

quiosco *m* newsstand 6

quisiera I would like 3

quitar: ... la mesa to clear the table 9; **quitarse** to take off (clothes, etc.) 5

R

rafting: practicar el... to go white-water rafting 11

rápidamente rapidly 5

rascacielos *m* skyscraper 6

ratón *m* mouse 1

recámara *f* bedroom 9

recepción *f* reception, front desk 8

recepcionista *m/f* receptionist 5

receta *f* prescription 8

recibir to receive 6

reciclar to recycle 11

recientemente recently 5

reclamo de equipajes *m, pl.* baggage claim 12

recoger to pick up, gather 11

recomendar (ie) to recommend 10

recordar (ue) to remember 10

recursos *m, pl.* **naturales** natural resources 11

refresco *m* soft drink 3

refrigerador *m* refrigerator 9

regalar to give (as a gift) 7

regalo *m* gift 7

registrarse to register 12

regresar to return 1

regular okay, so-so P

reírse (de) to laugh at 10

relámpago *m* lightning 11

religión *f* religion 1

reloj *m* clock 1; watch 7

remar to row 11

reparar to fix 13

repartidor/a *m/f* delivery person 5

repetir (i, i) to repeat 6

reportar to report 14

reportero/a reporter 14

resfriado *m* cold 8

residencia *f* **estudiantil** dormitory 1

resolver (ue) to resolve 9

responsable responsible 3

respuesta *f* answer 1

restaurante *m* restaurant 1

retirar take out, to withdraw 6

reunirse (con) to meet, get together 10

revisar to check 13

revista *f* magazine 6

rico/a rich 2

ridículo: es ... it's ridiculous 12

río *m* river 11

robar to rob 14

rojo/a red 4

romper to break 9; romper (con) to break up (with) 10

ropa f clothes, clothing 7; ropa f interior underwear 7

ropero m closet 7

rosado/a pink 4

rubio/a blond(e) 2

ruido m noise 9

ruso m Russian (language) 1

S

sábado m Saturday P

sábana f sheet 12

saber to know (facts, information) 4; to know how to (skills) 4

sacar la basura to take out the garbage 9; sacar fotos f, pl. to take photos 11; sacar una nota to get a grade 1; sacar los pasaportes to get passports 12; sacar una radiografía to x-ray 8; sacar sangre to draw blood 8

saco m de dormir sleeping bag 11

sal f salt 3

sala f living room 9; sala de espera waiting room 8; sala familiar family room 9

salchicha f sausage 3

salida f departure 12

salir to leave, go out 1; salir (con) to go out (with), date 10

salud f health 8

salvadoreño/a m/f, n., adj. Salvadorean P

sandalias f, pl. sandals 7

sandía f watermelon 3

sándwich m sandwich 3

se reflex. pron. yourself, himself, herself, themselves 5

secador m de pelo hairdryer 5

secadora f dryer 9

secar: ... los platos to dry the dishes 9; secarse to dry (oneself) 5

secretario/a m/f secretary 5

seguir (i, i) to continue, follow 13

segundo/a second 12; de segunda clase second class 13; segundo piso second floor 9

seguro/a safe 13

sello m stamp 6

selva f jungle 11

semáforo m traffic light 13

semana f week P; semana f que viene next week 4

sentarse (ie, i) to sit down 8

sentir (ie, i) to be sorry, regret 10; lo siento mucho I'm so sorry P;

sentirse (ie, i) to feel 8

separarse (de) to separate 10

septiembre September P

séptimo/a seventh 12

ser to be 1

serio/a serious 2

serpiente f snake 11

servicio m restroom 13; servicio de habitación room service 12

servilleta f napkin 9

servir (i, i) to serve 3

sexto/a sixth 12

SIDA m AIDS 14

silla f chair 1; silla de ruedas wheel chair 8

sillón m easy chair 9

simpático/a nice, likeable 2

sin without 3

sincero/a honest, sincere 10

sitio web m web site 1

sobre on 6; sobre m envelope 6

sobrepoblación f overpopulation 14

sobrina f niece 2

sobrino m nephew 2

sociología f sociology 1

¡Socorro! ¡Help! 13

sofá m sofa 9

solicitar to apply (job) 14

solicitud f application 14

soltero/a single 10

sombrero m hat 7

sonar (ue) to ring, to sound 5

sopa f soup 3

sótano m basement 9

su/sus his, her, its, your (formal), their 2

subir to go up 9; subirse a to get on, board 12

sucio/a dirty 7

suegra f mother-in-law 2

suegro m father-in-law 2

suelo m floor 9

suéter m sweater 7

sufrir to suffer 14

sugerir (ie, i) to suggest 10

suyo/a/os/as (of) his, (of) hers, (of) theirs, (of) yours (formal) 7

T

talla f size (clothing) 7

taller m mecánico shop 13

también also 3

tampoco neither, not either 6

tan: tan... como as...as 9; tan pronto como as soon as 14

tanque m tank 13

tanto: tanto como as much as 9; tanto/a/os/as... como as much/

many...as 9

taquilla f ticket window 13

tarde f afternoon P; buenas tardes good afternoon P; de la tarde P.M. (in the afternoon) P; por/en la tarde in the afternoon 1

tarea f homework, assignment, task 1

tarjeta f card; tarjeta de crédito credit card 6; tarjeta de embarque boarding pass 12; tarjeta postal post card 6; tarjeta telefónica calling card 10

tatuaje m tattoo 13

taxi m taxi 6

taza f cup 9

te dir. obj. you (informal) 5; ind. obj. you (to/for you) (informal) 7; ¿Te duele? Does it hurt? 8; te presento (informal) I want to introduce ... to you P; reflex. pron. yourself (informal) 5

té m tea 3

teatro m theater 6

techo m roof 9

teclado m keyboard 1

teléfono m celular cell phone 10

televisión f TV 1; ver la tele(visión) to watch TV 4

televisor m television set 1

temer to fear, be afraid of 10

temprano early 1

tenedor m fork 9

tener to have 2; tener ... años to be ... years old 2; tener calor/frío to be hot/cold 4; tener celos to be jealous 10; tener más cuidado to be (more) careful 13; tener éxito to be successful 14; tener ganas de + infinitivo to feel like (doing something) 4; tener hambre/sed to be hungry/thirsty 3; tener miedo to be afraid 11; tener prisa to be in a hurry 12; tener que + infinitivo to have to ... (do something) 4; tener sueño to be sleepy 5

tenis m tennis 4

tercer third 12

tercero/a third 12

terminar to finish 6

termómetro m thermometer 8

terrorismo m terrorism 14

ti obj. prep. you (informal) 6

tía f aunt 2

tiempo m weather 4; a tiempo on time 1

tienda f store 5; tienda de campaña tent 11; tienda f de ropa clothing store 5

tierra *f* earth, land 11
tijeras *f, pl.* scissors 5
tío *m* uncle 2
tiza *f* chalk 1
toalla *f* towel 5
tocar to play (instruments) 4
tocineta *f* bacon 3
tocino *m* bacon 3
todo/a/os/as *adj.:* toda la mañana all
  morning 1; toda la noche all night 1;
  toda la tarde all afternoon 1; todas
  las mañanas every morning 1; todas
  las noches every evening, night 1;
  todas las tardes every afternoon 1;
  todo el día all day 1; todos los días
  every day 1
todavía still, yet 3
tomar to take, drink 3; tomar apuntes
  m, pl. to take notes 1; tomar el sol to
  sunbathe 4; tomar fotos *f, pl.* to take
  photos 11
tomate *m* tomato 3
tonto/a foolish, silly 2
torcerse el tobillo *m* to sprain one's
  ankle 8
tormenta *f* storm 11
torta *f* cake 3
tos *f* cough 8
toser to cough 8
trabajador/a hardworking 2
trabajar to work 1; trabajar para... to
  work for... 5
trabajo *m* de tiempo completo full-
  time job 5; trabajo de tiempo parcial
  part-time job 5; trabajo *m* escrito
  paper (academic) 1; trabajo
  voluntario *m* volunteerism 14; en el
  trabajo at work 2
traer to bring 4
tráfico *m* traffic 13
traje *m* suit 7; traje de baño bathing
  suit 7
tranquilamente peacefully 5
tránsito *m* traffic 13
tratar de + *infinitivo* to try to (do
  something) 10
tren *m* train 13
triste sad 2
tú *subj.* you (*informal*) P
tu/tus your (*informal*) 2
tutor/a tutor 14
tuyo/a/os/as (of) yours (*informal*) 7

U

un/uno/una a 1; one P; un poco a
  little 2; una vez once, one time 8
unos/unas some 1
universidad *f* college/university 1

uña *f* fingernail 8
urgente: es ... it's urgent 12
uruguayo/a *m/f, n., adj.* Uruguayan P
usar to use 1
usted *subj.* you (*formal*) P; *obj. prep.*
  you (*formal*) 6
ustedes *subj.* you (*pl.*) P; *obj. prep.* you
  (*pl.*) 6
uva *f* grape 6

V

vaca *f* cow 11
vacaciones *f, pl.* vacation 11
vacuna *f* vaccination 8
valle *m* valley 11
vaqueros *m, pl.* jeans 7
vaso *m* glass (drinking) 9
VCR *m* VCR 1
vecino/a *m/f* neighbor 9
vejez old age 10
velocidad *f* speed 13
venda *f* bandage 8
vender to sell 3
venezolano/a *m/f, n., adj.* Venezuelan
  P
venir to come 4
ventana *f* window 1
ventanilla *f* window (airplane, train,
  car) 12
ver to see 4; ver la tele to watch TV 4
verano *m* summer 4
verdad: es ... it's true 12
verde green 4
verdura *f* vegetable 3
vestido *m* dress 7
vestirse (i) to get dressed 5
viajar to travel 11; viajar de mochila
  to backpack 11
viaje *m* a trip 13
víctima *f* victim 14
vida *f* life 10
videograbadora *f* VCR 1
viejo/a old 2
viernes Friday P
vinagre *m* vinegar 3
vino *m* wine 3
violencia *f* violence 14
visitar to visit 2
viudo/a *m/f* widower/widow 10
vivir to live 1
volar (ue) to fly 12
vólibol *m* volleyball 4
voluntario/a *m/f* volunteer 14
volver (ue) to return, to go back 3
vomitar to vomit 8
vómito *m* vomit 8
vosotros/as *m/f, subj.* you (*informal,
  pl., Sp.*) P; *obj. prep.* you (*informal,*

pl., Sp.) 6
votar (por) to vote (for) 14
vuelo *m* flight 12
vuestro/a/os/as your (*informal*) 2; (of)
  yours (*informal*) 7

Y

y and 2
ya already 5
yeso *m* cast 8
yo *subj.* I P

Z

zanahoria *f* carrot 3
zapatería *f* shoe store 6
zapatos *m, pl.* shoes 7; zapatos de
  tenis tennis shoes 7
zumo *m, pl.* juice 3

Índice

Credits

PHOTO CREDITS

Preliminary Chapter
Opener: Stuart Cohen/The Image Works. Page 13 (top): Getty Images News and Sport Services. Page 13 (far left): Gamma-Presse, Inc. Page 13 (left): Al Tielemans/SI/IPN/Aurora Photos. Page 13 (right): Bill Davila/Retna. Page 13 (far right): Sue Adler/Camera Press/Retna. Page 18: Robert Frerck/Odyssey Productions. Page 28 (top left): Gamma-Presse, Inc. Page 28 (top right): Getty Images News and Sport Services.

Chapter 1
Opener: Strauss/Curtis/Corbis Images. Page 47 (left): Robert Frerck/Odyssey Productions. Page 47 (right): Peter Menzel/Stock, Boston. Page 59 (left): Roger Antrobus/Corbis Images. Page 59 (right): Doug Wilson/Corbis Images. Page 59 (bottom): Robert Van Der Hilst/Stone/Getty Images. Page 61: Diego Rivera, Flower Day, 1925. Oil on canvas (58x47.5 inches). Photograph ©2003 Museum Associates/LACMA/Los Angeles County Museum of Art, Los Angeles County Fund.

Chapter 2
Opener: Rob Lewine/Corbis Images. Page 82: Odyssey Productions. Page 85 (top left): Michael Newman/PhotoEdit. Page 85 (top & center): Digital Vision/Getty Images. Page 85 (top right): Robert Frerck/Woodfin Camp & Associates. Page 85 (bottom left): Tony Freeman/PhotoEdit. Page 85 (bottom right): Suzanne L. Murphy/D.Donne Bryant. Page 86 (top): Courtesy Laila Dawson. Page 86 (center): Robert Frerck/Woodfin Camp & Associates. Page 86 (bottom): David McNew/Getty Images News and Sport Services. Page 90: Jose L. Palaez/Corbis Stock Market. Page 92: ©Getty Images News and Sport Services. Page 93 (top): Photo by Alfonzo Fernandez, San Antonio, Texas. Page 93 (bottom): Mario Algaze/The Image Works. Page 94 (top): Rudi Von Briel/PhotoEdit. Page 94 (center): John Neubauer/PhotoEdit. Page 95 (center): John Pugh, Siete Punto Uno. Photo courtesy John Pugh. Page 95 (bottom): Yreina Cervantez, La Ofrenca. Mural Toluca Street under First Street Bridge, Los Angeles. A Neighborhood Pride, Great Walls Unlimited project. ©SPARC.

Chapter 3
Opener: Digital Vision/Getty Images. Page 110: Courtesy Laila Dawson. Page 114: Chad Slattery/Stone/Getty Images. Page 117 (left): Robert Frerck/Odyssey Productions. Page 117 (right): Erik Rank/Foodpix. Page 118 (top left): John Lei/Stock, Boston. Page 118 (top right): David Simson/Stock, Boston. Page 118 (bottom left): Matthew Klein/Photo Researchers. Page 118 (bottom right): Courtesy Laila Dawson. Page 128: Hulton Archive/Getty Images. Page 129 (top): Courtesy Laila Dawson. Page 129 (center): Richard A. Cooke II/Stone/Getty Images. Page 129 (bottom): Richard During/Stone/Getty Images. Page 130 (top): Robert Frerck/Odyssey Productions. Page 130 (left): Russell Cheyne/Stone/Getty Images. Page 130 (center): ©Everton/The Image Works. Page 131: D. Donne Bryant Stock.

Chapter 4
Opener: Syracuse Newspapers/The Image Works. Page 149 (top): Pablo Corral Vega/Corbis Images. Page 149 (bottom): Owen Franken/Corbis Images. Page 152 (top left): Courtesy Laila Dawson. Page 152 (top right): Art Wolfe/Stone/Getty Images. Page 152 (center): ©AP/Wide World Photos. Page 152 (bottom left): ©Everton/The Image Works. Page 152 (bottom & center): Chip and Rosa Maria Peterson. Page 152 (bottom right): Michael Busselle/Stone/Getty Images. Page 160 (left): Bettmann/Corbis Images. Page 160 (top right): Jeremy Horner/Corbis Images. Page 160 (bottom right): ©AP/Wide World Photos. Page 161 (top): Guido Alberto Rossi/The Image Bank/Getty Images. Page 161 (center): Max & Bea Hunn/D. Donne Bryant Stock Photography. Page 161 (bottom): J.W. Mowbray/Photo Researchers. Page 162 (top): Robert Frerck/Odyssey Productions. Page 162 (bottom): Mark Bacon/Latin Focus. Page 163: Prensa Latina/Getty Images News and Sport Services.

Chapter 5
Opener: David Young-Wolff/PhotoEdit. Page 185 (top): Orban Thierry/Corbis Sygma. Page 185 (bottom): AFP/Corbis Images. Page 186: Robert Frerck/Odyssey Productions. Page 190: Courtesy Peter Cervoni. Page 193 (top): Peter Holmes/Age Fotostock America, Inc. Page 193 (left): Peter Bowater/Age Fotostock America, Inc. Page 193 (bottom): J.D. Dallet/Age Fotostock America, Inc. Page 194 (top left): Robert Frerck/Odyssey Productions. Page 194 (top right): Salvador Dali, Still Life; ©1996 Demart Pro Arte, Geneva/Artists Rights Society (ARS), New York/Salvador Dali Museum, St. Petersburg, FL/Lerner/SUPERSTOCK. Page 194 (left of center): Pedro Coll/Corbis Stock Market. Page 194 (center): Photofest. Page 195 (top): Robert Frerck/Odyssey Productions. Page 195 (bottom): Courtesy Laila Dawson.

Chapter 6
Opener: Javier Pierini/PhotoDisc, Inc./Getty Images. Page 214 (center): Courtesy Laila Dawson. Page 214 (bottom): Frank Scherschel/Getty Images News and Sport Services. Page 226: Robert Frerck/Odyssey Productions. Page 227 (top): Chad Ehlers/Stone/Getty Images. Page 227 (bottom): Courtesy Laila Dawson. Page 228 (top): Loren McIntyre. Page 228 (center): Kit Houghton/Corbis Images. Page 228 (bottom): Icon Sports Media. Page 229 (left): Alex Stewart/The Image Bank/Getty Images. Page 229 (right): Steve Benbow/Woodfin Camp & Associates. Page 230: Barnabas Bosshart/Corbis Images. Page 231: ©AP/Wide World Photos.

Chapter 7
Opener: Latin Stock. Page 246 (center): Suzanne Murphy/D. Donne Bryant Stock Photography. Page 246 (bottom): Chip Peterson and Rosa Maria de la Cueva Peterson. Page 247: Bryon Augustin/D. Donne Bryant Stock Photography. Page 261 (top): Robert Frerck/Odyssey Productions. Page 261 (bottom left): Ira Block/National Geographic Society. Page 261 (bottom & center): Ira Block/National Geographic Society. Page 261 (bottom right): Robert Frerck/Odyssey Productions. Page 262 (top): John Maier/The Image Works. Page 262 (left & center): George Holton/Photo Researchers. Page 262 (center): Ted Kerasote/Photo Researchers. Page 262 (right): Victor Englebert. Page 262 (bottom): Richard Smith/Corbis Sygma. Page 263 (top): William J. Jahoda/Photo Researchers. Page 263 (center): Courtesy Laila Dawson. Page 263 (bottom): Victor Englebert/Photo Researchers. Page 264: Ken Biggs/Stone/Getty Images. Page 265: Courtesy Laila Dawson.

Chapter 8
Opener: Peter Krogh/National Geographic Society. Page 273 (top): Yellow Dog Productions/The Image Bank/Getty Images. Page 273 (bottom): Mug Shots/Corbis Stock Market. Page 286 (top): Bill Ross/Corbis Images. Page 286 (center): Felicia Martinez/PhotoEdit. Page 298: Carlos Alvarez/Getty Images News and Sport Services. Page 299 (top): Joseph Standart/Corbis Stock Market. Page 299 (center): Victor Englebert. Page 300 (top right): Loris Barbazza/Stone/Getty Images. Page 300 (left): M. Algaze/The Image Works. Page 300 (center): Kimball Morrison/South American Pictures. Page 300 (right & center): ©AP/Wide World Photos. Page 300 (bottom right): Russell A. Mittermeier/Bruce Coleman, Inc.

Chapter 9
Opener: Tony Morrison/South American Pictures. Page 322: Timothy Ross/The Image Works. Pages 326 and 327 (top left, top right and bottom): Courtesy Laila Dawson. Page 327 (top & center): Jose L. Palaez/Corbis Stock Market. Page 330: DPPI/Icon Sports Media. Page

331 (top): Carlos Sanuvo/Bruce Coleman, Inc. Page 331 (center): Robert Fried/D. Donne Bryant Stock Photography. Page 331 (bottom): E. Caldwell/D.Donne Bryant. Page 332 (top): Courtesy Sartoroti, Ministry of Tourism of Uruguay. Reproduced with permission. Page 332 (center): Gary M. Prior/Getty Images News and Sport Services. Page 332 (bottom): Joe Viesti/Viesti Associates, Inc. Page 333: Pedro Figari, Baile Criollo; 61x82 cm, oil on canvas. Photo courtesy Museo Virtual de Artes El País. ©1997 El País.

Chapter 10
Opener: Paul Barton/Corbis Images. Page 354: Rony Liang/Bruce Coleman, Inc. Page 363 (center): David Hiser/Stone/Getty Images. Page 363 (bottom): Donne Bryant/D. Donne Bryant Stock Photography. Page 364 (top): Courtesy Laila Dawson. Page 364 (center): David Hiser/Stone/Getty Images. Page 364 (bottom left): Jon Kopaloff/Getty Images News and Sport Services. Page 364 (bottom right): Peter Chartrand/D. Donne Bryant Stock Photography. Page 365 (top): Jules Bucher/Photo Researchers. Page 365 (bottom): A. Farnsworth/The Image Works. Page 367: Courtesy The Textile Museum, Washington, D.C.

Chapter 11
Opener: Courtesy Costa Rica Expeditions, www.costaricaexpeditions.com. Page 375: ©Photodisk, Inc. Page 376: Courtesy Laila Dawson. Page 387 (bottom left): Ken Graham/Stone/Getty Images. Page 387 (bottom right): Peter Christopher/Masterfile. Page 388: Michael Fogden/Animals Animals. Page 396: ©AP/Wide World Photos. Page 397 (top): Courtesy Laila Dawson. Page 397 (center): Victor Englebert. Page 397 (bottom): D. Donne Bryant Stock Photography. Page 398 (top): Robert Frerck/Odyssey Productions. Page 398 (center left): Will & Deni McIntyre/Photo Researchers. Page 398 (center right): Danny Lehman/Corbis Images. Page 399 (top): Kevin Schafer/Corbis Images. Page 399 (bottom): Kevin Schafer/Corbis Images.

Chapter 12
Opener and page 416: Courtesy Trino Gonzalez. Page 422-423: Courtesy Joseph R. Farrell. Page 423: Pablo Corral V/Corbis Images. Page 428 (top): Odyssey Productions. Page 428 (center left): Robert Frerck/Odyssey Productions. Page 428 (bottom): Sylvain Grandadam/Stone/Getty Images. Page 432 (left): Robert Frerck/Odyssey Productions. Page 432 (center): Robert Frerck/Odyssey Productions. Page 432 (right): Ron May/Liaison Agency, Inc./Getty Images. Page 433 (left): Peter Menzel/Stock, Boston. Page 433 (right): Robert Frerck/Odyssey Productions. Page 434 (left): Pablo Picasso, Guernica, 1937. Art Resource NYC/Artists' Rights Society, New York. Page 434 (right): ©AP/Wide World Photos. Page 434 (bottom): B. Daemmrich/The Image Works. Page 435 (left): Art Resource. Page 435 (right): Goya y Lucientes, Francisco de Don Manuel Osorio Manrique de Zuñiga. Oil on canvas (127 x101.6cm). Photograph 1994 The Metropolitan Museum of Art. ©The Metropolitan Museum of Art, The Jules Bache Collection, 1949. Page 435 (bottom): Goya, El Quitasol, 1777. ©Museo del Prado, Madrid.

Chapter 13
Opener: Odyssey Productions. Page 445: Corbis Images. Page 456: ©Cover/The Image Works. Page 462: Courtesy Laila Dawson. Page 466 (top): Hugh Rogers. Page 466 (center): Courtesy Biblioteca Medicea Laurenziana. Page 467: Robert Frerck/Odyssey Productions. Page 468: Mary Evans Picture Library. Page 469: ©AP/Wide World Photos.

Chapter 14
Opener: Bob Daemmrich/The Image Works. Page 478: Mario Tama/Getty Images News and Sport Services. Page 483: Peter Chartrand/D.Donne Bryant. Page 490: Courtesy Michael Navarro. Page 495: James L. Amos/Corbis Images. Page 496 (top): Ted DeGrazia, Operation Arrowhead, 1972. Oil on linen. DeGrazia Foundation, Gallery in the Sun, Tucson, Arizona. Reproduced with permission. Page 496 (bottom): Courtesy Degolyer Library, Southern Methodist University. Page 497 (center): Mark E. Gibson/Corbis Images. Page 498: Robert Holmes/Corbis Images. Page 499 (top): Courtesy Laila Dawson. Page 499 (bottom): Art on File/Corbis Images.

TEXT CREDITS

We would like to thank the following for their permission to reprint the selections that appear in *Dicho y hecho*.
Page 163: **Herederos de Nicolás Guillén** for "Sensemayá" by Nicolás Guillén. Reprinted by permission.
Page 301: **Programa Editorial de la Universidad del Valle** for "El Amigo," by Miguel Fernando Caro G. from *Antología del cuento corto colombiano*. Reprinted by permission.
Page 469: **New Directions Publishing Corporation** for "Serpiente labrada sobre un muro," by Octavio Paz, from EARLY POEMS 1935-1939. Copyright ©1973. Reprinted by permission of New Directions Publishing Corp.

REALIA CREDITS

CHAPTER 1 *Page 37:* Reprinted by permission of Telmex. *Page 46:* Adapted by permission of Pontificia Universidad Católica del Ecuador.

CHAPTER 3 *Page 103:* ©Chef Merito 1998, all rights reserved. Reprinted by permission. *Page 126:* Printed by permission of Lario's Restaurant.

CHAPTER 5 *Page 171:* Created by Siboney U.S.A., International Hispanics Communications, Copyright Colgate-Palmolive Company, 1998. Reprinted by permission of Colgate-Palmolive Company.

CHAPTER 7 *Page 239:* Reprinted by permission of Buenhogar.

CHAPTER 8 *Page 279:* Printed by permission of Lario's Restaurant. *Page 299:* Permission requested.

CHAPTER 9 *Page 311:* Permission requested. *Page 328:* Permission requested. *Page 328:* Adapted by permission of Richard López at Puntaweb.

CHAPTER 10 *Page 358:* Reprinted by permission of La Nación. *Page 362:* Reprinted by permission of Revista IMAGEN.

CHAPTER 11 Page 391: Adapted by permission of Kempery Tours CIA, LTDA. *Page 394:* Permission requested.

CHAPTER 12 *Page 425:* Reprinted by permission of SAETA, Inc. *Page 428:* Reprinted by permission of Teatro Lope de Vega. *Page 429:* Reprinted by permission of el Parque de Atracciones-Madrid. *Page 429:* Reprinted by permission of Arrocería Puerto de Atocha y Restaurante Redondela.

CHAPTER 13 *Page 446:* Reprinted by permission of Maria Luisa O. de Montellano. *Page 448:* Reprinted by permission of BASF Española S.A. *Page 451:* ©Condorito/Editorial Televisa, S.A. de C.V. Reprinted by permission.

CHAPTER 14 *Page 479:* Information provided by Vega & Associates, publishers of the *Hispanic Yellow Pages* of Washington, DC; Maryland; and Virginia. Reprinted by permission.

Every attempt has been made to locate the copyright holder for the newspaper excerpt on page 231. Any further information would be welcomed by the publisher.

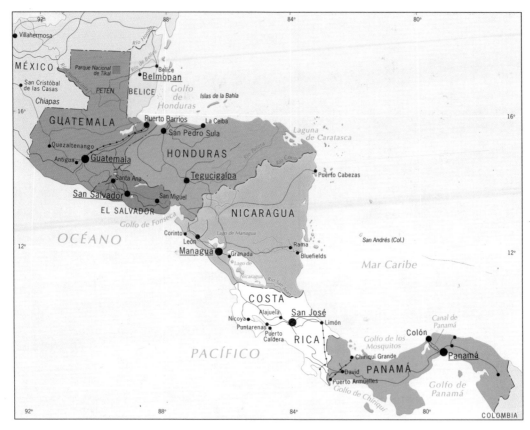

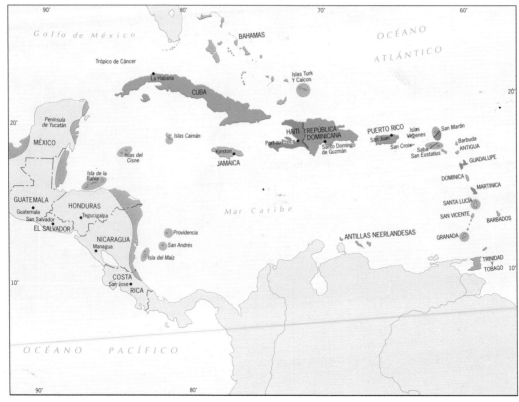